Discovering Computers Enhanced

Tools, Apps, Devices, and the Impact of Technology

ESSENTIALS

Dedication

With heartfelt thanks to my husband, Bill, and children, Jackie and Ricky ... for their endless support, devotion, assistance, understanding, and patience during my work on this and all other projects throughout my career. I love you all dearly.

Thanks also to Sue, Steve, Jennifer, and Mark. It's a pleasure to work with such a dedicated team.

— Misty E. Vermaat

Thanks to my family and friends for their support, encouragement, and patience. Special acknowledgement goes to my mother, Mandy, and to my professors at Purdue University, especially James Quasney, Ralph Webb, and Daniel Yovich, who taught me that keeping a positive mental attitude and striving for excellence are the keys to success.

— Susan L. Sebok

For my wife, Traci, and my children, Maddy and Sam, whose support and love are incredibly motivating. Thanks to my parents for their endless encouragement, and to Linda Linardos, who was instrumental in starting my writing career.

— Steven M. Freund

I would like to thank Mike, Emma, and Lucy for their support and inspiration, and Maggie for providing welcome distractions. Special thanks to my parents for being terrific role models.

— Jennifer T. Campbell

Thanks to my family and friends for their encouragement, and to my colleagues and students at Bentley University for their helpful feedback, which guided my contributions to this book. Thanks to Bentley University for providing me with an environment to learn and teach new technology.

— Mark Frydenberg

The author team also would like to thank our developmental editor, Lyn Markowicz, whose patience, attention to detail, and determination contributed in so many meaningful ways to this project.

SHELLY CASHMAN SERIES®

ENHANCED EDITION

Discovering Computers 2017

Tools, Apps, Devices, and the Impact of Technology

ESSENTIALS

VERMAAT | SEBOK | FREUND | CAMPBELL | FRYDENBERG

Shelly Cashman Series®

CENGAGE
Learning®

Australia • Brazil • Mexico • Singapore • United Kingdom • United States

Discovering Computers Essentials Enhanced: Tools, Apps, Devices, and the Impact of Technology
Misty E. Vermaat
Susan L. Sebok
Steven M. Freund
Jennifer T. Campbell
Mark Frydenberg

Product Director: Kathleen McMahon

Product Manager: Amanda Lyons

Managing Developer: Emma Newsom

Associate Content Developer:
Crystal Parenteau

Marketing Manager: Kristie Clark

Marketing Coordinator: William Guiliani

Manufacturing Planner: Julio Esperas

Senior Content Project Manager:
Matthew Hutchinson

Development Editor: Lyn Markowicz

Researcher: F. William Vermaat

Management Services: Lumina Datamatics, Inc.

Art Director: Jackie Bates, GEX

Text Design: Joel Sadagursky

Cover Design: Lisa Kuhn, Curio Press, LLC

Cover Photo: ©iStock.com/audioundwerbung

Illustrator: Lumina Datamatics, Inc.

Compositor: Lumina Datamatics, Inc.

Printer: RRD Menasha

© 2017 Cengage Learning

WCN: 01-100-101

For product information and technology assistance, contact us at
Cengage Learning Customer & Sales Support, 1-800-354-9706

For permission to use material from this text or product,
submit all requests online at **cengage.com/permissions**
Further permissions questions can be emailed to
permissionrequest@cengage.com

Library of Congress Control Number: 2015954308

ISBN-13: 978-1-305-65746-5

Cengage Learning
20 Channel Center Street
Boston, MA 02210
USA

Cengage Learning is a leading provider of customized learning solutions with office locations around the globe, including Singapore, the United Kingdom, Australia, Mexico, Brazil and Japan. Locate your local office at:
international.cengage.com/region

Cengage Learning products are represented in Canada by Nelson Education, Ltd.

Purchase any of our products at your local college bookstore or at our preferred online store at **www.cengagebrain.com**

Printed in the United States of America
Print Number: 02   Print Year: 2016

Discovering Computers Essentials Enhanced
Tools, Apps, Devices, and the Impact of Technology

Table of Contents at a Glance

Discovering Computers Essentials Enhanced
Tools, Apps, Devices, and the Impact of Technology

Table of Contents

CHAPTER **3**

Computers and Mobile Devices: Evaluating Options for Home and Work   **107**

CHAPTER **4**

Programs and Apps: Productivity, Graphics, Security, and Other Tools   **157**

CHAPTER **5**

Digital Security, Ethics, and Privacy: Threats, Issues, and Defenses   211

Web Development   FO 1

Table of Boxed Elements

DISCOVER MORE ONLINE WITH THESE FREE RESOURCES

HIGH-TECH TALK ARTICLES

HOW TO: YOUR TURN ASSIGNMENTS – APP ADVENTURES

Preface

The Shelly Cashman Series® offers the finest textbooks in computer education. We are proud of the fact that the previous seventeen editions of this textbook have been the most widely used in computer education. With this edition of *Discovering Computers Enhanced*, we have implemented improvements based on current computer trends and comments made by instructors and students. *Discovering Computers Essentials Enhanced*: *Tools, Apps, Devices, and the Impact of Technology* continues with the innovation, quality, and reliability you have come to expect from the Shelly Cashman Series.

In *Discovering Computers Essentials Enhanced*: *Tools, Apps, Devices, and the Impact of Technology* you will find an educationally sound, highly visual, interactive, and easy-to-follow pedagogy that, with the help of animated figures, relevant video, and interactive activities in the e-book, presents an in-depth treatment of introductory computer subjects. Readers will finish the course with a solid understanding of computers, how to use computers, and how to access information on the web.

Objectives of This Text, eReader, and CourseMate Web site

Discovering Computers Essentials Enhanced: *Tools, Apps, Devices, and the Impact of Technology* is intended for use as a stand-alone solution or in combination with an applications, Internet, or programming textbook in a full-semester introductory technology course. No experience with computers is assumed. The objectives of this offering are to:

- Provide skills for creating a web presence in a new Web Development appendix
- Present Windows 10 information to readers for currency
- Present the most-up-to-date technology in an ever-changing discipline
- Give readers an in-depth understanding of why computers are essential in business and society
- Teach the fundamentals of and terms associated with computers and mobile devices, the Internet, programs and apps, and digital safety and security
- Present the material in a visually appealing, interactive, and exciting manner that motivates readers to learn
- Provide exercises, assignments, and interactive learning activities that allow readers to learn by actually using computers, mobile devices, and the Internet
- Offer distance-education providers a textbook with a meaningful and exercise-rich digital learning experience

Hallmarks of Discovering Computers

To date, more than six million readers have learned about computers using *Discovering Computers Enhanced*. With the online integration and interactivity, step-by-step visual drawings and photographs, unparalleled currency, and the Shelly and Cashman touch, this book will make your computer concepts course exciting and dynamic. Hallmarks of Shelly Cashman Series *Discovering Computers Enhanced* include:

A Proven Pedagogy

Careful explanations of complex concepts, educationally-sound elements, and reinforcement highlight this proven method of presentation.

A Visually Appealing Book that Maintains Student Interest

The latest technology, photos, drawings, and text are combined artfully to produce a visually appealing and easy-to-understand book. Many of the figures include a step-by-step presentation, which simplifies the more complex technology concepts. Pictures and drawings reflect the latest trends in computer technology.

Latest Technologies and Terms

The technologies and terms readers see in *Discovering Computers Enhanced* are those they will encounter when they start using computers and mobile devices personally and professionally. Only the latest applications are shown throughout the book.

Web Integrated

This book uses the web as a major learning tool. The purpose of integrating the web into the book is to (1) offer students additional information and currency on important topics; (2) use its interactive capabilities to offer creative reinforcement; (3) make available alternative learning techniques with games and quizzes; (4) underscore the relevance of the web as a fundamental

Distinguishing Features

Discovering Computers Essentials Enhanced: Tools, Apps, Devices, and the Impact of Technology includes a variety of compelling features, certain to engage and challenge students, making learning with *Discovering Computers Essentials Enhanced* an enriched experience. These compelling features include:

- **NEW!** • **Introducing Today's Technologies.** This new introductory chapter as well as Windows 10 information detail how to succeed in this course by setting the stage for the rich resources available in the text and online to support learning.

- **NEW!** • **Technology Timeline.** This engaging visual provides milestones in technology history.

- **NEW!** • **Cloud and Skills Coverage.** An integrated approach to cloud computing and search skills appears throughout the text shows how to apply these concepts to learning.

- **NEW!** • **Career Coverage.** Career information is covered, including using social media to jumpstart your technology career.

- **NEW!** • **Focus On: Web Development.** This new Focus On appendix showcases fundamental information for creating a web presence.

- • **Strong Content.** Based on market research, assessment of organization of each chapter's content, *Discovering Computers Essentials Enhanced* has been restructured and reorganized to improve retention of material and promote transference of knowledge. The text's visually engaging presentation showcases current technology as well as course fundamentals in order to reinforce classroom and real-world applications.

- • **Balanced Presentation.** The print book provides students with what they need to know to be successful digital citizens in the classroom and beyond. Online resources address timely content and expand on the print text with content appropriate for Information Technology majors. Readers can choose to utilize this digital-only content, empowering each to fit the content to their specific needs and goals for the course.

- • **Thematic Approach.** Chapter boxes, marginal elements, and accompanying online content are linked by common themes to facilitate class discussions and help students make connections. These connections shed light on the integral role technology plays in business and society.

- • **Media Engagement.** Enrichment content is available online to enhance student knowledge and understanding through additional free resources and premium content. Developed by the authors, this content provides deeper understanding and encourages learning by doing, as well as offering practical skill development.

- • **Reinforcement and Support.** End-of-chapter student assignments offer students an exceptional learning solution in addition to significant practice opportunities in the form of study guide materials, flash cards, practice tests and critical thinking opportunities.

---

information tool that can be used in all facets of society; (5) introduce students to web-based research; and (6) offer instructors the opportunity to organize and administer their traditional campus-based or distance-education-based courses on the web using various learning management systems.

Extensive End-of-Chapter Student Assignments

A notable strength of *Discovering Computers Enhanced* is the extensive student assignments and activities at the end of each chapter. Well-structured student assignments can make the difference between students merely participating in a class and students retaining the information they learn. End-of-chapter student assignments include the following:

- • Study Guide exercises reinforce material for the exams
- • Key Terms page reviews chapter terms
- • Checkpoint exercises test knowledge of chapter concepts
- • How To: Your Turn exercises require that students learn new practical skills
- • Problem Solving exercises require that students seek solutions to practical technology problems
- • Internet Research exercises require that students search for information on the web
- • Critical Thinking exercises challenge student assessment and decision-making skills

Instructor Resources

The Instructor Resources include both teaching and testing aids.

Instructor's Manual   Includes lecture notes summarizing the chapter sections, figures and boxed elements found in every chapter, teacher tips, classroom activities, lab activities, and quick quizzes in Microsoft Word files.

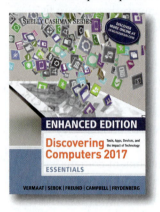

Syllabus   Customizable sample syllabi that cover policies, assignments, exams, and other course information.

Solutions to Exercises   Includes solutions for all end-of-chapter student assignments.

PowerPoint Presentations   A one-click-per-slide presentation system that provides PowerPoint slides for every subject in each chapter.

Test Bank and Test Engine   Cengage Learning Testing Powered by Cognero is a flexible, online system that allows you to author, edit, and manage test bank content from multiple Cengage Learning solutions and to create multiple test versions. It works on any operating system or browser with no special installs or downloads needed, allowing you to create tests from anywhere with Internet access. Multi-language support, an equation editor and unlimited metadata help ensure your tests are complete and compliant, and it enables you to import and export content into other systems. The *Discovering Computers Enhanced* Test Bank includes multiple for every chapter, featuring objective-based and critical thinking question types, and including page number references and figure references as appropriate.

Free Resources   Available on the student companion website accessed via www.cengagebrain.com, additional free resources for each chapter allow students to discover more materials and deeper content online to enrich learning.

Computer Concepts CourseMate

The Computer Concepts CourseMate for *Discovering Computers Enhanced* is the most expansive digital website for any computer concepts text in the market today. The content in the CourseMate solution is integrated into each page of the text, giving students easy access to current information on important topics, reinforcements activities, and alternative learning techniques.

These interactive activities are captured within the CourseMate EngagementTracker, making it easy to assess students' retention of concepts.

MindTap

Typical courses often require students to juggle a variety of print and digital resources, as well as an array of platforms, access codes, logins, and homework systems. Now all of those resources are available in one personal learning experience called MindTap. MindTap is a cloud-based, interactive, customizable, and complete online course. More than an e-book, and different than a learning management system, each MindTap course is built upon authoritative Cengage Learning content, accessible anytime, anywhere.

Additional Online Material

SAM: Skills Assessment Manager

Get workplace-ready with SAM, the market-leading proficiency-based assessment and training solution for Microsoft Office! SAM's active, hands-on environment helps students master Microsoft Office skills and computer concepts that are essential to academic and career success, delivering the most comprehensive online learning solution for your course.

Through skill-based assessments, interactive trainings, business-centric projects, and comprehensive remediation, SAM engages students in mastering the latest Microsoft Office programs on their own, giving instructors more time to focus on teaching. Computer concepts labs supplement instruction of important technology-related topics and issues through engaging simulations and interactive, auto-graded assessments. With enhancements, including streamlined course setup, more robust grading and reporting features, and the integration of fully interactive MindTap Readers containing Cengage Learning's premier textbook content, SAM provides the best teaching and learning solution for your course.

CourseCasts: Learning on the Go

Always available… always relevant   Our fast-paced world is driven by technology. You know because you are an active participant — always on the go, always keeping up with technological trends, and always learning new ways to embrace technology to power your life. Let CourseCasts, hosted by Ken Baldauf of Florida State University, be your guide to weekly updates in this ever-changing space. These timely, relevant podcasts are produced weekly and are available for download at http://coursecasts.course.com or directly from iTunes (search by CourseCasts). CourseCasts are a perfect solution to getting students (and even instructors) to learn on the go!

Visual Walkthrough of the Book

Current. Relevant. Innovative.

Chapter Opener
familiarize students with the
material in each chapter.

How To
features enable readers to learn
new practical skills.

Consider This
features provide readers with
critical thinking opportunities.

Mini Features
throughout the text explore
various real world topics to
deepen concept understanding.

Secure IT

features allow students to broaden their knowledge with details regarding security issues they will face.

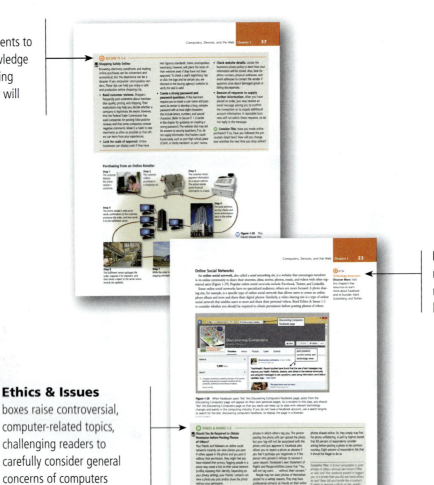

By The Way (BTW)

marginal elements assist readers in broadening their knowledge.

Ethics & Issues

boxes raise controversial, computer-related topics, challenging readers to carefully consider general concerns of computers in society.

Now You Should Know

feature provides assessment opportunity and integrates directly to chapter learning objectives to assess learning outcomes.

Chapter Summary

allows another review of materials presented in the chapter to reinforce learning and provide additional self-assessment opportunities.

Technology @ Work

features put chapter information to practical use and provide context within students' lives.

End-of-Chapter Student Assignments

Study Guide
materials reinforce chapter content.

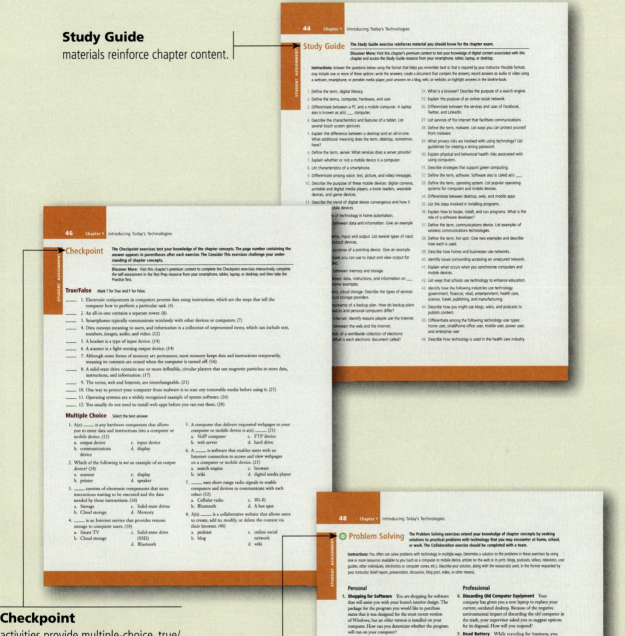

Checkpoint
activities provide multiple-choice, true/false, matching, and consider this exercises to reinforce understanding of the topics presented in the chapter.

Problem Solving
activities call on students to relate concepts to their own lives, both personally and professionally, as well as provide a collaboration opportunity.

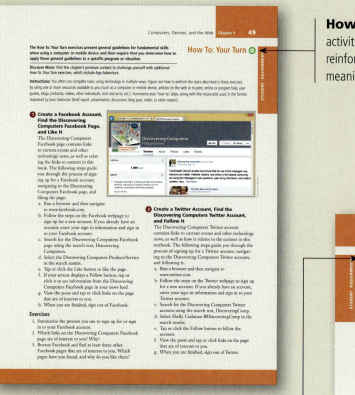

How To: Your Turn

activities enable readers to learn and to reinforce new practical skills with personally meaningful and applicable exercises.

Internet Research

exercises require follow-up research on the web and suggest writing a short article or presenting the findings of the research to the class.

Critical Thinking

activities provide opportunities for creative solutions to these thought-provoking activities presented in each chapter. The Critical Thinking exercises are constructed for class discussion, presentation, and independent research. The Collaboration exercise is designed for a team environment.

Visual Walkthrough of the Computer Concepts CourseMate, MindTap, and Free Resources

CourseMate

Introduce the most current technology into the classroom with the Computer Concepts CourseMate. An integrated MindTap eReader and a wide range of online learning games, quizzes, practice tests, and web links expand on the topics covered in the text with hands-on reinforcement. Visit www.cengagebrain.com to register your access code and access your course and the premium resources assigned by your instructor.

Engagement Tracker

Engagement Tracker makes assessing students easy by tracking student progress on the interactive activities. Clear and visual reports illustrate the class progress as a whole.

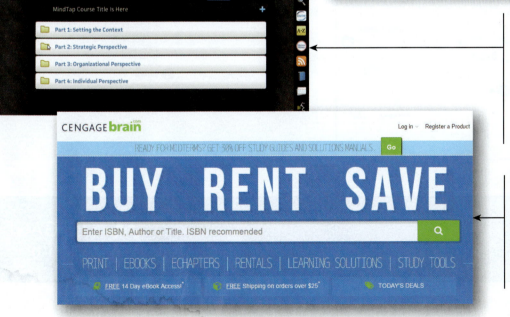

MindTap

MindTap is a personalized teaching experience with relevant assignments that guide students to analyze, apply, and improve thinking, allowing you to measure skills and outcomes with ease.

Free Resources on CengageBrain

Start with locating *Discovering Computers* on www.cengagebrain.com in order to access the free resources found on the student resources page.

Engage with CourseMate by Following These Easy Steps!

Purchase Access

1 Your course materials can be purchased at your campus bookstore or by visiting **www.cengagebrain.com** and searching for your course materials ISBN.

Register / Login

Visit **https://login.cengagebrain.com**

Three Options:

2a Registering your product? Enter your access code and select "Register" (then go to step 3).

2b Don't have a CengageBrain account? Select "Don't have an account" to create your account (then go to step 4).

2c Returning student who wants to login to a course? Enter your email address and password and select "Log In" (then go to step 8).

Create Account or Log In

3a If you're a new user, select "Create a New Account" (then go to step 4).

3b If you're a returning user, log in (then go to step 6).

Complete the Account Information Form

4 Complete the Account Information form and agree to the license agreement.

5 Select "Continue".

Select Your Institution

6 Select your institution.

7 Select "Search".

You're All Set!

8 Select the "Open" button next to the name of your course.

9 If your instructor has provided a Course Key, enter it here.

If your instructor has not provided a Course Key, you may begin accessing resources now.

That's it! You've successfully registered for CourseMate.

Please note: Directions are accurate at the time of printing, and steps may vary slightly depending upon when the web site is accessed.

Tap into **engagement**

MindTap empowers you to produce your best work—consistently.

MindTap is designed to help you master the material. Interactive videos, animations, and activities create a learning path designed by your instructor to guide you through the course and focus on what's important.

MindTap delivers real-world activities and assignments

that will help you in your academic life as well as your career.

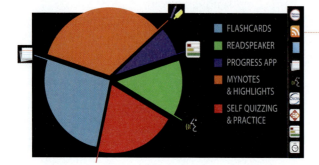

MindTap helps you stay organized and efficient

by giving you the study tools to master the material.

MindTap empowers and motivates

with information that shows where you stand at all times—both individually and compared to the highest performers in class.

"MindTap was very useful – it was easy to follow and everything was right there."
— Student, San Jose State University

"I'm definitely more engaged because of MindTap."
— Student, University of Central Florida

"MindTap puts practice questions in a format that works well for me."
— Student, Franciscan University of Steubenville

Tap into more info at: **www.cengage.com/mindtap**

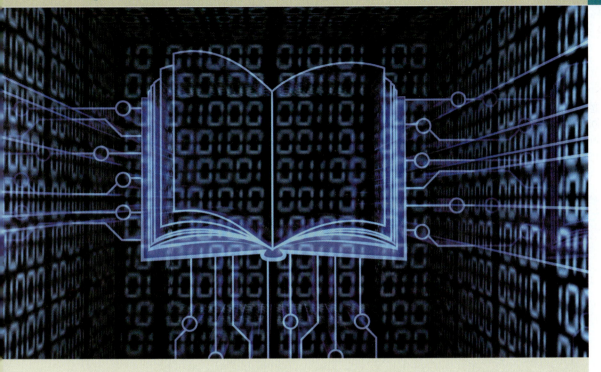

You can improve your digital literacy by reading this book and accessing its associated online content.

Introduction

This introductory chapter is designed to prepare you to succeed in this course. It begins with a discussion of browsing the web, followed by overview of the book and its associated additional online content, which familiarizes you with the meanings of references and symbols that appear throughout the book. Next is a brief buyer's guide that you can use to purchase a desktop, laptop, or tablet for use during the semester. Finally is an abbreviated set of exercises designed to acquaint you with the resources you will be expected to use in Chapter 1.

Keep in mind that this chapter uses a variety of terms that are described in more depth in Chapter 1 and throughout the book. These terms also are defined in this book's index. If you need additional information about a particular topic, refer to the appropriate chapter.

Browsing the Web

Each chapter in this book contains topics, elements, and assignments that presume you already know how to use a browser. As you may know, a browser is software that enables you to access and view webpages on a computer or mobile device that has an Internet connection. Some widely used browsers include Internet Explorer, Firefox, Safari, Edge, and Chrome. Read How To 1 for instructions about using a browser to display a webpage on a computer or mobile device.

⚙ HOW TO 1

Use a Browser to Display a Webpage
The following steps describe how to use a browser to display a webpage on a computer or mobile device:

1. Run a browser. (Chapter 1 discusses running programs and apps.)
2. If necessary, tap or click the address bar to select it and any previously displayed web address it may contain. (A web address is a unique address that identifies a webpage.)

3. In the address bar, type the web address of the webpage you want to visit and then press the ENTER key or tap or click the Go (or similar) button to display the web-page. For example, www.cengagebrain.com is a valid web address, which displays the CengageBrain webpage shown in the figure below. (Chapter 2 discusses the components of a web address.)
4. If necessary, scroll to view the entire webpage. You can scroll either by sliding

your finger across a touch screen or by using a pointing device, such as a mouse, to drag the scroll bar.
5. Tap or click links on the webpage to navigate to the link's destination.

⚙ **Consider This:** What should you do if the web address you enter does not display a webpage or you receive an error message?

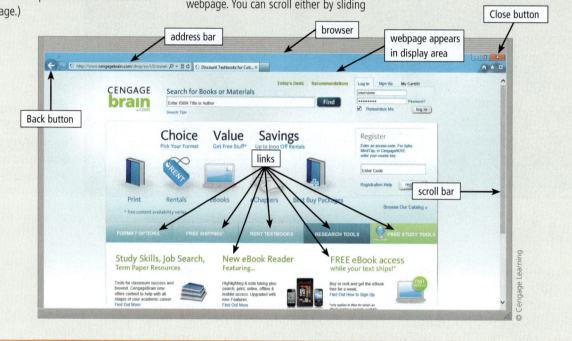

© Cengage Learning

⚙ CONSIDER THIS

What does the ⚙ icon mean that appears in the book?
This icon denotes that the questions or exercises that follow require critical thinking. Your instructor may assign or expect you to discuss in class any of these questions that appear throughout the chapters.

Book and Online Content

As a student in this course, you should be aware that the material located in the pages of this book includes content you should know to be successful as a student and as a digital citizen. Other content is available online only as free resources or premium content. The free resources are available at no additional cost with your book purchase, whereas the premium content may or may not have been included with your purchase, as determined by your instructor. Please see the preface or your instructor for details related to the location of the free resources and the premium content, as well as information about purchasing the premium content, if desired.

Free Resources   The free resources, which are available online, present (1) up-to-date content including current statistics, trends, models, products, programs, apps, etc., (2) content that elaborates on essential material in the book, or (3) content required for those students majoring in the information technology or computer science fields. When free resources are available for a topic in this book, they will be identified in one of two ways:

(a) Free resources icon (🖺): These icons precede chapter boxed elements to indicate that additional material is available in the free resources. The chapter boxed elements that may have associated free resources include the following (Figure 1):

- Ethics & Issues
- How To
- Secure IT
- Technology @ Work

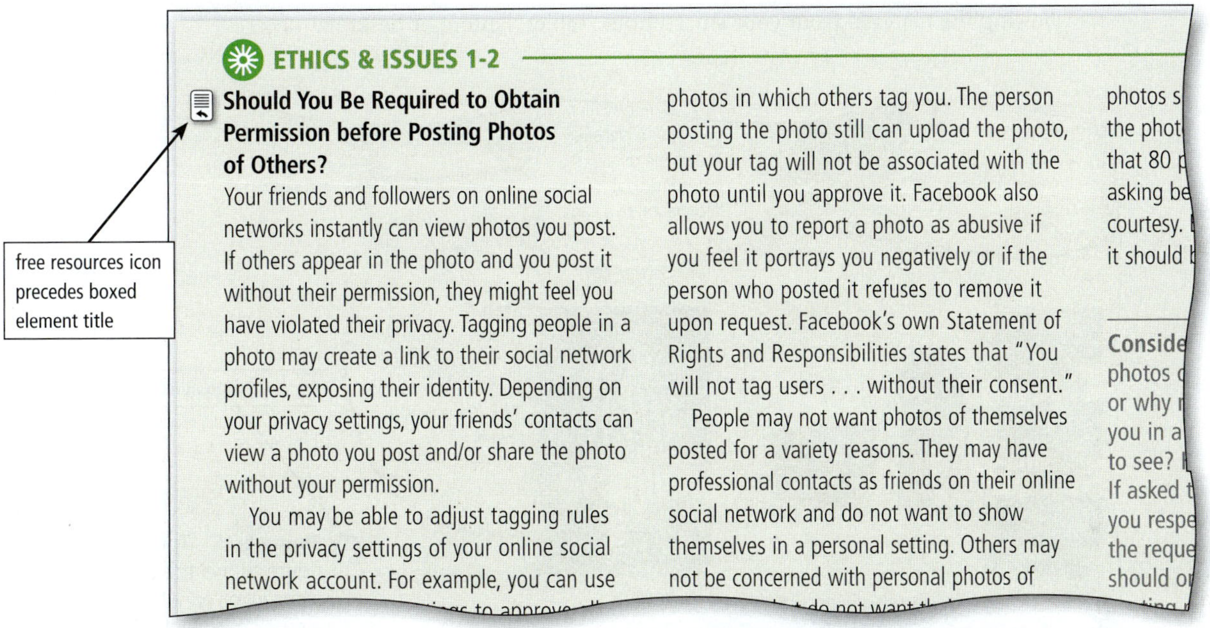

Figure 1   When you see the 🖺 icon to the left of a boxed element title or the phrase, it means you can find additional related online material in the free resources.

(b) **Discover More** reference: These references within the text and in the margins briefly identify the type of material you will find in the free resources. The Discover More references appear within the paragraphs of text in the chapter (Figure 2). The marginal elements that may have associated free resources include the following:

- High-Tech Talk
- Technology Innovator
- Technology Trend

🟠 BTW

Table of Boxed Elements
For a complete list of every print and online boxed element in this book, see the Table of Boxed Elements in the preface.

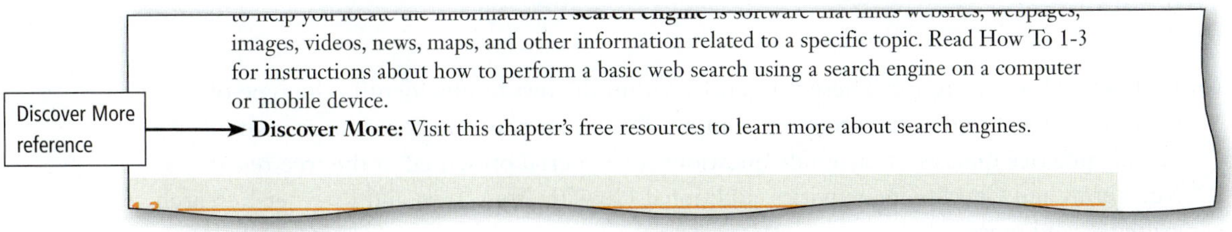

Figure 2   When you see the **Discover More** reference, it means you can find additional, related online content that will direct you either to material in the free resources or premium content.

Premium Content The premium content, which is available online, includes interactive activities, additional exercises, and other resources designed to enhance your learning experience, reinforce and test your knowledge of chapter concepts, or challenge you with additional assignments. When premium content is available for a topic in this book, it will be identified in one of two ways:

(a) Premium content icon ( ): These icons precede chapter figures and other elements to indicate that additional resources are available as premium content. The chapter elements with associated premium content include the following (Figure 3):

- Animation videos: View these animations to better understand some of the more complex figures in the book.
- Drag-and-drop activities: Practice these interactive activities to test your knowledge of a concept in a table or figure.
- Study Guide, Flash Cards, and Practice Test resources: Prepare for quizzes and exams by viewing the material from your smartphone, tablet, laptop, or desktop.

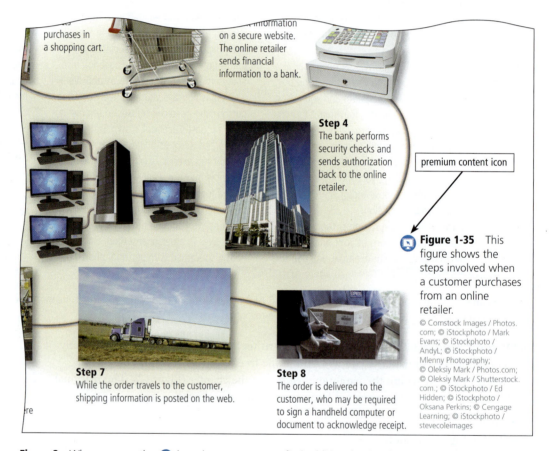

purchases in a shopping cart.

...information on a secure website. The online retailer sends financial information to a bank.

Step 4
The bank performs security checks and sends authorization back to the online retailer.

premium content icon

Figure 1-35 This figure shows the steps involved when a customer purchases from an online retailer.
© Comstock Images / Photos.com; © iStockphoto / Mark Evans; © iStockphoto / AndyL; © iStockphoto / Mlenny Photography; © Oleksiy Mark / Photos.com; © Oleksiy Mark / Shutterstock.com.; © iStockphoto / Ed Hidden; © iStockphoto / Oksana Perkins; © Cengage Learning; © iStockphoto / stevecoleimages

Step 7
While the order travels to the customer, shipping information is posted on the web.

Step 8
The order is delivered to the customer, who may be required to sign a handheld computer or document to acknowledge receipt.

Figure 3 When you see the icon, it means you can find additional, related online chapter resources in the premium content.

(b) **Discover More** reference: These references within the text briefly identify the type of material you will find in the premium content. Resources available as premium content include practice quizzes, study guide questions for material presented in the free resources, Key Terms and Checkpoint activities, additional How To: Your Turn and Internet Research exercises, and more.

Purchasing the Right Computer

As a student in a technology course, you might be thinking of purchasing a desktop, laptop, or tablet to help you with this course and future courses in your academic career. In addition to the information in this section, consider speaking with your instructors, as well as an academic advisor, to see if they have any specific recommendations for computers or mobile devices you might use in the courses you plan to take. If your academic institution has a store that sells computers, it also might have specific computer or mobile device recommendations, as well as a student discount program. Make sure the computer or mobile device you purchase is capable of running the software that you will need for your classes.

Step 1: Choose the Computer Type

Laptops, tablets, and desktops each serve a different purpose. It is important that you choose the type of computer best suited to your needs. This section briefly describes and identifies some of the pros and cons associated with each type of computer. See Chapter 3 for a more thorough discussion of computer types.

Laptops   A laptop is a thin, lightweight mobile computer with a screen in its lid and a keyboard in its base (Figure 4). Users who need or want to be able carry a computer from place to place may choose a laptop.

traditional laptop

ultrathin laptop

Figure 4   Two different types of laptops.
© Sergey Peterman / Shutterstock.com; © iStockphoto / Skip Odonnel; Source: Microsoft; Apple, Inc.

PROS

- Portable
- Uses less electricity than a desktop
- Contains a battery that can last at least several hours without being plugged in to an external power source
- Often more powerful than a tablet
- Contains several different types of ports
- All required components housed in a single unit (i.e., compact keyboard, touchpad, screen, speakers, etc.)
- Can support more types of external devices than tablets (i.e., full-sized keyboard, mouse, microphone, monitor, printer, scanner, webcam, speakers, etc.)
- Supports programs and apps specifically designed for desktops and laptops
- Can connect to a large monitor

CONS

- Might not be as powerful as high-end desktops
- May not support as much memory and hard drive space as desktops
- Contains fewer ports than desktops
- May support fewer external devices than desktops
- Not as easy for a user to upgrade or repair as desktops
- May not be as portable as tablets

Tablets   A tablet is a thin, lightweight mobile computer that has a touch screen (Figure 5). Users who do not need the power of a laptop but require a portable computer for basic tasks may choose a tablet.

Figure 5   One type of tablet.
© iStockphoto / franckreporter

PROS

- More portable than laptops
- Lightweight (most tablets weigh less than two pounds)
- Use less electricity than a desktop
- Battery life often is superior to laptops
- All required components housed in a single unit (touch screen, speakers, etc.)
- Can connect a removable keyboard
- Use thousands of free and fee-based apps
- Often are easier to use than desktops and laptops
- Built-in memory card slots can increase storage capacity

CONS

- Not as powerful as desktops and laptops
- Hardware cannot be upgraded
- Typically do not support the same types of apps as desktops and laptops
- Have limited multitasking capabilities
- More susceptible to damage because they frequently are moved from place to place
- Because a touch screen is the primary form of input, it may be difficult to enter large amounts of text on a tablet (unless an external keyboard is connected)
- Lack surface to rest wrists and arms, so ergonomic problems may develop

Desktops   A desktop is a computer designed to be in a stationary location, where all of its components fit on or under a desk or table (Figure 6). Users who may prefer desktops include those with basic home or office computing needs who do not require the portability of a mobile computer or those with high-end computing needs, such as 3-D gaming or HD video editing.

desktop with tower

all-in-one

Figure 6   Two different types of desktops.
© iStockphoto / Oleksiy Mark; Source: Microsoft; © iStockphoto / hocus-focus; Apple, Inc.

PROS

- Often more powerful than laptops and tablets
- Can connect to one or more large monitor(s)
- Contain several different types of ports or multiple duplicate ports
- Can accommodate more types of external devices than laptops and tablets (i.e., keyboard, mouse, microphone, monitor, printer, scanner, webcam, speakers, etc.)
- Often support more memory and hard drive capacity than laptops and tablets
- Support programs and apps specifically designed for desktops and laptops
- Relatively easy for a user to upgrade and repair

CONS

- Require several external, separate components, such as a keyboard, mouse, speakers, and sometimes the monitor
- High-end models can be more expensive than laptops and tablets
- Cannot run apps designed for mobile device operating systems, such as Android and iOS

Most students will find that a laptop or desktop is most suitable for their coursework or for gaming. In addition, they might choose a tablet to carry with them at other times because tablets are ideal for everyday tasks, such as searching the web, checking email messages, participating in video calls, and reading e-books.

Step 2: Choose the Operating System

An operating system is software (a program) that coordinates all the activities among computer components. Multiple operating systems exist for each type of device (Table 1). Deciding which operating system is best for you will be the next step in determining the specific brand of computer that ultimately meets your needs.

Certain courses may require specific applications (apps), and those applications may be available only on a specific operating system. For example, a course that teaches digital media might require an application that is available only for Mac OS. Table 2 illustrates the various categories of programs and apps. This section outlines the more common operating systems for each type of device. See Chapter 4 for a more thorough discussion of an operating system.

Table 1	Examples of Operating Systems by Category
Category	**Name**
Desktop	Windows
	OS X
	UNIX
	Linux
	Chrome OS
Mobile	Google Android
	Apple iOS
	Windows Phone

Table 2   Categories of Programs and Apps

Category	Sample Uses for Students
Communications	View course websites. Communicate via email with instructors and other students. Send and receive files. Facilitate and participate in online meetings with instructors and other students.
File, Disk, and System Management	Organize personal and school-related files. Copy and move files. Search for files.
Graphics and Media	Create digital media, such as images and movies. View multimedia course content, such as online lectures.
Personal Interest	Perform research using content from dictionaries, encyclopedias, etc. Learn through tutors and prepare for tests.
Productivity	Create research papers and other documents. Develop presentations to use in classes. Organize your academic and personal schedule.
Security	Protect your computer and schoolwork from viruses and other malicious software.

Laptops and Desktops   The two primary operating systems available on laptops and desktops are Windows (shown in Figure 7) and Mac OS (shown in Figure 8). While other operating systems, such as UNIX, Linux, and Chrome OS also are available, Windows and Mac OS are the most common. Some computers can run multiple operating systems. For example, Apple computers can run Windows and Linux in addition to Mac OS. Windows and Mac OS each offer a unique user experience; the best way to determine which one you are most comfortable with is to try using each one. Most stores that sell laptops and desktops will have some working models that you can evaluate. Make sure the operating system you decide to use also is capable of running the programs and apps required for your courses.

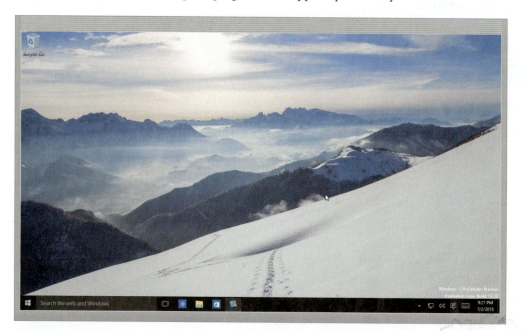

Figure 7   Windows operating system.
Source: Microsoft

Figure 8   Mac OS operating system.
Source: Apple, Inc.

Tablets   Tablets often include one of three operating systems: Android (Figure 9), iOS (Figure 10), or Windows (Figure 11). While Android and iOS are the most popular operating systems on tablets, the Windows operating system is increasing in popularity. Determine the types of apps you wish to use on the tablet and then determine which operating systems support those apps.

If you want your tablet to synchronize seamlessly with other computers and devices, such as a laptop, desktop, or smartphone, consider an operating system that is compatible with your other computer or device. For example, if you have an Android phone, you might prefer the Android operating system for your tablet. If you use an iPhone or iPod Touch, you might prefer the iOS operating system for your tablet.

Figure 9   Tablet running Android operating system.
© iStockphoto / PetkoDanov

Figure 10   Tablet running iOS operating system.
© iStockphoto / Hocus Focus Studio

Figure 11   Tablet running Windows operating system.
© Pieter Beens / Shutterstock.com

Step 3: Choose Configuration Options

The final step in choosing the best laptop, tablet, or desktop to meet your needs is to choose the specific configuration details. For example, you may have to choose the size of the display, amount of memory, storage capacity, and processor speed.

Display Screen Size   Display screens for computers are available in a variety of sizes (Figure 12). A laptop's screen typically can range from 11 to 17 inches, and a tablet's screen generally is between 7 and 12 inches. If you purchase a laptop or tablet, a smaller screen size will make the device lighter and more portable. For example, laptops with screens exceeding 15 inches typically are much heavier, which makes them less convenient to transport. Desktops often use a monitor as their display, with the size of screens on these monitors ranging from 13 inches to more than 30 inches.

If you primarily will be sending and receiving email messages, creating and editing documents using a word processing app, and browsing the web, a device with a smaller screen should meet your needs. If you require a larger screen to work with large documents or display multiple windows simultaneously, or if you want to experience less eyestrain with the contents appearing larger on the screen, consider a desktop or laptop display with a larger screen size. If you require touch functionality (and the operating system you plan to use supports it), purchase a screen that supports touch input. In addition, if you decide to purchase a laptop or desktop, you usually can connect a second monitor.

monitor display

laptop display

digital camera display

Figure 12   A variety of displays.
© cobalt88 / Shutterstock.com;
© Pawel Gaul / Photos.com

Memory   The amount of memory (RAM) installed in your laptop, tablet, or desktop will help determine the types of programs and apps that can run on the computer, as well as how many programs and apps can run simultaneously (Figure 13). If you are purchasing a laptop or desktop, review the system requirements for the programs and apps you plan to use, and make sure to purchase a computer with enough memory to meet those system requirements. For example, if the operating system you plan to use requires at least 4 GB (gigabytes) of memory, and you plan to use a word processing app that requires 4 GB of memory, you should purchase a laptop or desktop with at least 8 GB of memory. It is recommended that you purchase a computer with slightly more memory than you need at the present time. This enables you to use multiple programs and apps simultaneously and also accommodates programs and apps you might install and use at a later time.

Figure 13   Memory modules contain memory chips.
© TerryM / Shutterstock.com

Storage Capacity and Media   Laptops, tablets, desktops are available with various storage capacities. The higher the storage capacity, the more data and information you can keep on the computer or device. To determine the ideal storage capacity, add together the amount of storage space required for all the programs and apps you want to use. In addition, estimate the amount of space you might need to store the files you create. If you are planning to store digital media, such as audio, photos, and videos, make sure the storage device has sufficient space for those files as well. Try not to purchase a device with exactly the amount of storage space you anticipate needing. Always purchase more than you need so that you do not risk running out of space.

In addition to determining sufficient storage capacity for your needs, two main types of primary storage devices from which you may be able to choose include a hard disk (also called a hard drive) or an SSD (solid-state drive) (Figure 14). Hard disks use magnetic particles to store data, instructions, and information on one or more inflexible, circular platters. SSDs are flash memory storage devices that contain their own processors to manage their storage. Hard disks often are less expensive than SSDs and offer greater storage capacities. SSDs, however, are faster than hard disks and may be less susceptible to failure.

Figure 14   Two different types of storage devices.
© Andresr / Shutterstock.com; © roadk / Shutterstock.com

Processor Speed   If you are purchasing a laptop or desktop, you probably will have to determine the processor that will best meet your needs. Many different brands and models of processors are available (Figure 15). Review the system requirements for the programs and apps you want to run to determine the processor best suited to your needs. Because a variety of brands and models of processors exist, you may find it difficult to decide which one to purchase. When you are shopping for your laptop, tablet, or desktop, ask a sales associate to explain the differences among the various processors so that you can make an informed decision.

Step 4: Choose the Purchasing Option

You can purchase new computers and mobile devices in physical stores as well as from online retailers. Each purchasing option has advantages and disadvantages, and it is important to consider these before making a purchasing decision. If, after reading this section, you still do not have a strong preference to purchase from a physical store or an online retailer, compare costs from each for a computer with an identical or similar configuration.

Figure 15   Processor that might be found in a computer or device.
Courtesy of Intel Corporation

Physical Stores   A variety of computers and mobile devices are available for sale at physical stores. While physical stores offer the convenience of being able to shop for and bring home a computer or mobile device the same day, they have a limited inventory and available configuration options. Computers and mobile devices in retail stores are prebuilt and often cannot be customized at the store. For example, if you evaluate the various computers at a physical store and see a laptop you are considering, that laptop may be available in only one configuration. If you want to make changes to the hardware configuration (such as adding a larger hard drive), that would need to be done by a third party after you make the purchase. Some computer and mobile device manufacturers may void their warranty if a third party upgrades your computer or mobile device after the purchase has been made, so be sure to purchase a computer that adequately meets your needs.

Online Retailers Unlike physical stores, online retailers may offer greater configuration options for a computer or mobile device you are considering purchasing. For example, you may be able to completely customize a computer by choosing the exact processor, memory, and hard drive capacity. Online retailers also may offer prebuilt options, so consider the cost difference between purchasing a prebuilt computer and a customized computer with similar specifications. You may find that purchasing a prebuilt computer with a configuration slightly better than one you customized is less expensive. Prebuilt computers often may be less expensive because they are mass produced. If you purchase a computer from an online retailer, however, you will not be able to see the computer and evaluate it before purchase. In addition, it may take several days to several weeks before computers and mobile devices purchased from online retailers may arrive on your doorstep. If you receive the computer or mobile device and do not like it, returning or exchanging it may not be as easy as if you were to purchase it in a physical store.

✳ How To: Your Turn

The How To: Your Turn exercises present general guidelines for fundamental skills when using a computer or mobile device and then require that you determine how to apply these general guidelines to a specific program or situation.

Instructions: You often can complete tasks using technology in multiple ways. Figure out how to perform the tasks described in these exercises by using one or more resources available to you (such as a computer or mobile device, articles on the web or in print, online or program help, user guides, blogs, podcasts, videos, other individuals, trial and error, etc.). Summarize your 'how to' steps, along with the resource(s) used, in the format requested by your instructor (brief report, presentation, discussion, blog post, video, or other means).

1 **Get the Most out of Your Book**

Unlike many traditional textbooks, this book contains a variety of elements to help enrich your understanding of the concepts taught in the text. These elements include steps that teach you how to perform real-world tasks, current issues related to technology, and a variety of information to keep you secure while interacting with computers and mobile devices. The following steps guide you through the process of navigating this book and getting the most out of it.

a. Locate and read a How To box in Chapter 1 (or other chapter of your choice). How To boxes appear in shaded boxes with orange borders at the top and bottom. These boxes teach you how to perform real-world tasks that are related to the surrounding chapter content. Answer the question(s) at the bottom of the How To box.

b. Locate and read a Consider This box in Chapter 1 (or other chapter of your choice). Consider This boxes are identified by a green border at the top and bottom. These boxes contain common questions and answers that are related to the surrounding chapter content and often promote critical thinking.

c. Locate and read a Secure IT box in Chapter 1 (or other chapter of your choice). Secure IT boxes

appear in shaded boxes with orange borders at the top and bottom. These boxes contain information about security concerns and helpful safety and security tips that are related to the surrounding chapter content. Answer the question(s) at the bottom of the Secure IT box.

d. Locate and read an Ethics & Issues box in Chapter 1 (or other chapter of your choice). Ethics & Issues boxes appear in shaded boxes with orange borders at the top and bottom. These boxes contain information about current, relative ethical issues and present multiple sides of the issue. Answer the question(s) at the bottom of the Ethics & Issues box.

e. Locate and read a Mini Feature in Chapter 1 (or other chapter of your choice). Mini Features are one page in length and present interesting concepts that are related to the surrounding chapter text. Answer the question(s) at the bottom of the Mini Feature.

f. Locate and read a BTW element (BTW stands for "by the way"). BTW elements provide extra tidbits of information related to the chapter text and also may reference additional online content.

g. Locate and read an Internet Research element. These elements provide suggested search keywords to help you use a search engine to locate current information about the surrounding chapter text.

How To: Your Turn ✳

h. Locate and read the Technology @ Work box in Chapter 1 (or other chapter of your choice). Technology @ Work boxes are identified by purple borders at the top and bottom and provide information about how technology is used in various industries. Answer the question(s) at the bottom of the Technology @ Work box.

Exercises

1. What type of box or element described above is your favorite? Why? Which one is your least favorite? Why?
2. Describe ways that each type of box and element in the chapter can help enhance your understanding of the chapter contents.
3. Review the topics of the boxes in Chapter 1 (or other chapter of your choice). Which one is of most interest to you? Why?

2 **Access This Book's Free Resources**

This book's free resources contain a wealth of information that extends beyond what you learn by reading this book. The free resources also contain additional information about current technology developments and content required for those students majoring in the information technology or computer science fields.

You can access the free resources at the web address of www.cengagebrain.com. Once the book's free resources are displayed, select Chapter 1 to view the resources associated with that chapter. View the resources available with another chapter and notice the similarities between the types of content offered in Chapter 1 and the other chapter you chose.

Exercises

1. What exact steps did you take to access the free resources?
2. List and describe the different types of content present in the Chapter 1 free resources.

3. Do you feel the free resources will be useful to you and further enhance your understanding of computers and other technology? Why or why not?

3 **Sign Up for a Microsoft Account**

A Microsoft account provides access to resources to several Microsoft services. These services include access to resources, such as a free email account, cloud storage, a location to store information about your contacts, and an online calendar. You will need a Microsoft account to complete some of the exercises in this book. The following steps guide you through the process of signing up for a Microsoft account.

a. Run a browser and navigate to www.outlook.com.
b. Tap or click the link and then follow the on-screen instructions to sign up for a free Microsoft account.
c. Browse the resources available to you in your Microsoft account.
d. If assigned by your instructor, compose and send a new email message from your Microsoft account to your instructor stating that you have signed up for a Microsoft account successfully.
e. Add your instructor's contact information. Next, add contact information for at least three more people.
f. Add your birthday to the calendar.
g. Edit your Microsoft account profile to add more contact and work information.

Exercises

1. If necessary, navigate to and view your new outlook .com email account. What are some ways to prevent junk email messages using the mail settings? What is junk email?
2. What is OneDrive? How much space do you have available on OneDrive to post files?
3. How can you see yourself using the various features in your newly created Microsoft account?

✳ Internet Research

The Internet Research exercises broaden your understanding of chapter concepts by requiring that you search for information on the web.

Instructions: Use a search engine or another search tool to locate the information requested or answers to questions presented in the exercises. Describe your findings, along with the search term(s) you used and your web source(s), in the format requested by your instructor (brief report, presentation, discussion, blog post, video, or other means).

❶ Social Media

You likely have heard and seen the phrases, "Like us on Facebook" and "Follow us on Twitter." Facebook and Twitter are two websites that advertisers, organizations, celebrities, and many groups use to promote and share their products, causes, events, and interests. Millions of people have accounts on Facebook, Twitter, and many other websites known collectively as online social networks. You will learn about social media throughout this book and, in Chapter 1, will learn how to create Facebook and Twitter accounts. You then will view information on these websites and realize that social media can engage and connect the online social network community members effectively.

Research This: If you are signed in to your Facebook account, sign out. Run a browser and then navigate to www.facebook.com. What information is required to sign up for an account? Why does Facebook require a birthdate? Locate and then tap or click the About link. How many 'likes' does Facebook have? What is the content of the first post on this page? How many people 'liked' this first post, and how many people replied to it?

If you are signed in to your Twitter account, sign out. Navigate to www.twitter.com. Describe the contents of the cover photos. Tap or click the About link at the bottom of the page and read the information. What is the content of the three most recent Tweets?

❷ Search Skills

Searching in an E-Book

One advantage that e-books have over printed books is that you can search the text to locate specific content easily. To search within an e-book, locate its search box, often identified by a 'Search inside this book' (or similar) label. Type the word or phrase for which to search, and tap or click a search button. The search button usually contains the word Search or the word Go, or displays a magnifying glass icon. The reader will highlight or provide a list of occurrences where the search text appears within the e-book. You often can jump directly to the page where the word or phrase appears or tap or click buttons labeled Next or Previous (or displaying forward- and backward-pointing arrow icons) to navigate through the occurrences. Within the text, the key words appear highlighted.

A search box also may include options for narrowing down search results, such as limiting search results to a particular chapter. When you type a page number in a search box, some e-book readers will navigate to the location in the e-book corresponding to that page in the printed book.

Research This: Select any e-book to display on your computer or mobile device. Type a significant word from the title as your search text. Use the e-book reader's search feature to answer these questions: (1) Where on the screen, and in what format, does the e-book reader display search results? (2) What information do search results include to help you find the result you are seeking? (3) How do you navigate from one occurrence of the search term to the next? (3) How does the e-book display your search text within the book so that you can locate it easily?

If you are reading the *Discovering Computers* e-book, display it on your computer or mobile device. Enter appropriate search text into the search box for the *Discovering Computers* e-book reader to search for answers to each of these questions: (1) How many times does the word, Twitter, appear in Chapter 1? (2) Complete the sentence in Chapter 1 that begins, "Most e-book reader models have…" (3) What sentence contains the first occurrence of the word, laptop, in Chapter 1?

If you read both the *Discovering Computers* e-book and another e-book, compare the experience using both e-book readers. Which features are common to both? What differences did you notice?

❸ Security

The buyer's guide in this introductory chapter provides information you can use to purchase a laptop, tablet, or desktop. No matter which operating system you choose and how you configure the computer or device, you need to protect your investment from security risks. You will learn about these unwelcome intrusions, called malware, in Chapter 1 and throughout this book, but it is important to obtain malware protection when, or soon after, you purchase the computer or mobile device. You also should install the latest updates.

Research This: Visit a physical electronics store or view online retailers' websites to learn about software that helps prevent malware from infecting computers. Read the packaging or the product details or talk to employees to determine the names of three programs recommended or rated highly. What protections against Internet threats are offered? For example, do they safeguard your photos, music, and financial data, include updates and backup tasks, and offer parental controls? What is the cost, if any, of these programs and the updates? Do computer or mobile device manufacturers include this software with the original purchase? Which operating system is required? How much memory is required?

INTRODUCING TODAY'S TECHNOLOGIES:
Computers, Devices, and the Web

1

Technology provides access to the digital world around you.

"I use computers, mobile devices, and the web to do homework, look up information, check email, play games, post updates, talk to friends, upload photos, sync music, and so much more! I feel comfortable using technology. What more do I need to know?"

While you may be familiar with some of the content in this chapter, do you know how to . . .

- Use a touch screen?
- Configure social media privacy settings to prevent others from posting unauthorized photos of you?
- Ease eyestrain while working on a computer or mobile device?
- Protect your hearing when using earbuds or headphones?
- Back up computers and mobile devices?
- Perform a web search?
- Sync computers and mobile devices?
- Protect your computer from viruses and other malware?
- Shop safely online?
- Create a strong password?
- 'Like' the Discovering Computers page on Facebook and 'follow' it on Twitter?
- Connect to a wireless network?

In this chapter, you will discover how to perform these tasks along with much more information essential to this course. For additional content available that accompanies this chapter, visit the free resources and premium content. Refer to the Preface and the Intro chapter for information about how to access these and other additional instructor-assigned support materials.

© iStockPhoto / scanrail

✔ Objectives

After completing this chapter, you will be able to:

1 Differentiate among laptops, tablets, desktops, and servers

2 Describe the purpose and uses of smartphones, digital cameras, portable and digital media players, e-book readers, wearable devices, and game devices

3 Describe the relationship between data and information

4 Briefly explain various input options (keyboards, pointing devices, voice and video input, and scanners), output options (printers, displays, and speakers), and storage options (hard disks, solid-state drives, USB flash drives, memory cards, optical discs, and cloud storage)

5 Differentiate the web from the Internet, and describe the relationship among the web, webpages, websites, and web servers

6 Explain the purpose of a browser, a search engine, and an online social network

7 Briefly describe digital security risks associated with viruses and other malware, privacy, your health, and the environment

8 Differentiate between an operating system and applications

9 Differentiate between wired and wireless network technologies, and identify reasons individuals and businesses use networks

10 Discuss how society uses technology in education, government, finance, retail, entertainment, health care, science, travel, publishing, and manufacturing

11 Identify technology used by home users, small/home office users, mobile users, power users, and enterprise users

Today's Technology

In the course of a day, you may . . . complete a homework assignment and watch a streaming video using your laptop, flip through news headlines and make dinner reservations using your tablet, search for directions and the local weather forecast while listening to music on your smartphone, edit a video on a desktop computer, and share photos online from your digital camera with family and friends. These and many other technologies are an integral part of everyday life: at school, at home, and at work (Figure 1-1).

Technology can enable you to more efficiently and effectively access and search for information; share personal ideas, photos, and videos with friends, family, and others; communicate with and meet other people; manage finances; shop for goods and services; play games or access other sources of entertainment; keep your life and activities organized; and complete business activities. People who can accomplish these types of tasks using technology often are said to be tech savvy.

Because technology changes, you must keep up with the changes to remain digitally literate. *Digital literacy* involves having a current knowledge and understanding of computers, mobile devices, the web, and related technologies. This book presents the knowledge you need to be digitally literate today.

As you read this first chapter, keep in mind it is an overview. Most of the terms and concepts introduced in this chapter will be discussed in more depth later in the book.

Figure 1-1 People use a variety of computers, mobile devices, and apps everyday.

Computers

A **computer** is an electronic device, operating under the control of instructions stored in its own memory, that can accept data (*input*), process the data according to specified rules, produce information (*output*), and store the information for future use. Computers contain many electric, electronic, and mechanical components known as *hardware*.

Electronic components in computers process data using instructions, which are the steps that tell the computer how to perform a particular task. A collection of related instructions organized for a common purpose is referred to as software or a program. Using software, you can complete a variety of activities, such as search for information, type a paper, balance a budget, create a presentation, or play a game.

One popular category of computer is the personal computer. A *personal computer* (PC) is a computer that can perform all of its input, processing, output, and storage activities by itself and is intended to be used by one person at a time. Most personal computers today also can communicate with other computers and devices.

Types of personal computers include laptops, tablets, and desktops, with the first two sometimes called mobile computers. A *mobile computer* is a portable personal computer, designed so that a user can carry it from place to place. A *user* is anyone who interacts with a computer or mobile device, or utilizes the information it generates.

Discover More: Visit this chapter's free resources to learn more about electronic components and circuitry of a computer.

Laptops

A **laptop**, also called a *notebook computer*, is a thin, lightweight mobile computer with a screen in its lid and a keyboard in its base (Figure 1-2). Designed to fit on your lap and for easy transport, most laptops weigh up to 7 pounds (varying by manufacturer and specifications). A laptop that is less than one inch thick and weighs about three pounds or less sometimes is referred to as an ultrathin laptop. Most laptops can operate on batteries or a power supply or both.

screen

keyboard

hinges

Figure 1-2 A typical laptop has a keyboard in the base and a screen in the lid, with the lid attaching to the base with hinges.
© iStockphoto / Stephen Krow

Tablets

Usually smaller than a laptop but larger than a phone, a **tablet** is a thin, lighter-weight mobile computer that has a touch screen (read How To 1-1 for ways to interact with a touch screen). A popular style of tablet is the slate, which does not contain a physical keyboard (Figure 1-3). Like laptops, tablets run on batteries or a power supply or both; however, batteries in a tablet typically last longer than those in laptops.

Figure 1-3 A slate tablet.
© iStockphoto / franckreporter

⚙ HOW TO 1-1

Interact with a Touch Screen

You usually can interact with a touch screen using gestures. A *gesture* is a motion you make on a touch screen with the tip of one or more fingers or your hand. Touch screens are convenient because they do not require a separate device for input. Tablets and smartphones typically have touch screens.

The table below presents common ways to interact with a touch screen.

🖥 Touch Screen Gestures

Motion	Description	Common Uses
Tap	Quickly touch and release one finger one time	Activate a link (built-in connection) Press a button Run a program or app
Double-tap	Quickly touch and release one finger two times	Run a program or app Zoom in (show a smaller area on the screen, so that contents appear larger) at the location of the double-tap
Press and hold	Press and hold one finger to cause an action to occur, or until an action occurs	Display a shortcut menu (immediate access to allowable actions) Activate a mode enabling you to move an item with one finger to a new location
Drag, or *slide*	Press and hold one finger on an object and then move the finger to the new location	Move an item around the screen Scroll
Swipe	Press and hold one finger and then move the finger horizontally or vertically on the screen	Scroll Display a bar that contains commands on an edge of the screen
Stretch	Move two fingers apart	Zoom in (show a smaller area on the screen, so that contents appear larger)
Pinch	Move two fingers together	Zoom out (show a larger area on the screen, so that contents appear smaller)

✳ **Consider This:** In addition to the motions listed in the table, what other motions do you think a touch screen should support?

© Cengage Learning

✳ CONSIDER THIS

If a slate tablet has no keyboard, how do you type on it?

You can use your fingers to press keys on a keyboard that appears on the screen, called an *on-screen keyboard*, or you can purchase a separate physical keyboard that attaches to or wirelessly communicates with the tablet. You also may be able to speak into the tablet, and your spoken words will translate to typed text.

Internet Research

What is a virtual keyboard?

Search for: virtual keyboard

⚙ **BTW**

Desktop

The term, desktop, also sometimes is used to refer to an on-screen work area on laptops, tablets, and desktops.

Desktops and All-in-Ones

A **desktop**, or desktop computer, is a personal computer designed to be in a stationary location, where all of its components fit on or under a desk or table. On many desktops, the screen is housed in a display device (or simply display) that is separate from a tower, which is a case that contains the processing circuitry (Figure 1-4a). Another type of desktop called an **all-in-one** does not contain a tower and instead uses the same case to house the display and the processing circuitry (Figure 1-4b). Some desktops and all-in-ones have displays that support touch.

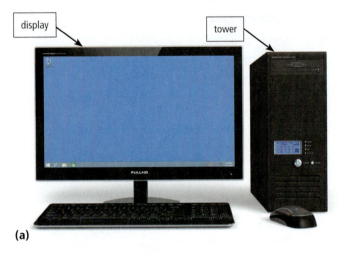

(a)   (b)   all-in-one   display   tower

Figure 1-4   Some desktops have a separate tower; all-in-ones do not.
© iStockphoto / Oleksiy Mark; Source: Microsoft; © iStockphoto / hocus-focus; Apple, Inc.

✳ **CONSIDER THIS**

Which type of computer — laptop, tablet, or desktop — is best?

It depends on your needs. Because laptops can be as powerful as the average desktop, more people today choose laptops over desktops so that they have the added benefit of portability. Tablets are ideal for those not needing the power of a laptop or for searching for information, communicating with others, and taking notes in lectures, at meetings, conferences, and other forums where a laptop is not practical. Desktops and all-in-ones often have larger displays than laptops or tablets, which make them well suited for developing software, editing large documents, or creating images and videos.

⚙ **BTW**

Online

When a computer or device connects to a network, it is said to be online.

Figure 1-5   A server provides services to other computers or devices on a network.
© iStockPhoto / GuidoVrola

Servers

A **server** is a computer dedicated to providing one or more services to other computers or devices on a network. A network is a collection of computers and devices connected together, often wirelessly. Services provided by servers include storing content and controlling access to hardware, software, and other resources on a network.

A server can support from two to several thousand connected computers and devices at the same time. Servers are available in a variety of sizes and types for both small and large business applications (Figure 1-5). Smaller applications, such as at home, sometimes use a high-end desktop as a server. Larger corporate, government, and web applications use powerful, expensive servers to support their daily operations.

Mobile and Game Devices

A *mobile device* is a computing device small enough to hold in your hand. Because of their reduced size, the screens on mobile devices are small — often between 3 and 5 inches.

Some mobile devices are Internet capable, meaning that they can connect to the Internet wirelessly. You often can exchange information between the Internet and a mobile device or between a computer or network and a mobile device. Popular types of mobile devices are smartphones, digital cameras, portable and digital media players, e-book readers, and wearable devices.

✹ CONSIDER THIS

Are mobile devices computers?

The mobile devices discussed in this section can be categorized as computers because they operate under the control of instructions stored in their own memory, can accept data, process the data according to specified rules, produce or display information, and store the information for future use.

Smartphones

A **smartphone** is an Internet-capable phone that usually also includes a calendar, an address book, a calculator, a notepad, games, and several other apps (which are programs on the smartphone). Other apps are available through an app store that typically is associated with the phone.

Smartphones typically communicate wirelessly with other devices or computers. With most smartphone models, you also can listen to music, take photos, and record videos.

Many smartphones have touch screens. Instead of or in addition to a touch screen, some smartphones have a keyboard that slides in and out from behind the phone (Figure 1-6). Others have built-in mini keyboards or keypads that contain both numbers and letters. Some are called a *phablet* because they combine the features of a smartphone with a tablet.

touch screen

slide out keyboard

🔵 **Figure 1-6**
Smartphones may have a touch screen and/or a slide out keyboard.
© iStockphoto / Moncherie;
© iStockPhoto / scanrail

Instead of calling someone's phone to talk, you can send messages to others by pressing images on an on-screen keyboard on the phone, keys on the phone's mini keyboard, or buttons on the phone's keypad. Four popular types of messages that you can send with smartphones include voice messages, text messages, picture messages, and video messages.

- A *voice mail message* is a short audio recording sent to or from a smartphone or other mobile device.
- A *text message* is a short note, typically fewer than 300 characters, sent to or from a smartphone or other mobile device.
- A *picture message* is a photo or other image, sometimes along with sound and text, sent to or from a smartphone or other mobile device.
- A *video message* is a short video clip, usually about 30 seconds, sent to or from a smartphone or other mobile device.

Read Ethics & Issues 1-1 to consider whether it should be legal to use a hands-free device, such as a smartphone, while driving.

✳ ETHICS & ISSUES 1-1

Should It Be Legal to Use a Hands-Free Device while Driving?
Your new vehicle includes a sophisticated hands-free system that enables you to connect a mobile device to the vehicle's sound system. In addition to making phone calls without holding your device, you also can use this technology to read and respond to email messages or to update your Facebook status using speech-to-text, which converts your spoken words to text. Is this technology safe to use?

The debate about hands-free device safety elicits different points of view from vehicle insurance companies, consumer safety groups, and the telecommunications industry. AAA (American Automobile Association) conducted a study to measure the mental effect of using hands-free devices while driving. The conclusions indicated that drivers using hands-free devices are distracted, miss visual clues, and have slower reaction times. The report also stated that 3000 fatalities occur each year due to the use of hands-free devices.

Critics say that using a hands-free device gives people a false sense of security. Others claim that drivers can be just as easily distracted if they are discussing business or emotional matters with passengers in the vehicle. Some states have outlawed any use of mobile phones while driving; others require drivers to use hands-free devices while driving. Lawmakers are attempting to regulate "distracted driving" caused by using hands-free devices. One issue that remains unclear is whether law enforcement has a right to look at a user's devices to determine whether they were used illegally.

Consider This: Do you think the government should be able to establish rules about hands-free device usage while driving? Why or why not? Do you believe you are distracted if you use hands-free devices while driving? Why or why not? Do you think auto manufacturers should continue to put hands-free device technology in vehicles? Why or why not?

Digital Cameras

A **digital camera** is a device that allows you to take photos and store the photographed images digitally (Figure 1-7). A smart digital camera also can communicate wirelessly with other devices and include apps similar to those on a smartphone. Many mobile computers and devices, such as tablets and smartphones, include at least one integrated digital camera.

Digital cameras typically allow you to review, and sometimes modify, images while they are in the camera. You also can transfer images from a digital camera to a computer or device, so that you can review, modify, share, organize, or print the images. Digital cameras often can connect to or communicate wirelessly with a computer, a Smart TV (discussed later in the chapter), a printer, or the Internet, enabling

Figure 1-7 With a digital camera, you can view photographed images immediately through a small screen on the camera to see if the photo is worth keeping.
Source: Samsung

⚡ Internet Research
What is a digital SLR camera?

Search for: digital slr camera

you to access the photos on the camera without using a cable. Some also can record videos. Many digital cameras also have built-in GPS (discussed later in this chapter), giving them the capability to record the exact location where a photo was taken and store these details with the photo.

Portable and Digital Media Players

A **portable media player** is a mobile device on which you can store, organize, and play or view digital media (Figure 1-8). *Digital media* includes music, photos, and videos. Thus, portable media players enable you to listen to music, view photos, and watch videos, movies, and television shows. With most, you transfer the digital media from a computer or the web, if the device is Internet capable, to the portable media player. Some enable you to play the media while it streams, that is, while it transfers to the player.

Portable media players usually require a set of *earbuds*, which are small speakers that rest inside each ear canal. Some portable media player models have a touch screen, while others have a pad that you operate with a thumb or finger, so that you can navigate through digital media, adjust volume, and customize settings. Some portable media players also offer a calendar, address book, games, and other apps (discussed later in this chapter).

Portable media players are a mobile type of digital media player. A *digital media player* or *streaming media player* is a device, typically used in a home, that streams digital media from a computer or network to a television, projector, or some other entertainment device.

Internet Research

What are popular digital media players?

Search for: digital media players

portable media player

earbuds

digital media player

Figure 1-8 Portable media players, such as the iPod shown here, typically include a set of earbuds. Digital media players stream media to a home entertainment device.
© iStockphoto / Sebastien Cote; © iStockPhoto / marvinh

E-Book Readers

An **e-book reader** (short for electronic book reader), or *e-reader*, is a mobile device that is used primarily for reading e-books (Figure 1-9). An *e-book*, or digital book, is an electronic version of a printed book, readable on computers and other digital devices. In addition to books, you typically can purchase and read other forms of digital media such as newspapers and magazines.

Most e-book reader models have a touch screen, and some are Internet capable. These devices usually are smaller than tablets but larger than smartphones.

Wearable Devices

A **wearable device** or *wearable* is a small, mobile computing consumer device designed to be worn (Figure 1-10). These devices often communicate with a mobile device or computer.

Wearable devices include activity trackers, smartwatches, and smartglasses. Activity trackers monitor heart rate, measure pulse, count steps, and track sleep patterns. In addition to keeping time, a smartwatch can communicate with a smart-phone to make and answer phone calls, read and send messages, access the web, play music, work with apps, such as fitness trackers and GPS, and more. With smartglasses, a user looks into an eyeglass-type device to view information or take photos and videos that are projected to a miniature screen in the user's field of vision.

Figure 1-9 An e-book reader.
© iStockPhoto

activity tracker

smartwatch

smartglasses

Figure 1-10 Activity trackers, smartwatches, and smartglasses are popular types of wearable devices.
© iStockPhoto / MileA;
© iStockPhoto / scanrail;
© iStockPhoto / ferrantraite

Game Devices

A **game console** is a mobile computing device designed for single-player or multiplayer video games. Gamers often connect the game console to a television so that they can view their gameplay on the television's screen (Figure 1-11). Many game console models are Internet capable and also allow you to listen to music and watch movies or view photos. Typically weighing between three and eleven pounds, the compact size of game consoles makes them easy to use at home, in the car, in a hotel, or any location that has an electrical outlet and a television screen.

A handheld game device is small enough to fit in one hand, making it more portable than the game console. Because of their reduced size, the screens are small — similar in size to some smartphone screens. Some handheld game device models are Internet capable and also can communicate wirelessly with other similar devices for multiplayer gaming.

game console handheld game device

Figure 1-11 Game consoles often connect to a television; handheld game devices contain a built-in screen.
© iStockPhoto / pagadesign; © iStockPhoto / AnthonyRosenberg

✳ **CONSIDER THIS**

Are digital cameras, portable media players, e-book readers, and handheld game devices becoming obsolete because more and more smartphones and tablets include their functionality?

Many smartphones and tablets enable you to take and store photos; store, organize, and play or view your digital media; read e-books; and play games. This trend of computers and devices with technologies that overlap, called **digital device convergence**, means that consumers may need fewer devices for the functionality that they require.

Still, consumers may purchase separate stand-alone devices (i.e., a separate digital camera, portable media player, etc.) for a variety of reasons. The stand-alone device (i.e., a digital camera) may have more features and functionality than the combined device offers (i.e., a smartphone). You might want to be able to use both devices at the same time; for example, you might send text messages on the phone while reading a book on an e-book reader. Or, you might want protection if your combined device (i.e., smartphone) breaks. For example, you still can listen to music on a portable media player if your smartphone becomes nonfunctional.

Mini Feature 1-1: Living Digitally — Gaming and Digital Home

Technology has made homes entertaining, efficient, and safe. Read Mini Feature 1-1 to learn how game devices provide entertainment and education, and home automation offers convenience and significant cost savings.

✵ MINI FEATURE 1-1

Gaming and Digital Home

Academic researchers developed the first video games in the 1950s as part of their studies of artificial intelligence and simulations, and their work was applied and expanded commercially to early home consoles and arcade games. The concept of home automation can be traced back to 1898 when Nikola Tesla invented the first remote control. The following sections describe how these two technologies are used today.

Gaming

Video gamers spend billions of dollars each year making the most of their downtime with game consoles and devices, with an estimated 5 billion people worldwide playing at least 45 hours per week. The popularity is due, in large part, to the social aspect of gathering families and friends to play together as a group or online with each other and those around the world. The wide variety of categories offers a gaming experience for practically everyone in genres such as adventure, education, fitness, puzzles, sports, role-playing, and simulation.

- **Obtaining Games:** Gamers have several options available for locating games. For tablets and smartphones, they can download games from an app store to a mobile computer or device. For game consoles, they can purchase or rent discs or other media that contain games; download or transfer them from online stores; or sign up for cloud services that stream or transfer games on demand.

- **Accessories and Input Techniques:** The more popular game consoles work with a wide variety of accessories and input techniques for directing movements and actions of on-screen players and objects. They include gamepads, voice commands, and fitness accessories, some of which are shown here. Although many games are played using a controller, several systems operate by allowing the player to be the controller.

© iStockphoto / Florea Marius Catalin; © iStockphoto / Brandon Alms; © iStockphoto / Lee Pettet; © iStockphoto / Craig Veltri; © Courtesy of DDR Game

Home Automation

New home builders and existing homeowners are integrating features that automate a wide variety of tasks, save time and money, and enhance the overall at-home environment.

- **Lighting:** Controlling lighting is one of the more common uses of technology in the home. Remotes turn light fixtures on and off, and motion sensors turn on lights when a car or a visitor approaches the driveway or walkway.

- **Thermostats:** Programmable thermostats adjust to seasonal needs and can be set to control temperatures in individual rooms. Homeowners can use their smartphones to monitor heating and cooling systems, adjust temperatures, and manage energy consumption.

- **Appliances**: Smart appliances, such as dishwashers, can be programmed to run at nonpeak electrical times. Coffeemakers can turn on at set times and shut off if an overheating coffeepot has been left on accidentally. Refrigerators can track expiration dates and create shopping lists.

- **Security:** Security systems can detect break-ins at doors and heat from fires, and they can send text and email messages to alert a homeowner when someone has entered or left the home. Surveillance cameras keep a watchful eye on the premises and interior rooms; homeowners can view the images on televisions and computers within the house or on a webpage when they are away from home, as shown in the figure.

© DavidEwingPhotography / Shutterstock.com; © Poulsons Photography / Shutterstock.com; © Anthony Berenyi / Shutterstock.com

- **Remotes:** Many people are turning to using their smartphones and tablets to control all the devices in the room. Users enjoy the convenience of customizing apps to operate their television, DVR, and security system and to perform other functions anywhere in the home.

Discover More: Visit this chapter's free resources to learn more about game genres, game controllers, remotes, programmable thermostats, smart appliances, security systems, and vacuum systems.

© iStockphoto / Christian J. Stewart; © Mmaxer / Shutterstock. com; © iStockphoto / Nastco; © ESPN; © Cengage Learning

✵ Consider This: How has your life become more efficient, safe, and enjoyable by using home automation and entertainment features? What are the advantages of playing games, and do they outweigh the disadvantages?

Data and Information

Computers process data (input) into information (output) and often store the data and resulting information for future use. *Data* is a collection of unprocessed items, which can include text, numbers, images, audio, and video. *Information* conveys meaning to users. Both business and home users can make well-informed decisions because they have instant access to information from anywhere in the world.

Many daily activities either involve the use of or depend on information from a computer. For example, as shown in Figure 1-12, computers process several data items to print information in the form of a cash register receipt.

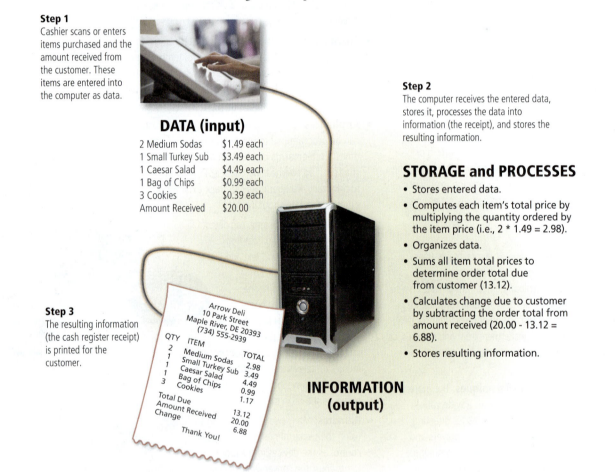

Step 1
Cashier scans or enters items purchased and the amount received from the customer. These items are entered into the computer as data.

DATA (input)

2 Medium Sodas	$1.49 each
1 Small Turkey Sub	$3.49 each
1 Caesar Salad	$4.49 each
1 Bag of Chips	$0.99 each
3 Cookies	$0.39 each
Amount Received	$20.00

Step 2
The computer receives the entered data, stores it, processes the data into information (the receipt), and stores the resulting information.

STORAGE and PROCESSES

- Stores entered data.
- Computes each item's total price by multiplying the quantity ordered by the item price (i.e., 2 * 1.49 = 2.98).
- Organizes data.
- Sums all item total prices to determine order total due from customer (13.12).
- Calculates change due to customer by subtracting the order total from amount received (20.00 - 13.12 = 6.88).
- Stores resulting information.

Step 3
The resulting information (the cash register receipt) is printed for the customer.

Arrow Deli
10 Park Street
Maple River, DE 20393
(734) 555-2939

QTY	ITEM	TOTAL
2	Medium Sodas	2.98
1	Small Turkey Sub	3.49
1	Caesar Salad	4.49
1	Bag of Chips	0.99
3	Cookies	1.17

Total Due 13.12
Amount Received 20.00
Change 6.88

Thank You!

INFORMATION (output)

Figure 1-12 A computer processes data into information. In this simplified example, the item ordered, item price, quantity ordered, and amount received all represent data (input). The computer processes the data to produce the cash register receipt (information, or output).
© Cengage Learning; © iStockphoto / Norman Chan; © bikeriderlondon / Shutterstock

BTW

Mobile Computer Input
If you prefer a full-sized keyboard to a laptop's keyboard or a tablet's on-screen keyboard, you can use a full-sized keyboard with your mobile computer. Likewise, if you prefer using a mouse instead of a touchpad, you can use a mouse with your mobile computer.

CONSIDER THIS ——————

Can you give another example of data and its corresponding information?
Your name, address, term, course names, course sections, course grades, and course credits all represent data that is processed to generate your semester grade report. Other information on the grade report includes results of calculations such as total semester hours, grade point average, and total credits.

Input

Users have a variety of input options for entering data into a computer, many of which involve using an input device. An **input device** is any hardware component that allows you to enter data and instructions into a computer or mobile device. The following sections discuss common input methods.

Keyboards   A *keyboard* contains keys you press to enter data and instructions into a computer or mobile device (Figure 1-13). All desktop keyboards have a typing area that includes letters of the alphabet, numbers, punctuation marks, and other basic keys. Some users prefer a wireless keyboard because it eliminates the clutter of a cord.

Keyboards for desktops contain more keys than keyboards on mobile computers and devices. To provide the same functionality as a desktop keyboard, many of the keys on mobile computers and devices serve two or three purposes. On a laptop, for example, you often use the same keys to type numbers and to show various areas on a screen, switching a key's purpose by pressing a separate key first.

Instead of a physical keyboard, users also can enter data via an on-screen keyboard or a virtual keyboard, which is a keyboard that projects from a device to a flat surface.

desktop keyboard

laptop keyboard

Figure 1-13 Users have a variety of options for entering typed text.
© skyfotostock / Shutterstock.com;
© Africa Studio / Shutterstock.com;
© iStockphoto /
kycstudio; © iStockphoto /
MorePixels; Courtesy of Virtek, Inc.

on-screen keyboard   mini keyboard   virtual keyboard

Pointing Devices   A pointing device is an input device that allows a user to control a small symbol on a screen, called the pointer. Desktops typically use a mouse as their pointing device, and laptops use a touchpad (Figure 1-14).

A *mouse* is a pointing device that fits under the palm of your hand comfortably. With the mouse, you control movement of the pointer and send instructions to the computer or mobile device. Table 1-1 identifies some of the common mouse operations. Like keyboards, some users prefer working with a wireless mouse.

A *touchpad* is a small, flat, rectangular pointing device that is sensitive to pressure and motion. To control the pointer with a touchpad, slide your fingertip across the surface of the pad. On most touchpads, you also can tap the pad's surface to imitate mouse operations, such as clicking.

Figure 1-14 A mouse and a touchpad.
© iStockphoto / PhotoTalk;
© iStockphoto / Michael Bodmann

mouse

touchpad

Table 1-1   Mouse Operations

Operation	Description	Common Uses
Point	Move the mouse until the pointer is positioned on the item of choice.	Position the pointer on the screen.
Click	Press and release the primary mouse button, which usually is the left mouse button.	Select or deselect items on the screen or start a program or feature.
Right-click	Press and release the secondary mouse button, which usually is the right mouse button.	Display a shortcut menu.
Double-click	Quickly press and release the primary mouse button twice without moving the mouse.	Start a program or program feature.
Drag	Point to an item, hold down the primary mouse button, move the item to the desired location on the screen, and then release the mouse button.	Move an object from one location to another or draw pictures.

Voice and Video Input Some mobile devices and computers enable you to speak data instructions using voice input and to capture live full-motion images using video input. With your smartphone, for example, you may be able to use your voice to send a text message, schedule an appointment, and dial a phone number. Or, you may opt for video calling instead of a voice phone call, so that you and the person you called can see each other as you chat on a computer or mobile device. As in this example, video input usually works in conjunction with voice input. For voice input, you use a microphone, and for video input you use a webcam (Figure 1-15).

A *microphone* is an input device that enables you to speak into a computer or mobile device. Many computers and most mobile devices contain built-in microphones. You also can talk into a *headset*, which contains both a microphone and a speaker. Many headsets can communicate wirelessly with the computer or mobile device. A *webcam* is a digital video (DV) camera that allows you to capture video and usually audio input for your computer or mobile device.

Figure 1-15 You can speak instructions into a microphone or wireless headset and capture live video on a webcam for a video call.
© iStockphoto / Stephen Krow; © iStockphoto / pierrephoto; © iStockphoto / Suprijono Suharjoto

Figure 1-16 A scanner.
© iStockphoto / Edgaras Marozas

Scanners A *scanner* is a light-sensing input device that converts printed text and images into a form the computer can process (Figure 1-16). A popular type of scanner works in a manner similar to a copy machine, except that instead of creating a paper copy of the document or photo, it stores the scanned document or photo electronically.

Output

Users have a variety of output options to convey text, graphics, audio, and video — many of which involve using an output device. An **output device** is any hardware component that conveys information from a computer or mobile device to one or more people. The following sections discuss common output methods.

Printers A **printer** is an output device that produces text and graphics on a physical medium, such as paper or other material (Figure 1-17). Printed content sometimes is referred to as a *hard copy* or *printout*. Most printers today print text and graphics in both black-and-white and color on a variety of paper types with many capable of printing lab-quality photos. A variety of printers support wireless printing, where a computer or other device communicates wirelessly with the printer.

A *3-D printer* can print solid objects, such as clothing, prosthetics, eyewear, implants, toys, parts, prototypes, and more. 3-D printers use a plastic substance that prints in layers to create a 3-D (three-dimensional) model.

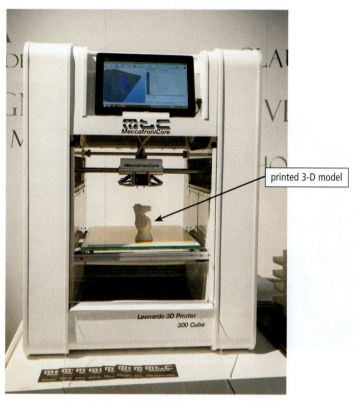

printed photo

printed 3-D model

Figure 1-17 A printer can produce a variety of printed output including photos and 3-D solid objects.
Courtesy of Epson America, Inc.; © iStockPhoto / Stefano Tinti

Displays A display is an output device that visually conveys text, graphics, and video information. Displays consist of a screen and the components that produce the information on the screen. The display for a desktop typically is a monitor, which is a separate, physical device. Mobile computers and devices typically integrate the display in their same physical case (Figure 1-18). Some displays have touch screens.

Home users sometimes use a digital television or a Smart TV as a display. A *Smart TV* is an Internet-enabled high-definition television (HDTV) from which you can use the Internet to watch video, listen to the radio, play games, and communicate with others — all while watching a television show.

smartphone display

digital camera display

tablet display

laptop display

monitor display

Figure 1-18 Displays vary depending on the computer or mobile device.
© iStockphoto / Sebastien Cote; © David Lentz / Photos.com; © Dmitry Rukhlenko / Photos.com; © Mrallen / Dreamstime.com; © Pakhnyushcha / Shutterstock.com

What can you do to ease eyestrain while using a computer or mobile device?
Position the display about 20 degrees below eye level. Clean the screen regularly. Blink your eyes every five seconds. Adjust the room lighting. Face into an open space beyond the screen. Use larger fonts or zoom the display. Take an eye break every 30 minutes. If you wear glasses, ask your doctor about computer glasses.

headphones

Figure 1-19 In a crowded environment where speakers are not practical, users can wear headphones to hear music, voice, and other sounds.
© iStockphoto / Photo_Alto

Speakers, Earbuds, and Headphones

Speakers allow you to hear audio, that is, music, voice, and other sounds. Most personal computers and mobile devices have a small internal speaker. Many users attach higher-quality speakers to their computers and mobile devices, including game consoles.

So that only you can hear sound, you can listen through earbuds (shown earlier in this chapter in Figure 1-8) or headphones, which cover or are placed outside of the ear (Figure 1-19). Both earbuds and headphones usually include noise-cancelling technology to reduce the interference of sounds from the surrounding environment. To eliminate the clutter of cords, users can opt for wireless speakers or wireless headphones. Read How To 1-2 to learn how to protect your hearing when using earbuds or headphones.

✳ **HOW TO 1-2**

Protect Your Hearing when Using Earbuds or Headphones
Using earbuds and headphones improperly can lead to permanent hearing loss. The following tips describe some ways to protect your hearing when using earbuds or headphones:

• If people standing next to you can hear the sound being transmitted through the earbuds or headphones you are wearing, decrease the volume until they no longer can hear it. The quieter the sounds, the less damage you will incur.

• If you intend to listen to music through earbuds or headphones for hours at a time, consider listening at only 30 percent maximum volume. Listening for extended periods of time at a high volume may be unsafe for your ears.

• Consider using a high-quality set of headphones. These headphones reduce your risk of developing hearing loss because the sound quality often is better and does not require you to turn up the volume as loud. Also, their design is better, allowing a closer fit and thus

reducing the necessary volume required for optimal listening.

• Consider using a set of earbuds or headphones that reduce outside noise. When the earbuds or headphones eliminate the external noise effectively, they can reduce the volume level needed. The lower the volume levels, the less potential hearing damage.

✳ **Consider This:** Do you prefer earbuds or headphones? Why? Do you think you turn the volume up too loud while listening to music through earbuds or headphones?

🌀 **Internet Research**

What types of headphones are available?

Search for: headphone reviews

Memory and Storage

Memory consists of electronic components that store instructions waiting to be executed and the data needed by those instructions. Although some forms of memory are permanent, most memory keeps data and instructions temporarily, which means its contents are erased when the computer is shut off.

Storage, by contrast, holds data, instructions, and information for future use. For example, computers can store hundreds or millions of student names and addresses permanently.

A computer keeps data, instructions, and information on **storage media**. Examples of local storage media includes hard disks, solid-state drives, USB (universal serial bus) flash drives, memory cards, and optical discs. The amount of storage for each type of storage media varies, but hard disks, solid-state drives, and optical discs usually hold more than USB flash drives and memory cards. Some storage media are portable, meaning you can remove the medium from one computer and carry it to another computer.

A **storage device** records (writes) and/or retrieves (reads) items to and from storage media. Storage devices often also function as a source of input and output because they transfer items from storage to memory and vice versa. Drives and readers/writers, which are types of storage devices, accept a specific kind of storage media. For example, a DVD drive (storage device) accepts a DVD (storage media).

Discover More: Visit this chapter's free resources to learn more about media storage capacity.

Hard Disks A *hard disk* is a storage device that contains one or more inflexible, circular platters that use magnetic particles to store data, instructions, and information. The entire device is enclosed in an airtight, sealed case to protect it from contamination. Laptops and desktops often contain at least one hard disk that is mounted inside the computer's case (Figure 1-20).

BTW
Disk vs. Disc
Disk is the term used to describe hard disks and other magnetic media, and disc is the term used to describe CDs, DVDs, and other optical media.

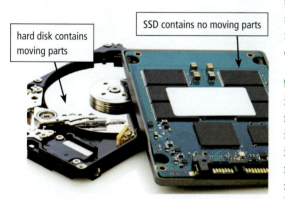

hard disk contains moving parts

SSD contains no moving parts

hard disk is positioned in base of laptop

Figure 1-21 A solid-state drive (SSD) is about the same size as a laptop hard disk.
© iStockphoto / Ludovit Repko

Solid-State Drives A *solid-state drive* (SSD) is a storage device that typically uses flash memory to store data, instructions, and information. Flash memory contains no moving parts, making it more durable and shock resistant than other types of media. For this reason, some manufacturers are using SSDs instead of hard disks in their laptops, tablets, and desktops (Figure 1-21).

Figure 1-20 A hard disk mounted inside a laptop's case.
© iStockphoto / Brian Balster

CONSIDER THIS

What is an external hard drive?
An external hard drive is a separate, portable, freestanding hard disk or SSD that usually connect to the computer with a cable (Figure 1-22). As with an internal hard disk or SSD, the entire external hard drive is enclosed in an airtight, sealed case.

external hard drive connected to laptop

Figure 1-22 A external hard drive is a separate, freestanding storage device.
© iStockphoto / murat sarica

BTW
Hard Drives
The term **hard drive** is used to collectively refer to hard disks and SSDs.

Figure 1-23 You insert a USB flash drive in a USB port on a computer.
© Pakhnyushcha / Shutterstock.com

USB Flash Drives A *USB flash drive* is a portable flash memory storage device that you plug in a USB port, which is a special, easily accessible opening on a computer or mobile device (Figure 1-23). USB flash drives are convenient for mobile users because they are small and lightweight enough to be transported on a keychain or in a pocket.

Memory Cards A *memory card* is removable flash memory, usually no bigger than 1.5 inches in height or width, that you insert in and remove from a slot in a computer, mobile device, or card reader/writer (Figure 1-24). With a card reader/writer, you can transfer the stored items, such as digital photos, from a memory card to a computer or printer that does not have a built-in card slot.

Figure 1-24
Computers and mobile devices use a variety of styles of memory cards to store documents, photos, and other items.
© Verisakeet / Fotolia;
© Sonar / Fotolia; Courtesy of Mark Frydenberg;
© uwimages / Fotolia

memory card in computer

memory card in digital camera

memory card in phone

memory card in card reader/writer, which is attached to computer

☀ **CONSIDER THIS**

What is the general use for each type of local storage media?
Hard disks and SSDs store software and all types of user files. A *file* is a named collection of stored data, instructions, or information and can contain text, images, audio, and video. Memory cards and USB flash drives store files you intend to transport from one location to another, such as a homework assignment or photos. Optical discs generally store software, photos, movies, and music.

Figure 1-25 You can insert a DVD in a DVD drive on a computer.
© iStockphoto / Hanquan Chen

Optical Discs An *optical disc* is a type of storage media that consists of a flat, round, portable metal disc made of metal, plastic, and lacquer that is written and read by a laser. CDs (compact discs) and DVDs (digital versatile discs) are two types of optical discs (Figure 1-25).

Cloud Storage Instead of storing data, instructions, and information locally on a hard drive or other media, some users opt for cloud storage. **Cloud storage** is an Internet service that provides remote storage to computer users. For example, Figure 1-26 shows JustCloud, which provides cloud storage solutions to home and business users.

Types of services offered by cloud storage providers vary. Some provide storage for specific types of media, such as photos, whereas others store any content and provide backup services. A **backup** is a duplicate of content on a storage medium that you can use in case the original is lost, damaged, or destroyed. Read Secure IT 1-1 for suggestions for backing up your computers and mobile devices.

Figure 1-26 JustCloud is an example of a website that provides cloud storage solutions to home and business users.
Source: JustCloud.com

☀ SECURE IT 1-1

Backing Up Computers and Mobile Devices

Power outages, hardware failure, theft, and many other factors can cause loss of data, instructions, or information on a computer or mobile device. To protect against loss, you should back up the contents of storage media regularly. Backing up can provide peace of mind and save hours of work attempting to recover important material in the event of a mishap.

A backup plan for laptop and desktop computers could include the following:

- Use a backup program, either included with your computer's operating system or one that you purchased separately, to copy the contents of your entire hard drive to a separate device.
- Regularly copy music, photos, videos, documents, and other important items to an external hard drive, a USB flash drive, or a DVD.
- Subscribe to a cloud storage provider.
- Schedule your files to be backed up regularly.

Backup plans for mobile devices are less specific. Apps for backing up your smartphone or tablet's content are available. You also can back up a mobile device to your computer's hard drive using synchronization software that runs on your computer (synchronization software is discussed later in this chapter). Some mobile device manufacturers, such as Apple, provide cloud storage solutions to owners of their devices. Other services allow subscribers to use another computer as a backup storage location. Overall, the best advice is to back up often using a variety of methods.

☀ **Consider This:** Do you back up files regularly? If not, why not? What would you do if you had no backup and then discovered that your computer or mobile device had failed?

cloud storage provider

Courtesy of Western Digital Corporation; © iStockphoto / Stephen Krow; © Cengage Learning

✔ **NOW YOU SHOULD KNOW**

Be sure you understand the material presented in the sections titled Today's Technology, Computers, Mobile and Game Devices, and Data and Information, as it relates to the chapter objectives.

Now you should know . . .

- Which type of computer might be suited to your needs (Objective 1)
- Why you would use a smartphone, digital camera, portable or digital media player, e-book reader, or wearable device, and which game software/apps you find interesting (Objective 2)
- How to recognize the difference between data and information (Objective 3)
- When you might use the various methods of input, output, and storage (Objective 4)

Discover More: Visit this chapter's premium content for practice quiz opportunities.

The Web

The World Wide Web (or web, for short) is a global library of information available to anyone connected to the Internet. The **Internet** is a worldwide collection of computer networks that connects millions of businesses, government agencies, educational institutions, and individuals (Figure 1-27).

❉ **CONSIDER THIS**

How do I access the Internet?

Businesses, called Internet service providers (ISPs), offer users and organizations access to the Internet free or for a fee. By subscribing to an ISP, you can connect to the Internet through your computers and mobile devices.

Figure 1-27 The Internet is the largest computer network, connecting millions of computers and devices around the world.

✳ CONSIDER THIS

Are the web and Internet the same?
No. The Internet provides more than three billion home and business users around the world access to a variety of services. The World Wide Web is one of the widely used services of the Internet. Other popular services include email, instant messaging, VoIP, and FTP (all discussed later in this chapter).

People around the world access the web to accomplish the following types of online tasks:

- Search for information
- Conduct research
- Communicate with and meet other people
- Share information, photos, and videos with others
- Access news, weather, and sports
- Participate in online training
- Shop for goods and services
- Play games with others
- Download or listen to music
- Watch videos
- Download or read books
- Make reservations

 BTW

Downloading
Downloading is the process of transferring content from a server on the Internet to a computer or mobile device.

The **web** consists of a worldwide collection of electronic documents. Each electronic document on the web is called a **webpage**, which can contain text, graphics, audio, and video (Figure 1-28). A **website** is a collection of related webpages, which are stored on a web server. A **web server** is a computer that delivers requested webpages to your computer or mobile device.

Webpages often contain links. A *link*, short for *hyperlink*, is a built-in connection to other documents, graphics, audio files, videos, webpages, or websites. To activate an item associated with a link, you tap or click the link. In Figure 1-27, for example, tapping or clicking the audio link connects to a live radio show so that you can hear the broadcast. A text link often changes color after you tap or click it to remind you visually that you previously have visited the webpage or downloaded the content associated with the link.

Links allow you to obtain information in a nonlinear way. That is, instead of accessing topics in a specified order, you move directly to a topic of interest. Some people use the phrase *surfing the web* to refer to the activity of using links to explore the web.

A **browser** is software that enables users with an Internet connection to access and view webpages on a computer or mobile device. Some widely used browsers include Internet Explorer, Firefox, Safari, Edge, and Google Chrome. Read How To 1 in the Succeeding in this Course chapter at the beginning of this book for instructions about using a browser to display a webpage on a computer or mobile device.

Figure 1-28 Webpages, such as the one shown here, can display text, graphics, audio, and video on a computer or mobile device. Pointing to a link on the screen typically changes the shape of the pointer to a small hand with a pointing index finger.
Source: WTMJ

Web Searching

A primary reason that people use the web is to search for specific information, including text, photos, music, and videos. The first step in successful searching is to identify the main idea or concept in the topic about which you are seeking information. Determine any synonyms, alternate spellings, or variant word forms for the topic. Then, use a search engine, such as Google, to help you locate the information. A **search engine** is software that finds websites, webpages, images, videos, news, maps, and other information related to a specific topic. Read How To 1-3 for instructions about how to perform a basic web search using a search engine on a computer or mobile device.

Discover More: Visit this chapter's free resources to learn more about search engines.

✺ HOW TO 1-3

Perform a Basic Web Search
The following steps describe how to use a search engine on a computer or mobile device to perform a basic web search:

1. Run a browser. (For instructions on running programs and apps, see How To 1-4 later in this chapter.)
2. Display the search engine's webpage on the screen by entering its web address in the address bar. For example, you could type google.com to access the Google search engine, bing.com to access the

Bing search engine, or yahoo.com to access the Yahoo! search engine.

3. Tap or click the Search box and then type the desired search text in the Search box. The more descriptive the search text, the easier it will be to locate the desired search results. As the figure shows, the search engine may provide search text suggestions as you type search text in the Search box.
4. To display search results based on your typed search text, press the ENTER key or tap or click the Search button. To display search results based on one of the suggestions provided

by the search engine, tap or click the desired search text suggestion.

5. Scroll through the search results and then tap or click a search result to display the corresponding webpage.
6. To return to the search results, tap or click the Back button in your browser or on your mobile device, which typically looks like a left-pointing arrow.

✺ **Consider This:** What search text would you enter to locate the admission criteria for your school?

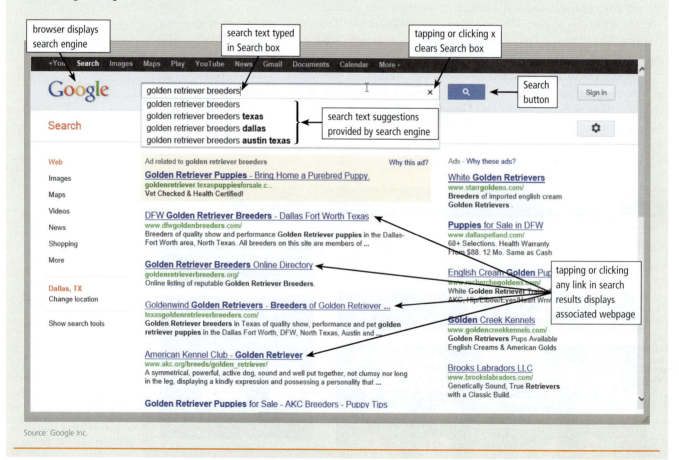

Source: Google Inc.

Online Social Networks

An **online social network**, also called a *social networking site*, is a website that encourages members in its online community to share their interests, ideas, stories, photos, music, and videos with other registered users (Figure 1-29). Popular online social networks include Facebook, Twitter, and LinkedIn.

Some online social networks have no specialized audience; others are more focused. A photo sharing site, for example, is a specific type of online social network that allows users to create an online photo album and store and share their digital photos. Similarly, a video sharing site is a type of online social network that enables users to store and share their personal videos. Read Ethics & Issues 1-2 to consider whether you should be required to obtain permission before posting photos of others.

BTW
Technology Innovators
Discover More: Visit this chapter's free resources to learn more about Facebook and its founder, Mark Zuckerberg, and Twitter.

Figure 1-29 When Facebook users 'like' this Discovering Computers Facebook page, posts from the Discovering Computers page will appear on their own personal pages. As a student in this class, you should 'like' the Discovering Computers page so that you easily can keep up to date with relevant technology changes and events in the computing industry. If you do not have a Facebook account, use a search engine to search for the text, discovering computers facebook, to display the page in a browser.
Source: Facebook

ETHICS & ISSUES 1-2

Should You Be Required to Obtain Permission before Posting Photos of Others?

Your friends and followers on online social networks instantly can view photos you post. If others appear in the photo and you post it without their permission, they might feel you have violated their privacy. Tagging people in a photo may create a link to their social network profiles, exposing their identity. Depending on your privacy settings, your friends' contacts can view a photo you post and/or share the photo without your permission.

You may be able to adjust tagging rules in the privacy settings of your online social network account. For example, you can use Facebook's privacy settings to approve all photos in which others tag you. The person posting the photo still can upload the photo, but your tag will not be associated with the photo until you approve it. Facebook also allows you to report a photo as abusive if you feel it portrays you negatively or if the person who posted it refuses to remove it upon request. Facebook's own Statement of Rights and Responsibilities states that "You will not tag users . . . without their consent."

People may not want photos of themselves posted for a variety reasons. They may have professional contacts as friends on their online social network and do not want to show themselves in a personal setting. Others may not be concerned with personal photos of themselves but do not want their children's photos shared online. Or, they simply may find the photo unflattering. A poll by Sophos stated that 80 percent of respondents consider asking before posting a photo to be common courtesy. Eight percent of respondents felt that it should be illegal to do so.

Consider This: Is it ever acceptable to post photos of others without permission? Why or why not? Has someone posted or tagged you in a photo that you did not want others to see? How did you handle the situation? If asked to remove a photo or tag, would you respect the person's feelings and honor the request? What restrictions and policies should online social networks have about posting photos of others?

✳ **CONSIDER THIS**

How do Facebook, Twitter, and LinkedIn differ?
With Facebook, you share messages, interests, activities, events, photos, and other personal information — called posts — with family and friends. You also can 'like' pages of celebrities, companies, products, etc., so that posts from others who like the same items will appear along with your other activities on Facebook. With Twitter, you 'follow' people, companies, and organizations in which you have an interest. Twitter enables you to stay current with the daily activities of those you are following via their Tweets, which are short posts (messages) that Twitter users broadcast for all their followers.

On LinkedIn, you share professional interests, education, and employment history, and add colleagues or coworkers to your list of contacts. You can include recommendations from people who know you professionally. Many employers post jobs using LinkedIn and consider information in your profile as your online resume.

Internet Communications

As mentioned earlier, the web is only one of the services on the Internet. Other services on the Internet facilitate communications among users, including the following:

- Email allows you to send messages to and receive messages and files from other users via a computer network.
- With messaging services, you can have a real-time typed conversation with another connected user (real-time means that both of you are online at the same time).
- VoIP (Voice over Internet Protocol) enables users to speak to other users over the Internet (discussed further in later chapters).
- With FTP (File Transfer Protocol), users can transfer items to and from other computers on the Internet (discussed further in later chapters).

Digital Security and Privacy

People rely on computers to create, store, and manage their information. To safeguard this information, it is important that users protect their computers and mobile devices. Users also should be aware of health risks and environmental issues associated with using computers and mobile devices.

Viruses and Other Malware

Malware, short for malicious software, is software that acts without a user's knowledge and deliberately alters the computer's or mobile device's operations. Examples of malware include viruses, worms, trojan horses, rootkits, spyware, adware, and zombies. Each of these types of malware attacks your computer or mobile device differently. Some are harmless pranks that temporarily freeze, play sounds, or display messages on your computer or mobile device. Others destroy or corrupt data, instructions, and information stored on the infected computer or mobile device. If you notice any unusual changes in the performance of your computer or mobile device, it may be infected with malware. Read Secure IT 1-2 for ways to protect computers from viruses and other malware.

Privacy

Nearly every life event is stored in a computer somewhere . . . in medical records, credit reports, tax records, etc. In many instances, where personal and confidential records were not protected properly, individuals have found their privacy violated and identities stolen. Some techniques you can use to protect yourself from identity theft include shredding financial documents before discarding them, never tapping or clicking links in unsolicited email messages, and enrolling in a credit monitoring service.

Adults, teens, and children around the world are using online social networks to share their photos, videos, journals, music, and other personal information publicly. Some of these unsuspecting, innocent computer users have fallen victim to crimes committed by dangerous strangers.

SECURE IT 1-2

Protection from Viruses and Other Malware

It is impossible to ensure a virus or malware never will attack a computer, but you can take steps to protect your computer by following these practices:

- **Use virus protection software.** Install a reputable antivirus program and then scan the entire computer to be certain it is free of viruses and other malware. Update the antivirus program and the virus signatures (known specific patterns of viruses) regularly.

- **Use a firewall.** Set up a hardware firewall or install a software firewall that protects your network's resources from outside intrusions.

- **Be suspicious of all unsolicited email and text messages.** Never open an email message unless you are expecting it, *and* it is from a trusted source. When in doubt, ask the sender to confirm the message is

legitimate before you open it. Be especially cautious when deciding whether to tap or click links in email and text messages or to open attachments.

- **Disconnect your computer from the Internet.** If you do not need Internet access, disconnect the computer from the Internet. Some security experts recommend disconnecting from the computer network before opening email attachments.

- **Download software with caution.** Download programs or apps only from websites you trust, especially those with music and video sharing software.

- **Close spyware windows.** If you suspect a pop-up window (a rectangular area that suddenly appears on your screen) may be spyware, close the window. Never tap or click an Agree or OK button in a suspicious window.

- **Before using any removable media, scan it for malware.** Follow this procedure even for shrink-wrapped software from major developers. Some commercial software has been infected and distributed to unsuspecting users. Never start a computer with removable media inserted in the computer unless you are certain the media are uninfected.

- **Keep current.** Install the latest updates for your computer software. Stay informed about new virus alerts and virus hoaxes.

- **Back up regularly.** In the event your computer becomes unusable due to a virus attack or other malware, you will be able to restore operations if you have a clean (uninfected) backup.

Consider This: What precautions do you take to prevent viruses and other malware from infecting your computer? What new steps will you take to attempt to protect your computer?

Protect yourself and your dependents from these criminals by being cautious in email messages and on websites. For example, do not share information that would allow others to identify or locate you, and do not disclose identification numbers, user names, passwords, or other personal security details. A user name is a unique combination of characters, such as letters of the alphabet or numbers, that identifies one specific user. A password is a private combination of characters associated with a user name. Read Secure IT 1-3 for tips on creating strong passwords.

SECURE IT 1-3

Creating Strong Passwords

A good password is easy for you to remember but difficult for criminals and password-breaking software to guess. Use these guidelines to create effective, strong passwords:

- **Personal information:** Avoid using any part of your first or last name, your family members' or pets' names, phone number, street address, license plate number, Social Security number, or birth date.

- **Length:** Use at least eight characters.

- **Difficulty:** Use a variety of uppercase and lowercase letters, numbers, punctuation marks, and symbols. Select characters located on different parts of the keyboard, not the ones you commonly use or that are adjacent to each other. Criminals often use software that converts common words to symbols, so their program might generate the passwords

GoToSleep and Go2Sleep as possibilities to guess.

- **Modify:** Change your password frequently, at least every three months.

- **Variation:** Do not use the same password for all websites you access. Once criminals have stolen a password, they attempt to use that password for other accounts they find on your computer or mobile device, especially banking websites.

- **Passphrase:** A passphrase, which is similar to a password, consists of several words separated by spaces. Security experts recommend misspelling a few of the words and adding several numerals. For example, the phrase, "Create a strong password," could become the passphrase, "Creaet a strang pasword42."

- **Common sequences:** Avoid numbers or letters in easily recognized patterns, such

as "asdfjkl;," "12345678," "09870987," or "abcdefg." Also, do not spell words backwards, use common abbreviations, or repeat strings of letters or numbers.

- **Manage:** Do not keep your passwords in your wallet, on a sheet of paper near your computer, or in a text file on your computer or mobile device. Memorize all of your passwords, or store them securely using a password management app on your computer or mobile device. Additional information about password management software is provided in Secure IT 5-3 in Chapter 5.

- **Test:** Use online tools to evaluate password strength.

Consider This: How strong are your passwords? How will you modify your passwords using some of these guidelines?

Health Concerns

Prolonged or improper computer and mobile device use can lead to injuries or disorders of the hands, wrists, elbows, eyes, neck, and back. Computer and mobile device users can protect themselves from these health risks through proper workplace design, good posture while at the computer, and appropriately spaced work breaks.

With the growing use of earbuds and headphones, some users are experiencing hearing loss. Ways to protect your hearing when using these devices were presented in How To 1-2 earlier in this chapter.

Two behavioral health risks are technology addiction and technology overload. Technology addiction occurs when someone becomes obsessed with using technology. Individuals suffering from technology overload feel distressed when deprived of computers and mobile devices. Once recognized, both technology addiction and technology overload are treatable disorders.

Environmental Issues

Manufacturing processes for computers and mobile devices along with *e-waste*, or discarded computers and mobile devices, are depleting natural resources and polluting the environment. When computers and mobile devices are stored in basements or other locations, disposed of in landfills, or burned in incinerators, they can release toxic materials and potentially dangerous levels of lead, mercury, and flame retardants.

Green computing involves reducing the electricity consumed and environmental waste generated when using a computer. Strategies that support green computing include recycling, using energy efficient hardware and energy saving features, regulating manufacturing processes, extending the life of computers, and immediately donating or properly disposing of replaced computers. When you purchase a new computer, some retailers offer to dispose of your old computer properly.

Discover More: Visit this book's premium content for the Internet Research: Green Computing exercise for each chapter in this book.

🟠 **BTW**

Technology Innovators
Discover More: Visit this chapter's free resources to learn about Microsoft and its founder, Bill Gates, Apple, and its cofounders, Steve Jobs and Steve Wozniak.

✳ **CONSIDER THIS**

How can you contribute to green computing?
Some habits you can alter that will help reduce the environmental impact of computing include the following:

1. Do not leave a computer or device running overnight.
2. Turn off your monitor, printer, and other devices when you are not using them.
3. Use energy efficient hardware.
4. Use paperless methods to communicate.
5. Recycle paper and buy recycled paper.
6. Recycle toner, computers, mobile devices, printers, and other devices.
7. Telecommute.
8. Use videoconferencing and VoIP for meetings.

Programs and Apps

Software, also called a **program**, consists of a series of related instructions, organized for a common purpose, that tells the computer what tasks to perform and how to perform them.

Two categories of software are system software and application software (or applications). System software consists of the programs that control or maintain the operations of the computer and its devices. Operating systems are a widely recognized example of system software. Other types of system software, sometimes called tools, enable you to perform maintenance-type tasks usually related to managing devices, media, and programs used by computers and mobile devices. The next sections discuss operating systems and applications.

Operating Systems

An *operating system* is a set of programs that coordinates all the activities among computer or mobile device hardware. It provides a means for users to communicate with the computer or mobile device and other software. Many of today's computers and mobile devices use a version of Microsoft's Windows, Apple's Mac OS, Apple's iOS, or Google's Android (Figure 1-30).

To use an application, your computer or mobile device must be running an operating system.

Applications

An **application** (or **app** for short) consists of programs designed to make users more productive and/or assist them with personal tasks. Browsers, discussed in an earlier section, are an example of an application that enables users with an Internet connection to access and view webpages. Table 1-2 identifies the categories of applications with samples of ones commonly used in each category.

Figure 1-30 Shown here are the Mac OS and Windows operating systems for laptops and desktops and the Android and iOS operating systems for smartphones. You interact with these operating system interfaces by tapping or clicking their icons or tiles.
Sources: Apple Inc.; Apple Inc.; Google Inc.; Microsoft.

Table 1-2 Categories of Applications

Category	Sample Applications	Sample Uses
Productivity	Word Processing	Create letters, reports, and other documents.
	Presentation	Create visual aids for presentations.
	Schedule and Contact Management	Organize appointments and contact lists.
	Personal Finance	Balance checkbook, pay bills, and track income and expenses.
Graphics and Media	Photo Editing	Modify digital photos, i.e., crop, remove red-eye, etc.
	Video and Audio Editing	Modify recorded movie clips, add music, etc.
	Media Player	View images, listen to audio/music, watch videos.
Personal Interest	Travel, Mapping, and Navigation	View maps, obtain route directions, locate points of interest.
	Reference	Look up material in dictionaries, encyclopedias, etc.
	Educational	Learn through tutors and prepare for tests.
	Entertainment	Receive entertainment news alerts, check movie times and reviews, play games.

(Continued)

Table 1-2 *Continued*

Category	Sample Applications	Sample Uses
Communications	Browser	Access and view webpages.
	Email	Send and receive messages.
	VoIP	Speak to other users over the Internet.
	FTP	Transfer items to and from other computers on the Internet.
Security	Antivirus	Protect a computer against viruses.
	Personal Firewall	Detect and protect against unauthorized intrusions.
	Spyware, Adware, and other Malware Removers	Detect and delete spyware, adware, and other malware.
File, System, and Disk Management	File Manager	Display and organize files on storage media.
	Search	Locate files and other items on storage media.
	Image Viewer	Display, copy, and print contents of graphics files.
	Screen Saver	Shows moving image or blank screen if no keyboard or mouse activity occurs.

© Cengage Learning; Courtesy of NCH Software; Source: Apple Inc.; Source: Google Inc.; Courtesy of AVG Technologies; Source: Microsoft

Discover More: Visit this chapter's free resources for an expanded Categories of Applications table.

Applications include programs stored on a computer, as well as those on a mobile device or delivered to your device over the Internet.

- A *desktop app* is an application stored on a computer.
- A *web app* is an application stored on a web server that you access through a browser.
- A *mobile app* is an application you download from a mobile device's app store or other location on the Internet to a smartphone or other mobile device.

Some applications are available as both a web app and a mobile app. In this case, you typically can sync (or match) the data and activity between the web app and the mobile app, which is discussed later in this chapter.

Discover More: Visit this book's premium content for the How To: Your Turn – App Adventure exercise for each chapter in this book.

Installing and Running Programs

Installing a program is the process of setting up the program to work with a computer or mobile device, printer, and/or other hardware. When you buy a computer or mobile device, it usually has some software, such as an operating system, preinstalled on its internal media so that you can use the computer or mobile device the first time you turn it on.

Installed operating systems often include applications such as a browser, media player, and calculator. To use additional desktop apps on a computer, you usually need to install the software. Mobile apps typically install automatically after you transfer the app's files to your mobile device from its website. You usually do not need to install web apps before you can run them.

Once installed, you run a program so that you can interact with it. When you instruct a computer or mobile device to run a program, the computer or mobile device *loads* it, which means the program's instructions are copied from storage to memory. Once in memory, the computer or mobile device can carry out, or execute, the instructions in the program so that you can use it.

You interact with a program through its user interface. The *user interface* controls how you enter data and instructions and how information is displayed on the screen. Often, you work with icons or tiles (shown in Figure 1-30 earlier in the chapter), which are miniature images that link to programs, media, documents, or other objects. Read How To 1-4 for instructions about locating, installing, and running programs and mobile apps.

✸ HOW TO 1-4

Locate, Install, and Run Programs and Mobile Apps
The following steps describe how to locate, install, and run programs and mobile apps:

Locate the Program or Mobile App

- Locate the program or mobile app to install. Programs are available from retail stores, websites, and from other online services such as Apple's App Store or Google Play. Mobile apps are available from your device's app store.

Download and/or Install the Program or Mobile App

- If you are installing a program on your computer from physical media such as a CD or DVD, insert the media in your computer. If the installation process does not start automatically, locate the installation program on the media and then double-tap or double-click the installation program.

- If the program or mobile app is available from a website or online store, download the application to your computer or mobile device. Once the download is complete, if the installation process does not start automatically, locate and then double-tap or double-click the downloaded file to begin the installation.

Run the Program or Mobile App

- You have various options for running a program or mobile app:

  - If you are using a computer, tap or click the program's tile or double-tap or double-click the program's icon in the desktop.

  - Display a list of all programs and apps on your computer or mobile device and then tap or click the icon representing the program to run (some computers may require you to double-tap or double-click the icon).

  - Use the search feature in the operating system to locate the newly installed program or app and then tap or click the search result to run the program or app.

✸ **Consider This:** After installing a mobile app, where are some locations you might look to find the new app's icon or tile?

✸ CONSIDER THIS

How do you know if a program will run on your computer?
When you buy a computer, you can find a list of the computer's specifications on the box, the manufacturer's website, or the order summary. Similarly, when you buy software, the box or the product's website will list specifications and minimum requirements for memory, speed, and more. Your computer's specifications should be the same as or greater than the software specifications. Ensure the software will run on your computer before making a purchase, because many retailers will not allow you to return software.

Developing Programs and Apps

A *software developer*, sometimes called a developer or programmer, is someone who develops programs and apps or writes the instructions that direct the computer or mobile device to process data into information. When writing instructions, a developer must be sure the program or app works properly so that the computer or mobile device generates the desired results. Complex programs can require thousands to millions of instructions.

Software developers use a programming language or application development tool to create programs and apps. Popular programming languages include C++, Java, JavaScript, Visual C#, and Visual Basic. Figure 1-31 shows some of the Visual Basic instructions a software developer may write to create a simple payroll program.

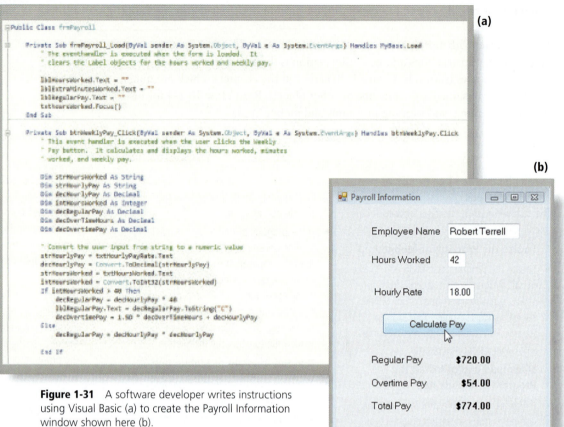

Figure 1-31 A software developer writes instructions using Visual Basic (a) to create the Payroll Information window shown here (b).
Source: © Cengage Learning

✓ NOW YOU SHOULD KNOW

Be sure you understand the material presented in the sections titled The Web, Digital Security and Privacy, and Programs and Apps, as it relates to the chapter objectives.
Now you should know . . .

- Why webpages use links (Objective 5)
- How to perform a basic web search (Objective 6)
- What risks you are exposed to as a result of your technology use and how you can minimize those risks (Objective 7)
- How to recognize an operating system and which programs and apps you might find useful (Objective 8)

Discover More: Visit this chapter's premium content for practice quiz opportunities.

Communications and Networks

Communications technologies are everywhere. Many require that you subscribe to an Internet service provider. With others, an organization such as a business or school provides communications services to employees, students, or customers.

In the course of a day, it is likely you use, or use information generated by, one or more of the communications technologies in Table 1-3.

Table 1-3 Uses of Communications Technologies

Type	Brief Description
Chat rooms	Real-time typed conversation among two or more people on a computers or mobile devices connected to a network
Email	Transmission of messages and files via a computer network
Fax	Transmission and receipt of documents over telephone lines
FTP	Permits users to transfer files to and from servers on the Internet
GPS	Navigation system that assists users with determining their location, ascertaining directions, and more
Instant messaging	Real-time typed conversation with another connected user where you also can exchange photos, videos, and other content
Internet	Worldwide collection of networks that links millions of businesses, government agencies, educational institutions, and individuals
Newsgroups	Online areas in which users have written discussions about a particular subject
RSS	Specification that enables web content to be distributed to subscribers
Videoconference	Real-time meeting between two or more geographically separated people who use a network to transmit audio and video
Voice mail	Allows users to leave a voice message for one or more people
VoIP	Conversation that takes place over the Internet using a telephone connected to a computer, mobile device, or other device
Wireless Internet access points	Enables users with computers and mobile devices to connect to the Internet wirelessly
Wireless messaging services	Send and receive wireless messages to and from smartphones, mobile phones, handheld game devices, and other mobile devices using text messaging and picture/video messaging

© Cengage Learning

Wired and Wireless Communications

Computer communications describes a process in which two or more computers or devices transfer (send and receive) data, instructions, and information over transmission media via a communications device(s). A **communications device** is hardware capable of transferring items from computers and devices to transmission media and vice versa. Examples of communications devices are modems, wireless access points, and routers. As shown in Figure 1-32, some communications involve cables and wires; others are sent wirelessly through the air.

Wired communications often use some form of telephone wiring, coaxial cable, or fiber-optic cables to send communications signals. The typically are used within buildings or underground between buildings.

Because it is more convenient than installing wires and cables, many users opt for wireless communications, which sends signals through the air or space. Examples of wireless communications technologies include Wi-Fi, Bluetooth, and cellular radio, which are discussed below:

- **Wi-Fi** uses radio signals to provide high-speed Internet and network connections to computers and devices capable of communicating via Wi-Fi.

combination modem/router/wireless access point

Internet

modem

Figure 1-32 Modems, wireless access points, and routers are examples of communications devices that enable communications between computers/mobile devices and the Internet. Notice that some computers and devices communicate via wires, and others communicate wirelessly.

© Cengage Learning; © iStockphoto / Petar Chernaev; © iStockphoto / Oleksiy Mark; © Patryk Kosmider / Shutterstock.com; © Pablo Eder / Shutterstock.com; © iStockphoto / 123render.; Source: Microsoft; © iStockphoto / aquarius83men

Most computers and many mobile devices, such as smartphones and portable media players, can connect to a Wi-Fi network.

- **Bluetooth** uses short-range radio signals to enable Bluetooth-enabled computers and devices to communicate with each other. For example, Bluetooth headsets allow you to connect a Bluetooth-enabled phone to a headset wirelessly.
- Cellular radio uses the cellular network to enable high-speed Internet connections to devices with built-in compatible technology, such as smartphones. Cellular network providers use the categories 3G, 4G, and 5G to denote cellular transmission speeds, with 5G being the fastest.

Wi-Fi and Bluetooth are both hot spot technologies. A *hot spot* is a wireless network that provides Internet connections to mobile computers and devices. Wi-Fi hot spots provide wireless network connections to users in public locations, such as airports and airplanes, train stations, hotels, convention centers, schools, campgrounds, marinas, shopping malls, bookstores, libraries, restaurants, coffee shops, and more. Bluetooth hot spots provide location-based services, such as sending coupons or menus, to users whose Bluetooth-enabled devices enter the coverage range.

Discover More: Visit this chapter's free resources to learn more about cellular transmissions.

Networks

A **network** is a collection of computers and devices connected together, often wirelessly, via communications devices and transmission media. Networks allow computers to share *resources*, such as hardware, software, data, and information. Sharing resources saves time and money. In many networks, one or more computers act as a server. The server controls access to the resources on a network. The other computers on the network, each called a client, request resources from the server (Figure 1-33). The major differences between the server and client computers are that the server typically has more power, more storage space, and expanded communications capabilities.

Many homes and most businesses and schools network their computers and devices. Most allow users to connect their computers wirelessly to the network. Users often are required to sign in to, or log on, a network, which means they enter a user name and password (or other credentials) to access the network and its resources. Read Ethics & Issues 1-3 to consider issues associated with unsecured networks.

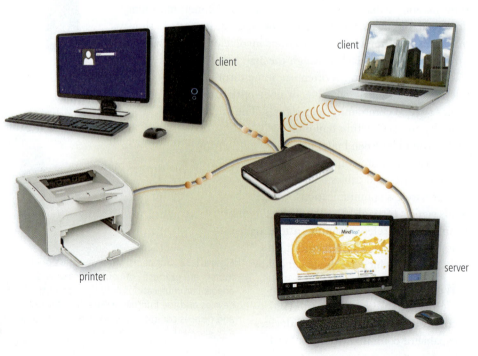

Figure 1-33   A server manages the resources on a network, and clients access the resources on the server. This network enables three separate computers to share the same printer, one wirelessly.

© iStockphoto / sweetym; Source: Microsoft;
© iStockphoto / Skip Odonnell; © Jennifer Nickert
/ Shutterstock.com; © Serg64 / Shutterstock.com;
© Oleksiy Mark / Shutterstock.com; Source: Cengage
Learning; © Cengage Learning

✹ ETHICS & ISSUES 1-3

Would You Connect to an Unsecured Network?

If you turn on your laptop and notice that you can connect to a nearby home or business's wireless network and access the Internet without a password, for free, you may find yourself in an ethical dilemma. Because they do not know how to secure a wireless network, many home and business users leave their networks open for use by anybody in their signal's range. Experts estimate that up to 35 percent of wireless connections are unsecured, leaving them open to hackers. (A hacker is someone who accesses a computer or network illegally.)

Criminals sometimes use unsecured wireless networks to cover up technology-related crimes. Others may steal connections to avoid the costs of Internet service. In other cases, a user's laptop or mobile device may connect automatically to an open wireless network, without the user's authorization or knowledge. If you are using an unsecured wireless network, hackers may be able to capture your passwords, hijack your accounts, or send spam or a virus.

The Electronic Communications Privacy Act (ECPA) states that it is not illegal "to intercept or access an electronic communication made through an electronic communication system that is configured so that such electronic communication is readily accessible to the general public." It is unclear whether this law refers to an unsecured home network or whether it pertains only to public hot spots, such as restaurants and libraries. Some lawmakers even support punishing those who leave their networks unsecured.

Consider This: Would you use your neighbor's unsecured wireless home network without permission? Why or why not? What would you do if you found out that someone was using your wireless home network without your permission? How should legal authorities address such abuse? What punishment should violators receive? Should those leaving their networks unsecured receive punishment, too? Why or why not?

Home Networks   Home networks save the home user money and provide many conveniences. Each networked computer or mobile device on a home network has the following capabilities:

- Connect to the Internet at the same time
- Share a single high-speed Internet connection
- Access photos, music, videos, and other content on computers and devices throughout the house
- Share devices such as a printer, scanner, or external hard drive
- Play multiplayer games with players on other computers and mobile devices in the house
- Connect game consoles to the Internet
- Subscribe to and use VoIP
- Interact with other devices in a smart home (such as thermostats, lighting controls, etc.)

Home networks usually are small, existing within a single structure, and use wireless technologies such as those shown previously in Figure 1-30. You do not need extensive knowledge of networks to set up a home network. You will need a communications device, such as a router, which usually includes setup instructions. Most operating systems also provide tools enabling you easily to connect all the computers and devices in your house.

Business Networks   Business and school networks can be small, such as in a room or building, or widespread, connecting computers and devices across a city, country, or the globe. Some reasons that businesses network their computers and devices together include the following:

- **Facilitate communications.** Using a network, employees and customers communicate efficiently and easily via email, messaging services, blogs, online social networks, video calls, online meetings, videoconferencing, VoIP, and more.
- **Share hardware.** In a networked environment, each computer on the network can access the hardware on the network, instead of providing each user with the same piece of hardware. For example, computer and mobile device users can access the laser printer on the network, as they need it.
- **Share data, information, and software.** In a networked environment, any authorized computer user can access data, information, and software stored on other computers on the network. A large company, for example, might have a database of customer information that any authorized user can access.

Mini Feature 1-2: Staying in Sync

If you use multiple computers and mobile devices throughout the day, keeping track of common files may be difficult. Read Mini Feature 1-2 to learn how to keep your computers and devices in sync with each other.

MINI FEATURE 1-2

Staying in Sync

Assume that each morning you begin the day by checking your appointment calendar on your home or office computer. That same calendar appears on your smartphone, so that you can view your schedule throughout the day. If you add, change, or delete appointments using the smartphone, however, you may need to update the calendar on your computer to reflect these edits. When you **synchronize**, or **sync**, computers and mobile devices, you match the files in two or more locations with each other, as shown in the figure below. Along with appointments, other commonly synced files from a smartphone are photos, email messages, music, apps, contacts, calendars, and ringtones.

Syncing can be a one-way or a two-way process. With a one-way sync, also called mirroring, you add, change, or delete files in a destination location, called the *target*, without altering the same files in the original location, called the *source*. For example, you may have a large collection of music stored on your home computer (the source), and you often copy some of these songs to your mobile device (the target). If you add or delete songs from your computer, you also will want to add or change these songs on your mobile device. If, however, you add or change the songs on your mobile device, you would not want to make these changes on your computer.

In two-way sync, any change made in one location also is made in any other sync location. For example,

you and your friends may be working together to create one document reflecting your combined ideas. This document could be stored on a network or on cloud storage on the Internet. Your collaboration efforts should reflect the latest edits each person has made to the file.

You can use wired or wireless methods to sync. In a wired setup, cables connect one device to another, which allows for reliable data transfer. While wireless syncing offers convenience and automation, possible issues include battery drain and low signal strength when the devices are not close to each other. Strategies for keeping your files in sync include the following:

- **Use a cable and software.** Syncing photos from a camera or a smartphone to a computer frees up memory on the mobile device and creates a backup of these files. You easily can transfer photos using a data sync cable and synchronization software. Be certain not to disconnect the mobile device from the computer until the sync is complete. You also can copy your photos and documents from the computer to a smartphone, an external hard drive, a USB flash drive, or some other portable storage device.

- **Use cloud storage.** Cloud storage can provide a convenient method of syncing files stored on multiple computers and accessing them from most devices with Internet access. Several cloud storage providers offer a small amount of storage space at no cost and additional storage for a nominal fee per month or per year. Each provider has specific features, but most allow users to share files with other users, preview file contents, set passwords, and control who has permission to edit the files.

- **Use web apps.** By using web apps for email, contacts, and calendars, your information is stored online, so that it is accessible anywhere you have an Internet connection and can sync with multiple devices.

Discover More: Visit this chapter's free resources to learn more about wired setups, wireless syncing, and cloud storage providers.

Consider This: Synchronization is an effective method of organizing and sharing common files. What files have you synced, such as photos, music, and email? Which sync method did you use?

© iStockphoto / 123render; Source: Microsoft; © iStockphoto / Moncherie;
© iStockphoto / Ivan Stevanovic; Courtesy of Western Digital Corporation

Technology Uses

Technology has changed society today as much as the industrial revolution changed society in the eighteenth and nineteenth centuries. People interact directly with technology in fields such as education, government, finance, retail, entertainment, health care, science, travel, publishing, and manufacturing.

Education/Mini Feature 1-3: Digital School

Educators and teaching institutions use technology to assist with education. Most equip labs and classrooms with laptops or desktops. Some even provide computers or mobile devices to students. Many require students to have a mobile computer or mobile device to access the school's network or Internet wirelessly, or to access digital-only content provided by a textbook publisher. To promote the use of technology in education, vendors often offer substantial student discounts on hardware and software.

Educators may use a course management system, sometimes called a learning management system, which is software that contains tools for class preparation, distribution, and management. For example, through the course management system, students access course materials, grades, assessments, and a variety of collaboration tools.

Many schools offer distance learning classes, where the delivery of education occurs at one place while the learning occurs at other locations. Distance learning courses provide time, distance, and place advantages for students who live far from a campus or work full time. A few schools offer entire degrees online. National and international companies offer distance learning training because it eliminates the costs of airfare, hotels, and meals for centralized training sessions.

Read Mini Feature 1-3 to learn about additional technologies integrated in the classroom.

 BTW

Technology @ Work
For more information about how technology is used in a variety of fields, read the Technology @ Work feature at the end of each chapter in this book.

BTW

Technology Trend
Discover More: Visit this chapter's free resources to learn about massive open online courses (MOOCs).

 Internet Research
How do educators use iTunes U?

Search for: itunes u

✷ **MINI FEATURE 1-3**

Digital School

Technology and education intersect in today's classrooms. Students can use a variety of devices, apps, and websites to collaborate and obtain content while teachers can share information in most content areas to engage students and enhance the learning process. Digital technology offers flexibility and a revised classroom setting.

- **Mobile devices and tablets:** Schools are updating their computer labs by eliminating rows of desktops and allowing students to bring their own devices into the room and also into their classrooms, a practice often referred to as *BYOD* (bring your own device). They connect their laptops and mobile devices to power and data; they then they use educational apps, store and share files, read digital books, and create content without leaving their desks.

- **Virtual field trips:** Virtual tours of museums, ancient sites, and galleries allow audiences to see exhibits, examine paintings, and explore historical objects. After viewing 360-degree panoramas of such places as Colonial Williamsburg and Machu Picchu, students can interact with experts via Twitter and videoconferencing.

- **Games and simulations:** Game design theory can help engage students and reinforce key

concepts. When students master one set of objectives in a particular topic, they can progress to more advanced levels. They can receive instant feedback and recognition for their accomplishments, collaborate with teammates, repeat play to achieve higher scores, and document their experiences. Researchers claim that students are more likely to pursue challenging subject matter when it is offered in a gaming setting.

- **Interactive whiteboards:** Teachers and students can write directly on an interactive display, shown in the figure, which is a touch-sensitive device resembling a dry-erase board. It displays images on a connected computer screen. Touch gestures are used to zoom, erase, and annotate displayed content.

- **Share projects:** Effective movies can bring the words in a textbook to life. Students can create scripts and then use animation software or a video camera to tell stories that apply the concepts they have learned

Used with permission of SMART Technologies ULC (www.smarttech. com). SMART Board and the SMART logo are trademarks of SMART Technologies ULC and may be registered in the European Union, Canada, the United States and other countries.

(continued)

and upload them to media sharing websites. They also can write blogs, design graphics, and conduct interviews to apply and share the concepts they have learned in the classroom.

- **3-D printers:** Low-cost 3-D printers created for the classroom and libraries are becoming popular, especially in science and engineering classes. Geology students can create topography models, biology students can examine cross sections of

organs, architecture students can print prototypes of their designs, and history students can create artifacts.

Discover More: Visit this chapter's free resources to learn more about the digital school.

☀ **Consider This:** Which digital technologies have you used in your classrooms? Did they help you learn and retain information presented? If so, how?

Government

Most government offices have websites to provide citizens with up-to-date information. People in the United States access government websites to view census data, file taxes, apply for permits and licenses, pay parking tickets, buy stamps, report crimes, apply for financial aid, and renew vehicle registrations and driver's licenses.

Employees of government agencies use computers as part of their daily routine. North American 911 call centers use computers to dispatch calls for fire, police, and medical assistance. Military and other agency officials use the U.S. Department of Homeland Security's network of information about domestic security threats to help protect against terrorist attacks. Law enforcement officers have online access to the FBI's National Crime Information Center (NCIC) through in-vehicle laptops, fingerprint readers, and mobile devices (Figure 1-34). The NCIC contains more than 15 million missing persons and criminal records, including names, fingerprints, parole/probation records, mug shots, and other information.

Figure 1-34 Law enforcement officials use computers and mobile devices to access emergency, missing person, and criminal records in computer networks in local, state, and federal agencies.
© iStockPhoto / jacomstephens

Finance

Many people and companies use online banking or finance software to pay bills, track personal income and expenses, manage investments, and evaluate financial plans. The difference between using a financial institutions' website versus finance software on your computer is that all your account information is stored on the bank's computer instead of your computer. The advantage is you can access your financial records from anywhere in the world.

Investors often use online investing to buy and sell stocks and bonds — without using a broker. With online investing, the transaction fee for each trade usually is much less than when trading through a broker.

Discover More: Visit this chapter's free resources to learn more about online investing.

Retail

You can purchase just about any product or service on the web, including groceries, flowers, books, computers and mobile devices, music, movies, airline tickets, and concert tickets. To purchase from an online retailer, a customer visits the business's storefront, which contains product descriptions, images, and a shopping cart. The shopping cart allows the customer to collect purchases. When ready to complete the sale, the customer enters personal data and the method of payment, which should be through a secure Internet connection. Figure 1-35 illustrates the steps involved when a customer purchases from an online retailer.

Many mobile apps make your shopping experience more convenient. Some enable you to manage rewards, use coupons, locate stores, or pay for goods and services directly from your phone or other mobile device. Other mobile apps will check a product's price and availability at stores in your local area or online. Read Secure IT 1-4 for tips about shopping safely online.

Discover More: Visit this chapter's free resources to learn more about mobile payments.

✳ SECURE IT 1-4

Shopping Safely Online

Browsing electronic storefronts and making online purchases can be convenient and economical, but the experience can be a disaster if you encounter unscrupulous vendors. These tips can help you enjoy a safe and productive online shopping trip.

- **Read customer reviews.** Shoppers frequently post comments about merchandise quality, pricing, and shipping. Their evaluations may help you decide whether a company is legitimate. Be aware, however, that the Federal Trade Commission has sued companies for posting false positive reviews and that some companies remove negative comments. Make it a habit to rate merchants as often as possible so that others can learn from your experiences.

- **Look for seals of approval.** Online businesses can display seals if they have met rigorous standards. Some unscrupulous merchants, however, will place the seals on their websites even if they have not been approved. To check a seal's legitimacy, tap or click the logo and be certain you are directed to the issuing agency's website to verify the seal is valid.

- **Create a strong password and password questions.** If the merchant requires you to create a user name and password, be certain to develop a long, complex password with at least eight characters that include letters, numbers, and special characters. (Refer to Secure IT 1-3 earlier in this chapter for guidance on creating a strong password.) The website also may ask for answers to security questions; if so, do not supply information that hackers could locate easily, such as your high school, place of birth, or family members' or pets' names.

- **Check website details.** Locate the business's privacy policy to learn how your information will be stored. Also, look for phone numbers, physical addresses, and email addresses to contact the vendor if questions arise about damaged goods or billing discrepancies.

- **Beware of requests to supply further information.** After you have placed an order, you may receive an email message asking you to confirm the transaction or to supply additional account information. A reputable business will not solicit these requests, so do not reply to the message.

✳ **Consider This:** Have you made online purchases? If so, have you followed the precautions listed here? How will you change your activities the next time you shop online?

Purchasing from an Online Retailer

Step 1 The customer displays the online retailer's storefront.

Step 2 The customer collects purchases in a shopping cart.

Step 3 The customer enters payment information on a secure website. The online retailer sends financial information to a bank.

Step 5 The online retailer's web server sends confirmation to the customer, processes the order, and then sends it to the fulfillment center.

Step 4 The bank performs security checks and sends authorization back to the online retailer.

Step 6 The fulfillment center packages the order, prepares it for shipment, and then sends a report to the server where records are updated.

Step 7 While the order travels to the customer, shipping information is posted on the web.
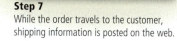

Step 8 The order is delivered to the customer, who may be required to sign a handheld computer or document to acknowledge receipt.

Figure 1-35 This figure shows the steps involved when a customer purchases from an online retailer.

Entertainment

You can use computers and mobile devices to listen to audio clips or live audio; watch video clips, television shows, or live performances and events; read a book, magazine, or newspaper; and play a myriad of games individually or with others. In some cases, you download the media from the web to a computer or mobile device so that you can watch, listen to, view, or play later. Some websites support *streaming*, where you access the media content while it downloads. For example, radio and television broadcasts often use streaming media to broadcast music, interviews, talk shows, sporting events, news, and other segments so that you can listen to the audio or view the video as it downloads to your computer. You also can create videos, take photos, or record audio and upload (transfer) your media content to the web to share with others, such as on an online social network.

✹ CONSIDER THIS

Can I make copies of songs or other media that I have purchased and downloaded from a legitimate website, such as iTunes?

You typically can make a copy as a personal backup, but you cannot share the copy with others in any format unless you have legal permission from the copyright owner to do so. That is, you cannot give someone a CD copy, nor can you share a digital file by posting it on the web or sending it as an email message.

⊙ BTW

Technology Trend

Discover More: Visit this chapter's free resources to learn what is meant by a QR code and how QR codes are used in the medical field.

Health Care

Nearly every area of health care today uses computers. Whether you are visiting a family doctor for a regular checkup, having lab work or an outpatient test, filling a prescription, or being rushed in for emergency surgery, the medical staff around you will be using computers for various purposes:

- Hospitals and doctors use computers and mobile devices to maintain and access patient records (Figure 1-36).
- Computers and mobile devices monitor patients' vital signs in hospital rooms and at home; patients use computers to manage health conditions, such as diabetes.
- Robots deliver medication to nurses' stations in hospitals.
- Computers and computerized devices assist doctors, nurses, and technicians with medical tests.
  - Doctors use the web and medical software to assist with researching and diagnosing health conditions.
  - Doctors use email, text messaging, and other communications services to correspond with patients.
  - Patients use computers and mobile devices to refill prescriptions, and pharmacists use computers to file insurance claims and provide customers with vital information about their medications.
  - Surgeons implant computerized devices, such as pacemakers, that allow patients to live longer.
  - Surgeons use computer-controlled devices to provide them with greater precision during operations, such as for laser eye surgery and robot-assisted heart surgery.
  - Medical staff create labels for medicine, hospital ID bracelets, and more, enabling staff to verify dosage and access patient records by scanning the label.

Figure 1-36 Doctors, nurses, technicians, and other medical staff use computers and computerized devices to assist with medical tests.

© iStockPhoto / Neustockimage

Science

All branches of science, from biology to astronomy to meteorology, use computers to assist them with collecting, analyzing, and modeling data. Scientists also use the Internet to communicate with colleagues around the world. Breakthroughs in surgery, medicine, and treatments often result from scientists' use of computers. Tiny computers now imitate functions of the central nervous system, retina of the eye, and cochlea of the ear. A cochlear implant allows a deaf person to distinguish sounds. Electrodes implanted in the brain stop tremors associated with Parkinson's disease.

A *neural network* is a system that attempts to imitate the behavior of the human brain. Scientists create neural networks by connecting thousands of processors together much like the neurons in the brain are connected. The capability of a personal computer to recognize spoken words is a direct result of scientific experimentation with neural networks.

Travel

Whether traveling by car or plane, your goal is to arrive safely at your destination. As you make the journey, you may interact with a navigation system or GPS, which uses satellite signals to determine a geographic location. GPS technology also assists people with creating maps, determining the best route between two points, locating a lost person or stolen object, monitoring a person's or object's movement, determining altitude, calculating speed, and finding points of interest. Vehicles manufactured today typically include some type of onboard navigation system (Figure 1-37). Many mobile devices, such as smartphones, also have built-in navigation systems.

In preparing for a trip, you may need to reserve a car, hotel, or flight. Many websites offer these services to the public where you can search for and compare flights and prices, order airline tickets, or reserve a rental car. You also can print driving directions and maps from the web.

Figure 1-37 Many vehicles include an onboard navigation system.
© kaczor58 / Shutterstock.com

Publishing

Many publishers of books, magazines, newspapers, music, film, and video make their works available online. Organizations and individuals publish their thoughts and ideas using a blog, podcast, or wiki.

- A *blog* is an informal website consisting of time-stamped articles (posts) in a diary or journal format, usually listed in reverse chronological order. Posts can contain text, photos, links, and more. For example, Figure 1-38 shows the Nutrition Blog Network, in which registered

blog posts

Figure 1-38 Any group or individual can create a blog, so that they can share thoughts and ideas.
Source: Nutrition Blog Network

BTW
High-Tech Talk
Discover More: Visit this chapter's free resources to learn how navigation systems, mobile phone trackers, and game consoles use triangulation to determine a location.

BTW
High-Tech Talk
Discover More: Visit this chapter's free resources to learn more about how neural networks work.

Internet Research

How can you create a blog?

Search for: create a blog

dietitians post articles about nutrition. As others read articles in your blog, you can enable them to reply with their own thoughts. A blog that contains video is called a video blog.

- Podcasts are a popular way to distribute audio or video on the web. A *podcast* is recorded media that users can download or stream to a computer or portable media player. Examples of podcasts include lectures, political messages, radio shows, and commentaries. Podcasters register their podcasts so that subscribers can select content to automatically download when they are connected.

- A *wiki* is a collaborative website that allows users to create, add to, modify, or delete the content via their browser. Many wikis are open to modification by the general public. The difference between a wiki and a blog is that users cannot modify original posts made by a blogger. Read Ethics & Issues 1-4 for an issue related to using wikis as a source for research.

ETHICS & ISSUES 1-4

Should Wikis Be Allowed as Valid Sources for Academic Research?

As wikis have grown in number, size, and popularity, many educators and librarians have shunned them as valid sources of research. While some wikis are tightly controlled with a limited number of contributors and expert editors, these wikis usually focus on narrowly defined, specialized topics. Most large, multi-topic online wikis, such as Wikipedia, often involve thousands of editors, many of whom remain anonymous.

Critics of wikis cite the lack of certified academic credentials by the editors, as well as potential political or gender bias by contributors. Wikis also are subject to vandalism. Vandals' motives vary; some

enter false information to discredit the wiki, and others for humorous results. On occasion, rival political factions have falsified or embellished wiki entries in an attempt to give their candidate an advantage. Some wiki supporters argue that most wikis provide adequate controls to correct false or misleading content quickly and to punish those who submit it. One popular wiki now requires an experienced editor to verify changes made to certain types of articles. Other wiki protection methods include locking articles from editing, creating a list of recently edited articles, enabling readers to report vandalism, and allowing people to be notified about changes to a wiki page that

they have edited or that is about them. Some proponents propose that people should use wikis as a starting point for researching a fact, but that they should verify the fact using traditional sources.

Consider This: Should instructors allow wikis as valid sources for academic research? Why or why not? Would you submit a paper to your instructor that cites a wiki as a source? Why or why not? What policies might wikis enforce that could garner more confidence from the public? If a wiki provided verification of the credentials of the author, would you trust the wiki more? Why or why not?

Figure 1-39 Automotive factories use industrial robots to weld car bodies.
© Small Town Studio / Shutterstock.com

Manufacturing

Computer-aided manufacturing (CAM) refers to the use of computers to assist with manufacturing processes, such as fabrication and assembly. Industries use CAM to reduce product development costs, shorten a product's time to market, and stay ahead of the competition. Often, robots carry out processes in a CAM environment. CAM is used by a variety of industries, including oil drilling, power generation, food production, and automobile manufacturing. Automobile plants, for example, have an entire line of industrial robots that assemble a car (Figure 1-39).

Special computers on the shop floor record actual labor, material, machine, and computer time used to manufacture a particular product. The computers process this data and automatically update inventory, production, payroll, and accounting records on the company's network.

Technology Users

Every day, people around the world use various technologies at home, at work, and at school. Depending on the hardware, software, and communications requirements, these users generally can be classified in one of five categories. Keep in mind that a single user may fall into more than one category.

- A *home user* is any person who spends time using technology at home. Parents, children, teenagers, grandparents, singles, couples, etc., are all examples of home users.
- A *small/home office user* includes employees of companies with fewer than 50 employees, as well as the self-employed who work from home. Small offices include local law practices, accounting offices, travel agencies, and florists.
- A *mobile user* includes any person who works with computers or mobile devices while away from a main office, home, or school. Examples of mobile users are sales representatives, real estate agents, insurance agents, meter readers, package delivery people, journalists, consultants, and students.
- A *power user* is a user who requires the capabilities of a powerful computer. Examples of power users include engineers, scientists, architects, desktop publishers, and graphic artists.
- An enterprise has hundreds or thousands of employees or customers who work in or do business with offices across a region, the country, or the world. Each employee or customer who uses computers, mobile devices, and other technology in the enterprise is an *enterprise user*. Read Ethics & Issues 1-5 to consider whether employees should be held accountable for their online social network posts.

⚹ ETHICS & ISSUES 1-5

Should Employees Be Held Accountable for Their Online Social Network Posts?
In addition to looking at your resume and scheduling an interview, a potential employer may search the web to find out information about you. A recent Career Builder survey found that 39 percent of employers look at applicants' use of online social networks, and 43 percent of those found information that caused them not to hire the applicant.

Once employed, your manager still may track your online activity. Companies are concerned about damaged reputations, or even lawsuits. Employee actions that worry their employers

include discussing company sales activity, griping about their managers or customers, or posting photos that show them taking part in unethical, illegal, or unsavory activities.

Social network-related firings have raised the question of whether companies should monitor employees' online social network activity. Accessing an employee's or a potential employee's social network profile also could have consequences for the company. If a company realizes that a person is a member of a minority group or has a disability, the company could face discrimination charges if it does not hire or later fires the employee. Privacy experts state that your online social network posts are your

own business. Debate about what falls under free speech is ongoing. Remember that you cannot delete easily what you post online. Whether or not you currently are searching for employment, online posts you make now can damage your future job prospects.

Consider This: What are the results when you search for yourself online? What steps can you take to clean up and protect your online reputation? Would you share social networking accounts or passwords with an employer or potential employer? Why or why not? Should companies monitor employees' accounts? Why or why not?

Table 1-4 illustrates the range of hardware, programs/apps, and communications forms used in each of these categories.

Table 1-4 Categories of Users

User	Sample Hardware	Sample Desktop Apps	Sample Mobile or Web Apps	Forms of Communications
All Users	– Smartphone – Digital camera – Printer	– Word processing – Schedule and contact management – Browser – Security	– Alarm clock – Calculator – News, weather, sports – Reference – Finance	– Email – Online social networks – Blogs
Home User	– Laptop, tablet, or desktop – Portable media player and earbuds or headphones – Game console – E-book reader – Wearable device – Webcam – Headset	– Personal finance – Photo and video editing – Media player – Educational – Entertainment	– Banking – Travel – Mapping – Navigation – Health and fitness – Retail – Media sharing – Educational	– Messaging – VoIP
Small/Home Office User	– Desktop(s) or laptop(s) – Server – Webcam – Scanner	– Spreadsheet – Database – Accounting	– Travel – Mapping	– Messaging – VoIP – FTP
Mobile User	– Laptop or tablet – Video projector – Wireless headset	– Note taking – Presentation – Educational – Entertainment	– Travel – Mapping – Navigation – Retail – Educational	
Power User	– Desktop – Scanner	– Desktop publishing – Multimedia authoring – Computer-aided design – Photo, audio, video editing		– FTP – Videoconferencing
Enterprise User	– Server – Desktop(s) or laptop(s) – Industry-specific handheld computer – Webcam – Scanner	– Spreadsheet – Database – Accounting	– Travel – Mapping – Navigation	– Messaging – VoIP – FTP – Videoconferencing

✔ **NOW YOU SHOULD KNOW** ─────────────────────────────────

Be sure you understand the material presented in the sections titled Communications and Networks, Technology Uses, and Technology Users, as it relates to the chapter objectives.
Now you should know . . .

- When you might use wired and wireless communications, and why you would use a network (Objective 9)
- How you would use technology in education, government, finance, retail, entertainment, health care, science, travel, publishing, and manufacturing (Objective 10)
- What types of hardware, software, and communications you could use at home, school, and work (Objective 11)

Discover More: Visit this chapter's premium content for practice quiz opportunities.

✔ Chapter Summary

Chapter 1 introduced you to basic computer concepts. You learned about laptops, tablets, desktops, servers, smartphones, digital cameras, portable media players, e-book readers, and game devices. The chapter introduced various methods for input, output, memory, and storage. It discussed the Internet, browsing and searching the web, and online social networks. Next, the chapter introduced digital security and safety risks and precautions, along with various types of programs, applications, communications, and networks. The many different uses of technology applications in society also were presented, along with types of users. This chapter is an overview. Many of the terms and concepts introduced will be discussed further in later chapters.

   Discover More: Visit this book's free resources for additional content that accompanies this chapter and also includes these features: Technology Innovators: Facebook/Mark Zuckerberg, Twitter, Microsoft/Bill Gates, and Apple/Steve Jobs/Steve Wozniak; Technology Trends: MOOCs and QR Codes in the Medical Field; and High-Tech Talks: Triangulation and Neural Networks.

Test your knowledge of chapter material by accessing the Study Guide, Flash Cards, and Practice Test resources from your smartphone, tablet, laptop, or desktop.

⚡ TECHNOLOGY @ WORK ─────────────────────────────────

Health Care

You are out running on a beautiful day, tracking your route and distance using a health and fitness app on a smartphone. While running, you accidentally step on uneven pavement and suffer an injury that requires a trip to an emergency room. Upon check-in, the employee at the front desk uses a tablet to record your personal data and symptoms. She also uses the tablet to verify that your insurance coverage is current and informs you of your co-payment amount. After waiting several minutes, a triage nurse takes your temperature and blood pressure and then asks a series of questions about your symptoms. The nurse also records this data in a tablet and asks you to remain in the waiting room until someone from the radiology department is available to perform a CT scan. The radiology department is located in a different area of the hospital, so the technicians watch a computer screen that displays a list of patients who currently are waiting for their services.

About 30 minutes later, a technician calls your name and escorts you to the radiology department for your CT scan. As she is performing the scan, a computer records the images that later will be reviewed by a physician. When the CT scan is complete, you return to the waiting room until a physician reviews the results. Once she receives the results and reviews them, a hospital employee takes you to a consultation room.

   The physician informs you that other than a few bumps and bruises, she believes that you have sustained no permanent damage and prescribes medication to help ease the pain. She then returns to a computer at the nurses' station and adds her diagnosis to the database that stores your medical records. She also sends your prescription electronically to the hospital's pharmacy. Once discharged, you visit the cashier to pay the bill. You then use a tablet to sign an electronic version of your discharge paperwork so that the hospital can store it

electronically. The hospital bills your insurance company electronically. If you owe a balance

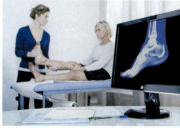
© Shutterstock / Image Point Fr

after the insurance company pays its portion, a computer at the hospital will generate a bill that will be mailed to you. After purchasing your medication and leaving the hospital, you realize that despite the hospital being busy, computers decreased the time of your visit by automating processes that otherwise would have been performed manually and reduced possible errors by storing all of your personal information centrally.

✺ **Consider This:** How else might computers and technology be used in the health care industry?

Study Guide

The Study Guide exercise reinforces material you should know for the chapter exam.

Discover More: Visit this chapter's premium content to test your knowledge of digital content associated with this chapter and access the Study Guide resource from your smartphone, tablet, laptop, or desktop.

Instructions: Answer the questions below using the format that helps you remember best or that is required by your instructor. Possible formats may include one or more of these options: write the answers; create a document that contains the answers; record answers as audio or video using a webcam, smartphone, or portable media player; post answers on a blog, wiki, or website; or highlight answers in the book/e-book.

1. Define the term, digital literacy.

2. Define the terms, computer, hardware, and user.

3. Differentiate between a PC and a mobile computer. A laptop also is known as a(n) ___ computer.

4. Describe the characteristics and features of a tablet. List several touch screen gestures.

5. Explain the difference between a desktop and an all-in-one. What additional meaning does the term, desktop, sometimes have?

6. Define the term, server. What services does a server provide?

7. Explain whether or not a mobile device is a computer.

8. List characteristics of a smartphone.

9. Differentiate among voice, text, picture, and video messages.

10. Describe the purpose of these mobile devices: digital cameras, portable and digital media players, e-book readers, wearable devices, and game devices.

11. Describe the trend of digital device convergence and how it applies to mobile devices.

12. Describe uses of technology in home automation.

13. Differentiate between data and information. Give an example of each.

14. Define the terms, input and output. List several types of input devices and output devices.

15. Describe the purpose of a pointing device. Give an example.

16. List the hardware you can use to input and view output for voice and video.

17. Differentiate between memory and storage.

18. A computer keeps data, instructions, and information on ___ media. Give some examples.

19. Define the term, cloud storage. Describe the types of services offered by cloud storage providers.

20. Describe components of a backup plan. How do backup plans for mobile devices and personal computers differ?

21. Describe the Internet. Identify reasons people use the Internet.

22. Differentiate between the web and the Internet.

23. The ___ consists of a worldwide collection of electronic documents. What is each electronic document called?

24. What is a browser? Describe the purpose of a search engine.

25. Explain the purpose of an online social network.

26. Differentiate between the services and uses of Facebook, Twitter, and LinkedIn.

27. List services of the Internet that facilitate communications.

28. Define the term, malware. List ways you can protect yourself from malware.

29. What privacy risks are involved with using technology? List guidelines for creating a strong password.

30. Explain physical and behavioral health risks associated with using computers.

31. Describe strategies that support green computing.

32. Define the term, software. Software also is called a(n) ___.

33. Define the term, operating system. List popular operating systems for computers and mobile devices.

34. Differentiate between desktop, web, and mobile apps.

35. List the steps involved in installing programs.

36. Explain how to locate, install, and run programs. What is the role of a software developer?

37. Define the term, communications device. List examples of wireless communications technologies.

38. Define the term, hot spot. Give two examples and describe how each is used.

39. Describe how homes and businesses use networks.

40. Identify issues surrounding accessing an unsecured network.

41. Explain what occurs when you synchronize computers and mobile devices.

42. List ways that schools use technology to enhance education.

43. Identify how the following industries use technology: government, financial, retail, entertainment, health care, science, travel, publishing, and manufacturing.

44. Describe how you might use blogs, wikis, and podcasts to publish content.

45. Differentiate among the following technology user types: home user, small/home office user, mobile user, power user, and enterprise user.

46. Describe how technology is used in the health care industry.

You should be able to define the Primary Terms and be familiar with the Secondary Terms listed below.

Key Terms

Discover More: Visit this chapter's premium content to view definitions for each term and access the Flash Cards resource from your smartphone, tablet, laptop, or desktop.

Primary Terms (shown in **bold-black** characters in the chapter)

all-in-one (6)	digital camera (8)	network (32)	storage media (17)
app (27)	digital device	online social network (23)	sync (34)
application (27)	convergence (10)	output device (14)	synchronize (34)
backup (18)	e-book reader (9)	portable media player (8)	tablet (4)
browser (21)	game console (10)	printer (14)	wearable device (9)
Bluetooth (32)	green computing (26)	program (26)	web (21)
cloud storage (18)	hard drive (17)	search engine (22)	web server (21)
communications	input device (12)	server (6)	webpage (21)
device (31)	Internet (20)	smartphone (7)	website (21)
computer (4)	laptop (4)	software (26)	Wi-Fi (31)
desktop (6)	memory (16)	storage device (17)	

Secondary Terms (shown in *italic* characters in the chapter)

3-D printer (15)	*hot spot (32)*	*point (13)*	*stretch (5)*
blog (39)	*hyperlink (21)*	*power user (41)*	*surfing the web (21)*
BYOD (35)	*information (12)*	*press and hold (5)*	*swipe (5)*
click (13)	*input (4)*	*printout (14)*	*tap (5)*
computer-aided manufacturing (40)	*keyboard (13)*	*resources (32)*	*target (34)*
data (12)	*link (21)*	*right-click (13)*	*text message (7)*
desktop app (28)	*loads (28)*	*scanner (14)*	*touchpad (13)*
digital literacy (2)	*malware (24)*	*slide (5)*	*USB flash drive (18)*
digital media (8)	*memory card (18)*	*small/home office user (41)*	*user (4)*
digital media player (9)	*microphone (14)*	*Smart TV (15)*	*user interface (29)*
double-click (13)	*mobile app (28)*	*social networking site (23)*	*video message (7)*
double-tap (5)	*mobile computer (4)*	*software developer (29)*	*voice mail message (7)*
downloading (21)	*mobile device (7)*	*solid-state drive (17)*	*wearable (9)*
drag (5, 13)	*mobile user (41)*	*source (34)*	*web app (28)*
earbuds (8)	*mouse (13)*	*streaming (38)*	*webcam (14)*
e-book (9)	*neural network (39)*	*streaming media player (9)*	*wiki (40)*
enterprise user (41)	*notebook computer (4)*		
e-reader (9)	*on-screen keyboard (5)*		
e-waste (26)	*operating system (27)*		
file (18)	*optical disc (18)*		
gesture (5)	*output (4)*		
hard copy (14)	*personal computer (4)*		
hard disk (17)	*phablet (7)*		
hardware (4)	*picture message (7)*		
headset (14)	*pinch (5)*		
home user (41)	*podcast (40)*		

all-in-one (6)

Checkpoint

The Checkpoint exercises test your knowledge of the chapter concepts. The page number containing the answer appears in parentheses after each exercise. The Consider This exercises challenge your understanding of chapter concepts.

Discover More: Visit this chapter's premium content to complete the Checkpoint exercises interactively; complete the self-assessment in the Test Prep resource from your smartphone, tablet, laptop, or desktop; and then take the Practice Test.

True/False   Mark T for True and F for False.

_T_ 1. Electronic components in computers process data using instructions, which are the steps that tell the computer how to perform a particular task. (4)

_F_ 2. An all-in-one contains a separate tower. (6)

_T_ 3. Smartphones typically communicate wirelessly with other devices or computers. (7)

_F_ 4. Data conveys meaning to users, and information is a collection of unprocessed items, which can include text, numbers, images, audio, and video. (12)

_T_ 5. A headset is a type of input device. (14)

_F_ 6. A scanner is a light-sensing output device. (14)

_T_ 7. Although some forms of memory are permanent, most memory keeps data and instructions temporarily, meaning its contents are erased when the computer is turned off. (16)

_F_ 8. A solid-state drive contains one or more inflexible, circular platters that use magnetic particles to store data, instructions, and information. (17)

_F_ 9. The terms, web and Internet, are interchangeable. (21)

_T_ 10. One way to protect your computer from malware is to scan any removable media before using it. (25)

_T_ 11. Operating systems are a widely recognized example of system software. (26)

_T_ 12. You usually do not need to install web apps before you can run them. (28)

Multiple Choice   Select the best answer.

1. A(n) _____ is any hardware component that allows you to enter data and instructions into a computer or mobile device. (12)
   a. output device
   c. **input device**
   b. communications device
   d. display

2. Which of the following is *not* an example of an output device? (14)
   a. **scanner**
   c. display
   b. printer
   d. speaker

3. _____ consists of electronic components that store instructions waiting to be executed and the data needed by those instructions. (16)
   a. Storage
   c. Solid-state drives
   b. Cloud storage
   d. **Memory**

4. _____ is an Internet service that provides remote storage to computer users. (18)
   a. Smart TV
   c. Solid-state drive (SSD)
   b. **Cloud storage**
   d. Bluetooth

5. A computer that delivers requested webpages to your computer or mobile device is a(n) _____. (21)
   a. VoIP computer
   c. FTP device
   b. **web server**
   d. hard drive

6. A _____ is software that enables users with an Internet connection to access and view webpages on a computer or mobile device. (21)
   a. search engine
   c. **browser**
   b. wiki
   d. digital media player

7. _____ uses short-range radio signals to enable computers and devices to communicate with each other. (32)
   a. Cellular radio
   c. Wi-Fi
   b. **Bluetooth**
   d. A hot spot

8. A(n) _____ is a collaborative website that allows users to create, add to, modify, or delete the content via their browser. (40)
   a. podcast
   c. online social network
   b. blog
   d. **wiki**

Checkpoint

Matching Match the terms with their definitions.

1. all-in-one (6)
2. server (6)
3. phablet (7)
4. digital device convergence (10)
5. touchpad (13)
6. storage device (17)
7. solid-state drive (17)
8. file (18)
9. software (26)
10. operating system (27)

a. term that describes the trend of computers and devices with technologies that overlap

b. mobile device that combines features of a smartphone and a tablet

c. storage device that typically uses flash memory to store data, instructions, and information

d. small, flat, rectangular pointing device that is sensitive to pressure and motion

e. set of programs that coordinates all the activities among computer or mobile device hardware

f. named collection of stored data, instructions, or information

g. type of desktop computer that does not contain a tower and instead uses the same case to house the display and the processing circuitry

h. series of related instructions, organized for a common purpose, that tells the computer what tasks to perform and how to perform them

i. computer that is dedicated to providing one or more services to other computers or devices on a network

j. component that records and/or retrieves items to and from storage media

✳ Consider This Answer the following questions in the format specified by your instructor.

1. Answer the critical thinking questions posed at the end of these elements in this chapter: Ethics & Issues (8, 23, 33, 40, 41), How To (5, 16, 22, 29), Mini Features (11, 34, 35), Secure IT (19, 25, 25, 37), and Technology @ Work (43).

2. What does it mean to be digitally literate, and why is it important? (2)

3. What are the different touch screen gestures and the actions they may cause to occur? (5)

4. What types of keyboards are available for smartphones and tablets? (5, 7)

5. In addition to books, what other digital media can be read on an e-book reader? (9)

6. In addition to keeping time, how might you use a smartwatch? (9)

7. Why might a consumer purchase separate stand-alone devices, such as smartphones, digital cameras, portable media players? (10)

8. How can you ease eyestrain while using a computer or mobile device? (16)

9. What types of files might you choose to store on a memory card or USB flash drive, rather than on a hard drive? (18)

10. What steps might you include in a backup plan? (19)

11. Why might you choose to use LinkedIn rather than Facebook? (24)

12. How might you know if your computer or mobile device is infected with malware? (24)

13. What types of software protect a computer from viruses and other malware? (25)

14. Why should you use a different password for all websites you access? (25)

15. How might you know if you are addicted to computers or suffer from technology overload? (26)

16. Why is green computing important? (26)

17. What steps can you take to contribute to green computing? (26)

18. What is the difference between system and application software? (26)

19. What are some examples of popular operating systems? (27)

20. How do desktop apps, web apps, and mobile apps differ? (28)

21. Where can you obtain programs or apps? (29)

22. What does a user interface control? (29)

23. What are some popular programming languages? (29)

24. Why might you opt for wireless communications? (31)

25. In a network, what is the major difference between a server and a client? (32)

26. When should you use a one-way sync or a two-way sync? (34)

27. What type of industries use computer-aided manufacturing (CAM)? (40)

✳ Problem Solving

The Problem Solving exercises extend your knowledge of chapter concepts by seeking solutions to practical problems with technology that you may encounter at home, school, or work. The Collaboration exercise should be completed with a team.

Instructions: You often can solve problems with technology in multiple ways. Determine a solution to the problems in these exercises by using one or more resources available to you (such as a computer or mobile device, articles on the web or in print, blogs, podcasts, videos, television, user guides, other individuals, electronics or computer stores, etc.). Describe your solution, along with the resource(s) used, in the format requested by your instructor (brief report, presentation, discussion, blog post, video, or other means).

Personal

1. **Shopping for Software** You are shopping for software that will assist you with your home's interior design. The package for the program you would like to purchase states that it was designed for the most recent version of Windows, but an older version is installed on your computer. How can you determine whether the program will run on your computer?

2. **Bad Directions** You are driving to your friend's house and are using your smartphone for directions. While approaching your destination, you realize that your smartphone app instructed you to turn the wrong way on your friend's street. How could this have happened?

3. **Bank Account Postings** While reviewing your checking account balance online, you notice that debit card purchases have not posted to your account for the past several days. Because you use online banking to balance your account, you become concerned about your unknown account balance. What steps will you take to correct this situation?

4. **Trial Expired** You have been using an app on your mobile device for a 30-day trial period. Now that the 30 days have expired, the app is requesting that you to pay to continue accessing your data. What are your next steps? What steps could you have taken to preserve your data before the trial period expired?

5. **Problematic Camera** After charging your digital camera battery overnight, you insert the battery and turn on the camera only to find that it is reporting a low battery. Seconds later, the camera shuts off automatically. What might be wrong?

Professional

6. **Discarding Old Computer Equipment** Your company has given you a new laptop to replace your current, outdated desktop. Because of the negative environmental impact of discarding the old computer in the trash, your supervisor asked you to suggest options for its disposal. How will you respond?

7. **Dead Battery** While traveling for business, you realize that you forgot to bring the battery charger for your laptop. Knowing that you need to use the laptop to give a presentation tomorrow, what steps will you take tonight to make sure you have enough battery power?

8. **Cannot Share Photos** You are attempting to send photos of a house for sale in an email message to your real estate partner. Each time you attempt to send the email message, you receive an automatic response stating that the files are too large. What are your next steps?

9. **Incorrect Sign-In Credentials** Upon returning to the office from a well-deserved two-week vacation, you turn on your computer. When you enter your user name and password, an error message appears stating that your password is incorrect. What are your next steps?

10. **Synchronization Error** You added appointments to the calendar on your computer, but these appointments are not synchronizing with your smartphone. Your calendar has synchronized with your smartphone in the past, but it has stopped working without explanation. What are your next steps?

Collaboration

11. **Technology in Health Care** Your primary care physician is moving from a shared office so that he can open his own practice. He mentioned that he would like to use technology in his office that not only will improve the patient experience, but also make his job easier. Form a team of three people to determine the types of technology your doctor can use in his new office. One team member should research ways that technology can help improve patient check-in and billing. Another team member should research the types of technology your doctor can use while he is working with patients, and the third team member should research any additional technology that can be used in the office to improve the patient experience. Compile your findings in a report and submit it to your instructor.

The **How To: Your Turn** exercises present general guidelines for fundamental skills when using a computer or mobile device and then require that you determine how to apply these general guidelines to a specific program or situation.

How To: Your Turn

Discover More: Visit this chapter's premium content to challenge yourself with additional How To: Your Turn exercises, which include App Adventure.

Instructions: You often can complete tasks using technology in multiple ways. Figure out how to perform the tasks described in these exercises by using one or more resources available to you (such as a computer or mobile device, articles on the web or in print, online or program help, user guides, blogs, podcasts, videos, other individuals, trial and error, etc.). Summarize your 'how to' steps, along with the resource(s) used, in the format requested by your instructor (brief report, presentation, discussion, blog post, video, or other means).

1 Create a Facebook Account, Find the Discovering Computers Facebook Page, and Like It

The Discovering Computers Facebook page contains links to current events and other technology news, as well as relating the links to content in this book. The following steps guide you through the process of signing up for a Facebook account, navigating to the Discovering Computers Facebook page, and liking the page.

Source: Facebook

a. Run a browser and then navigate to www.facebook.com.
b. Follow the steps on the Facebook webpage to sign up for a new account. If you already have an account, enter your sign-in information and sign in to your Facebook account.
c. Search for the Discovering Computers Facebook page using the search text, Discovering Computers.
d. Select the Discovering Computers Product/Service in the search results.
e. Tap or click the Like button to like the page.
f. If your screen displays a Follow button, tap or click it to see information from the Discovering Computers Facebook page in your news feed.
g. View the posts and tap or click links on the page that are of interest to you.
h. When you are finished, sign out of Facebook.

Exercises

1. Summarize the process you use to sign up for or sign in to your Facebook account.
2. Which links on the Discovering Computers Facebook page are of interest to you? Why?
3. Browse Facebook and find at least three other Facebook pages that are of interest to you. Which pages have you found, and why do you like them?

2 Create a Twitter Account, Find the Discovering Computers Twitter Account, and Follow It

The Discovering Computers Twitter account contains links to current events and other technology news, as well as how it relates to the content in this textbook. The following steps guide you through the process of signing up for a Twitter account, navigating to the Discovering Computers Twitter account, and following it.

a. Run a browser and then navigate to www.twitter.com.
b. Follow the steps on the Twitter webpage to sign up for a new account. If you already have an account, enter your sign-in information and sign in to your Twitter account.
c. Search for the Discovering Computers Twitter account using the search text, DiscoveringComp.
d. Select Shelly Cashman @DiscoveringComp in the search results.
e. Tap or click the Follow button to follow the account.
f. View the posts and tap or click links on the page that are of interest to you.
g. When you are finished, sign out of Twitter.

✳ How To: Your Turn

Exercises

1. Summarize the process you use to sign up for or sign in to your Twitter account.
2. How is the Discovering Computers Twitter account similar to the Discovering Computers Facebook page? How are they different?
3. Browse Twitter and find at least three other Twitter accounts to follow. Which ones have you found, and why do you like them?

3 **Connect to a Wireless Network**

Wireless networks are available in many homes and businesses. Connecting to a wireless network can provide you with high-speed access to the Internet and other network resources. The following steps guide you through the process of connecting to a wireless network from a computer or mobile device.

a. If necessary, turn on your computer or mobile device and make sure wireless functionality is enabled.
b. Obtain the name of the wireless network to which you want to connect. **Note:** *You should connect only to wireless networks for which you have permission*.
c. On your computer or mobile device, view the list of available wireless networks.
d. Select the wireless network to which you want to connect.

e. If necessary, enter the requested security information, such as an encryption key or a password.
f. Run a browser to test your connection to the wireless network.

Exercises

1. Why should you not connect to a wireless network unless you have permission?
2. What is the name of the wireless network to which you connected?
3. Why might you connect to a wireless network on your smartphone instead of using your mobile data plan?

4 **Manage Your Calendar**

Individuals are choosing to use calendars on computers and mobile devices to keep track of events in their personal and professional lives more easily. In addition, students might use calendars to keep track of their class schedules. The following steps guide you through the process of managing your computer or mobile device's calendar.

a. Run the calendar app (usually by tapping or clicking its icon or tile on the home screen).
b. To add a new appointment, tap or click the Add or New Appointment button or icon and then enter the title or subject of the appointment, its date, time, location, and other information. Tap or click the Save button or icon on the New Appointment screen to save the information to your calendar.
c. Specify repeating information for appointments that occur at the same time over multiple occurrences, such as a class that meets every Tuesday from 10:00 a.m. to 11:00 a.m.
d. View your appointments on a daily, weekly, or monthly calendar by tapping or clicking the appropriate choice in the calendar app.
e. To edit an appointment, meeting, or event on your calendar, open the item by tapping or clicking it, make the necessary changes and then save the changes.

combination modem/router/wireless access point

Internet

modem

© Cengage Learning; © iStockphoto / Petar Chernaev; © iStockphoto / Oleksiy Mark; © Patryk Kosmider / Shutterstock.com; © Pablo Eder / Shutterstock.com; © iStockphoto / 123render; Source: Microsoft; © iStock-photo / aquarius83men

f. To delete an appointment, meeting, or event on your calendar, open the item by tapping or clicking it, and then tap or click the button to delete it. If necessary, confirm the deletion. If you are attempting to delete a recurring item on the calendar, the calendar app may ask whether you want to delete the one occurrence, or the entire series of appointments, meetings, or events.

Exercises

© iStockphoto / Moncherie

1. In addition to your class schedule, what other recurring appointments might you add to your calendar?
2. Many calendar apps have a feature that can remind you of upcoming appointments in advance. How far in advance do you think you should be reminded of upcoming appointments?
3. How can you synchronize the calendar on your mobile device with the calendar on your home computer?

⑤ Back Up Photos from a Phone or Tablet

Many individuals take photos using mobile devices such as phones and tablets. Many, however, neglect to realize the importance of backing up these memories. A backup of the photos will be useful if you lose your mobile device, upgrade it to a newer model, or the device becomes damaged. While many mobile devices have built-in capabilities to back up photos to the cloud or to a desktop or laptop, it is important to make sure these features are configured properly. The following steps guide you through the process of backing up photos from a phone or tablet.

Backing Up to the Cloud

a. If necessary, install and sign in to an app on a phone or tablet that can back up photos to the cloud. Make sure the service you use gives you enough storage space for the photos you intend to upload.
b. Follow the instructions in the app and configure it to back up the photos at an interval of your choosing. Some options might include:
   • Back up all photos at certain intervals (such as one time per day or one time per week)
   • Back up photos as you take them
   • Back up photos stored in specific folders
c. If you are using a mobile device with a data plan, consider specifying whether you want the backup to occur only when you are connected to

How To: Your Turn ✳

Wi-Fi. Backing up using your phone or tablet's data plan may result in additional charges if you inadvertently exceed your quota.

d. Verify all photos have been backed up to the cloud service.

Backing Up to a Computer

a. Use the USB cable that came with your phone or tablet to connect it to the computer to which you want to back up the photos.
b. After the computer has recognized that a phone or tablet is connected, navigate to the drive on the computer representing the phone or tablet and then navigate to the folder containing the photos. If your phone or tablet stores pictures on both internal storage and a memory card, remember to back up your photos from both locations.
c. Drag the photos from the location on your phone or tablet to a folder on your computer that will store the backed up files.
d. When the files have finished backing up to the computer, close all open folder windows on the computer and then safely disconnect the phone or tablet from the computer.

© Dmitry Rukhlenko / Photos.com

Exercises

1. How often do you think you should back up your photos? Why?
2. When backing up photos, why might it be better to connect your phone or tablet to the computer using a cable instead of inserting the memory card from the phone or tablet into the computer?
3. Compare and contrast three apps or services that can back up photos from your phone or tablet to the cloud. Which one would you choose, and why?

✳ Internet Research

The Internet Research exercises broaden your understanding of chapter concepts by requiring that you search for information on the web.

Discover More: Visit this chapter's premium content to challenge yourself with additional Internet Research exercises, which include Search Sleuth, Green Computing, Ethics in Action, You Review It, and Exploring Technology Careers.

Instructions: Use a search engine or another search tool to locate the information requested or answers to questions presented in the exercises. Describe your findings, along with the search term(s) you used and your web source(s), in the format requested by your instructor (brief report, presentation, discussion, blog post, video, or other means).

❶ Making Use of the Web
Informational and Research

Informational and research websites contain factual information and include reference works such as libraries, encyclopedias, dictionaries, directories, and guides. More than 2.4 billion people worldwide use the Internet, and Google is one of the websites they visit most often. Google reports that people perform more than 100 billion searches every month using its Google Search. In How To 1 in the Succeeding in this Course chapter at the beginning of this book and How To 1-3 in this chapter, you learned how to use a browser to display a webpage on a computer or mobile device and to perform a basic web search using a search engine.

Research This: Using a browser and search engine, find the answers to the following questions. (1) Search for the top five informational websites and top five research websites. What types of information or research does each present? What search text did you use? (2) Visit Google's website and locate the company's early philosophy: "Ten things we know to be true." What are five of these values? What is the goal of the "Made with Code" initiative? (3) Visit the Engadget website and read at least three reviews of tablets. Create a table listing the product name, price, battery life, pros, and cons. (4) Locate articles about using hands-free devices for conversations while driving. Which states have passed legislation to restrict drivers' use of hands-free devices while driving? Describe the features found in the sophisticated hands-free system of one of this year's vehicles.

Google's mission is to organize the world's information and make it universally accessible and useful.

Products · Company · Management

Source: Google Inc.

❷ Social Media

Online social networks are a central communications tool and the primary source of news and information for many people. Historians place the birth of online social networking with the BBS (Bulletin Board System), where users communicated with a central computer and sent messages to other BBS members and also downloaded files and games. The next phase of online social networks evolved when CompuServe, AOL (America Online), and Prodigy were among the services linking people with similar interests. Today's online social networks share many of the same basic principles by allowing members to communicate common interests, play games, and share photos, videos, and music. Some of these online social networks are for personal use, while others are for entrepreneurs, business owners, and professionals to share job-related topics.

Research This: Compare the features of the top personal online social networks, and create a table listing the number of active members in the United States and worldwide, the number of years the sites have existed, the more popular features, and the amount of content, such as photos, news stories, and links, that is shared each month. What types of advertisements are featured in each of these sites? Which sites are marketed toward younger and older users? Then, research the online social networks used for business. How does their content differ from that found on the personal online social networks? How many companies use these sites as a recruiting tool? How many native languages are supported? How are professionals using these websites to find potential clients and business partners?

❸ Search Skills
Selecting Search Terms

Search text that you send to a search engine, such as Google, Bing, or Yahoo!, impacts the quality of your search results. Rather than typing a long question in the search box, you may improve your results if you select the question's most important words as your search text. For example, instead of typing the

Internet Research ✳

entire question "How many users currently are on Facebook?" as your search text, type the following as your search text: facebook users current. Many search engines consider common words — such as how, are, and on — as stop words, or words that a search engine ignores when performing a search.

Place the most specific or important word (facebook) first in your search text and then follow it with additional words to narrow the results. To see if rearranging the order of the words yields different results, type current users facebook. Some search results from both queries likely will overlap. Many search engines assist you by automatically completing terms as you type them and will display a list of popular alternatives from which you can select. Sometimes, replacing a search term with a synonym will improve your results. For example, try using the search text, facebook users, followed by the current year instead of the using the word, current. Most search engines are not case sensitive. (They do not distinguish between uppercase and lowercase characters.)

Source: Microsoft

Research This: Create search text using the techniques described above, and type it into a search engine to find answers to these questions. (1) What English words are stop words for Google? (2) What is the largest solid-state drive available? (3) How many hours per day on average do teens spend playing video games? (4) When is the next update to the Android mobile operating system expected to be released?

❹ Security

Secure IT 1-3 in this chapter offers advice about creating secure passwords when registering for websites. Despite suggestions and constant reminders from security experts to develop and then periodically change passwords, users continue to create weak passwords.

These common passwords are broken easily and, therefore, never should be used. For many years, the most common passwords have been the word, password, and the number sequences 123456 and 12345678.

Research This: Use a search engine to locate at least 2 different companies' lists of the 10 or 20 more common passwords in the past two years. Which passwords appear on both lists? Find a password-strength checking website and type three passwords to determine how easy or difficult they are to crack. Why do consumers continue to use these passwords despite repeated warnings to avoid them? Do you have accounts using one or more of these passwords? What advice is given for developing strong passwords, such as using the lyrics to the first line of a favorite song? How do the companies gather data to determine common passwords?

❺ Cloud Services
Cloud Storage (Iaas)

Cloud storage providers offer online access to hardware for storing files, and web and mobile apps to access, back up, and manage files. Cloud storage is an example of IaaS (infrastructure as a service), a service of cloud computing that allows individuals and businesses to use a vendor's hardware to manage their computing needs.

Cloud storage providers offer both free and paid service plans based on the amount of free storage, and some allow users to earn additional storage by recommending friends to use their services or by participating in promotional campaigns. Many cloud storage providers enable users to synchronize files across multiple devices, access files via mobile or web apps, share files with team members, and maintain previous versions of files. Some provide built-in access to web-based productivity software or integrate with third-party web and mobile apps.

Research This: (1) Use a search engine to find three popular cloud storage providers. Create accounts and try each for a period specified by your instructor. In a table, summarize their features, including amount of free storage available (offered or earned), restrictions on file sizes you can upload, ease of use of web and mobile apps, operating systems or devices supported, cost of paid plans, and additional services provided for a fee. (2) Many cloud storage providers offer several gigabytes of free storage to their users. What is the largest amount of free storage you can find? Who is the provider? Can you identify any drawbacks to using this service?

Critical Thinking

The Critical Thinking exercises challenge your assessment and decision-making skills by presenting real-world situations associated with chapter concepts. The Collaboration exercise should be completed with a team.

Instructions: Evaluate the situations below, using personal experiences and one or more resources available to you (such as articles on the web or in print, blogs, podcasts, videos, television, user guides, other individuals, electronics or computer stores, etc.). Perform the tasks requested in each exercise and share your deliverables in the format requested by your instructor (brief report, presentation, discussion, blog post, video, or other means).

1. Reactions to Software Problems

People who use computers and mobile devices sometimes experience problems with software, including operating systems, desktop apps, web apps, and mobile apps. Problems range from not being able to install or download the program or app to a computer or mobile device, to a program or an app producing unanticipated results. Depending on the situation, these problems can result in user stress. Many people believe reactions to software problems tend to be more extreme than reactions to problems with other tools.

Do This: Evaluate situations in which you have seen people react to program and app problems on their computers and mobile devices. Discuss how these users can reduce their frustration when dealing with such problems. Have you ever been frustrated by problems with a program or an app? How did you react? What did you do to solve the problem?

2. Energy Efficiency

Increases in energy prices lead many individuals to look at purchasing energy-efficient computers and devices. Energy-efficient models often look and perform similarly to equivalent computers or devices that use more energy.

Do This: Find two computers or devices of identical configuration, where the only difference is energy consumption. How much energy does the energy-efficient model save? Are energy-efficient computers and devices more or less expensive? Will the difference in cost (if any) affect your purchasing decision? How else might you be able to change your settings on your existing computer or device to save energy? Use the web to locate articles that recommend energy-efficient products and that provide tips about additional ways to save energy.

3. Case Study

Amateur Sports League   You are the new manager for a nonprofit amateur soccer league. The previous manager tracked all of the data on paper. You realize that using technology will increase your efficiency and enable you to communicate better with the board of directors, coaches, and players. At the board's next meeting, you will share ideas of how you will use technology.

Do This: To prepare for the meeting, you compile the following: differences between input and output, a list of the types of data you can use as input, and a list of the types of information you can produce as output. You include the types of computers, mobile devices, and other technologies you will use to enter data and produce the information. Incorporate your own experiences and user reviews of the devices. Compile your findings.

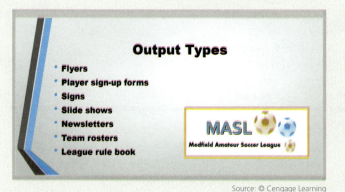

Collaboration

4. Recommending Technology Solutions   People use computers and mobile devices in a variety of fields, including travel, manufacturing, and more. Although the way people use computers and mobile devices varies, each use involves hardware, programs and apps, and some type of communications method, such as the Internet or cellular network.

Do This: Form a three-member team and choose a field in which you all are interested. Assign one member to investigate hardware, another to investigate programs and apps, and the third member to investigate communications methods used in the field. Locate user reviews and articles by industry experts. Each team member should develop a list of related items that may be used. After the investigation, create a hypothetical business or organization in the field. Recommend specific hardware, programs or apps, and communications capabilities that would be best for the network or organization. Include comparisons of specific items, as well as costs. Be sure to summarize your investigations, describe the hypothetical business or organization, and outline and support your recommendations.

CONNECTING AND COMMUNICATING ONLINE: The Internet, Websites, and Media

The Internet provides a variety of ways to communicate online.

"I use the Internet and web to shop for bargains, browse Google for all sorts of information, manage my fantasy sports teams, download music, check email on my phone, and so much more! What more could I gain from using the Internet?"

While you may be familiar with some of the content in this chapter, do you know how to . . .

- Use a public Wi-Fi hot spot safely?
- Register a domain name?
- Identify a cybersquatter?
- Browse the web safely?
- Tag digital content?
- Protect yourself from identity theft?
- Improve search results?
- Publish a website?
- Download digital media from online services?
- Set up a personal VoIP service?
- Combat cyberbullying?
- Determine your IP address?
- Search for a job online?

In this chapter, you will discover how to perform these tasks along with much more information essential to this course. For additional content available that accompanies this chapter, visit the free resources and premium content. Refer to the Preface and the Intro chapter for information about how to access these and other additional instructor-assigned support materials.

✔ Objectives

After completing this chapter, you will be able to:

1 Discuss the evolution of the Internet

2 Briefly describe various broadband Internet connections

3 Describe the purpose of an IP address and its relationship to a domain name

4 Describe features of browsers and identify the components of a web address

5 Describe ways to compose effective search text

6 Explain benefits and risks of using online social networks

7 Describe uses of various types of websites: search engines; online social networks; informational and research; media sharing; bookmarking; news, weather, sports, and other mass media; educational; business, governmental, and organizational; blogs; wikis and collaboration; health and fitness; science; entertainment; banking and finance; travel and tourism; mapping; retail and auctions; careers and employment; e-commerce; portals; content aggregation; and website creation and management

8 Explain how the web uses graphics, animation, audio, video, and virtual reality

9 Explain how email, email lists, Internet messaging, chat rooms, online discussions, VoIP, and FTP work

10 Identify the rules of netiquette

The Internet

One of the major reasons business, home, and other users purchase computers and mobile devices is for Internet access. The **Internet** is a worldwide collection of networks that connects millions of businesses, government agencies, educational institutions, and individuals. Each of the networks on the Internet provides resources that add to the abundance of goods, services, and information accessible via the Internet.

Today, billions of home and business users around the world access a variety of services on the Internet using computers and mobile devices. The web, messaging, and video communications are some of the more widely used Internet services (Figure 2-1). Other Internet services include chat rooms, discussion forums, and file transfer. To enhance your understanding of Internet services, the chapter begins by discussing the history of the Internet and how the Internet works and then explains each of these services.

Evolution of the Internet

The Internet has its roots in a networking project started by the Pentagon's Advanced Research Projects Agency (ARPA), an agency of the U.S. Department of Defense. ARPA's goal was to build a network that (1) allowed scientists at different physical locations to share information and work together on military and scientific projects and (2) could function even if part of the network were disabled or destroyed by a disaster such as a nuclear attack. That network, called *ARPANET*, became functional in September 1969, linking scientific and academic researchers across the United States.

The original ARPANET consisted of four main computers, one each located at the University of California at Los Angeles, the University of California at Santa Barbara, the Stanford Research Institute, and the University of Utah. Each of these computers served as a host on the network. A *host*, more commonly known today as a server, is any computer that provides services and connections to other computers on a network. Hosts often use high-speed communications to transfer data and messages over a network. By 1984, ARPANET had more than 1,000 individual computers linked as hosts. Today, millions of hosts connect to this network, which now is known as the Internet.

access information

send or post messages

videoconference or video call

Figure 2-1 People around the world use the Internet in daily activities, such as accessing information, sending or posting messages, and conversing with others from their computers and mobile devices.

Source: Library of Congress; © artjazz / Shutterstock; © iStockphoto / Chesky_W; © iStockPhoto / pictafolio; © iStockphoto / Blend_Images; © Andrey_Popov / Shutterstock; © Bloomua / Shutterstock

The Internet consists of many local, regional, national, and international networks. Both public and private organizations own networks on the Internet. These networks, along with phone companies, cable and satellite companies, and the government, all contribute toward the internal structure of the Internet.

Discover More: Visit this chapter's free resources to learn about Internet2.

✺ CONSIDER THIS

Who owns the Internet?

No single person, company, institution, or government agency owns the Internet. Each organization on the Internet is responsible only for maintaining its own network.

The World Wide Web Consortium (*W3C*), however, oversees research and sets standards and guidelines for many areas of the Internet. The mission of the W3C is to ensure the continued growth of the web. Nearly 400 organizations from around the world are members of the W3C, advising, defining standards, and addressing other issues.

⚡ **Internet Research**

Which organizations are members of the World Wide Web Consortium?

Search for: w3c members

Connecting to the Internet

Users can connect their computers and mobile devices to the Internet through wired or wireless technology and then access its services free or for a fee. With wired connections, a computer or device physically attaches via a cable or wire to a communications device, such as a modem, that transmits data and other items over transmission media to the Internet. For wireless connections, many mobile computers and devices include the necessary built-in technology so that they can transmit data and other items wirelessly. Computers without this capability can use a wireless modem or other communications device that enables wireless connectivity. A *wireless modem*, for example, uses a wireless communications technology (such as cellular radio, satellite, or Wi-Fi) to connect to the Internet. Figure 2-2 shows examples of modems. The wireless modem shown in the figure is known as a *dongle*, which is a small device that connects to a computer and enables additional functions when attached.

Today, users often connect to the Internet via *broadband* Internet service because of its fast data transfer speeds and its always-on connection. Through broadband Internet service, users can download webpages quickly, play online games, communicate in real time with others, and more. Table 2-1 shows examples of popular wired and wireless broadband Internet service technologies for home and small business users.

Figure 2-2 Using a modem is one way to connect computers and mobile devices to the Internet.

Courtesy of Zoom Telephonics Inc; © Oleksiy Mark / Shutterstock.com; Source: Microsoft; © Kristina Postnikova / Shutterstock.com; Kristina Postnikova / Shutterstock.com; © Cengage Learning; © DR / Fotolia

Table 2-1   Popular Broadband Internet Service Technologies

	Technology	Description
Wired	Cable Internet service	Provides high-speed Internet access through the cable television network via a cable modem
	DSL (digital subscriber line)	Provides high-speed Internet connections through the telephone network via a DSL modem
	Fiber to the Premises (FTTP)	Uses fiber-optic cable to provide high-speed Internet access via a modem
Wireless	**Wi-Fi** (wireless fidelity)	Uses radio signals to provide high-speed Internet connections to computers and devices with built-in Wi-Fi capability or a communications device that enables Wi-Fi connectivity
	Mobile broadband	Offers high-speed Internet connections over the cellular radio network to computers and devices with built-in compatible technology (such as 3G, 4G, or 5G) or a wireless modem or other communications device
	Fixed wireless	Provides high-speed Internet connections using a dish-shaped antenna on a building, such as a house or business, to communicate with a tower location via radio signals
	Satellite Internet service	Provides high-speed Internet connections via satellite to a satellite dish that communicates with a satellite modem

© Cengage Learning

Many public locations, such as shopping malls, coffee shops, restaurants, schools, airports, hotels, and city parks have Wi-Fi hot spots. Recall that a **hot spot** is a wireless network that provides Internet connections to mobile computers and devices. Although most hot spots enable unrestricted or open access, some require that users agree to terms of service, obtain a password (for example, from the hotel's front desk), or perform some other action in order to connect to the Internet. Read Secure IT 2-1 for ways to use a public Wi-Fi hot spot safely.

⊛ SECURE IT 2-1

Using Public Wi-Fi Hot Spots Safely

Connecting wirelessly to a public hot spot at your local coffee shop or at the airport can be convenient and practical. Using this free service can be risky, however, because cyber-criminals may lurk in public Wi-Fi hot spots, hoping to gain access to confidential information on your computer or mobile device. Follow these guidelines for a safer browsing experience:

- **Avoid typing passwords and financial information.** Identity thieves are on the lookout for people who sign in to accounts, enter their credit card account numbers in shopping websites, or conduct online banking transactions. If you must type this personal information, be certain the website's web address begins with "https," signifying a secure connection. If the website's web address changes to "http," indicating an unsecure connection,

sign out to end your Internet session immediately.

- **Sign out of websites.** When finished using an account, sign out of it and close the window.

- **Disable your wireless connection.** If you have finished working online but still need to use the computer, disconnect from the wireless connection.

- **Do not leave your computer or mobile device unattended.** It may seem obvious, but always stay with your computer or mobile device. Turning your back to talk with a friend or to refill your coffee gives thieves a few seconds to steal sensitive information that may be displayed on the screen.

- **Beware of over-the-shoulder snoopers.** The person sitting behind you may be watching or using a camera

phone to record your keystrokes, read your email messages and online social network posts, and view your photos and videos.

⊛ **Consider This:** How will you apply these precautions the next time you use a public Wi-Fi hot spot? Should businesses post signs alerting customers about Wi-Fi security issues?

© DeiMosz / Shutterstock.com

Home and small business users can share and provide wireless Internet connections by creating their own Wi-Fi hot spot through a communications device in the home or business that is connected to broadband Internet service. Instead of a stationary Wi-Fi hot spot, some users opt to create mobile hot spots through mobile broadband Internet service via a separate communications device or a tethered Internet-capable device (Figure 2-3). *Tethering* transforms a smartphone or Internet-capable tablet into a portable communications device that shares its Internet access with other computers and devices wirelessly. Users may pay additional fees for mobile hot spot and tethering services.

Internet Research

What is a MiFi device?

Search for: mifi

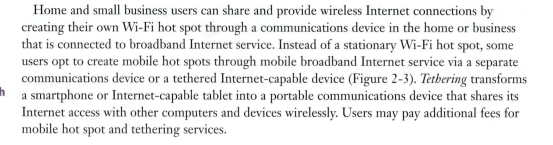

communications device as a mobile hot spot

tethered smartphone as a mobile hot spot

mobile broadband Internet service

Internet

mobile hot spot range

Figure 2-3 You can create a mobile hot spot using a communications device or by tethering a smartphone.

Courtesy of Verizon Wireless; © figarro / Can Stock Photo; © iStockphoto / Dane Wirtzfeld; © amfoto / Shutterstock.com; © Alex Staroseltsev / Shutterstock.com; Source: Microsoft; © Cengage Learning

Employees and students typically connect their computers and mobile devices to the Internet wirelessly through a business or school network, which, in turn, usually connects to a high-speed Internet service. When away from the office, home, or school, mobile users often access the Internet using Wi-Fi, mobile hot spots, or tethering services. Hotels and airports often provide wireless Internet connections as a free service to travelers. Many hotels have computers in their lobbies for customers to check email, browse the web, or print travel documents. Customers often bring their laptops or tablets to coffee shops, restaurants, libraries, hotels, and malls that offer free Wi-Fi as a service to their patrons.

CONSIDER THIS

Does everyone use broadband Internet?

No. Some home users connect computers and devices to the Internet via slower-speed dial-up access because of its lower cost or because broadband access is not available where they live. Dial-up access takes place when a modem in a computer connects to the Internet via a standard telephone line that transmits data and information using an *analog* (continuous wave pattern) signal.

Internet Service Providers

An **Internet service provider** (**ISP**), sometimes called an Internet access provider, is a business that provides individuals and organizations access to the Internet free or for a fee. ISPs often charge a fixed amount for an Internet connection, offering customers a variety of plans based on desired speeds, bandwidth, and services. In addition to Internet access, ISPs may include additional services, such as email and online storage.

Bandwidth represents the amount of data that travels over a network. A higher bandwidth means more data transmits. Data sizes typically are stated in terms of megabytes and gigabytes. A *megabyte* (**MB**) is equal to approximately one million characters, and a *gigabyte* (**GB**) is equal to approximately one billion characters. Table 2-2 shows approximate data usage for various Internet activities.

⊙ BTW
Byte
A byte is the basic storage unit on a computer or mobile device and represents a single character.

Table 2-2 Data Usage Examples

Activity	Quantity	Approximate Data Usage
Send and receive email messages (with no attachments)	100 messages	3–6 MB
Post on online social networks (text only)	100 posts	25–50 MB
Upload or download photos	50 photos	50 MB
Send and receive email messages (with attachments)	100 messages	0.75–1 GB
Visit webpages	200 visits	1 GB
Talk with others using VoIP (without video)	1 hour	1.25 GB
Listen to streaming music	1 hour	1–2 GB
Play online games	1 hour	1.75 GB
Watch smaller, standard-quality streaming video	1 hour	2–5 GB
Download apps, games, music, e-books	25 downloads	3 GB
Talk with others using VoIP (with video)	1 hour	5–7.5 GB
Watch HD streaming video	1 hour	5–20 GB

© Cengage Learning

🕖 Internet Research
Can I check the speed of my Internet connection?
Search for: internet speed test

❋ CONSIDER THIS

Does the term data have multiple meanings?

In the technology field, as discussed in Chapter 1, data can refer to unprocessed items that computers often process into information. Data also refers to the content that is stored on media or transmitted over a network. For example, when you select a data plan for your smartphone, the mobile service provider typically limits the amount of data (number of bytes) you can transfer each month depending on the plan you selected.

Wi-Fi networks often provide free Internet access, while some charge a daily or per use fee. Instead of locating a hot spot, some users prefer to subscribe to a mobile service provider, such as Verizon Wireless, so that they can access the Internet wherever they have mobile phone access. A **mobile service provider**, sometimes called a wireless data provider, is an ISP that offers wireless Internet access to computers and mobile devices with the necessary built-in wireless capability (such as Wi-Fi), wireless modems, or other communications devices that enable wireless connectivity. An antenna on or built into the computer or device, wireless modem, or communications device typically sends signals through the airwaves to communicate with a mobile service provider.

Discover More: Visit this chapter's free resources to learn more about Internet service providers.

How Data Travels the Internet

Computers and devices connected to the Internet work together to transfer data around the world using servers and clients and various wired and wireless transmission media. On the Internet, your computer or device is a client that can access data and services on a variety of servers. Wired transmission media includes phone line, coaxial cable, and fiber-optic cable. Wireless transmission media includes radio waves and satellite signals.

The inner structure of the Internet works much like a transportation system. Just as interstate highways connect major cities and carry the bulk of the automotive traffic across the country, several main transmission media carry the heaviest amount of **traffic**, or communications activity, on the Internet. These major carriers of network traffic are known collectively as the *Internet backbone*.

In the United States, the transmission media that make up the Internet backbone exchange data at several different major cities across the country. That is, they transfer data from one network to another until reaching the final destination (Figure 2-4).

How a Home User's Request for a Webpage Might Travel the Internet Using Cable Internet Service

Step 1
You send a request to the Internet. For example, you enter the web address of a webpage you want to visit in the address bar of your browser.

Step 2
A cable modem transfers the computer's digital signals to the cable television line in your house.

Step 3
Your request (digital signals) travels through cable television lines to a central cable system, which is shared by up to 500 homes in a neighborhood.

Step 4
The central cable system sends your request over high-speed fiber-optic lines to the cable operator, who often also is the ISP.

Step 6
The server retrieves the requested webpage and sends it back through the Internet backbone to your computer.

Step 5
The ISP routes your request through the Internet backbone to the destination server (in this example, the server that contains the requested webpage).

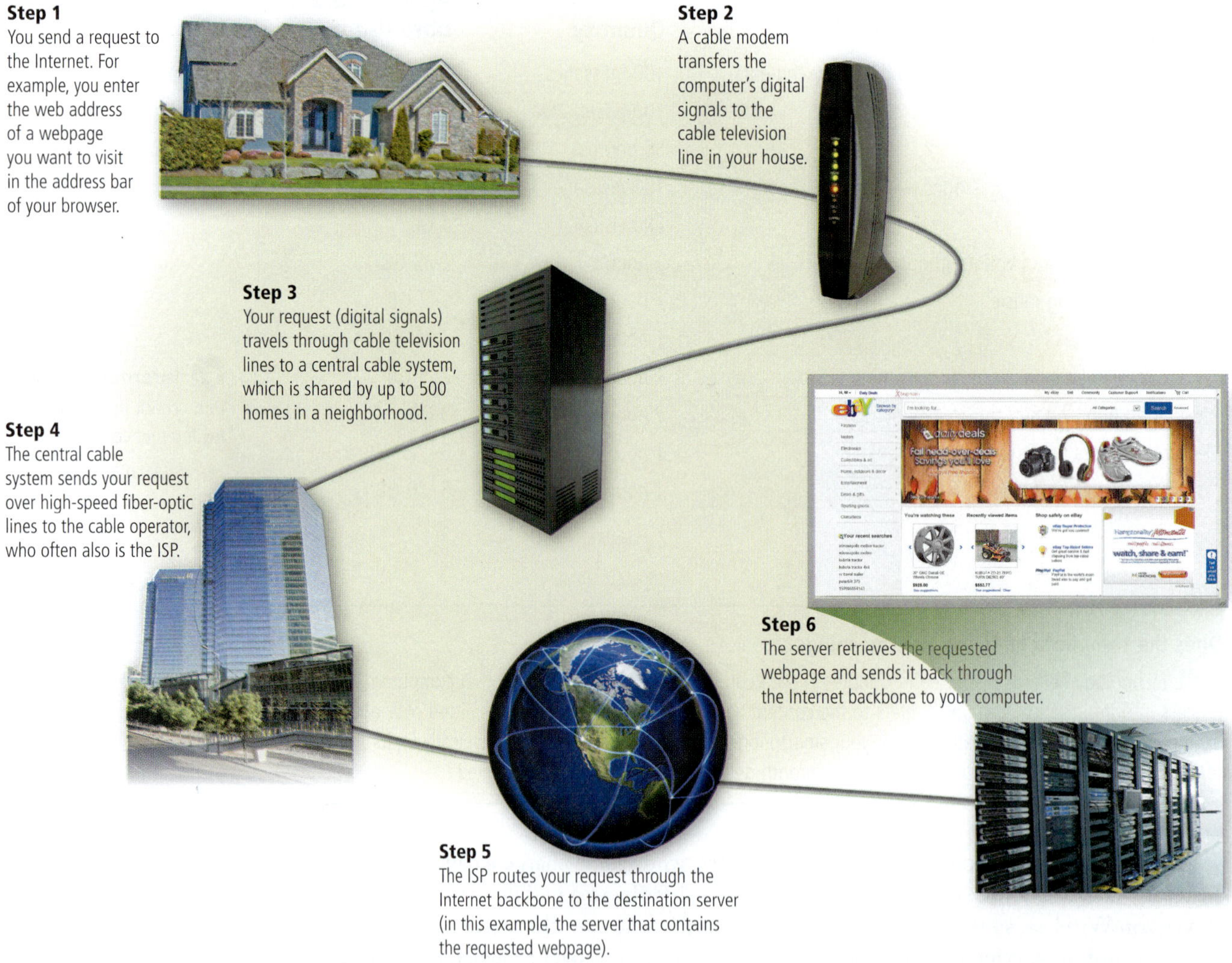

Figure 2-4 This figure shows how a home user's request for eBay's webpage might travel the Internet using cable Internet service.
© romakoma / Shutterstock.com; © Pablo Eder / Shutterstock.com; © dotshock / Shutterstock.com; © TonyV3112 / Shutterstock.com; © iStockPhoto / loops7; © iStockphoto / luismmolina; Source: eBay

IP Addresses and Domain Names

The Internet relies on an addressing system much like the postal service to send data to a computer or device at a specific destination. An **IP address**, short for Internet Protocol address, is a sequence of numbers that uniquely identifies the location of each computer or device connected to the Internet.

The Internet uses two IP addressing schemes: IPv4 and IPv6. Due to the growth of the Internet, the original IPv4 addresses began dwindling in availability. The IPv6 scheme increased the available number of IP addresses exponentially. Because lengthy IP addresses can be difficult to remember, the Internet supports domain names. A **domain name** is a text-based name that corresponds to the IP address of a server that hosts a website (Figure 2-5). A domain name is part of the web address that you type in a browser's address bar to access a website.

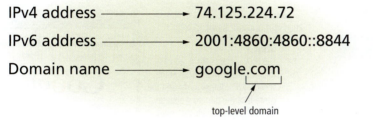

IPv4 address ⟶ 74.125.224.72
IPv6 address ⟶ 2001:4860:4860::8844
Domain name ⟶ google.com
top-level domain

Figure 2-5 The IPv4 and IPv6 addresses, along with the domain name for Google's website.
© Cengage Learning

The suffix of the domain name, called the *top-level domain* (*TLD*), identifies the type of organization associated with the domain. In Figure 2-5, for example, the .com is the TLD. Table 2-3 lists some of the original TLDs. New TLDs are being introduced to give individuals and businesses flexibility and creativity when purchasing domain names. For example, .museum, .technology, .name, and .biz have been introduced as TLDs within recent years.

The organization that approves and controls TLDs is called *ICANN* (pronounced EYE-can), which stands for Internet Corporation for Assigned Names and Numbers. For websites outside the United States, the suffix of the domain name may include a country code TLD (*ccTLD*), which is a two-letter country code, such as au for Australia. For example, www.philips.com.au is the domain name for Philips Australia. Read How To 2-1 to learn how to register a domain name.

Table 2-3	Original TLDs
TLD	**Intended Purpose**
.com	Commercial organizations, businesses, and companies
.edu	Educational institutions
.gov	Government agencies
.mil	Military organizations
.net	Network providers or commercial companies
.org	Nonprofit organizations

Discover More: Visit this chapter's free resources for an expanded table of popular TLDs.
© Cengage Learning

⚙ **HOW TO 2-1**

Register a Domain Name
Individuals and companies register domain names so that people can find their websites easily using a browser. You register a domain name through a *registrar*, which is an organization that sells and manages domain names. When creating a website to post online, register a domain name that is easy to remember so that visitors can navigate to your website quickly. The following steps describe how to register a domain name.

1. Run a browser.
2. Use a search engine to locate a domain name registrar and then navigate to the

website. You may want to evaluate several domain name registrars before deciding which one to use. Domain name registrars often offer various pricing models for registering domain names.

3. Perform a search on the domain name registrar's website for the domain name you wish to register. If the domain name is not available or costs too much, continue searching for a domain name that is available and within your price range, or explore various TLDs. For example, if the domain name you wish to register is not available or too expensive with the

".com" TLD, consider using another TLD such as ".net" or ".org."

4. Follow the steps on the domain name registrar's website to select and complete the purchase and registration of the desired domain name.

⚙ **Consider This:** What domain name based on your name would you register for your personal website? If your preferred domain name is not available, what are three alternative domain names you would consider?

BTW
High-Tech Talk
Discover More: Visit this chapter's free resources to learn more about DNS servers.

The *domain name system* (DNS) is the method that the Internet uses to store domain names and their corresponding IP addresses. When you enter a domain name (i.e., google.com) in a browser, a DNS server translates the domain name to its associated IP address so that the request can be routed to the correct computer (Figure 2-6). A *DNS server* is a server on the Internet that usually is associated with an ISP. Read Ethics & Issues 2-1 to consider issues related those who purchase unused or lapsed domain names for nefarious purposes.

How a Browser Displays a Requested Webpage

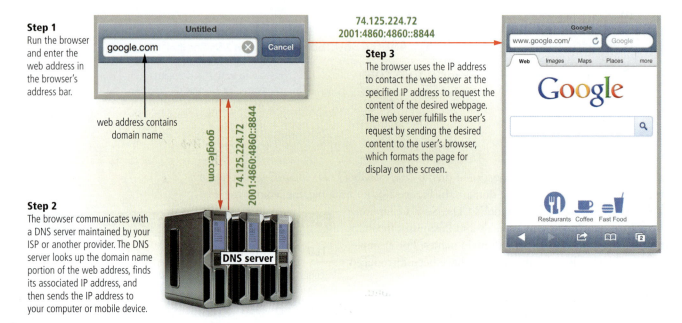

Step 1
Run the browser and enter the web address in the browser's address bar.

web address contains domain name

Step 2
The browser communicates with a DNS server maintained by your ISP or another provider. The DNS server looks up the domain name portion of the web address, finds its associated IP address, and then sends the IP address to your computer or mobile device.

DNS server

74.125.224.72
2001:4860:4860::8844

Step 3
The browser uses the IP address to contact the web server at the specified IP address to request the content of the desired webpage. The web server fulfills the user's request by sending the desired content to the user's browser, which formats the page for display on the screen.

Figure 2-6 This figure shows how a user's entered domain name (google.com) uses a DNS server to display a webpage (Google, in this case).
Apple Inc.; © Cengage Learning; © Cengage Learning; © Sashkin / Shutterstock.com; Source: Google Inc.

⚙ ETHICS & ISSUES 2-1

Should Cybersquatters Be Prosecuted?

You learn from a registrar that a domain name containing your company name is not available. When you enter the web address in a browser, a webpage appears that contains ads, false content, or a notice that the domain is available for purchase, likely by a cyber-squatter. Cybersquatters purchase unused or lapsed domain names so that they can profit from selling them. Cybersquatters sometimes will sell you the domain name, but some take advantage of people trying to reach a more popular website to promote their own business or needs. One example is when a politician registered several domain names that included his opponent's names and redirected them to his own campaign website.

Website owners periodically must renew domain names. Cybersquatters look for out-of-date registrations and buy them so that the original website owner must buy them back. Cybersquatters often purchase domain names with common words, alternate spellings of trademarked terms, or celebrity names. With the constant increase of new TLDs, cybersquatting cases are on the rise. Experts recommend purchasing your domain name with as many TLDs as you can afford, as well as to register your own name and that of your children.

More than 15 years ago, lawmakers enacted the *Anticybersquatting Consumer Protection Act* (ACPA). The ACPA's goal is to protect trademark owners from having

to pay a cybersquatter for a domain name that includes their trademark. To win a case against a cybersquatter, the owners must prove that the cybersquatters acted in bad faith, meaning they tried knowingly to profit from purchasing a domain name with a trademarked term, or a common misspelling or nickname of a trademarked term. Critics say that the ACPA prohibits free speech and free market.

Consider This: Should cybersquatting be illegal? Why or why not? Is it ethical to profit from cybersquatting? Why or why not? How should companies protect their brands when registering for domain names?

The World Wide Web

While the Internet was developed in the late 1960s, the World Wide Web emerged in the early 1990s as an easier way to access online information using a browser. Since then, it has grown phenomenally to become one of the more widely used services on the Internet.

As discussed in Chapter 1, the **World Wide Web** (**WWW**), or **web**, consists of a worldwide collection of electronic documents. Each electronic document on the web is called a **webpage**, which can contain text, graphics, animation, audio, and video. Some webpages are static (fixed); others are dynamic (changing). Visitors to a *static webpage* all see the same content each time they view the webpage. With a *dynamic webpage*, by contrast, the content of the webpage generates each time a user displays it. Dynamic webpages may contain customized content, such as the current date and time of day, desired stock quotes, weather for a region, or ticket availability for flights. The time required to download a webpage varies depending on the speed of your Internet connection and the amount of graphics and other media involved.

A **website** is a collection of related webpages and associated items, such as documents and photos, stored on a web server. A **web server** is a computer that delivers requested webpages to your computer or mobile device. The same web server can store multiple websites.

As web technologies matured in the mid-2000s, industry experts introduced the term *Web 2.0* to refer to websites that provide a means for users to share personal information (such as online social networks), allow users to modify website content (such as wikis), and provide applications through a browser (such as web apps).

Navigating the Web

Recall from Chapter 1 that a **browser** is an application that enables users with an Internet connection to access and view webpages on a computer or mobile device. Internet-capable mobile devices such as smartphones use a special type of browser, called a *mobile browser*, which is designed for their smaller screens and limited computing power. Many websites can detect if you are accessing their content on a mobile device (Figure 2-7).

BTW

Web vs. Internet
Recall that the terms web and Internet should not be used interchangeably. The World Wide Web is a service of the Internet.

BTW

Technology Innovator
Discover More: Visit this chapter's free resources to learn about Tim Berners-Lee (creator of the World Wide Web).

multiple tabs open in browser window

website on desktop browser

website on mobile browser

Figure 2-7 Many websites, such as the Centers for Disease Control and Prevention shown here, provide a mobile version that is designed specifically for display on a mobile browser.
Source: Centers for Disease Control and Prevention

When you run a browser, it may retrieve and display a starting webpage, sometimes called a home page. The initial home page that is displayed is specified in the browser. You can change your browser's home page at any time through its settings, options, or similar commands.

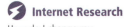 **Internet Research**

How do I change my browser's home page?

Search for: change browser home page

Another use of the term, **home page**, refers to the first page that is displayed on a website. Similar to a book cover or a table of contents, a website's home page provides information about its purpose and content. Many websites allow you to personalize the home page so that it contains areas of interest to you.

Current browsers typically support **tabbed browsing**, where the top of the browser shows a tab (similar to a file folder tab) for each webpage you display (shown in Figure 2-7). To move from one displayed webpage to another, you tap or click the tab in the browser. Tabbed browsing allows users to have multiple home pages that automatically are displayed when the browser runs. You also can organize tabs in a group, called a tab group, and save the group as a favorite, so that at any time you can display all tabs at once.

Because some websites attempt to track your browsing habits or gather personal information, current browsers usually include a feature that allows you to disable and/or more tightly control the dissemination of your browsing habits and personal information. Read Secure IT 2-2 for safe browsing tips.

⚙ SECURE IT 2-2

Safe Browsing Techniques

Browsing the web is similar to crossing a busy street: you need to exercise caution and look carefully for unexpected traffic. Cybercriminals are on the lookout to prey upon unsuspecting users, so you should follow these guidelines when browsing:

- **Verify the website is safe.** Type the website address of your email, banking, online social network, and other personal accounts directly in a browser; never visit these websites merely by tapping or clicking links found in email messages. Before you sign in, double-check the web address to verify it is correct. Most browsers change the color of the address bar to verify the website is legitimate. Also, check that the web address begins with https instead of the less secure http, and look for a closed padlock symbol beside it.
- **Turn off location sharing.** At times, you may want allow *location sharing*, which gives websites access to your current location. This feature is handy when you want to obtain current weather conditions or use a navigation app. This information could be misused

by dishonest individuals, however, so it is recommended you turn off location sharing.

- **Clear your browsing history.** A copy of every website you visit is stored in the browser's *cache* (pronounced cash) folder. If you perform online banking or view your credit card transactions, the cache could contain personal information, such as passwords and account numbers. You can specify to clear cache automatically each time you close a browser.
- **Never store passwords.** Many browsers can store your passwords so that you do not need to type them each time you visit the same websites. Although you may consider this feature a convenience, keep in mind that anyone who accesses your computer can view these secure websites easily using your account information.
- **Use a phishing filter.** *Phishing* is a scam in which a perpetrator attempts to obtain your personal and/or financial information. Many browsers include a *phishing filter*, which is a program that warns or blocks you from potentially fraudulent or suspicious websites.
- **Enable a pop-up or pop-under blocker.** Malicious software creators can develop a

pop-up ad or pop-under ad, which are Internet advertisements that suddenly appear in a new window on top of or behind a webpage displayed in a browser. A **pop-up blocker** is a filtering program that stops pop-up ads from displaying on webpages; similarly a **pop-under blocker** stops pop-under ads. Many browsers include these blockers. You also can download them from the web at no cost.

- **Use private browsing.** Prevent people using your computer or mobile device from seeing the websites you viewed or searches you conducted by using *private browsing*. The browser discards passwords, temporary Internet files, data entered into forms, and other information when you exit the browser.
- **Use a proxy server.** To protect your online identity, use a *proxy server*, which is another computer that screens all your incoming and outgoing messages. The proxy server will prevent your browsing history, passwords, user names, and other personal information from being revealed.

✴ **Consider This:** Which pop-ups have you encountered while browsing? What new techniques will you use to browse the web safely?

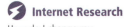 **Internet Research**

Does the browser war have a winner?

Search for: browser wars

Mini Feature 2-1: Browsers

The decision of which browser to use is a topic of discussion among computer experts and novices alike. Read Mini Feature 2-1 to learn about features of specific browsers.

✳ MINI FEATURE 2-1

Browsers

All browsers can retrieve and display webpages, but their features and ease of use vary. Many factors can affect the decision to choose the browser that best fits your needs.

Configuring Options

Users can customize some settings to improve their browsing experience, such as those listed below.

- **Favorites**, also called *bookmarks*, are links to preferred websites. When you add a website to the list of favorites, you can visit that website simply by tapping or clicking its name in a list instead of typing its web address. Favorites can be organized into folders, alphabetized, and sorted by date or how frequently you view the websites.

- Security features, such as filters and secure connections, help protect you from fraudulent and malicious websites that might attempt to steal your identity and personal information. These features also can block websites you do not want to be displayed and can instruct the browser to save passwords.

- Privacy features help prevent thieves from accessing information about your browsing history, such as websites you have visited, data about your browsing session, and content you have seen on specific webpages.

Obtaining Browsers

A browser often is included in the operating system of a computer or mobile device. For example, many computer manufacturers include Edge or Internet Explorer when they install Windows and include Safari when they install Mac OS. Use a search engine to locate the browser you want to install, and visit its website to download the most recent version. Most browsers are available for download at no cost. Keep your browser up to date to prevent security holes. You can set your browser to perform updates automatically.

Making a Decision

Selecting the best browser for your needs involves some careful thought. You may decide to install several and then use each one for specific needs. Perform some research to compare browsers and then consider the following factors:

- How old is your computer or mobile device? A newer browser may not work properly on older hardware.

- How much memory is in your computer or mobile device? Some browsers work best with a lot of memory.

- Which operating system are you using? Some browsers are available for specific operating systems. For example, Internet Explorer and Edge are available only for Windows operating systems.

- What do you want the browser to do? Some browsers are best suited for performing simple searches, while others excel when running websites containing media.

Specific Browsers

- **Chrome:** Google's Chrome was first released in 2008. This free browser is available for Windows and Mac OS and must be downloaded and installed. Chrome has independent tabbed browsing; if one tab develops a problem, the other tabs continue to function.

- **Firefox:** Developed by the Mozilla Corporation for Windows, Mac OS, and Linux, Firefox is known for its extensive array of plug-ins (discussed later in the chapter). This free browser was first released in 2004 and must be downloaded and installed. It has enhanced privacy and security features, a spelling checker, tabbed browsing, and a password manager.

- **Internet Explorer:** Internet Explore is a free browser, available primarily for Microsoft Windows and comes pre-installed. First released in 1995, features protection against it phishing and malware, and settings to delete information about searches performed and webpages visited.

- **Edge:** Edge is a Microsoft web browser included in the Windows 10 operating system. It is the default browser for Windows 10 on most devices, and is not compatible with prior versions of Windows. Features include integration with Cortana and OneDrive, along with annotation and reading tools.

- **Opera:** This second-oldest browser is free, fast, and small. Used on both computers and mobile devices, Opera must be downloaded and installed. It began as a research project in Norway in 1994 and introduced several features found on most of today's browsers.

- **Safari:** Preinstalled on Apple computers and devices, Safari has been the default browser for Mac OS since 2003 and is relatively new to Windows. The browser has built-in sharing with online social networks, fast performance, parental controls, and ease of use.

Mobile Browsers

Many browsers are included by default with some mobile devices and smartphones. Their features vary greatly. Some allow users to zoom and use keyboard shortcuts with most websites, while others display only websites optimized for mobile devices. The more popular mobile browsers are Chrome, Firefox, Internet Explorer, Edge, Safari, and Opera Mini.

Discover More: Visit this chapter's free resources to learn more about filters and secure connections, shareware websites, research to compare browsers, and specific browsers.

✳ **Consider This:** Which browser or browsers have you used? Would you consider using another browser? Why or why not? When first invented, their only function was to browse the web. Can you recommend a more descriptive name for today's browsers?

Chrome

Firefox

Internet Explorer

Edge

Opera

Safari

Google Inc; Mozilla Foundation; Microsoft; Opera Software; Apple Inc

🔵 Internet Research
What is the Silk browser?
Search for: silk browser

Web Addresses

A webpage has a unique address, called a **web address** or *URL* (Uniform Resource Locator). For example, the web address of http://www.nps.gov identifies the U.S. Department of the Interior National Park Service home page. A browser retrieves a webpage using its web address.

If you know the web address of a webpage, you can type it in the address bar of the browser. For example, if you type the address http://www.nps.gov/history/places.htm in the address bar and then press the ENTER key or tap or click the Search, Go, or similar button, the browser downloads and displays the associated webpage (Figure 2-8). The path, history/places.htm, in this web address identifies a webpage that is specified in a file named places.htm, which is located in a folder named history on the server that hosts the nps.gov website. When you enter this web address, after obtaining the IP address for the nps.gov domain name, the browser sends a request to the web server to retrieve the webpage named places.htm, and delivers it to your browser to be displayed.

✳ **CONSIDER THIS** ─────────────────────────────────────

Although you entered the web address correctly, your screen does not match Figure 2-8. Why?

Organizations may update or redesign their websites, which may cause your screens to look different from those shown in this book.

──

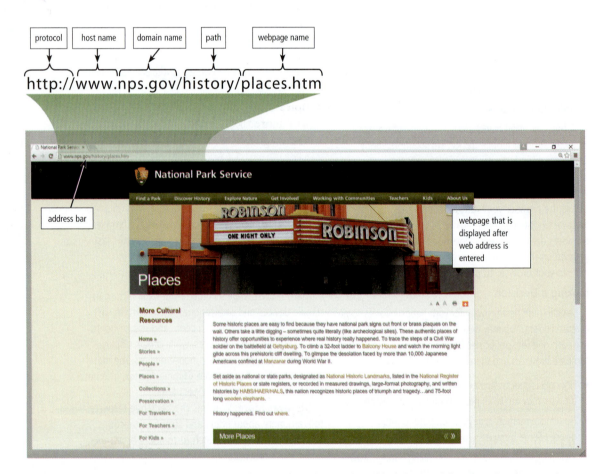

Figure 2-8 After entering http://www.nps.gov/history/places.htm in the address bar and then pressing the ENTER key or tapping or clicking the Search, Go, or similar button in a browser, the U.S. Department of the Interior National Park Service home page is displayed.

Source: National Park Service U.S. Department of the Interior

A web address consists of a protocol, domain name, and sometimes the host name, path to a specific webpage, or file name of the webpage. The *http*, which stands for Hypertext Transfer Protocol, is a set of rules that defines how webpages transfer on the Internet. Many web addresses begin with http:// as the protocol. The text between the protocol and the domain name, called the host name, identifies the type of Internet server or the name of the web server. The www, for example, indicates a web server.

❋ CONSIDER THIS

Do you need to type the protocol and host name in a web address?
Many browsers and websites do not require that you enter the http:// or the host name www in the web address. For example, you could enter nps.gov instead of http://www.nps.gov. As you begin typing a web address or if you enter an incorrect web address, browsers often display a list of similar addresses or related websites from which you can select. If, however, the host name is not www, you will need to type the host name as part of the web address. For example, the web address of schools.nyc.gov for the New York City schools website does not contain a www and thus requires entry of the entire web address.

When you enter a web address in a browser, you request, or pull, information from a web server. Another way users can pull content is by subscribing to a *web feed*, which contains content that has changed on a website. Mass media, blogs, and online social networks often provide web feeds, saving users the time spent checking the websites for updated content. Most browsers contain the capability to read web feeds.

Internet Research
How do I read web feeds?
Search for: rss reader

Discover More: Visit this chapter's free resources to learn about Internet protocols.

Web Apps and Mobile Apps

Recall from Chapter 1 that a *web app* is an application stored on a web server that you access through a browser. Users typically interact with web apps directly on a website, sometimes referred to as the host. Web app hosts usually provide storage for users' data and information on their servers, known as *cloud storage*.

Many web app hosts provide free access to their software. Others offer part of their web app free and charge for access to a more comprehensive program. Many include advertisements in the free version and charge for an advertisement-free version. Some allow you to use the web app free and pay a fee when a certain action occurs. For example, you can prepare your tax return for free, but if you elect to print it or file it electronically, you pay a minimal fee.

A *mobile app* is an application you download from a mobile device's app store or other location on the Internet to a smartphone or other mobile device. Mobile apps often take advantage of features of the device, such as touch screens, digital cameras, microphones, and embedded GPS receivers, to enable you to enter and capture data.

❋ CONSIDER THIS

What are GPS receivers?
GPS (global positioning system) is a navigation system that consists of one or more earth-based receivers that accept and analyze signals sent by satellites in order to determine the receiver's geographic location. A **GPS receiver** is a handheld, mountable, or embedded device that contains an antenna, a radio receiver, and a processor. Most smartphones include embedded GPS receivers so that users can determine their location, obtain directions, and locate points of interest. Read Ethics & Issues 2-2 to consider issues related to apps that track your location.

GPS receivers determine their location on Earth by analyzing at least 3 separate satellite signals from 24 satellites in orbit.

Discover More: Visit the High-Tech Talk in Chapter 1's free resources to learn about how GPS receivers use triangulation.

⚙ ETHICS & ISSUES 2-2

Should Apps Be Allowed to Track Your Location?

When you install an app on your smartphone, you unintentionally may be allowing the app to send personal data. Apps can transmit your location, as well as the time you spend using the app. Apps also can collect personal information, including gender and birth year, if you access the app through an online social network profile. Although apps often present an option to review their security policies, some track user data without permission, or require you to enable tracking before you can use the app. You may see the results of tracking in the ads you see when browsing the web or using an app. Other apps may track your location without your knowledge, such as apps that parents use to pinpoint a child's whereabouts.

If you search for driving directions, coupons, or restaurant tips based on your current location or past activities, you might be using apps that openly use this type of tracking. For example, a check-in app posts your location to online social networks, and another app enables you to locate friends by tracking their Bluetooth signals. Even when you opt to share data, use of these types of apps is not without risk. When people use location-tracking apps, for instance, they run the risk of someone stalking or robbing them. One positive use of location-tracking apps is with emergency services. Lawmakers have struggled with whether law enforcement officials can use location-tracking without a user's knowledge. The U.S. Supreme Court recently ruled that police must get a warrant before searching a user's phone or reading text messages.

Consider This: Should app makers be able to require you to enable tracking or track your activity without your knowledge? Why or why not? Should the police be able to track GPS data without warrants? Why or why not? Would you use apps that post your location to your online social network profile or otherwise alert others of your whereabouts? Why or why not?

🌐 Internet Research

What are popular mobile apps?

Search for: top mobile apps

Web apps and mobile apps often work together (Figure 2-9). You might access your cloud storage website from a laptop or desktop. The cloud storage website hosts web apps to upload, download, browse, organize, and view files. The website also may provide a mobile app that you install on a smartphone so that you can access the same information or perform the same tasks from a mobile device. Because the data and information for each app is stored on cloud storage, all data is synchronized and accessible from anywhere you have an Internet connection, regardless of the computer or device used. The functionality of the app across computers and devices generally is the same, although the mobile app sometimes has fewer features. Some tasks may be easier to accomplish on one device or the other. For example, if a lot of typing is required, you may opt to use the web app on a laptop so that you can use a standard keyboard.

Discover More: Visit this chapter's free resources to learn more about mobile device app stores.

web app on Smart TV

web app on browser window

mobile app on tablet

mobile app on smartphone

Figure 2-9 Web and mobile apps often work together, enabling you to access your content from a variety of computers and devices.
Courtesy of Microsoft Corporation

✓ **NOW YOU SHOULD KNOW** ────────────────────

Be sure you understand the material presented in the sections titled The Internet, Connecting to the Internet, and The World Wide Web, as it relates to the chapter objectives.
Now you should know...

- Why you interact with hosts and networks on the Internet (Objective 1)
- Which broadband Internet service and ISP is best suited to your needs (Objective 2)
- How a browser works with domain names and IP addresses when you enter a web address (Objectives 3 and 4)
- Which browser(s) you would use and why (Objective 4)

Discover More: Visit this chapter's premium content for practice quiz opportunities.

Types of Websites

The web contains several types of websites: search engines; online social networks; informational and research; media sharing; bookmarking; news, weather, sports, and other mass media; educational; business, governmental, and organizational; blogs; wikis and collaboration; health and fitness; science; entertainment; banking and finance; travel and tourism; mapping; retail and auctions; careers and employment; e-commerce; portals; content aggregation; and website creation and management. Many websites fall into more than one of these types. All of these websites can be accessed from computers or mobile devices but often are formatted differently and may have fewer features on mobile devices.

Search Engines

A web **search engine** is software that finds websites, webpages, images, videos, news, maps, and other information related to a specific topic. You also can use a search engine to solve mathematical equations, define words, and more.

Thousands of search engines are available. Some search engines, such as Bing, Google, and Yahoo!, are helpful in locating information on the web for which you do not know an exact web address or are not seeking a specific website. Those that work with GPS devices or services are location based, meaning they display results related to the device's current geographical position. For example, your smartphone may be able to display all gas stations within a certain distance of your current location. Some search engines restrict searches to a specific type of information, such as jobs or recipes.

Search engines typically allow you to search for one or more of the following items:

- Images: photos, diagrams, and drawings
- Videos: home videos, music videos, television programs, and movie clips
- Maps: maps of a business or address, or driving directions to a destination
- Audio: music, songs, recordings, and sounds
- Publications: news articles, journals, and books
- People or Businesses: addresses and phone numbers
- Blogs: specific opinions and ideas of others

Search engines require that you enter a word or phrase, called *search text*, to describe the item you want to find. Search text can be broad, such as spring break destinations, or more specific, such as walt disney world. If you misspell search text, search engines typically correct the misspelling or identify alternative search text. Some also provide suggested search text, links, and/or images as you type your search text.

Depending on your search text, search engines may respond with thousands to billions of search results, sometimes called *hits*. The content of the search results varies depending on the type of information you are seeking and your search text. Some search results contain links to webpages or articles; others are media, such as images or videos. Most search engines sequence the search results based on how close the words in the search text are to one another in the titles and descriptions of the results. Thus, the first few links probably contain more relevant information.

If you enter a phrase with spaces between the words in search text, most search engines display results that include all of the keywords. Because keywords describe content, search

BTW
Technology Innovators
Discover More: Visit this chapter's free resources to learn about Yahoo! and Google.

Internet Research
What is a natural language search engine?
Search for: natural language search

Internet Research
What is a search engine spider?
Search for: search engine spider

results exclude articles, conjunctions, and other similar words (e.g., to, the, and). Table 2-4 lists some operators you can use in search text to refine searches. Instead of working with operators to refine search text, many search engines provide an advanced search feature or search tools that assist with limiting search results based on items such as date, TLD, language, etc.

Table 2-4 Search Engine Operators

Operator	Description	Examples	Explanation
Space or +	Display search results that include specific words.	art + music art music	Results have both words, art and music, in any order,
OR	Display search results that include only one word from a list.	dog OR puppy	Results have either the word, dog, or the word, puppy.
		dog OR puppy OR canine	Results have the word, dog, or the word, puppy, or the word, canine.
( )	Combine search results that include specific words with those that include only one word from a list.	Kalamazoo Michigan (pizza OR subs)	Results include both words, Kalamazoo Michigan, and either the word, pizza, or the word, subs.
–	Exclude a word from search results.	automobile-convertible	Results include the word, automobile, but do not include the word, convertible.
" "	Search for an exact phrase in a certain order.	"19th century literature"	Results include the exact phrase, 19th century literature.
*	Substitute characters in place of the asterisk.	writer*	Results include any word that begins with the text, writer (e.g., writer, writers, writer's)

© Cengage Learning

✺ CONSIDER THIS

How can you improve search results?
You may find that many items listed in the search results have little or no bearing on the item you are seeking. You can eliminate superfluous items in search results by carefully crafting search text and use search operators to limit search results. Other techniques you can use to improve your searches include the following:
- Use specific nouns.
- Put the most important terms first in the search text.
- List all possible spellings, for example, email, e-mail.
- Before using a search engine, read its Help information.
- If the search is unsuccessful with one search engine, try another.
- Practice search techniques by performing the Internet Research: Search Skills exercise in each chapter of this book.

Subject Directories   A *subject directory* classifies webpages in an organized set of categories, such as sports or shopping, and related subcategories. A subject directory provides categorized lists of links arranged by subject. Using a subject directory, you locate a particular topic by tapping or clicking links through different levels, moving from the general to the specific. A disadvantage with a subject directory is that users sometimes have difficulty deciding which categories to choose as they work through the menus of links presented.

Discover More: Visit this chapter's free resources to learn more about search engines and subject directories.

Mini-Feature 2-2: Online Social Networks

Recall from Chapter 1 that an **online social network**, or *social networking site*, is a website that encourages members in its online community to share their interests, ideas, stories, photos, music, and videos with other registered users. Some online social networks also enable users to communicate through text, voice, and video chat, and play games together online. You interact with an online social network through a browser or mobile app on your computer or mobile device. Read Mini Feature 2-2 for features and uses of popular online social networks.

✴ **MINI FEATURE 2-2**

Online Social Networks

People you know through personal and professional circles form your social networks. You share common interests, work or spend leisure time together, and know many of one another's friends. Online social networks allow you to manage your social networks online.

Your account on an online social network includes profile information, such as your name, location, photos, and personal and professional interests. You might create accounts on several online social networks to separate your personal and professional activities. Online social networks allow you to view the profiles of other users and designate them as your *friends* or contacts. Some sites, such as Facebook and LinkedIn, require friends to confirm a friendship, while others, such as Twitter and Google+, allow users to follow one another without confirmation.

© iStockphoto / temizyurek

You can expand your online social network by viewing your friends' friends and then, in turn, designating some of them as your friends. Friends of your friends and their friends form your *extended contacts*.

- Extended contacts on a personal online social network such as Facebook can introduce you to others at your college or from your hometown, connect you with long-distance friends or relatives, or enable you to stay in touch with those who have interests similar to yours.

- Extended contacts on a professional online social network such as LinkedIn can introduce you to people who work at companies where you might be seeking employment. You can share employment history and skills in your profile, enabling potential employers who look at your profile to learn about your specific skills.

Read Secure IT 2-3 for tips about securing your privacy when using online social networks.

Personal Uses

Personal uses of online social networks include sharing photos and videos, greetings, or status updates.

© iStockphoto / Lentz Photography

A *status update* informs friends about what you are doing. You can *like*, or show appreciation for, online content such as photos or videos on online social networks such as Facebook and Google+. When you do, people who see the same content will know that you liked it, and the person who posted it is notified. All of your updates, likes, posts, and events appear in the activity stream associated with your account. Activity updates from friends may appear on a separate page associated with your account, often called a *news feed*.

On many online social networks, updates can include hashtags to identify their topics. A *hashtag* is a word(s) preceded by a # symbol that describes or categorizes a post. Users can search for posts on a topic by searching for a hashtag. Some online social networks list trending topics based on popular hashtags. Many television broadcasts, advertisements, and businesses post hashtags to encourage viewers and customers to share comments on Twitter or Facebook.

When accessing an online social network with a GPS-enabled mobile device, the location where you check in may be revealed as part of a status update. An online social network's mobile app can share your location with friends, find others nearby, and alert you to promotional deals from local businesses.

Follow button

© iStockphoto / hocus-focus

Business Uses

Businesses use online social networks to connect with their customers, provide promotional offers, and offer targeted advertising. For example, users who recommend online content about travel services may see travel-related advertising on their online social network's webpage.

Businesses also use data from online social networks to better connect with and understand customers. They can review comments from customers about their experiences using companies' products or services. Monitoring these feeds continuously gives companies immediate feedback from customers.

Nonprofit organizations use online social networks to promote activities and causes, accept donations, and allow volunteers to contact one another online.

Discover More: Visit this book's chapter's free resources to learn more about specific online social network websites and mobile apps.

✴ **Consider This:** How can businesses and individuals use online social networks to bring people together in support of a common goal? What benefits and risks are involved when using online social networks?

⚙ SECURE IT 2-3

Privacy and Security Risks with Online Social Networks

Online social networks can be excellent places to share messages, photos, and videos. They can, however, be risky places to divulge personal information. Follow these tips to help protect against thieves who are following the network traffic and attempting to invade private facets of your life.

- **Register with caution.** During the registration process, provide only necessary information. Do not disclose your birthdate, age, place of birth, or the city where you currently are living. If an email address is required, consider using a new address so that the online social network cannot access your email address book. Online social networks occasionally ask users to enter their email address and password to determine if their friends also are members of the network. In turn, the network obtains access to contacts in your address book and can send spam (unsolicited email messages) to your friends.

- **Manage your profile.** Check for privacy settings, usually found on the Settings or Options tabs, to set permissions so that you can control who can review your profile and photos, determine how people can search for you and make comments, and if desired, block certain people from viewing your page. Be aware that online social networks may change privacy settings. Periodically check your settings to ensure you have the most up-to-date settings.

- **Choose friends carefully.** You may receive a friend request that appears to be from someone you know. In reality, this message may originate from an identity thief who created a fake profile in an attempt to obtain your personal information. Confirm with the sender that the request is legitimate.

- **Limit friends.** While many online social networks encourage the practice, do not try to gather too many friends in your social network. Some experts believe that a functional online social network should not exceed 150 people. Occasionally review what your friends are posting about you.

- **Divulge only relevant information.** Write details about yourself that are relevant to the reasons you are participating in an online social network. When posting information, be aware that the message may be accessible publicly and associated with your identity permanently. Do not post anything you would not want to be made public.

- **Be leery of urgent requests for help.** Avoid responding to emergency pleas for financial assistance from alleged family members. In addition, do not reply to messages concerning lotteries you did not enter and fabulous deals that sound too good to be true.

- **Read the privacy policy.** Evaluate the website's privacy policy, which describes how it uses your personal information. For example, if you watch a video while signed in to your account, an external website or app may have access to this information and post this activity as an entry in both your activity stream and your friends' news feeds.

❋ **Consider This:** Should online social networks do a better job of telling their users what information is safe or unsafe to share? What role should parents play in overseeing their child's involvement in online social networks?

Informational and Research

An informational and research website contains factual information. Examples include libraries, encyclopedias, dictionaries, directories, guides (Figure 2-10), and other types of reference. You can find guides on numerous topics, such as health and medicine, research paper documentation styles, and grammar rules. Many of the other types of websites identified in this section also are used to research information.

Figure 2-10 You can research health conditions from your symptoms on a medical website, such as WebMD.
Source: WebMD, LLC

Media Sharing

A *media sharing site* is a website that enables members to manage and share media such as photos, videos, and music. These websites are sometimes called photo sharing sites, video sharing sites (Figure 2-11), and music sharing sites, respectively. Media sharing sites, which may be free or charge a fee, provide a quick and efficient way to upload, organize, store, share, and download media.

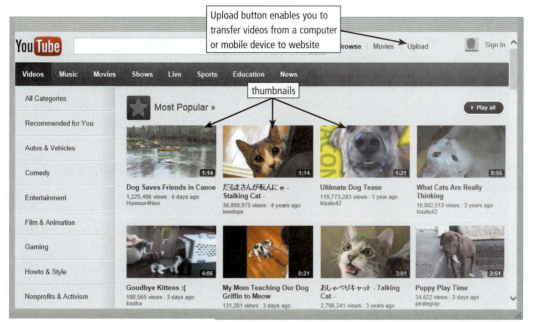

Figure 2-11   YouTube is an example of a video sharing site. You tap or click the thumbnail to view the video.
Source: YouTube, Inc.

✳ CONSIDER THIS

Why would you use a media sharing site instead of an online social network?
Although the lines between media sharing sites and online social networks are becoming blurred, some users chose a traditional media sharing site if they simply want to post photos, videos, or music to share with others and do not require the full functionality of an online social network. Before you allow someone to take your photo or record video of you, however, remember that the photo or video may be posted on a media sharing site. These photos or videos may be accessible publicly and associated with your identity for a long time. Also, once posted, you may be giving up certain rights to the media. Further, do not post photos or videos that are protected by copyright.

Bookmarking

A *bookmarking site* is a website that enables members to organize, tag, and share links to media and other online content (Figure 2-12). A **tag** is a short descriptive label that you assign to webpages, photos, videos, blog posts, email messages, and other digital content so that it is easier locate at a later time. Many websites and web apps support tagging, which enables users to organize their online content. Read How To 2-2 to learn how to tag digital content.

✳ **BTW**

Technology Trend
Discover More: Visit this chapter's free resources to learn more about uses of bookmarking sites.

Figure 2-12   Pinterest is an example of a bookmarking site.

✳ HOW TO 2-2

Tag Digital Content

When you post digital content online, it is a good idea to tag the content so that it is easy for you and others to locate and organize. After you have uploaded digital content to a media sharing site, follow the instructions on the website to apply tags to the digital content you uploaded. Consider the following suggestions when tagging digital content:

• Apply tags to all digital media, such as photos, music, and videos.

• If you are using multiple tags to identify one file, separate each tag with a separator. The website to which you are posting will inform you how to separate multiple tags (such as a space, comma, or semicolon).

• Choose tags that are descriptive of the content you are posting. For example, if you are posting a photo from a recent family vacation to Hammonasset Beach State Park, you might choose

"Hammonasset" and "vacation" as two of your tags for this photo.

• After you have tagged the digital content, perform a search on the media sharing site for your content, using the tags as your search criteria, to verify your content is displayed as intended.

✳ **Consider This:** Why else is it important to tag digital content? What tags might you assign to your favorite song in your music library?

Discover More: Visit this chapter's free resources to learn more about websites that support tagging.

✳ CONSIDER THIS

What are the various kinds of social media?

Social media consists of content that users create and share online, such as photos, videos, music, links, blog posts, Tweets, wiki entries, podcasts, and status updates. Social media websites facilitate the creation or publishing of social media online and include media sharing sites (for photo, video, and audio files), bookmarking sites, blogs and microblogs, wikis, podcasts, online social networks, and online gaming sites.

✳ BTW

Technology Innovator
Discover More: Visit this chapter's free resources to learn about Arianna Huffington (founder of *The Huffington Post* news website).

News, Weather, Sports, and Other Mass Media

News, weather, sports, and other mass media websites contain newsworthy material, including stories and articles relating to current events, life, money, politics, weather (Figure 2-13), and sports. You often can customize these websites so that you can receive local news or news about specific topics. Some provide a means to send you alerts, such as weather updates or sporting event scores, via text or email messages.

News on the web is not replacing the newspaper but enhancing it and reaching different populations. Although some exist solely online, many magazines and newspapers sponsor websites that provide summaries of printed articles, as well as articles not included in the printed versions. Newspapers, magazines, and television and radio stations often have corresponding news, weather, or sports websites and mobile apps. Read Ethics & Issues 2-3 to consider the issues related to using fake names on websites.

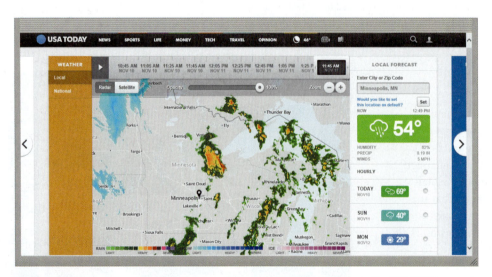

Figure 2-13 Forecasts, radar, and other weather conditions are available on the WEATHER webpage on USA TODAY's website.
Source: Gannett

ETHICS & ISSUES 2-3

Is It Ethical to Use a Fake Name or ID on a Website?

You are signing up for an account on an online social network, an online dating website, or a news website that enables you to post comments. Should you use your real name?

Many argue that it is harmless to protect your anonymity by using a fake name but believe that it is not right to create a fake profile to mislead others or leave malicious comments on a website. The latter has become so prevalent that terms have emerged to describe this behavior. For example, *catfishing* is when someone creates a fake online social network or online dating profile and forms relationships with unsuspecting users. A *troll* is a user who

posts negative, inflammatory comments on a blog post or article with the intent of inciting other users.

One website creates very thorough, but completely fake, personas, which include email addresses, Social Security numbers, phone numbers, and more. Although law enforcement has raised concerns over the potential misuses of fake profiles, it technically is legal, even though the names and personas are not real. Legitimate uses for fake name generators include testers of large databases, such as ones for hospitals.

Facebook currently requires members to use their real names. Twitter's policy is that anyone can create a fake account, but it has a verification process to identify the official account of a celebrity or public

figure. Most fake Twitter accounts are harmless, and often are flattering. Although some argue that creating a fake account constitutes identity theft, unless the intent is to harm or embarrass the real person, it is not unethical or illegal. When a journalist created a fake account for a politician and posted discriminatory quotes and Tweets in the politician's name, many considered it an ethics violation, because journalists are supposed to report the truth.

Consider This: Is it ever acceptable to use a fake name online? Why or why not? Is it unethical to create fake personas for others to use? Why or why not? Should websites require you to use a real name, or have a verification process? Why or why not?

Educational

An educational website offers exciting, challenging avenues for formal and informal teaching and learning. The web contains thousands of tutorials from learning how to fly airplanes to learning how to cook a meal. For a more structured learning experience, companies provide online training to employees, and colleges offer online classes and degrees. Instructors often use the web to enhance classroom teaching by publishing course materials, grades, and other pertinent class information.

Business, Governmental, and Organizational

A business website contains content that increases brand awareness, provides company background or other information, and/or promotes or sells products or services. Nearly every enterprise has a business website. Examples include Allstate Insurance Company, Apple Inc., General Motors Corporation, Kraft Foods Inc., and Walt Disney Company.

Most United States government agencies have websites providing citizens with information, such as census data, or assistance, such as filing taxes (Figure 2-14). Many other types of organizations use the web for a variety of reasons. For example, nonprofit organizations raise funds for a cause and advocacy groups present their views or opinions.

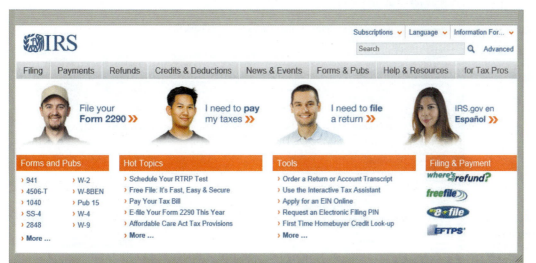

Figure 2-14
Government agencies, such as the IRS webpage shown here, have websites providing assistance and information to citizens.
Source: IRS

Tweets present current events and technology news

Figure 2-15 When you 'follow' @DiscoveringComp on Twitter, you will see Tweets such as those shown here posted by the Discovering Computers user "Shelly Cashman", in your account's timeline, along with Tweets from others whom you are following. As a student in this class, you should 'follow' @DiscoveringComp so that you easily can keep current with relevant technology changes and events in the computing industry.
Source: Twitter

Blogs

As described in Chapter 1, a **blog** (short for weblog) is an informal website consisting of time-stamped articles, or posts, in a diary or journal format, usually listed in reverse chronological order. The term *blogosphere* refers to the worldwide collection of blogs. A blog that contains video sometimes is called a video blog, or vlog. A *microblog* allows users to publish short messages usually between 100 and 200 characters, for others to read. The collection of a user's Tweets, or posts on Twitter, for example, forms a microblog (Figure 2-15).

✳ **CONSIDER THIS** ──────────────

How can you locate Tweets about certain topics?
When searching Twitter, you can use hashtags to find related posts. Similarly, you can tag any word(s) in your Tweets by typing it as a hashtag, such as #election.

───────────────────────────

Similar to an editorial section in a newspaper, blogs reflect the interests, opinions, and personalities of the author, called the **blogger**, and sometimes website visitors. Blogs have become an important means of worldwide communications. Businesses create blogs to communicate with employees, customers, and vendors. They may post announcements of new information on a corporate blog. Teachers create blogs to collaborate with other teachers and students. Home users create blogs to share aspects of their personal lives with family, friends, and others.

Wikis and Collaboration

Whereas blogs are a tool for publishing and sharing messages, wikis enable users to organize, edit, and share information. A **wiki** is a type of collaborative website that allows users to create, add, modify, or delete the website content via a browser. Wikis can include articles, documents, photos, or videos. Some wikis are public, accessible to everyone (Figure 2-16). Others are private so that content is accessible only to certain individuals or groups. Many companies, for example, set up wikis as an intranet for employees to collaborate on projects or access information, procedures, and documents. (An *intranet* is an internal network that uses Internet technologies.)

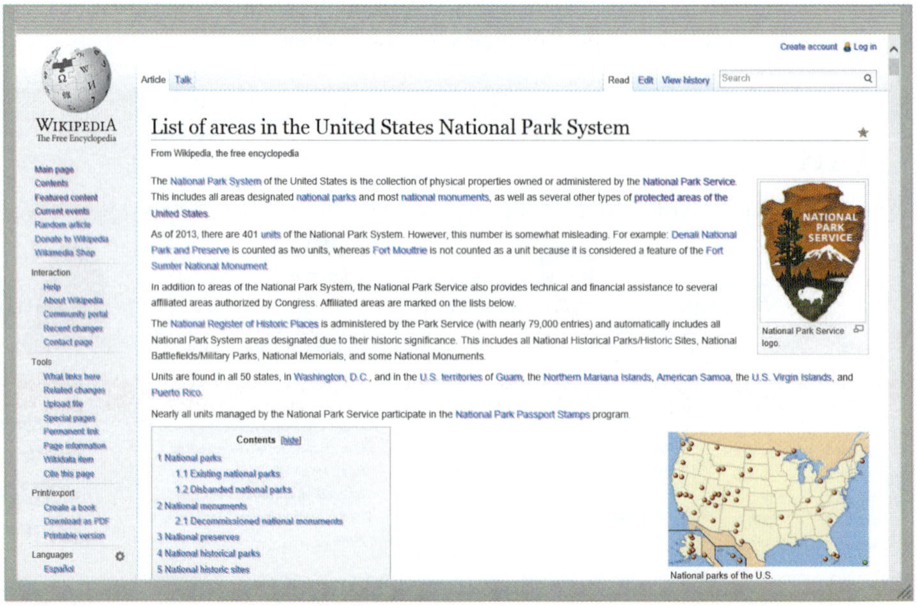

Figure 2-16 Wikipedia is a popular public wiki.
Source: Wikimedia Foundation

Contributors to a wiki typically must register before they can edit content or add comments. Wikis usually hold edits on a webpage until an editor or website manager can review them for accuracy. Unregistered users typically can review the content but cannot edit it or add comments.

Other types of collaboration sites enable users to share and edit any type of project — including documents, photos, videos, designs, prototypes, schedules, and more, often at the same time. On these websites, comments or edits are seen by other connected users. Most of these websites also enable users to communicate via chat windows, and some provide a whiteboard.

Discover More: Visit this chapter's free resources to learn more about public wikis and other collaboration websites.

Internet Research
Have errors been found in Wikipedia?
Search for: wikipedia factual errors

Health and Fitness

Many websites provide up-to-date medical, fitness, nutrition, or exercise information for public access. Some offer users the capability of listening to health-related seminars and discussions. Consumers, however, should verify the online information they read with a personal physician. Health service organizations store your personal health history, including prescriptions, lab test results, doctor visits, allergies, and immunizations. Doctors use the web to assist with researching and diagnosing health conditions.

Science

Several websites contain information about space exploration, astronomy, physics, earth sciences, microgravity, robotics, and other branches of science. Scientists use online social networks to collaborate on the web. Nonprofit science organizations use the web to seek public donations to support research.

Entertainment

An entertainment website offers music, videos, shows, performances, events, sports, games, and more in an interactive and engaging environment. Many entertainment websites support streaming media. **Streaming** is the process of transferring data in a continuous and even flow, which allows users to access and use a file while it is transmitting. You can listen to streaming audio or watch streaming video, such as a live performance or broadcast, as it downloads to your computer, mobile device, or an Internet-connected television.

Sophisticated entertainment websites often partner with other technologies. For example, you can cast your vote on a television show via your phone or online social network account.

Banking and Finance

Online banking and online trading enable users to access their financial records from anywhere in the world, as long as they have an Internet connection. Using online banking, users can access accounts, pay bills, transfer funds, calculate mortgage payments, and manage other financial activities from their computer or mobile device (Figure 2-17). With online trading, users can invest in stocks, options, bonds, treasuries, certificates of deposit, money market accounts, annuities, mutual funds, and so on, without using a broker. Read Secure IT 2-4 for tips about protecting your bank accounts and other personal information from identity theft.

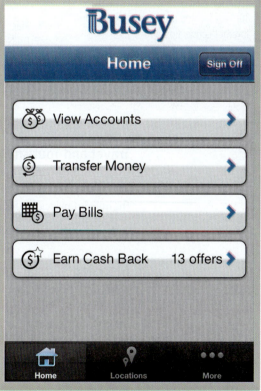

Figure 2-17   Many banks, such as Busey shown here, provide mobile versions of their online banking website so that users can manage financial accounts from their smartphones.
Source: First Busey Corporation

SECURE IT 2-4

Protecting Yourself from Identity Theft

The fastest growing crime in the United States is identity theft. More than nine million people fall victim each year, with the unauthorized use of an existing credit card accounting for much of the problem. The National Crime Victimization Survey reports that household identity theft losses amount to more than $13 billion each year, and that figure does not account for the aggravation and time required to repair the accounts. Practice these techniques to thwart attempts to steal your personal data:

- Do not tap or click links in or reply to spam for any reason.
- Install a personal firewall (software that protects network resources from outside intrusions).
- Clear or disable web cookies (small text files that web servers store on a computer) in your browser. This action might prevent some cookie-based websites from functioning, but you will be able to decide which cookies to accept or reject.
- Turn off file and printer sharing on your Internet connection.
- Set up a free email account. Use this email address for merchant forms.

- Sign up for email filtering through your ISP or use an anti-spam program.
- Shred financial documents before you discard them.
- Provide only the required information on website forms.
- Avoid checking your email or performing banking activities on public computers. These computers are notorious for running *keyloggers*, which record keystrokes in a hidden file, and other tracking software. If you must use a public computer for critical activities, be certain to sign out of any password-protected website and to clear the browser's cache.
- Request a free copy of your medical records each year from the Medical Information Bureau.
- Obtain your credit report once a year from each of the three major credit reporting agencies and correct any errors. Enroll in a credit monitoring service.
- Request, in writing, to be removed from mailing lists.
- Place your phone number on the National Do Not Call Registry.
- Avoid shopping club and buyer cards.

- Do not write your phone number on charge or credit receipts. Ask merchants not to write this number or any other personal information, especially your Social Security number and driver's license number, on the back of your personal checks.
- Do not preprint your phone number or Social Security number on personal checks.
- Fill in only the required information on rebate, warranty, and registration forms.
- Learn how to block your phone number from displaying on the receiver's system.

If your identity has been stolen, immediately change any passwords that may have been compromised. If you have disclosed your debit or credit card numbers, contact your financial institutions. You also should visit the Federal Trade Commission website or call the FTC help line.

Consider This: Do you know anyone who has been a victim of identity theft? What steps will you take to protect your identity using some of these guidelines?

Travel and Tourism

Travel and tourism websites enable users to research travel options and make travel arrangements. On these websites, you typically can read travel reviews, search for and compare flights and prices, order airline tickets, book a room, or reserve a rental car.

Discover More: Visit this chapter's free resources to learn more about travel websites.

Mapping

Several mapping website and web apps exist that enable you to display up-to-date maps by searching for an address, postal code, phone number, or point of interest (such as an airport, lodging, or historical site). The maps can be displayed in a variety of views, including terrain, aerial, maps, streets, buildings, traffic, and weather. These websites also provide directions when a user enters a starting and destination point (Figure 2-18). Many work with GPS to determine where a user is located, eliminating the need for a user to enter the starting point and enabling the website to recommend nearby points of interest.

Discover More: Visit this chapter's free resources to learn more about mapping web apps.

Figure 2-18   Using mapping web apps, such as Google Maps shown here, you can obtain driving directions from one destination to another.
Source: Google Inc.

Retail and Auctions

You can purchase just about any product or service on the web, a process that sometimes is called *e-retail* (short for electronic retail). To purchase online, the customer visits the business's *electronic storefront*, which contains product descriptions, images, and a shopping cart (Figure 2-19). The *shopping cart* allows the customer to collect purchases. When ready to complete the sale, the customer enters personal data and the method of payment, which should be through a secure Internet connection.

Figure 2-19   Shown here is Amazon's storefront for Professional and Technical Books.
Source: Amazon.com, Inc.

With an **online auction**, users bid on an item being sold by someone else. The highest bidder at the end of the bidding period purchases the item. eBay is one of the more popular online auction websites.

☼ CONSIDER THIS ─────────────────────────────

Is it safe to enter financial information online?
As an alternative to entering credit card, bank account, or other financial information online, some shopping and auction websites allow consumers to use an online payment service such as PayPal. To use an online payment service, you create an account that is linked to your credit card or funds at a financial institution. When you make a purchase, you use your online payment service account, which transfers money for you without revealing your financial information.

Careers and Employment

You can search the web for career information and job openings. Job search websites list thousands of openings in hundreds of fields, companies, and locations. This information may include required training and education, salary data, working conditions, job descriptions, and more. In addition, many organizations advertise careers on their websites.

When a company contacts you for an interview, learn as much about the company and the industry as possible before the interview. Many have websites with detailed company profiles.

Discover More: Visit this chapter's free resources to learn more about job search websites.

E-Commerce

E-commerce, short for electronic commerce, is a business transaction that occurs over an electronic network, such as the Internet. Anyone with access to a computer or mobile device, an Internet connection, and a means to pay for purchased goods or services can participate in e-commerce. Some people use the term *m-commerce* (mobile commerce) to identify e-commerce that takes place using mobile devices. Popular uses of e-commerce by consumers include shopping and auctions, finance, travel, entertainment, and health.

Three types of e-commerce websites are business-to-consumer, consumer-to-consumer, and business-to-business.

- *Business-to-consumer (B2C) e-commerce* consists of the sale of goods and services to the general public, such as at a shopping website.
- *Consumer-to-consumer (C2C) e-commerce* occurs when one consumer sells directly to another, such as in an online auction.
- *Business-to-business (B2B) e-commerce* occurs when businesses provide goods and services to other businesses, such as online advertising, recruiting, credit, sales, market research, technical support, and training.

Portals

A **portal** is a website that offers a variety of Internet services from a single, convenient location (Figure 2-20). A wireless portal is a portal designed for Internet-capable mobile devices. Most portals offer these free services: search engine; news, sports, and weather; web publishing; yellow pages; stock quotes; maps; shopping; and email and other communications services.

Discover More: Visit this chapter's free resources to learn more about portals.

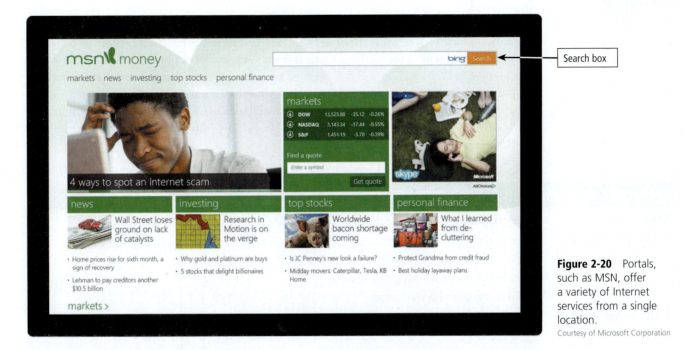

Figure 2-20 Portals, such as MSN, offer a variety of Internet services from a single location.
Courtesy of Microsoft Corporation

Content Aggregation

A **content aggregation** website or web app, sometimes called a *curation website*, allows users to collect and compile content from a variety of websites about a particular topic or theme (Figure 2-21). Types of content that may be compiled includes news, reviews, images, videos, podcasts (discussed later in this chapter), and blogs. Content aggregation websites save users time because they need to visit only one website (the content aggregation website) instead of visiting multiple websites to obtain information.

Discover More: Visit this chapter's free resources to learn more about content aggregation websites.

Figure 2-21 A content aggregation web app that compiles news from a variety of online sources.
Source: SmallRivers

Website Creation and Management

By creating their own websites, businesses and individuals can convey information to billions of people. The content of the webpages ranges from news stories to product information to blogs to surveys. Web creation and management sites provide tools that support the steps in **web publishing**, which is the creation and maintenance of websites. To create a website, you do not have to be a computer programmer. For the small business or home user, web publishing is fairly easy as long as you have the proper tools. Table 2-5 outlines the five main steps in web publishing.

Table 2-5   Steps in Web Publishing

Step	Description
1. Plan the website.	Identify the purpose of the website and the characteristics of the people you want to visit the website. Determine ways to differentiate your website from other similar ones. Decide how visitors will navigate the website. Register the desired domain name.
2. Design the website.	Design the appearance and layout of elements on the website. Decide colors and formats. Determine content for links, text, graphics, animation, audio, video, virtual reality, and blogs. You may need specific hardware, such as a digital camera, webcam, video camera, scanner, and/or audio recorder. You also may need software that enables you to create images or edit photos, audio, and video.
3. Create the website.	To create a website, you have several options: a. Use the features of a word processing program that enable you to create basic webpages from documents containing text and graphics. b. Use a *content management system*, which is a tool that assists users with creating, editing, and hosting content on a website. c. Use website authoring software to create more sophisticated websites that include text, graphics, animation, audio, video, special effects, and links. d. More advanced users create sophisticated websites by using a special type of software, called a text editor, to enter codes that instruct the browser how to display the text, images, and links on a webpage. e. For advanced features, such as managing users, passwords, chat rooms, and email, you may need to purchase specialized website management software.
4. Host the website.	Options for transferring the webpages from your computer to a web server include the following: a. A *web hosting service* provides storage space on a web server for a reasonable monthly fee. b. Many ISPs offer web hosting services to their customers for free or for a monthly fee. c. Online content management systems usually include hosting services for free or for a fee, depending on features and amount of storage used.
5. Maintain the website.	Visit the website regularly to ensure its contents are current and all links work properly. Create surveys on the website to test user satisfaction and solicit feedback. Run analytics to track visitors to the website and measure statistics about its usage.

BTW

Technology Trend
Discover More: Visit this chapter's free resources to learn more about responsive web design.

Some websites are dedicated to one portion of web publishing; others provide a variety of web publishing tools, including website design, content management, web hosting, website marketing, website analytics, survey development, and more. Because users view websites on a variety of computers and devices, many website developers use an approach called **responsive web design** (RWD) that adapts the layout of the website to fit the screen on which it is being displayed.

Discover More: Visit this chapter's free resources to learn more about website creation and management.

Can you assume that content on a website is correct and accurate?

No. Any person, company, or organization can publish a webpage on the Internet. No one oversees the content of these webpages.

Use the criteria below to evaluate a website or webpage before relying on its content.

• Affiliation: A reputable institution should support the website without bias in the information.

• Audience: The website should be written at an appropriate level.

• Authority: The website should list the author and the appropriate credentials.

• Content: The website should be well organized and the links should work.

• Currency: The information on the webpage should be current.

• Design: The pages at the website should download quickly, be visually pleasing, and be easy to navigate.

• Objectivity: The website should contain little advertising and be free of bias.

✓ NOW YOU SHOULD KNOW

Be sure you understand the material presented in the section titled Types of Websites as it relates to the chapter objectives. *Now you should know …*

• How to enter search text and improve your search results (Objective 5)

• How you can benefit from online social networks (Objective 6)

• When you would use specific types of websites (Objective 7)

• How you can publish your own website (Objective 7)

Discover More: Visit this chapter's premium content for practice quiz opportunities.

Digital Media on the Web

Most webpages include *multimedia*, which refers to any application that combines text with media. Media includes graphics, animation, audio, video, and/or virtual reality. The sections that follow discuss how the web uses these types of media.

Graphics

A **graphic** is a visual representation of nontext information, such as a drawing, chart, or photo. Many webpages use colorful graphics to convey messages (Figure 2-22). As shown in the figure, some websites use thumbnails on their pages because larger graphics can be time-consuming to display. A *thumbnail* is a small version of a larger image. You usually can tap or click a thumbnail to display the image in full size.

Figure 2-22 Many webpages use colorful graphics to convey messages. For example, the variety of colors, images, shapes, and thumbnails on the San Diego Zoo webpage visually separate and draw attention to areas of the webpage, making the webpage more dynamic and enticing.

Source: Zoological Society of San Diego

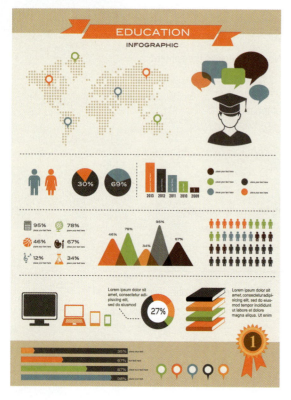

Figure 2-23 An infographic presents complex concepts at a glance.
© Marish / Shutterstock

The web often uses infographics to present concepts, products, and news. An *infographic* (short for information graphic) is a visual representation of data or information, designed to communicate quickly, simplify complex concepts, or present patterns or trends (Figure 2-23). Many forms of infographics exist: maps, signs, charts, and diagrams.

Of the graphics formats for displaying images on the web (Table 2-6), the JPEG and PNG formats are more common. *JPEG* (pronounced JAY-peg) is a compressed graphics format that attempts to reach a balance between image quality and file size. With JPG files, the more compressed the file, the smaller the image and the lower the quality. *PNG* (pronounced ping) is a patent-free compressed graphics format that restores all image details when the file is viewed. That is, the PNG format does not lose image quality during compression.

 **Table 2-6   Graphics Formats Used on the Web**

Abbreviation	Name	Uses
BMP	Bitmap	Desktop backgrounds Scanned images
GIF	Graphics Interchange Format	Images with few colors Simple diagrams Shapes
JPEG	Joint Photographic Experts Group	Digital camera photos Game screenshots Movie still shots
PNG	Portable Network Graphics	Comic-style drawings Line art Web graphics
TIFF	Tagged Image File Format	Photos used in printing industry

© Cengage Learning

CONSIDER THIS

What is a PDF file?
PDF, which stands for Portable Document Format, is an electronic image format by Adobe Systems that mirrors the appearance of an original document. Users can view a PDF without needing the software that originally created the document.

Animation   Many webpages use *animation*, which is the appearance of motion created by displaying a series of still images in sequence. For example, text that animates by scrolling across the screen can serve as a ticker to display stock updates, news, sports scores, weather, or other information. Web-based games often use animation.

Audio

On the web, you can listen to audio clips and live audio. *Audio* includes music, speech, or any other sound. Simple applications consist of individual audio files available for download to a computer or device. Once downloaded, you can play (listen to) the content of these files. Read How To 2-3 for instructions about downloading digital media from online services. Other applications use streaming audio so that you can listen to the audio while it downloads.

Internet Research
What other formats for images and graphics are used on the web?
Search for: web image formats

BTW
Compressed Files
Compressed files take up less storage space. Smaller file sizes result in faster downloading of webpages because small files transmit faster than large files.

Internet Research
How do you subscribe to an iTunes podcast?
Search for: subscribe itunes podcast

⚙ HOW TO 2-3

Download Digital Media from Online Services

Online services make various forms of digital media available, such as books, music, movies, and apps. You typically can use a program, such as iTunes, or an app, such as the Google Play Store, to access digital media. Digital media also may be available from these services' websites. The following steps describe how to download digital media from online services when you know the name or keyword(s) for the digital media you want to find.

1. On a computer or mobile device, run the program or app from which the digital media is available. If a program or app is not accessible easily, navigate to the online service using a browser.

2. Enter the name or keyword(s) in the Search box.

3. Tap or click the Search button to perform the search.

4. Navigate through the search results and then tap or click the search result for the item you want to download.

5. Locate and then tap or click the Download button or link to download the digital media to your computer or mobile device.

The following steps describe how to browse for and download digital media.

1. On your computer or mobile device, run the program or app from which the digital media is available. If a program or app is not accessible easily, navigate to the online service using a browser.

2. Tap or click the category corresponding to the type of digital media you want to browse. Common categories include music, movies, books, and apps.

3. Browse the items in the category.

4. When you find an item you want to download, tap or click the item to display additional information.

5. Look for and then tap or click the Download button or link to download the digital media to your computer or mobile device.

✷ **Consider This:** In addition to the online services listed in this box, what are three additional resources from which you can download digital media?

Audio files are compressed to reduce their file sizes. For example, the *MP3* format reduces an audio file to about one-tenth its original size, while preserving much of the original quality of the sound.

To listen to an audio file on your computer, you need special software called a *media player*. Most current operating systems contain a media player; for example, the Windows operating system includes Windows Media Player (Figure 2-24). Some audio files, however, might require you to download a media player. Media players available for download include iTunes and RealPlayer. You can download media players free from the web.

Discover More: Visit this chapter's free resources to learn more about audio file formats.

Figure 2-24 Windows Media Player is a popular media player, through which you can listen to music and watch video.
Source: Microsoft Corporation

Video

On the web, you can view video clips or watch live video. *Video* consists of images displayed in motion. Most video also has accompanying audio. You also can upload, share, or view video clips at a video sharing site. Educators, politicians, and businesses use video blogs and video podcasts to engage students, voters, and consumers.

Simple video applications on the web consist of individual video files, such as movie or television clips, that you must download completely before you can play them on a computer or mobile device. Video files often are compressed because they are quite large in size. Videos posted to the web often are short in length, usually less than 10 minutes, because they can take a long time to download. As with streaming audio files, streaming video files allows you to view longer or live videos by playing them as they download to your computer.

Discover More: Visit this chapter's free resources to learn more about video file formats.

Virtual Reality   **Virtual reality** (VR) is the use of computers to simulate a real or imagined environment that appears as a three-dimensional (3-D) space. VR involves the display of 3-D images that users explore and manipulate interactively. Using special VR software, a developer

Internet Research
What is a Smart TV?
Search for: smart tv

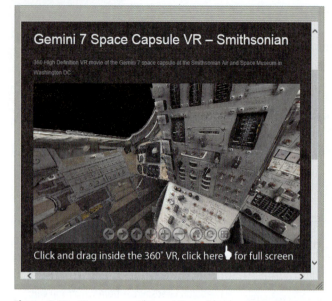

Figure 2-25 Users can explore a VR world using a touch screen or their input device. For example, users can explore the inside of the Gemini 7 space capsule, located at the Smithsonian Air and Space Museum in Washington, D.C., from their computer or mobile device.
Source: World VR

Internet Research
What is HTML5?
Search for: html5

creates an entire 3-D environment that contains infinite space and depth, called a VR world (Figure 2-25). A VR world on the web, for example, might show a house for sale where potential buyers walk through rooms in the VR house by sliding their finger on a touch screen or moving an input device forward, backward, or to the side.

In addition to games and simulations, many practical applications of VR also exist. Science educators create VR models of molecules, organisms, and other structures for students to examine. Companies use VR to showcase products or create advertisements. Architects create VR models of buildings and rooms so that clients can see how a completed construction project will look before it is built.

Plug-Ins

Most browsers have the capability of displaying basic multimedia elements on a webpage. Sometimes, however, a browser requires an additional program, called a plug-in, to display multimedia. A *plug-in*, or add-on, is a program that extends the capability of a browser. For example, your browser may require Adobe Reader to view and print PDF files. You typically can download plug-ins at no cost from various websites. Some plug-ins run on all sizes of computers and mobile devices; others have special versions for mobile devices.

Some mobile devices and browsers, however, do not support plug-ins. For this reason, web designers are using newer technologies to create websites that display correctly in both desktop and mobile browsers; these technologies generally do not require the use of plug-ins to display media.

Discover More: Visit this chapter's free resources to learn more about plug-ins.

Other Internet Services

As previously mentioned, the web is only one of the many services on the Internet. Other Internet services include the following: email, email lists, Internet messaging, chat rooms, online discussions, VoIP (Voice over IP), and FTP (File Transfer Protocol).

Email

Email (short for electronic mail) is the transmission of messages and files via a computer network. Email was one of the original services on the Internet, enabling scientists and researchers working on government-sponsored projects to communicate with colleagues at other locations.

You use an **email program** to create, send, receive, forward, store, print, and delete email messages. Email programs are available as desktop apps, web apps, and mobile apps. An email message can be simple text or can include an attachment such as a document, a graphic, an audio clip, or a video clip.

Just as you address a letter when using the postal system, you address an email message with the email address of your intended recipient. Likewise, when someone sends you a message, he or she must have your email address.

An *email address* is a combination of a user name and a domain name that identifies a user so that he or she can receive Internet email. A **user name** is a unique combination of characters, such as letters of the alphabet and/or numbers, that identifies a specific user. Your user name must be different from the other user names in the same domain. For example, a user named Rick Claremont whose server has a domain name of esite.com might want to select rclaremont as his user name. If esite.com already has an rclaremont (for Rita Claremont) user name, then Rick will have to select a different user name, such as rick.claremont or rclaremont2.

Sometimes, organizations decide the format of user names for new users so that the user names are consistent across the company. In many cases, however, users select their own user names, often selecting a nickname or any other combination of characters for their user name. Many users select a combination of their first and last names so that others can remember it easily.

In an Internet email address, an @ (pronounced at) symbol separates the user name from the domain name. Your service provider supplies the domain name. A possible email address for Rick Claremont would be rclaremont@esite.com, which would be read as follows: R Claremont at e site dot com. Most email programs allow you to create a *contacts folder*, which contains a list of names, addresses, phone numbers, email addresses, and other details about people with whom you communicate.

Figure 2-26 illustrates how an email message may travel from a sender to a receiver. When you send an email message, an outgoing mail server determines how to route the message through the Internet and then sends the message. As you receive email messages, an incoming mail server holds the messages in your mailbox until you use your email program to retrieve them. Most email programs have a mail notification alert that informs you via a message and/or sound when you receive a new email message(s).

Discover More: Visit this chapter's free resources to learn more about email programs.

✳ CONSIDER THIS

What are good practices to follow when using email?

1. Keep messages brief.
2. Respond to messages promptly.
3. Use proper grammar, spelling, and punctuation.
4. Never respond to unsolicited messages.
5. Use meaningful subject lines.
6. Read the message before you send it.
7. Use email when you want a permanent record of a communication.

How an Email Message May Travel from a Sender to a Receiver

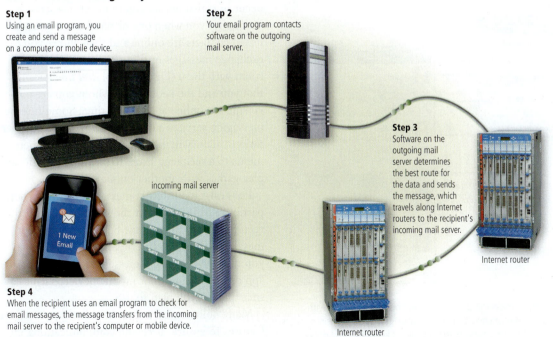

Step 1
Using an email program, you create and send a message on a computer or mobile device.

Step 2
Your email program contacts software on the outgoing mail server.

Step 3
Software on the outgoing mail server determines the best route for the data and sends the message, which travels along Internet routers to the recipient's incoming mail server.

incoming mail server

Internet router

Step 4
When the recipient uses an email program to check for email messages, the message transfers from the incoming mail server to the recipient's computer or mobile device.

Internet router

Figure 2-26   This figure shows how an email message may travel from a sender to a receiver.

Email Lists

An **email list**, or electronic mailing list, is a group of email addresses used for mass distribution of a message. When a message is sent to an email list, each person on the list receives a copy of the message in his or her mailbox. You *subscribe* to an email list by adding your email address to the mailing list, which is stored on a list server. To remove your name, you *unsubscribe* from the mailing list.

The original use of email lists, such as *LISTSERV*, allowed any subscriber to send a message, which created a discussion-type forum among all subscribers via email. Many mailing lists today, such as in Figure 2-27, however, are one-way communications and do not allow subscribers to send messages.

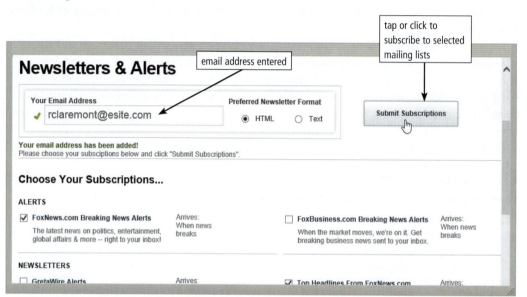

Figure 2-27 When you subscribe to a mailing list, you and all others in the list receive messages from the website. Shown here is a user who receives newsletters and alerts from FoxNews.com.
Source: FOX News Network, LLC

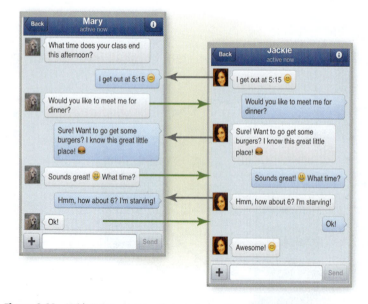

Figure 2-28 With Internet messaging services, you and the person(s) with whom you are conversing are online at the same time. The conversation appears on all parties' screens at the same time. Shown here is Facebook messenger.
© iStockphoto / Petar Chernaev; © Cengage Learning; © iStockphoto / Oleksiy Mark; © Cengage Learning

Internet Messaging

Internet messaging services, which often occur in real-time, are communications services that notify you when one or more of your established contacts are online and then allows you to exchange messages or files or join a private chat room with them (Figure 2-28). *Real time* means that you and the people with whom you are conversing are online at the same time. Some Internet messaging services support voice and video conversations, allow you to send photos or other documents to a recipient, listen to streaming music, and play games with another online contact.

For real-time Internet messaging to work, both parties must be online at the same time. Also, the receiver of a message must be willing to accept messages. To use an Internet messaging service, you may have to install messenger software or an app on the computer or mobile device, such as a smartphone, you plan to use.

Many online social networks include a messaging feature. To ensure successful communications, all individuals on the friend list need to use the same or a compatible messenger.

Discover More: Visit this chapter's free resources to learn more about Internet messaging services.

Chat Rooms

A **chat** is a real-time typed conversation that takes place on a computer or mobile device with many other online users. A **chat room** is a website or application that permits users to chat with others who are online at the same time. A server echoes the user's message to everyone in the chat room. Anyone in the chat room can participate in the conversation, which usually is specific to a particular topic. Businesses sometimes use chat rooms to communicate with customers.

As you type on your keyboard, others connected to the same chat room server also see what you have typed (Figure 2-29). Some chat rooms support voice chats and video chats, in which people hear or see each other as they chat. Most browsers today include the capability to connect to a chat server.

Figure 2-29   As you type, others in the same chat room see what you have typed.
Attribution: © ARENA Creative / Shutterstock.com; © Cengage Learning; © topseller / Shutterstock.com; © Alex Staroseltsev / Shutterstock.com; © Oleksiy Mark / Shutterstock.com; © Oleksiy Mark / Shutterstock.com; © Tom Wang / Shutterstock.com; © vlad_star / Shutterstock.com; © artjazz / Shutterstock.com

Online Discussions

An **online discussion**, or *discussion forum*, is an online area in which users have written discussions about a particular subject (Figure 2-30). To participate in a discussion, a user posts a message, called an article, and other users read and reply to the message. A *thread*, or threaded discussion, consists of the original article and all subsequent related replies.

Some discussion forums require that you enter a user name and password to participate in the discussion. For example, an online discussion for students taking a college course may require a user name and password to access the discussion. This ensures that only students in the course

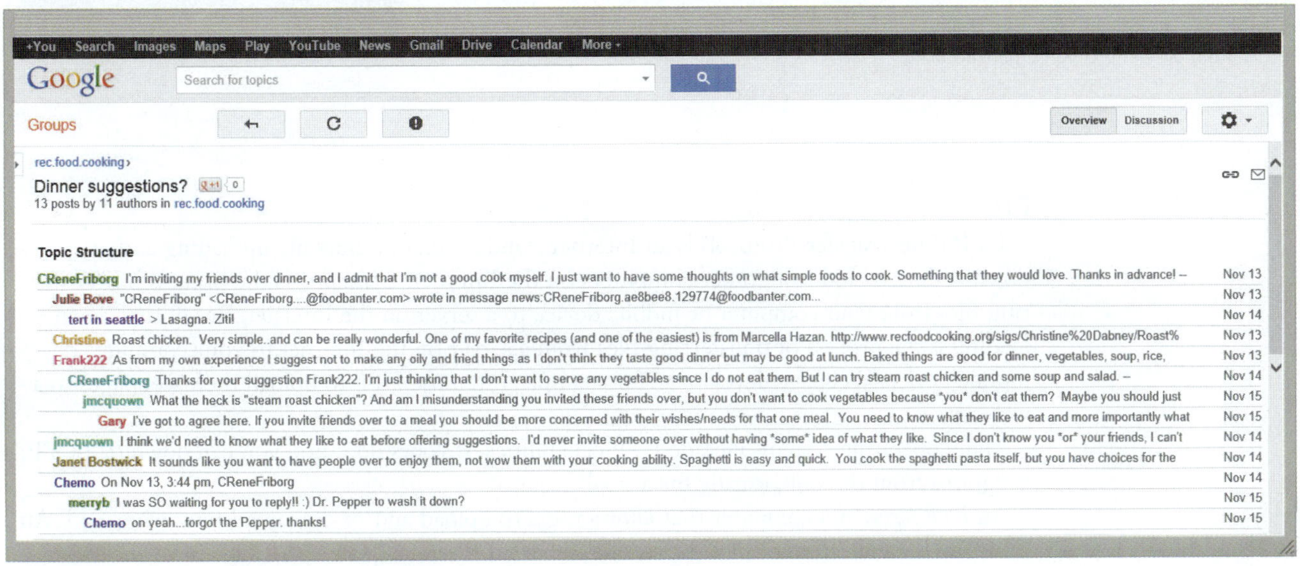

Figure 2-30   Users in an online discussion read and reply to other users' messages.
Source: Google Inc.

participate in the discussion. Posts in an online discussion usually are stored for a certain amount of time, such as a semester, in this example.

VoIP

VoIP, short for Voice over IP (Internet Protocol), enables users to speak to other users via their Internet connection. That is, VoIP uses the Internet (instead of the public switched telephone network) to connect a calling party to one or more local or long-distance called parties.

To place an Internet phone call, you need a broadband Internet connection, a microphone and speaker, both of which are included with a standard computer or mobile device, and VoIP software, such as Skype. Some VoIP services require that you purchase a separate phone and VoIP router, and subscribe to their service. Others offer certain services free and require a subscription for additional services. Read How To 2-4 for instructions about how to set up a personal VoIP service and make a call.

⚙ HOW TO 2-4

📃 Set Up a Personal VoIP Service and Make a Call

VoIP services enable you to make free video or voice calls to others around the world. In many cases, the person you are calling also must use the same VoIP service. The following steps describe how to set up a VoIP service and make a call.

1. If you do not know the VoIP service you want to use, search for a program or app that enables you to place and receive VoIP calls.

2. If necessary, download the program or app for the VoIP service you will use.

3. Most VoIP services require you to have an account with their service before you can place or receive a call. When you start the VoIP program or app, search for the button or link to create a new account.

Follow the steps in the program or app to finish creating the account.

4. Once the account has been created, if necessary, sign in to the VoIP service with your user name and password.

5. Make sure the person you are calling also has an account with the same VoIP service. You should know at least one person using this service to successfully place a call. VoIP services typically allow you to locate and call someone by entering their user name or adding them to your list of contacts. If necessary, add the person you want to call to your list of contacts.

6. On the list of contacts, select the person you want to call and then tap or click the appropriate button to place the call.

7. When the other person answers, you can start your voice or video call.

8. When you are ready to end the call, tap or click the button to end the call.

9. When you are finished using the VoIP service, you should sign out of and exit the VoIP program or app.

✷ **Consider This:** Survey your friends and family to see if they use a VoIP service. If so, which service is the most popular among them?

Source: Microsoft

FTP

FTP (File Transfer Protocol) is an Internet standard that permits file uploading and downloading to and from other computers on the Internet. *Uploading* is the process of transferring files from your computer or mobile device to a server on the Internet. Recall that downloading is the process of transferring files from a server on the Internet to your computer or mobile device. Webpage developers, for example, often use FTP to upload their webpages to a web server.

Many operating systems include FTP capabilities. If yours does not, you can download FTP programs from the web, usually for a small fee.

An *FTP server* is a computer that allows users to upload and/or download files using FTP. An FTP site is a collection of files that reside on an FTP server. Many FTP sites have *anonymous FTP*, whereby anyone can transfer some, if not all, available files. Some FTP sites restrict file transfers to those who have authorized accounts (user names and passwords) on the FTP server.

Discover More: Visit this chapter's free resources to learn more about FTP programs.

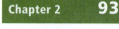

Mini Feature 2-3: Digital Communications

Home users, small/home office users, mobile users, power users, and enterprise users interact with technology for many reasons, including communication, productivity, and information. Read Mini Feature 2-3 for examples of how a home user might interact with digital communications.

✳ **MINI FEATURE 2-3**

Digital Communications

This scenario, which assumes you are a home user with a busy family, presents situations and questions regarding technology use during a single day.

7:30 a.m. You notice a leaky pipe under the kitchen sink. Your regular plumber recently has retired. On your smartphone, you run an app that enables you to use search criteria, GPS, and user reviews. You find a local plumber who has many positive reviews and tap the phone number on the smartphone touch screen to place the call. You leave a message explaining the problem and asking the plumber to call you back.
✳ How can you evaluate reviews for authenticity and bias? How might an app provider use your location information in ways you have not authorized?

8:45 a.m. The plumber calls you back to schedule an appointment time. You open your laptop and use the electronic calendar web app your entire family uses to keep track of appointments. You find a time that works for both of you and update the electronic calendar.
✳ What features enable multiple people, such as a family or small business, to use an electronic calendar? What issues may occur from using a shared calendar?

10:00 a.m. You have a freelance job blogging for a local florist. You are required to post twice weekly to the florist's blog about agreed-upon topics. You use a wiki to confirm the symbolic meaning of different types of roses so that you can include that in your next blog post. You sign in to the blog's content management system and submit your post to the blog.
✳ What responsibility do bloggers have to post accurate, verified information? Should users rely on wikis to verify content?

Credit TK

11:00 a.m. While you are driving to a doctor's appointment, you receive several text messages on your smartphone. You use your Bluetooth headset and your smartphone's speech-to-text feature to respond to the text messages without taking your eyes off of the road.
✳ Is it legal in your state to use hands-free devices while driving? What, if any, are the consequences of noncompliance?

1:00 p.m. Back at home, you flip through today's mail. You received a bill for your monthly mortgage payment. Using your laptop, you navigate to your bank's website

and schedule a recurring payment for the mortgage to ensure you never will be late on a payment.
✳ What precautions should you take when accessing financial information and authorizing payments on the web?

5:30 p.m. Unsure of what to make for dinner, you use your tablet to view recipes you bookmarked on a bookmarking site. You verify that you have the ingredients on hand and follow the recipe on your tablet as you prepare dinner.
✳ Who owns the content posted to social networking or bookmarking sites? What risks are involved with using these types of websites?

Credit TK

8:30 p.m. While helping your daughter with her math homework, you discover a website that includes the answers to questions asked in her textbook. You have a discussion with your daughter about ethical issues surrounding posting and using that type of content.
✳ Should students receive punishment for using answers they find on a website?

9:00 p.m. You sit down to watch your favorite vocal competition

Credit TK

reality show, streaming live through your Smart TV. The show enables you to send a text message to vote for your favorite contestant. You debate between two popular singers, then finally send your vote via text message.
✳ How else do TV, movie, and other entertainment websites use the Internet to interact with viewers or listeners?

10:30 p.m. You use the calendar app on your smartphone to confirm your schedule for tomorrow and then head to bed.
✳ How does technology enhance the daily life of a home user?

Discover More: Visit this chapter's free resources for additional scenarios for small/home office users, mobile users, power users, and enterprise users.

Netiquette

Netiquette, which is short for Internet etiquette, is the code of acceptable behaviors users should follow while on the Internet; that is, it is the conduct expected of individuals while online. Netiquette includes rules for all aspects of the Internet, including the web, social media, Internet messaging, chat rooms, online discussions, and FTP. Figure 2-31 outlines some of the rules of netiquette, with respect to online communications. Read Ethics & Issues 2-4 to consider issues related to an extreme misuse of online communications — online bullying.

Discover More: Visit this chapter's free resources to learn more about emoticons.

Netiquette Guidelines for Online Communications
Golden Rule: Treat others as you would like them to treat you.

Be polite. Avoid offensive language.

Avoid sending or posting *flames*, which are abusive or insulting messages. Do not participate in *flame wars*, which are exchanges of flames.

Be careful when using sarcasm and humor, as it might be misinterpreted.

Do not use all capital letters, which is the equivalent of SHOUTING!

Use **emoticons** to express emotion. Popular emoticons include:

:) Smile	:| Indifference	:o Surprised	:(Frown	:\ Undecided	;) Wink

Use abbreviations and acronyms for phrases:

BTW	by the way	IMHO	in my humble opinion	FWIW	for what it's worth
FYI	for your information	TTFN	ta ta for now	TYVM	thank you very much

Clearly identify a *spoiler*, which is a message that reveals an outcome to a game or ending to a movie or program.

Be forgiving of other's mistakes.

Read the *FAQ* (frequently asked questions), if one exists.

Figure 2-31 Some of the rules of netiquette, with respect to online communications.
© Cengage Learning

✳ ETHICS & ISSUES 2-4

Who Is Responsible for Monitoring Cyberbullying?

Sending or forwarding threatening text messages, posting embarrassing or altered pictures of someone without his or her permission, or setting up a fake online social network page where others make cruel comments and spread rumors about someone all are examples of cyberbullying. *Cyberbullying* is harassment using technology, often involving teens and preteens. Unlike verbal bullying, the perpetrators can hide behind the anonymity of the Internet and can reach a wide audience quickly. Victims cannot just walk away or ignore bullying that comes in the form of text messages, email, or online social network posts.

Cyberbullying often takes place outside of school hours on personal devices or computers not owned or monitored by a school. Yet the ramifications affect the victim at school. Schools struggle to come up with policies. Many schools are adopting policies that include consequences for any form of student-to-student bullying, even using nonschool resources, if it contributes to a hostile environment for any student or group of students. Some schools specify that students who retaliate against anyone who reports instances of bullying or cyberbullying will receive punishment.

Anti-bullying laws vary from state to state and often do not include specific language about cyberbullying. One argument against criminalizing cyberbullying is the protection of free speech. Awareness campaigns, school policies, and parent monitoring of technology use are some ways to attempt to prevent cyberbullying. These methods are not always effective. The impact on the victim can lead to poor grades, health issues, mental health concerns, and even suicide.

Consider This: Should schools be responsible for punishing students who cyberbully other students outside of school? Why or why not? What role can parents play in reducing cyberbullying? What are the positive and negative aspects of the freedom to be anonymous on the Internet?

✔ NOW YOU SHOULD KNOW

Be sure you understand the material presented in the sections titled Digital Media on the Web, Other Internet Services, and Netiquette as it relates to the chapter objectives.
Now you should know …

- Why you use media on the web (Objective 8)
- How you can benefit from using email, email lists, Internet messaging, chat rooms, discussion forums, VoIP, and FTP (Objective 9)
- What rules you should follow in online communications (Objective 10)

Discover More: Visit this chapter's premium content for practice quiz opportunities.

✔ Chapter Summary

This chapter presented the evolution of the Internet, along with various ways to connect to the Internet, how data travels the Internet, and how the Internet works with domain names and IP addresses. It discussed the web at length, including topics such as browsing, navigating, web addresses, web apps and mobile apps, searching, and online social networks. It presented various types of websites and media on the web. It also introduced other services available on the Internet, such as email, email lists, Internet messaging, chat rooms, online discussions, VoIP, and FTP. Finally, the chapter listed rules of netiquette.

Discover More: Visit this chapter's free resources for additional content that accompanies this chapter and also includes these features: Technology Innovators: Tim Berners-Lee, Yahoo! and Google, Arianna Huffington, and LinkedIn; Technology Trends: Uses of Bookmarking Sites and Responsive Web Design; and High-Tech Talks: IP Addresses and DNS Servers.

Test your knowledge of chapter material by accessing the Study Guide, Flash Cards, and Practice Test resources from your smartphone, tablet, laptop, or desktop.

⚡ TECHNOLOGY @ WORK

Transportation

What is transportation like without computers and mobile devices? Delivery drivers use clipboards to hold their records. Human navigators use paper maps to track routes for pilots. Ship captains rely solely on experience to navigate through shallow waters. Today, the transportation industry relies heavily on computer and mobile device usage.

Many vehicles include onboard navigation systems to help you navigate from one location to another. Some of these systems provide other services, such as dispatching roadside assistance, unlocking the driver's side door if you lock the keys in your vehicle, and tracking the vehicle if it is stolen.

The shipping and travel industries identify items during transport using bar codes, which are identification codes that consist of lines and spaces of different lengths. When you ship a package, the shipping company, such as UPS or FedEx, places a bar code on the package to indicate its destination to a computer. Because a package might travel to its destination by way of several trucks, trains, and airplanes,

computers automatically route the package as efficiently as possible. You are able to visit a website or sign up for text message notifications to track a package's progress during shipment.

When you travel by airplane, baggage handling systems ensure that your luggage reaches its destination on time. When you check in your baggage at the airport, a bar code identifies the airplane on which the bags should be placed. If you change planes, automated baggage handling systems route your bags to connecting flights with very little, if any, human intervention. When the bags reach their destination, they are routed automatically to the baggage carousel in the airport's terminal building.

Pilots of high-technology commercial, military, and space aircraft today work in a glass cockpit, which features computerized instrumentation, navigation, communications, weather reports, and an autopilot. The electronic flight information shown on high-resolution displays is designed to reduce pilot workload, decrease fatigue, and enable pilots to concentrate on flying safely.

Boats and ships also are equipped with computers that include detailed electronic maps, which help the captain navigate, as well as calculate the water depth and provide a layout of the underwater surface so that the captain can avoid obstructions.

As you travel the roadways, airways, and waterways, bear in mind that computers often are responsible for helping you to reach your destination as quickly and safely as possible.

Consider This: In what other ways do computers and technology play a role in the transportation industry?

Digital Vision / Getty Images

Study Guide

The Study Guide exercise reinforces material you should know for the chapter exam.

Discover More: Visit this chapter's premium content to **test your knowledge of digital content** associated with this chapter and **access the Study Guide resource** from your smartphone, tablet, laptop, or desktop.

Instructions: Answer the questions below using the format that helps you remember best or that is required by your instructor. Possible formats may include one or more of these options: write the answers; create a document that contains the answers; record answers as audio or video using a webcam, smartphone, or portable media player; post answers on a blog, wiki, or website; or highlight answers in the book/e-book.

1. Explain how ARPANET contributed to the growth of the Internet.
2. Describe the role of a host on a network.
3. Identify the role of the W3C.
4. Define the terms, dongle and broadband. List popular wired and wireless broadband Internet services.
5. State the purpose of a hot spot, and list tips for using hot spots safely.
6. ISP stands for _____.
7. Briefly describe how data and information travel the Internet.
8. Describe the purpose and composition of an IP address. Differentiate between IPv4 and IPv6.
9. Define the term, domain name. List general steps to register for a domain name.
10. Identify the purpose of several generic TLDs. Identify ICANN's role with TLDs.
11. Describe how and why cybersquatters register domain names.
12. State the purpose of a DNS server.
13. Differentiate between static and dynamic webpages.
14. Distinguish among the web, a webpage, a website, and a web server.
15. Explain the purpose of a browser. Describe the function of tabbed browsing.
16. List ways you can browse safely.
17. Name examples of popular browsers for personal computers and mobile devices.
18. Define the term, web address. Name a synonym.
19. Name and give examples of the components of a web address.
20. Describe the purpose of a web feed.
21. Explain the relationship between web and mobile apps.
22. Describe the purpose of GPS receivers, and why manufacturers embed them in smartphones.
23. Explain the risks and concerns involved in letting apps track your location. List any benefits.
24. Describe how to use a search engine. What are some ways you can refine a search?
25. Besides webpages, identify other items a search engine can find.
26. Differentiate between a search engine and a subject directory.
27. Explain how to use an online social network for personal or business use.

28. List ways to use online social networks securely.
29. Describe the purpose of these types of websites: informational and research; media sharing; bookmarking; news, weather, sports, and other mass media; educational; business, governmental, and organizational; blogs; wikis and collaboration; health and fitness; science; entertainment; banking and finance; travel and tourism; mapping; retail and auctions; careers and employment; e-commerce; portals; content aggregation; and website creation and management.
30. Is it ethical to use a fake name online? Why or why not? List techniques to protect yourself from identity theft.
31. Describe the uses of tags. List steps to tag digital content.
32. Define the term, e-commerce. Differentiate among B2C, C2C, and B2B e-commerce.
33. List uses and benefits of content aggregation websites and apps.
34. Identify and briefly describe the steps in web publishing.
35. The _____ web design approach adapts the layout of the website to fit the screen on which it is displayed.
36. List the seven criteria for evaluating a website's content.
37. _____ refers to any application that combines text with media.
38. Explain how webpages use graphics, animation, audio, video, virtual reality, and plug-ins.
39. Define the terms, thumbnail and infographic.
40. Name the types of graphics formats used on the web and how they use compression.
41. List general steps to download digital media.
42. Describe the purpose of these Internet services and explain how each works: email, email lists, messaging, chat rooms, online discussions, VoIP, and FTP.
43. Describe the components of an email address.
44. _____ refers to Internet communications in which both parties communicate at the same time.
45. List steps to set up a personal VoIP service and make a call.
46. Describe how a home user interacts with digital communications.
47. Define the term, netiquette.
48. Describe cyberbullying, and explain why it is difficult to catch the perpetrators.
49. Describe how the transportation industry uses technology.

You should be able to define the Primary Terms and be familiar with the Secondary Terms listed below.

Key Terms

Discover More: Visit this chapter's premium content to view definitions for each term and to access the Flash Cards resource from your smartphone, tablet, laptop, or desktop.

Primary Terms (shown in **bold-black** characters in the chapter)

blog (78)
blogger (78)
browser (65)
chat (91)
chat room (91)
Chrome (67)
content aggregation (83)
domain name (63)
e-commerce (82)
Edge (67)
email (88)
email list (90)
email program (88)
emoticons (94)
favorites (67)

Firefox (67)
FTP (92)
GB (61)
GPS (70)
GPS receiver (70)
graphic (85)
home page (66)
hot spot (59)
Internet (56)
Internet Explorer (67)
Internet messaging (90)
Internet service provider (ISP) (61)
IP address (62)
MB (61)
mobile service provider (61)

netiquette (94)
online auction (82)
online discussion (91)
online social network (72)
Opera (67)
PDF (86)
pop-up blocker (66)
pop-under blocker (66)
portal (82)
responsive web design (84)
Safari (67)
search engine (71)
social media (76)
streaming (79)
tabbed browsing (66)
tag (75)

traffic (62)
user name (88)
virtual reality (87)
VoIP (92)
web (65)
web address (68)
web publishing (84)
web server (65)
webpage (65)
website (65)
wiki (78)
World Wide Web (WWW) (65)

Secondary Terms (shown in *italic* characters in the chapter)

analog (60)
animation (86)
anonymous FTP (92)
Anticybersquatting Consumer Protection Act (64)
ARPANET (56)
audio (86)
bandwidth (61)
blogosphere (78)
bookmarks (67)
bookmarking site (75)
broadband (58)
business-to-business (B2B) e-commerce (82)
business-to-consumer (B2C) e-commerce (82)
cable Internet service (59)
cache (66)
catfishing (77)
ccTLD (63)
cloud storage (69)
consumer-to-consumer (C2C) e-commerce (82)
contacts folder (89)
content management system (84)
curation website (83)
cyberbullying (94)
discussion forum (91)
DNS server (64)
domain name system (DNS) (64)
dongle (58)

DSL (59)
dynamic webpage (65)
electronic storefront (81)
e-retail (81)
email address (88)
extended contacts (73)
FAQ (94)
Fiber to the Premises (FTTP) (59)
fixed wireless (59)
flames (94)
flame wars (94)
friends (73)
FTP server (92)
gigabyte (61)
hashtag (73)
hits (71)
host (56)
http (69)
ICANN (63)
infographic (86)
Internet backbone (62)
intranet (78)
JPEG (86)
keyloggers (80)
like (73)
LISTSERV (90)
location sharing (66)
m-commerce (82)
media player (87)
media sharing site (75)
megabyte (61)

microblog (78)
mobile app (69)
mobile broadband (59)
mobile browser (65)
MP3 (87)
multimedia (85)
news feed (73)
phishing (66)
phishing filter (66)
plug-in (88)
PNG (86)
pop-up ad (66)
pop-under ad (66)
private browsing (66)
proxy server (66)
real time (90)
registrar (63)
satellite Internet service (59)
search text (71)
shopping cart (81)
social networking site (72)

spoiler (94)
static webpage (65)
status update (73)
subscribe (90)
subject directory (72)
tethering (60)
thread (91)
thumbnail (85)
top-level domain (TLD) (63)
troll (77)
unsubscribe (90)
uploading (93)
URL (68)
video (87)
W3C (58)
Web 2.0 (65)
web app (69)
web feed (69)
web hosting service (64)
Wi-Fi (59)
wireless modem (58)

wiki (78)

Checkpoint

The Checkpoint exercises test your knowledge of the chapter concepts. The page number containing the answer appears in parentheses after each exercise. The Consider This exercises challenge your understanding of chapter concepts.

Discover More: Visit this chapter's premium content to **complete the Checkpoint exercises** interactively; complete the **self-assessment in the Test Prep resource** from your smartphone, tablet, laptop, or desktop; and then **take the Practice Test.**

True/False   Mark T for True and F for False.

T ___ 1. No single person or government agency controls or owns the Internet. (58)

T **F** ___ 2. The W3C is responsible for maintaining all networks and content on the Internet. (58)

T ___ 3. Users typically pay additional fees for mobile hot spot and tethering services. (60)

F ___ 4. A gigabyte (GB) is the basic storage unit on a computer or mobile device and represents a single character. (61)

T ___ 5. A dynamic webpage's contents generate each time a user displays the page. (65)

T ___ 6. Most browsers are available for download at no cost. (67)

T ___ 7. Mobile apps sometimes have fewer features than a web app. (69)

F ___ 8. A subject directory is software that finds websites, webpages, images, videos, maps, and other information related to a specific topic. (71)

T ___ 9. When you post digital content online, it is a good idea to tag it so that it is easy to locate and organize. (76)

___ 10. The term, blogosphere, refers to the worldwide collection of blogs. (78)

T **F** ___ 11. Tethering is the process of transferring data in a continuous and even flow, which allows users to access and use a file while it is transmitting. (79)

F ___ 12. One way to protect yourself from identity theft online is to retain all your cookies in your browser. (80)

Multiple Choice   Select the best answer.

1. A(n) _____ is any computer that provides services and connections to other computers on a network. (56)
   - **a. host**
   - b. client
   - c. FTP site
   - d. subject directory

2. A(n) _____ is a sequence of numbers that uniquely identifies the location of each computer or device connected to the Internet. (62)
   - a. Internet backbone
   - b. domain name
   - **c. IP address**
   - d. ccTLD

3. You register a domain name through _____, which is an organization that sells and manages domain names. (63)
   - a. a cybersquatter
   - **b. a registrar**
   - c. ICANN
   - d. an ISP

4. The _____ is the method the Internet uses to store domain names and their corresponding IP addresses. (64)
   - **a. domain name system (DNS)**
   - b. top-level domain (TLD)
   - c. File Transfer Protocol (FTP)
   - d. W3C

5. One way to protect your identity while browsing is to use a(n) _____, which is another computer that screens all your incoming and outgoing messages. (66)
   - a. password
   - b. anonymous FTP
   - c. phishing filter
   - **d. proxy server**

6. _____ is a set of rules that defines how webpages transfer on the Internet. (69)
   - a. Top-level domain
   - **b. Hypertext Transfer Protocol**
   - c. IPv4
   - d. Web 2.0

7. A(n) _____ website contains factual material, such as libraries, encyclopedias, dictionaries, directories, guides, and other types of reference. (74)
   - a. wikis and collaboration
   - b. media sharing
   - c. business
   - **d. informational and research**

8. A _____ is a website that offers a variety of Internet services from a single, convenient location. (82)
   - a. LISTSERV
   - b. microblog
   - **c. portal**
   - d. cache

Checkpoint

Matching   Match the terms with their definitions.

(handwritten answers at left: E, I/A, A/I, G, J, H, D, B, F, C)

1. tethering (60)
2. Internet backbone (62)
3. domain name (63)
4. web server (65)
5. tag (75)
6. catfishing (77)
7. wiki (78)
8. curation website (83)
9. chat (91)
10. cyberbullying (94)

a. text-based name that corresponds to the IP address of a server that hosts a website

b. website or web app that allows users to collect and compile content from a variety of websites about a particular topic or theme

c. harassment, often involving teens and preteens, using technology

d. collaborative website that allows users to create, add, modify, or delete website content via a browser

e. technique that transforms a smartphone or Internet-capable tablet into a portable communications device that shares its Internet access with other computers and devices wirelessly

f. real-time typed conversation that takes place on a computer or mobile device with many other online users

g. computer that delivers requested webpages to your computer or mobile device

h. online practice of creating a fake profile to form relationships with unsuspecting users

i. term used to refer to the major carriers of network traffic

j. short descriptive label that you assign to digital content so that it is easier to locate at a later time

✳ Consider This   Answer the following questions in the format specified by your instructor.

1. Answer the critical thinking questions posed at the end of these elements in this chapter: Ethics & Issues (64, 70, 77, 94), How To (63, 76, 87, 92), Mini Features (67, 73, 93), Secure IT (59, 66, 74, 80), and Technology @ Work (95).
2. What were ARPA's original goals? (56)
3. What are the advantages of using a broadband Internet service? (58)
4. What is the relationship between domain names and IP addresses? (62)
5. Is cybersquatting ethical? Why or why not? (64)
6. What is a cybersquatter? (64) What is the goal of the Anticybersquatting Consumer Protection Act (ACPA)? (64)
7. How does a static webpage differ from a dynamic webpage? (65)
8. How does using a proxy server help protect your online identity? (66)
9. What are some safe browsing techniques? (66)
10. What are some popular mobile browsers? (67)
11. How do GPS receivers track their location on earth? (70)
12. What are the advantages and risks associated with allowing an app to track your location? (70)
13. What techniques can you use to improve search results? (72)
14. What precautions can you take to minimize privacy and security risks associated with online social networks? (74)
15. Would you use a public computer to check email or do online banking? Why or why not? What are the risks? (80)
16. How do e-commerce and m-commerce differ? (82)
17. What should you determine during the planning stage of a website? (84)
18. What steps are involved in web publishing? (84)
19. What are some criteria you can use to evaluate a website or webpage before relying on its content? (85)
20. How do JPEG and PNG formats differ? (86)
21. What are some practical applications of virtual reality? (88)
22. Where can you obtain plug-ins? (88)
23. Besides the web, what other Internet services are available? (88)
24. What are some good practices to follow when using email? (89)
25. What elements do you need to place an Internet phone call? (92)
26. What is anonymous FTP? (92)
27. What activities might be considered cyberbullying? (94)

✳ Problem Solving

The Problem Solving exercises extend your knowledge of chapter concepts by seeking solutions to practical problems with technology that you may encounter at home, school, work, or with nonprofit organizations. The Collaboration exercise should be completed with a team.

Instructions: You often can solve problems with technology in multiple ways. Determine a solution to the problems in these exercises by using one or more resources available to you (such as a computer or mobile device, articles on the web or in print, blogs, podcasts, videos, television, user guides, other individuals, electronics or computer stores, etc.). Describe your solution, along with the resource(s) used, in the format requested by your instructor (brief report, presentation, discussion, blog post, video, or other means).

Personal

1. Cyberbullying Message While reviewing the email messages in your email account, you notice one that you interpret as cyberbullying. You do not recognize the sender of the email message, but still take it seriously. What are your next steps?

2. Unsolicited Friend Requests You recently signed up for an account on the Facebook online social network. When you log in periodically, you find that people you do not know are requesting to be your friend. How should you respond?

3. Unexpected Search Engine A class project requires that you conduct research on the web. After typing the web address for Google's home page and pressing the ENTER key, your browser redirects you to a different search engine. What could be wrong?

4. Images Do Not Appear When you navigate to a webpage, you notice that no images are appearing. You successfully have viewed webpages with images in the past and are not sure why images suddenly are not appearing. What steps will you take to show the images?

5. Social Media Password Your social media password has been saved on your computer for quite some time and the browser has been signing you in automatically. After deleting your browsing history and saved information from your browser, the online social network began prompting you again for your password, which you have forgotten. What are your next steps?

Source: Twitter

Professional

6. Suspicious Website Visits The director of your company's information technology department sent you an email message stating that you have been spending an excessive amount of time viewing websites not related to your job. You periodically visit websites not related to work, but only on breaks, which the company allows. How does he know your web browsing habits? How will you respond to this claim?

7. Automatic Response When you return from vacation, a colleague informs you that when she sent email messages to your email address, she would not always receive your automatic response stating that you were out of the office. Why might your email program not respond automatically to every email message received?

8. Email Message Formatting A friend sent an email message containing a photo to your email account at work. Upon receiving the email message, the photo does not appear. You also notice that email messages never show any formatting, such as different fonts, font sizes, and font colors. What might be causing this?

9. Mobile Hot Spot Not Found Your supervisor gave you a mobile hot spot to use while you are traveling to a conference in another state. When you attempt to connect to the hot spot with your computer, tablet, and phone, none of the devices is able to find any wireless networks. What might be the problem, and what are your next steps?

10. Sporadic Email Message Delivery The email program on your computer has been displaying new messages only every hour, on the hour. Historically, new email messages would arrive and be displayed immediately upon being sent by the sender. Furthermore, your coworkers claim that they sometimes do not receive your email messages until hours after you send them. What might be the problem?

Collaboration

11. Technology in Transportation Your project team has been assigned to present a business proposal to a group of potential investors. Because the presentation will take place in Kansas City, Missouri, you will need to transport people and ship some materials to that location. Form a team of three people and determine how to use technology to ship materials and how to make travel arrangements. One team member should research the steps required to use a website to make flight reservations, one team member should determine the steps necessary to print a package shipping label from his or her computer and track the package while it is en route, and another team member should find directions from Kansas City International Airport to a nearby hotel.

The How To: Your Turn exercises present general guidelines for fundamental skills when using a computer or mobile device and then require that you determine how to apply these general guidelines to a specific program or situation.

How To: Your Turn ✳

Discover More: Visit this chapter's premium content to **challenge yourself with this additional How To: Your Turn exercises**, which include App Adventure.

Instructions: You often can complete tasks using technology in multiple ways. Figure out how to perform the tasks described in these exercises by using one or more resources available to you (such as a computer or mobile device, articles on the web or in print, online or program help, user guides, blogs, podcasts, videos, other individuals, trial and error, etc.). Summarize your 'how to' steps, along with the resource(s) used, in the format requested by your instructor (brief report, presentation, discussion, blog post, video, or other means).

❶ Determine Your IP (Internet Protocol) Address

Knowing a computer or mobile device's IP address can help you identify it on a network and can help you troubleshoot any problems you may experience connecting to the Internet or other computers and devices on your network. The following steps guide you through the process of determining your IP address.

a. Run a browser and then navigate to a search engine of your choice.

b. Search for a website that can determine your IP address and then navigate to one of these websites.

c. Your IP address should be displayed upon navigating to the website. If it does not, return to the search results and navigate to a different site.

or

a. Run a browser and then navigate to a search engine of your choice.

b. Search for a website that explains how to determine the IP address for your specific operating system and version.

c. View the search results and then navigate to the website that provides you with the best guidance.

d. Follow the instructions on your computer or mobile device to determine the IP address.

Source: Microsoft Corporation

Exercises

1. Summarize the process you used to determine your IP address.
2. What is your IP address?
3. Is it possible for a computer to have more than one IP address at the same time? Why or why not?

❷ Participate in an Online Auction

Online auctions allow consumers to bid on products that other people are selling. If you are the highest bidder at the end of the bidding period, you often can arrange payment through the online auction. The following steps guide you through the process of participating in an online auction. **WARNING: Do not purchase or bid on an item if you do not intend to purchase it. If you win the auction, you legally may be obligated to provide payment for the item.**

a. Run a browser and then navigate to www.ebay.com.

b. Tap or click the link to register for a new account.

c. Enter the requested information to create the account.

d. Search for an item on which you would like to bid. If you want to browse items in a specific category instead, tap or click the link to browse for items by category.

e. When the search results appear, tap or click an item that interests you to see more details about the item.

f. Review the item details to determine whether you would like to bid on this item. If the item does not interest you, return to the search results and select another item.

g. The seller may have a "Buy It Now" option that allows you to purchase the item immediately at a predetermined price. Alternatively, you can bid on the item by making an offer. The highest bidder at the end of the auction will win the item. **Remember: If you bid on and win an item, you are obligated to provide payment.**

h. You will be notified if you are the winning bidder when the auction closes. At that time, follow the instructions to arrange to pay the seller.

i. When you are finished, sign out of eBay.

✸ How To: Your Turn

Exercises

1. What item(s) did you view? If the buyer had the "Buy It Now" option available, do you think the asking price was fair?
2. Would you purchase an item from an online auction? Why or why not?
3. What items might you post for sale on an online auction?

Source: eBay

3 **View and Manage Data Usage**

Many people have limited data plans, so it is important to know how to view the amount of data you have used on your phone or tablet when you are not connected to the Internet using a Wi-Fi connection. If you are using a phone or tablet where Wi-Fi is available, you should strongly consider using the Wi-Fi connection not only to limit data plan usage, but also to experience faster speed. If you find that your data usage is high each month, you may be able to see which apps are using the most data and adjust usage of those apps accordingly. The following steps guide you through the process of viewing and managing data usage.

a. Display the settings on your mobile device.
b. Select the option to view data usage.
c. If necessary, tap the option to display a list of apps and how much data each app uses. If necessary, select the time period for which you want to see the data usage.
d. If you notice an app using a large amount of data, tap the app to see details for that app. If necessary, disable background data transfer for the app. Background data transfer is data the app downloads and uploads even while you are not actively using the app.
e. If you want your mobile device to notify you when you are approaching your monthly data limit, set the necessary notification option and select a value under your monthly data limit in the appropriate area.

f. If you want your mobile device to turn off data (this does not include Wi-Fi) when you reach a certain limit, set the necessary option and then select a value that is just less than your monthly data limit to ensure you never reach or exceed the limit.
g. Save all changes.

Exercises

1. Do you have a data limit on your mobile data plan? If so, what is it?
2. When you enter an area with Wi-Fi, do you configure your mobile device to connect to the Wi-Fi? Why or why not?
3. Review the mobile data usage on your mobile device. Which app uses the most data? Which app uses the least data?

Source: Google Inc.

4 **Search for a Job Online**

If you know the company for which you would like to work, you may be able to visit that company's website and search for a webpage with current job postings. If you would like to search for openings in multiple companies, consider using a job search website. The following steps guide you through the process of searching for a job online.

a. Run a browser.
b. Use a search engine to locate a job search website and then navigate to the website.
c. Many job search websites allow you to search for jobs by criteria, such as keyword, category or location. If

How To: Your Turn ✸

you are searching for a job in a specific field, enter relevant keyword(s) (i.e., software developer) or select an appropriate category (i.e., technology). To limit your search results to a specific geographical area, specify a location (i.e., Atlanta).

d. Some websites allow you to search for jobs based on additional criteria, such as company, salary, job type, education, and experience. Specify these additional criteria by performing an advanced search.

e. After entering the job search criteria, start the search.

f. When the search results appear, scroll through the results. To find out more about a particular job, tap or click the job listing.

g. If desired, follow the instructions in the job listing to apply for the job.

Exercises

1. Review three job search websites. Which one did you like the best? Why?

2. Which keywords would you use on a job search website to search for a job in your desired field?

3. Before completing this exercise, have you ever searched for a job online? Do you think it is better to search for a job using a job search website, or by vising company websites directly and viewing their job postings? Justify your answer.

❺ Send Email Messages Using Various Email Programs and Web Apps

The process required to send an email message using a computer or mobile device from various email programs and web apps is very similar. The following steps guide you through the process of sending email messages using various email programs and web apps.

a. Run the email program or navigate to the email web app on your computer or mobile device.

b. Locate and then tap or click the button to compose a new email message.

c. Type the recipient's email address in the To text box. If you are sending the email message to multiple recipients, separate each email address with a semicolon (;).

d. If you would like to send a carbon copy of the email message to one or

more people, type their email address(es) in the Cc text box (which stands for carbon copy).

e. To send a copy of the email message to someone while hiding his or her email address from the other recipients, enter his or her email address in the Bcc text box (which stands for blind carbon copy). The email recipients listed in the To or Cc text boxes will not be able to see the recipients you specified in the Bcc text box.

f. Enter a descriptive subject in the Subject text box. It is not good practice to leave the subject blank when you send an email message because the recipient's email server may place messages without a subject in a spam or junk mail folder.

g. Type the body of the email message in the appropriate area.

h. If your email program supports it, check the spelling of your email message and correct any errors found.

i. Tap or click the Send button, which sends the email message to everyone listed in the To, Cc, and Bcc text boxes.

Exercises

1. Under what circumstances might you want to send a blind carbon copy of an email message to one or more people?

2. Send an email message to your instructor and put your email address in the Cc text box. Use an appropriate subject and tell your instructor you have successfully completed this exercise.

3. Search for and evaluate three web apps that can send and receive email. Which one is your favorite, and why?

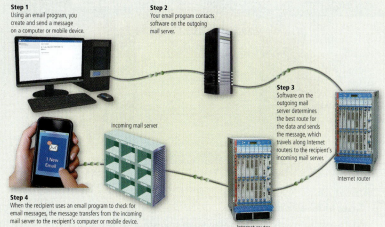

How an Email Message May Travel from a Sender to a Receiver

Step 1
Using an email program, you create and send a message on a computer or mobile device.

Step 2
Your email program contacts software on the outgoing mail server.

Step 3
Software on the outgoing mail server determines the best route for the data and sends the message, which travels along Internet routers to the recipient's incoming mail server.

Step 4
When the recipient uses an email program to check for email messages, the message transfers from the incoming mail server to the recipient's computer or mobile device.

incoming mail server

Internet router

Internet router

✳ Internet Research

The Internet Research exercises broaden your understanding of chapter concepts by requiring that you search for information on the web.

Discover More: Visit this chapter's premium content to **challenge yourself with additional Internet Research exercises**, which include Search Sleuth, Green Computing, Ethics in Action, You Review It, and Exploring Technology Careers.

Instructions: Use a search engine or another search tool to locate the information requested or answers to questions presented in the exercises. Describe your findings, along with the search term(s) you used and your web source(s), in the format requested by your instructor (brief report, presentation, discussion, blog post, video, or other means).

❶ Making Use of the Web

Online Social Networks and Media Sharing

Every second, an average of 5,700 Tweets and 41,000 Facebook posts are created. With these impressive numbers, it is no wonder that online social media have become ubiquitous throughout the world. Twitter, Facebook, and other online social networks, especially those featured in Mini Feature 2-2 in this chapter, are popular among users of all ages. Likewise, media sharing sites, such as YouTube, which is shown in Figure 2-11 in this chapter, are popular means of managing and sharing photos, videos, and music.

Research This: Visit two of the websites discussed in Mini Feature 2-2 or other online social networks and create a profile if you do not currently have one. What personal information is required to join? Does either website ask for personal information that you are uncomfortable sharing? How does the content of these two websites differ? Which features are beneficial for casual users, and which are targeted toward business or professional users? Then, visit two social media sites. What personal information is required to join? Are these websites supported by advertisements? Locate the instructions for posting media. Are these instructions straightforward? Do these websites impose a limit on the number and/or size of media files a user can post?

newspapers, advertisements generally are not used to fund the majority of operating costs, nor are users required to pay monthly or annual fees for basic services that they receive at no cost. One method that social media sites use to generate start-up and ongoing subsidies is through venture capitalists' funding. These investors scrutinize business plans and market trends in an effort to locate Internet start-up companies with the potential to generate substantial returns. Once the businesses are running, additional monies are needed to maintain and improve the websites. At this point, some websites display advertisements. The charge for companies to place an advertisement generally increases as the number of subscribers grows. Another method of generating income is to charge users for accessing premium content. Online dating services use this tactic successfully, for they allow people to browse online profiles free of charge but require them to pay to contact a potential dating match.

Research This: Locate venture capitalists who are seeking Internet start-up companies. Which criteria do they use to make investment decisions? Who are the successful venture capitalists, and which companies have they funded? Which types of advertisements are displayed on specific social media and online social networks? How does the content of these ads pertain to the demographics and interests of users?

Source: Facebook

❷ Social Media

Most social media companies have invested millions of dollars to develop and maintain their websites. Unlike other commercial media, such as television, radio, and

❸ Search Skills

Understand Search Results

Search results display the most relevant results first. Search results may include links to websites, news stories, images, videos, maps, and information from Wikipedia and other online databases. Results also may show links to similar searches, related people, or posts from online social networks or social media sites.

Because many search engines rely on advertising for revenue, some search results are paid advertisements. Companies and organizations may pay search providers to display links to their websites prominently in the

Internet Research ✹

search results when search text contains words relevant to their products and services. Paid ads often appear at the top or along the side of a search results page. A search results page may display an icon or use shading to specify that the search result is an advertisement.

When evaluating the reliability of search results, consider the sources of the information provided. Specialized information such as medical advice or stock performance should come from recognizable sources in those areas, while you might rely on reviews from customers when selecting a restaurant or purchasing a smartphone.

Source: Google.

Research This: Type each search text phrase listed in the paragraph below into the search boxes in Bing, Google, and Yahoo! and then take a screenshot of the first page of search results from each. Compare them, identifying ads, news, images, videos, social media results, information from online databases, search tools, and common links that both search engines returned. Which search engine's results do you find more useful in each case? Why?

Type the following search text: (1) internet service providers, (2) google corporate headquarters, (3) flights from boston to los angeles, and (4) identity theft.

4 Security

Cybercriminals may lurk in public Wi-Fi hot spots, as you learned in Secure IT 2-1 in this chapter. These thieves also may be on the lookout for customers entering their PIN at keypads near cash registers

or at ATMs. Body heat from fingers touching the keys remains for a short time, and a device with infrared-scanning capabilities can detect which keys are warmer than others. This device, which is readily available for purchase at cell phone accessories stores, snaps on the back of cell phones. It captures the thermal heat signatures, with the most recently touched keys glowing red and the cooler keys glowing light green. The thief, therefore, knows which keys comprise the PIN and the sequence of numbers by looking at the intensity of colors on the infrared scan.

Research This: How much does a thermal imaging cell phone case cost? Which brand of phone is more commonly used to capture thermal imaging? What steps can consumers take to thwart thieves using infrared scanning? Which key materials are less apt to retain the thermal signatures: metal, rubber, or plastic? Researchers from which university published a paper discussing thermal camera-based attacks?

5 Cloud Services
Collaboration and Productivity (SaaS)
Microsoft's Office Online and Google Docs are online productivity suites for creating documents, presentations, spreadsheets, and other projects. Microsoft and Google offer these apps as part of their respective cloud storage services. Because documents are stored on the cloud, you can access them from any computer or device connected to the Internet.

These are examples of SaaS (software as a service), a service of cloud computing that allows access to software using a browser, without the need to install software on a computer or device. As providers update their software, users receive the latest version upon signing in. SaaS apps often allow users to collaborate and share their work with other users. Many providers offer SaaS titles at no cost; others require users to purchase a subscription or pay a fee for the features they use.

Research This: (1) Sign up for accounts on Microsoft OneDrive and Google Drive to create and store documents with Office Online and Google Docs. With each app, create a document, share it with another user, and edit it simultaneously. What is an advantage of sharing documents over sending the files by email to collaborators? (2) How do Microsoft Office Online and Google Docs compare with Microsoft Office installed on your computer? What features are available on the cloud that are not possible on a desktop version?

✷ Critical Thinking

The Critical Thinking exercises challenge your assessment and decision-making skills by presenting real-world situations associated with chapter concepts. The Collaboration exercise should be completed with a team.

Instructions: Evaluate the situations below, using personal experiences and one or more resources available to you (such as articles on the web or in print, blogs, podcasts, videos, television, user guides, other individuals, electronics or computer stores, etc.). Perform the tasks requested in each exercise and share your deliverables in the format requested by your instructor (brief report, presentation, discussion, blog post, video, or other means).

1. Mobile Browser Comparison

Although most mobile devices include a mobile browser, users have the option of downloading and installing other browsers.

Source: Google, Inc.

Do This: Evaluate and compare reviews of at least four mobile browsers, such as Android, Firefox, Opera, Safari, or Silk. Discuss the major differences among the browsers you researched, including number and types of features, which devices are compatible, how they display webpages, security features, and the speed at which they perform. Discuss any experiences you or your classmates have had with various browsers. Include in your discussion which mobile browser you would recommend and why.

2. Acceptable Use Policy

Most businesses provide Wi-Fi and Internet access, as well as compatible computers or devices, to employees while they are at work. While the intention is for employees to use the Internet for work-related purposes, employees often find it easy to become distracted with other activities on the Internet, such as social media, checking personal email messages, playing games, or visiting websites for entertainment. These activities can degrade Internet access for others or lead to poor performance, as well as expose the company to malware or other risks. Many businesses create an acceptable use policy (AUP) that outlines how employees should use the Internet. It also may outline consequences for unauthorized Internet use.

Do This: Locate two AUPs published online. Compare the two policies and then create a policy you believe would be fair to employees of a small business. Include guidelines for Internet use during breaks, use of smartphones, and restrictions for using social media.

3. Case Study

Amateur Sports League   You are the new manager for a nonprofit amateur soccer league. The league needs a website. You prepare information about the website to present to the board of directors.

Do This: First, you plan the website by determining its purpose and audience. Use a search engine to locate two sports league websites, and print their home pages. Identify what you like and do not like about each. Think about the design of your website, and select the colors you would recommend. Describe the types of media you would include on the webpage and give specific examples, such as a logo, photos or a slide show, or links to videos. Make a sketch of the home page layout, including navigation, media, and text. Research content management systems. Evaluate whether you could use a preformatted template to meet your needs, and find what types of customization options are available. Determine whether you need a separate ISP for hosting the website, and calculate the costs. List ways you will maintain and update the site content. Compile your findings.

Collaboration

4. Website Evaluation   You and three teammates want to open a new chain of fast food sandwich shops. You envision a website that includes a menu, nutritional options, and allergy information, and that has regular promotions and special offers.

Do This: With your teammates, evaluate existing fast food and sandwich websites by comparing the advantages and disadvantages of each. Assign each member the task of evaluating one chain. Team members should print the home page of the assigned website and evaluate each restaurants' website. Pay particular attention to the following areas: (1) design, (2) ease of use, (3) menu, (4) nutritional information, (5) allergy information, (6) special offers, (7) location information and directions, and (8) hours and contact information. Summarize your evaluations and rank the websites in terms of their effectiveness. Be sure to include brief explanations supporting your rankings.

COMPUTERS AND MOBILE DEVICES:
Evaluating Options for Home and Work

3

People use or interact with a variety of computers or mobile devices every day.

"I use my laptop at home and school and an all-in-one at work. I send messages and access the Internet on my smartphone, take photos with my digital camera, and read books on my e-book reader. What more do I need to know about computers and mobile devices?"

While you may be familiar with some of the content in this chapter, do you know how to …

- Protect computers and devices from malware infections?
- Determine which mobile computer, desktop, or mobile device to purchase?
- Safely use an ATM?
- Rent a movie using a DVD kiosk?
- Help eliminate e-waste?
- Use a mobile device safely in a public area?
- Identify a DisplayPort or an HDMI port?
- Pair Bluetooth devices?
- Connect your phone to a Wi-Fi network to save data charges?
- Protect your hardware from theft, vandalism, and failure?
- Prevent technology-related tendonitis or CTS?
- Tell if you are addicted to technology?
- Manage power for your computers and mobile devices

In this chapter, you will discover how to perform these tasks along with much more information essential to this course. For additional content available that accompanies this chapter, visit the free resources and premium content. Refer to the Preface and the Intro chapter for information about how to access these and other additional instructor-assigned support materials.

© iStockPhoto / German

✔ Objectives

After completing this chapter, you will be able to:

1 Describe the characteristics and uses of laptops, tablets, desktops, and all-in-ones

2 Describe the characteristics and types of servers

3 Differentiate among POS terminals, ATMs, and self-service kiosks

4 Describe cloud computing and identify its uses

5 Describe the characteristics and uses of smartphones, digital cameras, portable and digital media players, e-book readers, and wearable devices

6 Describe the characteristics of and ways to interact with game devices, including gamepads, joysticks and wheels, dance pads, and motion-sensing controllers

7 Identify uses of embedded computers

8 Differentiate a port from a connector, identify various ports and connectors, and differentiate among Bluetooth, Wi-Fi, and NFC wireless device connections

9 Identify safeguards against hardware theft and vandalism and hardware failure

10 Discuss ways to prevent health-related injuries and disorders caused from technology use, and describe ways to design a workplace ergonomically

Computers and Mobile Devices

As Chapter 1 discussed, a **computer** is an electronic device, operating under the control of instructions stored in its own memory, that can accept data (input), process the data according to specified rules, produce information (output), and store the information for future use. A **mobile device** is a computing device small enough to hold in your hand. Types of computers and mobiles devices include laptops, tablets, and desktops; servers and terminals; smartphones, digital cameras, e-book readers, portable and digital media players, and wearable devices; game devices; and embedded computers. Figure 3-1 shows a variety of computers and mobile devices.

In addition to discussing features, functions, and purchasing guidelines of computers and mobile devices, this chapter also presents ways to connect peripheral devices, protect computers and mobile devices from theft and failure, and minimize your health risks while using computers and mobile devices.

Mobile Computers and Desktops

A **mobile computer** is a portable personal computer, such as a laptop or tablet, designed so that a user easily can carry it from place to place, whereas a desktop is designed to be in a stationary location. A *personal computer* (PC) is a mobile computer or desktop that can perform all of its input, processing, output, and storage activities by itself and is intended to be used by one person at a time. Personal computers often are differentiated by the type of operating system they use, with Windows and Mac operating systems leading the market share. Companies such as Acer, Dell, Lenovo, HP (Hewlett-Packard), and Samsung sell personal computers that use the Windows operating system, and Apple sells personal computers that use the Mac operating system. Other operating systems for personal computers include Linux and Chrome OS.

Read Secure IT 3-1 for suggestions about how to avoid malware infections on your computers and mobile devices.

🔆 BTW

Peripheral Devices

A *peripheral device* is a device you connect to a computer or mobile device to expand its capabilities. Examples include a keyboard, mouse, microphone, monitor, printer, scanner, external hard drive, webcam, and speakers.

🔆 BTW

The term PC sometimes is used to describe a computer that runs a Windows operating system.

gure 3-1 Computers and mobile devices are available in a variety of shapes and sizes.

SECURE IT 3-1

Avoid Malware Infections

Some websites contain tempting offers to download free games and music, install toolbars that offer convenience, enter contests, and receive coupons on your computers or mobile devices. Danger, however, may lurk in those files, for they secretly could install malware with effects ranging from a mild annoyance to a severe problem such as identity theft. Recall that malware is malicious software that acts without your knowledge and deliberately alters operations of your computer or mobile device. As a general rule, do not install or download unfamiliar software. Follow these guidelines to minimize the chance of your computer or mobile device becoming infected with malware:

- **Social media:** Malware authors often focus on social media, with the goal of stealing personal information, such as passwords, profiles, contact lists, and credit card account details. Their websites urge unsuspecting users to take surveys, tap or click links to obtain free merchandise and games, and download antivirus programs. Ignore these deceitful tactics.

- **Email:** Spam (unsolicited email messages) can be loaded with malware, but even email messages from friends can be a

culprit. If the message does not contain a subject line or contains links or an attachment, exercise caution. One option is to save the attachment to your computer so that antivirus software can scan the file for possible malware before you open it. Your best practice is to avoid opening suspicious messages at all costs.

- **Flash memory storage:** Colleagues and friends may hand you a USB flash drive or memory card with software, photos, and other files. Scan these media with security software before opening any files.

- **Pop-up windows:** At times, a window may open suddenly (called a pop-up window), with a warning that your computer is infected with a virus or that a security breach has occurred, and then make an urgent request to download free software to scan your computer or mobile device and correct the alleged problem. Beware. Many of these offers actually are rogue security software that will infect a computer.

- **Websites:** Websites you visit or pop-up windows may present instructions to download new software or update current programs installed on a computer or mobile device. If you are uncertain of their legitimacy, exit and research the software

by reading reviews online before you decide to install it.

- **Software:** Occasionally, some seemingly safe software attempts to install malware. Even worse, some software touted as offering malware protection actually installs more malware. Always obtain software from reputable sources and, if possible, update software directly from manufacturers' websites. Consider using the custom installation option to ensure that only the desired software is installed. Read the permissions dialog boxes that are displayed on your screen before tapping or clicking the OK or Agree buttons. If you are uncertain about the messages you are viewing, cancel the installation.

- **Smartphones:** Malware creators are targeting smartphones, particularly those using the Android operating system. While an estimated 80 percent of all smartphones are unprotected now, savvy users are obtaining protection from malware attacks. Read reviews before downloading antimalware apps from trusted sources.

Consider This: What online activities might cause malware to be installed on your computer? Which specific websites provide reputable antimalware apps for mobile devices? What new techniques will you use to avoid malware?

CONSIDER THIS

What is inside a personal computer?

The electronic components and circuitry of a personal computer usually are part of or are connected to a motherboard (Figure 3-2). A *motherboard*, sometimes called a system board, is the main circuit board of the personal computer. Many electronic components attach to the motherboard; others are built into it. Two main components on the motherboard are the processor and memory. Many motherboards also integrate sound, video, and networking capabilities. A *processor*, also called a *CPU* (central processing unit), is the electronic component that interprets and carries out the basic instructions that operate a computer. Memory consists of electronic components that store instructions waiting to be executed and data needed by those instructions.

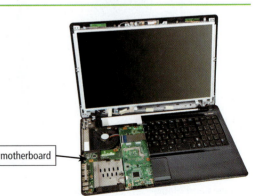

Figure 3-2 Shown here is a partial motherboard in a laptop.
© rawgroup / Fotolia

Internet Research

What is a computer chip?

Search for: computer chip

Laptops, Tablets, and Other Mobile Computers

A **laptop**, also called a *notebook computer*, is a thin, lightweight mobile computer with a screen in its lid and a keyboard in its base (Figure 3-3). Designed to fit on your lap and for easy transport, most laptops weigh up to 7 pounds (varying by manufacturer and specifications) and can be as powerful as the average desktop.

Laptops have input devices, such as a keyboard, touchpad, and webcam; output devices, such as a screen and speakers; a storage device(s), such as a hard drive and maybe an optical disc drive; and usually built-in wireless communications capability. Some laptops have touch screens. Most can operate on batteries or a power supply or both. Read Ethics & Issues 3-1 to consider issues related to laptops and other devices with cameras.

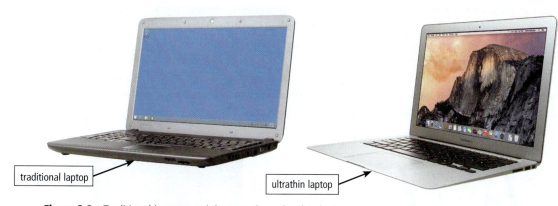

traditional laptop

ultrathin laptop

Figure 3-3   Traditional laptops weigh more than ultrathin laptops.
© Sergey Peterman / Shutterstock.com; © iStockphoto / Skip Odonnell; Microsoft; Apple, Inc.

❋ **ETHICS & ISSUES 3-1**

What Punishment for Webcam Spying Is Appropriate?

Microphones, digital cameras, and webcams have many practical and harmless uses. These technologies also can leave you open to spying. For example, one school district used software, which was supposed to track the school-distributed laptops in case of theft, to take photos and screen captures of students. In another instance, a person noticed that when she gave a customer service rep access to her computer, he turned on her webcam without asking for her permission.

Cybercriminals can use spy tools that take photos, or record video or audio, without turning on a light or other notification that

indicates your camera or microphone is in use. The Flame virus is one way for spy tools to infect your computer. Security experts recommend using a sticker to cover your webcam, and inserting a dummy plug in the microphone port when you are not using it. These technologies also allow people to take photos or videos in a public setting and share them without your knowledge. A director at the American Civil Liberties Union stated that when you are in a public place, people have the right to photograph you. Privacy advocates criticize *Google Street View*, however, which takes images captured using moving vehicles equipped with GPS and cameras and then creates a

panoramic view of an area, including people entering and exiting buildings or relaxing on a beach.

Many states' laws do not cover these types of acts. Massachusetts, however, recently passed a law that made secretly taking photos or videos that focused on people's private body parts a criminal offense. Lawmakers continue to debate and expand current laws, as well as pass new ones.

Consider This: Should webcam spying punishments be comparable to other types of spying? Why or why not? What kind of privacy should you expect when you are in a public place?

Ultrathin laptops weigh less than traditional laptops, usually have a longer battery life, and generally run the Windows operating system. In order to minimize their thickness, many ultrathin laptops have fewer ports than traditional laptops, do not include an optical disc drive, and often require the use of special dongles to attach cables that connect to external displays or a network. (Recall that a dongle is a small device that connects to a computer and enables additional functions when attached.)

Tablets   Usually smaller than a laptop but larger than a phone, a **tablet** is a thin, lighter-weight mobile computer that has a touch screen.

Two popular form factors (shapes and sizes) of tablets are the slate and convertible (Figure 3-4). Resembling a letter-sized pad, a *slate tablet* is a type of tablet that does not contain a physical keyboard. A *convertible tablet* is a tablet that has a screen it its lid and a keyboard in its base, with the lid and base connected by a swivel-type hinge. You can use a convertible tablet like a traditional laptop, or you can rotate the display and fold it down over the keyboard so that it looks like a slate tablet. As with laptops, tablets run on batteries or a power supply or both; however, batteries in a tablet typically last longer than those in laptops.

Some tablets include a *stylus*, which looks like a small ink pen, that you can use instead of a fingertip to enter data, make selections, or draw on a touch screen. A stylus may include buttons you can press to simulate clicking a mouse. As an alternative to interacting with the touch screen, some users prefer to purchase a separate physical keyboard that attaches to or wirelessly communicates with the tablet (shown with the slate tablet in Figure 3-4).

Tablets are useful especially for taking notes in class, at meetings, at conferences, and in other forums where the standard laptop is not practical. Because slate tablets can have a more durable construction, they often are used in the medical field and other areas where exposure to germs, heat, humidity, dust, and other contaminants is greater.

⊛ BTW

Pens
Some tablet manufacturers refer to a stylus as a pen.

slate tablet in stand

magnetic keyboard cover

convertible tablet

stylus

Figure 3-4   Examples of slate and convertible tablets.
Courtesy of Microsoft; © iStockPhoto / rasslava

⊛ CONSIDER THIS

What is a phablet?
Some manufacturers use the term, *phablet*, to refer to a device that combines features of a smartphone with a tablet (Figure 3-5). These devices are larger than smartphones but smaller than full-sized tablets. The screen on a phablet usually measures five to seven inches diagonally. Some include a stylus.

Figure 3-5   A phablet combines features of a smartphone and a tablet.
© iStockPhoto / Krystian Nawrocki

Handheld Computers

A *handheld computer* is a computer small enough to fit in one hand. Many handheld computers communicate wirelessly with other devices or computers. Some handheld computers have miniature or specialized keyboards. Others have a touch screen and also include a stylus for input.

Many handheld computers are industry-specific and serve the needs of mobile employees, such as parcel delivery people or warehouse employees (Figure 3-6), whose jobs require them to move from place to place. Handheld computers often send data wirelessly to central office computers.

Figure 3-6   This handheld computer is a lightweight computer that enables warehouse employees to take inventory and check supplies.
© iStockphoto / Ermin Gutenberger

Mini Feature 3-1: Mobile Computer Buyer's Guide

If you need computing capability while traveling and during lectures or meetings, you may find a laptop or tablet to be an appropriate choice. Read Mini Feature 3-1 for tips to consider when purchasing a mobile computer.

✳ MINI FEATURE 3-1

Mobile Computer Buyer's Guide

With the abundance of mobile computer manufacturers, research each before making a purchase. The following are purchasing considerations unique to mobile computers.

© iStockPhoto / vtls

1. **Determine which mobile computer form factor fits your needs.** Consider a tablet or ultrathin laptop if you require a lightweight device and the most mobility. If you require additional ports or want the computer's capabilities to be more comparable to a desktop, consider purchasing a traditional laptop.

2. **Consider a mobile computer with a sufficiently large screen.** Laptops and tablets are available with various screen sizes. For example, most traditional and ultrathin laptop screens range in size from 11 to 18 inches, while most tablet screens range in size from 7 to 12 inches.

3. **Experiment with different keyboards and pointing devices.** Mobile computers often vary in size, and for that reason have different keyboard layouts. Familiarize yourself with the keyboard layout of the computer you want to purchase, and make sure it is right for you. If you have large fingers, for example, you should not purchase a computer with a small, condensed keyboard. Laptops typically include a touchpad to control the pointer. Tablets have a touch screen and an on-screen keyboard.

4. **Consider processor, memory, and storage upgrades at the time of purchase.** As with a desktop, upgrading a mobile computer's memory and internal storage may be less expensive at the time of initial purchase. Some internal storage is custom designed for mobile computer manufacturers, meaning an upgrade might not be available in the future.

5. **The availability of built-in ports and slots is important.** Determine which ports and slots (discussed later in this chapter) you require on the mobile computer. If you plan to transfer photos from a digital camera using a memory card, consider a mobile computer with a built-in card slot compatible with your digital camera's memory card. If you plan to connect devices such as a printer or USB flash drive to your mobile computer, consider purchasing one with a sufficient number of USB ports. In addition, evaluate mobile computers with ports enabling you to connect an external monitor.

6. **If you plan to use your mobile computer for a long time without access to an electrical outlet, or if the battery life for the mobile computer you want to purchase is not sufficient, consider purchasing a second battery.** Some mobile computers, such as most tablets and ultrathin laptops, have built-in batteries that can be replaced only by a qualified technician. In that case, you might look into options for external battery packs or power sources.

7. **Purchase a well-padded and well-designed carrying case that is comfortable and ergonomic.** An amply padded carrying case will protect your mobile computer from the bumps it may receive while traveling. A well-designed carrying case will have room for accessories such as USB flash drives, pens, and paperwork. Although a mobile computer may be small enough to fit in a handbag, make sure that the bag has sufficient padding to protect the computer. Test the carrying case with the laptop inside to ensure it is comfortable and ergonomic.

8. **If you plan to connect your mobile computer to a video projector, make sure the mobile computer is compatible with the video projector.** You should check, for example, to be sure that your mobile computer will allow you to display an image on the screen and projection device at the same time. Also, ensure that the mobile computer has the ports required or that you have the necessary dongle and cables to connect to the video projector.

Discover More: Visit this chapter's free resources to learn more about mobile computer manufacturers, form factors, screens, keyboards, pointing devices, upgrades, batteries, carrying cases, and video projectors.

✳ **Consider This:** Based on your current computing needs, should you purchase a traditional laptop, ultrathin laptop, or tablet? What are the specifications of the mobile computer you would purchase?

Desktops and All-in-Ones

A **desktop**, or desktop computer, is a personal computer designed to be in a stationary location, where all of its components fit on or under a desk or table (Figure 3-7). Components that typically occupy space outside of a desktop include peripheral devices such as a keyboard, mouse, and webcam (input devices); speakers and printer (output devices); external hard drive (storage device); and possibly a router and/or modem (communications devices). Depending on the form factor of the desktop, it may also require an external monitor.

Some people use the term, *system unit*, to refer to the case that contains and protects the motherboard, internal hard drive, memory, and other electronic components of the computer from damage. A desktop may have a system unit tower that is a separate device from a monitor. A *tower*, which is made of metal or plastic, is a frame that houses the system unit on a desktop. Towers are available in a variety of form factors. Although they can range in height from 12 inches to 30 inches or more, the trend is toward smaller desktop tower form factors. An **all-in-one** (AIO) or *all-in-one desktop*, by contrast, does not have a tower and instead houses the display, system unit, and possibly an optical drive, in the same case.

⚙ **BTW**

Monitor Speakers
Many monitors have integrated speakers.

⚙ **BTW**

Technology Innovators
Discover More: Visit this chapter's free resources to learn about Dell and its founder, Michael Dell.

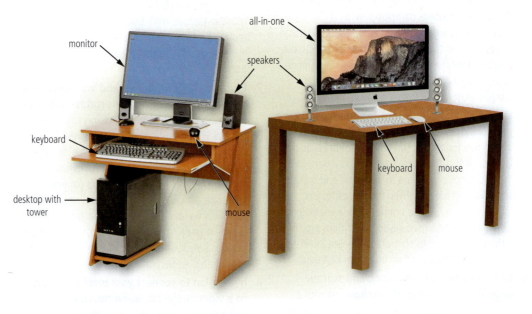

Figure 3-7 The desktop with a tower shown in this figure is a Windows computer, and the all-in-one is a Mac computer.
© George Dolgikh / Shutterstock. com; © iStockphoto / Skip Odonnell; © iStockphoto / Evgeny Kuklev; © Cengage Learning; Microsoft; Apple, Inc.

✳ **CONSIDER THIS**

Who uses desktops?
Home and business users who do not require the portability of a mobile computer may work with desktops for their everyday computing needs. Gaming enthusiasts often choose a *gaming desktop*, which offers high-quality audio, video, and graphics with optimal performance for sophisticated single-user and networked or Internet multiplayer games. Power users may work with a high-end desktop, sometimes called a *workstation*, that is designed to handle intense calculations and sophisticated graphics. For example, architects use powerful desktops to design buildings and homes, and graphic artists use them to create computer-animated special effects for full-length motion pictures and video games. Some users configure a desktop to function as a server on a network (servers are discussed later in this chapter).

⚡ **Internet Research**
Which movies use computer animation?

Search for: movies using computer animation

Mini Feature 3-2: Desktop Buyer's Guide

Desktops are a suitable option if you work mostly in one place and have plenty of space in a work area. Read Mini Feature 3-2 for tips to consider when purchasing a desktop.

 BTW
High-Tech Talk
Discover More: Visit this chapter's free resources to learn how touch screens use capacitive, resistive, surface wave, and other technologies to sense touch.

MINI FEATURE 3-2

Desktop Buyer's Guide

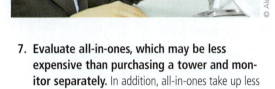
© Alexey Salo / Photos.com

Today, desktop manufacturers emphasize desktop style by offering bright colors, trendy displays, and theme-based towers so that the computer looks attractive if it is in an area of high visibility. If you have decided that a desktop is most suited to your technology needs, the next step is to determine specific software, hardware, peripheral devices, and services to purchase, as well as where to buy the computer. The following considerations will help you determine the appropriate desktop to purchase.

1. **Determine the specific software to use on the desktop.** Decide which software contains the features necessary for the tasks you want to perform. Your hardware requirements depend on the minimum requirements of the software you plan to use on the desktop.

2. **Know the system requirements of the operating system.** Determine the operating system you want to use because this also dictates hardware requirements. If, however, you purchase a new desktop, chances are it will include the latest version of your preferred operating system (Windows, Mac OS, or Linux).

3. **Look for bundled software.** Purchasing software at the same time you purchase a desktop may be less expensive than purchasing the software at a later date.

4. **Avoid purchasing the least powerful desktop available.** Technology changes rapidly, which means a desktop that seems powerful enough today may not serve your computing needs in the future. Purchasing a desktop with the most memory, largest hard drive capacity, and fastest processor you can afford will help delay obsolescence.

5. **Consider upgrades to the keyboard, mouse, monitor, printer, microphone, and speakers.** You use these peripheral devices to interact with the desktop, so make sure they meet your standards.

6. **Consider a touch screen monitor.** A touch screen monitor will enable you to interact with the latest operating systems and apps using touch input.

7. **Evaluate all-in-ones, which may be less expensive than purchasing a tower and monitor separately.** In addition, all-in-ones take up less space and often look more attractive than desktops with separate towers.

8. **If you are buying a new desktop, you have several purchasing options:** buy directly from a school bookstore, a local computer dealer, or a large retail store, or order from a vendor by mail, phone, or the web. Each purchasing option has its advantages. Explore each option to find the best combination of price and service.

9. **Be aware of additional costs.** Along with the desktop itself, you also may need to make extra purchases. For example, you might purchase computer furniture, an uninterruptable power supply (UPS) or surge protector (discussed later in the chapter), an external hard drive, a printer, a router, or a USB flash drive.

10. **If you use your computer for business or require fast resolution of major computer problems, consider purchasing an extended warranty or a service plan through a local dealer or third-party company.** Most extended warranties cover the repair and replacement of computer components beyond the standard warranty.

Discover More: Visit this chapter's free resources to learn more about desktop manufacturers, software, upgrades, touch screen monitor options, all-in-ones, hidden costs, and warranties.

Consider This: Shop around for a desktop that meets your current needs. Which desktop would you purchase? Why?

Table 3-1 Dedicated Servers

Type	Main Service Provided
Application server	Stores and runs apps
Backup server	Backs up and restores files, folders, and media
Database server	Stores and provides access to a database
Domain name server	Stores domain names and their corresponding IP addresses
File server (or storage server)	Stores and manages files
FTP server	Stores files for user upload or download via FTP
Game server	Provides a central location for online gaming
Home server	Provides storage, Internet connections, or other services to computers and devices in a household
List server	Stores and manages email lists
Mail server	Stores and delivers email messages
Network server	Manages network traffic
Print server	Manages printers and documents being printed
Web server	Stores and delivers requested webpages to a computer via a browser

© Cengage Learning

Servers

A **server** is a computer dedicated to providing one or more services to other computers or devices on a network. Services provided by servers include storing content and controlling access to hardware, software, and other resources on a network. In many cases, a server accesses data, information, and programs on another server. In other cases, personal computers, devices, or terminals (discussed in the next section) access data, information, and programs on a server. Servers can support from two to several thousand connected computers or devices at the same time.

Some servers, called dedicated servers, perform a specific service and can be placed with other dedicated servers to perform multiple services (Table 3-1). Each type of dedicated server uses software designed specifically to manage its service. Dedicated servers typically require a faster processor, more memory, and additional storage.

Servers typically include a processor, memory, storage, and network connections. Depending on its function, a server may or may not require a monitor or an input device. Some servers are controlled from remote computers. Form factors for servers include rack server, blade server, and tower server, which are shown in Figure 3-8 and briefly described below.

- A *rack server*, sometimes called a rack-mounted server, is a server that is housed in a slot (bay) on a metal frame (rack). A rack can contain multiple servers, each in a different bay. The rack is fastened in place to a flat surface.
- A *blade server* is a server in the form of a single circuit board, or blade. The individual blades insert in a blade server chassis that can hold many blades. Like a rack server, the chassis is fastened in place to a flat surface.
- A *tower server* is a server built into an upright cabinet (tower) that stands alone. The tower can be similar in size and shape to a desktop tower or larger.

✺ CONSIDER THIS

Which server should you use?
Home or small business users and organizations with ample floor space often choose tower servers. (Some home users even use a desktop tower or powerful laptop to act as a home server.) Data centers and other organizations looking to conserve floor space often choose rack servers or blade servers. Organizations that require a large quantity of servers usually opt for blade servers.

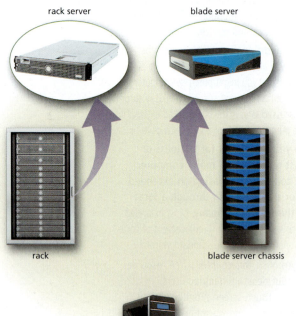

rack server

blade server

rack

blade server chassis

tower server

Figure 3-8 Shown here are a rack server, blade server, and tower server.
© iStockphoto / Godfried Edelman; © iStockphoto / luismmolina; © iStockphoto / evirgen;
© iStockphoto / Alexander Shirokov; © iStockphoto / luismmolina

Some organizations use virtualization to improve utilization of technology. *Virtualization* is the practice of sharing or pooling computing resources, such as servers and storage devices. *Server virtualization* uses software to enable a physical server to emulate the hardware and computing capabilities of one or more servers, known as virtual servers. Users can use software to configure the storage, processing power, memory, operating system, and other characteristics of virtual servers. From the end user's point of view, a virtual server behaves just like a physical server. The advantages are that a virtual server can be created and configured quickly, does not require a new physical server, and is easier to manage. Cloud computing, discussed later in this chapter, uses server virtualization.

Major corporations use server farms, mainframes, or other types of servers for business activities to process everyday transactions (Figure 3-9). A *server farm* is a network of several servers together in a single location. Server farms make it possible to combine the power of multiple servers. A *mainframe* is a large, expensive, powerful server that can handle hundreds or thousands of connected users simultaneously. Enterprises use server farms, mainframes, or other large servers to bill millions of customers, prepare payroll for thousands of employees, and manage millions of items in inventory.

Figure 3-9   Server farms and mainframes can handle thousands of connected computers and process millions of instructions per second.
© Sashkin / Shutterstock.com

Terminals

A *terminal* is a computer, usually with limited processing power, that enables users to send data to and/or receive information from a server, or host computer. The host computer processes the data and then, if necessary, sends information (output) back to the terminal. Terminals may include a monitor and/or touch screen, keyboard, and memory.

A *thin client* is a terminal that looks like a desktop but has limited capabilities and components. Because thin clients typically do not contain a hard drive, they run programs and access data on a network or the Internet. Public locations, such as libraries and schools, and enterprises sometimes use thin clients because they cost less, are easier to maintain, last longer, use less power, and are less susceptible to malware attacks than desktops.

Special-purpose terminals perform specific tasks and contain features uniquely designed for use in a particular industry. Three widely used special-purpose terminals are point-of-sale (POS) terminals, ATMs, and self-service kiosks.

Point-of-Sale Terminals

The location in a retail or grocery store where a consumer pays for goods or services is the point of sale (POS). Most retail stores use a *POS terminal* to record purchases, process credit or debit cards, and update inventory.

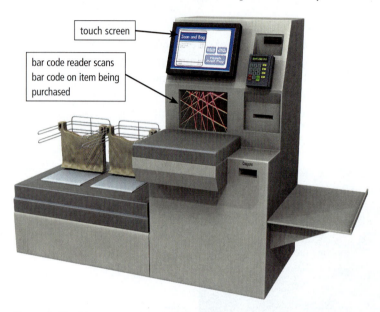

touch screen

bar code reader scans bar code on item being purchased

Figure 3-10   Many grocery stores offer self-service checkouts, where consumers use POS terminals to scan purchases, scan their store or saver card and coupons, and then pay for the goods.
© Valentyna Chukhlyebova / Shutterstock; © iStockPhoto / 00one

In a grocery store, the POS terminal is a combination of an electronic cash register, bar code reader, and printer (Figure 3-10). A *bar code reader* is an input device that uses laser beams to read bar codes on products. When the checkout clerk or customer scans the bar code on the grocery item, the computer uses the manufacturer name and item numbers to look up the price of the item and the complete product name. Then, the price of the item shows on the display device, the name of the item and its price print on a receipt, and the item being sold is recorded so that the inventory can be updated. Thus, the output from a POS terminal serves as input to other computers to maintain sales records, update inventory, verify credit, and perform other activities associated with the sales transactions that are critical to running the business. Some POS terminals are Internet capable, which allows updates to inventory at geographically separate locations.

Many POS terminals handle credit card or debit card payments. After swiping your card through the reader, the POS terminal connects to a system that authenticates the purchase. Once the transaction is approved, the terminal prints a receipt for the customer.

ATMs

An *ATM* (automated teller machine) is a self-service banking terminal that connects to a host computer through a network (Figure 3-11). Banks place ATMs in public locations, including grocery stores, convenience stores, retail outlets, shopping malls, sports and concert venues, and gas stations, so that customers can access their bank accounts conveniently.

Using an ATM, people withdraw and deposit money, transfer funds, or inquire about an account balance. Some ATMs have a touch screen; others have special buttons or keypads for entering data. To access a bank account, you insert a plastic bank card in the ATM's card reader. The ATM asks you to enter a numeric password, called a *PIN* (personal identification number), which verifies that you are the holder of the bank card. When your transaction is complete, the ATM prints a receipt for your records. Read Secure IT 3-2 for ATM safety tips.

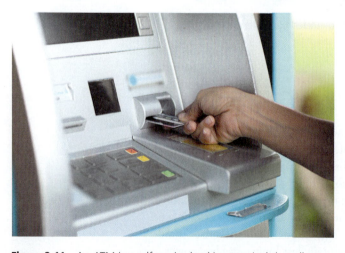

Figure 3-11   An ATM is a self-service banking terminal that allows customers to access their bank accounts.
© bankerwin / Fotolia

SECURE IT 3-2

ATM Safety

Visiting an ATM to withdraw or deposit money is convenient, but it also is ripe with potential for criminal activity. Avoid being a victim by exercising common sense and following these guidelines.

- **Location:** Choose an ATM in a well-lit public area away from bushes and dividers and near the entrance of a building. If using a drive-up ATM, keep the engine running and doors locked, roll windows up while waiting for the ATM to process your request, and leave adequate room to maneuver between your vehicle and the one in the lane in front of you. Observe your surroundings and be suspicious of people sitting in vehicles or loitering nearby.

- **ATM card and PIN:** Handle the ATM card like cash by keeping it in a safe location and storing it in a protective sleeve. Do not write the PIN on the back of the card or store it in a text file on your smartphone; instead, memorize the numbers. (For information about password manager apps, read Secure IT 5-3 in Chapter 5.) Report a lost or stolen card immediately.

- **Transaction:** Minimize time by having the ATM card ready as you approach the machine. Do not allow people to watch your activity. Cover the keypad or screen with one hand as you enter the PIN, and use your body to block as much of the area as possible. If the ATM screen appears different, behaves unusually, or offers options with which you are unfamiliar or uncomfortable, cancel the transaction and leave the area.

- **Be suspicious of skimmers:** Thieves can capture a credit card number and PIN by placing a *skimmer* on an ATM (shown in the figure) or on other self-service stations, such as gas pumps, where users swipe their credit cards for payment. Sophisticated skimmers are Bluetooth enabled or are entire panels placed directly on top of the ATM faces and are virtually undetectable. Less-technical devices are false card readers secured to the card slot with double-sided tape and a hidden camera or an overlay on the keypad. Many ATMs have security stickers informing customers to notify attendants if the seal is broken.

- **Valuables:** Expensive clothes and jewelry can be incentives to potential assailants. Dress modestly and leave jewels at home.

- **Exiting:** Do not count cash in public; immediately put it in your pocket or fold it in your hand. If you receive a receipt, take it with you and do not discard it in a trash can near the area. As you leave, be certain you are not being followed. If you suspect someone is tracking you, immediately walk to a populated area or business, or drive to a police or fire station.

- **Statements:** Review your balances and bank statements frequently. Be certain all deposits and withdrawals are listed, and look for unusual or unfamiliar activity.

skimmer

© photobeginner / Shutterstock

Consider This: Which of these tips do you follow, and how will you change your behavior the next time you visit an ATM or other self-service stations? Which ATMs in your neighborhood appear to be in safe locations?

Self-Service Kiosks

A self-service *kiosk* is a freestanding terminal that usually has a touch screen for user interaction. Table 3-2 identifies several widely used self-service kiosks. Because users interact with self-service kiosks independently, without a salesperson nearby, it is important the kiosk is simple and easy to use. In many cases, a web app or mobile app can extend or enhance the capability of the kiosk. For example, you can reserve an item via the app on a computer or mobile device and then use the kiosk to finalize the transaction.

Internet Research

What is a mobile boarding pass?

Search for: mobile boarding pass

Table 3-2	Self-Service Kiosks
Type	**Typical Services Provided**
Financial kiosk	Pay bills, add minutes to phone plans, add money to prepaid cards, and perform other financial activities.
Photo kiosk	Print photos from digital images. Some allow editing of digital photos. Users may print directly at the kiosk or may send an order to a photo lab to be printed.
Ticket kiosk	Print tickets. Located in airports, amusement parks, movie theaters, rental companies, and train stations.
Vending kiosk	Dispense item after payment is received. Examples include DVD rentals and license plate renewals.
Visitor kiosk	Manage and track visitors upon check-in. Located in businesses, schools, hospitals, and other areas where access is controlled or registration is required.

© Cengage Learning

A *DVD kiosk*, for example, is a self-service DVD rental machine that connects to a host computer through a network (Figure 3-12). DVD kiosks are associated with a particular vendor. To rent a movie online, for example, a customer establishes an account or connects to an existing account on the vendor's website, selects the desired movie, and then chooses a nearby DVD kiosk where the movie will be picked up. Customers also usually can select movies directly at the DVD kiosk via a touch screen or some other input device on the kiosk. After presenting identifying information and swiping a credit card through the reader, the DVD kiosk dispenses the rented movie to the customer. The customer returns it to any of the vendor's nationwide DVD kiosks, at which time the customer's account is charged a fee based on the time elapsed.

Figure 3-12 A DVD kiosk is a self-service DVD rental terminal.
Courtesy of Redbox

Supercomputers

A *supercomputer* is the fastest, most powerful computer — and the most expensive (Figure 3-13). Supercomputers are capable of processing many trillions of instructions in a single second. With weights that exceed 100 tons, these computers can store more than 20,000 times the data and information of an average desktop.

Applications requiring complex, sophisticated mathematical calculations use supercomputers. For example, large-scale simulations and applications in medicine, aerospace, automotive design, online banking, weather forecasting, nuclear energy research, and petroleum exploration use a supercomputer.

Internet Research

How is the fastest supercomputer used?

Search for: fastest supercomputer

Figure 3-13 Supercomputers can process more than one quadrillion instructions in a single second.
Los Alamos National Laboratory

✅ NOW YOU SHOULD KNOW

Be sure you understand the material presented in the sections titled Computers and Mobile Devices, Mobile Computers and Desktops, Servers, Terminals, and Supercomputers, as it relates to the chapter objectives. *Now you should know . . .*

- What you should consider when purchasing a desktop or mobile computer (Objective 1)
- When you would use specific types of servers (Objective 2)
- How you use a POS terminal, ATM, and self-service kiosk (Objective 3)

Discover More: Visit this chapter's premium content for practice quiz opportunities.

Cloud Computing

Cloud computing refers to an environment that provides resources and services accessed via the Internet (Figure 3-14). Resources include email messages, schedules, music, photos, videos, games, websites, programs, web apps, servers, storage, and more. Services include accessing software, storing files online, and configuring an environment of servers for optimal performance. That is, instead of accessing these resources and services locally, you access them on the cloud. For example, you use cloud computing capabilities when you store or access documents, photos, videos, and other media online; use programs and apps online (i.e., email, productivity, games, etc.); and share ideas, opinions, and content with others online (i.e., online social networks).

🔆 **BTW**

The Cloud
The cloud-shaped symbol, which today universally represents cloud computing, stems from early diagrams that visually portrayed the Internet as a cloud, intangible and widespread.

Figure 3-14 Users access resources on the cloud through their Internet connections.

Businesses use cloud computing to more efficiently manage resources, such as servers and programs, by shifting usage and consumption of these resources from a local environment to the Internet. For example, an employee working during the day in California could use computing resources located in an office in Paris that is closed for the evening. When the company uses the computing resources, it pays a fee that is based on the amount of computing time and other resources it consumes, much in the way that consumers pay utility companies for the amount of electricity used.

Cloud computing allows a company to diversify its network and server infrastructure. Some cloud computing services automatically add more network and server capacity to a company's website as demand for services of the website increases. The network and server capacity may be duplicated around the world so that, for example, an outage of a single server does not affect the company's operations.

Internet Research

How secure is the cloud?

Search for: cloud privacy issues

✳ CONSIDER THIS

Are all cloud services available to everyone?
Some cloud services are public and others are private. A public cloud is made available free or for a fee to the general public or a large group, usually by a cloud service provider. A private cloud is dedicated to a single organization. Some cloud services are hybrid, combining two or more cloud types.

Discover More: Visit this chapter's free resources to learn more about business uses of cloud computing and cloud service providers.

Mobile Devices

A mobile device is a computing device small enough to hold in your hand. Because of their reduced size, the screens on mobile devices are small — often between 3 and 5 inches. Popular types of mobile devices are smartphones, digital cameras, portable and digital media players, e-book readers, and wearable devices. Read Ethics & Issues 3-2 to consider issues related to recycling computers and mobile devices.

✳ ETHICS & ISSUES 3-2

Should Recycling of Electronics Be Made Easier?
As technology advances and prices fall, many people think of computers and mobile devices as disposable. Worldwide, consumers generate an estimated 20 to 50 million tons of e-waste annually. (Recall that e-waste consists of discarded computers and mobile devices.) E-waste releases lead, mercury, barium, and other elements into soil and water.

Electronics recycling is known as eCycling. Only about 12 percent of e-waste is eCycled. Electronics recycling can take several forms: reusing parts; creating new products from old products; or melting down or reducing parts to basic elements or materials.

Many not-for-profit organizations, retail websites, mobile service providers, and big box retailers offer reselling and eCycling options. Several electronics companies allow you to trade your device for a gift certificate. The Sustainable Materials Management (SMM) Electronics Challenge promotes eCycling by certifying recycling businesses that meet or pass qualification guidelines. Other companies focus exclusively on eCycling. One business has developed automated kiosks that tell you what your device is worth, connect you to a buyer, take your device, and dispense cash back on the spot. The U.S. Environmental Protection Agency (EPA) lists eCycling, reselling, and donation resources on its website.

A large amount of e-waste pollutes developing countries that may accept the materials for profit. A proposed federal bill, supported by many electronics manufacturers and resellers, makes it illegal for companies to export e-waste to developing countries. Currently, several states have laws that mandate eCycling.

Consider This: Should the government, manufacturers, or users be responsible for recycling of obsolete equipment? Why? What impact does exporting toxic waste have on developing nations? Should the state or federal government mandate an eCycling program for electronics? Why or why not?

Smartphones

A **smartphone** is an Internet-capable phone that usually also includes a calendar, an address book, a calculator, a notepad, games, browser, and numerous other apps. In addition to basic phone capabilities, many smartphones include these features:

- Send and receive email messages and access the web — via Wi-Fi or a mobile data plan
- Communicate wirelessly with other devices or computers
- Function as a portable media player
- Include a built-in digital camera
- Talk directly into the smartphone's microphone or into a Bluetooth headset that wirelessly communicates with the phone
- Conduct live video calls, where the parties can see each other as they speak
- Receive GPS signals to determine a user's current location
- Synchronize data and information with a computer or another mobile device
- Support voice control so that you can speak instructions to the phone and it speaks responses back to you
- Connect to external devices wirelessly, such as via BlueTooth
- Serve as a wireless access point

Many smartphones have touch screens. Instead of or in addition to an on-screen keyboard, some have a built-in mini keyboard on the front of the phone or a keyboard that slides in and out from behind the phone. Others have keypads that contain both numbers and letters. Some also include a stylus.

BTW

High-Tech Talk
Discover More: Visit this chapter's free resources to learn how voice recognition technology works.

✷ CONSIDER THIS

How do you type text messages on a phone that has only a numeric keypad and no touch screen?
Each key on the keypad represents multiple characters, which are identified on the key. For example, the 2 key on the phone's keypad displays the letters a, b, and c on the key's face. On many phones, you cycle through the number, letters, and other symbols associated with a particular key by pressing a key on the keypad multiple times. To type the word, hi, for instance, you would press the 4 key (labeled with the letters g, h, and i) twice to display the letter h, pause momentarily to advance the cursor, and then press the 4 key three times to display the letter i.

A variety of options are available for typing on a smartphone (Figure 3-15). Many can display an *on-screen keyboard*, where you press keys on the screen using your fingertip or a stylus. Some phones support a *swipe keyboard app*, on which users enter words by tracing a path on an on-screen keyboard with their fingertip or stylus from one letter to the next in a continuous motion. With other phones, you press letters on the phone's keyboard or keypad. Some phones use *predictive text*, where you press one key on the keyboard or keypad for each letter in a word, and software on the phone predicts the word you want. Swipe keyboard apps and predictive text save users time when entering text on the phone.

on-screen keyboard

swipe keyboard app

mini keyboard

keypad

slide out keyboard

portable keyboard

virtual keyboard

speech to text

Figure 3-15 A variety of options for typing on a smartphone.

Instead of typing on a phone's keyboard or keypad, users can enter text via a *portable keyboard*, which is a full-sized keyboard that communicates with a smartphone via a dock, cables, or wirelessly. Some portable keyboards physically attach to and remove from the device; others are wireless. Another option is a *virtual keyboard* that projects an image of a keyboard on a flat surface. Finally, some phones work with apps that convert your spoken word to text.

Messaging Services   With messaging services, users can send and receive messages to and from smartphones, mobile phones, handheld game devices, other mobile devices, and computers. The type of messages you send depends primarily on the services offered by the mobile service provider that works with the phone or other mobile device you select. Many users have unlimited wireless messaging plans, while others pay a fee per message sent or received. Messaging services include text and picture/video.

With text messaging service, or *SMS* (*short message service*), users can send and receive short text messages, typically fewer than 300 characters, on a phone or other mobile device or computer. Text message services typically provide users with several options for sending and receiving messages, including:

- Mobile to mobile: Send a message from your mobile device to another mobile device.
- Mobile to email: Send a message from your mobile device to any email address.
- Mobile to provider: Send a message by entering a *common short code* (*CSC*), which is a four- or five-digit number assigned to a specific content or mobile service provider, sometimes followed by the message, for example, to a vote for a television program contestant or donate to a charity.
- Web to mobile: Send a message from a website to a mobile device or notification from a website to a mobile device with messages of breaking news and other updates, such as sports scores, stock prices, weather forecasts, incoming email messages, game notifications, and more.

✳ CONSIDER THIS

What is the difference between push and pull notifications?
A *push notification*, sometimes called a server push, is a message that initiates from the sending location (such as a server) without a request from the receiver. With a *pull notification*, by contrast, receiver requests information from the sending location.

With picture messaging service, users can send photos and audio files, as well as short text messages, to a phone or other mobile device or computer. With video messaging services, users can send short video clips, usually about 30 seconds in length, in addition to all picture messaging services. Smartphones and other mobile devices with picture/video messaging services, also called *MMS* (*multimedia message service*), typically have a digital camera built into the device. Users who expect to receive numerous picture/video messages should verify the phone has sufficient memory. Picture/video message services typically provide users these options for sending and receiving messages:

- Mobile to mobile: Send the picture/video from your mobile device to another mobile device.
- Mobile to email: Send the picture/video from your mobile device to any email address.

Internet Research

What messaging apps are recommended?

Search for: best messaging apps

If you send a picture message to a phone that does not have picture/video messaging capability, the phone usually displays a text message directing the user to a webpage that contains the picture/video message. Some online social networks allow you to send a picture/video message directly to your online profile.

✳ CONSIDER THIS

Do you need a messaging service to send a text or picture/video message?
Instead of using a messaging plan from your mobile service provider, you can use a mobile messaging app to send and receive text, picture, and other message from users. Many messaging apps also provide group chat capabilities. Most messaging apps can be downloaded to your mobile device at no cost.

Voice mail, which functions much like an answering machine, allows someone to leave a voice message for one or more people. Unlike answering machines, however, a computer in the voice mail system converts an analog voice message into digital form. Once digitized, the message is stored in a voice mailbox. A voice mailbox is a storage location on a hard drive in the voice mail system. To help users manage voice mail messages, some systems offer visual voice mail. With *visual voice mail*, users can view message details, such as the length of calls and, in some cases, read message contents instead of listening to them. Some voice mail systems can convert a voice mail message to a text message for display on a computer or mobile device, such as a smartphone, which you then can manage like any other text message.

Messaging services and voice mail systems also may be able to send messages to groups of phone numbers or email addresses. Read Secure IT 3-3 for tips about safely using smartphones and other mobile devices in public.

Discover More: Visit this chapter's free resources to learn more about speech to text.

BTW
Analog vs. Digital
Human speech is analog because it uses continuous (wave form) signals that vary in strength and quality. Most computers and electronic devices are digital, which use only two discrete states: on and off.

SECURE IT 3-3

Safe Mobile Device Use in Public Areas

Sending a text message, updating a Facebook status, posting a Tweet, selecting a new playlist, and checking email messages are tasks you may perform using a mobile device many times each day. They all require some concentration as you focus on the device, usually while looking downward, and they distract you from events occurring around you. Using technology responsibly and safely can prevent theft and injuries.

One common method of thwarting a smartphone thief is to avoid using the phone to check the time. Potential thieves randomly ask people for the correct time. If a person stops and takes a phone out of a pocket or purse, the thief glances at the make and model and decides if it is worth snatching.

Bus stops and train stations are common places for mobile device theft. People in these locations tend to use their smartphones to check schedules, send text messages, and make phone calls. Headphones and earbuds are giveaways that you are using a mobile device and may not be focused on your surroundings. Recent studies show that more than 100 mobile phones are stolen every minute in the United States. Thieves are likely to snatch the devices while the doors are closing just before the train or bus departs from a station so that the victim is unable to pursue the thief. To decrease the chance of theft or pickpocketing, keep your mobile device(s) in a front pocket or in a zippered backpack. Keep your head up and stay aware of your surroundings. If possible, when in public, avoid using accessories that

indicate the type of device to which they are connected.

Cognitive psychologists have studied the effects of inattentional blindness, which occurs when a person's attention is diverted while performing a natural activity, such as walking. The researchers have determined that diverted attention is particularly pronounced when people are talking on a mobile phone and, to a lesser extent, using a portable media player. Emergency room reports indicate that distracted walking accidents are on the rise, especially when people trip over cracks in sidewalks or run into fixed objects, such as parked cars and telephone poles.

Consider This: Do you know anyone who has had a mobile device stolen? If so, how did the theft occur? Have you ever experienced inattentional blindness or distracted walking?

Digital Cameras

A **digital camera** is a mobile device that allows users to take photos and store the photographed images digitally. A *smart digital camera* also can communicate wirelessly with other devices and can include apps similar to those on a smartphone. Mobile computers and devices, such as smartphones and tablets, often include at least one integrated digital camera.

CONSIDER THIS

Do you need a digital camera if you have a camera built into your mobile phone?
If you use a camera only for posts on social media sites, then you may choose to use your mobile phone's built-in camera. If, however, you want increased zoom capabilities, more powerful flash, image stabilization, manual control of settings, and to reduce the drain on your phone's battery, then you may want to opt for a separate digital camera.

In addition to cameras built into phones and other devices, types of digital cameras include point-and-shoot cameras and SLR cameras (Figure 3-16). A *point-and-shoot camera* is an affordable and lightweight digital camera with lenses built into it and a screen that displays an approximation of the image to be photographed. Point-and-shoot cameras, which range in size and features, provide acceptable quality photographic images for the home or small office user. An *SLR camera* (single-lens reflex camera), by contrast, is a high-end digital camera that has interchangeable lenses and uses a mirror to display on its screen an exact replica of the image to be photographed. SLR cameras are much heavier and larger than point-and-shoot cameras. They also can be quite expensive, with a variety of available lens sizes and other attachments.

 **Figure 3-16**   SLR digital cameras have lenses and other attachments, whereas the lenses on point-and-shoot cameras are built into the device. Many smartphones also have built-in digital cameras.
© iStockphoto / andrew-thief;
© Pawel Gaul / Photos.com;
© iStockphoto / Stephen Krow;
Courtesy of Samsung

Most point-and-shoot cameras include zoom and autofocus capability, use a built-in flash, store images on memory cards, and enable you to view and sometimes edit images directly on the camera. Many can take video in addition to still photos. Some are equipped with GPS, giving them the capability to record the exact location where a photo was taken and then store these details with the photo. Others are waterproof. Figure 3-17 illustrates how a point-and-shoot digital camera might work.

Internet Research

What is an SD card?

Search for: sd card information

How a Digital Camera Might Work

Step 1
Point to the image to photograph and take the photo. Light passes into the lens of the camera.

Step 2
The image is focused on a chip called a *charge-coupled device* (*CCD*).

Step 3
The CCD generates an analog signal that represents the image.

Step 4
The analog signal is converted to a digital signal by an analog-to-digital converter (ADC).

Step 5
A processor in the camera adjusts the quality of the image and usually stores the digital photo on media inserted in the camera.

Figure 3-17   This figure shows how a point-and-shoot digital camera might work.
© iStockphoto / David Birkbeck;
© iStockphoto / David Birkbeck;
© Johan Larson / Shutterstock.com;
Courtesy of Kingston Technology Company, Inc

Smart digital cameras include all the features of point-and-shoot cameras and also enable you to connect wirelessly via Wi-Fi. Using the wireless capability, you instantly can save captured photos or videos on a networked computer or the cloud, share them on your online social network, upload them to a video sharing site, send them via email, and more. With a smart digital camera, you typically can download apps (just like on a smartphone) from an app store.

Digital cameras store captured images on storage media in the camera or on some type of memory card. Although most cameras enable you to review, edit, print, and share photos directly from the camera, some users prefer to transfer photos from a digital camera or the memory card to a computer's hard drive to perform these tasks.

Photo Quality   Resolution affects the quality of digital camera photos. **Resolution** is the number of horizontal and vertical pixels in a display. A *pixel* (short for picture element) is the smallest element in an electronic image (Figure 3-18). Digital camera resolution typically is stated in *megapixels* (*MP*), or millions of pixels. For example, a 16 MP resolution means 16 million pixels. The greater the number of pixels the camera uses to capture a picture, the better the quality of the picture but the larger the file size and the more expensive the camera. Most digital cameras provide a means to adjust the resolution. At a lower resolution, you can capture and store more images in the camera.

The actual photographed resolution is known as the *optical resolution*. Some manufacturers state enhanced resolution, instead of, or in addition to, optical resolution. The *enhanced resolution* usually is higher because it uses a special formula to add pixels between those generated by the optical resolution. Be aware that some manufacturers compute a digital camera's megapixels from the enhanced resolution, instead of optical resolution.

Discover More: Visit this chapter's free resources to learn more about resolution.

BTW
Technology Innovator
Discover More: Visit this chapter's free resources to learn about Sony (multinational technology corporation).

pixel

Figure 3-18   A pixel is the smallest element in an electronic image.
© Lingong / Dreamstime.com

Portable and Digital Media Players

A **portable media player** is a mobile device on which you can store, organize, and play or view digital media (Figure 3-19). Smartphones and other mobile devices often can function as a portable media player. Portable media players enable you to listen to music; view photos; watch videos, movies, and television shows; and even record audio and video. Some include a digital camera and also offer a calendar, address book, games, and other apps. Others communicate wirelessly with other devices or computers and enable you to synchronize your digital media with a computer, another mobile device, or cloud storage.

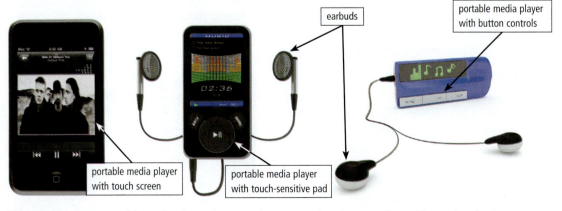

earbuds

portable media player with button controls

portable media player with touch screen

portable media player with touch-sensitive pad

Figure 3-19   Some portable media players have touch screens; others have touch-sensitive pads or buttons that enable you to access your media library.
© iStockphoto / Stephen Krow; © iStockphoto / rzelich; © iStockphoto / AleksVF

⚙ **BTW**

EarPods
Apple uses the term, *EarPods*, to refer to earbuds they designed to match the shape of the human ear.

Portable media players usually require a set of *earbuds*, which are small speakers that rest inside each ear canal. Available in a variety of sizes and colors, some portable media player models have a touch screen. Others have a *touch-sensitive pad*, which is an input device that contains buttons and/or wheels you operate with a thumb or finger. Using the touch-sensitive pad, you can scroll through and play music; view pictures; watch videos or movies; navigate through song, picture, or movie lists; display a menu; adjust volume; customize settings; and perform other actions. Some portable media players have only button controls.

Portable media players are a mobile type of digital media player. A **digital media player** or *streaming media player* is a device, typically used in a home, that streams digital media from a computer or network to a television, projector, or some other entertainment device (Figure 3-20). Some can stream from the Internet, enabling users to access video on websites. Some users opt for a digital media player instead of subscribing to cable or satellite subscription services to watch television programs.

Your collection of stored digital media is called a *media library*. Portable media players and some digital media players house your media library on a storage device in the player and/or on some type of memory card. With most, you transfer the digital media from a computer or the Internet, if the device is Internet capable, to the player's media library. Read How To 2-3 in Chapter 2 for instructions about how to download digital media from online services.

digital media player

Figure 3-20 A digital media player streams media to a home entertainment device.
Courtesy of Apple, Inc.

Mini Feature 3-3: Mobile Device Buyer's Guide

When purchasing a smartphone, digital camera, or portable or digital media player, you should consider several factors. Read Mini Feature 3-3 for tips to consider when purchasing these mobile devices.

⚙ **MINI FEATURE 3-3**

Mobile Device Buyer's Guide

Mobile devices such as smartphones, digital cameras, and portable and digital media players are extremely popular. Research the manufacturers and then consider the following guidelines before purchasing a mobile device.

Smartphone Purchase Guidelines

1. Choose a mobile service provider and plan that satisfies your needs and budget. Choose a sufficient voice, text, and data plan that is appropriate.

2. Decide on the size, style, and weight of the smartphone that will work best for you.

3. Determine whether you prefer an on-screen keyboard, keypad, or mini keyboard.

4. Select a smartphone that is compatible with the program you want to use for synchronizing your email messages, contacts, calendar, and other data.

5. Choose a smartphone with sufficient battery life that meets your lifestyle.

6. Make sure your smartphone has enough memory and storage for contacts, email messages, photos, videos, and apps.

7. Consider purchasing accessories such as extra batteries, earbuds, screen protectors, and carrying cases.

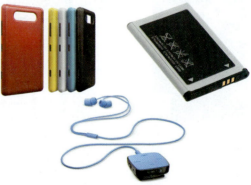

Digital Camera Purchase Guidelines

1. Determine the type of digital camera that meets your needs, such as a point-and-shoot camera or SLR camera.

2. Choose a camera with an appropriate resolution.

3. Evaluate memory cards, because different cameras require different memory cards.

© iStockphoto / tomprout

4. Consider a camera with built-in photo editing features.

5. Make sure that you can see the screen easily.

6. If the photos you plan to take will require you to zoom, choose a camera with an appropriate optical zoom.

7. Purchase accessories such as extra batteries and battery chargers, extra memory cards, lenses, and carrying cases.

© iStockphoto / Vasiliki Varvaki

Portable or Digital Media Player Purchase Guidelines

1. Choose a device with sufficient storage capacity for your media library and apps.

2. Consider how the portable or digital media player will connect to the Internet. Some devices connect using a wired and/or wireless connection. Choose a player that is compatible with the type of connection you can provide.

3. Read reviews about sound quality. If you are purchasing a portable device, consider higher-quality earbuds, headphones, or external speakers.

© iStockphoto / Olga Popova;
© iStockphoto / Olga Popova;
© Terry Morris / Photos.com

4. Select a player that is compatible with other devices you already own.

5. Consider additional memory cards to increase the storage capacity of your portable or digital media player.

6. Consider the accessories. If your portable or digital media player connects to a television or other display, consider purchasing a keyboard so that you can type easily. If the device is portable, consider additional batteries or a protective case.

Discover More: Visit this chapter's free resources to learn more about smartphone, digital camera, and portable and digital media player manufacturers and specifications.

✳ **Consider This:** Although most smartphones also can function as digital media players and digital cameras, would you have a separate digital media player and digital camera? Why?

E-Book Readers

An **e-book reader** (short for electronic book reader), or *e-reader*, is a mobile device that is used primarily for reading e-books and other digital publications (Figure 3-21). An *e-book*, or digital book, is an electronic version of a printed book, readable on computers and other mobile devices. Digital publications include books, newspapers, and magazines. Mobile computers and devices that display text also can function as e-book readers.

E-book readers usually are smaller than tablets but larger than smartphones. Most e-book reader models can store thousands of books, have a touch screen, and are Internet capable with built-in wireless technology. You use an on-screen keyboard to navigate, search, make selections, take notes, and highlight. Some have a *text-to-speech feature*, where the device speaks the contents of the printed page. E-book readers are available with an electronic paper black-and-white screen or with a color screen. Most have settings to adjust text size and

Figure 3-21 E-book readers enable you to read e-books and other digital publications such as newspapers and magazines.
© iStockPhoto / Petar Chernaev

BTW
Electronic Paper Screen
Some users of e-books prefer the electronic paper black-and-white screen over the models with color screens because the electronic paper resembles a paper page from a book.

for various lighting conditions, such as bright sunlight or dim lighting. Batteries usually have a long life, providing more than 75 hours of use before needing to be recharged.

Similar to how a portable media player stores digital media, e-book readers store digital publications in a library on a storage device in the e-book reader and/or on memory cards. You typically transfer the digital publication from a computer or the Internet, if the device is Internet capable, to the e-book reader. Read How To 2-3 in Chapter 2 for instructions about how to download digital media from online services.

Discover More: Visit this chapter's free resources to learn more about e-book readers.

✹ CONSIDER THIS

Do you need a separate e-book reader if you have a tablet or other device that can function as an e-book reader?
If you want the flexibility of reading on one device while using a tablet or other device for separate tasks, you will want to purchase a separate e-book reader. Also, e-book readers have a design suited for optimal readability of on-screen text and a longer battery life.

Internet Research
Which activity trackers are the most widely used?
Search for: popular activity trackers

Wearable Devices

A **wearable device** or *wearable* is a small, mobile computing device designed to be worn by a consumer (Figure 3-22). These devices often communicate with a mobile device or computer using Bluetooth. Three popular types of wearable devices are activity trackers, smartwatches, and smartglasses.

activity tracker communicates with health fitness app on smartphone

smartwatch wirelessly communicates with compatible smartphone

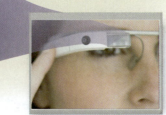

smartglasses, such as Google Glass shown here, respond to voice instruction to access note taking and other apps

Figure 3-22 Three popular wearable devices include activity trackers, smartwatches, and smartglasses.
© iStockPhoto / Petar Chernaev; © iStockPhoto / Chesky_W; © iStockPhoto / scanrail; © iStockPhoto / Wavebreak; Source: Google Inc

An *activity tracker* is a wearable device that monitors fitness-related activities such as distance walked, heart rate, pulse, calories consumed, and sleep patterns. These devices typically sync, usually wirelessly, with a web or mobile app on your computer or mobile device to extend the capability of the wearable device.

A *smartwatch* is a wearable device that, in addition to keeping time, can communicate wirelessly with a smartphone to make and answer phone calls, read and send messages, access the web, play music, work with apps such as fitness trackers and GPS, and more. Most include a touch screen.

Smartglasses, also called *smart eyewear*, are wearable head-mounted eyeglass-type devices that enable the user to view information or take photos and videos that are projected to a miniature screen in the user's field of vision. For example, the device wearer could run an app while wearing smartglasses that display flight status information when he or she walks into an airport. Users control the device

Internet Research
How does augmented reality apply to smartglasses?
Search for: augmented reality

through voice commands or by touching controls on its frame. Some smartglasses also include mobile apps, such as fitness trackers and GPS.

Discover More: Visit this chapter's free resources to learn more about wearable devices.

Game Devices

A **game console** is a mobile computing device designed for single-player or multiplayer video games. Gamers often connect the game console to a television or a monitor so that they can view gameplay on the screen. Some models also allow you to listen to music and watch movies or view photos. Typically weighing between 3 and 11 pounds, many game console models include storage for games and other media. Optical disc drives in the game consoles provide access to games and movies on optical disc. Some use memory cards and accept USB flash drives. Game consoles that are Internet capable enable gamers to download games, stream games or movies, and play with others online. Some gamers connect keyboards or webcams so that they more easily can send text messages or conduct video chats with other gamers.

A **handheld game device** is a small mobile device that contains a screen, speakers, controls, and game console all in one unit. Some include a stylus. Some handheld game device models have touch screens and built-in digital cameras. Some are Internet capable for down-loading games and apps. Most handheld game devices can communicate wirelessly with other similar devices for multiplayer gaming.

With a game console or computer video game, players direct movements and actions of on-screen objects via a controller, voice, or air gestures. Game controllers include gamepads, joysticks and wheels, dance pads, and a variety of motion-sensing controllers (Figure 3-23). The following list describes each of these types of game controllers. Most communicate via wired or wireless technology.

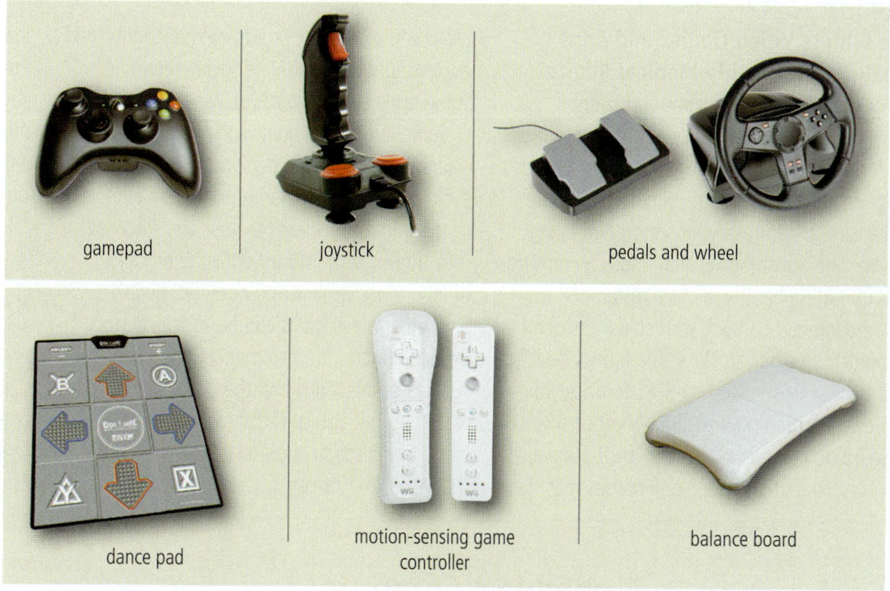

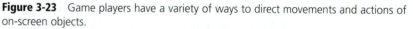

gamepad   joystick   pedals and wheel

dance pad   motion-sensing game controller   balance board

Figure 3-23 Game players have a variety of ways to direct movements and actions of on-screen objects.
© iStockphoto / peng wu; © aquariagirl1970 / Shutterstock.com; © George Dolgikh / Shutterstock.com; Courtesy of DDR Game; © iStockphoto / Florea Marius Catalin; © Stuartkey / Dreamstime.com

- A *gamepad*, which is held with both hands, controls the movement and actions of players or objects in video games or computer games. On the gamepad, users press buttons with their thumbs or move sticks in various directions to trigger events. Several gamepads can communicate with the game console simultaneously for multiplayer gaming.
- Users running flight and driving simulation software often use a joystick or wheel. A *joystick* is a handheld vertical lever, mounted on a base, that you move in different directions to control the actions of the simulated vehicle or player. The lever usually includes buttons, called triggers, that you press to initiate certain events. A *wheel* is a steering-wheel-type input device that users turn to simulate driving a car, truck, or other vehicle. Most wheels also include foot pedals for acceleration and braking actions.
- A *dance pad* is a flat, electronic device divided into panels that users press with their feet in response to instructions from a music video game. These games test the user's ability to step on the correct panel at the correct time, following a pattern that is synchronized with the rhythm or beat of a song.

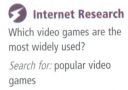
Internet Research

Which video games are the most widely used?

Search for: popular video games

- *Motion-sensing game controllers* allow users to guide on-screen elements with air gestures, that is, by moving their body or a handheld input device through the air. Some motion-sensing game controllers are sold with a particular type of game; others are general purpose. Sports games, for example, use motion-sensing game controllers, such as baseball bats and golf clubs. With general-purpose motion-sensing game controllers, you simulate batting, golfing, and other actions with a universal handheld device or no device at all.
- Other controllers include those used for music and fitness games. Controllers that resemble musical instruments, such as guitars, drums, keyboards, and microphones work with music video games that enable game players to create sounds and music by playing the instrument. Fitness games often communicate with a *balance board*, which is shaped like a weight scale and contains sensors that measure a game player's balance and weight. Read Ethics & Issues 3-3 to consider whether games and apps are qualified to provide medical advice.

Discover More: Visit this chapter's free resources to learn more about game devices.

ETHICS & ISSUES 3-3

Are Fitness Video Games and Apps Qualified to Provide Medical Advice?
Most video games and smartphone apps provide a workout only for your fingers. A host of games and apps, however, attempt to track calories, suggest workout routines, and more. Because you can take your smartphone anywhere, one advantage is that apps can provide tips for eating healthfully at a restaurant, act as a pedometer to track your steps, and send reminders to exercise. Wearable fitness devices can track your steps or use GPS to trace your route when running or biking. Another advantage is you can receive instant feedback and support from fitness apps and games that

allow you to post workouts, calorie counts, and even weight loss to online social networks. Some apps even reward you for working out.

Some critics find fault with these apps, claiming that medical personnel have not evaluated either the game or app developers, or the games and apps themselves. Because they do not take into account the amount of lean muscle mass and body fat, health and weight loss goals can be miscalculated. Experts say that games that simulate sports, such as tennis, burn half the calories you would burn if you participated in the actual sport. Some medical professionals also note that apps do not consider a participant's

medical history when recommending activities. Proponents of fitness-related games and apps say that the games encourage people to be more active and can provide positive feedback, especially the elderly and children who might otherwise not get much physical activity.

Consider This: Should game and app developers provide medical advice? Why or why not? Can fitness-related games provide a quality workout? Can an app give accurate calorie recommendations? Why or why not? As long as the games make people more active, should you ignore a games' shortcomings? Why or why not?

Embedded Computers

An **embedded computer** is a special-purpose computer that functions as a component in a larger product. Embedded computers are everywhere — at home, in your car, and at work. The following list identifies a variety of everyday products that contain embedded computers.

- **Consumer electronics:** Mobile phones, digital phones, digital televisions, cameras, video recorders, DVD players and recorders, answering machines
- **Home automation devices:** Thermostats, sprinkling systems, security systems, vacuum systems, appliances, lights
- **Automobiles:** Antilock brakes, engine control modules, electronic stability control, airbag control unit, cruise control, navigation systems and GPS receivers
- **Process controllers and robotics:** Remote monitoring systems, power monitors, machine controllers, medical devices
- **Computer devices and office machines:** Keyboards, printers, fax and copy machines

Because embedded computers are components in larger products, they usually are small and have limited hardware. These computers perform various functions, depending on the requirements of the product in which they reside. Embedded computers in printers, for example, monitor the amount of paper in the tray, check the ink or toner level, signal if a paper jam has occurred, and so on. Figure 3-24 shows some of the many embedded computers in vehicles. Read Ethics & Issues 3-4 to consider whether in-vehicle technology fosters a false sense of security.

Smartphone apps, such as the OnStar RemoteLink app shown here, remotely start the engine, unlock doors, stream music through the vehicle's sound system, display driving directions, and more.

Cars equipped with wireless communications capabilities, called *telematics*, include features such as navigation systems, remote diagnosis and alerts, and Internet access.

Adaptive cruise control systems detect if vehicles in front of you are too close and, if necessary, adjust the vehicle's throttle, may apply brakes, and/or sound an alarm.

Tire pressure monitoring systems send warning signals if tire pressure is insufficient.

Advanced airbag systems have crash-severity sensors that determine the appropriate level to inflate the airbag, reducing the chance of airbag injury in low-speed accidents.

Electronic stability control automatically applies brakes, and may reduce engine power, when you lose control of steering or traction.

Drive-by-wire systems sense pressure on the gas pedal and communicate electronically to the engine how much and how fast to accelerate.

Figure 3-24 Some of the embedded computers designed to improve your safety, security, and performance in today's vehicles.

© Nir Levy / Shutterstock.com; © Santiago Cornejo / Shutterstock.com; © iStockphoto / narvikk; © iStockphoto / kenneth-cheung; © iStockPhoto / Marcin Laska; © iStockPhoto / pagadesign; Source: OnStar, LLC

✳ ETHICS & ISSUES 3-4

Does In-Vehicle Technology Foster a False Sense of Security?

Embedded computers in vehicles can guide you when backing out of a driveway, warn you if a vehicle or object is in your blind spot, or alert you to unsafe road conditions. Apps can track gas mileage or notify you when your car needs an oil change or other services. Recently, all new cars were required to include electronic stability control, which can assist with steering the car in case of skidding, and backup cameras. Other technologies adjust vehicle speed or headlight usage, and can even activate the brakes.

All of this technology is intended to make driving safer.

Critics of in-vehicle technology claim that it can provide drivers with a false sense of security. If you rely on a sensor for assistance while backing up, parking, or changing lanes, for example, you may miss other obstructions that could cause a crash. Reliance on electronic stability control or other crash-avoidance technologies may cause you to drive faster than conditions allow or to pay less attention to the distance between your vehicle and others.

The effect on new, teen drivers is especially of concern. If teens learn to drive using vehicles

equipped with features such as video rearview mirrors, they may be unable to drive older, less-equipped vehicles safely. Many apps and devices help parents protect their teens while driving. Apps can program mobile devices to block incoming calls or text messages while the vehicle is moving. GPS can track a vehicle's location and speed. Sensors can monitor seatbelt usage and number of passengers in the vehicle.

Consider This: Does in-vehicle technology make driving safer? Why or why not? What basic skills should all drivers have, regardless of their vehicle's technology?

✳ CONSIDER THIS

Can embedded computers use the Internet to communicate with other computers and devices?

Many already do, on a small scale. For example, a Smart TV enables you to browse the web, stream video from online media services, listen to Internet radio, communicate with others on social media sites, play online games, and more — all while watching a television show.

A trend, called the *Internet of Things*, describes an environment where processors are embedded in every product imaginable (things), and those 'things' communicate with one another via the Internet (i.e., alarm clocks, coffeemakers, apps, vehicles, refrigerators, phones, washing machines, doorbells, streetlights, thermostats, navigation systems, etc.). For example, when your refrigerator detects the milk is low, it sends your phone a text message that you need milk and adds a 'buy milk' task to your scheduling app. On the drive home, your phone determines the closest grocery store that has the lowest milk price and sends the address of that grocery store to your vehicle's navigation system, which, in turn, gives you directions to the store. In the store, your phone directs you to the dairy aisle, where it receives an electronic coupon from the store for the milk. Because this type of environment provides an efficient means to track or monitor status, inventory, behavior, and more — without human intervention — it sometimes is referred to as machine-to-machine (M2M) communications. For additional information about the Internet of Things, read Mini Feature 6-1 in Chapter 6.

Putting It All Together

BTW

Technology Trend
Discover More: Visit this chapter's free resources to learn about volunteer computing, where you can donate your computer's resources to promote scientific research projects.

Industry experts typically classify computers and mobile devices in six categories: personal computers (desktop), mobile computers and mobile devices, game consoles, servers, supercomputers, and embedded computers. A computer's size, speed, processing power, and price determine the category it best fits. Due to rapidly changing technology, however, the distinction among categories is not always clear-cut. Table 3-3 summarizes the categories of computers discussed on the previous pages.

Table 3-3 Categories of Computers and Mobile Devices

Category	Physical Size	Number of Simultaneously Connected Users	General Price Range
Personal computers (desktop)	Fits on a desk	Usually one (can be more if networked)	Several hundred to several thousand dollars
Mobile computers and mobile devices	Fits on your lap or in your hand	Usually one	Less than a hundred dollars to several thousand dollars
Game consoles	Small box or handheld device	One to several	Several hundred dollars or less
Servers	Small cabinet to room full of equipment	Two to thousands	Several hundred to several million dollars
Supercomputers	Full room of equipment	Hundreds to thousands	Half a million to several billion dollars
Embedded computers	Miniature	Usually one	Embedded in the price of the product

© Cengage Learning

✔ NOW YOU SHOULD KNOW

Be sure you understand the material presented in the sections titled Cloud Computing, Mobile Devices, Game Devices, Embedded Computers, and Putting It All Together, as it relates to the chapter objectives.
Now you should know . . .

- When you are using cloud computing (Objective 4)
- What you should consider when purchasing a mobile device (Objective 5)
- What types of controllers you might use with game consoles (Objective 6)
- When you are using an embedded computer (Objective 7)

Discover More: Visit this chapter's premium content for practice quiz opportunities.

BTW

Instead of the term, port, the term, *jack*, sometimes is used to identify audio and video ports (i.e., audio jack or video jack).

Ports and Connections

Computers and mobile devices connect to peripheral devices through ports or by using wireless technologies. A **port** is the point at which a peripheral device (i.e., keyboard, printer, monitor, etc.) attaches to or communicates with a computer or mobile device so that the peripheral device can send data to or receive information from the computer or mobile device. Most computers and mobile devices have ports (Figure 3-25). Some ports have a micro or mini version for mobile devices because of the smaller sizes of these devices.

A **connector** joins a cable to a port. A connector at one end of a cable attaches to a port on the computer or mobile device, and a connector at the other end of the cable attaches to a port on the peripheral device. Table 3-4 shows a variety of ports you may find on a computer or mobile device. USB and Thunderbolt are more general-purpose ports that allow connections to a wide variety of devices; other ports are more specific and connect a single type of device.

Figure 3-25   Most computers and mobile devices have ports so that you can connect the computer or device to peripherals.
Courtesy of Gateway; © Ultraone / Dreamstime.com; Courtesy of Lenovo; © iStockphoto / Nikada; © eduard ionescu / Shutterstock

Table 3-4   Popular Ports and Connectors

Port Type	Connector Photo	Port Photo	Port Type	Connector Photo	Port Photo
DisplayPort (audio/video)			Mini USB		
DVI (digital video interface)			Mini HDMI (audio/video)		
HDMI (audio/video)			Network (Ethernet)		
Headphones			Speaker		
Lightning			Thunderbolt		
Microphone			USB (Type A)		
Micro USB			USB (Type B)		
Mini DisplayPort			VGA		

Discover More: Visit this chapter's free resources for an expanded list of ports and connectors.

© Cengage Learning; © Steveheap / Dreamstime.com; © iStockphoto / Hans Martens; © iStockphoto / Ksenia Krylova; © iStockphoto / Lusoimages; © Jorge Salcedo / Shutterstock.com; © Aarrows / Dreamstime.com; © iStockphoto / Lusoimages; © Pcheruvi / Dreamstime.com; © iStockphoto / Potapova Vaeriya; © iStockphoto / Jivko Kazakov; © iStockphoto / TimArbaev; © iStockphoto / Ashok Rodrigues; © iStockphoto / Jon Larson; © Aarrows / Dreamstime.com; © iStockphoto / Denis Sokolov; © Germán Ariel Berra / Shutterstock.com; © Aarrows / Dreamstime.com; © iStockphoto / Li Ding; © iStockphoto / TimArbaev; © iStockphoto / Matthew Brown; © Jorge Salcedo /Shutterstock.com; © Pcheruvi / Dreamstime.com; © Anton Malcev / Photos.com; © iStockphoto / alexander kirch; © iStockphoto / Nick Smith; © iStockphoto / Mohamed Badawi; © Jorge Salcedo /Shutterstock © iStockphoto / Brandon Laufenberg; © getIT / Shutterstock.com; © stavklem / Shutterstock.com; © iStockphoto / Lusoimages; © lexan / Shutterstock; © iStockPhoto / NikiLitov; © iStockPhoto / Peter Hermus; © Jarp / Fotolia; Courtesy of Samsung

USB Ports

A **USB port**, short for universal serial bus port, can connect up to 127 different peripheral devices together with a single connector. Devices that connect to a USB port include the following: card reader, digital camera, external hard drive, game console, joystick, modem, mouse, optical disc drive, portable media player, printer, scanner, smartphone, digital camera, speakers, USB flash drive, and webcam. In addition to computers and mobile devices, you find USB ports in vehicles, airplane seats, and other public locations.

Several USB versions have been released, with newer versions (i.e., USB 3.0) transferring data and information faster than earlier ones (i.e., USB 2.0). Newer versions are *backward compatible*, which means they support older USB devices as well as newer ones. Keep in mind, though, that older USB devices do not run any faster in a newer USB port. In addition to transferring data, cables plugged into USB ports also may be able to transfer power to recharge many smartphones and tablets. Newer versions of USB can charge connected mobile devices even when the computer is not in use.

To attach multiple peripheral devices using a single USB port, you can use a USB hub. A *USB hub* is a device that plugs in a USB port on the computer or mobile device and contains multiple USB ports, into which you plug cables from USB devices. Some USB hubs are wireless. That is, a receiver plugs into a USB port on the computer and the USB hub communicates wirelessly with the receiver. Read Secure IT 3-4 for tips when using USB charging stations.

✳ SECURE IT 3-4

Public USB Charging Stations — Safe or Not?

Although you might be tempted to recharge your smartphone or mobile device at a public charging station, think twice before plugging your USB cable into the charging kiosk's port. The station may be *juice jacking*, which occurs when a hacker steals data from or transfers malware to the device via a USB cable at a charging station. (A hacker is someone who accesses a computer or network illegally.)

This process is possible because the USB cable is used for two purposes: supplying power and syncing data. It can occur within one minute after plugging into the charger.

Anything on the device is susceptible, including photos, contacts, and music, and some malware can create a full backup of your data, leaving you prone to identity theft. Once the phone or mobile device is infected, it can continue to transmit data via Wi-Fi. Security experts claim that the only method of erasing this malware is to restore the device to its factory settings.

Charging stations are common in airports, business centers, and conference rooms. While most are safe, you can reduce the possibility of juice jacking by taking these precautions:

- Use a travel charger, also called a power bank, which can recharge a device several times before needing recharging itself.

- Keep the phone or mobile device locked so that it requires a password to sync data with another device. Turning off the device while charging may not provide sufficient protection against accessing the storage media.

- Use a power-only USB cable that does not allow data transmission.

✳ **Consider This:** Should warning signs be posted by public charging stations? Would you use a public charging kiosk if your smartphone or mobile device was running low on battery power?

Discover More: Visit this chapter's free resources to learn more about USB versions.

Port Replicators and Docking Stations

Instead of connecting peripheral devices directly to ports on a mobile computer, some mobile users prefer the flexibility of port replicators and docking stations. A *port replicator* is an external device that provides connections to peripheral devices through ports built into the device. The mobile user accesses peripheral devices by connecting the port replicator to a USB port or a special port on the mobile computer. Port replicators sometimes disable ports on the mobile computer to prevent conflicts among the devices on the computer and port replicator.

A docking station is similar to a port replicator, but it has more functionality. A *docking station*, which is an external device that attaches to a mobile computer or device, contains a power connection and provides connections to peripheral devices (Figure 3-26). Docking stations also may include slots for memory cards, optical disc drives, and other devices. With the mobile computer or device in the docking station, users can work with a full-sized keyboard, a mouse, and other desktop peripheral devices from their laptop or tablet.

Wireless Device Connections

Instead of connecting computers and mobile devices to peripheral devices with a cable, some peripheral devices use wireless communications technologies, such as Bluetooth, Wi-Fi, and NFC.

Bluetooth **Bluetooth** technology uses short-range radio signals to transmit data between two Bluetooth-enabled computers or devices. In addition to computers, mobile devices

Figure 3-26 Docking stations often are used with tablets and other mobile computers, providing connections to peripheral devices.
Courtesy of Fujitsu Technology Solutions; © Cengage Learning

and many peripheral devices, such as a mouse, keyboard, printer, or headset, and many vehicles and consumer electronics are Bluetooth enabled. Bluetooth devices have to be within about 33 feet of each other, but the range can be extended with additional equipment. If you have a computer that is not Bluetooth enabled, you can purchase a Bluetooth wireless port adapter that will convert an existing USB port into a Bluetooth port. Read How To 3-1 for instructions about setting up two Bluetooth devices to communicate with each other.

⚙ HOW TO 3-1

Pair Bluetooth Devices
Before two Bluetooth devices will communicate with each other, they might need to be paired. *Pairing* is the process of initiating contact between two Bluetooth devices and allowing them to communicate with each other. It is important to have the documentation for the Bluetooth devices you are pairing readily available. The following steps will help you pair two Bluetooth devices.

1. Make sure the devices you intend to pair are charged completely or plugged into an external power source.

2. Turn on the devices to pair, ensuring they are within your immediate reach.

3. If necessary, enable Bluetooth on the devices you are pairing.

4. Place one device in *discoverable mode*, which means it is waiting for another Bluetooth device to locate its signal. If you are connecting a smartphone to a Bluetooth headset, for example,

the smartphone would need to be in discoverable mode.

5. Refer to the other device's documentation and follow the necessary steps to locate the discoverable device from the other device you are pairing.

6. After no more than about 30 seconds, the devices should initiate communications.

7. You may be required to enter a passkey (similar to a PIN) on one device for the other device with which you are pairing. For example, if you are pairing a smartphone with a Bluetooth headset, you may be required to enter the Bluetooth headset's passkey on the smartphone. In this case, you would refer to the Bluetooth headset's documentation to obtain the passkey. Common passkeys are 0000 and 1234.

8. After entering the correct passkey, the two devices should be paired successfully.

✳ **Consider This:** Why is a passkey required when pairing two Bluetooth devices? Do you need to pair Bluetooth devices before each use?

Wi-Fi Short for wireless fidelity, **Wi-Fi** uses radio signals that conform to 802.11 standards, which were developed by the Institute of Electrical and Electronics Engineers (IEEE).

Computers and devices that have the appropriate Wi-Fi capability can communicate via radio waves with other Wi-Fi computers or devices. Most mobile computers and devices are Wi-Fi enabled, along with routers and other communications devices. For successful Wi-Fi communications in open or outdoor areas free from interference, the Wi-Fi computers or devices should be within 300 feet of each other. In closed areas, the wireless range is about 100 feet. To obtain communications at the maximum distances, you may need to install extra hardware. Read How To 3-2 for instructions about connecting a phone to a Wi-Fi network.

⊛ HOW TO 3-2

Connect Your Phone to a Wi-Fi Network to Save Data Charges

Many of today's data plans limit the amount of data you can transfer each month on your mobile service provider's network. Connecting a smartphone to a Wi-Fi network enables you to transfer data without using your phone's data plan and risking costly overages. The following steps describe how to connect your phone to a Wi-Fi network.

1. Make sure you are in a location where a Wi-Fi network is available. Obtain any necessary information you need to connect to the Wi-Fi network.

2. Navigate to the settings on your phone.

3. Locate and enable Wi-Fi in your phone's settings.

4. When your phone displays a list of available wireless networks, choose the network to which you want to connect.

5. If necessary, enter any additional information, such as a password, required to connect to the network.

6. Your phone should indicate when it successfully is connected to the network.

7. When you are finished using the Wi-Fi connection or are not within range of the Wi-Fi network, disable Wi-Fi on your phone to help conserve battery life.

⊛ **Consider This:** If you have a data plan allowing unlimited data and you are within range of a Wi-Fi network, is it better to use your mobile service provider's network or the Wi-Fi network? Why?

Google Inc.

NFC **NFC** (near field communications) uses close-range radio signals to transmit data between two NFC-enabled devices. Examples of NFC-enabled devices include smartphones, digital cameras, computers, televisions, and terminals. Other objects, such as credit cards and tickets, also use NFC technology. For successful communications, the devices either touch or are within an inch or two of each other.

Discover More: Visit this chapter's free resources to learn more about transfer rates of wireless communications technologies and 802.11 standards.

⊛ CONSIDER THIS

What are some uses of NFC devices?

- Pay for goods and services (i.e., smartphone to terminal)
- Share contacts, photos, and other files (i.e., smartphone to smartphone or digital camera to television)
- Download apps (i.e., computer to smartphone)
- Gain access or admittance (i.e., smartphone to terminal)

Protecting Hardware

Users rely on computers and mobile devices to create, store, and manage important information. Thus, you should take measures to protect computers and devices from theft, vandalism, and failure.

Hardware Theft and Vandalism

Companies, schools, and other organizations that house many computers are at risk of hardware theft and vandalism, especially those with smaller computers that easily can fit in a backpack or briefcase. Mobile users are susceptible to hardware theft because the size and weight of their computers and devices make them easy to steal. Thieves may target laptops of company executives so that they can use the stolen computer to access confidential company information illegally.

To help reduce the chances of theft, companies and schools use a variety of security measures. Physical access controls, such as locked doors and windows, usually are adequate to protect the equipment. Many businesses, schools, and some homeowners install alarm systems for additional security. School computer labs and other facilities with a large number of semifrequent users often attach additional physical security devices, such as cables that lock the equipment to a desk, cabinet, or floor. Mobile users sometimes lock their mobile computers temporarily to a stationary object, for example, a table in a hotel room. Small locking devices also exist that require a key to access a hard drive or optical disc drive.

Users also can install a security or device-tracking app on their mobile computers and devices. Some security apps shut down the computer and sound an alarm if the computer moves beyond a specified distance. Others can be configured to photograph the thieves when they use the computer. Device-tracking apps use GPS, Wi-Fi, IP addresses, and other means to determine the location of a lost or stolen computer or device.

Users can configure computers and mobile devices to require identification before allowing access. For example, you can require entry of a user name and password to use the computer or device. Some computers and mobile devices have built-in or attached fingerprint readers (Figure 3-27), which can be used to verify a user's identity before allowing access. A *fingerprint reader* captures curves and indentations of a fingerprint. This type of security does not prevent theft, but it renders the computer or device useless if it is stolen.

Discover More: Visit this chapter's free resources to learn more about device-tracking apps.

Internet Research

How prevalent is theft of mobile devices?

Search for: mobile device theft

BTW

Lost Computers or Devices
You usually can instruct the password screen to display your name and phone number, so that a Good Samaritan can return a lost computer or device to you.

© iStockphoto / CHUYN

Figure 3-27 Some mobile computers and devices include fingerprint readers, which can be used to verify a user's identity.

fingerprint reader

Hardware Failure

Hardware can fail for a variety of reasons: aging hardware; random events, such as electrical power problems; and even errors in programs or apps. Not only could hardware failure require you to replace or repair a computer or mobile device, but it also can cause loss of software, data, and information.

One of the more common causes of system failure is an electrical power variation, which can cause loss of data and loss of equipment. If computers and mobile devices are connected to a network, a single power disturbance can damage multiple devices at once. Electrical disturbances that can cause damage include undervoltages and overvoltages.

- An **undervoltage** occurs when the electrical supply or voltage drops, often defined as more than five percent, below the normal volts. A *brownout* is a prolonged (more than a minute) undervoltage. A *blackout* is a complete power failure. Undervoltages can cause data loss but generally do not cause equipment damage.

- An **overvoltage**, or **power surge**, occurs when the incoming electrical supply or voltage increases, often defined as more than five percent, above the normal volts. A momentary overvoltage, called a *spike*, occurs when the increase in power lasts for less than one millisecond (thousandth of a second). Uncontrollable disturbances such as lightning bolts can cause spikes. Overvoltages can cause immediate and permanent damage to hardware.

To protect against electrical power variations, use a surge protector. A **surge protector**, also called a *surge suppressor*, uses electrical components to provide a stable current flow and minimize the chances of an overvoltage reaching the computer and other electronic equipment (Figure 3-28). Sometimes resembling a power strip, the computer and other devices plug in the surge protector, which plugs in the power source.

Figure 3-28 Circuits inside a surge protector safeguard against electrical power variations.
© iStockPhoto / missisya

The surge protector absorbs small overvoltages — generally without damage to the computer and equipment. To protect the computer and other equipment from large overvoltages, such as those caused by a lightning strike, some surge protectors stop working completely when an overvoltage reaches a certain level. Surge protectors also usually protect the computer from undervoltages. No surge protectors are 100 percent effective. Large power surges can bypass the protector. Repeated small overvoltages can weaken a surge protector permanently. Some experts recommend replacing a surge protector every two to three years.

For additional electrical protection, some users connect an uninterruptible power supply to the computer. An **uninterruptible power supply (UPS)** is a device that contains surge protection circuits and one or more batteries that can provide power during a temporary or permanent loss of power (Figure 3-29). A UPS connects your computer and a power source. Read How To 3-3 for purchasing suggestions regarding surge protectors and UPSs.

Figure 3-29 If power fails, a UPS uses batteries to provide electricity for a limited amount of time.
© rendeep kumar r / Shutterstock

HOW TO 3-3

Evaluate Surge Protectors and UPSs
Electrical power surges are a part of everyday life, and they are especially prevalent during thunderstorms and peak energy consumption periods. These unavoidable occurrences can damage or ruin sensitive electronic equipment. The processor in a computer is particularly sensitive to fluctuations in current. Two devices can help protect electronic components: a surge protector and an uninterruptible power supply (UPS).

Purchase the best surge protector you can afford. Typically, the amount of protection offered by a surge protector is proportional to its cost. That is, the more expensive the surge protector, the more protection it offers. When evaluating surge protectors and UPSs, they should meet or exceed these specifications:

- Sufficient outlets to accommodate each device needing protection
- Individual on/off switch for each device
- Built-in fuse
- UL 1449 rating that ensures quality control and testing
- Joule rating of at least 600
- Indicator light showing the device is functioning properly
- Warranty for damages to any connected equipment
- Low clamping voltage
- High energy-absorption rating
- Low response time, preferably less than ten nanoseconds
- Protection for a modem, communications lines, and cables

Consider This: What other factors might you consider while evaluating surge protectors? Why?

CONSIDER THIS

What other measures can organizations implement if their computers must remain operational at all times?
Some companies use duplicate components or duplicate computers to protect against hardware failure. A *fault-tolerant computer* has duplicate components so that it can continue to operate when one of its main components fail. Airline reservation systems, communications networks, ATMs, and other systems that must be operational at all times use duplicate components, duplicate computers, or fault-tolerant computers.

Health Concerns of Using Technology

The widespread use of technology has led to some important user health concerns. You should be proactive and minimize your chance of risk.

Repetitive Strain Injuries

A *repetitive strain injury* (*RSI*) is an injury or disorder of the muscles, nerves, tendons, ligaments, and joints. Technology-related RSIs include tendonitis and carpal tunnel syndrome.

- Tendonitis is inflammation of a tendon due to repeated motion or stress on that tendon.
- Carpal tunnel syndrome (CTS) is inflammation of the nerve that connects the forearm to the palm of the hand.

Repeated or forceful bending of the wrist can cause tendonitis of the wrist or CTS. Symptoms of tendonitis of the wrist include extreme pain that extends from the forearm to the hand, along with tingling in the fingers. Symptoms of CTS include burning pain when the nerve is compressed, along with numbness and tingling in the thumb and first two fingers.

Long-term computer work can lead to tendonitis or CTS. Factors that cause these disorders include prolonged typing, prolonged mouse usage, or continual shifting between the mouse and the keyboard. If untreated, these disorders can lead to permanent physical damage.

✳ CONSIDER THIS

What can you do to prevent technology-related tendonitis or CTS?

Follow these precautions:

- Take frequent breaks to exercise your hands and arms (Figure 3-30).

- Do not rest your wrists on the edge of a desk. Instead, place a wrist rest between the keyboard and the edge of your desk.

- Place the mouse at least six inches from the edge of the desk. In this position, your wrist is flat on the desk.

- Minimize the number of times you switch between the mouse and the keyboard.

- Keep your forearms and wrists level so that your wrists do not bend.

- Avoid using the heel of your hand as a pivot point while typing or using the mouse.

- Keep your shoulders, arms, hands, and wrists relaxed while you work.

- Maintain good posture.

- Stop working if you experience pain or fatigue.

Hand Exercises

- Spread fingers apart for several seconds while keeping wrists straight.
- Gently push back fingers and then thumb.
- Dangle arms loosely at sides and then shake arms and hands.

Figure 3-30   To reduce the chance of developing tendonitis or carpal tunnel syndrome, take frequent breaks during computer sessions to exercise your hands and arms.

© iStockphoto / Denis Kartavenko; © Oleksiy Mark / Shutterstock.com; © Cengage Learning

Other Physical Risks

With the growing use of earbuds and headphones in computers and mobile devices, some users are experiencing hearing loss. Read How To 3-4 for guidelines for evaluating earbuds and headphones.

Computer vision syndrome (*CVS*) is a technology-related health condition that affects eyesight. You may have CVS if you have sore, tired, burning, itching, or dry eyes; blurred or double vision after prolonged staring at a display device; headache or sore neck; difficulty shifting focus between a display device and documents; difficulty focusing on the screen image; color fringes or after-images when you look away from the display device; and increased sensitivity to light. Eyestrain associated with CVS is not thought to have serious or long-term consequences. Figure 3-31 outlines some techniques you can follow to ease eyestrain.

People who spend their workday using the computer sometimes complain of lower back pain, muscle fatigue, and emotional fatigue. Lower back pain sometimes is caused from poor posture. Always sit properly in the chair while you work. To alleviate back pain, muscle fatigue, and emotional fatigue, take a 15- to 30-minute break every 2 hours — stand up, walk around, stretch, and relax.

Techniques to Ease Eyestrain

- Every 10 to 15 minutes, take an eye break.
  - Look into the distance and focus on an object for 20 to 30 seconds.
  - Roll your eyes in a complete circle.
  - Close your eyes and rest them for at least one minute.
- Blink your eyes every five seconds.
- Place your display about an arm's length away from your eyes with the top of the screen at or below eye level.
- Use large fonts.
- If you wear glasses, ask your doctor about computer glasses.
- Adjust the lighting.

Figure 3-31 Following these tips may help reduce eyestrain while using technology.
© grublee / Shutterstock.com

HOW TO 3-4

Evaluate Earbuds and Headphones
Earbuds and headphones are used to listen to music and other audio files on computers and mobile devices. Selecting the proper product not only depends on the style you prefer, but also the type of audio you will be playing. Prices for earbuds and headphones can range from only a few dollars to several hundred dollars, so it is important to know what you are purchasing. The following guidelines describe what to look for when evaluating earbuds and headphones.

- Determine which style you prefer. Earbuds rest inside your ear, while headphones rest over your ear. Experiment with both types and determine which is more comfortable for you.
- Determine the quality you desire. If you listen to music casually and typically do not notice variations in sound quality, a higher-end product might not be necessary. Alternatively, if sound quality is important, you may consider a more expensive set. Note that a higher price does not always indicate better quality; read online product reviews for information about the sound quality of various products.
- Decide whether you would like a noise cancelling feature. *Noise cancelling* helps block external noise while you are listening to the audio on your device. Noise cancelling headphones sometimes require batteries, and you are able to turn the noise cancelling feature on and off. If you will be listening to audio in locations where you also need to hear what is going on around you, consider purchasing a product without this feature.

Consider This: Based on your preferences and needs, which type of product (earbuds or headphones) is best for you? Locate a product online that meets your specifications. What brand is it? How much does it cost? Where is this product available?

Internet Research

What is a text neck?

Search for: text neck

Another way to help prevent these injuries is to be sure your workplace is designed ergonomically. **Ergonomics** is an applied science devoted to incorporating comfort, efficiency, and safety into the design of items in the workplace. Ergonomic studies have shown that using the correct type and configuration of chair, keyboard, display, and work surface helps users work comfortably and efficiently and helps protect their health (Figure 3-32). You can hire an ergonomic consultant to evaluate your workplace and recommend changes.

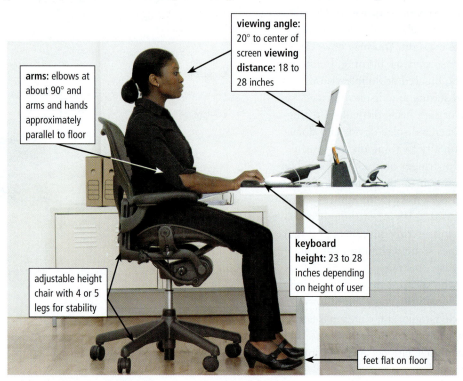

viewing angle: 20° to center of screen **viewing distance:** 18 to 28 inches

arms: elbows at about 90° and arms and hands approximately parallel to floor

keyboard height: 23 to 28 inches depending on height of user

adjustable height chair with 4 or 5 legs for stability

feet flat on floor

Figure 3-32 A well designed work area should be flexible to allow adjustments to the height and build of different individuals.
© Science Photo Library / Alamy

Behavioral Health Risks

Some technology users become obsessed with computers, mobile devices, and the Internet. **Technology addiction** occurs when technology use consumes someone's entire social life. Technology addiction is a growing health problem, but it can be treated through therapy and support groups.

People suffering from *technology overload* feel distressed when deprived of technology, even for a short length of time, or feel overwhelmed with the amount of technology they are required to manage. To cope with the feelings of distraction and to control the impact that technology can have on work and relationships, set aside technology-free time.

✹ CONSIDER THIS

How can you tell if you are addicted to technology?
Symptoms of a user with technology addiction include the following:

- Craves computer time
- Overjoyed when using a computer or mobile device
- Unable to stop using technology
- Irritable when not using technology
- Neglects family and friends
- Problems at work or school

NOW YOU SHOULD KNOW

Be sure you understand the material presented in the sections titled Ports and Connections, Protecting Hardware, and Health Concerns of Using Technology as it relates to the chapter objectives.
Now you should know...

- How you can connect a peripheral device to a computer or mobile device (Objective 8)
- How you can protect your hardware from theft, vandalism, and failure (Objective 9)
- How you can minimize your risk of health-related injuries and disorders that can result from using technology (Objective 10)

Discover More: Visit this chapter's premium content for practice quiz opportunities.

Chapter Summary

This chapter presented characteristics of and purchasing guidelines for laptops, tablets, desktops, smartphones, digital cameras, and portable and digital media players. It also discussed servers, supercomputers, point-of-sale terminals, ATMs, self-service kiosks, e-book readers, wearable devices, game devices, embedded computers, and cloud computing. It presented a variety of ports and connections, ways to protect hardware, and health concerns of using technology use along with preventive measures.

Discover More: Visit this chapter's free resources for additional content that accompanies this chapter and also includes these features: Technology Innovators: Samsung, Dell/Michael Dell, Sony, and Nintendo; Technology Trends: Bitcoin and Volunteer Computing; and High-Tech Talks: Touch Screen Technology and Voice Recognition Technology.

Test your knowledge of chapter material by accessing the Study Guide, Flash Cards, and Practice Test resources from your smartphone, tablet, laptop, or desktop.

TECHNOLOGY @ WORK

Energy Management

When you walk into your office at the start of a new day, you give little thought to the fact that the lights are on and the temperature is comfortable. For all you know, the air conditioner and lighting were on all night; however, energy management systems are hard at work conserving energy and reducing energy costs. When you return home, you also might take for granted the fact that your dryer automatically stops when it senses that your clothes are dry, or that your dishwasher or washing machine uses only enough water to sufficiently clean its contents. Individuals in the energy management field always are looking for ways to use technology to manage energy use.

Building automation systems are devices that can control various building components, such as complex air conditioning systems and lighting systems. Building automation systems adjust these components to provide a comfortable, safe working environment without wasting energy. For example, in an office building where employees all work weekdays from 8:00 a.m. until 5:00 p.m., the building automation system might prompt the air conditioner to turn on one or two hours before the first employees arrive. After the employees leave for the day, the air conditioner either may turn off for the evening or maintain a higher temperature to conserve energy. Some systems used in hotel rooms may include motion sensors that turn off the air conditioner if they sense no motion or noise in the room. Cruise ship cabins and hotel rooms with doors to a balcony may automatically shut down the air conditioner if the door is left open. Air conditioning systems often are one of the largest consumers of energy, and money spent toward automating one of these systems often can be recovered in smaller electricity bills. In addition to controlling the air conditioning system, building automation systems also can control and monitor lighting. Many newer buildings include motion and sound sensors in each room and automatically turn off lights when the rooms are unoccupied. Lighting in common areas of these buildings might turn off after hours when the building is unoccupied. Alternatively, if the building has plenty of natural light coming in, sensors automatically can turn off lights when sufficient sunlight is available, or turn on the lights when the sunlight decreases.

The energy management field has made significant advancements because of computer technologies. Businesses not only are able to reduce their energy costs, but they also are conserving energy at the same time.

Consider This: In what other ways do computers and technology play a role in the energy management field?

© Viktor Gladkov / Shutterstock

Study Guide

The Study Guide exercise reinforces material you should know for the chapter exam.

Discover More: Visit this chapter's premium content to **test your knowledge of digital content** associated with this chapter and **access the Study Guide resource** from your smartphone, tablet, laptop, or desktop.

Instructions: Answer the questions below using the format that helps you remember best or that is required by your instructor. Possible formats may include one or more of these options: write the answers; create a document that contains the answers; record answers as audio or video using a webcam, smartphone, or portable media player; post answers on a blog, wiki, or website; or highlight answers in the book/e-book.

1. List types of computers and mobile devices.
2. Describe how personal computers often are differentiated.
3. Explain how to avoid malware infections.
4. Define the term, motherboard.
5. Describe the roles of the processor and memory.
6. Differentiate among traditional and ultrathin laptops, tablets, phablets, and handheld computers.
7. To interact with a tablet, you may use a touch screen or a(n) _____.
8. List steps to protect yourself from webcam spying.
9. List considerations when purchasing a mobile computer. Explain the importance of built-in ports and slots.
10. A(n) _____ desktop may be less expensive and take up less space.
11. Identify types of desktop users and explain how each user's computer needs may differ.
12. Identify how you can purchase the appropriate desktop computer for your needs.
13. Describe the purpose and functions of a server. Differentiate among rack, blade, and tower servers.
14. Define virtualization as it relates to servers. Define the terms, server farm and mainframe.
15. Define the terms, terminal and thin client. List the advantages of a thin client.
16. Identify situations where POS terminals, ATMs, and self-service kiosks might be used. List ATM safety guidelines.
17. A(n) _____ is used to solve complex, sophisticated mathematical calculations, such as those used in petroleum exploration.
18. List cloud computing resources. Describe how businesses use cloud computing to manage resources.
19. List types of mobile devices. Describe features of a smartphone.
20. Explain the issues surrounding the recycling of e-waste.
21. Identify methods for typing on a smartphone.
22. List options provided by text, picture/video message, and voicemail services.
23. Distinguish between push and pull notifications.
24. _____ occurs when a person's attention is diverted, such as by talking on a mobile phone.
25. Describe the types of digital cameras, how they store captured images, and how to transfer photos to a computer.
26. Explain how resolution affects digital picture quality.
27. Identify the features of portable media and digital media players.
28. List considerations when purchasing different types of mobile devices.
29. List features of e-book readers and wearable devices.
30. Identify types of game controllers.
31. Explain whether fitness video games are an effective form of exercise.
32. List products that contain embedded computers. List the disadvantages of in-vehicle technology.
33. Describe the trend, the Internet of Things.
34. Describe categories of computers and mobile devices, and identify general characteristics of size, user type, and price.
35. Explain how a computer uses ports and connectors.
36. List devices that connect to a USB port. Explain risks of using public USB charging stations.
37. Define the term, backward compatible.
38. Distinguish between a port replicator and a docking station.
39. Describe the following technologies: Bluetooth, Wi-Fi, and NFC.
40. _____ is the process of initiating contact between two Bluetooth devices.
41. List steps to connect your phone to a Wi-Fi network.
42. List methods for securing against hardware theft and vandalism.
43. Define the terms, undervoltage and overvoltage, and explain how each can damage a computer or data.
44. Describe the purposes of surge protectors and UPS devices. Explain the purpose a fault-tolerant computer.
45. Identify causes and types of repetitive strain injuries. List symptoms of CVS.
46. List guidelines for evaluating earbuds and headphones.
47. Describe the role of ergonomics in a workplace.
48. List symptoms of technology addiction. Define the term, technology overload.
49. Describe how technology is used in the energy management industry.

Key Terms

You should be able to define the Primary Terms and be familiar with the Secondary Terms listed below.

Discover More: Visit this chapter's premium content to **view definitions** for each term and to **access the Flash Cards resource** from your smartphone, tablet, laptop, or desktop.

Primary Terms (shown in **bold-black** characters in the chapter)

all-in-one (114)
Bluetooth (137)
cloud computing (121)
computer (108)
computer vision syndrome (143)
connector (135)
desktop (114)
digital camera (125)
digital media player (128)

e-book reader (129)
embedded computer (132)
ergonomics (144)
game console (131)
handheld game device (131)
laptop (111)
mobile computer (108)
mobile device (108)

NFC (138)
overvoltage (140)
port (134)
portable media player (127)
power surge (140)
resolution (127)
server (116)
smartphone (123)
surge protector (140)

tablet (112)
technology addiction (144)
undervoltage (140)
uninterruptible power supply (UPS) (140)
USB port (136)
wearable device (130)
Wi-Fi (138)

Secondary Terms (shown in *italic* characters in the chapter)

all-in-one desktop (114)
activity tracker (130)
application server (116)
ATM (118)
backup server (116)
backward compatible (136)
balance board (132)
bar code reader (118)
blackout (140)
blade server (116)
brownout (140)
building automation systems (145)
charge-coupled device (CCD) (126)
common short code (CSC) (124)
convertible tablet (112)
CPU (110)
CVS (143)
dance pad (131)
database server (116)
discoverable mode (137)
docking station (136)
domain name server (116)
DVD kiosk (120)
earbuds (128)
EarPods (128)
e-book (129)
enhanced resolution (127)
e-reader (129)
fault-tolerant computer (141)
file server (116)
fingerprint reader (139)
FTP server (116)
game server (116)
gamepad (131)
gaming desktop (114)
Google Street View (111)

handheld computer (112)
home server (116)
Internet of Things (133)
jack (134)
joystick (131)
juice jacking (136)
kiosk (119)
list server (116)
mail server (116)
mainframe (117)
media library (128)
megapixel (MP) (127)
MMS (multimedia message service) (124)
motherboard (110)
motion-sensing game controller (132)
network server (116)
noise cancelling (143)
notebook computer (111)
on-screen keyboard (123)
optical resolution (127)
pairing (137)
peripheral device (108)
personal computer (108)
phablet (112)
PIN (118)
pixel (127)
point-and-shoot camera (125)
port replicator (136)
portable keyboard (124)
POS terminal (118)
predictive text (123)
print server (116)
processor (111)
pull notification (124)
push notification (124)

rack server (116)
repetitive strain injury (RSI) (142)
server farm (117)
server virtualization (117)
slate tablet (112)
SLR camera (125)
smart digital camera (125)
smart eyewear (130)
smartglasses (130)
smartwatch (130)
SMS (short message service) (124)
spike (140)
storage server (116)
streaming media player (128)
stylus (112)
supercomputer (120)
surge suppressor (140)
swipe keyboard app (123)
system unit (114)
technology overload (144)

telematics (133)
terminal (117)
text-to-speech feature (129)
thin client (117)
touch-sensitive pad (128)
tower (114)
tower server (116)
ultrabook (111)
USB hub (136)
virtual keyboard (124)
virtualization (117)
visual voice mail (125)
voice mail (125)
wearable (130)
web server (116)
wheel (131)
workstation (114)

phablet (112)

Checkpoint

The Checkpoint exercises test your knowledge of the chapter concepts. The page number containing the answer appears in parentheses after each exercise. The Consider This exercises challenge your understanding of chapter concepts.

Discover More: Visit this chapter's premium content to **complete the Checkpoint exercises** interactively; complete the **self-assessment in the Test Prep resource** from your smartphone, tablet, laptop, or desktop; and then **take the Practice Test**.

True/False   Mark T for True and F for False.

_____ 1. Malware authors often focus on social media, with the goal of stealing personal information. (110)

_____ 2. The disadvantages of a virtual server are that it is difficult to manage and takes a long time to create and configure. (117)

_____ 3. A mainframe is a small terminal that looks like a desktop, but has limited capabilities and components. (117)

_____ 4. Thin clients contain powerful hard drives. (117)

_____ 5. Applications requiring complex, sophisticated mathematical calculations use mainframes. (120)

_____ 6. Most computers and electronic devices are analog, which use only two discrete states: on and off. (125)

_____ 7. SLR cameras are much heavier and larger than point-and-shoot cameras. (125)

_____ 8. Because embedded computers are components in larger products, they usually are small and have limited hardware. (132)

_____ 9. Instead of the term, port, the term, connector, sometimes is used to identify audio and video ports. (134)

_____ 10. Newer versions of USB are backward compatible, which means they support only new USB devices, not older ones. (136)

_____ 11. A port replicator is an external device that provides connections to peripheral devices through ports built into the device. (136)

_____ 12. Because the processor in a computer is particularly sensitive to fluctuations in current, you always should use a surge protector. (141)

Multiple Choice   Select the best answer.

1. Which of the following is *not* true of ultrathin laptops? (111)
   a. They weigh less than traditional laptops.
   b. They have a shorter battery life.
   c. Many have fewer ports than traditional laptops.
   d. They do not include an optical disc drive.

2. Some people use the term _____ to refer to the case that contains and protects the motherboard, internal hard drive, memory, and other electronic components of the computer from damage. (114)
   a. system unit
   b. phablet
   c. thin client
   d. USB hub

3. Power users may work with a high-end desktop, sometimes called a(n) _____, that is designed to handle intense calculations and powerful graphics. (114)
   a. laptop
   b. gaming desktop
   c. server farm
   d. workstation

4. Services provided by _____ include storing content and controlling access to hardware, software, and other resources on a network. (116)
   a. jacks
   b. servers
   c. fault-tolerant computers
   d. mainframes

5. A dedicated server that backs up and restores files, folders, and media is referred to as a _____. (116)
   a. web server
   b. file server
   c. storage server
   d. backup server

6. A four- or five-digit number assigned to a specific content or mobile service provider is referred to as a(n) _____. (124)
   a. CSC
   b. MMS
   c. SMS
   d. SLR

7. A(n) __ is a special-purpose computer that functions as a component in a larger product. (132)
   a. server
   b. embedded computer
   c. thin client
   d. ultrabook

8. A(n) _____ can connect up to 127 different peripheral devices together with a single connector. (136)
   a. SLR device
   b. USB port
   c. port replicator
   d. docking station

Checkpoint

Matching Match the terms with their definitions.

_____ 1. peripheral device (108)

_____ 2. motherboard (110)

_____ 3. CPU (110)

_____ 4. slate tablet (112)

_____ 5. phablet (112)

_____ 6. server virtualization (117)

_____ 7. thin client (117)

_____ 8. kiosk (119)

_____ 9. push notification (124)

_____ 10. fault-tolerant computer (141)

a. term used to refer to a device that combines the features of a smartphone with a tablet

b. computer with duplicate components so that it can continue to operate when one of its main components fail

c. tablet that does not contain a physical keyboard

d. component you connect to a computer or mobile device to expand its capabilities

e. terminal that looks like a desktop but has limited capabilities and components

f. the use of software to enable a physical server to emulate the hardware and computing capabilities of one or more servers

g. electronic component that interprets and carries out the basic instructions that operate a computer

h. freestanding terminal that usually has a touchscreen for user input

i. message that initiates from a sending location without a request from the receiver

j. the main circuit board of a personal computer

✹ Consider This Answer the following questions in the format specified by your instructor.

1. Answer the critical thinking questions posed at the end of these elements in this chapter: Ethics & Issues (111, 122, 132, 133), How To (137, 138, 141, 143), Mini Features (113, 115, 128), Secure IT (110, 119, 125, 136), and Technology @ Work (145).

2. How do malware authors use social media to spread infection? (110)

3. What are the two main components of the motherboard? (110)

4. How do ultrathin laptops differ from traditional laptops? (111)

5. What privacy issues have arisen with webcams in mobile devices? (111)

6. What are the two types of tablets? (112)

7. What is a stylus? (112)

8. What is in the system unit? (114)

9. What are the features of a gaming desktop? (114)

10. Who might use a workstation? (114)

11. What additional requirements are associated with a dedicated server? (116)

12. What are the three form factors for servers? (116)

13. What are the advantages of virtual servers? (117)

14. How does a POS terminal serve as input? (118)

15. What are some examples of self-serve kiosks? (119)

16. How does cloud computing allow businesses to more efficiently manage resources? (122)

17. What are three types of cloud computing? (122)

18. What information might you receive from a web to mobile text message? (124)

19. For what purpose is a common short code (CSC) used? (124)

20. How do push notifications differ from pull notifications? (124)

21. How do SLR cameras differ from point-and-shoot cameras? (125)

22. What is the difference between enhanced and optical resolution? (127)

23. What are three popular wearable devices? (130)

24. Why are embedded computers usually small with limited hardware? (132)

25. What are some types of ports you might find on a computer or mobile device? (135)

26. What is the purpose of a docking station? (137)

27. What is necessary before two Bluetooth devices can communicate? (138)

28. Why might you want to connect your phone to a Wi-Fi network? (138)

29. How does a surge protector work? What is the purpose of an uninterruptible power supply? (140)

30. How can you prevent RSIs and CTS? (142)

✹ Problem Solving

The Problem Solving exercises extend your knowledge of chapter concepts by seeking solutions to practical problems with technology that you may encounter at home, school, or work. The Collaboration exercise should be completed with a team.

Instructions: You often can solve problems with technology in multiple ways. Determine a solution to the problems in these exercises by using one or more resources available to you (such as a computer or mobile device, articles on the web or in print, blogs, podcasts, videos, television, user guides, other individuals, electronics or computer stores, etc.). Describe your solution, along with the resource(s) used, in the format requested by your instructor (brief report, presentation, discussion, blog post, video, or other means).

Personal

1. **Slow Computer Performance**   Your computer is running exceptionally slow. Not only does it take the operating system a long time to start, but programs also are not performing as well as they used to perform. How might you resolve this?

2. **Faulty ATM**   When using an ATM to deposit a check, the ATM misreads the amount of the check and credits your account the incorrect amount. What can you do to resolve this?

Source: Google

3. **Wearable Device Not Syncing**   Your wearable device synchronized with your smartphone this morning when you turned it on, but the two devices no longer are synchronized. What might be wrong, and what are your next steps?

4. **Battery Draining Quickly**   Although the battery on your smartphone is fully charged, it drains quickly. In some instances when the phone shows that the battery has 30% remaining, it shuts down immediately. What might be wrong?

5. **Potential Virus Infection**   While using your laptop, a message is displayed stating that your computer is infected with a virus and you should tap or click a link to download a program designed to remove the virus. How will you respond?

Professional

6. **Excessive Phone Heat**   While using your smartphone, you notice that throughout the day it gets extremely hot, making it difficult to hold up to your ear. What steps can you take to correct this problem?

7. **Server Not Connecting**   While traveling on a business trip, your phone suddenly stops synchronizing your email messages, calendar information, and contacts. Upon further investigation, you notice an error message stating that your phone is unable to connect to the server. What are your next steps?

8. **Mobile Device Synchronization**   When you plug your smartphone into your computer to synchronize the data, the computer does not recognize that the smartphone is connected. What might be the problem?

9. **Cloud Service Provider**   Your company uses a cloud service provider to back up the data on each employee's computer. Your computer recently crashed, and you need to obtain the backup data to restore to your computer; however, you are unable to connect to the cloud service provider's website. What are your next steps?

10. **Connecting to a Projector**   Your boss asked you to give a presentation to your company's board of directors. When you enter the boardroom and attempt to connect your laptop to the projector, you realize that the cable to connect your laptop to the projector does not fit in any of the ports on your laptop. What are your next steps?

Collaboration

11. **Technology in Energy Management**   Your science instructor is teaching a lesson about how technology has advanced the energy management field. Form a team of three people to prepare a brief report about how technology and energy management are connected. One team member should research how computers play a role in conserving energy. Another team member should research other types of technology present in today's homes and buildings that can conserve energy, and the third team member should research other benefits (such as cost savings) resulting from proper energy management.

The How To: Your Turn exercises present general guidelines for fundamental skills when using a computer or mobile device and then require that you determine how to apply these general guidelines to a specific program or situation.

How To: Your Turn ✹

Discover More: Visit this chapter's premium content to **challenge yourself with additional How To: Your Turn exercises**, which include App Adventure.

Instructions: You often can complete tasks using technology in multiple ways. Figure out how to perform the tasks described in these exercises by using one or more resources available to you (such as a computer or mobile device, articles on the web or in print, online or program help, user guides, blogs, podcasts, videos, other individuals, trial and error, etc.). Summarize your 'how to' steps, along with the resource(s) used, in the format requested by your instructor (brief report, presentation, discussion, blog post, video, or other means).

❶ Synchronize a Device

Synchronizing a mobile device with the cloud or a computer provides a backup location for your data

© iStockPhoto / Krystian Nawrocki

should your device fail, or become lost or stolen. While companies such as Google and Apple typically will allow you to download your purchased apps again free of charge, you also should synchronize your data so that it is available in the event a problem with your device arises. The following steps guide you through the process of synchronizing a device.

Synchronize with the Cloud

a. Search for an app compatible with your device that allows you to synchronize the data on your device with the cloud. Some device manufacturers, such as Apple, provide a service to synchronize your device with the cloud.

b. If necessary, download and install the app.

c. The first time you run the app, you may need to enter some personal information so that you are able to sign in and access your data in the future.

d. Configure the app to synchronize at your desired interval. If you are synchronizing a smartphone, keep in mind that synchronizing with the cloud will require a data plan. Be sure your data plan supports the amount of data that will be synchronized.

e. Once you have configured the synchronization settings successfully, select the option to manually synchronize your device at this time.

Synchronize with a Computer

a. Install and run the app designed to synchronize your device with your computer. For instance, iTunes is used to synchronize Apple devices with a computer.

b. Connect the device to the computer using the synchronization cable provided.

c. When the synchronization is complete, a message will inform you that it is safe to disconnect the device. Do not disconnect the device before the synchronization is complete, as that may damage the data on the device.

Retrieve Synchronized Data

If you lose your device or the data on your device, you can retrieve the data previously synchronized. To retrieve data synchronized previously, follow the instructions in the program or app used to synchronize your data.

Exercises

1. What type of device are you attempting to synchronize? What programs and apps are available to synchronize your device with the cloud? What programs and apps are available to synchronize your device with a computer?

2. Which program or app did you use to synchronize your device? Why did you choose that program or app instead of the others?

3. How long did it take to synchronize your device? What data on your device did the program or app synchronize?

❷ Find, Download, and Read an E-Book on an E-Book Reader

Most e-book readers enable you to find and download new e-books without having to connect to a computer first. To search for and download an e-book, you need to establish an Internet connection through either Wi-Fi or a mobile data plan. The following steps guide you through the process of finding, downloading, and reading an e-book on an e-book reader.

a. Turn on your e-book reader and establish an Internet connection.

b. Navigate to the store on your e-book reader where you can search for and download e-books.

c. Locate the option to search available e-books and then enter the desired search text. You usually can search by the book's title, author, or genre.

✹ How To: Your Turn

d. Perform the search and then browse the search results for the book you want to download and install.

e. Select the option to download the book. Please note that many books cost money to download. If your payment information was entered previously, you may be charged for downloading this e-book. If you do not want to be charged, locate and download an e-book that is free.

f. When the download is complete, return to your list of installed e-books.

g. Select the e-book you have just downloaded to read the e-book.

Exercises

1. What type of e-book reader do you have? Are you happy with the selection of e-books on your e-book reader?

2. In addition to e-book readers, what other types of devices allow you to read e-books?

3. Do e-books cost more or less than traditional print books? What are the advantages and disadvantages of using e-books?

© iStockPhoto / Petar Chernaev

❸ Manage Power for Mobile Computers and Devices

Configuring power management settings on mobile computers and devices will help ensure your battery life is maximized. The following steps guide you through the process of configuring power management features on mobile computers and devices.

a. Display the Control Panel or Settings on your mobile computer or device.

b. Tap or click the option to display power management or battery settings.

c. If necessary, select a power plan setting to view or modify.

d. Make the necessary adjustments to the settings that affect power consumption. For example, configure the display to dim or turn off after 30 seconds of inactivity. This will allow you enough time to read what is on the screen without having to touch the screen or move the mouse.

e. Save all changes.

Exercises

1. What power management settings have you configured on your mobile computer or device?

2. Compare battery life on your device before and after configuring power management settings. Have you noticed an improvement in battery life? If so, how vmuch?

3. What other power management settings are you able to configure on your mobile computer or device?

Google Inc.

How To: Your Turn ✸

4 Use your Mobile Device Ergonomically

Individuals are using various mobile devices, such as phones and tablets, more frequently, and using these devices ergonomically can help prevent unnecessary injury. The following guidelines will help you use your mobile device ergonomically:

- Use shortcuts and abbreviations whenever possible to avoid excessive hand movement.
- Make sure your hands, wrists, and arms are at a natural angle, and avoid holding the device in a position that causes discomfort.
- Use hands-free devices and voice recognition features whenever possible to avoid hand movement.
- Do not use the device for extended periods of time without taking frequent breaks.
- Avoid resting the device on your lap during use.
- Sit in an upright position or stand when using the device.
- Consider using a separate keyboard and mouse if you will be interacting with the device extensively.
- Use the device in a setting with natural light.

Exercises

1. Have you been following the above guidelines while using mobile computers and devices? If not, what have you been doing differently?
2. What types of health risks might nonergonomic use of a mobile device pose?
3. What are some additional guidelines you can follow to help minimize health risks while using your mobile device?

© Marcin Balcerzak / Shutterstock

5 Transfer Media from a Mobile Device to a Computer

Many individuals take photos and record videos using mobile devices such as digital cameras, smartphones, and tablets. After taking the photos and recording the videos, transferring them to a computer allows you easily to create backup copies, edit the media, and create digital albums. The following steps describe multiple ways to transfer media from a mobile device to a computer.

To transfer photos from a mobile device to a computer using a memory card:

a. Safely remove the memory card from the mobile device.
b. Properly insert the memory card into the appropriate memory card slot on the computer.
c. When the computer detects the memory card, navigate to the location of the media to transfer.
d. Select the files to transfer and then drag them to the destination folder on the computer.
e. Use the operating system's "Eject" or "Safely Remove" feature to remove the memory card from the computer safely and insert it back in the mobile device.

To transfer photos from a mobile device to a computer using a USB cable:

a. Connect the cable to the mobile device and to the computer.
b. When the computer detects the mobile device, navigate to the location on the mobile device containing the media to transfer.
c. Select the files to transfer and then drag them to the destination folder on the computer.
d. Disconnect the USB cable from the computer and from the mobile device.

   Some mobile devices also allow you to transfer media using wireless technologies, such as Bluetooth and Wi-Fi. The steps required to transfer photos wirelessly vary greatly for each device. Thus, read your mobile device's documentation to see if and how you can transfer media to your computer wirelessly. Be aware that transferring photos using your mobile data plan could increase your data charges. Consider using Wi-Fi or Bluetooth to transfer the media.

Exercises

1. Of the above techniques, which way do you find is easiest to transfer media from your mobile device to a computer? Why?
2. What other technologies might you be able to use to transfer media from a mobile device to a computer?
3. Would you rather transfer media from your mobile device to a computer, or transfer it to the cloud? Why?

✹ Internet Research

The Internet Research exercises broaden your understanding of chapter concepts by requiring that you search for information on the web.

Discover More: Visit this chapter's premium content to **challenge yourself with additional Internet Research exercises**, which include Search Sleuth, Green Computing, Ethics in Action, You Review It, and Exploring Technology Careers.

Instructions: Use a search engine or another search tool to locate the information requested or answers to questions presented in the exercises. Describe your findings, along with the search term(s) you used and your web source(s), in the format requested by your instructor (brief report, presentation, discussion, blog post, video, or other means).

① Making Use of the Web
Retail and Auctions

E-retailers are changing the ways consumers shop for goods. One market research firm reports that nearly three-fourths of shoppers complete one-half of all their transactions online. As shoppers grow increasingly loyal to e-commerce, retail websites have become more sophisticated, and brick-and-mortar stores have adapted to the online presence. Nearly 90 percent of smartphone owners use their devices to compare prices, locate promotional offers, and determine directions and store hours.

Online auctions offer another convenient method of shopping for and selling practically anything imaginable. Most auction sites organize products in categories and provide photos and descriptions. eBay is one of thousands of Internet auction websites and is the world's largest personal online trading community. In addition, craigslist is a free online equivalent of classified advertisements.

Research This: (a) Visit two retail websites and search for the latest e-book readers. Which features do these websites offer compared with the same offerings in brick-and-mortar stores? What are the advantages and disadvantages of shopping online? What policies do these websites offer for returning items? Which items have you purchased online?

(b) Visit an auction website and search for two objects pertaining to your favorite musical artist, sports team, or celebrity. For example, search for an autographed photo or ticket stubs. Describe these two items. How many people have bid on these items? Who are the sellers? What are the opening and current bids?

② Social Media

Businesses know that using social media is an efficient and effective method of building brand loyalty and promoting the exchange of ideas. The informal communication between consumers and company representatives can help maintain credibility and promote trust. According to a recent study, more than 70 percent of American Internet users visit online social networks, and 65 percent of these people discover particular brands, products, and services by reading material posted on these websites. Twitter, Facebook, and other social media often are used to befriend customers, give a positive feeling about services and goods, engage readers, and market new ideas. Subscribers share their opinions, thoughts, and experiences, either positive or negative, through product and service reviews.

Research This: Visit at least three Twitter, Facebook, or other online social network sites and review the content. How many Twitter followers or Facebook 'likes' does the website have? Identify three organizations, businesses, products, or causes that have a presence on Facebook, Twitter, or other online social networks. How many followers or fans do they have? Which posts are engaging and promote positive attitudes about the company and the products or services offered? How many user-generated reviews and product ratings are shown? How do the online social networks encourage sharing opinions? In which ways do the companies respond to and interact with followers and fans? If negative posts are written, does the company respond professionally and positively?

③ Search Skills
Search Operators

Search engines provide operators, or special symbols, that will help narrow down search results. Use quotation marks around search text to search for an exact word or phrase. For example, type the following as your search text: "wireless communications technologies" (be sure to include the quotation marks) to search for those three words in that exact order. Search results will display matching pages with the quoted search phrase highlighted or in bold.

Source: eBay

Internet Research ✳

To match one or more words in a phrase, you can use an asterisk (*), also called a wildcard operator, as part of your search text. Each asterisk represents one or more words. For example, type the following as your search text: "wireless * technologies" (with the quotation marks) to find search results that match wireless communications technologies, wireless Internet technologies, wireless and related technologies, and others. If you are searching for a phrase or quotation with many words, consider using the asterisk wildcard operator in place of some of the words in the search text. This technique is useful if you have a quotation, and you want to find out who said it or where it may have appeared.

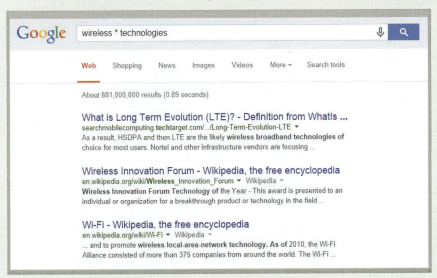

Source: Google

Research This: Create search queries using quotation marks and/or the wildcard operator to answer the following questions and use a search engine to find the answers. (1) Someone once said, "Life is not fair, get used to it." Who was it? (2) What are three websites containing digital camera reviews? (3) How do businesses use near field communications? (4) Find five different words that complete the phrase, handheld ___ devices, by typing appropriate search text into a search engine.

4 Security

Surge protectors and uninterruptible power supplies offer protection from electrical power surges, as you learned in the Protecting Hardware section of this chapter. While these surges are part of everyday life, they are more likely to occur during thunderstorms and peak energy consumption periods. These unavoidable occurrences can damage or ruin sensitive electronic equipment. The processor in a computer is particularly sensitive to the fluctuations in current. When shopping for a surge protector, purchase the best product you can afford. Typically, the amount of protection offered by a surge protector is proportional to its cost. That is, the more expensive the surge protector, the more protection it offers.

Research This: Visit an electronics store or view websites with a variety of surge protectors from several manufacturers. Read the packaging or specifications to determine many of the features. Compare at least three surge protectors by creating a table using these headings: manufacturer, model, price, Joule rating (a Joule is the unit of energy the device can absorb before it can be damaged; the higher the Joule rating, the better the protection), warranty, energy-absorption rating, response time, and other features. Which surge protector do you recommend? Why?

5 Cloud Services
Data Providers and Mashups (DaaS)

The web has made it possible for many information providers to make business, housing, weather, demographic, and other data available on demand to third parties. Accessing online data on demand is an example of DaaS (data as a service), a service of cloud computing that provides current data over the Internet for download, analysis, or use in new applications.

Mashups are apps that combine data from one or more online data providers. Mapping mashups are popular because users can visualize locations associated with data originating from a variety of online sources, including real estate listings, crime statistics, current Tweets, live traffic conditions, or digital photos.

Research This: (1) Use a search engine to find two different online data markets. Write a report sharing the sources or focus of information each provides, the availability of visualization tools to preview data, and how developers can access or incorporate the data into their own apps and websites. (2) Use a search engine to find a popular mapping mashup based on data from one of the sources listed above, or another topic. Identify the provider of the data and the provider of the maps on which the data is displayed. (3) Use a search engine to find an app or website that will help you create your own map mashup showing locations of your online data: Facebook friends, Flickr or Instagram photos, or Tweets. Take a screenshot of the mashup you made.

Critical Thinking

The Critical Thinking exercises challenge your assessment and decision-making skills by presenting real-world situations associated with chapter concepts. The Collaboration exercise should be completed with a team.

Instructions: Evaluate the situations below, using personal experiences and one or more resources available to you (such as articles on the web or in print, blogs, podcasts, videos, television, user guides, other individuals, electronics or computer stores, etc.). Perform the tasks requested in each exercise and share your deliverables in the format requested by your instructor (brief report, presentation, discussion, blog post, video, or other means).

1. Technology Purchases

You are the director of information technology at a company that specializes in designing and selling customizable sportswear for local high school and college sports teams. Most of the technology equipment is out of date and must be replaced. You need to evaluate the requirements of individual employees so that you can order replacements.

Do This: Determine the type of computer or mobile device that might be most appropriate for the following employees: a graphic designer who exclusively works in the office, a cashier who is responsible for assisting customers with purchases, and a sales representative who travels to various locations and needs wireless communications capabilities. Consider the varying requirements of each, including mobility, security, and processing capabilities. Discuss various options that might work for each user, and considerations when purchasing each type of device.

2. Game Devices

You manage a youth recreation center and have been given a grant to purchase a game console and accessories, along with fitness games, for use at the center.

Do This: Use the web to research three popular recent game consoles. Choose five characteristics to compare the game consoles, such as Internet capabilities, multiplayer game support, storage capacity, television connection, and game controllers. Research fitness games for each console and what accessories are needed to run the games. Determine the goals of each game, such as skill-building, weight loss, or entertainment. Read user reviews of each game, as well as professional reviews by gaming industry experts. If possible, survey your friends and classmates to learn about their experiences with each game, such as heart rate while playing the games, any fitness goals reached, and their enjoyment of the game.

3. Case Study

Amateur Sports League You are the new manager for a nonprofit amateur soccer league. The league would like to purchase a digital camera to upload pictures of players, games, and fundraising events to its Facebook page and its website.

Do This: You need to prepare information about digital camera options to present to the board of directors. First, research the cost and quality differences between point-and-shoot cameras and SLR cameras. Use the web to find a recent model of both camera types and compare the reviews, as well as the costs, for each. Make a list of additional features, such as video capabilities, editing capabilities, lens, megapixels, GPS, flash, and zoom. Determine how each camera stores the images, the amount of storage available, and how to transfer images to a computer or mobile device. Explore whether software is included with the camera that can be used to edit, store, or organize the images after they are transferred to a computer. Compare your findings with the camera capabilities of a recent model smartphone. Determine what type of camera would be best for the league's needs and the capabilities that are most important.

Courtesy of Samsung

Collaboration

4. National Security Uses for Technology Technology is an integral part of military operations. Many military research projects use simulators that resemble civilian computer games. Your company has been contacted by the Department of Defense for a research project.

Do This: Form a four-member team, and then form two two-member groups. Assign each group one of the following topics to research: (1) How have mobile computers and cloud computing affected issues of national security? (2) How can the utilization of microchips worn by soldiers, or wearable computers, be integrated into civilian use? Meet with your team and discuss your findings. Determine any advantages or disadvantages, as well as any legal ramifications that may arise.

PROGRAMS AND APPS: Productivity, Graphics, Security, and Other Tools

4

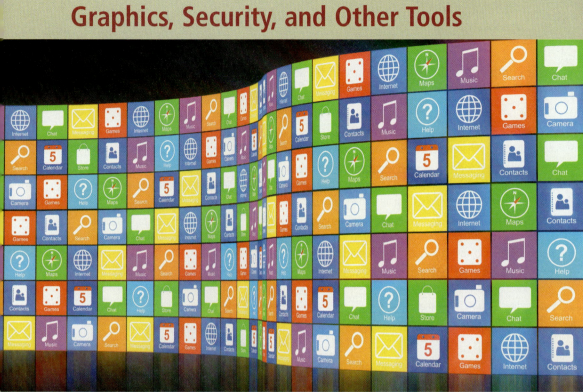

People use a variety of programs and apps on their computers and mobile devices.

"I use my computer and mobile devices to complete homework assignments, pay bills, edit digital photos, post social media updates, and play games. I also use an antivirus program. What other programs and apps could I need?"

While you may be familiar with some of the content in this chapter, do you know how to …

- Determine safe websites for downloading software?
- Ensure you are not plagiarizing Internet content?
- Safely use a personal finance app?
- Use project management software?
- Avoid risks when using payment apps?
- Edit and share photos?
- Use voice command personal assistant apps?
- Identify different types of viruses and malware?
- Recognize a virus hoax?
- Protect your smartphone against malware threats?
- Recognize a phishing message?
- Uninstall a program or remove an app?
- Compress and uncompress files and folders?

In this chapter, you will discover how to perform these tasks along with much more information essential to this course. For additional content available that accompanies this chapter, visit the free resources and premium content. Refer to the Preface and the Intro chapter for information about how to access these and other additional instructor-assigned support materials.

✓ Objectives

After completing this chapter, you will be able to:

1   Identify the general categories of programs and apps

2   Describe how an operating system interacts with applications and hardware

3   Differentiate among the ways you can acquire programs and apps: retail, custom, web app, mobile app, mobile web app, shareware, freeware, open source, and public-domain

4   Identify the key features of productivity applications: word processing, presentation, spreadsheet, database, note taking, calendar and contact management, project management, accounting, personal finance, legal, tax preparation, document management, support services, and enterprise computing

5   Identify the key features of graphics and media applications: computer-aided design, desktop publishing, paint/image editing, photo editing and photo management, video and audio editing, multimedia and website authoring, media player, and disc burning

6   Identify the uses of personal interest applications: lifestyle, medical, entertainment, convenience, and education

7   Identify the purpose of software used in communications

8   Identify the key features of security tools: personal firewall, antivirus programs, malware removers, and Internet filters

9   Identify the key features of file, disk, and system management tools: file manager, search, image viewer, uninstaller, disk cleanup, disk defragmenter, screen saver, file compression, PC maintenance, and backup and restore

Programs and Apps

Using programs and apps, you can accomplish a variety of tasks on computers and mobile devices (Figure 4-1). Recall from Chapter 1 that a **program**, or **software**, consists of a series of related instructions, organized for a common purpose, that tells the computer what tasks to perform and how to perform them. An **application**, or **app**, sometimes called *application software*, consists of programs designed to make users more productive and/or assist them with personal tasks.

An *operating system* is a set of programs that coordinates all the activities among computer or mobile device hardware. Other programs, often called *tools* or *utilities*, enable you to perform maintenance-type tasks usually related to managing devices, media, and programs used by computers and mobile devices. The operating system and other tools are collectively known as *system software* because they consist of the programs that control or maintain the operations of the computer and its devices.

Role of the Operating System

To use applications, such as a browser or word processing program on a desktop or laptop, your computer must be running an operating system. Similarly, a mobile device must be running an operating system to run a mobile app, such as a navigation or payment app. Desktop operating systems include Mac OS, Windows, Linux, and Chrome OS. Mobile operating systems include Android, iOS, and Windows Phone. The operating system, therefore, serves as the interface between the user, the applications and other programs, and the computer's or mobile device's hardware (Figure 4-2).

🌀 **Internet Research**
Which mobile operating system is the most widely used?

Search for: mobile operating system market share

Figure 4-1 Users work with a variety of programs and apps, some of which are shown in this figure.

© Cengage Learning; Courtesy of NCH Software; Source: Apple Inc.; Source: Google Inc.; Courtesy of AVG Technologies; Source: Microsoft

An Example of How an Operating System Interacts with a User, an Application, and Hardware

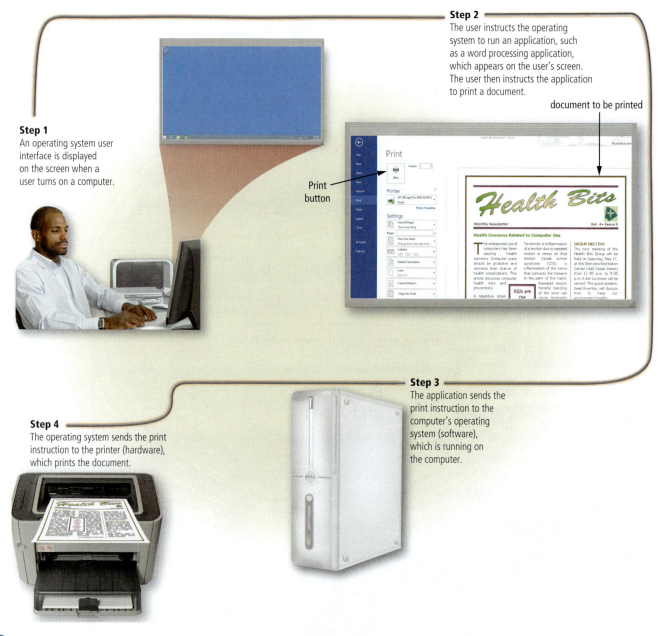

Step 2
The user instructs the operating system to run an application, such as a word processing application, which appears on the user's screen. The user then instructs the application to print a document.

document to be printed

Step 1
An operating system user interface is displayed on the screen when a user turns on a computer.

Print button

Step 3
The application sends the print instruction to the computer's operating system (software), which is running on the computer.

Step 4
The operating system sends the print instruction to the printer (hardware), which prints the document.

Figure 4-2 This figure shows how the operating system is the interface between the user, the application, and the hardware.
© photoguy_76 / Fotolia; © Cengage Learning; © restyler / Shutterstock.com; © StockLite / Shutterstock; Source: Microsoft

Each time you start a computer or mobile device, the operating system is loaded (copied) from the computer's hard drive or mobile device's storage media into memory. Once the operating system is loaded, it coordinates all the activities of the computer or mobile device. This includes running applications and transferring data among input and output devices and memory. While the computer or mobile device is running, the operating system remains in memory.

Discover More: Visit this chapter's free resources to learn more about desktop and mobile operating systems.

Obtaining Software

Software is available in a variety of forms: retail, custom, web app, mobile app, mobile web app, shareware, freeware, open source, and public domain.

- *Retail software* is mass-produced, copyrighted software that meets the needs of a wide variety of users, not just a single user or company. Some retail software, such as an operating system, is preinstalled on new computers and mobile devices. You also can purchase retail software from local stores and on the web. With online purchases, you may be able to download purchased programs immediately instead of waiting for the software to arrive by mail.
- *Custom software* performs functions specific to a business or industry. Sometimes a company cannot locate retail software that meets its unique requirements. In this case, the company may use software developers to create tailor-made custom software. Custom software usually costs more than retail software.
- A *web app* is an application stored on a web server that you access through a browser. Users typically interact with web apps directly by visiting a website, but some web apps also can be accessed locally offline. Many websites provide free access to their apps. Some charge a one-time fee, while others charge recurring monthly or annual subscription fees. You may be able to use part of a web app free and pay for access to a more comprehensive program or pay a fee when a certain action occurs.
- A *mobile app* is an application you download from a mobile device's app store, sometimes called a *marketplace*, or other location on the Internet to a smartphone or other mobile device. Some mobile apps are preinstalled on a new mobile computer or device. Many mobile apps are free; others have a minimal cost — often less than a few dollars.
- A *mobile web app* is a web app that is optimized for display in a browser on a mobile device, regardless of screen size or orientation. Many app developers opt for web delivery because they do not have to create a different version for each mobile device's app store. Many web apps use a responsive design, which means the app displays properly on any computer or device.
- *Shareware* is copyrighted software that is distributed at no cost for a trial period. To use a shareware program beyond that period, you send payment to the software developer or you might be billed automatically unless you cancel within a specified period of time. Some developers trust users to send payment if software use extends beyond the stated trial period. Others render the software useless if no payment is received after the trial period expires. In some cases, a scaled-down version of the software is distributed free, and payment entitles the user to the fully functional product.
- *Freeware* is copyrighted software provided at no cost by an individual or a company that retains all rights to the software. Thus, software developers typically cannot incorporate freeware in applications they intend to sell. The word, free, in freeware indicates the software has no charge.
- *Open source software* is software provided for use, modification, and redistribution. This software has no restrictions from the copyright holder regarding modification of the software's internal instructions and its redistribution. Open source software usually can be downloaded from a web server on the Internet, often at no cost. Promoters of open source software state two main advantages: users who modify the software share their improvements with others, and customers can personalize the software to meet their needs.
- *Public-domain software* has been donated for public use and has no copyright restrictions. Anyone can copy or distribute public-domain software to others at no cost.

Thousands of shareware, freeware, and public-domain programs are available on the Internet for users to download. Examples include communications, graphics, and game programs. Read Secure IT 4-1 for tips about safely downloading shareware, freeware, or public-domain software.
Discover More: Visit this chapter's free resources to learn more about software availability.

⚙ SECURE IT 4-1

📄 Safe Downloading Websites

Websites tempt potential customers with catchy offers for software promising to speed up the computer or to obtain the latest versions of games and music. The temptation to download shareware, freeware, and public-domain software is high, especially when the cost of such useful or fun programs is free or extremely reasonable. This action could be dangerous, however, because some of these websites are filled with virus-infected software just waiting to be installed on an unsuspecting user's computer or mobile device.

Before downloading any software, consider these factors when locating and evaluating shareware, freeware, or public-domain websites:

- Search for popular shareware, freeware, and public-domain download websites.

The software generally is organized into evaluation categories, such as outstanding and recommended, or grouped into purpose, such as tools and gaming.

- Look for websites with programs for your particular type of computer or mobile device. Some websites exclusively offer Windows- or Apple-based products.
- Obtain the latest versions of shareware, freeware, and public-domain software. Many developers update their programs frequently in an effort to include new features and to thwart viruses. The newest versions, therefore, often are safer and easier to use than previous versions.
- Locate websites with a variety of programs in a specific category. For example, if you need antivirus software, you can search

to find which shareware, freeware, and public-domain software is available.

- Read ratings for and reviews of products. Often, comments from users provide guidance in selecting the most desirable software for your needs.

If you follow these tips, you may find shareware, freeware, and public-domain software to be one of the best software bargains in the marketplace.

⚙ **Consider This:** Have you ever used or downloaded programs or apps from a shareware, freeware, or public-domain software website? If so, what software did you acquire? If not, would you consider locating shareware, freeware, or public-domain software for your particular needs? Why or why not?

⚙ CONSIDER THIS

What is software as a service?

Software as a service (SaaS) describes a computing environment where an Internet server hosts and deploys applications. Editing projects or photos, sending email messages, and managing finances are common consumer tasks of SaaS applications. For an exercise related to SaaS, see the Internet Research: Cloud Services exercise at the end of this chapter.

Installing Software

Recall from Chapter 1 that you typically need to install desktop apps on a computer. Installing is the process of setting up the software to work with a computer, printer, and other hardware. Mobile apps typically install automatically after you download the app from the device's app store. You usually do not need to install web apps before you can use them, but you may need to install plug-ins, such as Java or Flash, so that the web apps work.

During installation of software or before the first use, a program or app may ask you to register and/or activate the software. *Software registration* typically is optional and usually involves submitting your name and other personal information to the software manufacturer or developer. Registering the software often entitles you to product support. *Product activation* is a technique that some software manufacturers use to ensure that you do not install the software on more computers than legally licensed. Usually, the software can be run a preset number of times, has limited

BTW

Syncing Apps
When you install an app on one computer or device, it also will install automatically on any other computers and devices on the same subscription plan.

functionality, or does not function until you activate it via the Internet or by phone. Thus, activation is a required process for programs that request it. Some software allows multiple activations; for example, you can install it and run it on a laptop and a desktop. Registering and/ or activating software also usually entitles you to free program updates for a specified time period, such as a year.

Many desktop and mobile apps use an *automatic update* feature, where the updates can be configured to download and install automatically. With web apps, by contrast, you always access the latest version of the software.

✳ CONSIDER THIS

What is a license agreement?

A *license agreement,* sometimes called an end-user license agreement (*EULA*), is the right to use a program or app. The license agreement provides specific conditions for use of the software, which a user typically must accept before using the software (Figure 4-3). Unless otherwise specified by a license agreement, you do not have the right to copy, loan, borrow, rent, or in any way distribute programs or apps. Doing so is a violation of copyright law; it also is a federal crime.

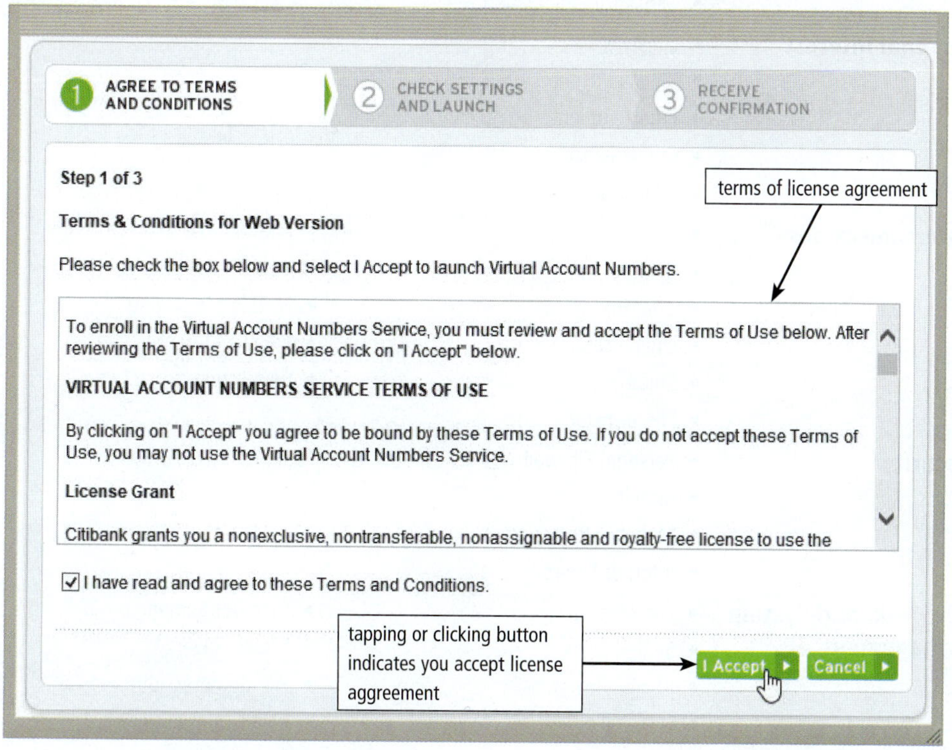

Figure 4-3 A user must accept the terms in a license agreement before using the software.
Source: Citigroup Inc

Categories of Programs and Apps

With programs and apps, you can work on a variety of projects — such as creating letters, memos, reports, and other documents; developing presentations; preparing and filing taxes; drawing and altering images; recording and enhancing audio and video clips; obtaining directions or maps; playing games individually or with others; composing email and other messages; protecting computers and mobile devices from malware; organizing media; locating files; and much more. Table 4-1 categorizes popular categories of programs and apps by their general use.

Table 4-1 Programs and Apps by Category

Category	Types of Programs and Apps	
Productivity (Business and Personal)	• Word Processing • Presentation • Spreadsheet • Database • Note Taking • Calendar and Contact Management • Project Management	• Accounting • Personal Finance • Legal • Tax Preparation • Document Management • Support Services • Enterprise Computing
Graphics and Media	• Computer-Aided Design (CAD) • Desktop Publishing • Paint/Image Editing • Photo Editing and Photo Management • Clip Art/Image Gallery	• Video and Audio Editing • Multimedia and Website Authoring • Media Player • Disc Burning
Personal Interest	• Lifestyle • Medical • Entertainment • Convenience • Education	
Communications	• Blog • Browser • Chat Room • Online Discussion • Email • File Transfer	• Internet Phone • Internet Messaging • Mobile Messaging • Videoconference • Web Feeds
Security	• Personal Firewall • Antivirus • Malware Removers • Internet Filters	
File, Disk, and System Management	• File Manager • Search • Image Viewer • Uninstaller • Disk Cleanup	• Disk Defragmenter • Screen Saver • File Compression • PC Maintenance • Backup and Restore

✳ CONSIDER THIS

Are the categories of programs and apps shown in Table 4-1 mutually exclusive?

Programs and apps listed in one category may be used in other categories. For example, photo editing applications, which appear in the graphics and media category, often also are used for business or personal productivity. Additionally, the programs and apps in the last three categories (communications; security; and file, disk, and system management) often are used in conjunction with or to support programs and apps in the first three categories (productivity, graphics and media, and personal interest). For example, email appears in the communications category but also is a productivity application.

Productivity Applications

Productivity applications can assist you in becoming more effective and efficient while performing daily activities at work, school, and home. Productivity applications include word processing, presentation, spreadsheet, database, note taking, calendar and contact management, project management, accounting, personal finance, legal, tax preparation, document management, and enterprise computing.

A variety of manufacturers offer productivity apps in each of these areas, ranging from desktop to mobile to web apps. Many have a desktop version and a corresponding mobile version adapted for smaller screen sizes and/or touch screens.

Developing Projects

With productivity applications, users often create, edit, format, save, and distribute projects. Projects include documents, presentations, spreadsheets, notes, calendars, contact lists, budgets, and more.

During the process of developing a project, you likely will switch back and forth among the following activities.

1. When you *create* a project, you enter text or numbers, insert images, add contacts, schedule appointments, and perform other tasks using a variety of input methods, such as a keyboard, a mouse, touch, or voice.
2. To *edit* a project means to make changes to its existing content. Common editing tasks include inserting, deleting, cutting, copying, and pasting.
   a. Inserting involves adding text, images, or other content.
   b. Deleting involves removing text, images, or other content.
   c. Cutting is the process of removing content and storing it in a temporary storage location, called a *clipboard*.
   d. Copying is the process of placing content on a clipboard, with the content remaining in the project. Read Ethics & Issues 4-1 for a discussion about unethical copying.
   e. Pasting is the process of transferring content from a clipboard to a specific location in a project.

⚹ ETHICS & ISSUES 4-1

What Can Schools and Employers Do to Prevent Internet Plagiarism?
The Internet has made it easier for students and employees to plagiarize; in contrast, it also provides tools that schools and employers can use to detect illegal copying. Schools often have specific rules about what constitutes plagiarism. Employees, such as journalists, are expected to follow ethical guidelines when copying or citing content.

The Internet offers many ways for students to cheat intentionally, including websites that allow you to purchase a research paper. Students may not realize that copying information without properly citing it also is plagiarism. Students who intentionally plagiarize blame competition. Teachers have several tools to catch plagiarists,

including services that compare papers to others on the Internet and produce a report highlighting content resembling previously published writing.

A journalist might be expected not only to produce multiple articles daily but also to use social media to keep readers engaged. This pressure tempts some journalists to copy content, sometimes without giving credit or linking to the original source. The laws against plagiarism are the same whether copying content from a respected news source, a personal blog, or social media. The pressures of time and expectations of content can create high-profile cases of plagiarism that affect not only the journalist but the news source for which he or she writes.

Some argue that the best way to prevent cheating is to educate. First, teach the values and discuss the consequences of cheating. Next, teach how to cite sources properly and summarize information. Before copying or paraphrasing another person's work, contact him or her to request permission. When in doubt, check with a librarian, editor, or instructor.

Consider This: How should educators and employers deal with plagiarism? Should schools use a paper-comparison service in an attempt to stop cheating? Why or why not? Does linking to the original source excuse a journalist who copies content? Why or why not?

3. When users *format* a project, they change its appearance. Formatting is important because the overall look of a project significantly can affect its capability to communicate information clearly. Examples of formatting tasks are changing the font, font size, and font style (Figure 4-4).
    a. A *font* is a name assigned to a specific design of characters. Cambria and Calibri are examples of fonts.
    b. *Font size* indicates the size of the characters in a particular font. Font size is gauged by a measurement system called points. A single point is about 1/72 of an inch in height.
    c. A *font style* adds emphasis to a font. Bold, italic, underline, and color are examples of font styles.
4. During the process of creating, editing, and formatting a project, the computer or mobile device holds it in memory. To keep the project for future use requires that you save it. When you *save* a project, the computer transfers the project from memory to a local storage medium, such as a USB flash drive or hard drive, or cloud storage, so that you can retrieve it later.
5. You can distribute a project as a hard copy or electronically. A *hard copy* is information that exists on a physical medium, such as paper. To generate a hard copy, you *print* a project. Sending electronic files via email or posting them for others to view, on websites for example, saves paper and printer supplies. Many users opt for electronic distribution because it contributes to green computing.

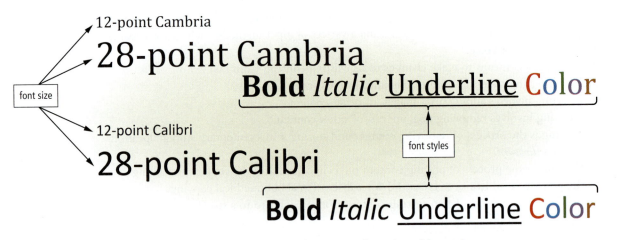

Figure 4-4   The Cambria and Calibri fonts are shown in two font sizes and a variety of font styles.
© Cengage Learning

✳ **CONSIDER THIS** —————————————————————————

How often should you save a project, and why do some apps not require you save?
Saving at regular intervals, such as every 5 or 10 minutes, ensures that the majority of your work will not be lost in the event of a power loss or system failure. Many programs have an AutoSave feature that automatically saves open projects at specified time intervals, such as every 10 minutes.

Some web and mobile apps, such as online productivity apps, save your work instantly as you type. These apps and the document both are stored on the cloud. Thus, the app automatically saves your changes to a cloud server with every keystroke.

✳ **CONSIDER THIS** —————————————————————————

What is a clip art/image gallery?
Applications often include a **clip art/image gallery**, which is a collection of clip art and photos. Some applications contain links to additional clips available on the web or are available as web apps. You also can purchase clip art/image gallery software that contains thousands of images.

In addition to clip art and photos, many clip art/image galleries provide fonts, animations, sounds, video clips, and audio clips. You can use the images, fonts, and other items from the clip art/image gallery in all types of projects, including documents, brochures, worksheets, and slide shows.

Word Processing

Word processing software, sometimes called a word processor, is an application that allows users to create and manipulate documents containing mostly text and sometimes graphics (Figure 4-5). Millions of people use word processing software on their computers and mobile devices every day to develop documents such as letters, memos, reports, mailing labels, newsletters, and webpages.

A major advantage of using word processing software is that it enables users to change their written words easily. Word processing software also has many features to make documents look professional and visually appealing. For example, you can change the font, size, and color of characters; apply special effects, such as three-dimensional shadows; use built-in styles to format documents; and organize text in newspaper-style columns.

Most word processing software allows users to incorporate graphics, such as digital photos and clip art, in documents. In Figure 4-5, a user inserted an image of a tractor in the document. With word processing software, you easily can modify the appearance of an image after inserting it in the document.

You can use word processing software to define the size of the paper on which to print and to specify the margins. A feature, called wordwrap, allows users to type words in a paragraph continually without pressing the ENTER key at the end of each line. While you edit a paragraph or change the paragraph margins, the words in the paragraph automatically wrap, or reflow within the para- graph. As you type more lines of text than can be displayed on the screen, the top portion of the document moves upward, or scrolls, off the screen.

Internet Research

What are the guidelines for writing business letters?

Search for: business letter writing

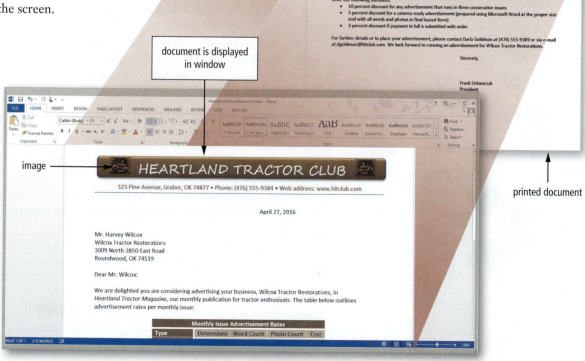

document is displayed in window

image

printed document

Figure 4-5   Word processing software enables users to create professional and visually appealing documents.
Microsoft; © Cengage Learning

Figure 4-6 This presentation created with presentation software consists of five slides.
Source: Microsoft; © Cengage Learning

Word processing software typically includes tools to assist you with the writing process. For example, a spelling checker reviews the spelling of individual words, sections of a document, or the entire document. A grammar checker detects passive voice, run-on sentences, and grammatical errors. A format checker identifies extraneous spaces, capitalization errors, and more.

Discover More: Visit this chapter's free resources to learn more about word processing software and features.

Presentation

Presentation software is an application that allows users to create visual aids for presentations to communicate ideas, messages, and other information to a group. The presentations can be viewed as slides, sometimes called a *slide show*, that are displayed on a large monitor or on a projection screen from a computer or mobile device (Figure 4-6).

Presentation software typically provides a variety of predefined presentation formats that define complementary colors for backgrounds, text, and graphical accents on the slides. This software also provides a variety of layouts for each individual slide such as a title slide, a two-column slide, and a slide with clip art, a chart, a table, or a diagram. In addition, you can enhance any text, charts, and graphics on a slide with 3-D effects, animation, and other special effects, such as shading, shadows, and textures.

When building a presentation, users can set the slide timing so that the presentation automatically displays the next slide after a preset delay. Presentation software allows you to apply special effects to the transition between slides. One slide, for example, might fade away as the next slide appears.

Presentation software typically includes a clip gallery that provides images, photos, video clips, and audio clips to enhance presentations. Some audio and video editing applications work with presentation software, providing users with an easy means to record and insert video, music, and audio commentary in a presentation.

You can view or print a finished presentation in a variety of formats, including a hard copy outline of text from each slide and handouts that show completed slides. Presentation software also incorporates features such as checking spelling, formatting, researching, and creating webpages from existing slide shows.

Discover More: Visit this chapter's free resources to learn more about presentation software.

Spreadsheet

Spreadsheet software is an application that allows users to organize data in columns and rows and perform calculations on the data. These columns and rows collectively are called a **worksheet**. Most spreadsheet software has basic features to help users create, edit, and format worksheets. A spreadsheet file also is known as a workbook because it can contain thousands of related individual worksheets. Data is organized vertically in columns and horizontally in rows on each worksheet (Figure 4-7).

Each worksheet usually can have thousands of columns and rows. One or more letters identify each column, and a number identifies each row. Only a small fraction of these columns and rows are visible on the screen at one time. Scrolling through the worksheet displays different parts of it on the screen.

A cell is the intersection of a column and row. The spreadsheet software identifies cells by the column and row in which they are located. For example, the intersection of column B and row 4 is referred to as cell B4. As shown in Figure 4-7, cell B4 contains the number, $1,000.29, which represents the wages for January.

Many of the worksheet cells shown in Figure 4-7 contain a number, called a value, that can be used in a calculation. Other cells, however, contain formulas that generate values. A formula performs calculations on the data in the worksheet and displays the resulting value in a cell, usually the cell containing the formula. When creating a worksheet, you can enter your own formulas. In Figure 4-7, for example, cell B17 could contain the formula =B9+B10+B11+B12+ B13+B14+B15+B16, which would add (sum) the contents of cells B9, B10, B11, B12, B13, B14, B15, and B16. That is, this formula calculates the total expenses for January.

A *function* is a predefined formula that performs common calculations, such as adding the values in a group of cells or generating a value such as the time or date. For example, the function =SUM(B9:B16) instructs the spreadsheet application to add all of the numbers in the range of cells B9 through B16. Spreadsheet applications contain many built-in functions.

One of the more powerful features of spreadsheet software is its capability to recalculate the rest of the worksheet when data in a cell changes. Spreadsheet software's capability of recalculating data also makes it a valuable budgeting, forecasting, and decision-making tool. Another standard feature of spreadsheet software is charting, which depicts the data in graphical form, such as bar charts or pie charts. A visual representation of data through charts often makes it easier for users to see at a glance the relationship among the numbers.

Discover More: Visit this chapter's free resources to learn more about spreadsheet software and built-in functions.

BTW

Formulas
In many spreadsheet apps, a formula begins with an equal sign (=).

BTW

Technology Innovator
Discover More: Visit this chapter's free resources to learn about Dan Bricklin (cocreator of the first spreadsheet program).

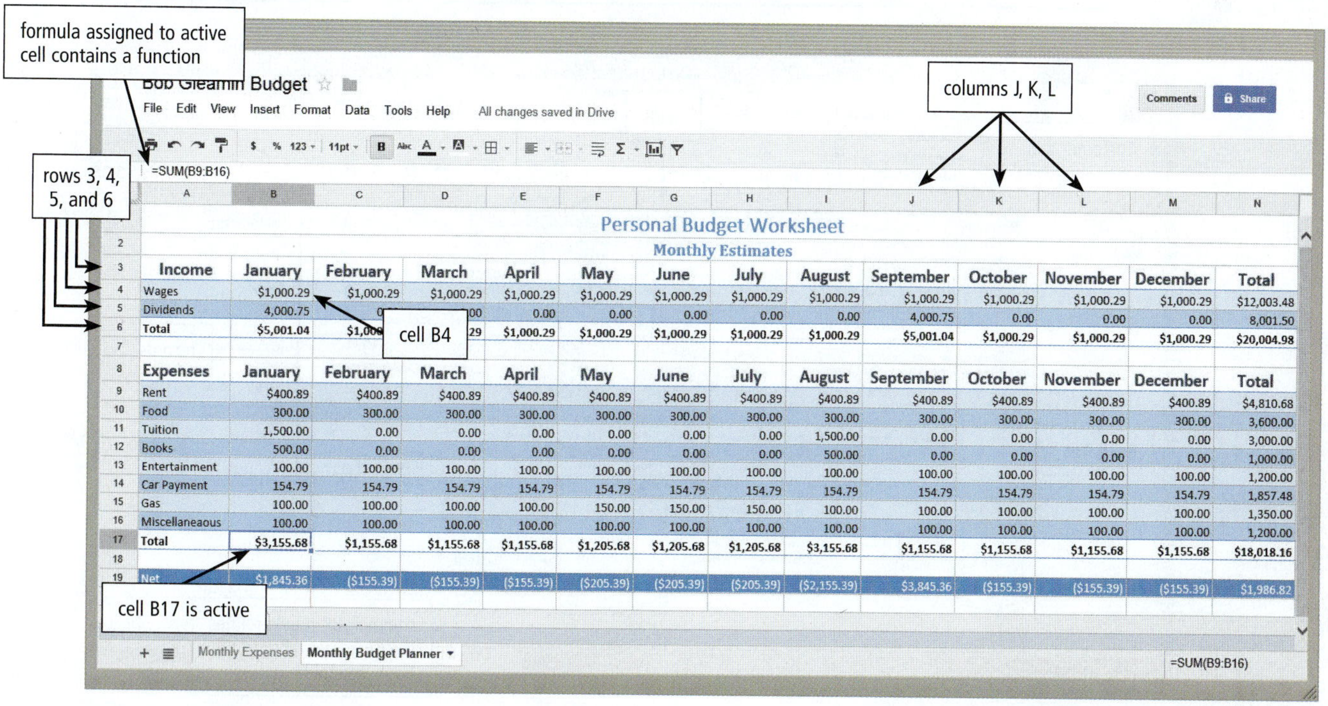

Figure 4-7   With spreadsheet software, you create worksheets that contain data arranged in columns and rows, and you can perform calculations on the data in the worksheets.
Source: Google Inc.

BTW

Web Databases
You likely interact with many databases without realizing it. For example, much of the information you access on the web — including photos, videos, movies, job listings, reservation details, and class registrations — is stored in databases.

BTW

High-Tech Talk

Discover More: Visit this chapter's free resources to learn how to filter data in database and spreadsheet programs.

Database

A **database** is a collection of data organized in a manner that allows access, retrieval, and use of that data. In a manual database, you might record data on paper and store it in a filing cabinet. With a database stored electronically, such as the one shown in Figure 4-8, the computer stores the data on a storage medium, such as a hard drive or optical disc, or on cloud storage.

Database software is an application that allows users to create, access, and manage a database. Using database software, you can add, change, and delete data in a database; sort and retrieve data from the database; and create forms and reports using the data in the database.

With most personal computer database programs, a database consists of a collection of tables, organized in rows and columns. Each row, called a record, contains data about a given item in the database, which is often a person, product, object, or event. Each column, called a field, contains a specific category of data within a record. The Publishing database shown in Figure 4-8 consists of two tables: a Customer table and a Book Rep table. The Customer table contains 15 records (rows), each storing data about one customer. The customer data is grouped into 10 fields (columns): CU # (customer number), Customer Name, Street, City, State, Postal Code, Amount Paid, Current Due, Returns, and BR # (book rep number). The Current Due field, for instance, contains the amount of money the customer owes the publisher. The Customer and Book Rep tables relate to each other through a common field, BR # (book rep number).

Users run queries to retrieve data. A query is a request for specific data from the database. For example, a query might request a list of customers whose balance is greater than $20,000. After obtaining the results of a query, database applications can present them on the screen, send them to a printer, or save them in a file.

✷ **CONSIDER THIS**

When should you use a database instead of a spreadsheet program?
Although databases and spreadsheets both store data, these programs have different purposes and capabilities. Spreadsheet programs are ideal for calculating results or creating charts from value in the worksheet. You should use a database program, however, if want to collect, reorganize and filter data, and/or create reports from the data.

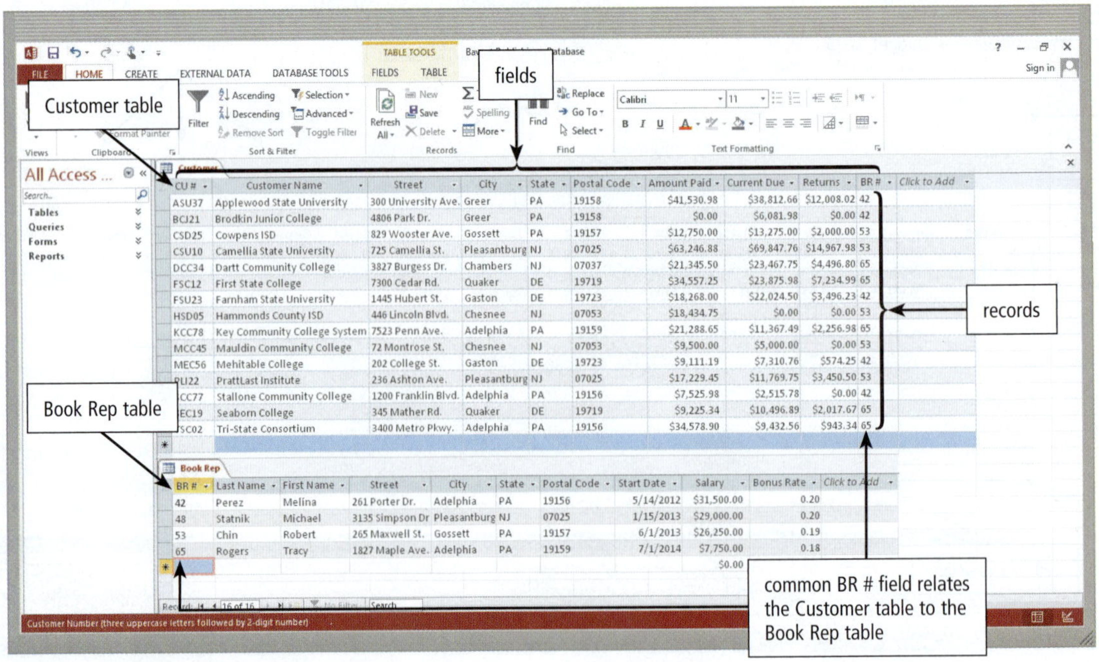

Figure 4-8 This database contains two tables: one for customers and one for book reps. The Customer table has 15 records and 10 fields; the Book Rep table has 4 records and 10 fields.
Source: Microsoft

Discover More: Visit this chapter's free resources to learn more about personal computer database programs.

Note Taking

Note taking software is an application that enables users to enter typed text, handwritten comments, drawings, sketches, photos, and links anywhere on a page and then save the page as part of a notebook (Figure 4-9). Users also can include audio recordings as part of their notes. Some enable users to sync their notes to the cloud so that they can access the notes on any computer or mobile device. Many note taking applications also include a calendar feature.

Users find note taking software convenient during meetings, class lectures and conferences, and in libraries and other settings that previously required pencil and paper for recording thoughts and discussions.

Discover More: Visit this chapter's free resources to learn more about note taking applications.

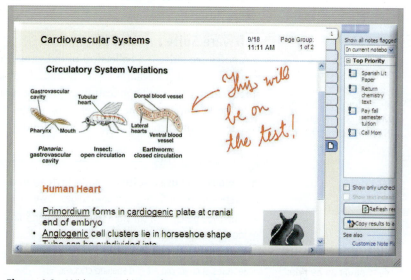

Figure 4-9 With note taking software, mobile users can handwrite notes, draw sketches, insert photos and links, and type text.
Source: Microsoft

Calendar and Contact Management

Calendar and contact management software is an application that helps you organize your calendar, keep track of contacts, and share this information with other users, who can view it on their computers and mobile devices (Figure 4-10). This software provides a way for individuals and workgroups to organize, find, view, and share appointment and contact information easily. Although sometimes available separately, calendar and contact management software often exists as a unit in a single program. Many email applications include calendar and contact management features.

Figure 4-10 Users can share schedules with other users via calendar and contact management applications.
Google Inc.

🔘 **BTW**

Technology Trend

Discover More: Visit this chapter's free resources to learn about the note taking app, Evernote.

Calendar and contact management applications enable you to synchronize information. This means that all of your computers and mobile devices, along with your organization's server or cloud storage, have the latest version of any updated information.

Discover More: Visit this chapter's free resources to learn more about calendar and contact management applications.

Software Suite

A **software suite** is a collection of individual related applications available together as a unit. Productivity software suites typically include, at a minimum, word processing, presentation, spreadsheet, and email applications. While several productivity suites are designed to be installed on a local computer, some are web apps and/or mobile web apps that enabling you to share and collaborate with projects stored on the cloud.

✹ CONSIDER THIS

Why would you use a software suite instead of a stand-alone application?
Software suites offer three major advantages: lower cost, ease of use, and integration.

- When you purchase a software suite, the suite usually costs significantly less than purchasing each application individually, or as stand-alone applications.
- Software suites provide ease of use because the applications in the suite normally use a consistent interface and share features, such as clip art and spelling checker.
- Applications in a software suite often are integrated, which makes it easy to share information among them. For example, you can copy a chart created from a worksheet in a spreadsheet program and paste it into a slideshow in the presentation software.

Discover More: Visit this chapter's free resources to learn more about software suites.

Project Management

Project management software is an application that allows a user to plan, schedule, track, and analyze the events, resources, and costs of a project. Project management software helps users manage project variables, allowing them to complete a project on time and within budget. A marketing manager, for example, might use project management software to schedule the processes required in a product launch (Figure 4-11). Read How To 4-1 to learn how you can manage a project using project management software.

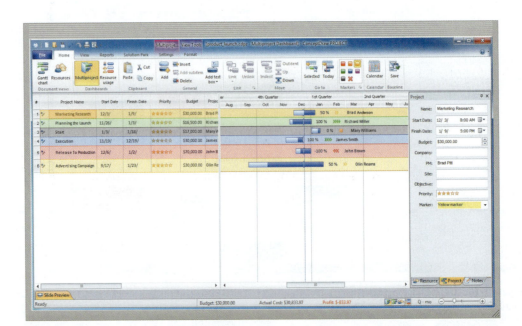

Figure 4-11 With project management software, you can plan and schedule the tasks and processes required in a project.
Courtesy of CS Odessa

⚙ HOW TO 4-1

📝 Manage a Project Using Project Management Software

Several project management programs and apps exist that are both free and fee based. Project management programs and apps are designed for projects of specific sizes, so be sure to research the various programs and apps on the market and choose one that best suits your needs. To manage a project using project management software, follow these steps:

1. Make sure you understand the project in its entirety, as well as the steps you must take to bring the project to completion.

2. Determine the date by which the project must be completed.

3. Verify you have the appropriate resources (people and materials) to complete the project. If you do not have the necessary resources, you should obtain them.

4. Determine the order of the steps that must be taken to bring the project to completion. Identify steps that must be taken before other steps, as well as steps that can be completed at the same time as other steps.

5. Verify the feasibility of the plan.

6. During the project, it will be necessary to update the progress and possibly adjust dates. Changes to the project and its dates should be communicated to the entire project team.

✳ **Consider This:** Do you think project management software can help individuals complete a project more quickly? Why or why not?

✳ CONSIDER THIS

Does the term, project, have two meanings in the technology field?
Yes. As discussed earlier in this chapter, a project can be a deliverable you create using application software, such as a document, presentation, spreadsheet, notes, calendar, contact list, budget, and more. A project also describe the collection of tasks and processes required to develop a solution to a problem.

Accounting

Accounting software is an application that helps businesses of all sizes record and report their financial transactions. With accounting software, business users perform accounting activities related to the general ledger, accounts receivable, accounts payable, purchasing, invoicing (Figure 4-12), and payroll functions. Accounting software also enables business users to write and print checks, track checking account activity, and update and reconcile balances on demand.

Most accounting software supports online credit checks, bill payment, direct deposit, and payroll services. Some offer more complex features, such as job costing and estimating, time tracking, multiple company reporting, foreign currency reporting, and forecasting the amount of raw materials needed for products. The cost of accounting software for small businesses ranges from less than one hundred to several thousand dollars. Accounting software for large businesses can cost several hundred thousand dollars.

Discover More: Visit this chapter's free resources to learn more about accounting software.

Figure 4-12 Accounting software helps businesses record and report their financial transactions.
Courtesy of Intuit

Personal Finance

Personal finance software is a simplified accounting application that helps home users and small/home office users balance their checkbooks, pay bills, track personal income and expenses, verify account balances, transfer funds, track investments, and evaluate financial plans (Figure 4-13). Personal finance software helps determine where, and for what purpose, you are spending money so that you can manage your finances.

Most personal finance software includes financial planning features, such as analyzing home and personal loans, preparing income taxes, and managing retirement savings. Other features include managing home inventory and setting up budgets. Most of these applications also offer a variety of online services, such as online banking and online investing. Read Secure IT 4-2 for safety tips when using personal finance apps on your smartphone or other mobile device.

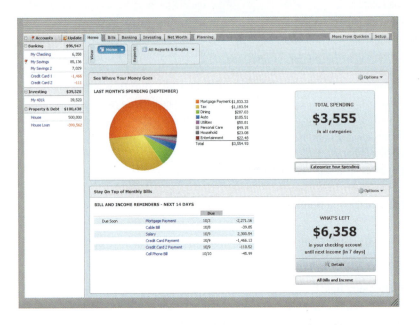

Figure 4-13   Personal finance software assists home users with tracking personal accounts.
Courtesy of Intuit

⚙ SECURE IT 4-2

📋 Using Personal Finance Apps Safely

Personal finance apps offer convenient and easy methods to pay bills, deposit checks, examine account balances, verify payments, and transfer funds. They also are a magnet for cybercriminals to snatch an unsuspecting user's personal information and send it to someone else anywhere in the world, who then can use the information for monetary transactions. Nearly one-third of malware banking apps target customers in the United States with malicious instructions that invade their smartphones and gain access to information stored on their devices. Users in Brazil, Australia, and France also are becoming extremely popular targets for banking thieves. By using caution and common sense, however, users can take steps to safeguard their funds and their identities by following these practices:

- **Evaluate the apps.** Fraudulent apps may resemble legitimate apps from financial institutions. They often, however, are riddled with misspellings and awkward sentences. In addition, legitimate companies rarely promote downloading an app from a pop-up or pop-under advertisement. If you desire an app from a bank or other financial institution, visit that company's website for instructions about downloading and installing its authentic apps.

- **Use strong passwords to access the apps.** Many of the more secure personal finance apps have dual passwords that involve typing a string of characters and also validating a picture. In addition, be certain to password protect your mobile device.

- **Guard your smartphone.** At least 100 smartphones are lost or stolen every minute in the United States according to MicroTrax, an asset protection company. With that figure in mind, store as little personal information as possible on your phone so that if the mobile device is lost, the chance of having your identity stolen and your accounts compromised is lessened. Also install software to locate your lost or stolen device and to erase its content remotely.

- **Verify the transactions.** Always verify your transactions by scrutinizing monthly statements. In addition, periodically check balances and alert your financial institution if any activity seems abnormal.

☀ **Consider This:** Have you used finance apps? If so, which ones? When making transactions, do you follow some of the tips described in this box? If not, would you consider downloading an app to complete some common banking transactions? Why or why not?

Legal

Legal software is an application that assists in the preparation of legal documents and provides legal information to individuals, families, and small businesses (Figure 4-14). Legal software provides standard contracts and documents associated with buying, selling, and renting property; estate planning; marriage and divorce; and preparing a will or living trust. By answering a series of questions or completing a form, the legal software tailors the legal document to specific needs. Read Ethics & Issues 4-2 to consider whether an attorney should review documents created with legal software.

Discover More: Visit this chapter's free resources to learn more about legal software.

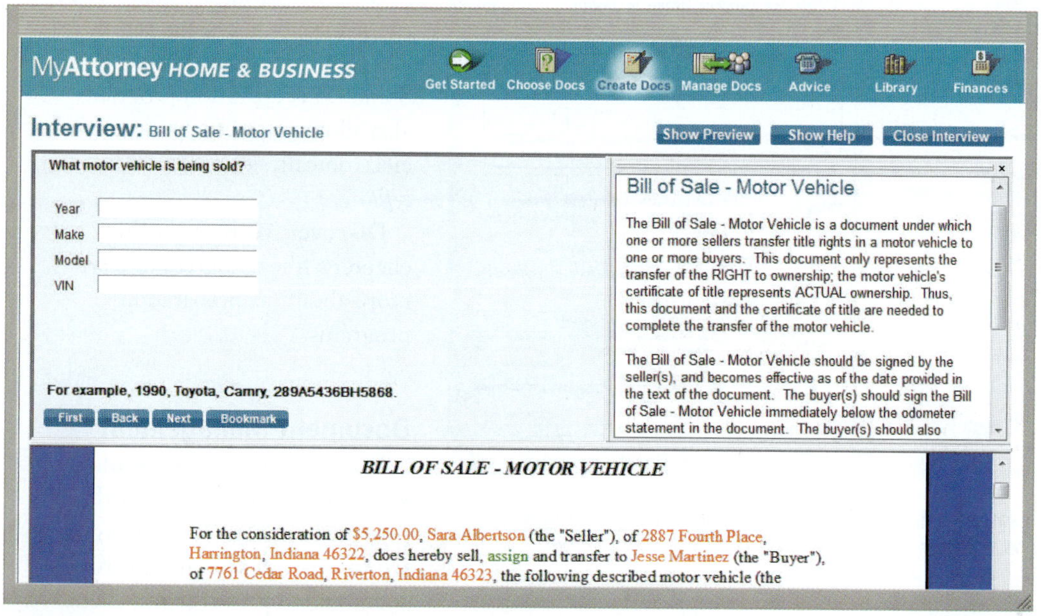

Figure 4-14   Legal software assists individuals, families, and small businesses in the preparation of legal documents.
Source: Avanquest Software

ETHICS & ISSUES 4-2

Should an Attorney Review Documents Created with Legal Software?

If you want to sublet your apartment or buy or sell a used car, should you seek legal help? Hiring an attorney to create a lease or sale agreement can cost hundreds of dollars. Legal software or website services, on the other hand, typically cost less than $100 and sometimes are free. While it is tempting to opt for the route that will save money, you should evaluate the program to make sure it is up to date, addresses the latest laws and provisions that are specific to your state, and includes a legal dictionary. If you use a program that is out of date or creates an incomplete or invalid legal document, the cost for an attorney to correct the document could exceed the amount you originally spent on the program.

A lease that you create or sign regarding subletting or renting an apartment should have provisions for payment of any damages, breaking or extending the agreement, and who is responsible for routine maintenance and repair. In some states, the property owner must disclose any mold, lead paint, or water quality issues. Sales agreements, such as for used cars, should include language that protects the buyer from undisclosed damage to the car, as well as clearly specify any further responsibility of the car seller.

Attorneys caution against using legal software unless you intend to have an attorney review the document. Not only can they validate the accuracy of the document, attorneys claim they can provide for gaps in the software; further, they are versed in laws specific to your state or circumstance. Others argue that any legal document is better than a verbal agreement and can protect both parties.

Consider This: Would you use legal software to create a legal document? Why or why not? Would you sign a legal document created with software without consulting an attorney? Why or why not? How do mistakes made as a result of using legal software differ from mistakes that result from human error?

Tax Preparation

Tax preparation software is an application that can guide individuals, families, or small businesses through the process of filing federal and state taxes (Figure 4-15). These programs forecast tax liability and offer money-saving tax tips, designed to lower your tax bill. After you answer a series of questions and complete basic forms, the software creates and analyzes your tax forms to search for missed potential errors and deduction opportunities.

Once the forms are complete, you can print any necessary paperwork; then, they are ready for filing. Some tax preparation programs also allow you to file your tax forms electronically, a process called *e-filing*.

Discover More: Visit this chapter's free resources to learn more about tax preparation programs.

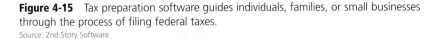

Figure 4-15 Tax preparation software guides individuals, families, or small businesses through the process of filing federal taxes.
Source: 2nd Story Software

Document Management

Document management software is an application that provides a means for sharing, distributing, and searching through documents by converting them into a format that can be viewed by any user. The converted document, which mirrors the original document's appearance, can be viewed and printed without the software that created the original document. Some document management software allows users to edit content and add comments to the converted document (Figure 4-16).

Many businesses use document management software to share and distribute company brochures, literature, and other documents electronically. Home users distribute flyers, announcements, and graphics electronically. A popular electronic image file format that document management software uses to save converted documents is **PDF** (Portable Document Format), developed by Adobe Systems.

Figure 4-16 Users can edit content and add comments to a converted document.
Source: Adobe Systems Incorporated

To view and print a PDF file, you need Adobe Reader software, which can be downloaded free from Adobe's website.

Discover More: Visit this chapter's free resources to learn more about document management software.

✷ CONSIDER THIS

Can you create a PDF file only in document management applications?
No. Many productivity applications, such as word processing and spreadsheet programs, provide a method of saving a project as a PDF. This enables other users to view your document without requiring the application that created the project.

Enterprise Computing

A large organization, commonly referred to as an enterprise, requires special computing solutions because of its size and geographic distribution. A typical enterprise consists of a wide variety of departments, centers, and divisions — collectively known as functional units. Nearly every enterprise has the following functional units: human resources, accounting and finance, engineering or product development, manufacturing, marketing, sales, distribution, customer service, and information technology.

Software used in functional units is not mutually exclusive; however, each functional unit in an enterprise uses specific software, as outlined below.

- Human resources software manages employee information, such as pay rate, benefits, personal information, performance evaluations, training, and vacation time.
- Accounting software manages everyday transactions, such as sales and payments to suppliers. Finance software helps managers budget, forecast, and analyze.
- Engineering or product development software allows engineers to develop plans for new products and test their product designs.
- Manufacturing software assists in the assembly process, as well as in scheduling and managing the inventory of parts and products.
- Marketing software allows marketing personnel to create marketing campaigns, target demographics, and track their effectiveness.
- Sales software enables the salesforce to manage contacts, schedule meetings, log customer interactions, manage product information, and take customer orders.
- Distribution software analyzes and tracks inventory and manages product shipping status.
- Customer service software manages the day-to-day interactions with customers, such as phone calls, email messages, web interactions, and messaging sessions.
- Information technology staff use a variety of programs and apps to maintain and secure the hardware and software in an enterprise.

Discover More: Visit this chapter's free resources to learn more about software used in an enterprise.

Mini Feature 4-1: Web and Mobile Apps for Personal and Business Productivity

A variety of applications provide a service intended to make business or personal tasks easier to accomplish. Some applications focus on a single service, while others provide several services in a single application. Read Mini Feature 4-1 to learn about some popular web and mobile apps for personal and business productivity.

⚙ **MINI FEATURE 4-1**

Web and Mobile Apps for Personal and Business Productivity

Whether you are checking appointments, sending or reading email messages, arranging travel, banking or looking up information online, making a purchase, scanning QR (quick response) codes or bar codes, or checking in with friends on online social networks, web and mobile apps can assist your personal and business productivity.

Calendar and Email

Maintaining a calendar and checking email messages are common tasks of calendar and email web and mobile apps. Calendar apps keep track of your appointments and synchronize information entered on a mobile device with your online or desktop calendar software. Email mobile apps integrate with your device's address book to display names from your device's contact list that match a recipient's name as you type it, and with your device's photo gallery for sending photos.

Source: Kayak

Travel

Purchasing flights, hotels, rental cars, or travel services is a common online task for personal and business travelers. Travel apps display available options and allow you to filter results. Many allow you to share travel plans with your online social networks.

Financial

You can access bank accounts or investments using a financial app. Financial mobile apps track expenses as you spend money and notify you when a bill is due. To help secure information, financial mobile apps can disable access if your device is stolen or lost. Some banking mobile apps allow you to upload a photo of a check taken with the device's camera to process the deposit.

Reference

Dictionaries, encyclopedias, books, and directories are available online as reference apps. Many have associated mobile apps that format information for mobile devices, or take advantage of their features. For example, rather than typing a search term in a dictionary web app to look up its definition, a mobile app also might offer voice input. On the mobile version of an encyclopedia app, you might shake the device to display random topics or redisplay the app's home

screen. Some reference mobile apps also can download information directly to your phone for offline access.

Retail

Online marketplaces and payment services support buying and selling items and transferring funds from one party to another. Marketplace apps enable customers to research products, enter or examine product reviews, and make purchases. A retail store mobile app might use a device's GPS to offer special deals closest to the customer's location. You also might use a device's camera to scan a product's bar code and then place the item in a shopping cart. Payment services allow customers to send money or pay for items using mobile devices. Read Secure IT 4-3 for safety tips when using payment apps.

Scanning

Scanning apps use a mobile device's camera to scan a QR code or bar code. A **QR code** is a square-shaped graphic that represents a web address or other information. A QR code reader app scans a QR code, and then displays its corresponding information. A bar code scanner reads a bar code and may provide product information, price, or reviews. Some supermarkets provide shopping apps for customers to scan bar codes of items they purchase.

© iStockPhoto / franckreporter

These apps create a customized shopping list, ordering items by their aisle location in the store, to provide a more efficient shopping experience.

Online Social Networks

Many users connect with family, friends, and coworkers using online social network mobile apps. Online social network web apps often integrate instant messaging and video chat communications. Online social network mobile apps allow users to include photos and videos from their device in their updates easily.

✳ **Consider This:** Compare the web and mobile versions of the same app for personal and business productivity. Which features are common to both? Which features in the mobile version are not found in the web version? Which features in the web version are not found in the mobile version? Why do you think the developers made these decisions? Which features would you like to see that are missing from either version of the app?

Discover More: Visit this chapter's free resources to learn more about web and mobile apps for personal and business productivity.

⚙ SECURE IT 4-3

📑 Avoiding Risks Using Payment Apps

Paying for coffee at the local coffee shop or buying tools at the hardware store has become streamlined with the advent of mobile payment apps. More than 15 percent of Starbucks transactions are accomplished using a smartphone app instead of using cash or credit card, and many merchants are accepting this form of payment as mobile wallet apps become more secure. The users enjoy the convenience of maintaining control when they scan their phone at the checkout counter instead of handing a credit card to a clerk. This security factor becomes even more pronounced at restaurants, where unscrupulous employees can take credit cards away from the table and then have full access to the personal information on the cards.

Mobile payment providers state that using their apps is more secure than using plastic credit cards. The apps use a payment system on phones equipped with an *NFC chip*, which stores data that is transmitted to a contactless terminal and verified as a legitimate sale. A smartphone user never enters an account number at the cash register because all financial information is stored on the mobile payment system. If, however, an unauthorized charge is made, the Electronic Fund Transfer Act protects users as long as the claim is made promptly, generally within two days.

If you use your smartphone to make purchases, follow this advice from the security experts:

- Use a password on your phone.
- Select a payment app that requires you to enter a password to start the transaction.
- Choose a payment app that issues a receipt so that you can verify every purchase.

- Be vigilant about checking mobile transactions against monthly statements from the credit card company.

✹ **Consider This:** Should additional merchants allow payments using mobile apps? Should merchants be required to pay when customers use payment apps, like they do when customers use credit cards? Why or why not? Where would you like to pay for transactions using your smartphone?

Google Inc.

✔ NOW YOU SHOULD KNOW

Be sure you understand the material presented in the sections titled Programs and Apps and Productivity Applications as it relates to the chapter objectives.
Now you should know …

- What categories of programs and apps you might find on a computer or mobile device (Objective 1)
- Why you need an operating system on computers and mobile devices (Objective 2)
- How you can obtain software (Objective 3)
- Which productivity applications might be suited to your needs (Objective 4)

Discover More: Visit this chapter's premium content for practice quiz opportunities.

Graphics and Media Applications

In addition to productivity applications, many people work with software designed specifically for their field of work. Power users, such as engineers, architects, desktop publishers, and graphic artists, often use sophisticated software that allows them to work with graphics and media. Many of these applications incorporate user-friendly interfaces or scaled-down versions, making it possible for the home and small business users also to create projects using these types of programs.

Graphics and media applications include computer-aided design, desktop publishing, paint/image editing, photo editing and photo management, video and audio editing, multimedia and website authoring, media players, and disc burning.

Figure 4-17 Architects use CAD software to design building structures.
© iStockPhoto / GordanD

Computer-Aided Design

Computer-aided design (CAD) software is a type of application that assists professionals and designers in creating engineering, architectural, and scientific designs and models. For example, engineers create design plans for vehicles and security systems. Architects design building structures and floor plans (Figure 4-17). Scientists design drawings of molecular structures.

Three-dimensional CAD programs allow designers to rotate designs of 3-D objects to view them from any angle. Some CAD software even can generate material lists for building designs.

Home and small business users work with less sophisticated design and modeling software. These applications usually contain thousands of predrawn plans that users can customize to meet their needs. For example, *home design/landscaping software* is an application that assists users with the design, remodeling, or improvement of a home, deck, or landscape.

Discover More: Visit this chapter's free resources to learn more about CAD software.

Desktop Publishing

Desktop publishing software (DTP software) is an application that enables designers to create sophisticated publications that contain text, graphics, and many colors. Professional DTP software is ideal for the production of high-quality color projects such as textbooks, corporate newsletters, marketing literature, product catalogs, and annual reports. Designers and graphic artists can print finished publications on a color printer, take them to a professional printer, or post them on the web in a format that can be viewed by those without DTP software.

Home and small business users create newsletters, brochures, flyers, advertisements, postcards, greeting cards, letterhead, business cards, banners, calendars, logos, and webpages using personal DTP software (Figure 4-18). Although many word processing programs include DTP features, home and small business users often prefer to create DTP projects using DTP software because of its enhanced features. These programs typically guide you through the development of a project by asking a series of questions. Then, you can print a finished publication on a color printer or post it on the web.

Many personal DTP programs also include paint/image editing software and photo editing and photo management software (discussed next), enabling users to embellish their publications with images.

Discover More: Visit this chapter's free resources to learn more about professional and personal DTP software.

Figure 4-18 With personal DTP software, such as Microsoft Publisher shown here, home users can create newsletters.
Courtesy of Joy Starks; Source: Microsoft

Paint/Image Editing

Graphic artists, multimedia professionals, technical illustrators, and desktop publishers use paint software and image editing software to create and modify graphics, such as those used in DTP projects and webpages. **Paint software**, also called *illustration software*, is an application that allows users to draw pictures, shapes, and other graphics with various on-screen tools, such as a pen, brush, eyedropper, and paint bucket. **Image editing software** is an application that provides the capabilities of paint software and also includes the capability to enhance and modify existing photos and images.

Modifications can include adjusting or enhancing image colors, adding special effects such as shadows and glows, creating animations, and image stitching (combining multiple images into a larger image).

Paint/image editing software for the home or small business user provides an easy-to-use interface; includes various simplified tools that allow you to draw pictures, shapes, and other images (Figure 4-19); and provides the capability of modifying existing graphics and photos. These products also include many templates to assist you in adding images to projects, such as greeting cards, banners, calendars, signs, labels, business cards, and letterhead.

Discover More: Visit this chapter's free resources to learn more about paint and image editing software.

BTW
Built-In Image Editing
Word processing, presentation, and other productivity applications usually include basic image editing capabilities.

Figure 4-19 Home users can purchase affordable paint/image editing programs that enable them to draw images.
DrawPlus X5 © Serif (Europe) Ltd, | www.serif.com

Photo Editing and Photo Management

Photo editing software is a type of image editing software that allows users to edit and customize digital photos. With photo editing software, users can retouch photos, crop images, remove red-eye, erase blemishes, restore aged photos, add special effects, enhance image quality, change image shapes, color-correct images, straighten images, remove or rearrange objects in a photo, add layers, and more (Figure 4–20). Many applications also provide a means for creating digital photo albums.

Figure 4-20 With photo editing software, users can edit digital photos, such as by adjusting the appearance of images as shown here.
PhotoPlus X6 © Serif (Europe) Ltd | www.serif.com

When you purchase a digital camera, it usually includes photo editing software. Many digital cameras also include basic photo editing software so that you can edit the image directly on the camera. Read How To 4-2 for instructions about editing and sharing photos. Read Ethics & Issues 4-3 to consider issues related to altering digital photos.

With **photo management software**, you can view, organize, sort, catalog, print, and share digital photos. Some photo editing software includes photo management functionality. Many online photo storage services enable you to create scrapbooks — selecting photos, adding captions, selecting backgrounds, and more.

⊙ BTW
Technology Trend
Discover More: Visit this chapter's free resources to learn about the photo sharing app, Instagram.

⊙ **HOW TO 4-2**

Edit and Share Photos
When you take a photo using a digital camera or smartphone, you sometimes may want to edit the photo to remove unwanted areas, correct imperfections, or change its file size. Many apps allow you to edit photos easily. Several are simple to use and do not require advanced photo editing experience. Before editing a photo, you first should make a backup of the original photo. The table below describes common ways to edit photos using a photo editing app.

After you have edited a photo to your satisfaction, you may want to share the photo with others. Many mobile devices, such as smartphones and tablets, as well as most photo editing apps, have built-in options that allow you to share photos. To share a photo on a mobile device or from within a photo editing app, follow these steps:

1. Open the photo to share.
2. Select the sharing option in the photo editing app or on the mobile device.
3. Choose the method by which to share the photo. Common ways to share

photos include sending the photo as an email attachment, posting the photo to an online social network or photo sharing site, and sending the photo as a picture message to another mobile device.

⊛ **Consider This:** Examine your digital camera or other mobile device with a camera feature. Which of the photo editing features discussed here does it have? Did you notice any photo editing features in addition to those listed here?

ACTION	PURPOSE	STEPS
Crop	Removes unwanted areas of a photo	1. Select cropping tool. 2. Adjust photo border to define area(s) of the photo to keep and discard.
Remove red-eye	Removes the appearance of red eyes caused by the camera flash	1. Select red-eye removal tool. 2. Tap or click areas of the photo with the red-eye effect or drag a border around the affected areas.
Resize	Changes the physical dimensions of the photo	1. Select resizing tool. 2. Drag sizing handles to increase or decrease the photo's dimensions or type the desired height and width in the appropriate text boxes.
Compress	Decreases the photo's file size	1. Select option to compress photo. 2. Choose desired level of compression.
Adjust sharpness	Increases or decreases crispness of objects in the photo	1. Select option to adjust sharpness. 2. Drag sharpness slider to desired value or type the desired sharpness level into appropriate text box.
Adjust brightness	Adjusts lightness or darkness in the photo	1. Select option to adjust brightness. 2. Drag brightness slider to desired value or type the desired brightness level into appropriate text box.
Adjust contrast	Adjusts the difference in appearance between light and dark areas of the photo	1. Select option to adjust contrast. 2. Drag contrast slider to desired value or type the desired contrast level into appropriate text box.

Is It Ethical to Alter Digital Photos?

Many commercial artists, photojournalists, and creators of magazine covers and billboards use photo editing software to alter digital photos. Artists use photo editing software to enhance digital photos by changing colors, adding or removing objects, and more. When does photo manipulation become unethical?

In several high-profile cases, news sources published intentionally altered photos that misrepresented the facts, in one case publishing photos of an aging world leader edited to remove his hearing aid. One school received criticism when it altered necklines on yearbook photos to be more modest.

Real estate agents on occasion have altered photos of homes for online listings or print brochures. Also making news are celebrity or model photos that artists retouch to change their physical appearance.

The National Press Photographers Association expresses reservations about digital altering and subscribes to the following belief: "As [photo]journalists we believe the guiding principle of our profession is accuracy; therefore, we believe it is wrong to alter the content of a photo in any way ... that deceives the public." Yet, some insist that the extent to which a photo "deceives the public" is in the eye of the beholder. Many differentiate between

technical manipulation to improve photo quality and an intent to deceive. Some governments are attempting to legislate photo manipulation. One country banned a magazine in which a celebrity's appearance appeared visibly altered. Some celebrities refuse to allow airbrushing or other manipulation of photos of them.

Consider This: Is it ethical to alter digital photos? Why or why not? Does the answer depend on the reason for the alteration, the extent of the alteration, or some other factor? Should magazines stop altering pictures of people to change their appearance? Why or why not?

Video and Audio Editing

Video editing software is an application that allows professionals to modify a segment of a video, called a clip. For example, users can reduce the length of a video clip, reorder a series of clips, or add special effects such as words that move across the screen. Video editing software typically includes audio editing capabilities. **Audio editing software** is an application that enables users to modify audio clips, produce studio-quality soundtracks, and add audio to video clips (Figure 4-21). Most television shows and movies are created or enhanced using video and audio editing software.

Many home users work with easy-to-use video and audio editing software, which is much simpler to use than its professional counterpart, for small-scale movie making projects. With these programs, home users can edit home movies, add music or other sounds to the video, and share their movies on the web. Some operating systems include video editing and audio editing applications.

Discover More: Visit this chapter's free resources to learn more about video and audio editing software.

Figure 4-21 With audio editing software, users modify audio clips.
Source: Adobe Systems Incorporated

Multimedia and Website Authoring

Multimedia authoring software allows users to combine text, graphics, audio, video, and animation in an interactive application (Figure 4-22). With this software, users control the placement of text and images and the duration of sounds, video, and animation. Once created, multimedia presentations often take the form of interactive computer-based presentations or web-based presentations designed to facilitate learning, demonstrate product functionality, and elicit direct user participation. Training centers, educational institutions, and online magazine publishers use multimedia authoring software to develop interactive applications. These applications may be distributed on an optical disc, over a local area network, or via the Internet as web apps.

Website authoring software helps users of all skill levels create related webpages that include graphics, video, audio, animation, special effects with interactive content, and blog posts. In addition, many website authoring programs allow users to organize, manage, and maintain websites. Website authoring software often has capabilities of multimedia authoring software.

✸ **CONSIDER THIS**

What is computer-based or web-based training?

Computer-based training (*CBT*) is a type of education in which students learn by using and completing exercises with instructional software. *Web-based training* (*WBT*) is a type of CBT that uses Internet technology to deliver the training. CBT and WBT typically consist of self-directed, self-paced instruction about a topic so that the user becomes actively involved in the learning process instead of being a passive recipient of information. Beginning athletes use CBT programs to learn the intricacies of participating in a sport. The military and airlines use CBT simulations to train pilots to fly in various conditions and environments. WBT is popular in business, industry, and schools for teaching new skills or enhancing existing skills of employees, teachers, and students.

Discover More: Visit this chapter's free resources to learn more about multimedia and website authoring software.

Figure 4-22   Multimedia authoring software allows you to create dynamic presentations that include text, graphics, audio, video, and animation.
Courtesy of Matchware Inc.

Media Player

A **media player** is a program that allows you to view images and animations, listen to audio, and watch video files on your computer or mobile device (Figure 4-23). Media players also may enable you to organize media files by genre, artist, or other category; create playlists; convert files to different formats; connect to and purchase media from an online media store or market-place; stream radio stations' broadcasting over the Internet; download podcasts; burn audio CDs; and transfer media to portable media players.

Discover More: Visit this chapter's free resources to learn more about media players.

Figure 4-23   A media player.
Source: Rhapsody

Disc Burning

Disc burning software writes text, graphics, audio, and video files on a recordable or rewritable disc. This software enables home users easily to back up contents of their hard drive on an optical disc (CD/DVD) and make duplicates of uncopyrighted music or movies. Disc burning software usually also includes photo editing, audio editing, and video editing capabilities.

Personal Interest Applications

Countless desktop, mobile, and web apps are designed specifically for lifestyle, medical, entertainment, convenience, or education activities. Most of the programs in this category are relatively inexpensive; many are free. Some applications focus on a single service, while others provide several services in a single application.

- Lifestyle applications: Access the latest news or sports scores, check the weather forecast, compose music, research genealogy, find recipes, or locate nearby restaurants, gas stations, or points of interest.
- Medical applications: Research symptoms, establish a fitness or health program, track exercise activity, refill prescriptions, count calories, or monitor sleep patterns.

- Entertainment applications: Listen to music or the radio, view photos, watch videos or shows, read a book or other publication, organize and track fantasy sports teams, and play games individually or with others.
- Convenience applications: Obtain driving directions or your current location, remotely start your vehicle or unlock/lock the doors, set an alarm or timer, check the time, calculate a tip, use your phone as a flashlight, or use a personal assistant that acts on your voice commands (read How To 4-3 for instructions about using personal assistant apps).
- Education applications: Access how-to guides, learn or fine-tune a particular skill, follow a tutorial, run a simulation, assist children with reading and other elementary skills, or support academics.

⚙ HOW TO 4-3

Use Features in Voice Command Personal Assistant and Mobile Search Apps
Many mobile operating systems include a virtual personal assistant that processes voice commands and performs certain tasks. Some mobile search apps also act on spoken commands.. For example, you can issue voice commands to set an alarm, add an appointment to your calendar, send a text message, or run an app. The following table describes ways to use features in voice command personal assistant apps:

Task	Sample Voice Command(s)
Change phone settings	"Turn on Wi-Fi." "Turn off Bluetooth."
Dial a number	"Call Madelyn's Cell." "Call Mom Home." "Dial 407-555-8275."
Obtain information	"When was George Washington born?" "How many ounces are in a pound?" "What is the closest Chinese restaurant?"
Obtain driving instructions	"Navigate to 123 Main Street, Orlando, Florida." "Navigate to The Home Depot." "Navigate to Manchester, New Hampshire."
Perform a search	"What is the gas mileage for a Ford Explorer?" "Search butterfly lifespan."
Run an app	"Run calendar." "Run email."
Schedule a meeting	"Schedule a meeting with Traci at the library at 3:00 p.m. tomorrow."
Send a text message	"Text Samuel meet me at the pool."
Set a reminder	"Remind me to go grocery shopping tomorrow."
Set a timer	"Set timer for five minutes."
Set an alarm	"Set an alarm for 6:00 a.m. tomorrow." "Set an alarm for 6:30 a.m. every weekday."

🌼 **Consider This:** What other voice commands are available on your phone? Do you use voice commands? Why or why not?

Mini Feature 4-2: Web and Mobile Apps for Media and Personal Interest

A variety of applications provide a service intended to make media and personal interest tasks easier to accomplish. Some applications focus on a single service, while others provide several services in a single application. Read Mini Feature 4-2 to learn about some popular web and mobile apps for media and personal interests.

Web and Mobile Apps for Media and Personal Interests

Whether sharing, viewing, and purchasing media, such as photos; streaming audio and video; or playing games by yourself or with others, countless web and mobile apps are available to meet your needs. You also can use web and mobile apps to look up news, sports, and weather; obtain maps and directions; help you reach your health and fitness goals; and assist you with academic objectives.

Media Sharing

With media sharing mobile apps, you use the digital camera on your mobile device to take quality photos and/or videos and then instantly can share the photos or videos on online social networks. Using the corresponding media sharing web app, you can categorize, tag, organize, and rank the media posted by you, your friends, and your contacts.

Instagram

Streaming Audio and Video

Podcasts, video blogs, clips or episodes from a television show, or even entire movies are available through a variety of streaming media web and mobile apps. Some services are available only with membership, and may charge a monthly fee. Others are free, but include ads. Streaming media enables you to view and listen to content without downloading it to your computer or device, saving valuable disc or media storage space.

Gaming

Game web and mobile apps often offer a social component, enabling you to chat within the game environment, find friends who play the same game apps, and post your scores on social media. Word, puzzle, and board games are just some examples of apps you can play by yourself or with friends or others using the same apps.

News, Sports, and Weather

Many apps provide access to the latest news, stories, current events, sports scores, sporting events, and weather forecasts. Some of these mobile apps use GPS technology to provide current or customized information based on the location of your mobile device. You also can configure these apps to deliver text messages and other types of alerts to your device when certain events occur, such as when a football team scores a touchdown or when severe weather is near.

Mapping

Using your mobile device's GPS capability, you can use mapping mobile apps to obtain directions, maps, and recommendations for restaurants or other points of interest based on your current location. Some mapping apps even help you to locate friends based on their GPS signals (if they enable you to do so). Others allow you to share your current location on social media using a check-in feature. Web apps help you decide on a route, print directions or a map, and even find amenities along your route, such as public rest stops or restaurants.

Health and Fitness

Losing weight, training for a race, or following a low-calorie diet are some uses of health and fitness apps. Using a mobile device as a pedometer or GPS receiver can help you count your steps or create a map of a route you run and then update your profile with the data it tracked. You can use corresponding web apps to chart and analyze your progress, schedule your next workout, or determine the next steps

MyFitnessPal LLC

to reach your goals. These apps also can help plan your meals and track the nutritional value of food you consume.

Academic

If you need to study terms or topics, flash card apps can provide reinforcement. This book's premium content for example, has an accompanying Flash Cards app designed to improve your retention of chapter key terms. Schools often subscribe to educational apps that provide students with games, quizzes, and lessons about course topics. Using these apps, teachers can keep track of students' progress and pinpoint areas where they may need extra help. You also can access complete college or high school courses and take advantage of free or fee-based digital content provided by publishers and teachers.

Discover More: Visit this chapter's free resources to learn more about web and mobile apps for media and personal interests.

✸ **Consider This:** Which web and mobile apps have you used for media sharing; streaming audio and video; gaming; news, sports, and weather; mapping; health and fitness; and education? Will you try others after reading this mini feature? Why or why not?

⚙ **BTW**
Mobile Communications Apps
Most of the communications apps in Table 4-2 are available as mobile apps, as well.

Communications Applications

One of the main reasons people use computers is to communicate and share information with others. Earlier chapters presented a variety of communications applications, which are summarized in Table 4-2. Read Ethics & Issues 4-4 to consider whether your email provider should be allowed to read or scan your email messages.

Table 4-2 Communications Applications

Blog
- Time-stamped articles, or posts, in diary or journal format, usually listed in reverse chronological order
- Bloggers (author) use blogging software to create/maintain blog
  - Some blog services provide blogging software so users do not have to install it on their own servers

Internet Phone
- Allows users to speak to other users via an Internet connection
- Requires a microphone, a speaker, a high-speed Internet connection, and VoIP software
  - Some subscription services also require a separate phone and VoIP router
  - With a webcam, some services also support video chat or videoconferences

Browsing
- Allows users to access and view webpages on the Internet
- Requires browser
  - Integrated in most operating systems
  - Alternative browsers are available on the web for download, usually for free

Internet Messaging
- Real-time exchange of messages, files, images, audio, and/or video with another online user
- Requires messaging software
  - Integrated in some operating systems
  - Available for download on the web, usually for free, or available as a browser plug-in
  - Included with some paid ISPs

Chat
- Real-time, online typed conversation with one or more users
- Requires chat client software
  - Integrated in some operating systems and most browsers
  - Available for download on the web, usually for free
  - Included with some paid ISPs
  - Built into some websites

Mobile Messaging
- Short text, picture, or video messages sent and received, mainly on mobile devices
- May require messaging plan from mobile service provider
  - Requires messaging software
  - Integrated in most mobile devices
  - Available for download on the web, usually for free

Online Discussion
- Online areas where users have written discussions
- May require a reader program
- Integrated in some operating systems, email programs, and browsers

Videoconference
- Meeting between geographically separated people who use a network to transmit video/audio
- Requires videoconferencing software, a microphone, a speaker, and a webcam

Email
- Messages and files sent via a network, such as the Internet
- Requires an email program
  - Integrated in many software suites and operating systems
  - Available free at portals on the web
  - Included with a paid ISP
  - Can be purchased separately

Web Feeds
- Keeps track of changes made to blogs by checking feeds
- Requires a feed reader
  - Integrated in some email programs and browsers
  - Available for download on the web, usually for free

File Transfer
- Method of uploading files to and downloading files from servers on the Internet
- May require an FTP client program
  - Integrated in some operating systems
  - Available for download on the web; many free or open source alternatives are available
  - Many applications (such as web editing software) that require frequent transfer of files to the Internet have built-in FTP capabilities

Should Your Email Provider Be Allowed to Read or Scan Your Email?

When using any email program or service, you expect the app to scan incoming and outgoing mail to prevent the spread of malware. One web-based email service recently released a service update that includes automatic scanning of all email messages in order to provide targeted advertisements. Privacy experts point out that the scan includes all email messages sent or received, whether or not both the sender and recipient subscribe to the service.

Ad-supported web services, including email, often collect information in your profile, as well as your search results and other Internet activity. When you agree to

use these services, you give consent to this type of monitoring. In this case, the extent of the monitoring exceeds the policies of other web-based services. In a court filing, one email provider stated that users of web-based services have no "reasonable expectation" of privacy with respect to the content of email messages.

A further complication to this instance is that many educational institutions use this service for email, collaboration software, and more. The service admits to collecting data from students, even when the school has opted out of ad displays. Laws are unclear whether collecting student data is legal. Several schools have joined to create a class-action lawsuit against the provider. Many

argue that collection of student data, which could include grades received and more, is a violation of the Family Educational Rights and Privacy Act (FERPA). Although FERPA predates cloud-based Internet services, it states that "schools must have written permission from the parent or eligible student in order to release any information from a student's education record."

Consider This: Should an email service provider disclose data collection practices? Why or why not? Is it ethical for an email provider to scan email sent by a nonsubscriber? Why or why not? Is collecting student data a violation of FERPA? Why or why not?

✔ NOW YOU SHOULD KNOW

Be sure you understand the material presented in the sections titled Graphics and Media Applications, Personal Interest Applications, and Communications Applications, as it relates to the chapter objectives.
Now you should know ...

- When you might use a graphics or media application (Objective 5)
- Which personal interest applications you would find useful (Objective 6)
- When you are interacting with communications applications (Objective 7)

Discover More: Visit this chapter's premium content for practice quiz opportunities.

Security Tools

To protect your computers and mobile devices, you can use one or more security tools. Security tools include personal firewalls, antivirus programs, malware removers, and Internet filters. Although some of these tools are included with the operating system, you also can purchase stand-alone programs that offer improvements or added functionality.

Personal Firewall

A **personal firewall** is a security tool that detects and protects a personal computer and its data from unauthorized intrusions (Figure 4-24). Personal firewalls constantly monitor all transmissions to and from a computer or mobile device and may inform a user of attempted intrusions. When connected to the Internet, your computer or mobile device is vulnerable to attacks from

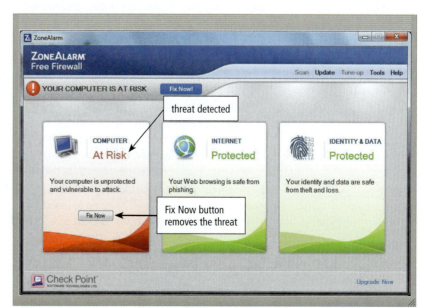

Figure 4-24 This personal firewall detected a threat to the computer and provided a means to remove the threat.
Courtesy of Checkpoint Software Technologies Ltd.

hackers who try to access a computer or network illegally. These attacks may destroy your data, steal information, damage your computer, or carry out some other malicious action.

✳ CONSIDER THIS

What is a hardware firewall?

A *hardware firewall* is a device intended to stop network intrusions before they attempt to affect your computer or network maliciously. Many routers also can function as a hardware firewall.

Discover More: Visit this chapter's free resources to learn more about personal firewalls.

Mini Feature 4-3: Viruses and Malware

A computer **virus** is a potentially damaging program that affects a computer or device negatively by altering the way it works. This occurs without the user's knowledge or permission. Once the virus is in a computer or device, it can spread and may damage your files, programs and apps, and operating system. Read Mini Feature 4-3 to learn more about viruses and other malware.

✳ MINI FEATURE 4-3

Viruses and Malware

Viruses do not generate by chance. The programmer of a virus, known as a virus author, intentionally writes a virus program. Writing a virus program usually requires significant programming skills. The virus author ensures the virus can replicate itself, conceal itself, monitor for certain events, and then deliver its payload. A *payload* is the destructive event or prank the virus delivers. Viruses can infect all types of computers and devices. Most variations of viruses have two phases involved in their execution: infection and delivery.

The first step in the infection phase is activation of the virus. The most common way viruses spread is by users running infected programs or apps. During the infection phase, viruses typically perform one or more of the following actions:

1. First, a virus replicates by attaching itself to program files. A macro virus hides in a macro, which is a standard feature of many productivity applications, such as word processing and spreadsheet apps. A boot sector virus targets the computer's start-up files. A file virus attaches itself to program files. The next time an infected program or app is run, the virus executes and infects the computer or device.

2. Viruses conceal themselves to avoid detection. A stealth virus disguises itself by hiding in fake code sections, which it inserts within working code in a file. A polymorphic virus actually changes its code as it delivers the infection.

3. Finally, viruses watch for a certain condition or event and activate when that condition or event occurs. The event might be starting the computer or device, or reaching a date on the system clock. A logic bomb activates when it detects a specific condition

(say, a name deleted from the employee list). A time bomb is a logic bomb that activates on a particular date or time. If the triggering condition does not exist, the virus simply replicates.

During the delivery phase, the virus unleashes its payload, which might be a harmless prank that displays a meaningless message — or it might be destructive, corrupting or deleting data and files. The most dangerous viruses do not have an obvious payload. Instead, they quietly modify files. One way antivirus software detects computer viruses is by monitoring files for unknown changes.

In addition to viruses, other malware includes worms, trojan horse programs, and rootkits.

- A *worm* resides in active memory and replicates itself over a network to infect computers and devices, using up system resources and possibly shutting down the system.

- A *trojan horse* is a destructive program disguised as a real program, such as a screen saver. When a user runs a seemingly innocent program, a trojan horse hiding inside can capture information, such as user names and passwords, from your computer or enable someone to control your computer remotely. Unlike viruses, trojan horses do not replicate themselves.

- A *rootkit* is a program that easily can hide and allow someone to take full control of your computer from a remote location, often for nefarious purposes. For example, a rootkit can hide in a folder on your computer. The folder appears empty because the rootkit has instructed your computer not to display the contents of the folder. Rootkits can be very dangerous and often require special software to detect and remove.

Studies show that malware can infect an unprotected computer within minutes after connecting to the Internet. Due to the increasing threat of viruses attacking your computer, it is more important than ever to protect your computer from viruses and other malware. Secure IT 1-2 in Chapter 1 lists steps you can follow to protect your computer from a virus infection.

Discover More: Visit this chapter's free resources to learn more about file viruses, polymorphic viruses, rootkits, and antivirus software.

Consider This: If your computer or mobile device is infected with a virus or malware, how will you know? How will you find instructions for removing a virus?

Signs of Virus Infection

- An unusual message or image is displayed on the computer screen.
- An unusual sound or music plays randomly.
- The available memory is less than what should be available.
- A program or file suddenly is missing.
- An unknown program or file mysteriously appears.
- The size of a file changes without explanation.
- A file becomes corrupted.
- A program or file does not work properly.
- System properties change.
- The computer operates much slower than usual.

© Cengage Learning

Antivirus Programs

To protect a computer from virus attacks, users should install an antivirus program and keep it updated by purchasing revisions or upgrades to the software. An **antivirus program** protects a computer against viruses by identifying and removing any computer viruses found in memory, on storage media, or on incoming files (Figure 4-25). Antivirus programs scan for programs that attempt to modify a computer's start-up files, the operating system, and other programs that normally are read from but not modified. In addition, many antivirus programs automatically scan files downloaded from the web, email attachments, opened files, and all types of removable media inserted in the computer or mobile device.

If an antivirus program identifies an infected file, it attempts to remove the malware. If the antivirus program cannot remove the infection, it often quarantines the infected file. A *quarantine* is a separate area of a hard drive that holds the infected file until the infection can be removed. This step ensures other files will not become infected. Quarantined files remain on your computer or mobile device until you delete them or restore them.

Most antivirus programs also include protection against other malware, such as worms, trojan horses, and spyware. When you purchase a new computer, it may include a trial version of antivirus software. Many email servers also have antivirus programs installed to check incoming and outgoing email messages for viruses and other malware. Read Secure IT 4-4 for tips about recognizing virus hoaxes.

BTW

Antivirus and Malware Detection Programs
You should run only one antivirus program on your computer but can run more than one malware detection program.

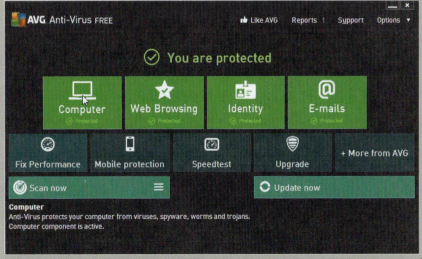

Figure 4-25 An antivirus program scans memory, media, and incoming email messages and attachments for viruses and attempts to remove any viruses it finds.
Courtesy of Checkpoint Software Technologies Ltd.

📄 **Recognizing Virus Hoaxes**

Computer hoaxes spread across the Internet in record time and often are the source of urban legends. These hoaxes take several forms and often disappear for months or years at a time, only to resurface some time later.

Most alarming to some users are the computer virus hoaxes that warn the computer is infected and needs immediate attention. Some warnings state the problem is so severe that the computer or device will explode or that the entire hard drive will be erased in a matter of seconds. The warnings cite prominent companies, such as Microsoft and Intel Security. These messages claim to offer a solution to the problem, generally requesting a fee for a program to download. Snopes.com compiles these hoaxes and describes their sources and histories.

In reality, these fake messages are generated by unscrupulous scammers preying upon gullible people who panic and follow the directions in the message. These users divulge credit card information and then often download files riddled with viruses.

If you receive one of these virus hoaxes, never respond to the message. Instead, delete it. Most importantly, never forward it to an unsuspecting friend or coworker. If you receive the virus hoax from someone you know, send him or her a separate email message with information about the hoax.

⊛ **Consider This:** Have you ever received a virus hoax? If so, what action did you take?

⊛ **CONSIDER THIS**

How do antivirus programs detect viruses?
Many antivirus programs identify viruses by looking for virus signatures. A *virus signature,* also called a virus definition, is a known specific pattern of virus code. Computer users should update their antivirus program's signature files regularly. This extremely important activity allows the antivirus program to protect against viruses written since the antivirus program was released and/or its last update. Most antivirus programs contain an automatic update feature or regularly prompts users to download the updated virus signatures, usually at least once a week. The vendor usually provides this service to registered users at no cost for a specified time.

Discover More: Visit this chapter's free resources to learn more about antivirus programs.

Spyware, Adware, and Other Malware Removers

Spyware is a type of program placed on a computer or mobile device without the user's knowledge that secretly collects information about the user and then communicates the information it collects to some outside source while the user is online. Some vendors or employers use spyware to collect information about program usage or employees. Internet advertising firms often collect information about users' web browsing habits. Spyware can enter your computer when you install a new program, through a graphic on a webpage or in an email message, or through malware.

Adware is a type of program that displays an online advertisement in a banner or pop-up or pop-under window on webpages, email messages, or other Internet services. Sometimes, Internet advertising firms hide spyware in adware.

A **spyware remover** is a type of program that detects and deletes spyware and similar programs. An **adware remover** is a program that detects and deletes adware. Malware removers detect and delete spyware, adware, and other malware. Read Secure IT 4-5 for measures you can take to protect your mobile device from malware.

⊛ **CONSIDER THIS**

Are cookies spyware?
A *cookie* is a small text file that a web server stores on your computer. Cookie files typically contain data about you, such as your user name, viewing preferences, or shopping cart contents. Cookies are not considered spyware because website programmers do not attempt to conceal the cookies.

Discover More: Visit this chapter's free resources to learn more about malware removers.

⚙ SECURE IT 4-5

📧 Malware Risks to Mobile Devices

Practically every smartphone is vulnerable to hacking attacks. Threats to smartphones and mobile devices are growing in record numbers due to the rising popularity of these products and the variety of marketplace sources for downloading apps.

Often the malware is disguised as a popular app and steals personal and sensitive information and phone numbers. It also can allow hackers to control the mobile device from remote locations. Once the hacker takes over the device, all the information on it is available, including passwords and account numbers. One of the fastest growing threats within mobile apps is *toll fraud malware*, which is a malicious mobile app that uses a variety of fraudulent schemes to charge unsuspecting users for premium messaging services.

Smartphone users can take several precautions to guard against malware threats. They include:

- Read reviews of apps and the companies that create them before downloading the apps to your mobile device.
- Use mobile malware and antivirus protection.
- Turn off location-based apps that track your movements.
- Do not connect to unknown wireless networks.
- Keep the operating system up to date.
- Enable the screen lock feature, and use a strong password to unlock the device.
- Reset the mobile device before selling or trading it in.
- Practice the same safe computing measures you take on your home computer.

✳ **Consider This:** Which of these guidelines do you follow now when using your smartphone or mobile device? How will you modify your usage after reading these tips?

Internet Filters

Filters are programs that remove or block certain items from being displayed. Four widely used Internet filters are anti-spam programs, web filters, phishing filters, and pop-up and pop-under blockers.

Anti-Spam Programs   **Spam** is an unsolicited email message or posting sent to many recipients or forums at once. Spam is considered Internet junk mail. The content of spam ranges from selling a product or service, to promoting a business opportunity, to advertising offensive material. Spam also may contain links or attachments that contain malware.

An **anti-spam program** is a filtering program that attempts to remove spam before it reaches your inbox or forum. If your email program does not filter spam, many anti-spam programs are available at no cost on the web. ISPs often filter spam as a service for their subscribers.

Web Filters   **Web filtering software** is a program that restricts access to certain material on the web. Some restrict access to specific websites; others filter websites that use certain words or phrases. Many businesses use web filtering software to limit employee's web access. Some schools, libraries, and parents use this software to restrict access to websites that are not educational.

Phishing Filters   **Phishing** is a scam in which a perpetrator sends an official looking email message that attempts to obtain your personal and/or financial information (Figure 4-26). Some phishing messages ask you to reply with your information; others direct you to a phony website or a pop-up or pop-under window that looks like a legitimate website, which then collects your information.

A **phishing filter** is a program that warns or blocks you from potentially fraudulent or suspicious websites. Some browsers include phishing filters.

🔵 Internet Research

What are current phishing scams?

Search for: recent phishing scams

Figure 4-26   An example of a phishing email message.
Source: Andrew Levine

Pop-Up and Pop-Under Blockers   A *pop-up ad* is an Internet advertisement that suddenly appears in a new window on top of a webpage. Similarly, a *pop-under ad* is an Internet advertisement that is hidden behind the browser window so that it will be viewed when users close their browser windows. A **pop-up blocker** or **pop-under blocker** is a filtering program that stops pop-up or pop-under ads from displaying on webpages. Many browsers include these blockers. You also can download pop-up and pop-under blockers from the web at no cost.

   Discover More: Visit this chapter's free resources to learn more about Internet filters.

File, Disk, and System Management Tools

To perform maintenance-type tasks related to managing a computer, its devices, or its programs, you can use one or more file, disk, and system management tools. Functions provided by these tools include the following: managing files, searching, viewing images, uninstalling software, cleaning up disks, defragmenting disks, setting up screen savers, compressing files, maintaining a personal computer, and backing up files and disks. Although some of these tools are included with the operating system, you also can purchase stand-alone programs that offer improvements or added functionality.

File Manager

   A **file manager** is a tool that performs functions related to file management. Some of the file management functions that a file manager performs are displaying a list of files on a storage medium (Figure 4-27); organizing files in folders; and copying, renaming, deleting, moving, and sorting files. A **folder** is a specific named location on a storage medium that contains related files. Operating systems typically include a file manager.

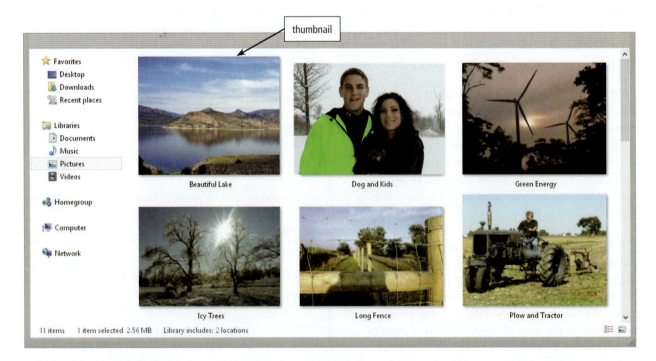

Figure 4-27   With a file manager, you can view files containing documents, photos, and music. In this case, thumbnails of photos are displayed.
Source: Microsoft

Search

A **search tool** is a program, usually included with an operating system, that attempts to locate a file, contact, calendar event, app or any other item stored on your computer or mobile device based on criteria you specify (Figure 4-28). The criteria could be a word(s), date, location, and other similar properties. Search tools can look through documents, photos, music, calendars, contacts, and other items on your computer or mobile device and/or on the Internet, combining search results in a single location.

Search tools typically use an index to assist with locating items quickly. An *index* stores a variety of information about a file, including its name, date created, date modified, author name, and so on. When you enter search criteria, instead of looking through every file and folder on the storage medium, the search tool looks through the index first to find a match. Each entry in the index contains a link to the actual file on the storage media for easy retrieval.

Image Viewer

An **image viewer** is a tool that allows users to display, copy, and print the contents of a graphics file, such as a photo (Figure 4-29). With an image viewer, users can see images without having to open them in a paint or image editing program. Many image viewers include some photo editing capabilities. Most operating systems include an image viewer.

Figure 4-28 This search displays all files on the mobile device that match the search critieria, Map. Notice the search results show map apps, email with a map, and a calendar event.
Source: Apple Inc

Figure 4-29 An image viewer allows users to see the contents of a photo file.
Source: Microsoft

Uninstaller

An **uninstaller** is a tool that removes a program, as well as any associated entries in the system files. When you install a program, the operating system records the information it uses to run the software in the system files. The uninstaller deletes files and folders from the hard drive, as well as removes program entries from the system files. Read How To 4-4 for instructions about uninstalling programs and removing apps from your computers and mobile devices.

HOW TO 4-4

Uninstall a Program or Remove an App

You may choose to uninstall a program or remove an app from your computer or mobile device for a variety of reasons. For example, you may uninstall a program if you need more space on your hard drive, or if you no longer have a use for that program. Uninstalling unwanted programs and apps will keep your hard drive free from clutter and maximize your computer or mobile device's performance. The following steps describe how to uninstall a program or remove an app.

Windows

1. Open the Control Panel.
2. Tap or click the option to uninstall a program.

3. Tap or click to select the program to uninstall.
4. Tap or click the Uninstall button and then follow the prompts on the screen.

Mac

1. Open the Finder.
2. Tap or click Applications in the left pane.
3. Scroll to display the app you wish to uninstall.
4. Drag the app's icon to the Trash.

iPhone, iPad, or iPod Touch

1. Press and hold the icon for the app you wish to delete until the app icons begin to animate.

2. Tap the X on the icon for the app you wish to delete to remove the app from your device.

Android

1. Display the Settings menu.
2. Tap the command to display a list of installed applications.
3. Tap the application to uninstall.
4. Tap the Uninstall button.
5. Tap the OK button.

⚙ **Consider This:** In addition to the reasons stated here, what other reasons might you choose to uninstall an app from your computer or mobile device?

⚙ CONSIDER THIS

Can you use a file manager to delete a program?

If an uninstaller exists and you remove software from a computer by deleting the files and folders associated with the program without running the uninstaller, the system file entries might not be updated. This may cause the operating system to display error messages when you start the computer.

Disk Cleanup

A **disk cleanup** tool searches for and removes unnecessary files (Figure 4-30). Unnecessary files may include downloaded program files, temporary Internet files, deleted files, and unused program files. Operating systems usually include a disk cleanup tool.

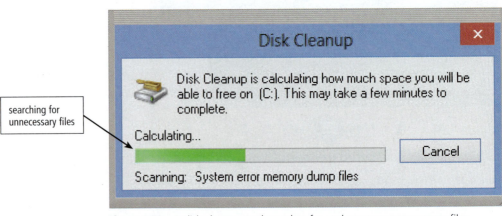

searching for unnecessary files

Figure 4-30 A disk cleanup tool searches for and removes unnecessary files.
Source: Microsoft

Disk Defragmenter

A **disk defragmenter** is a tool that reorganizes the files and unused space on a computer's hard disk so that the operating system accesses data more quickly and programs run faster. When an operating system stores data on a disk, it places the data in the first available sector (a storage location on a disk in the shape of an arc). The operating system attempts to place data in sectors that are contiguous (next to each other), but this is not always possible. When the contents of a file are scattered across two or more noncontiguous sectors, the file is fragmented.

Fragmentation slows down file access and, thus, the performance of the entire computer. Defragmenting the disk, or reorganizing it so that the files are stored in contiguous sectors, solves this problem (Figure 4-31). Operating systems usually include a disk defragmenter.

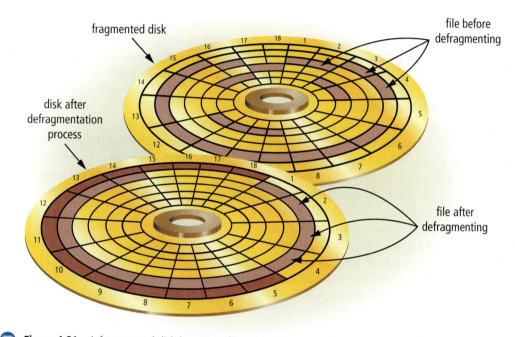

Figure 4-31   A fragmented disk has many files stored in noncontiguous sectors. Defragmenting reorganizes the files so that they are located in contiguous sectors, which speeds access time.
© Cengage Learning

BTW

SSDs
Defragmenting is necessary only on hard disks. You do not need to defragment an SSD (solid-state drive).

Screen Saver

A **screen saver** is a tool that causes a display device's screen to show a moving image or blank screen if no keyboard or mouse activity occurs for a specified time. When you press a key on the keyboard, tap the screen, or move the mouse, the screen saver disappears and the screen returns to the previous state.

✹ **CONSIDER THIS** ────────────

What is the purpose of a screen saver?

Screen savers originally were developed to prevent a problem called ghosting, in which images could be etched permanently on a monitor's screen. Although ghosting is not as severe of a problem with today's displays, manufacturers continue to recommend that users install screen savers for this reason. Screen savers also are popular for security, business, and entertainment purposes. To secure a computer, users configure their screen saver to require a password to deactivate.

File Compression

A **file compression tool** shrinks the size of a file(s). A compressed file takes up less storage space than the original file. Compressing files frees up room on the storage media. You may need to compress a file so that it will fit on a smaller storage medium, such as a USB flash drive. Attaching a compressed file to an email message, for example, reduces the time needed for file transmission. Uploading and downloading compressed files to and from the Internet reduces the file transmission time.

BTW
High-Tech Talk
Discover More: Visit this chapter's free resources to learn about compression algorithms.

Compressed files sometimes are called **zipped files**. When you receive or download a compressed file, you must uncompress it. To **uncompress** (or unzip or expand) a file, you restore it to its original form. Some operating systems include file compression and uncompression capabilities.

Discover More: Visit this chapter's free resources to learn more about file compression tools.

PC Maintenance

A **PC maintenance tool** is a program that identifies and fixes operating system problems, detects and repairs drive problems, and includes the capability of improving a computer's performance. Additionally, some personal computer maintenance utilities continuously monitor a computer while you use it to identify and repair problems before they occur.

Backup and Restore

A **backup tool** allows users to copy, or back up, selected files or the contents of an entire storage medium to another storage location, such as another hard drive, optical disc, USB flash drive, or cloud storage (Figure 4-32). During the backup process, the backup tool monitors progress and alerts you if it needs additional media, such as another disc. Many backup programs compress files during the backup process. By compressing the files, the backup program requires less storage space for the backup files than for the original files.

Because they are compressed, you usually cannot use backup files in their backed up form. In the event you need to use a backup file, a **restore tool** reverses the process and returns backed up files to their original form. Backup tools work with a restore tool. You should back up files and disks regularly in the event your originals are lost, damaged, or destroyed.

Discover More: Visit this chapter's free resources to learn more about backup tools.

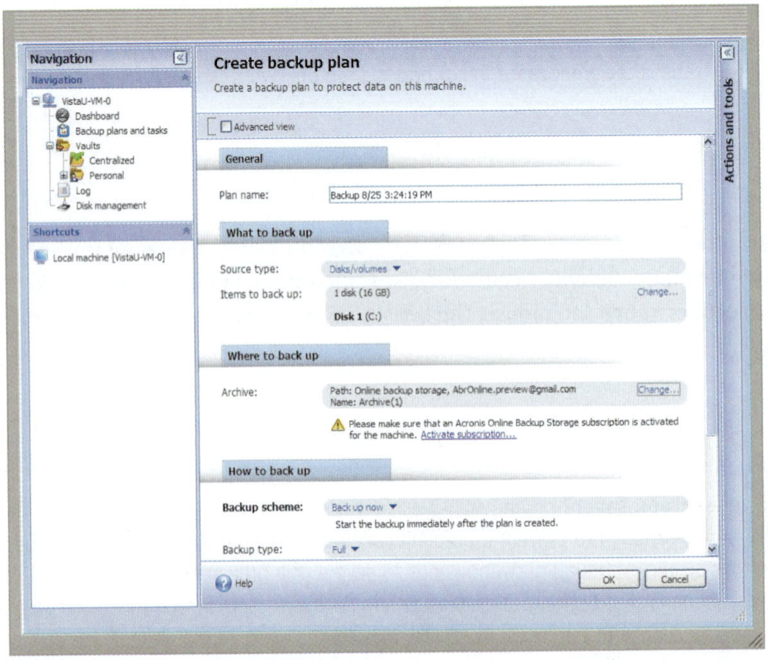

Figure 4-32 A backup tool allows users to copy files, folders, or the entire contents from one storage medium to another location.
Source: Acronis

✔ NOW YOU SHOULD KNOW

Be sure you understand the material presented in the sections titled Security Tools and File, Disk, and System Management Tools as it relates to the chapter objectives.
Now you should know ...

- Why you should use personal firewalls, antivirus programs, malware removers, and Internet filters (Objective 8)
- Which file, disk, and system management tools you would find useful (Objective 9)

Discover More: Visit this chapter's premium content for practice quiz opportunities.

✔ Chapter Summary

This chapter presented a variety of programs and apps available for computers and mobile devices. You learned about the role of the operating system and the various ways software is distributed. The chapter presented the features of a variety of productivity applications, graphics and media applications, and personal interest applications. It reviewed several communications applications and then presented features of a variety of security tools and file, disk, and system management tools.

Discover More: Visit this chapter's free resources for additional content that accompanies this chapter and also includes these features: Technology Innovators: Dan Bricklin, Google/Sergey Brin/Larry Page, Adobe Systems, and eBay/PayPal; Technology Trends: Evernote, Instagram, and iTunes U; and High-Tech Talks: Filtering Data and Compression Algorithms.

Test your knowledge of chapter material by accessing the Study Guide, Flash Cards, and Practice Test resources from your smartphone, tablet, laptop, or desktop.

⚡ TECHNOLOGY @ WORK

📄 Entertainment

Do you wonder how music on the radio sounds so perfectly in tune, how animated motion pictures are created, or how one controls and technology lighting during a concert? Not only does the entertainment industry rely on computers and technology to advertise and sell their services, computers also assist in other aspects, including audio and video composition, lighting control, computerized animation, and computer gaming.

Entertainment websites provide music and movies you can purchase and download to your computer or mobile device; live news broadcasts, performances, and sporting events; games you can play with other online users; and much more.

As early as 1951, computers were used to record and play music. Today, computers play a much larger role in the music industry. For example, if you are listening to a song on the radio and notice that not one note is out of tune, it is possible that a program or app was used to change individual notes without altering the rest of the song.

Many years ago, creating cartoons or animated motion pictures was an extremely time-consuming task because artists were responsible for sketching thousands of drawings by hand. Currently, artists use computers to create these drawings in a fraction of the time, which significantly reduces the time and cost of development. Technology also is used in other areas of movie production to add visual effects.

Technology also is used in the gaming industry. While some game developers create games from scratch, others might use game engines that simplify the development process. For example, LucasArts created the GrimE game engine, which is designed to create adventure games.

During a concert, lighting technicians use computer programs to control lights by turning them off and on, changing their color, or changing their placement at specified intervals. In fact, once a performance begins, the technicians often merely are standing by, monitoring the computer as it performs most of the

work. A significant amount of time and effort, however, is required to program the computer to execute its required tasks during a live show.

The next time you listen to a song, watch a movie, play a game, or attend a concert, think about the role technology plays in contributing to your entertainment.

✳ **Consider This:** How else might computers and technology be used in the entertainment industry?

© Horizons WWP / Alamy

Study Guide

The Study Guide exercise reinforces material you should know for the chapter exam.

Discover More: Visit this chapter's premium content to **test your knowledge of digital content** associated with this chapter and **access the Study Guide resource** from your smartphone, tablet, laptop, or desktop.

Instructions: Answer the questions below using the format that helps you remember best or that is required by your instructor. Possible formats may include one or more of these options: write the answers; create a document that contains the answers; record answers as audio or video using a webcam, smartphone, or portable media player; post answers on a blog, wiki, or website; or highlight answers in the book/e-book.

1. List categories of programs and apps. _____ is another word for program.

2. Define these terms: operating system, tools, and system software.

3. List examples of desktop and mobile operating systems.

4. Describe how an operating system interacts with the computer.

5. _____ software performs functions specific to a business or industry.

6. Differentiate among web apps, mobile apps, and mobile web apps.

7. List any restrictions for shareware, freeware, open source, and public-domain software.

8. Explain considerations for safely downloading software and apps.

9. Describe steps to register and activate software.

10. Explain the purpose of a license agreement.

11. List types of productivity applications.

12. Describe the activities that occur during project development.

13. Differentiate among font, font size, and font style.

14. Explain the impact of the Internet on plagiarism.

15. Applications often include a(n) _____ gallery, which is a collection of clip art and photos.

16. Identify functions of the following software: word processing, presentation, spreadsheet, database, note taking, calendar and contact management, software suite, project management, accounting, personal finance, legal, tax preparation, and document management.

17. Identify tools word processing programs provide that can assist you when writing.

18. Define the following terms: worksheet and function.

19. Describe when you should use a database and when to use a spreadsheet.

20. List advantages of using a software suite.

21. Identify ways you can manage a project using project management software.

22. List safety considerations when using personal finance apps.

23. Describe issues that might arise when using legal software.

24. Name the types of software used by various functional units in an enterprise.

25. Identify functions of the following apps: calendar and email, scanning, financial, reference, retail, travel, and online social networks.

26. Identify risks when using payment apps.

27. Identify functions of the following software: computer-aided design, desktop publishing, paint/image editing, photo editing and photo management, video and audio editing, multimedia and website authoring, media player, and disc burning.

28. List ways to edit digital photos. Identify issues surrounding altered digital photos.

29. _____ authoring software allows users to combine text, graphics, audio, video, and animation in an interactive application.

30. Define the terms, CBT and WBT.

31. List types of personal interest applications.

32. Describe ways to use voice command personal assistant apps.

33. Identify functions of the following apps: media sharing; streaming audio and video; game; news, sports, and weather; mapping; health and fitness; and academic.

34. Identify types of communications applications.

35. List issues surrounding an email provider scanning users' emails.

36. Identify functions of the following tools: personal firewalls, hardware firewalls, antivirus programs, malware removers, and Internet filters.

37. Describe ways a virus infects programs or apps.

38. List types of malware. Identify signs of a virus infection.

39. Explain the risks of and how to avoid computer virus hoaxes.

40. A virus _____ is a known specific pattern of virus code. Differentiate between spyware and adware.

41. Identify ways to avoid malware when using a mobile device.

42. List and describe four types of Internet filters.

43. Identify functions of the following tools: file manager, search, image viewer, uninstaller, disk cleanup, disk defragmenter, screen saver, file compression, PC maintenance, and backup and restore.

44. Define the terms, folder and index.

45. List steps to uninstall a program or remove an app.

46. Describe the disk defragmentation process.

47. Compressed files are sometimes called _____ files.

48. List storage media for backups.

49. Describe uses of technology in the entertainment industry.

You should be able to define the Primary Terms and be familiar with the Secondary Terms listed below.

Key Terms

Discover More: Visit this chapter's premium content to **view definitions** for each term and to **access the Flash Cards resource** from your smartphone, tablet, laptop, or desktop

Primary Terms   (shown in **bold-black** characters in the chapter)

accounting software (173)
adware remover (192)
anti-spam program (193)
antivirus program (191)
app (158)
application (158)
audio editing software (183)
backup tool (198)
calendar and contact management software (171)
clip art/image gallery (166)
computer-aided design (180)
database (170)
database software (170)
desktop publishing software (180)

disc burning software (185)
disk cleanup (196)
disk defragmenter (197)
document management software (176)
file compression tool (198)
file manager (194)
folder (194)
image editing software (181)
image viewer (195)
legal software (175)
media player (185)
multimedia authoring software (184)
note taking software (171)
paint software (181)
PC maintenance tool (198)

PDF (176)
personal finance software (174)
personal firewall (189)
phishing (193)
phishing filter (193)
photo editing software (181)
photo management software (182)
pop-under blocker (194)
pop-up blocker (194)
presentation software (168)
program (158)
project management software (172)
QR code (178)
restore tool (198)
screen saver (197)
search tool (195)
software (158)

software suite (172)
spam (193)
spreadsheet software (168)
spyware remover (192)
tax preparation software (176)
uncompress (198)
uninstaller (195)
video editing software (183)
virus (190)
web filtering software (193)
website authoring software (184)
word processing software (167)
worksheet (168)
zipped files (198)

Secondary Terms   (shown in *italic* characters in the chapter)

adware (192)
application software (158)
automatic update (163)
brightness (182)
clipboard (165)
compress (182)
computer-based training (CBT) (184)
contrast (182)
cookie (192)
create (165)
crop (182)
custom software (161)
edit (165)
e-filing (176)
EULA (163)
font (166)
font size (166)
font style (166)
format (166)
freeware (161)
function (169)

hard copy (166)
hardware firewall (190)
home design/landscaping software (180)
illustration software (181)
index (195)
license agreement (163)
marketplace (161)
mobile app (161)
mobile web app (161)
NFC chip (179)
open source software (161)
operating system (158)
payload (190)
pop-under ad (194)
pop-up ad (194)
print (166)
product activation (162)
productivity applications (165)
public-domain software (161)
quarantine (191)
red-eye (182)

resize (182)
retail software (161)
rootkit (190)
save (165)
security suite (189)
shareware (161)
sharpness (182)
slide show (168)
software as a service (SaaS) (162)
software registration (162)
spyware (192)

system software (158)
toll fraud malware (193)
tools (158)
trial version (161)
trojan horse (190)
utilities (158)
virus signature (192)
web app (161)
web-based training (WBT) (184)
worm (190)

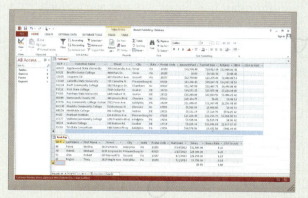

database software (170)

Checkpoint

The Checkpoint exercises test your knowledge of the chapter concepts. The page number containing the answer appears in parentheses after each exercise. The Consider This exercises challenge your understanding of chapter concepts.

Discover More: Visit this chapter's premium content to **complete the Checkpoint exercises** interactively; complete the **self-assessment in the Test Prep resource** from your smartphone, tablet, laptop, or desktop; and then **take the Practice Test.**

True/False   Mark T for True and F for False.

F 1. Application software serves as the interface between the user, the apps, and the computer's or mobile device's hardware. (158)

T 2. While a computer or mobile device is running, the operating system remains in memory. (160)

F 3. Open source software is mass-produced, copyrighted software that meets the needs of a wide variety of users. (161)

T 4. When downloading shareware, freeware, or public-domain software, it is good practice to seek websites with ratings for and reviews of products. (162)

T 5. With web apps, you always access the latest version of the software. (163)

F 6. With database software, users run functions to retrieve data. (170)

T 7. Software suites offer three major advantages: lower cost, ease of use, and integration. (172)

T 8. A PDF file can be viewed and printed without the software that created the original document. (176)

T 9. The military and airlines use CBT simulations to train pilots to fly in various conditions and environments. (184)

T 10. A router also can function as a hardware firewall. (190)

F 11. A worm is a destructive program designed as a real program. (190)

F 12. Cookies typically are considered a type of spyware. (192)

Multiple Choice   Select the best answer.

1. _____ software performs functions specific to a business or industry. (161)
   a. Retail
   b. Open source
   c. Shareware
   d. Custom ✓

2. A(n) _____ is the right to use a program or app. (163)
   a. license agreement ✓
   b. product activation
   c. software registration
   d. automatic update

3. _____ software is an application that allows users to organize data in columns and rows and perform calculations on the data. (168)
   a. Spreadsheet ✓
   b. Database
   c. Presentation
   d. Document management

4. Mobile payment apps use a payment system on phones equipped with a(n) _____, which stores data that is transmitted to a contactless terminal and verified as a legitimate sale. (179)
   a. QR chip
   b. EULA
   c. NFC chip ✓
   d. trojan horse

5. _____ is a type of application that assists professionals and designers in creating engineering, architectural, and scientific designs and models. (180)
   a. Enterprise software
   b. CAD software ✓
   c. Public-domain software
   d. A software suite

6. The term _____ refers to removing unwanted areas of a photo. (182)
   a. crop ✓
   b. snip
   c. compress
   d. shrink

7. A(n) _____ is a device intended to stop network intrusions before they attempt to affect your computer or network maliciously. (190)
   a. anti-spam program
   b. pop-under blocker
   c. hardware firewall ✓
   d. quarantine drive

8. _____ is a small text file that a web server stores on your computer. (192)
   a. A pop-under blocker
   b. A cookie ✓
   c. Adware
   d. Spyware

Checkpoint

Matching   Match the terms with their definitions.

D __ 1. tools (158)

B __ 2. shareware (161)

E __ 3. software as a service (162)

I __ 4. QR code (178)

G __ 5. CBT (184)

F __ 6. personal firewall (189)

A __ 7. payload (190)

C __ 8. worm (190)

J __ 9. quarantine (191)

H __ 10. phishing (193)

a. destructive event or prank a virus was created to deliver

b. copyrighted software that is distributed at no cost for a trial period

c. malware that resides in active memory and replicates itself over a network to infect computers and devices, using up the system resources and possibly shutting down the system

d. program that enables you to perform maintenance-type tasks usually related to managing devices, media, and programs used by computers and mobile devices

e. computing environment where an Internet server hosts and deploys applications

f. security tool that detects and protects a personal computer and its data from unauthorized intrusions

g. type of education in which students learn by using and completing exercises with instructional software

h. scam in which a perpetrator sends an official looking email message that attempts to obtain personal and/or financial information

i. square-shaped graphic that represents a web address or other information

j. separate area of a hard drive that holds an infected file until the infection can be removed

✳ Consider This   Answer the following questions in the format specified by your instructor.

1. Answer the critical thinking questions posed at the end of these elements in this chapter: Ethics & Issues (165, 175, 183, 189), How To (173, 182, 186, 196), Mini Features (178, 187, 190), Secure IT (162, 174, 179, 192, 193), and Technology @ Work (199).

2. What is the role of the operating system? (158)

3. What is system software? (158)

4. What are the advantages of open source software? (161)

5. Why do app developers opt for web delivery? (161)

6. What is the difference between software registration and product activation? (162)

7. What activities does a license agreement restrict? (163)

8. What does it mean to edit a project? (165)

9. What is the clipboard? (165)

10. What is meant by font style? (166)

11. How often should you save a project? (166)

12. How does a spreadsheet organize data? (169)

13. How are cells identified in a spreadsheet? (169)

14. When might you choose to use a database instead of a spreadsheet? (170)

15. What features are included in personal finance software? (174)

16. What steps can you take to safeguard your funds and identity when using personal finance apps? (174)

17. Who might use CAD? (180)

18. Should journalists edit or enhance digital photos? Why or why not? (183)

19. What tasks can you accomplish using mapping apps? (187)

20. How does a personal firewall protect your computer? (189)

21. What happens during the delivery phase of a virus? (190)

22. How do a virus, worm, trojan horse, and rootkit differ? (190)

23. In reference to malware, what is a quarantine? (191)

24. What is a phishing scam? (193)

25. Why is spam potentially dangerous? (193)

26. What are the different types of file, disk, and system management tools? (194)

27. How does a search tool locate a file on your computer or mobile device? (195)

28. What is a fragmented disk? (197)

29. How does fragmentation affect a computer's performance? (197)

30. What tasks does a PC maintenance tool perform? (198)

✳ Problem Solving

The Problem Solving exercises extend your knowledge of chapter concepts by seeking solutions to practical problems with technology that you may encounter at home, school, work, or with nonprofit organizations. The Collaboration exercise should be completed with a team.

Instructions: You often can solve problems with technology in multiple ways. Determine a solution to the problems in these exercises by using one or more resources available to you (such as a computer or mobile device, articles on the web or in print, blogs, podcasts, videos, television, user guides, other individuals, electronics or computer stores, etc.). Describe your solution, along with the resource(s) used, in the format requested by your instructor (brief report, presentation, discussion, blog post, video, or other means).

Personal

1. Antivirus Program Not Updating   You are attempting to update your antivirus program with the latest virus definitions, but you receive an error message. What steps will you take to resolve this issue?

2. Operating System Does Not Load   Each time you turn on your computer, the operating system attempts to load for approximately 30 seconds and then the computer restarts. You have tried multiple times to turn your computer off and on, but it keeps restarting when the operating system is trying to load. What are your next steps?

3. Unwanted Programs   When you displayed a list of programs installed on your computer so that you could uninstall one, you noticed several installed programs that you do not remember installing. Why might these programs be on your computer?

Source: Microsoft

4. News Not Updating   Each morning, you run an app on your smartphone to view the news for the current day. For the past week, however, you notice that the news displayed in the app is out of date. In fact, the app now is displaying news that is nearly one week old. Why might the app not be updating? What are your next steps?

5. Incompatible App   You are using your Android tablet to browse for apps in the Google Play store. You found an app you want to download, but you are unable to download it because a message states it is incompatible with your device. Why might the app be incompatible with your device?

Professional

6. Videoconference Freezes   While conducting a videoconference with colleagues around the country, the audio sporadically cuts out and the video freezes. You have attempted several times to terminate and then reestablish the connection, but the same problem continues to occur. What might be the problem?

7. License Agreement   You are planning to work from home for several days, but you are unsure of whether you are allowed to install a program you use at work on your home computer. What steps will you take to determine whether you are allowed to install the software on your home computer?

8. Low on Space   The computer in your office is running low on free space. You have attempted to remove as many files as possible, but the remaining programs and files are necessary to perform your daily job functions. What steps might you take to free enough space on the computer?

9. Unacceptable File Size   Your boss has asked you to design a new company logo using a graphics application installed on your computer. When you save the logo and send it to your boss, she responds that the file size is too large and tells you to find a way to decrease the file size. What might you do to make the image file size smaller?

10. Disc Burning Not Working   While attempting to back up some files on your computer on an optical disc, the disc burning software on your computer reports a problem and ejects the disc. When you check the contents of the disc, the files you are trying to back up are not there. What might be wrong?

Collaboration

11. Technology in Entertainment   The film department at a local high school is considering developing a movie and has asked for your help. The film teacher would like to incorporate technology wherever possible, in hopes that it would decrease the cost of the movie's production. Form a team of three people to determine what technology can be used to assist in the movie's production. One team member should research the type of technology that can be used during the filming process. Another team member should research the types of hardware and software available for editing footage, and the third team member should research the hardware and software requirements for producing and distributing the media.

The How To: Your Turn exercises present general guidelines for fundamental skills when using a computer or mobile device and then require that you determine how to apply these general guidelines to a specific program or situation.

How To: Your Turn ✳

Discover More: Visit this chapter's premium content to challenge yourself with **additional How To: Your Turn exercises**, which include App Adventure.

Instructions: You often can complete tasks using technology in multiple ways. Figure out how to perform the tasks described in these exercises by using one or more resources available to you (such as a computer or mobile device, articles on the web or in print, online or program help, user guides, blogs, podcasts, videos, other individuals, trial and error, etc.). Summarize your 'how to' steps, along with the resource(s) used, in the format requested by your instructor (brief report, presentation, discussion, blog post, video, or other means).

1 Obtain Help about Programs and Apps

Multiple ways are provided to obtain help while using the programs and apps on a computer or mobile device. The program or app developer usually includes a Help feature in the program and/or online. In addition, third parties often post resources online that can provide further assistance. The following steps describe how to obtain help about various programs and apps using various methods.

Help System

You typically can access help in a program or app using one of the following methods:

- Tap or click the Help or Information icon in the program or app. The appearance of Help or Information icons may vary, but typically they are identified by a question mark or the letter 'i' formatted in italic.
- Navigate the program or app's menu to locate the Help command.
- If you are using a program or app on a Windows laptop or desktop, press the F1 key on the keyboard to display Help content.

Online Help

Online help usually is available from the program or app developer. The following steps describe how to obtain online help.

a. Navigate to the program or app developer's website.
b. Locate, and then tap or click a Help or Support link.
c. Select the program or app for which you wish to obtain help to display the help information.

Searching for Help

In addition to obtaining help from within a program or app or on the developer's website, you also can search the web for help as described in the following steps.

a. Navigate to a search engine, such as google.com or yahoo.com.
b. Type the program or app name, as well as the type of help for which you are searching, as the search text, and then press the ENTER key or tap or click the Search (or a similar) button.
c. Scroll through the search results and then tap or click the search result to display more information. Be aware that not all help originates from reputable or accurate sources.

Exercises

1. Under what circumstances would you use each of these methods to obtain help with a program or app you are using?
2. Compare and contrast the different methods of obtaining help. Which method do you think is the best? Why?
3. What are some reputable websites that can provide you with help for the operating system installed on your computer? Why do you consider them reputable?

2 Compress/Uncompress Files and Folders

You may want to compress files if your hard drive is running out of available space. While the operating system may be able to compress some files by 50 percent or more, other files' sizes may not decrease significantly when they are compressed. Compressed files typically are stored by default in a file with a .zip file extension. The following steps describe how to compress a file or folder and then uncompress (expand or extract) the compressed file.

a. Press and hold or right-click the file(s) or folders you wish to compress to display a shortcut menu.
b. Tap or click the option to compress the file(s) or folder(s). (You may need to select a Send to or other command to display the compression options.)
c. If necessary, type the desired file name for the compressed file.

Uncompressing (or expanding) compressed files or folders returns them to their original form. The following steps uncompress a compressed file.

a. Double-tap or double-click the compressed file.
b. If necessary, tap or click the option to uncompress (expand or extract) the file.

or

a. Press and hold or right-click the compressed file to display a shortcut menu.
b. Tap or click the option to uncompress (expand or extract) the file.

✳ How To: Your Turn

Exercises

1. In addition to the operating system's built-in functionality to compress files and folders, what other programs and apps exist that can compress files and folders?
2. In addition to trying to free space on your storage device, for what other reasons might you want to compress files and folders?
3. Try compressing various types of files on your hard drive, such as a Word document and an image. Compare the file sizes before and after compression. What did you notice with each type of file?

❸ View Current Virus Threats

One important way to protect your computer or mobile device from viruses is to be aware of current threats. Several websites exist that not only provide a list of current virus threats but also describe how best to protect your computer or mobile device from these threats. As new virus threats are introduced, it is important to make sure your antivirus program is updated and running properly. The following steps describe how to view a list of current virus threats.

a. Run a browser and then navigate to a search engine of your choice.
b. Perform a search for websites that display current virus threats.
c. Review the search results and visit at least two websites that display current virus threats.
d. View the list of virus threats on each of these websites.

or

a. Run a browser and then navigate to a search engine of your choice.
b. Perform a search for websites created by companies that make antivirus software. Some companies that make antivirus software include Symantec, McAfee, and Microsoft.
c. Navigate to one of these company's websites and then search for a link to a webpage displaying current virus threats.
d. Tap or click the link to display current virus threats.

Courtesy of Checkpoint Software Technologies Ltd.

Exercises

1. Which websites did you access? Compare these websites and determine which you think provided the most helpful information. Why, in your opinion, does the website you chose provide the best information?
2. Has your computer or mobile device ever been infected with a virus? If so, what steps have you taken to remove the virus?
3. Is your computer or mobile device adequately protected from viruses? What steps do you take to keep your computer safe?

❹ Back Up Your Computer

Backing up your computer is an important way to protect your programs, apps, and data from loss. The frequency at which people back up their computers can vary. For instance, if you create and modify a lot of files on your computer, you may choose to back up your computer frequently. If you rarely use your computer or primarily use your computer for answering email messages and browsing the web, you might not back up your computer as often. The following steps guide you through the process of backing up a computer.

a. Decide which backup program you wish to use. Some operating systems have built-in tools you can use to back up a computer, or you can install a third-party program.
b. Run the program you will use to back up the computer.
c. If necessary, connect the storage device, such as an external hard drive, you will use to store the backup. If you plan to store the backup on an optical disc or another hard drive that already is installed, you will not need to connect an additional storage device.
d. Make sure the storage medium has enough available space for the backed up files. If you are storing the backup on optical discs, make sure you have enough optical discs for the backup.
e. Select the type of backup (full, incremental, differential, or selective) you wish to perform.
f. If you are performing a selective backup, choose the files, programs, and apps you wish to include in the backup.
g. Run the backup. The backup process may take up to several hours, depending on the number of files you are including in the backup.
h. If you are storing the backup on optical discs, the backup program may prompt you to insert new, blank optical discs throughout the backup process.

How To: Your Turn

i. When the backup is complete, store the backup in a safe location. In the event you lose data or information on the computer, you will need to retrieve the backup.

following steps describe how to share your online calendar.

a. If necessary, run a browser and navigate to an online calendar.

b. Display the calendar's settings.

c. Select the option to display the calendar's sharing settings.

d. Specify with whom you want to share the calendar.

e. Determine your sharing settings for each person. For example, you may select whether a person only can view your calendar or view and edit your calendar. You also can select the level of detail you want to share with others. For example, you can share the times you are free or busy, or you can share the specific details for each appointment.

f. If necessary, repeat the two previous steps for each additional person with whom you wish to share the calendar.

g. Save the settings.

h. Verify the people with whom you shared the calendar are able to access the calendar.

Source: Acronis

Exercises

1. How often do you feel you should back up your computer? Justify your answer.

2. Which storage medium do you feel is most appropriate for your backup? Justify your answer.

3. Research at least three programs that you can use to back up your computer. Which programs did you research? Which program or app do you feel is the best? Why?

Exercises

1. For what other reasons might you share your calendar?

2. In addition to the steps outlined previously, in what other ways can you share your calendar online?

3. In addition to sharing online calendars, is it possible to share calendars you create in programs such as Microsoft Outlook? If so, how?

5 **Share Your Online Calendar**

If you keep track of your meetings, appointments, and other obligations using an online calendar, you might want to share your calendar with others so that they know when you are available. For instance, you might want to share your calendar with fellow employees so that they can verify your availability before scheduling meetings. Your family members may share their calendars with one another so that it is easier to plan family events when everyone is available. The

Google Inc.

✳ Internet Research

The Internet Research exercises broaden your understanding of chapter concepts by requiring that you search for information on the web.

Discover More: Visit this chapter's premium content to **challenge yourself with additional Internet Research exercises**, which include Search Sleuth, Green Computing, Ethics in Action, You Review It, and Exploring Technology Careers.

Instructions: Use a search engine or another search tool to locate the information requested or answers to questions presented in the exercises. Describe your findings, along with the search term(s) you used and your web source(s), in the format requested by your instructor (brief report, presentation, discussion, blog post, video, or other means).

1 Making Use of the Web
Website Creation and Management

Retailers and organizations realize the importance of having a website to promote their goods and services. An online presence helps a business connect with an audience and ultimately builds trust and respect. Innovative and dynamic websites deliver information to current and potential customers and clients. Creating these websites requires a methodology of planning, designing, creating, hosting, and maintaining. A business must identify the website's purpose, demographics of the target audience, appropriate content and functionality, page layout, and usability. Once the website is implemented, it must be monitored to determine usage. Logs list the number of visitors, the browsers they used, and usage patterns. In addition, the website should be maintained to update content and features.

Products are available to help build and manage a website. Most offer well-designed templates that can be customized to accommodate specific personal and business needs. They can include calendars, photos, videos, maps, and blogs. Some of these design and management tools, such as those offered on Google Sites, are available at no cost, while others require fees for specific features, such as technical support or exclusive designs.

Research This: Visit Google Sites and two other online content management systems for building websites. Compare these web apps by creating a table using these headings: Name, Number of Templates, Price, Maximum Storage, Customer Support, and Features. The Features column could include the availability of items such as customizable color schemes, e-commerce, drag and drop, website logs and analytics, and mobile editing. Which website builder would you choose if you were creating a website? Why?

2 Social Media

Gaming via social media has seen explosive growth in recent years, especially among adult males. Exponential gaming growth has spawned companion businesses that facilitate and manage the gaming experience. Some mobile and desktop apps provide gamers a portal for tracking all their online gaming results in a central location that can be shared with friends and others with similar game interests. These apps integrate with the major Internet messaging services, have personalized news feeds, and incorporate a "suggestion" engine for new game discoveries. Many gaming blogs offer game tricks, work-arounds, and hidden features. Beginning gamers can engage their minds during downtime and expand their circle of online friends.

Research This: Visit at least two online social networks for gamers. How many games are shown? Which topics are featured in community discussions and live chats? Are rewards available? If so, what are they? Which online leagues and tournaments are offered? What are some of the latest news articles about specific games and the gaming industry? Have you participated in gaming online social networks? If so, which ones?

Google Inc.

Internet Research ✷

3 **Search Skills**

Narrowing Your Search Results

One strategy for narrowing search results is to specify what you are or are not looking for as part of your search text. Precede words with a plus sign (+) if you want to ensure that they appear in your search results, and precede a word with a minus sign (-) if you want to exclude that word from search results. For example, typing the phrase, windows +microsoft, will search for information about the operating system; typing the phrase, windows –microsoft, also will find information about windows that are made of glass.

Include the keyword, and, between words or phrases in search text if you want search results to include both words or phrases, or the keyword, or, if search results containing either word or phrase are acceptable. Group terms with parentheses to clarify search text. For example, type the phrase, iPhone and "Steve Jobs" (including the quotation marks), to search for articles about the inventor of the iPhone. Type the phrase, (iPhone or iPad) and "Steve Jobs" (including the parentheses and quotation marks), to search for information about iPhone or iPad devices that also mentions Steve Jobs.

Google, Inc.

Research This: Create search text using the techniques described above or in previous Search Skills exercises, and type it in a search engine to answer these questions. (1) What is an open source FTP application that has versions for both Windows and Mac? (2) Other than TurboTax, what are two examples of online tax preparation software? (3) Find reviews comparing Internet Explorer, Edge, Chrome, and Firefox browsers. (4) What are the more popular calendar management and task management apps on Google Play?

4 **Security**

Virus hoaxes are widespread and sometimes cause panic among Internet users. Secure IT 4-4 in this chapter gives advice on recognizing and avoiding virus hoaxes. Snopes.com provides further insight on the sources and variations of a wide variety of rumors, deceptions, and folklore.

Research This: Visit snopes.com and type the search text phrase, virus hoaxes & realities, in the Search box at the top of the page. Review the list of the more recent real (indicated by a green dot) and false (indicated by a red dot) rumors circulating on the Internet. Which are the three newest actual warnings, and which are the three latest virus hoaxes? What harm is predicted to occur if a user downloads each of these real or false viruses or views a website laden with malware? What is the origin of the website's name, Snopes?

5 **Cloud Services**

Photo Editing (SaaS)

Online photo editing apps provide browser-based capabilities to modify digital images, and often contain many similar features as their desktop counterparts. They are an example of SaaS (software as a service), a service of cloud computing that provides access to software solutions accessed through a browser. In addition to drawing shapes, touching up colors, and adding filters to images, online photo editing apps allow users to access, store, and share their photos on the cloud. Online photo editing apps often include the ability to share photos with friends easily by sending a link, or posting the photo to online social networks.

Research This: (1) Use a search engine to research various online photo editing apps. Compare the features of two of them as you explore their capabilities. Summarize your findings in a table, regarding image formats you can import or save, sharing capabilities, special editing features, and ways to organize photos online. Which features take advantage of the fact that the app is cloud based? (2) If you have access to computers running two different operating systems, such as Windows and Mac, try running the photo editing app in a browser on both computers. What similarities and differences do you notice between the two versions?

Critical Thinking

The Critical Thinking exercises challenge your assessment and decision-making skills by presenting real-world situations associated with chapter concepts. The Collaboration exercise should be completed with a team.

Instructions: Evaluate the situations below, using personal experiences and one or more resources available to you (such as articles on the web or in print, blogs, podcasts, videos, television, user guides, other individuals, electronics or computer stores, etc.). Perform the tasks requested in each exercise and share your deliverables in the format requested by your instructor (brief report, presentation, discussion, blog post, video, or other means).

1. File, Disk, and System Management Tools

You are the director of information technology at a company that frequently hires student interns. The interns tend to have limited experience with using file, disk, and system management tools. As part of your job, you lead workshops that teach the interns the many tasks and functions they can perform using these tools.

Do This: Choose three categories of tools, such as disk cleanup, PC maintenance, and file compression. Determine whether your computer's operating system includes these tools. Use the web to research popular tools for each category, whether they can be purchased separately or if they are available only as part of an operating system, and the costs for each tool. Choose one program from each category, and read user reviews and articles by industry experts. Describe situations where you would use each type of tool. Share any experiences you have with using the tools.

2. Web and Mobile App Comparison

You recently purchased a new smartphone and want to research mobile apps that also have accompanying web apps.

Do This: Choose three categories of apps, and find an example for each that has both a free web and mobile version. Read user reviews of each app, and search for articles by industry experts. Research any known safety risks for the apps. If you determine the app is safe, have access to the appropriate device, and would like to test the mobile app, you can download it

to a smartphone or other mobile device. Try accessing the web app on a computer. Using your experience or research, note the differences in functionality between the web and mobile app. Is one or the other easier to use? Why or why not?

3. Case Study

Amateur Sports League You are the new manager for a nonprofit amateur soccer league. The league needs productivity software in order to keep track of participant and budget information and to prepare flyers. You prepare information about productivity software options to present to the board of directors.

Do This: Use the web to research popular word processing, spreadsheet, and accounting software. Choose three programs from each category. List common features of each, find pricing information, and note any feedback or ratings by users. Which programs would you recommend? Why? Describe the steps involved in developing a project, creating a flyer for the league as an example. Identify possible uses the league may have for the spreadsheet and accounting software. Compile your findings.

Source: © Cengage Learning

Collaboration

4. Educational Program and App Effectiveness

The principal of the local elementary school has recommended that educational apps should play a major role in the learning process, believing that these apps enable students to learn at their own pace. Some enable teachers to track an individual student's progress and understanding.

Do This: Form a three-member team and research the use of educational apps. Each member of your team should choose a different type of app, such as flash cards, testing, or CBT. List the advantages and disadvantages of using that type of app. If possible, download or access a free version of an educational app from each category and spend some time using it. Read user reviews of popular apps, and search for articles by industry experts. Would you recommend using an app for educational purposes? Why or why not? Meet with your team, and discuss and compile your findings.

DIGITAL SECURITY, ETHICS, AND PRIVACY:
Threats, Issues, and Defenses

5

Users should take precautions to protect their digital content.

"I am careful when browsing the web, use antivirus software, and never open email messages from unknown senders. I use a cloud storage provider to back up my computer and mobile devices. What more do I need to know about digital safety and security?"

While you may be familiar with some of the content in this chapter, do you know how to . . .

- Avoid risks when playing online games?
- Determine if an email message has been spoofed?
- Tell if your computer or device is functioning as a zombie?
- Set up a personal firewall?
- Protect computers and devices from viruses and other malware?
- Protect your passwords?
- Use two-step verification?
- Prevent your data from being lost on the cloud?
- Follow a disaster recovery plan?
- Secure your wireless network?
- Safeguard your hardware and data from a disaster?
- Protect against a phishing scam?
- Protect yourself from social engineering scams?
- Evaluate your electronic profile?

In this chapter, you will discover how to perform these tasks along with much more information essential to this course. For additional content available that accompanies this chapter, visit the free resources and premium content. Refer to the Preface and the Intro chapter for information about how to access these and other additional instructor-assigned support materials.

© iStockPhoto / Vertigo3d

Digital Security Risks

Today, people rely on technology to create, store, and manage their critical information. Thus, it is important that computers and mobile devices, along with the data and programs they store, are accessible and available when needed. It also is crucial that users take measures to protect or safeguard their computers, mobile devices, data, and programs from loss, damage, and misuse. For example, organizations must ensure that sensitive data and information, such as credit records, employee and customer data, and purchase information, is secure. Home users must ensure that their credit card numbers are secure when they make online purchases.

A **digital security risk** is any event or action that could cause a loss of or damage to computer or mobile device hardware, software, data, information, or processing capability. The more common digital security risks include Internet and network attacks, unauthorized access and use, hardware theft, software theft, information theft, and system failure (Figure 5-1).

While some breaches to digital security are accidental, many are intentional. Some intruders do not disrupt a computer or device's functionality; they merely access data, information, or programs on the computer or mobile device before signing out. Other intruders indicate some evidence of their presence either by leaving a message or by deliberately altering or damaging data.

Cybercrime

An intentional breach to digital security often involves a deliberate act that is against the law. Any illegal act involving the use of a computer or related devices generally is referred to as a **computer crime**. The term **cybercrime** refers to online or Internet-based illegal acts such as distributing malicious software or committing identity theft. Software used by cybercriminals sometimes is called *crimeware*. Today, combating cybercrime is one of the FBI's top priorities.

unauthorized access
and use

intercepting
wireless
communications

Internet and
network attacks

http://www.

Virus Alert!
Warning! Threat detected!
A malicious item has been detected

virus attack

hardware theft

stolen computer

Digital
Security
Risks

system failure

lightning strike

software theft

illegal copying

information theft

stolen identity

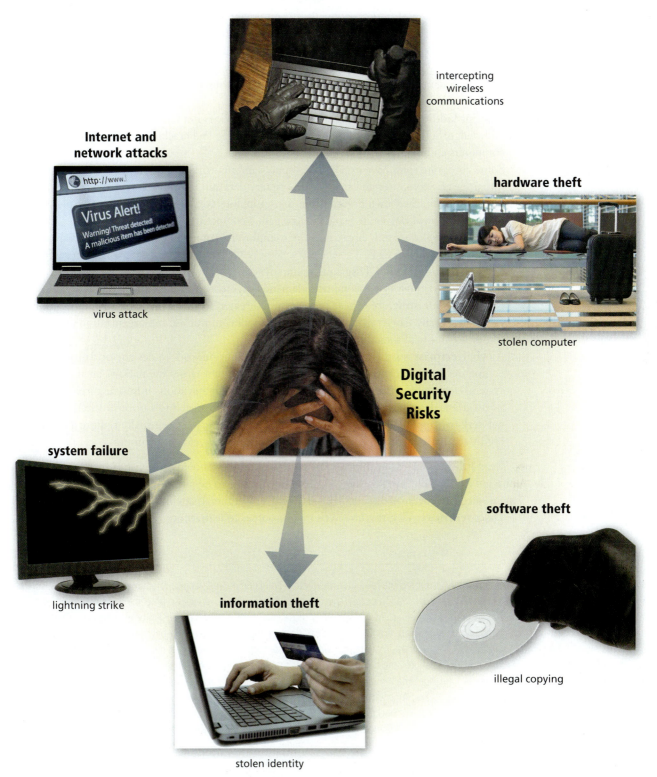

Figure 5-1   Computers and mobile devices, along with the data and programs they store, are exposed to several types of digital security risks.

© jamdesign / Fotolia; © iStockPhoto / BrianAJackson; © VRD / Fotolia; © iStockPhoto / Kenishirotie; © Cengage Learning; © JUPITER IMAGES/ Brand X /Alamy

Perpetrators of cybercrime typically fall into one of these basic categories: hacker, cracker, script kiddie, corporate spy, unethical employee, cyberextortionist, and cyberterrorist.

- The term **hacker**, although originally a complimentary word for a computer enthusiast, now has a derogatory meaning and refers to someone who accesses a computer or network illegally. Some hackers claim the intent of their security breaches is to improve security.

- A **cracker** also is someone who accesses a computer or network illegally but has the intent of destroying data, stealing information, or other malicious action. Both hackers and crackers have advanced computer and network skills.

Internet Research

How do script kiddies use malware?

Search for: script kiddie malware

- A **script kiddie** has the same intent as a cracker but does not have the technical skills and knowledge. Script kiddies often use prewritten hacking and cracking programs to break into computers and networks.

- Some corporate spies have excellent computer and networking skills and are hired to break into a specific computer and steal its proprietary data and information, or to help identify security risks in their own organization. Unscrupulous companies hire corporate spies, a practice known as corporate espionage, to gain a competitive advantage.

- Unethical employees may break into their employers' computers for a variety of reasons. Some simply want to exploit a security weakness. Others seek financial gains from selling confidential information. Disgruntled employees may want revenge.

- A **cyberextortionist** is someone who demands payment to stop an attack on an organization's technology infrastructure. These perpetrators threaten to expose confidential information, exploit a security flaw, or launch an attack that will compromise the organization's network — if they are not paid a sum of money.

- A **cyberterrorist** is someone who uses the Internet or network to destroy or damage computers for political reasons. The cyberterrorist might target the nation's air traffic control system, electricity-generating companies, or a telecommunications infrastructure. The term, *cyberwarfare*, describes an attack whose goal ranges from disabling a government's computer network to crippling a country. Cyberterrorism and cyberwarfare usually require a team of highly skilled individuals, millions of dollars, and several years of planning.

Read Ethics & Issues 5-1 to consider how cybercriminals should be punished. Some organizations hire individuals previously convicted of computer crimes to help identify security risks and implement safeguards because these individuals know how criminals attempt to breach security.

Discover More: Visit this chapter's free resources to learn more about cybercriminals.

✳ ETHICS & ISSUES 5-1

How Should Cybercriminals Be Punished?
A hacker received a 10-year jail sentence for selling credit card information from several large corporations, costing one company approximately $200 million. In another case, a hacker accessed the personal online accounts of celebrities, as well as people he knew, and distributed revealing photos and information. He also received 10 years in jail, in part for the emotional distress his actions caused his victims. Do these sentences seem too harsh? Some legal experts point out that the punishment given to some hackers is not in line with crimes of a violent nature.

In addition to the extent of the punishment, other issues surrounding

cybercrime laws include whether an action is defamation or free speech and who should be punished, the hacker or those who were hacked. If a hacker's actions damage the reputation of another via libel or slander, should the hacker be prosecuted under the defamation law or be protected under the First Amendment? A *hacktivist*, which is a type of hacker whose actions are politically or socially motivated, believes his or her actions should be protected under the First Amendment. Should companies whose systems have been breached be punished for their lax security? The Federal Trade Commission (FTC) has fined companies whose security flaws enabled hackers to access their systems.

Legislators have made efforts to define and prevent cybercrime, both with new laws and the expansion of existing laws. Cybercrime laws vary between states and countries, making it difficult to establish what is illegal. Determining who has jurisdiction over a case can create more legal hassles. For example, which area is responsible for determining punishment: where the victim(s) resides or where the criminal lives?

Consider This: Should hacktivism be punishable? Why or why not? Should corporations be liable for damages caused by hackers? Why or why not? Should hackers receive comparable punishment to violent criminals? Why or why not?

Internet and Network Attacks

Information transmitted over networks has a higher degree of security risk than information kept on an organization's premises. In an organization, network administrators usually take measures to protect a network from security risks. On the Internet, where no central administrator is present, the security risk is greater. Internet and network attacks that jeopardize security include malware, botnets, denial of service attacks, back doors, and spoofing.

Malware

Recall that **malware**, short for *malicious software*, consists of programs that act without a user's knowledge and deliberately alter the operations of computers and mobile devices. Table 5-1 summarizes common types of malware, all of which have been discussed in previous chapters. Some malware contains characteristics in two or more classes. For example, a single threat could contain elements of a virus, worm, and trojan horse.

Malware can deliver its *payload*, or destructive event or prank, on a computer or mobile device in a variety of ways, such as when a user opens an infected file, runs an infected program, connects an unprotected computer or mobile device to a network, or when a certain condition or event occurs, such as the computer's clock changing to a specific date. A common way that computers and mobile devices become infected with viruses and other malware is through users opening infected email attachments (Figure 5-2). Read Secure IT 5-1 to learn about how malware can affect online gaming.

Internet Research
Does a list of known malware exist?
Search for: malware list

Table 5-1   Common Types of Malware

Type	Description
Virus	A potentially damaging program that affects, or infects, a computer or mobile device negatively by altering the way the computer or device works without the user's knowledge or permission.
Worm	A program that copies itself repeatedly, for example in memory or on a network, using up resources and possibly shutting down the computer, device, or network.
Trojan horse	A program that hides within or looks like a legitimate program. Unlike a virus or worm, a trojan horse does not replicate itself to other computers or devices.
Rootkit	A program that hides in a computer or mobile device and allows someone from a remote location to take full control of the computer or device.
Spyware	A program placed on a computer or mobile device without the user's knowledge that secretly collects information about the user and then communicates the information it collects to some outside source while the user is online.
Adware	A program that displays an online advertisement in a banner, pop-up window, or pop-under window on webpages, email messages, or other Internet services.

Discover More: Visit this chapter's free resources to learn more about malware.

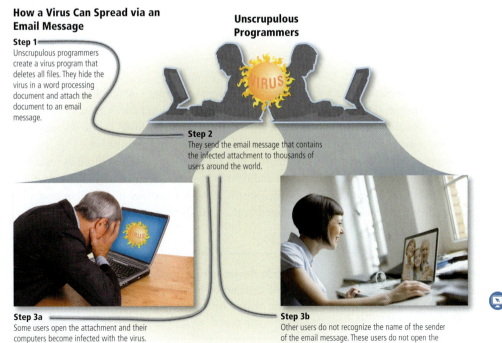

How a Virus Can Spread via an Email Message

Unscrupulous Programmers

Step 1
Unscrupulous programmers create a virus program that deletes all files. They hide the virus in a word processing document and attach the document to an email message.

Step 2
They send the email message that contains the infected attachment to thousands of users around the world.

Step 3a
Some users open the attachment and their computers become infected with the virus.

Step 3b
Other users do not recognize the name of the sender of the email message. These users do not open the email message — instead they immediately delete the email message and continue using their computers. These users' computers are not infected with the virus.

Figure 5-2 This figure shows how a virus can spread via an email message.
© Cengage Learning;
© iStockphoto / Steve Cukrov;
© iStockphoto / Casarsa

⚙ **CONSIDER THIS** ────────────────────────────────

What if you cannot remove malware?
In extreme cases, in order to remove malware from a computer or mobile device, you may need to erase, or reformat, an infected computer's hard drive, or reset a mobile device to its factory settings. For this reason, it is critical you have uninfected (clean) backups of all files. Consider creating recovery media when you purchase a new computer, and be sure to keep all installation media in the event you need to reinstall the computer's operating system and your apps. Seek advice from a technology specialist before performing a format or reformat instruction on your media.

🌀 **Internet Research**

What are the latest malware threats?

Search for: malware news

⚙ **SECURE IT 5-1** ────────────────────────────────

📃 **Play It Safe to Avoid Online Gaming Risks**

Gamers often understand general security issues regarding online behavior, but they may not be aware of a different set of technology and social risks they may encounter as they interact in the online world. Anyone experiencing the joys of playing games online or playing games with others through online services should realize that thieves and hackers lurking behind the scenes may take advantage of security holes and vulnerabilities that can turn a gaming session into a nightmare.

Viruses, worms, and malware can be hidden in downloaded game files, mobile apps, email message attachments, and messaging software. In addition, messages on online social networks may encourage gamers to visit fraudulent websites filled with malware. If the game requires a connection to the Internet, then any computer connected to the game's

server is subject to security cyberthreats. Thieves can take control of a remote computer that does not have a high level of security protection and use it to control other computers, or they could break into the computer and install malware to discover personal information.

Malicious users know that the gaming community uses social media intensely, so they also create accounts and attempt to mislead uninformed users into revealing personal information. The thieves may claim to have software updates and free games, when they really are luring users to bogus websites that ask users to set up profiles and accounts.

Gamers should follow these practices to increase their security:

- Before downloading any software or apps, including patches to games, or disclosing any private details, check the developer to be certain the website or the person making the request is legitimate.

- Read the permissions notices to learn what information is being requested or being collected. Avoid games requiring passwords to be saved to an online account on a smartphone.

- Exercise extreme caution if the game requires ActiveX or JavaScript to be enabled or if it must be played in administrator mode.

- Use a firewall and make exceptions to allow only trusted individuals to access your computer or mobile device when playing multiplayer online games.

- Do not share personal information with other gamers whom you meet online.

⚙ **Consider This:** Have you played online games or downloaded gaming apps and followed the advice listed here? How will you change your gaming behavior now that you are aware of specific security threats?

Botnets

A **botnet**, or *zombie army*, is a group of compromised computers or mobile devices connected to a network, such as the Internet, that are used to attack other networks, usually for nefarious purposes. A compromised computer or device, known as a **zombie**, is one whose owner is unaware the computer or device is being controlled remotely by an outsider.

A *bot* is a program that performs a repetitive task on a network. Cybercriminals install malicious bots on unprotected computers and devices to create a botnet. The perpetrator then uses the botnet to send spam via email, spread viruses and other malware, or commit a distributed denial of service attack (discussed in the next section).

⚙ **CONSIDER THIS** ────────────────────────────────

How can you tell if your computer or mobile device is functioning as a zombie?
Your computer or mobile device may be a zombie if you notice an unusually high drive activity, a slower than normal Internet connection, or connected devices becoming increasingly unresponsive. The chances of your computer or devices becoming part of a botnet greatly increase if your devices are not protected by an effective firewall.

Denial of Service Attacks

A **denial of service attack** (**DoS attack**) is an assault whose purpose is to disrupt computer access to an Internet service, such as the web or email. Perpetrators carry out a DoS attack in a variety of ways. For example, they may use an unsuspecting computer to send an influx of confusing data messages or useless traffic to a computer network. The victim computer network slows down considerably and eventually becomes unresponsive or unavailable, blocking legitimate visitors from accessing the network.

A more devastating type of DoS attack is the *distributed DoS attack* (*DDoS attack*) in which a zombie army is used to attack computers or computer networks. DDoS attacks have been able to stop operations temporarily at numerous websites, including powerhouses such as Yahoo!, eBay, Amazon.com, and CNN.com.

The damage caused by a DoS or DDoS attack usually is extensive. During the outage, retailers lose sales from customers, news websites and search engines lose revenue from advertisers, and time-sensitive information may be delayed. Repeated attacks could tarnish reputations, causing even greater losses.

Internet Research
Are DoS attacks still prevalent?
Search for: news of dos attacks

✳ CONSIDER THIS

Why would someone execute a Dos or DDoS attack?
Perpetrators have a variety of motives for executing a DoS or DDoS attack. Hactivists, or those who disagree with the beliefs or actions of a particular organization, claim political anger motivates their attacks. Some perpetrators use the attack as a vehicle for extortion. Others simply want the recognition, even though it is negative.

Back Doors

A **back door** is a program or set of instructions in a program that allows users to bypass security controls when accessing a program, computer, or network. Once perpetrators gain access to unsecure computers, they often install a back door or modify an existing program to include a back door, which allows them to continue to access the computer remotely without the user's knowledge. A rootkit can be a back door. Some worms leave back doors, which have been used to spread other worms or to distribute spam from the unsuspecting victim computers.

Programmers often build back doors into programs during system development. These back doors save development time because the programmer can bypass security controls while writing and testing programs. Similarly, a computer repair technician may install a back door while troubleshooting problems on a computer. If a programmer or computer repair technician fails to remove a back door, a perpetrator could use the back door to gain entry to a computer or network.

Spoofing

Spoofing is a technique intruders use to make their network or Internet transmission appear legitimate to a victim computer or network. Two common types of spoofing schemes are IP and email spoofing.

- *IP spoofing* occurs when an intruder computer fools a network into believing its IP address is associated with a trusted source. Perpetrators of IP spoofing trick their victims into interacting with the phony website. For example, the victim may provide confidential information or download files containing viruses, worms, or other malware.
- *Email spoofing* occurs when the sender's address or other components of an email header are altered so that it appears that the email message originated from a different sender. Email spoofing commonly is used in virus hoaxes, spam, and phishing scams (Figure 5-3). Read How To 5-1 to learn about how to determine if an email message has been spoofed.

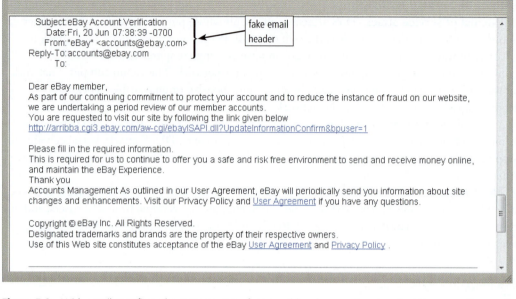

Figure 5-3 With email spoofing, the components of an email header are altered so that it appears the email message originated from a different sender.
Source: Privacy Rights Clearinghouse

HOW TO 5-1

Determine If an Email Message Has Been Spoofed

Spoofed email messages appear to originate from one source, but in reality originate from another source. Spoofed email messages often are sent by nefarious people attempting to obtain personal information. For example, an email message appearing to be sent from a reputable source, such as your financial institution, may ask you to reply with personal information, such as a password, Social Security number, or account number. If you reply, you will be sending personal information to an unknown third party that could use

the information to steal your identity, make unauthorized purchases, and more. The following steps describe some ways to determine if an email message has been spoofed.

- The email message requests personal information, such as account numbers, passwords, Social Security numbers, and credit card numbers.
- The email message contains spelling and/or grammatical errors.
- The email message encourages you to tap or click a link that takes you to another website.

- The header in the email message contains a different domain in the MessageID than the domain of the supposed sender.
- The "From" and "Reply-To" email addresses do not match.

If you ever are unsure of whether an email message was spoofed, contact the supposed sender either via phone or a new email message (do not reply to the original email message) to verify the authenticity of the message.

Consider This: Have you ever received a spoofed email message? Did you know it was spoofed? What steps did you take?

Safeguards against Internet and Network Attacks

Methods that protect computers, mobile devices, and networks from attacks include the following:

- Use antivirus software.
- Be suspicious of unsolicited email attachments.
- Scan removable media for malware before using it.
- Implement firewall solutions.
- Back up regularly.

Secure IT 1-2 in Chapter 1 provided some measures you can take to protect your computers and mobile devices from malware. Read Secure IT 5-2 for additional tips to protect home users against Internet and network attacks. The next section discusses firewalls in more depth.

BTW

Antivirus Programs
In addition to protecting against viruses and other malware, many antivirus programs also include protection from DoS and DDoS attacks.

SECURE IT 5-2

Protection from Viruses and Other Malware

It is impossible to ensure a virus or malware never will attack a computer, but you can take steps to protect your computer by following these practices:

- **Use virus protection software.** Install a reputable antivirus program and then scan the entire computer to be certain it is free of viruses and other malware. Update the antivirus program and the virus signatures (known specific patterns of viruses) regularly.

- **Use a firewall.** Set up a hardware firewall or install a software firewall that protects your network's resources from outside intrusions.

- **Be suspicious of all unsolicited email and text messages.** Never open an email message unless you are expecting it, *and* it is from a trusted source. When in doubt, ask the sender to confirm the message is legitimate before you open it. Be especially cautious when deciding whether to tap or click links in email and text messages or to open attachments.

- **Disconnect your computer from the Internet.** If you do not need Internet access, disconnect the computer from the Internet. Some security experts recommend disconnecting from the computer network before opening email attachments.

- **Download software with caution.** Download programs or apps only from websites you trust, especially those with music and video sharing software.

- **Close spyware windows.** If you suspect a pop-up or pop-under window may be spyware, close the window. Never tap or click an Agree or OK button in a suspicious window.

- **Before using any removable media, scan it for malware.** Follow this procedure even for shrink-wrapped software from major developers. Some commercial software has been infected and distributed to unsuspecting users. Never start a computer with removable media inserted in the computer unless you are certain the media are uninfected.

- **Keep current.** Install the latest updates for your computer software. Stay informed about new virus alerts and virus hoaxes.

- **Back up regularly.** In the event your computer becomes unusable due to a virus attack or other malware, you will be able to restore operations if you have a clean (uninfected) backup.

Consider This: What precautions do you take to prevent viruses and other malware from infecting your computer? What new steps will you take to attempt to protect your computer?

CONSIDER THIS

How can you determine if your computer or mobile device is vulnerable to an Internet or network attack?

You could use an **online security service,** which is a web app that evaluates your computer or mobile device to check for Internet and email vulnerabilities. The online security service then provides recommendations of how to address the vulnerabilities.

Organizations requiring assistance or information about Internet security breaches can contact or visit the website for the *Computer Emergency Response Team Coordination Center*, or *CERT/CC*, which is a federally funded Internet security research and development center.

Discover More: Visit this chapter's free resources to learn more about online security services.

Firewalls

A **firewall** is hardware and/or software that protects a network's resources from intrusion by users on another network, such as the Internet. All networked and online users should implement a firewall solution.

Organizations use firewalls to protect network resources from outsiders and to restrict employees' access to sensitive data, such as payroll or personnel records. They can implement a firewall solution themselves or outsource their needs to a company specializing in providing firewall protection.

Large organizations often route all their communications through a proxy server, which typically is a component of the firewall. A *proxy server* is a server outside the organization's network that controls which communications pass in and out of the organization's network. That is, a proxy server carefully screens all incoming and outgoing messages. Proxy servers use a variety of screening techniques. Some check the domain name or IP address of the message for legitimacy. Others require that the messages have digital signatures (discussed later in this chapter).

BTW
Technology Innovators
Discover More: Visit this chapter's free resources to learn about AVG, Intel Security, and Symantec (security product developers).

Home and small/home office users often protect their computers with a personal firewall. As discussed in Chapter 4, a **personal firewall** is a software firewall that detects and protects a personal computer and its data from unauthorized intrusions. Personal firewalls constantly monitor all transmissions to and from the computer and may inform a user of any attempted intrusions. Both Windows and Mac operating systems include firewall capabilities, including monitoring Internet traffic to and from installed applications. Read How To 5-2 for instructions about setting up a personal firewall.

Some small/home office users purchase a hardware firewall, such as a router or other device that has a built-in firewall, in addition to or instead of a personal firewall. Hardware firewalls stop malicious intrusions before they attempt to affect your computer or network. Figure 5-4 illustrates the purpose of hardware and software firewalls.

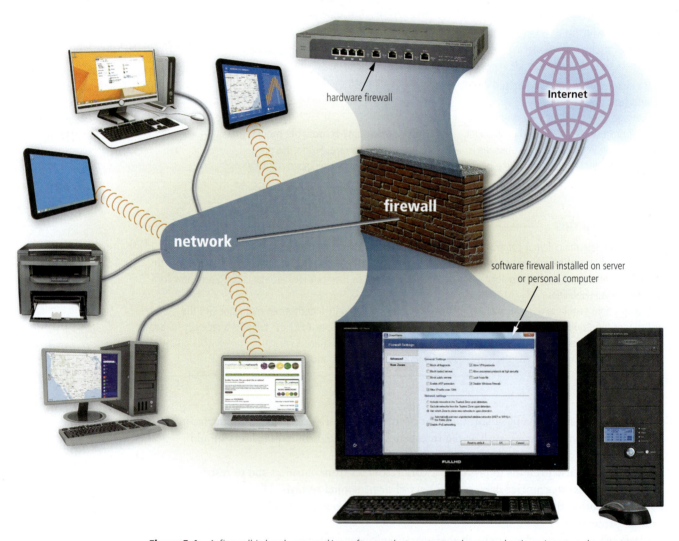

Figure 5-4 A firewall is hardware and/or software that protects a home or business's network resources from intrusion by users on another network, such as the Internet.

Courtesy of NETGEAR; © Cengage Learning; Courtesy of CheckPoint Software Technologies; © iStockphoto / Skip Odonnell; Source: Nutrition Blog Network; © iStockphoto / 123render; Source: Microsoft; © Iakov Filimonov / Shutterstock.com; © iStockphoto / Oleksiy Mark; Source: Microsoft; © iStockphoto / Ayaaz Rattansi; Source: Microsoft; © iStockphoto / Oleksiy Mark; Source: Microsoft; © Cengage Learning; Microsoft

⚙ **HOW TO 5-2**

📑 **Set Up a Personal Firewall**
A personal firewall is a program that helps protect your computer from unauthorized access by blocking certain types of communications. For example, if somebody knows the IP address of your computer and attempts to access it using a browser or other program, the personal firewall can be configured to deny the incoming connection. The following steps describe how to set up a personal firewall.

1. Locate and purchase a personal firewall. You can purchase personal firewalls online and in stores that sell software. Many operating systems include a personal firewall. Computers typically can have only one active personal firewall running at a time. If you purchase a personal firewall, you may need to disable the one that is included with the operating system.

2. If you purchase a personal firewall, follow the instructions to install the program on your computer.

3. Run the personal firewall.

4. If necessary, ensure the personal firewall is enabled.

5. Review the settings for the incoming and outgoing rules. Incoming rules display programs and services that are allowed to access your computer. Outgoing rules display programs and services on your computer that are allowed to communicate with other computers and mobile devices on your network or the Internet.

6. Back up or export your current list of incoming and outgoing rules. If your computer does not function properly after you adjust the rules (in Steps 7 and 8), you will be able to restore the current rules.

7. Adjust your incoming rules to disallow devices, programs, and services you do not want accessing your computer. Be careful adjusting these settings, as adding or removing rules may hinder a legitimate program's capability to work properly.

8. Adjust your outgoing rules to allow only appropriate programs on your computer to communicate with other computers and mobile devices on your network or the Internet. Examples include a browser, email program, or other communications programs.

9. Save your settings.

10. Test programs on your computer that require Internet access. If any do not function properly, restore the list of rules you backed up or exported in Step 6.

11. Exit the personal firewall.

⚙ **Consider This:** Which programs on your computer should have access to the Internet? Which programs should not?

Unauthorized Access and Use

Unauthorized access is the use of a computer or network without permission. *Unauthorized use* is the use of a computer or its data for unapproved or possibly illegal activities.

Home and business users can be a target of unauthorized access and use. Unauthorized use includes a variety of activities: an employee using an organization's computer to send personal email messages, an employee using the organization's word processing software to track his or her child's soccer league scores, or a perpetrator gaining access to a bank computer and performing an unauthorized transfer.

Safeguards against Unauthorized Access and Use

Organizations take several measures to help prevent unauthorized access and use. At a minimum, they should have a written *acceptable use policy* (*AUP*) that outlines the activities for which the computer and network may and may not be used. An organization's AUP should specify the acceptable use of technology by employees for personal reasons. Some organizations prohibit such use entirely. Others allow personal use on the employee's own time, such as a lunch hour. Whatever the policy, an organization should document and explain it to employees. The AUP also should specify the personal activities, if any, that are allowed on company time. For example, can employees check personal email messages or respond to personal text messages during work hours?

To protect your personal computer from unauthorized intrusions, you should disable file and printer sharing in your operating system (Figure 5-5). This security measure attempts to ensure that others cannot access your files or your printer. You also should be sure to use a firewall. The following sections address other techniques for protecting against unauthorized access and use. The technique(s) used should correspond to the degree of risk that is associated with the unauthorized access.

Figure 5-5   To protect files on your device's hard drive from hackers and other intruders, turn off file and printer sharing on your device.
Source: Microsoft

Access Controls

Many organizations use access controls to minimize the chance that a perpetrator intentionally may access or an employee accidentally may access confidential information on a computer, mobile device, or network. An *access control* is a security measure that defines who can access a computer, device, or network; when they can access it; and what actions they can take while accessing it. In addition, the computer, device, or network should maintain an *audit trail* that records in a file both successful and unsuccessful access attempts. An unsuccessful access attempt could result from a user mistyping his or her password, or it could result from a perpetrator trying thousands of passwords.

Organizations should investigate unsuccessful access attempts immediately to ensure they are not intentional breaches of security. They also should review successful access for irregularities, such as use of the computer after normal working hours or from remote computers. The security program can be configured to alert a security administrator whenever suspicious or irregular activities are suspected. In addition, an organization regularly should review users' access privilege levels to determine whether they still are appropriate.

User Names and Passwords

A **user name** — also called a *user ID* (identification), log on name, or sign in name — is a unique combination of characters, such as letters of the alphabet or numbers, that identifies one specific user. A **password** is a private combination of characters associated with the user name that allows access to certain computer resources.

Figure 5-6 Many websites that maintain personal and confidential data, such as Citibank's credit card system, require a user to enter a user name (user ID) and password.
Source: Citigroup Inc

🔅 BTW

Single Sign On
When you enter your user name into a *single sign on* account, such as for Microsoft, Google, Twitter, and Facebook, you automatically are signed in to other accounts and services. Many also recognize your information to provide additional customized content.

Most operating systems that enable multiple users to share computers and devices or that access a home or business network require users to enter a user name and a password correctly before they can access the data, information, and programs stored on a computer, mobile device, or network. Many systems that maintain financial, personal, and other confidential information also require a user name and password as part of their sign-in procedure (Figure 5-6).

Some systems assign a user name and/or password to each user. For example, a school may use a combination of letters from a student's first and last names as a user name. For example, Brittany Stearn's user name might be stearns_brit. Some websites use your email address as the user name. Information technology (IT) departments may assign passwords so that they have a record in case the employee leaves or forgets the password.

With other systems, users select their own user names and/or passwords. Many users select a combination of their first and last names for their user names. Many online social networks, media sharing sites, and retail and other websites allow you to choose your own user name. You might select a name that is formed from parts of your real name or nickname and possibly some numbers, if the name you want is taken (such as britstearns04). If you wish to remain more anonymous, choose a user name that combines common words, or reflects your interests (such as guitarboston27).

Once you select a password, change it frequently. Read Secure IT 1-3 in Chapter 1 for tips about creating strong passwords. Do not disclose your password to anyone or write it on a slip of paper kept near the computer, especially taped to the monitor or under the keyboard. Email and telemarketing scams often ask unsuspecting users to disclose their credit card numbers, so be wary if you did not initiate the inquiry or phone call. Read Secure IT 5-3 for tips about using a password manager.

⚙ SECURE IT 5-3

📄 Safely Use a Password Manager

If you use the same password to access your banking, shopping, online social networks, and school accounts, you are not alone. Many people think one password is sufficient protection for all their vital online accounts, but cyberthieves are aware of this flawed thinking and take advantage of this practice. Security experts recommend using different user names and passwords for every account and changing the passwords frequently.

Keeping track of all these accounts can be an overwhelming task. A *password manager*, also called a *password organizer*, is a convenient service that stores all your account information securely. Once you select a service, you download and install the software and create one master password. The first time you view a password-protected website and enter your user name and password, the password manager saves this information. The next time you visit one of these websites or apps, the software supplies the account information automatically. Password managers use two-step verification and advanced encryption techniques (discussed later in this chapter) to ensure information is stored securely.

Some managers offer the option to generate random passwords, which have a unique combination of jumbled numbers and letters that are difficult for criminals to steal, for each account. Other features include the ability to auto-fill information, such as your name, address, and phone number, on forms and to provide a hint if you have forgotten your master password.

Password manager services can be free to use or may require a small annual fee. Some security experts recommend using a service that charges a fee, stating that these companies may provide more features. Before using any manager, call the company and ask about security measures, the ability to sync with multiple mobile devices, 24-hour customer service via live chat or phone, and limits on the number of passwords that can be saved.

✳ **Consider This:** Do you use a password manager? If so, do you feel secure storing all your sign in and password information in this service? If not, how do you keep track of your passwords?

✳ CONSIDER THIS

Why do some websites allow you to use your email address as a user name?
No two users can have the same email address; that is, your email address is unique to you. This means you can use your email address and password from one website to validate your identity on another website. Facebook, Google, and Twitter, for example, are three popular websites that provide authentication services to other applications. By using your email address from one of these websites to access other websites, you do not have to create or remember separate user names and passwords for the various websites you visit.

In addition to a user name and password, some systems ask users to enter one of several pieces of personal information. Such items can include a grandparent's first name, your favorite food, your first pet's name, or the name of the elementary school you attended. These items should be facts that you easily remember but are not easy for others to discover about you when using a search engine or examining your profiles on online social networks. As with a password, if the user's response does not match information on file, the system denies access.

Passphrase   Instead of passwords, some organizations use passphrases to authenticate users. A *passphrase* is a private combination of words, often containing mixed capitalization and punctuation, associated with a user name that allows access to certain computer resources. Passphrases, which often can be up to 100 characters in length, are more secure than passwords, yet can be easy to remember because they contain words.

PIN   A **PIN** (personal identification number), sometimes called a *passcode*, is a numeric password, either assigned by a company or selected by a user. PINs provide an additional level of security. Select PINs carefully and protect them as you do any other password. For example, do not use the same four digits, sequential digits, or dates others could easily determine, such as birth dates.

⚙ BTW
Default Passwords
If a program or device has a default or preset password, such as admin, be sure to change it to prevent unauthorized access.

✳ CONSIDER THIS

Why do some websites display distorted characters you must reenter along with your password?

These websites use a CAPTCHA, which stands for Completely Automated Public Turing test to tell Computers and Humans Apart. A *CAPTCHA* is a program developed at Carnegie Mellon University that displays an image containing a series of distorted characters for a user to identify and enter in order to verify that user input is from humans and not computer programs (Figure 5-7).

A CAPTCHA is effective in blocking computer-generated attempts to access a website, because it is difficult to write programs for computers to detect distorted characters, while humans generally can recognize them. For visually impaired users or if words are too difficult to read, the CAPTCHA text can be read aloud; you also have the option of generating a new CAPTCHA.

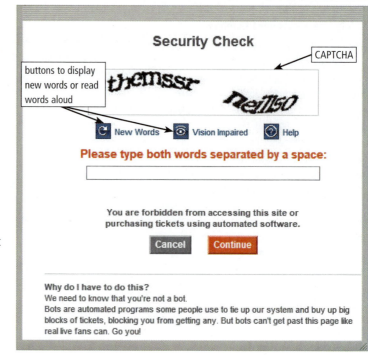

Figure 5-7 To continue with the ticket order process at the Ticketmaster website, the user must enter the characters in the CAPTCHA, which consists of the letters, themssr neillso, in this case.
Source: Carnegie Mellon University

Possessed Objects

A possessed object is any item that you must possess, or carry with you, in order to gain access to a computer or computer facility. Examples of possessed objects are badges, cards, smart cards, and keys. The card you use in an ATM (automated teller machine), for example, is a possessed object that allows access to your bank account.

Biometric Devices

A **biometric device** authenticates a person's identity by translating a personal characteristic, such as a fingerprint, into a digital code that is compared with a digital code stored in a computer or mobile device verifying a physical or behavioral characteristic. If the digital code in the computer or mobile device does not match the personal characteristic code, the computer or mobile device denies access to the individual.

Biometric devices grant access to programs, computers, or rooms using computer analysis of some biometric identifier. Examples of biometric devices and systems include fingerprint readers, face recognition systems, hand geometry systems, voice verification systems, signature verification systems, iris recognition systems, and retinal scanners.

Fingerprint Reader A **fingerprint reader**, or fingerprint scanner, captures curves and indentations of a fingerprint (Figure 5-8). Organizations use fingerprint readers to secure doors, computers, and software. With the cost of fingerprint readers often less than $100, some home and small business users install fingerprint readers to authenticate users before they can access a personal computer.

Figure 5-8 A fingerprint reader.
© Flynavyjp / Dreamstime.com

The reader also can be set up to perform different functions for different fingers; for example, one finger starts a program and another finger shuts down the computer. External fingerprint readers usually plug into a USB port.

Some laptops, smartphones, and smartwatches have a built fingerprint reader. Using their fingerprint, users can unlock the computer or device, sign in to programs and websites via their fingerprint instead of entering a user name and password, and on some devices, even test their blood pressure and heart rate.

Discover More: Visit this chapter's free resources to learn more about fingerprint readers.

✳ CONSIDER THIS

What is a lock screen?

A *lock screen* is a screen that restricts access to a computer or mobile device until a user performs a certain action. Some simply require a user swipe the screen to unlock the screen. Others verify a user's identity by requiring entry of a password, PIN, or passcode; a fingerprint scan; or a gesture swipe (Figure 5-9). Gestures are motions users make on a touch screen with the tip of one or more fingers or their hand. For example, to unlock the screen on a phone, a user could connect the dots on the screen using a pattern previously defined by the user.

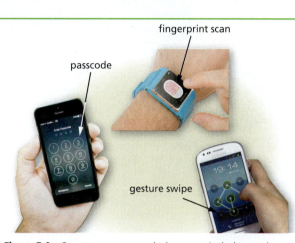

passcode • fingerprint scan • gesture swipe

Figure 5-9 Some ways users unlock screens include entering a passcode, scanning a fingerprint, and swiping a gesture.
© iStockPhoto / franckreporter; © Alexey Boldin / Shutterstock; © iStockPhoto / Carpe89

Face Recognition System

A *face recognition system* captures a live face image and compares it with a stored image to determine if the person is a legitimate user. Some buildings use face recognition systems to secure access to rooms. Law enforcement, surveillance systems, and airports use face recognition to protect the public. Some mobile devices use face recognition systems to unlock the device. Face recognition programs are becoming more sophisticated and can recognize people with or without glasses, makeup, or jewelry, and with new hairstyles.

Hand Geometry System

A *hand geometry system* measures the shape and size of a person's hand (Figure 5-10). Because hand geometry systems can be expensive, they often are used in larger companies to track workers' time and attendance or as security devices. Colleges use hand geometry systems to verify students' identities. Daycare centers and hospital nurseries use them to identify parents who pick up their children.

Voice Verification System

A *voice verification system* compares a person's live speech with their stored voice pattern. Larger organizations sometimes use voice verification systems as time and attendance devices. Many companies also use this technology for access to sensitive files and networks. Some financial services use voice verification systems to secure phone banking transactions.

Signature Verification System

A *signature verification system* recognizes the shape of your handwritten signature, as well as measures the pressure exerted and the motion used to write the signature. Signature verification systems use a specialized pen and tablet. Signature verification systems often are used to reduce fraud in financial institutions.

✳ BTW
Technology Trend
Discover More: Visit this chapter's free resources to learn more about uses of face recognition technology.

Figure 5-10 A hand geometry system verifies identity based on the shape and size of a person's hand.
Courtesy of Ingersoll Rand Security Technologies

✳ CONSIDER THIS

Do retailers use a signature verification system for credit card purchases?

No. With a credit card purchase, users sign their name on a signature capture pad using a stylus attached to the device. Software then transmits the signature to a central computer, where it is stored. Thus, the retailers use these systems simply to record your signature.

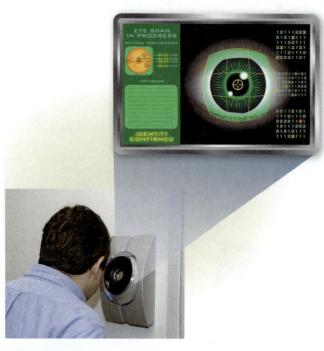

Iris Recognition System

High security areas use iris recognition systems. The camera in an iris recognition system uses iris recognition technology to read patterns in the iris of the eye (Figure 5-11). These patterns are as unique as a fingerprint. Iris recognition systems are quite expensive and are used by government security organizations, the military, and financial institutions that deal with highly sensitive data. Some organizations use retinal scanners, which work similarly but instead scan patterns of blood vessels in the back of the retina.

Figure 5-11 An iris recognition system.
© iStockPhoto / NKND200; © Robert F. Balazik / Shutterstock.com; © Cengage Learning

---

✳ CONSIDER THIS

How popular are biometric devices?
Biometric devices are gaining popularity as a security precaution because they are a virtually foolproof method of identification and authentication. For example, some grocery stores, retail stores, and gas stations use *biometric payment*, where the customer's fingerprint is read by a fingerprint reader that is linked to a payment method, such as a checking account or credit card. Users can forget their user names and passwords. Possessed objects can be lost, copied, duplicated, or stolen. Personal characteristics, by contrast, are unique and cannot be forgotten or misplaced.

Biometric devices do have disadvantages. If you cut your finger, a fingerprint reader might reject you as a legitimate user. Hand geometry readers can transmit germs. If you are nervous, a signature might not match the one on file. If you have a sore throat, a voice recognition system might reject you. Many people are uncomfortable with the thought of using an iris scanner.

⚙ BTW
Two-Step Verification
Users should register a landline phone number, alternate email address, or other form of contact beyond a mobile phone number so that they still can access their accounts even if they lose their mobile phone.

⚡ **Internet Research**
Which websites use two-step verification?
Search for: two-step verification websites

Two-Step Verification

In an attempt to further protect personal data and information from online thieves, many organizations such as financial institutions or universities that store sensitive or confidential items use a two-step verification process. With **two-step verification**, also known as *two-factor verification*, a computer or mobile device uses two separate methods, one after the next, to verify the identity of a user.

ATMs (automated teller machines) usually requires a two-step verification. Users first insert their ATM card into the ATM (Step 1) and then enter a PIN (Step 2) to access their bank account. Most debit cards and some credit cards use PINs. If someone steals these cards, the thief must enter the user's PIN to access the account.

Another use of two-step verification requires a mobile phone and a computer. When users sign in to an account on a computer, they enter a user name and a password (Step 1). Next, they are prompted to enter another authentication code (Step 2), which is sent as a text or voice message or via an app on a smartphone (Figure 5-12). This second code generally is valid for a set time, sometimes only for a few hours. If users do not sign in during this time limit, they must repeat the process and request another verification code. Microsoft and Google commonly use two-step verification when you sign in to their websites. If you sign in from a device you use frequently, you can elect to bypass this step.

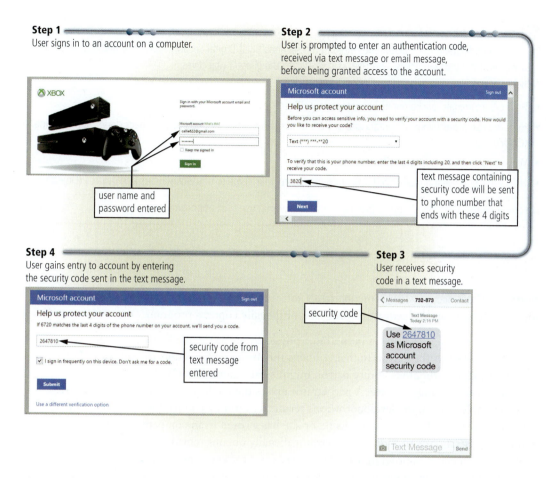

Step 1
User signs in to an account on a computer.

user name and password entered

Step 2
User is prompted to enter an authentication code, received via text message or email message, before being granted access to the account.

text message containing security code will be sent to phone number that ends with these 4 digits

Step 4
User gains entry to account by entering the security code sent in the text message.

security code from text message entered

Step 3
User receives security code in a text message.

security code

Figure 5-12   This figure shows an example of two-step authentication.
Source: Microsoft

✺ CONSIDER THIS

Can users circumvent the two-step verification process?
Users may be able to specify a computer as a trusted device during a two-step verification so that future sign-in attempts on that same computer will bypass the two-step verification. Only limited-use computers in safe areas should be identified as a trusted device.

Digital Forensics

   Digital forensics, also called *cyberforensics*, is the discovery, collection, and analysis of evidence found on computers and networks. Digital forensics involves the examination of media, programs, data and log files on computers, mobile devices, servers, and networks. Many areas use digital forensics, including law enforcement, criminal prosecutors, military intelligence, insurance agencies, and information security departments in the private sector.

   A digital forensics examiner must have knowledge of the law, technical experience with many types of hardware and software products, superior communication skills, familiarity with corporate structures and policies, a willingness to learn and update skills, and a knack for problem solving.

🟠 BTW
High-Tech Talk
Discover More: Visit this chapter's free resources to learn more about digital forensics.

✅ **NOW YOU SHOULD KNOW** ——————————————————

Be sure you understand the material presented in the sections titled Digital Security Risks, Internet and Network Attacks, and Unauthorized Access and Use, as it relates to the chapter objectives.
Now you should know …

- How cybercriminals' backgrounds and intent vary (Objective 1)
- How you can protect your computers and devices from malware, botnets, DoS attacks, back doors, and spoofing (Objective 2)
- Why you should use a firewall (Objective 2)
- How you can prevent unauthorized users from accessing your home or office computers and devices (Objective 3)

Discover More: Visit this chapter's premium content for practice quiz opportunities.

Software Theft

Software theft occurs when someone steals software media, intentionally erases programs, illegally registers and/or activates a program, or illegally copies a program.

- Physically stealing software: A perpetrator physically steals the media that contains the software, or steals the hardware that contains the media that contains the software. For example, an unscrupulous library patron might steal a game CD/DVD.
- Intentionally erasing software: A perpetrator erases the media that contains the software. For example, a software developer who is terminated from a company may retaliate by removing or disabling the programs he or she has written from company computers.
- Illegal registration/activation: A perpetrator illegally obtains registration numbers and/ or activation codes. A program called a *keygen*, short for key generator, creates software registration numbers and sometimes activation codes. Some unscrupulous individuals create and post keygens so that users can install software without legally purchasing it.
- Illegal copying: A perpetrator copies software from manufacturers. **Software piracy**, often referred to simply as **piracy**, is the unauthorized and illegal duplication of copyrighted software. Piracy is the most common form of software theft.

 BTW

BSA
To promote understanding of software piracy, a number of major worldwide software companies formed the *Business Software Alliance* (*BSA*). The BSA operates a website and antipiracy hotlines around the world.

Safeguards against Software Theft

To protect software media from being stolen, owners should keep original software boxes and media or the online confirmation of purchased software in a secure location, out of sight of prying eyes. All computer users should back up their files and drives regularly, in the event of theft. When some companies terminate a software developer or if the software developer quits, they escort the employee off the premises immediately. These companies believe that allowing terminated employees to remain on the premises gives them time to sabotage files and other network procedures.

Many manufacturers incorporate an activation process into their programs to ensure the software is not installed on more computers than legally licensed. During the **product activation**, which is conducted either online or by phone, users provide the software product's identification number to associate the software with the computer or mobile device on which the software is installed. Usually, the software can be run a preset number of times, has limited functionality, or does not function until you activate it.

To further protect themselves from software piracy, software manufacturers issue users license agreements. As discussed in Chapter 4, a **license agreement** is the right to use software. That is, you do not own the software. The most common type of license included with software purchased by individual users is a *single-user license agreement*, also called an *end-user license agreement* (*EULA*). The license agreement provides specific conditions for use of the software, which a user must accept before using the software. These terms usually are displayed when you install

 **Internet Research**

What are the penalties for piracy?

Search for: piracy penalties

the software. Use of the software constitutes acceptance of the terms on the user's part. Figure 5-13 identifies the conditions of a typical single-user license agreement.

To support multiple users' access of software, most manufacturers sell network versions or site licenses of their software, which usually costs less than buying individual stand-alone copies of the software for each computer. A *network license* is a legal agreement that allows multiple users to access the software on the server simultaneously. The network license fee usually is based on the number of users or the number of computers attached to the network. A *site license* is a legal agreement that permits users to install the software on multiple computers — usually at a volume discount.

Discover More: Visit this chapter's free resources to learn more about license agreements.

Typical Conditions of a Single-User License Agreement

You can…
- Install the software on only one computer or device. (Some license agreements allow users to install the software on a specified number of computers and/or mobile devices.)
- Make one copy of the software as a backup.
- Give or sell the software to another individual, but only if the software is removed from the user's computer first.

You cannot…
- Install the software on a network, such as a school computer lab.
- Give copies to friends and colleagues, while continuing to use the software.
- Export the software.
- Rent or lease the software.

Figure 5-13 A user must accept the terms of a license agreement before using the software.
© Cengage Learning

✳ **CONSIDER THIS**

Can you install software on work computers or work-issued smartphones?

Many organizations and businesses have strict written policies governing the installation and use of software and enforce their rules by checking networked or online computers or mobile devices periodically to ensure that all software is licensed properly. If you are not completely familiar with your school's or employer's policies governing installation of software, check with the information technology department or your school's technology coordinator.

Information Theft

Information theft occurs when someone steals personal or confidential information. Both business and home users can fall victim to information theft. An unethical company executive may steal or buy stolen information to learn about a competitor. A corrupt individual may steal credit card numbers to make fraudulent purchases. Information theft often is linked to other types of cybercrime. For example, an individual first might gain unauthorized access to a computer and then steal credit card numbers stored in a firm's accounting department.

Safeguards against Information Theft

Most organizations will attempt to prevent information theft by implementing the user identification and authentication controls discussed earlier in this chapter. These controls are best suited for protecting information on computers located on an organization's premises. To further protect information on the Internet and networks, organizations and individuals use a variety of encryption techniques.

Encryption

Encryption is the process of converting data that is readable by humans into encoded characters to prevent unauthorized access. You treat encrypted data just like any other data. That is, you can store it or send it in an email message. To read the data, the recipient must **decrypt**, or decode it. For example, users may specify that an email application encrypt a message before sending it securely. The recipient's email application would need to decrypt the message in order for the recipient to be able to read it.

In the encryption process, the unencrypted, readable data is called *plaintext*. The encrypted (scrambled) data is called *ciphertext*. An *encryption algorithm*, or *cypher*, is a set of steps that can convert readable plaintext into unreadable ciphertext. A simple encryption algorithm might switch the order of characters or replace characters with other characters. Encryption programs typically use more than one encryption algorithm, along with an encryption key. An *encryption key* is a set of characters that the originator of the data uses to encrypt the plaintext and the recipient of the data uses to decrypt the ciphertext.

Two basic types of encryption are private key and public key. With *private key encryption*, also called *symmetric key encryption*, both the originator and the recipient use the same secret key to encrypt and decrypt the data. *Public key encryption*, also called *asymmetric key encryption*, uses two encryption keys: a public key and a private key (Figure 5-14). Public key encryption software generates both the private key and the public key. A message encrypted with a public key can be decrypted only with the corresponding private key, and vice versa. The public key is made known to message originators and recipients. For example, public keys may be posted on a secure webpage or a public-key server, or they may be emailed. The private key, by contrast, should be kept confidential.

Some operating systems and email programs allow you to encrypt the contents of files and messages that are stored on your computer. You also can purchase an encryption program to encrypt files. Many browsers use encryption when sending private information, such as credit card numbers, over the Internet.

Mobile users today often access their company networks through a virtual private network. When a mobile user connects to a main office using a standard Internet connection, a *virtual private network* (*VPN*) provides the mobile user with a secure connection to the company network server, as if the user has a private line. VPNs help ensure that data is safe from being intercepted by unauthorized people by encrypting data as it transmits from a laptop, smartphone, or other mobile device.

Discover More: Visit this chapter's free resources to learn more about encryption algorithms and programs.

An Example of Public Key Encryption

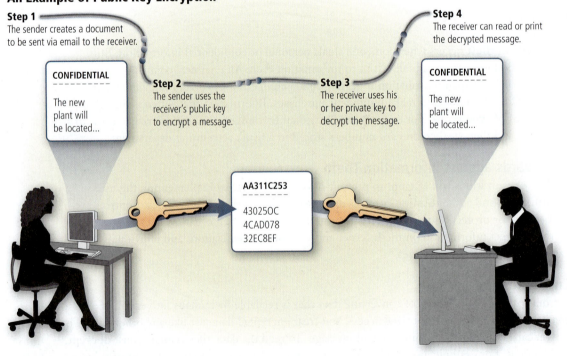

Step 1
The sender creates a document to be sent via email to the receiver.

Step 2
The sender uses the receiver's public key to encrypt a message.

Step 3
The receiver uses his or her private key to decrypt the message.

Step 4
The receiver can read or print the decrypted message.

CONFIDENTIAL
The new plant will be located...

CONFIDENTIAL
The new plant will be located...

AA311C253
43025OC
4CAD078
32EC8EF

Figure 5-14   This figure shows an example of public key encryption.
© Cengage Learning

Digital Signatures and Certificates

A **digital signature** is an encrypted code that a person, website, or organization attaches to an electronic message to verify the identity of the message sender. Digital signatures often are used to ensure that an impostor is not participating in an Internet transaction. That is, digital signatures can help to prevent email forgery. A digital signature also can verify that the content of a message has not changed.

A **digital certificate** is a notice that guarantees a user or a website is legitimate. E-commerce applications commonly use digital certificates. Browsers often display a warning message if a website does not have a valid digital certificate.

A website that uses encryption techniques to secure its data is known as a **secure site** (Figure 5-15). Web addresses of secure sites often begin with https instead of http. Secure sites typically use digital certificates along with security protocols.

✳ CONSIDER THIS

Who issues digital certificates?

A *certificate authority* (*CA*) is an organization that issues digital certificates. Each CA is a trusted third party that takes responsibility for verifying the sender's identity before issuing a certificate. Individuals and companies can purchase digital certificates from one of more than 35 online CA providers. The cost varies depending on the desired level of data encryption, with the strongest levels recommended for financial and e-commerce transactions.

Discover More: Visit this chapter's free resources to learn more about security protocols, digital certificates and signatures, and CA providers.

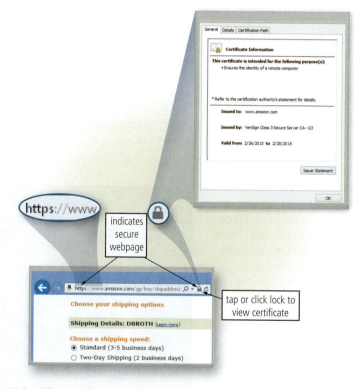

Figure 5-15   Web addresses of secure sites, such as the Amazon.com checkout, often begin with https instead of http. Browsers also often display a lock symbol in the window, which you usually can tap or click to see the associated digital certificate.
Source: Amazon.com and Microsoft

Mini Feature 5-1: Cloud Data Privacy

Privacy and security concerns arise when consumers and businesses consider moving their data to an online storage service. Read Mini Feature 5-1 to learn about privacy issues surrounding cloud data storage. Read Ethics & Issues 5-2 to consider who is responsible for data left on the cloud.

⚙ **MINI FEATURE 5-1**

Cloud Data Privacy

Privacy and security concerns arise when consumers and businesses consider moving their data to an online storage service. While the cloud offers a tremendous amount of storage space at a relatively low cost, the security of data and the reliability of cloud companies trigger concerns.

When people register for a cloud computing service, they sign a written contract or tap or click an online OK or Agree button to affirm they read and understand the terms of the agreement. Any data saved on the cloud is entrusted to the third-party provider, which has a legal obligation to protect the data from security breaches. The company also must guard against data loss due to physical disasters, such as power outages, cooling failures, and fire. When data has been compromised, many states require the company to disclose the issue to the data owner promptly.

The Cloud Security Alliance (CSA) warns of hackers who register for the service with a credit card or for a free trial period and then unleash malware in an attempt to gain access to passwords. Because the registration and validation procedure for accessing the cloud is relatively anonymous, authorities can have difficulty locating the abusers.

Another concern arises when transferring data over a network to the cloud. When the data is traveling to or from a computer and the cloud service, it is subject to interception. To minimize risk, security experts emphasize that the web address of the website you are visiting must begin with https, and the data should be encrypted and authenticated.

Law enforcement's access to the data raises another security issue. Email messages stored on a private server belong to the company or individual who owns the computer, so law enforcement officials must obtain a search warrant to read a particular user's messages. In contrast, law enforcement officials can access email messages stored on the cloud by requesting the information from the company that owns the cloud service. The user might not be notified of the search until up to 90 days after the search occurred; moreover, the search may occur without limitations and may include continuous monitoring of an individual's email communications.

International laws and industry regulations protect sensitive and personal data. Germany has some of the strictest cloud data privacy laws, and, in general, the European Union's privacy regulations are more

protective that those in the United States. In much of Europe, for example, consumers must agree to have their personal information collected, and they can review the data for accuracy. The education, health care, and financial services industries in the United States have strict data privacy regulations that affect cloud storage. For example, the Family Educational Rights and Privacy Act (FERPA) regulates the confidentiality of students' educational records, so colleges must obtain students' consent to share data with cloud storage providers and other third parties.

Cloud storage companies have increased their privacy and security features in recent years. Many allow consumers and businesses to protect files with passwords or require two-step authentication to access files, to delete data if a mobile device has been stolen or lost, and to delete data that has been stored past an expiration date.

Discover More: Visit this chapter's free resources to learn more about cloud security breaches, international laws and industry regulations, and protecting online data.

⚙ **Consider This:** How much of your personal data is stored on the cloud? Do you have concerns about the security of this data? Have you ever received a notice that any of your online data has been compromised? Should online social networks or email providers give more explicit notice that data is stored on the cloud? Should law enforcement officials be able to access your data without your consent? Why or why not?

© iStockPhoto / maxkabakov

⚙ BTW
Technology Trend
Discover More: Visit this chapter's free resources to learn more about cloud security.

Hardware Theft, Vandalism, and Failure

Users rely on computers and mobile devices to create, store, and manage important information. As discussed in Chapter 3, you should take measures to protect computers and devices from theft, vandalism, and failure.

Hardware theft is the act of stealing digital equipment. Hardware vandalism involves defacing or destroying digital equipment. Hardware can fail for a variety of reasons: aging hardware, natural or man-made disasters, or random events such as electrical power problems, and even errors in programs or apps. Figure 5-16 summarizes the techniques you can use to safeguard hardware from theft, vandalism, and failure.

Hardware Theft and Vandalism Safeguards
- Physical access controls (i.e., locked doors and windows)
- Alarm system
- Physical security devices (i.e., cables and locks)
- Device-tracking app

Hardware Failure Safeguards
- Surge protector
- Uninterruptible power supply (UPS)
- Duplicate components or duplicate computers
- Fault-tolerant computer

Figure 5-16 Summary of safeguards against hardware theft, vandalism, and failure.
© Cengage Learning; © iStockphoto / Norebbo

Backing Up — The Ultimate Safeguard

To protect against data loss caused by hardware/software/information theft or system failure, users should back up computer and mobile device files regularly. As previously described, a **backup** is a duplicate of a file, program, or media that can be used if the original is lost, damaged, or destroyed; and to **back up** a file means to make a copy of it. In the case of system failure or the discovery of corrupted files, you **restore** the files by copying the backed up files to their original location on the computer or mobile device.

If you choose to back up locally, be sure to use high-quality media. A good choice for a home user might be optical discs or an external hard drive. Keep your backup media in a fireproof and heat-proof safe or vault, or offsite. *Off-site* means in a location separate from where you typically store or use your computer or mobile device. Keeping backup copies off-site minimizes the chance that a single disaster, such as a fire, would destroy both the original and the backup media. An off-site location can be a safe deposit box at a bank, a briefcase, or cloud storage or cloud backup.

Cloud storage provides storage to customers, usually along with synchronization services but often on smaller amounts of data. By contrast, cloud backup provides only backup and retrieval services, but generally provides continuous data protection (discussed next) to the cloud. More customers are opting for cloud backup because it saves them the cost of maintaining hardware (Figure 5-17).

 BTW

Technology Innovator
Discover More: Visit this chapter's free resources to learn about the device-tracking app, LoJack.

Backup programs are available from many sources. Most operating systems include a backup program. Backup devices, such as external disk drives, also include backup programs. Numerous stand-alone backup tools exist. Cloud storage providers may offer backup services. Users of a cloud backup service install software on their computers that backs up files to the cloud as they are modified.

Figure 5-17 Cloud storage, such as Carbonite shown here, is a popular method for off-site backups.
Source: Carbonite, Inc.

Business and home users can perform four types of backup: full, differential, incremental, or selective. A fifth type, continuous data protection, often is used only by large enterprises to back up data to an in-house network storage device purchased and maintained by the enterprise. Cloud backup services, a sixth option, are providing continuous data protection capabilities at a lower cost. Table 5-2 summarizes the purpose, advantages, and disadvantages of each of these backup methods.

Some users implement a three-generation backup policy to preserve three copies of important files. The *grandparent* is the oldest copy of the file. The *parent* is the second oldest copy of the file. The *child* is the most recent copy of the file. When a new backup is performed, the child becomes the parent, the parent becomes the grandparent, and the media on which the grandparent copy was stored may be erased and reused for a future backup.

Table 5-2 Various Backup Methods

Type of Backup	Description	Advantages	Disadvantages
Full backup	Copies all of the files on media in the computer.	Fastest recovery method. All files are saved.	Longest backup time.
Differential backup	Copies only the files that have changed since the last full backup.	Fast backup method. Requires minimal storage space to back up.	Recovery is time-consuming because the last full backup plus the differential backup are needed.
Incremental backup	Copies only the files that have changed since the last full or incremental backup.	Fastest backup method. Requires minimal storage space to back up. Only most recent changes saved.	Recovery is most time-consuming because the last full backup and all incremental backups since the last full backup are needed.
Selective backup	Users choose which folders and files to include in a backup.	Fast backup method. Provides great flexibility.	Difficult to manage individual file backups. Least manageable of all the backup methods.
Continuous data protection (CDP)	All data is backed up whenever a change is made.	The only real-time backup. Very fast recovery of data.	Very expensive and requires a great amount of storage.
Cloud backup	Files are backed up to the cloud as they change.	Cloud backup provider maintains backup hardware. Files may be retrieved from anywhere with an Internet connection on any device.	Requires an Internet connection, otherwise files are marked for backup when the computer goes back online.

Mini Feature 5-2: Disaster Recovery

A **disaster recovery plan** is a written plan that describes the steps an organization would take to restore its computer operations in the event of a disaster. Read Mini Feature 5-2 to learn about steps an organization takes in the event of a disaster.

✦ MINI FEATURE 5-2

Disaster Recovery

A disaster can be natural or man-made (hackers, viruses, etc.). Each company and each department or division within an organization usually has its own disaster recovery plan. The following scenario illustrates how an organization might implement a disaster recovery plan.

Rosewood Associates is a consulting firm that helps clients use social media for marketing and customer outreach. Last week, a fire broke out in the office suite above Rosewood. The heat and smoke, along with water from the sprinkler system, caused extensive damage. As a result, Rosewood must replace all computers, servers, and storage devices. Also, the company lost all of the data it had not backed up.

Rosewood currently backs up its systems daily to an internal server and weekly to a remote cloud server. Because of damage to the internal server, the company lost several days of data. Rosewood does not have a plan for replacing hardware. Thus, they will lose several additional days of productivity while purchasing, installing, and configuring new hardware.

To minimize the chance of this type of loss in the future, the company hired you as a consultant to help create a disaster recovery plan. You first discuss the types of disasters that can strike, as shown in the table. You then explain that the goal of a disaster recovery plan is to prevent, detect, and correct system threats, and to restore the most critical systems first.

A disaster recovery plan typically contains these four components: emergency plan, backup plan, recovery plan, and test plan.

Emergency Plan: An emergency plan specifies the steps Rosewood will take as soon as a disaster strikes. The emergency plan is organized by type of disaster, such as fire, flood, or earthquake, and includes:

1. Names and phone numbers of people and organizations to notify (company management, fire and police department, clients, etc.)
2. Computer equipment procedures, such as equipment or power shutoff, and file removal; employees should follow these procedures only if it is safe to do so
3. Employee evacuation procedures
4. Return procedures (who can enter the facility and what actions they are to perform)

Backup Plan: The backup plan specifies how Rosewood will use backup files and equipment to resume computer operations, and includes:

1. The location of backup data, supplies, and equipment
2. Who is responsible for gathering backup resources and transporting them to an alternate computer facility
3. The methods by which data will be restored from cloud storage

Considerations for Disaster Recovery

Disaster Type	What to Do First	What Might Occur	What to Include in the Plan
Natural (earthquake, hurricane, tornado, etc.)	Shut off power Evacuate, if necessary Pay attention to advisories Do not use phone lines if lightning occurs	Power outage Phone lines down Structural damage to building Road closings, transportation interruptions Flooding Equipment damage	Generator Satellite phone, list of employee phone numbers Alternate worksite Action to be taken if employees are not able to come to work/leave the office Wet/dry vacuums Make and model numbers and vendor information to get replacements
Man-made (hazardous material spill, terrorist attacks, fire, hackers, malware, etc.)	Notify authorities (fire departments, etc.) of immediate threat Attempt to suppress fire or contain spill, if safe to do so Evacuate, if necessary	Data loss Dangerous conditions for employees Criminal activity, such as data hacking and identity theft Equipment damage	Backup data at protected site Protective equipment and an evacuation plan Contact law enforcement Make and model numbers and vendor information to obtain replacements

© Cengage Learning

4. A schedule indicating the order and approximate time each application should be up and running

Recovery Plan: The recovery plan specifies the actions Rosewood will take to restore full computer operations. As with the emergency plan, the recovery plan differs for each type of disaster. You recommend that Rosewood set up planning committees. Each committee would be responsible for different forms of recovery, such as replacing hardware or software.

Test Plan: The test plan includes simulating various levels of disasters and recording Rosewood's ability to recover. You run a test in which the employees follow the steps in the disaster recovery plan. The test uncovers a few needed recovery actions not specified in the plan, so you modify the plan. A few days later, you run another test without giving the employees any advance notice to test the plan again.

Discover More: Visit this chapter's free resources to learn more about lost productivity, backup plans, and alternate computer facilities.

✦ **Consider This:** For what kinds of natural and man-made disasters should a company plan? What roles can cloud storage providers play in helping to recover from a disaster? How involved should employees be in developing and testing disaster recovery plans?

© iStockphoto / Hans Laubel;
© iStockphoto / William Sen;
© Gewoldi / Photos.com

Wireless Security

Billions of home and business users have laptops, smartphones, and other mobile devices to access the Internet, send email and Internet messages, chat online, or share network connections — all wirelessly. Home users set up wireless home networks. Mobile users access wireless networks in hot spots at airports, hotels, shopping malls, bookstores, restaurants, and coffee shops. Schools have wireless networks so that students can access the school network using their mobile computers and devices as they move from building to building (Figure 5-18).

Although wireless access provides many conveniences to users, it also poses additional security risks. Some perpetrators connect to other's wireless networks to gain free Internet access; others may try to access an organization's confidential data.

To access a wireless network, the individual must be in range of the wireless network. Some intruders intercept and monitor communications as they transmit through the air. Others connect to a network through an unsecured wireless access point (WAP) or combination router/WAP. Read How To 5-3 for instructions about ways to secure a wireless network, in addition to using firewalls.

Figure 5-18 Wireless access points or routers around campus allow students to access the school network wirelessly from their classrooms, the library, dorms, and other campus locations.
© Robert Kneschke / Shutterstock.com; © iStockphoto / CEFutcher; © Natalia Siverina / Shutterstock.com; © Downunderphoto / Fotolia; © Natalia Siverina / Shutterstock.com; © Cengage Learning

---

✦ HOW TO 5-3

Secure Your Wireless Network

When you set up a wireless network, it is important to secure the network so that only your computers and mobile devices can connect to it. Unsecured wireless networks can be seen and accessed by neighbors and others nearby, which may make it easier for them to connect to and access the data on the computers and mobile devices on your network. The following list provides suggestions for securing your wireless network.

- Immediately upon connecting your wireless access point and/or router, change the password required to access administrative features. If the password remains at its default setting, others may possibly be able to connect to and configure your wireless network settings.

- Change the *SSID* (service set identifier), which is a network name, from the default to something that uniquely identifies your network, especially if you live in close proximity to other wireless networks.

- Do not broadcast the SSID. This will make it more difficult for others to detect your

wireless network. When you want to connect a computer or mobile device to your wireless network, it will be necessary to enter the SSID manually.

- Enable an encryption method such as WPA2 (Wi-Fi Protected Access 2), and specify a password or passphrase that is difficult for others to guess. The most secure passwords and passphrases contain more than eight characters, uppercase and lowercase letters, numbers, and special characters.

- Enable and configure the MAC (Media Access Control) address control feature. A *MAC address* is a unique hardware identifier for your computer or device. The *MAC address control* feature specifies the computers and mobile devices that can connect to your network. If a computer or device is not specified, it will not be able to connect.

- Choose a secure location for your wireless router so

that unauthorized people cannot access it. Someone who has physical access to a wireless router can restore factory defaults and erase your settings.

✵ **Consider This:** In addition to safeguarding the data and information on your computers from others, why else might it be a good idea to secure your wireless network?

Home	Wi-Fi	LAN	WWAN	Security	Advanced	▮▮ Verizon EvDO Rev.Ae	Dormant	▮▮▮

Wi-Fi

Wi-Fi Profiles	
Current Profile	Secure
Selected Profile	Secure ⌄
Network Name (SSID)	smith ✕
802.11 Mode	802.11g + 802.11b ⌄
WMM (Wi-Fi Multimedia)	Off ⌄
	With older Droids and devices that aren't working, use "Backward compatibility".
Channel	Auto ⌄
Security	WPA2 ⌄
Authentication	Open Access ⌄
Network Key	68c2c067
	8 ~ 63 ASCII characters For greater security, use a mixture of digits, upper case, lower case, and other symbols

Update Profile Apply Revert

Source: Verizon Wireless

Can you detect if someone is accessing your wireless home network?
If you notice the speed of your wireless connection is slower than normal, it may be a sign that someone else is accessing your network. You also may notice indicator lights on your wireless router flashing rapidly when you are not connected to your wireless network. Most wireless routers have a built-in utility that allows you to view the computers currently connected to your network. If you notice a computer that does not belong to you, consult your wireless router's documentation to determine how to remove it from the network.

Mini Feature 5-3: Mobile Security

As the number of smartphones and mobile devices in use increases, the possibility of security breaches and lost devices increases proportionally. Read Mini Feature 5-3 to learn about ways you can protect sensitive and personal data on your mobile devices.

⚙ MINI FEATURE 5-3

Mobile Security

The consequences of losing a smartphone or mobile device are significant given the amount of storage and the variety of personal and business data stored. Symantec, one the world's leading online security companies, projects that only one-half of lost or stolen phones eventually will be returned to their owners. Chances are that the people who find the missing phones likely will have viewed much of the content on the devices in a quest to find the owners and possibly to gain access to private information.

The goal, therefore, for mobile device users is to make their data as secure as possible. Follow these steps to protect sensitive and personal data and to fight mobile cybercrime.

- **Be extra cautious locating and downloading apps.** Any device that connects to the Internet is susceptible to mobile malware. Cyberthieves target apps on widely used phones and tablets. Popular games are likely candidates to house malware, and it often is difficult to distinguish the legitimate apps from the fake apps. Obtain mobile device apps from well-known stores, and before downloading anything, read the descriptions and reviews. Look for

misspellings and awkward sentence structure, which could be clues that the app is fake. If something looks awry, do not download. Scrutinize the number and types of permissions the app is requesting. If the list seems unreasonable in length or in the personal information needed, deny permission and uninstall the app.

- **Use a PIN.** Enable the passcode feature on a mobile device as the first step in stopping prying eyes from viewing contents. This four-to-eight-digit code adds a layer of protection. Only emergency functions can be accessed without entering the correct sequence of numbers. This strong code should not be information easily guessed, such as a birthday.

- **Turn off GPS tracking.** GPS technology can track the mobile device's location as long as it is transmitting and receiving signals to and from satellites. This feature is helpful to obtain directions from your current location, view local news and weather reports, find a lost device, summon emergency personnel, and locate missing children. Serious privacy concerns can arise, however, when the technology is used in malicious ways, such as to stalk individuals or trace their whereabouts. Unless you want to allow others to follow your locations throughout the day, disable the GPS tracking feature until needed.

- **Use mobile security software.** Protection is necessary to stop viruses and spyware and to safeguard personal and business data. Mobile security apps can allow you to lock your mobile device and SIM card remotely, erase the

turn off location services until needed

© iStockphoto / Henk Badenhorst; © iStockphoto / Marcello Bortolino;
© Cengage Learning

(Continued)

memory, and activate the GPS function. Other apps prevent cyberthieves from hijacking your phone and taking pictures, making recordings, placing calls to fee-imposed businesses, and sending infected messages to all individuals in your contact list. Look for security software that can back up data to a cloud account, set off a screeching alarm on the lost or stolen mobile device, offer live customer service, and provide theft, spam, virus, and malware protection.

- **Avoid tapping or clicking unsafe links.** Tapping or clicking an unknown link can lead to malicious websites. If you receive a text message from someone you do not know or an invitation to tap or click a link, resist the urge to fulfill the request. Your financial institution never will send you a message requesting you to enter your account user name and password. Malicious links can inject malware on the mobile

device to steal personal information or to create toll fraud, which secretly contacts wireless messaging services that impose steep fees on a monthly bill.

Discover More: Visit this chapter's free resources to learn more about methods to protect your mobile device and personal information.

Consider This: As the number of smartphones and mobile devices in use increases, the possibility of security breaches and lost devices increases proportionally. How can manufacturers and wireless carriers emphasize the importance of mobile security and convince users to take the precautions suggested in this mini feature? What mobile security safeguards have you taken to protect your smartphone or mobile device? What steps will you take after reading this mini feature?

NOW YOU SHOULD KNOW

Be sure you understand the material presented in the sections titled Software Theft; Information Theft; Hardware Theft, Vandalism, and Failure; Backing Up – The Ultimate Safeguard; and Wireless Security as it relates to the chapter objectives.

Now you should know …

- What actions you are allowed according to a software license agreement (Objective 4)
- Why you would want to use encryption, digital signatures, or digital certificates (Objective 5)
- How you can protect your hardware from theft, vandalism, and failure (Objective 6)
- Which backup method is most suited to your needs (Objective 7)
- How you can protect your wireless communications (Objective 8)

Discover More: Visit this chapter's premium content for practice quiz opportunities.

Ethics and Society

As with any powerful technology, computers and mobile devices can be used for both good and bad intentions. The standards that determine whether an action is good or bad are known as ethics.

Technology ethics are the moral guidelines that govern the use of computers, mobile devices, information systems, and related technologies. Frequently discussed areas of computer ethics are unauthorized use of computers, mobile devices, and networks; software theft (piracy); information accuracy; intellectual property rights; codes of conduct; green computing; and information privacy. The questionnaire in Figure 5-19 raises issues in each of these areas.

Previous sections in this chapter discussed unauthorized use of computers, mobile devices and networks, and software theft (piracy). The following sections discuss issues related to information accuracy, intellectual property rights, codes of conduct, green computing, and information privacy.

Your Thoughts?

		Ethical	Unethical
1.	An organization requires employees to wear badges that track their whereabouts while at work.	☐	☐
2.	A supervisor reads an employee's email message.	☐	☐
3.	An employee uses his computer at work to send email messages to a friend.	☐	☐
4.	An employee sends an email message to several coworkers and blind copies his supervisor.	☐	☐
5.	An employee forwards an email message to a third party without permission from the sender.	☐	☐
6.	An employee uses her computer at work to complete a homework assignment for school.	☐	☐
7.	The vice president of your Student Government Association (SGA) downloads a photo from the web and uses it in a flyer recruiting SGA members.	☐	☐
8.	A student copies text from the web and uses it in a research paper for his English Composition class.	☐	☐
9.	An employee sends political campaign material to individuals on her employer's mailing list.	☐	☐
10.	As an employee in the registration office, you have access to student grades. You look up grades for your friends, so that they do not have to wait for grades to be posted online.	☐	☐
11.	An employee makes a copy of software and installs it on her home computer. No one uses her home computer while she is at work, and she uses her home computer only to finish projects from work.	☐	☐
12.	An employee who has been laid off installs a computer virus on his employer's computer.	☐	☐
13.	A person designing a webpage finds one on the web similar to his requirements, copies it, modifies it, and publishes it as his own webpage.	☐	☐
14.	A student researches using only the web to write a report.	☐	☐
15.	In a society in which all transactions occur online (a cashless society), the government tracks every transaction you make and automatically deducts taxes from your bank account.	☐	☐
16.	Someone copies a well-known novel to the web and encourages others to read it.	☐	☐
17.	A person accesses an organization's network and reports to the organization any vulnerabilities discovered.	☐	☐
18.	Your friend uses a neighbor's wireless network to connect to the Internet and check email.	☐	☐
19.	A company uses recycled paper to print a 50-page employee benefits manual that is distributed to 425 employees.	☐	☐
20.	An employee is fired based on the content of posts on his or her online social network.	☐	☐

Figure 5-19 Indicate whether you think the situation described is ethical or unethical. Be prepared to discuss your answers.
© Cengage Learning

Information Accuracy

Information accuracy is a concern today because many users access information maintained by other people or companies, such as on the Internet. Do not assume that because the information is on the web that it is correct. As discussed in Chapter 2, users should evaluate the value of a webpage before relying on its content. Be aware that the organization providing access to the information may not be the creator of the information. Read Secure IT 5-4 to consider the risks associated with inaccurate data.

SECURE IT 5-4

Risks Associated with Inaccurate Data

Mapping and navigation software is invaluable for locating unfamiliar destinations. Problems arise, however, when satellite images are outdated or when the desired address cannot be found on a map. Inaccurate data can result in lost revenues for businesses when potential customers cannot find the storefront. It also has caused accidents when drivers followed turn-by-turn GPS directions and drove the wrong way on one-way streets, made illegal turns, or ended at ponds where a road stopped.

Business owners can report incorrect address data to some mapping services. They can, for example, state that the satellite image needs updating, their address has changed, the directions are incorrect, or the street names are inaccurate. In some cases,

the maps and addresses are updated quickly, often within a day.

Data entry errors also can lead to lost business, lawsuits, and expenses. In an extreme example, a $125 million Mars Climate Orbiter spacecraft was lost in space because Lockheed Martin engineers performed calculations using English units (pounds) to fire the thrusters guiding the spacecraft, but NASA engineers assumed the data was in metric units (Newtons) and sent the spacecraft 60 miles off course. In another unit conversion error, an axle broke on a Space Mountain roller coaster car at Tokyo Disneyland because it was the wrong size; the error occurred when engineers performed calculations to convert the original Space Mountain master plan from English units to metric units.

In the business world, mistakes can occur when software has not been updated or when employees are overworked, distracted, or faced with repetitive tasks. Software should have safeguards to verify valid data has been entered, such as checking that phone numbers have 10 numeric characters. Data cleaning software can eliminate duplicate database records, locate missing data, and correct discrepancies.

Consider This: Have you ever used a mapping app or website and encountered incorrect information? Would you consider notifying mapping companies of errors in their satellite images or directions? What steps can companies take to help employees enter data accurately?

Figure 5-20 This digitally edited photo shows a fruit that looks like an apple on the outside and an orange on the inside.
© Cengage Learning.

Internet Research

What is meant by fair use?

Search for: fair use definition

Internet Research

What is creative commons?

Search for: creative commons

In addition to concerns about the accuracy of computer input, some individuals and organizations raise questions about the ethics of using computers to alter output, primarily graphic output, such as a retouched photo. With graphics equipment and software, users easily can digitize photos and then add, change (Figure 5-20), or remove images.

Intellectual Property Rights

Intellectual property (IP) refers to unique and original works, such as ideas, inventions, art, writings, processes, company and product names, and logos. *Intellectual property rights* are the rights to which creators are entitled for their work. Certain issues arise surrounding IP today because many of these works are available digitally and easily can be redistributed or altered without the creator's permission.

A *copyright* gives authors, artists, and other creators of original work exclusive rights to duplicate, publish, and sell their materials. A copyright protects any tangible form of expression.

A common infringement of copyright is piracy, where people illegally copy software, movies, and music. Many areas are not clear-cut with respect to the law, because copyright law gives the public fair use to copyrighted material. The issues surround the phrase, fair use, which allows use for educational and critical purposes. This vague definition is subject to widespread interpretation and raises many questions:

- Should individuals be able to download contents of your website, modify it, and then put it on the web again as their own?
- Should a faculty member have the right to print material from the web and distribute it to all members of the class for teaching purposes only?
- Should someone be able to scan photos or pages from a book, publish them on the web, and allow others to download them?
- Should someone be able to put the lyrics of a song on the web?
- Should students be able to take term papers they have written and post them on the web, making it tempting for other students to download and submit them as their own work?

These issues with copyright law led to the development of *digital rights management* (DRM), a strategy designed to prevent illegal distribution of movies, music, and other digital content.

Codes of Conduct

A **code of conduct** is a written guideline that helps determine whether a specification is ethical/unethical or allowed/not allowed. An IT code of conduct focuses on acceptable use of technology. Employers and schools often specify standards for the ethical use of technology in an IT code of conduct and then distribute these standards to employees and students (Figure 5-21). You also may find codes of conduct online that define acceptable forms of communications for websites where users post commentary or other communications, such as blogs, wikis, online discussions, and so on.

Sample IT Code of Conduct

1. Technology may not be used to harm other people.
2. Employees may not meddle in others' files.
3. Employees may use technology only for purposes in which they have been authorized.
4. Technology may not be used to steal.
5. Technology may not be used to bear false witness.
6. Employees may not copy or use software illegally.
7. Employees may not use others' technology resources without authorization.
8. Employees may not use others' intellectual property as their own.
9. Employees shall consider the social impact of programs and systems they design.
10. Employees always should use technology in a way that demonstrates consideration and respect for fellow humans.

Figure 5-21   Sample IT code of conduct employers may distribute to employees.
© Cengage Learning; © iStockphoto / Oleksiy Mark

Green Computing

People use, and often waste, resources such as electricity and paper while using technology. Recall from Chapter 1 that **green computing** involves reducing the electricity and environmental waste while using computers, mobile devices, and related technologies. Figure 5-22 summarizes measures users can take to contribute to green computing.

Personal computers, displays, printers, and other devices should comply with guidelines of the ENERGY STAR program. The United States Department of Energy (DOE) and the United States Environmental Protection Agency (EPA) developed the *ENERGY STAR program* to help reduce the amount of electricity used by computers and related devices. This program encourages manufacturers to create energy-efficient devices. For example, many devices switch to sleep or power save mode after a specified number of inactive minutes or hours. Computers and devices that meet the ENERGY STAR guidelines display an ENERGY STAR label (shown in Figure 5-22).

Enterprise data centers and computer facilities consume large amounts of electricity from computer hardware and associated devices and utilities, such as air conditioning, coolers, lighting, etc. Organizations can implement a variety of measures to reduce electrical waste:

Green Computing Tips

1. Conserve Energy
   a. Use computers and devices that comply with the ENERGY STAR program.
   b. Do not leave a computer or device running overnight.
   c. Turn off the monitor, printer, and other devices when not in use.

2. Reduce Environmental Waste
   a. Use paperless methods to communicate.
   b. Recycle paper and buy recycled paper.
   c. Recycle toner and ink cartridges, computers, mobile devices, printers, and other devices.
   d. Telecommute.
   e. Use videoconferencing and VoIP for meetings.

Figure 5-22   A list of suggestions to make computing healthy for the environment.
US Environmental Protection Agency, ENERGY STAR program; © Roman Sotola / Shutterstock.com; © Cengage Learning

- Consolidate servers by using virtualization.
- Purchase high-efficiency equipment.
- Use sleep modes and other power management features for computers and devices.
- Buy computers and devices with low power consumption processors and power supplies.
- When possible, use outside air to cool the data center or computer facility.

Some organizations continually review their *power usage effectiveness* (PUE), which is a ratio that measures how much power enters the computer facility or data center against the amount of power required to run the computers and devices.

 **Internet Research**

Where can I recycle outdated electronics?

Search for: recycle old electronics

Should you save out-of-date computers and devices?
Users should not store obsolete computers and devices in their basement, storage room, attic, warehouse, or any other location. Computers, monitors, and other equipment contain toxic materials and potentially dangerous elements including lead, mercury, and flame retardants. In a landfill, these materials release into the environment. Recycling and refurbishing old equipment are much safer alternatives for the environment. Manufacturers can use the millions of pounds of recycled raw materials to make products such as outdoor furniture and automotive parts. Before recycling, refurbishing, or discarding your old computer, be sure to erase, remove, or destroy its hard drive so that the information it stored remains private.

Discover More: Visit this chapter's free resources to learn more about the ENERGY STAR program.

How to Safeguard Personal Information

1. Fill in only necessary information on rebate, warranty, and registration forms.
2. Do not preprint your phone number or Social Security number on personal checks.
3. Have an unlisted or unpublished phone number.
4. If you have Caller ID, find out how to block your number from displaying on the receiver's system.
5. Do not write your phone number on charge or credit receipts.
6. Ask merchants not to write credit card numbers, phone numbers, Social Security numbers, and driver's license numbers on the back of your personal checks.
7. Purchase goods with cash, rather than credit or checks.
8. Avoid shopping club and buyer cards.
9. If merchants ask personal questions, find out why they want to know before releasing the information.
10. Inform merchants that you do not want them to distribute your personal information.
11. Request, in writing, to be removed from mailing lists.
12. Obtain your credit report once a year from each of the three major credit reporting agencies (Equifax, Experian, and TransUnion) and correct any errors.
13. Request a free copy of your medical records once a year from the Medical Information Bureau.
14. Limit the amount of information you provide to websites. Fill in only required information.
15. Install a cookie manager to filter cookies.
16. Clear your history file when you are finished browsing.
17. Set up a free email account. Use this email address for merchant forms.
18. Turn off file and printer sharing on your Internet connection.
19. Install a personal firewall.
20. Sign up for email filtering through your ISP or use an anti-spam program.
21. Do not reply to spam for any reason.
22. Surf the web anonymously or through an anonymous website.

Figure 5-23 Techniques to keep personal data private.
© iStockphoto / Norebbo; © Cengage Learning

Information Privacy

Information privacy refers to the right of individuals and companies to deny or restrict the collection, use, and dissemination of information about them. Organizations often use huge databases to store records, such as employee records, medical records, financial records, and more. Much of the data is personal and confidential and should be accessible only to authorized users. Many individuals and organizations, however, question whether this data really is private. That is, some companies and individuals collect and use this information without your authorization. Websites often collect data about you, so that they can customize advertisements and send you personalized email messages. Some employers monitor your computer usage and email messages.

Figure 5-23 lists measures you can take to make your personal data more private. The following sections address techniques companies and employers use to collect your personal data.

Discover More: Visit this chapter's free resources to learn more about your credit report.

Electronic Profiles

When you fill out a printed form, such as a magazine subscription or contest entry, or an online form to sign up for a service, create a profile on an online social network, or register a product warranty, the merchant that receives the form usually stores the information you provide in a database. Likewise, every time you tap or click an advertisement on the web or perform a search online, your information and preferences enter a database. Some merchants may sell or share the contents of their databases with national marketing firms and Internet advertising firms. By combining this data with information from public records, such as driver's licenses and vehicle registrations, these firms can create an electronic profile of individuals. Electronic profiles may include personal details, such as your age, address, phone number, marital status, number and ages of dependents, interests, and spending habits.

Direct marketing supporters claim that using information in this way lowers overall selling costs, which lowers product prices. Critics contend that the information in an electronic profile reveals more about an individual than anyone has a right to know. They argue that companies should inform people if they plan to provide personal information to others, and people should have the right to deny such use. Many websites allow people to specify whether they want their personal information shared or preferences retained (Figure 5-24).

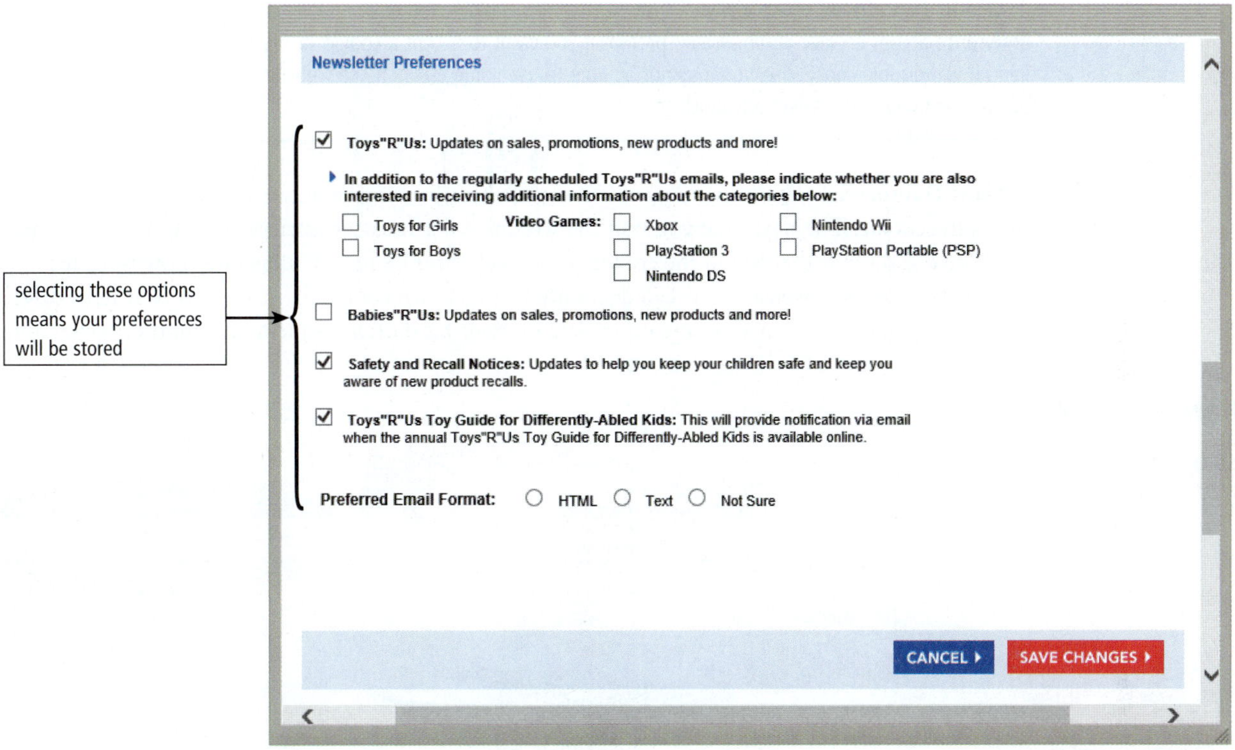

Figure 5-24   Many companies, such as Toys"R"Us shown here, allow users to specify whether they want the company to retain their preferences.
Source: Geoffrey, LLC

Cookies

A **cookie** is a small text file that a web server stores on your computer. Cookie files typically contain data about you, such as your user name, postal code, or viewing preferences. Websites use cookies for a variety of purposes:

- Most websites that allow for personalization use cookies to track user preferences. These cookies may obtain their values when a user fills in an online form requesting personal information. Some websites, for example, store user names in cookies in order to display a personalized greeting that welcomes the user, by name, back to the website. Other websites allow users to customize their viewing experience with preferences, such as local news headlines, the local weather forecast, or stock quotes.
- Some websites use cookies to store user names and/or passwords, so that users do not need to enter this information every time they sign in to the website.
- Online shopping sites generally use a *session cookie* to keep track of items in a user's shopping cart. This way, users can start an order during one web session and finish it on another day in another session. Session cookies usually expire after a certain time, such as a week or a month.

- Some websites use cookies to track how often users visit a site and the webpages they visit while at the website.
- Websites may use cookies to target advertisements. These websites store a user's interests and browsing habits in the cookie.

⚙ **CONSIDER THIS** ───────────────────────────────

Do websites ever sell information stored in cookies?
Some websites sell or trade information stored in your cookies to advertisers — a practice many believe to be unethical. If you do not want personal information distributed, you should limit the amount of information you provide to a website or adjust how your browser handles cookies. You can regularly clear cookies or set your browser to accept cookies automatically, prompt if you want to accept a cookie, or disable all cookie use. Keep in mind if you disable cookie use, you may not be able to use some e-commerce websites. As an alternative, you can purchase software that selectively blocks cookies.

Many commercial websites send a cookie to your browser; your computer's hard drive then stores the cookie. The next time you visit the website, your browser retrieves the cookie from your hard drive and sends the data in the cookie to the website. Figure 5-25 illustrates how websites work with cookies. A website can read data only from its own cookie file stored on your hard drive. That is, it cannot access or view any other data on your hard drive — including another cookie file.

How Cookies Work

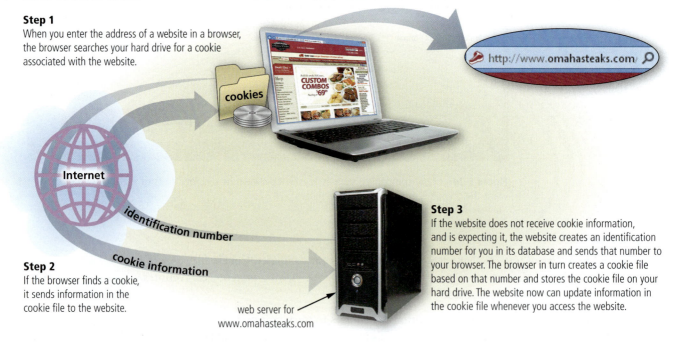

Step 1
When you enter the address of a website in a browser, the browser searches your hard drive for a cookie associated with the website.

Step 2
If the browser finds a cookie, it sends information in the cookie file to the website.

Step 3
If the website does not receive cookie information, and is expecting it, the website creates an identification number for you in its database and sends that number to your browser. The browser in turn creates a cookie file based on that number and stores the cookie file on your hard drive. The website now can update information in the cookie file whenever you access the website.

web server for www.omahasteaks.com

Figure 5-25 This figure shows how cookies work.
© Alex Staroseltsev / Shutterstock.com; Source: Omaha Steaks International, Inc; © iStockphoto / Norman Chan; © Cengage Learning

Phishing

Recall from Chapter 4 that **phishing** is a scam in which a perpetrator sends an official looking email message that attempts to obtain your personal and/or financial information. These messages look legitimate and request that you update credit card numbers, Social Security numbers, bank account numbers, passwords, or other private information. Read How To 5-4 for instructions about protecting yourself from phishing scams.

✹ HOW TO 5-4

Protect against a Phishing Scam

Phishing scams can be perpetrated via email messages, websites, and even on the phone. The following guidelines will help protect you against a phishing scam.

Phone Scams

- If you receive a phone call from someone claiming to be from a company with which you do business, record his or her name and the time of the call. Do not disclose personal or financial information to the caller. If the caller is offering a product or service and is requesting a payment, call the company back at the number you have on file, and ask to be transferred to the person who called you initially.

- Whenever possible, enter your payment information on secure websites instead of reading credit card numbers or bank account information on the phone. You never know whether the caller is recording your payment information to use later for malicious purposes.

Email Scams

- If you receive an email message from someone requesting you to verify online account or financial information, do not reply with this information.

- Never tap or click links in email messages, even if the message appears to be from someone you know. Nor should you copy and paste the link from the email message to a browser. Instead, type the link's web address into a browser's address bar manually, and make sure you type it correctly. If you are visiting your financial institution's website, make sure the web address you enter matches the web address you have on file for them.

- Do not reply to email messages asking you for financial assistance — even if the email message appears to originate from someone you know. If you receive this type of email message from someone you know, call the person to verify the message's authenticity.

Website Scams

- When visiting a website, such as your financial institution's website, that will require you to enter confidential information, be sure to type the web address correctly. Typing it incorrectly may take you to a phishing website where the information you enter can be collected by an unknown party.

- Make sure websites requiring your confidential information use the https://protocol.

- Websites with misspellings, poor grammar, or formatting problems may indicate a phishing website. Do not enter personal or financial information on a website that looks suspicious.

- Enable the *phishing filter* in your browser that can warn or block you from potentially fraudulent or suspicious websites.

✹ **Consider This:** Have you experienced a phishing scam? If so, how did it attempt to trick you into providing personal or financial information? How did you respond?

Clickjacking is yet another similar scam. With *clickjacking*, an object that can be tapped or clicked — such as a button, image, or link — on a website, pop-up ad, pop-under ad, or in an email message or text message contains a malicious program. When a user taps or clicks the disguised object, a variety of nefarious events may occur. For example, the user may be redirected to a phony website that requests personal information, or a virus may download to the computer or mobile device. Browsers typically include clickjacking protection.

⚡ **Internet Research**
Which phishing scams are prevalent?
Search for: recent phishing scams

Spyware and Adware

Recall from Chapter 4 that **spyware** is a program placed on a computer or mobile device without the user's knowledge that secretly collects information about the user and then communicates the information it collects to some outside source while the user is online. Some vendors or employers use spyware to collect information about program usage or employees. Internet advertising firms often collect information about users' web browsing habits. Spyware can enter your computer when you install a new program, through malware, or through a graphic on a webpage or in an email message.

Adware is a program that displays an online advertisement in a banner, a pop-up window, or pop-under window on webpages, email messages, or other Internet services. Adware on mobile phones is known as *madware*, for mobile adware. Sometimes, spyware is hidden in adware.

To remove spyware and adware, you can obtain spyware removers, adware removers, or malware removers that can detect and delete spyware and adware. Some operating systems and browsers include spyware and adware removers.

Social Engineering

As related to the use of technology, **social engineering** is defined as gaining unauthorized access to or obtaining confidential information by taking advantage of the trusting human nature of some victims and the naivety of others. Some social engineers trick their victims into revealing confidential information, such as user names and passwords, on the phone, in person, or on the Internet. Techniques they use include pretending to be an administrator or other authoritative figure, feigning an emergency situation, or impersonating an acquaintance. Social engineers also obtain information from users who do not destroy or conceal information properly. These perpetrators sift through company dumpsters, watch or film people dialing phone numbers or using ATMs, and snoop around computers or mobile devices looking for openly displayed confidential information.

To protect yourself from social engineering scams, follow these tips:

- Verify the identity of any person or organization requesting personal or confidential information.
- When relaying personal or confidential information, ensure that only authorized people can hear your conversation.
- When personal or confidential information appears on a computer or mobile device, ensure that only authorized people can see your screen.
- Shred all sensitive or confidential documents.
- After using a public computer, clear the cache in its browser.
- Avoid using public computers to conduct banking or other sensitive transactions.

Privacy Laws

The concern about privacy has led to the enactment of federal and state laws regarding the storage and disclosure of personal data, some of which are shown in Table 5-3. Common points in some of these laws are as follows:

1. Information collected and stored about individuals should be limited to what is necessary to carry out the function of the business or government agency collecting the data.
2. Once collected, provisions should be made to protect the data so that only those employees within the organization who need access to it to perform their job duties have access to it.
3. Personal information should be released outside the organization collecting the data only when the person has agreed to its disclosure.
4. When information is collected about an individual, the individual should know that the data is being collected and have the opportunity to determine the accuracy of the data.

Read Ethics & Issues 5-3 to consider the legal issues surrounding your digital footprint.

Table 5-3 Major U.S. Government Laws Concerning Privacy

Law	Purpose
Children's Internet Protection Act	Protects minors from inappropriate content when accessing the Internet in schools and libraries
Children's Online Privacy Protection Act (COPPA)	Requires websites to protect personal information of children under 13 years of age
Computer Abuse Amendments Act	Outlaws transmission of harmful computer code such as viruses
Digital Millennium Copyright Act (DMCA)	Makes it illegal to circumvent antipiracy schemes in commercial software; outlaws sale of devices that copy software illegally
Electronic Communications Privacy Act (ECPA)	Provides the same right of privacy protection of the postal delivery service and phone companies to various forms of electronic communications, such as voice mail, email, and mobile phones
Financial Modernization Act	Protects consumers from disclosure of their personal financial information and requires institutions to alert customers of information disclosure policies
Freedom of Information Act (FOIA)	Enables public access to most government records
HIPAA (Health Insurance Portability and Accountability Act)	Protects individuals against the wrongful disclosure of their health information
PATRIOT (Provide Appropriate Tools Required to Intercept and Obstruct Terrorism)	Gives law enforcement the right to monitor people's activities, including web and email habits
Privacy Act	Forbids federal agencies from allowing information to be used for a reason other than that for which it was collected

Discover More: Visit this chapter's free resources to learn about more privacy laws.

⚙ **ETHICS & ISSUES 5-3**

Do You Have the Right to Be Digitally Forgotten?

Privacy experts, such as The Institute for Responsible Online and Cell-Phone Communication (IROC2), warn that "Your digital activity is public and permanent" and is available permanently to anyone using a search engine. Does it have to be? Do you have a "right to be forgotten" as was ruled by a court in the European Union recently?

In this case, the court ordered a popular search engine to remove links to information that was "inadequate, irrelevant, or no longer relevant." The content in question included many factual articles published by a major news source. Examples included stories about a university student arrested for driving while intoxicated and a referee who lied about a mistake. Free speech advocates criticize the law. They state that a government should not be able to deny access to accurate information. Others argue that a person should be able to request removal of information that is damaging to his or her reputation. Some are concerned that negative incidents may be necessary information for an employer to know about a job seeker, or for those considering a relationship with another person. You can never truly delete your digital footprint because everything you do online has the potential to be forwarded, captured as a screenshot, or archived in databases.

Among the debated issues is whether the rights of a private citizen should differ from those of a public figure. Many argue that different rules apply for celebrities, politicians, and others who choose such professions. Some feel that the responsibility rests on search engines to provide methods that enable individuals to comment on, explain, or select what information is displayed when they are the subject of an Internet search. For example, Google developed the Google Inactive Account Manager, where you can specify what happens to your data after a period of inactivity.

Consider This: Does a government have a right to legislate search engine links? Why or why not? In what, if any, situations should individuals be able to request removal of digital content? Should search engines provide users with tools to control what information about them appears? Why or why not?

Employee Monitoring

Employee monitoring involves the use of computers, mobile devices, or cameras to observe, record, and review an employee's use of a technology, including communications such as email messages, keyboard activity (used to measure productivity), and websites visited. Many programs exist that easily allow employers to monitor employees. Further, it is legal for employers to use these programs.

⚙ **CONSIDER THIS**

Do employers have the right to read employee email messages?
Actual policies vary widely. Some organizations declare that they will review email messages regularly, and others state that email messages are private. In some states, if a company does not have a formal email policy, it can read email messages without employee notification.

Content Filtering

One of the more controversial issues that surround the Internet is its widespread availability of objectionable material, such as prejudiced literature, violence, and obscene photos. Some believe that such materials should be banned. Others believe that the materials should be filtered, that is, restricted.

Content filtering is the process of restricting access to certain material. Many businesses use content filtering to limit employees' web access. These businesses argue that employees are unproductive when visiting inappropriate or objectionable websites. Some schools, libraries, and parents use content filtering to restrict access to minors. Content filtering opponents argue that banning any materials violates constitutional guarantees of free speech and personal rights. Read Ethics & Issues 5-4 to consider whether content filtering violates first amendment rights.

✳ ETHICS & ISSUES 5-4

Does Content Filtering in a Public Library Violate First Amendment Rights?

Among the resources libraries offer are Internet-enabled computers. The use of content filtering software on library computers controls the type of information a patron can access. Free speech advocates argue that this violates the First Amendment because it restricts library patrons from viewing certain websites and content.

The Children's Internet Protection Act (CIPA) requires that schools and libraries use content filtering software in order to receive certain federal funds. The purpose of CIPA is to restrict access to objectionable material, protect children when communicating online,

prohibit children from sharing personal information, and restrict children's identities or accounts being hacked. Proponents of CIPA claim it is necessary to protect children. CIPA does allow libraries to turn off the filters, if an adult patrons requests it. Some libraries use content filtering software on computers used only by children.

Critics of content filtering software argue that the programs do not always work as intended. They can overfilter content, blocking information or education websites based on a single word. Some websites and services that filtering software may block include online social networks, or software platforms, such as Google Drive, which students may need to access to submit assignments.

Conversely, they can underfilter content, which could result in access to webpages with inappropriate media. Others argue that it gives unequal access to students doing research who rely on library computers to do schoolwork and those who have unfiltered Internet access at home.

Libraries typically have a policy stating acceptable use of the Internet. Libraries' policies also should state whether they use content filtering software, so that the patrons are aware.

Consider This: Is it fair for a government to require that libraries use content filtering software? Why or why not? Do free speech laws cover content on the Internet? Why or why not?

Web filtering software is a program that restricts access to specified websites. Some also filter sites that use specific words (Figure 5-26). Others allow you to filter email messages, chat rooms, and programs. Many Internet security programs include a firewall, antivirus program, and filtering capabilities combined. Browsers also often include content filtering capabilities.

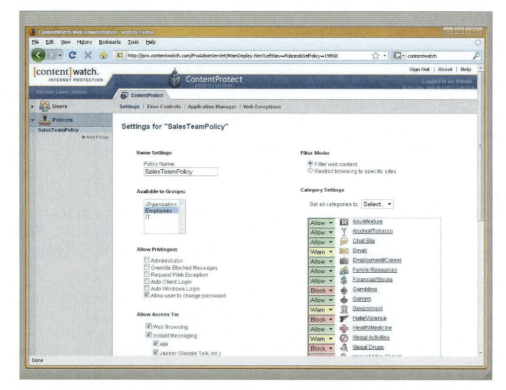

Figure 5-26   Web filtering software restricts access to specified websites.
Courtesy of ContentWatch, Inc.

✅ NOW YOU SHOULD KNOW

Be sure you understand the material presented in the sections titled Ethics and Society and Information Privacy as it relates to the chapter objectives.
Now you should know ...

- What issues you might encounter with respect to information accuracy, intellectual property, codes of conduct, and green computing (Objective 9)
- How you can make your personal data more private (Objective 10)
- Why your computer might have a cookie (Objective 10)

Discover More: Visit this chapter's premium content for practice quiz opportunities.

✅ Chapter Summary

This chapter presented a variety of digital security risks. You learned about cybercrime and cybercriminals. The chapter discussed risks and safeguards associated with Internet and network attacks, unauthorized access and use, software theft, information theft, and hardware theft, vandalism, and failure. It presented various backup strategies and methods of securing wireless communications. You learned about ethical issues in society and various ways to protect the privacy of personal information.

Discover More: Visit this chapter's free resources for additional content that accompanies this chapter and also includes these features: Technology Innovators: AVG, Intel Security, Symantec, and LoJack; Technology Trends: Uses of Face Recognition Technology and Cloud Security; and High-Tech Talks: Digital Forensics and Encryption Algorithms.

Test your knowledge of chapter material by accessing the Study Guide, Flash Cards, and Practice Test resources from your smartphone, tablet, laptop, or desktop.

⚡ TECHNOLOGY @ WORK

National and Local Security

Since 2001, the federal government, local governments, businesses, and individuals have been implementing aggressive new security measures because of the increase in terrorist activity. A security threat can exist anywhere, and it is nearly impossible for humans alone to protect the country. As a result, technology now assists governments, law enforcement officials, business owners, and other individuals with monitoring and maintaining security.

Advancements in computer vision enable computers to monitor indoor and outdoor areas that might be subject to a high volume of criminal activity. For example, some cities are installing cameras in problematic areas. A program analyzes the output from the camera and can determine whether two or more people in close proximity to one another might be engaged in a physical confrontation. If the computer detects suspicious behavior, it automatically notifies local law enforcement.

Computers also use facial recognition to identify individuals who do not belong in a particular area. For example, one theme park takes a picture of individuals they escort out of and ban from the park. As visitors walk from their cars to the park, surveillance cameras positioned in strategic locations scan visitors' faces and compare them with the database containing images of those who are banned from the park. If the computer finds a match, it alerts a security officer who then can investigate the situation. Thousands of people visit theme parks each day, and computers make it easier to perform the otherwise impossible task of identifying those who might be trespassing.

The federal government, particularly the Department of Homeland Security, uses a computerized No Fly List to track individuals who are not authorized to travel on commercial flights within the United States. When an individual makes a reservation, a computer compares his or her name to the names on the No Fly List. If the computer finds a match, the individual must prove that he or she is not the person on the list before being allowed to board an aircraft.

Whether you are walking outside, visiting an attraction, or traveling, the chances are good that computers are, in some way, ensuring your safety.

✴ **Consider This:** In what other ways do computers and technology play a role in national and local security?

© Dariusz Markowski / Photos.com

Study Guide

The Study Guide exercise reinforces material you should know for the chapter exam.

Discover More: Visit this chapter's premium content to **test your knowledge of digital content** associated with this chapter and **access the Study Guide resource** from your smartphone, tablet, laptop, or desktop.

Instructions: Answer the questions below using the format that helps you remember best or that is required by your instructor. Possible formats may include one or more of these options: write the answers; create a document that contains the answers; record answers as audio or video using a webcam, smartphone, or portable media player; post answers on a blog, wiki, or website; or highlight answers in the book/e-book.

1. Define the terms, digital security risk, computer crime, cybercrime, and crimeware.

2. Differentiate among hackers, crackers, script kiddies, cyberextortionists, and cyberterrorists. Identify issues with punishing cybercriminals.

3. List common types of malware. A(n) ___ is the destructive event or prank malware delivers.

4. Identify risks and safety measures when gaming.

5. Define these terms: botnet, zombie, and bot.

6. Describe the damages caused by and possible motivations behind DoS and DDoS attacks.

7. A(n) ___ allows users to bypass security controls when accessing a program, computer, or network.

8. Define the term, spoofing. How can you tell if an email is spoofed?

9. List ways to protect against Internet and network attacks.

10. Describe the purpose of an online security service.

11. Define the terms, firewall and proxy server. List steps to set up a personal firewall.

12. Give examples of unauthorized access and use of a computer or network.

13. Identify what an AUP should specify. Why might you disable file and printer sharing?

14. Explain how an organization uses access controls and audit trails.

15. Differentiate among user names, passwords, passphrases, and pass codes.

16. List tips for using a password manager safely.

17. What is a single sign on account? PIN stands for ___.

18. Describe the purpose of a CAPTCHA.

19. Define the terms, possessed objects and biometric devices.

20. What is the purpose of a lock screen?

21. Describe how companies use the following recognition, verification, or payment systems: fingerprint, face, hand, voice, signature, and iris. List disadvantages of biometric devices.

22. Explain the two-step verification process.

23. Define the term, digital forensics. Name areas in which digital forensics are used.

24. Define the terms, software theft, keygen, and software piracy. Identify methods to prevent software theft.

25. Explain the process of product activation.

26. Describe the following license agreement types: single- or end-user, network, and site. List conditions provided in a license agreement.

27. Give examples of information theft. How can you protect yourself from information theft?

28. Describe the functions of an encryption algorithm and an encryption key. Differentiate between private and public key encryption.

29. Unencrypted data is called ___; encrypted data is called ___.

30. Describe the purpose of a VPN.

31. Define these terms: digital signature, digital certificate, and secure site.

32. List concerns and responsibilities regarding cloud data storage and privacy.

33. Describe what occurs during hardware theft or vandalism.

34. Define the terms, backup and restore.

35. List six types of backups. Describe the three-generation backup policy.

36. Identify the components of a disaster recovery plan.

37. Describe security risks associated with wireless access. Identify ways to secure your wireless network.

38. List guidelines to protect your mobile device data.

39. Describe technology ethics, information accuracy, intellectual property rights, copyrights, and codes of conduct.

40. Describe issues surrounding inaccurate data.

41. List measures users can take to contribute to green computing.

42. Explain how companies, websites, and employers might infringe on your right to information privacy.

43. Describe how the following techniques are used to collect personal data: electronic profiles, cookies, phishing, clickjacking, spyware, adware, and madware.

44. How can you protect against phishing scams?

45. Identify methods to protect yourself from social engineering scams.

46. List examples of privacy laws. Should you be able to remove personal information from the Internet? Why or why not?

47. Describe what a company might track when monitoring employees.

48. Define and identify issues surrounding content and web filtering.

49. Describe uses of technology in the national and local security industry.

You should be able to define the Primary Terms and be familiar with the Secondary Terms listed below.

Key Terms

Discover More: Visit this chapter's premium content to **view definitions** for each term and to access the Flash Cards **resource** from your smartphone, tablet, laptop, or desktop.

Primary Terms (shown in **bold-black** characters in the chapter)

adware (244)	decrypt (229)	green computing (241)	restore (233)
back door (217)	denial of service attack	hacker (214)	script kiddie (214)
back up (233)	(DoS attack) (217)	information privacy (242)	secure site (231)
backup (233)	digital certificate (231)	information theft (229)	social engineering (245)
biometric device (224)	digital forensics (227)	license agreement (228)	software piracy (228)
botnet (216)	digital security risk (212)	malware (215)	software theft (228)
code of conduct (241)	digital signature (231)	online security service	spoofing (217)
computer crime (212)	disaster recovery plan	(219)	spyware (215)
content filtering (247)	(234)	password (222)	technology ethics (238)
cookie (243)	employee monitoring	personal firewall (220)	two-step verification (226)
cracker (214)	(247)	phishing (244)	user name (242)
cybercrime (212)	encryption (229)	PIN (223)	web filtering software
cyberextortionist (214)	fingerprint reader (224)	piracy (228)	(248)
cyberterrorist (214)	firewall (219)	product activation (228)	zombie (216)

Secondary Terms (shown in *italic* characters in the chapter)

acceptable use policy (AUP) (231)	*differential backup (234)*	*network license (229)*	*SSID (236)*
access control (222)	*digital rights management (240)*	*off-site (233)*	*symmetric key encryption (230)*
adware (215)	*distributed DoS attack (DDoS*	*parent (234)*	*trojan horse (215)*
asymmetric key encryption (230)	*attack) (217)*	*passcode (223)*	*two-factor verification (226)*
audit trail (222)	*email spoofing (217)*	*passphrase (223)*	*unauthorized access (221)*
biometric payment (226)	*encryption algorithm (230)*	*password manager (223)*	*unauthorized use (221)*
bot (216)	*encryption key (230)*	*password organizer (223)*	*user ID (222)*
Business Software Alliance	*end-user license agreement*	*payload (215)*	*virtual private network*
(BSA) (228)	*(EULA) (228)*	*phishing filter (244)*	*(VPN) (230)*
CAPTCHA (224)	*ENERGY STAR program (241)*	*plaintext (230)*	*virus (215)*
CERT/CC (219)	*face recognition system (225)*	*power usage effectiveness*	*voice verification system (225)*
certificate authority (CA) (231)	*full backup (234)*	*(PUE) (241)*	*worm (215)*
child (234)	*grandparent (234)*	*private key encryption (230)*	*zombie army (216)*
ciphertext (230)	*hacktivist (214)*	*proxy server (219)*	
clickjacking (245)	*hand geometry system (225)*	*public key encryption (230)*	
cloud backup (234)	*incremental backup (234)*	*rootkit (215)*	
Computer Emergency Response Team	*intellectual property (IP) (240)*	*selective backup (234)*	
Coordination Center (219)	*intellectual property rights (240)*	*session cookie (243)*	
continuous data protection	*IP spoofing (217)*	*signature verification*	
(CDP) (234)	*keygen (228)*	*system (225)*	
copyright (240)	*lock screen (225)*	*single sign on (222)*	
crimeware (212)	*MAC address (236)*	*single-user license*	
cyberforensics (227)	*MAC address control (236)*	*agreement (228)*	
cyberwarfare (214)	*madware (245)*	*site license (229)*	
cypher (230)	*malicious software (215)*	*spyware (215)*	

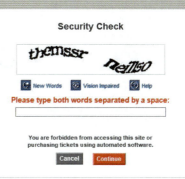

CAPTCHA (224)

Checkpoint

The Checkpoint exercises test your knowledge of the chapter concepts. The page number containing the answer appears in parentheses after each exercise. The Consider This exercises challenge your understanding of chapter concepts.

Discover More: Visit this chapter's premium content to **complete the Checkpoint exercises interactively;** complete the **self-assessment in the Test Prep resource** from on your smartphone, tablet, laptop, or desktop; and then **take the Practice Test.**

True/False   Mark T for True and F for False.

F   1. Any illegal act involving the use of a computer or related devices generally is referred to as a crimeware. (212)

F   2. A rootkit displays an online advertisement in a banner or pop-up window on webpages, email, or other Internet services. (215)

T   3. Viruses, worms, and other malware can be hidden in downloaded game files and mobile apps. (216)

T   4. An audit trail records in a file both successful and unsuccessful access attempts. (222)

T   5. It is good practice to change your password frequently. (222)

T   6. Intentionally erasing software would be considered software theft. (228)

F   7. A typical license agreement allows you to rent or lease the software. (229)

F   8. Unencrypted, readable data is called ciphertext. (230)

F   9. Private key encryption also is called asymmetric key encryption. (230)

T   10. VPNs encrypt data to help ensure that the data is safe from being intercepted by unauthorized people. (230)

T   11. When data is traveling to or from a computer to a cloud service, it is subject to interception. (232)

F   12. A good practice to secure your wireless network is to immediately broadcast the SSID. (236)

Multiple Choice   Select the best answer.

1. A _____ is someone who demands payment to stop an attack on an organization's technology infrastructure. (214)
   a. cyberterrorist
   b. script kiddie
   c. cracker
   d. cyberextortionist

2. _____ is a program that hides in a computer or mobile device and allows someone from a remote location to take full control of the computer or device. (215)
   a. A rootkit
   b. Spyware
   c. A trojan horse
   d. Adware

3. A _____ is a program or set of instructions in a program that allows users to bypass security controls when accessing a program, computer, or network. (217)
   a. zombie
   b. botnet
   c. back door
   d. session cookie

4. An employee using an organization's computer to send personal email messages might be an example of _____. (221)
   a. cybercrime
   b. hardware vandalism
   c. intellectual property rights violation
   d. unauthorized access and use

5. A _____ is a private combination of words, often up to 100 characters in length and containing mixed capitalization and punctuation, associated with a user name that allows access to certain computer resources. (223)
   a. passphrase
   b. private key
   c. passcode
   d. encryption algorithm

6. A(n) _____ is a set of characters that the originator of the data uses to encrypt the text and the recipient of the data uses to decrypt the text. (230)
   a. cipher
   b. plaintext
   c. public key
   d. encryption key

7. A(n) _____ backup method is the only real-time back up, providing very fast recovery of data. (234)
   a. selective
   b. full
   c. incremental
   d. continuous data protection

8. Online shopping websites generally use a _____ to keep track of items in a user's shopping cart. (243)
   a. phishing filter
   b. session cookie
   c. location sharing algorithm
   d. keygen

Checkpoint

Matching   Match the terms with their definitions.

H 1. script kiddie (214)

A 2. zombie (216)

C 3. bot (216)

B 4. spoofing (217)

I 5. access control (222)

G 6. keygen (228)

E 7. digital certificate (231)

J 8. technology ethics (238)

F 9. digital rights management (240)

D 10. cookie (243)

a. compromised computer or device whose owner is unaware the computer or device is being controlled remotely by an outsider

b. technique intruders use to make their network or Internet transmission appear legitimate to a victim computer or network

c. program that performs a repetitive task on a network

d. small text file that a web server stores on your computer

e. notice that guarantees a user or website is legitimate

f. strategy designed to prevent illegal distribution of movies, music, and other digital content

g. program that creates software registration numbers and sometimes activation codes

h. hacker who does not have the technical skills and knowledge of a cracker

i. security measure that defines who can access a computer, device, or network; when they can access it; and what actions they can take while accessing it

j. moral guidelines that govern the use of computers, mobile devices, information systems, and related technologies

✳ Consider This   Answer the following questions in the format specified by your instructor.

1. Answer the critical thinking questions posed at the end of these elements in this chapter: Ethics & Issues (214, 233, 246, 247), How To (218, 221, 236, 244), Mini Features (232, 235, 237), Secure IT (216, 219, 223, 240), and Technology @ Work (249).

2. What are some common digital security risks? (212)

3. How does a hacker differ from a cracker? (214)

4. What is cyberwarfare? (214)

5. What is a hacktivist? (214)

6. How does malware deliver its payload? (215)

7. What is a botnet? (216)

8. What practices should gamers follow to increase their security? (216)

9. What is the purpose of a DoS attack? (217)

10. Why would a programmer or computer repair technician build a back door? (217)

11. How is email spoofing commonly used? (217)

12. What are methods to protect computers, mobile devices, and networks from attacks? (218)

13. Who would an organization requiring assistance or information about Internet security breach contact? (219)

14. What screening techniques do proxy servers use? (219)

15. How does unauthorized access differ from unauthorized use? (221)

16. What is a single sign-on account? (222)

17. What is a password manager? (223)

18. Are passphrases more secure than passwords? Why or why not? (223)

19. How are fingerprint readers used with personal computers and mobile devices? (225)

20. What conditions are found in a typical single-user license agreement? (229)

21. Who issues digital certificates? (231)

22. What is meant by a three-generation backup policy? (234)

23. What should you include in a disaster recovery plan for natural disasters? What should you include for man-made disasters? (235)

24. What steps can you take to secure your wireless network? (236)

25. How can mobile security apps protect your mobile device data? (237)

26. What are some questions that arise surrounding fair use with respect to copyrighted material? (240)

27. What role does the ENERGY STAR program play in green computing? (241)

28. For what purposes do websites use cookies? (243)

29. What is clickjacking? (245)

✳ Problem Solving

The Problem Solving exercises extend your knowledge of chapter concepts by seeking solutions to practical problems with technology that you may encounter at home, school, work, or with nonprofit organizations. The Collaboration exercise should be completed with a team.

Instructions: You often can solve problems with technology in multiple ways. Determine a solution to the problems in these exercises by using one or more resources available to you (such as a computer or mobile device, articles on the web or in print, blogs, podcasts, videos, television, user guides, other individuals, electronics or computer stores, etc.). Describe your solution, along with the resource(s) used, in the format requested by your instructor (brief report, presentation, discussion, blog post, video, or other means).

Personal

1. No Browsing History While using the browser on your tablet, you realize that it is not keeping a history of websites you have visited. Why might this be happening, and what is the first step you will take to correct this problem?

2. Phishing Scam You just received an email message from someone requesting personal identification information. Believing the message was legitimate, you provided the requested information to the original sender. You now realize, however, that you might have fallen victim to a phishing scam. What are your next steps?

Source: Privacy Rights Clearinghouse

3. Suspicious File Attachment You receive an email message that appears to be from someone you know. When you try to open the attachment, nothing happens. You attempt to open the attachment two more times without any success. Several minutes later, your computer is running slower and you are having trouble running apps. What might be wrong?

4. Antivirus Software Outdated After starting your computer and signing in to the operating system, a message is displayed stating that your virus definitions are out of date and need to be updated. What are your next steps?

5. Laptop's Physical Security You plan to start taking your laptop to school so that you can record notes in class. You want to make sure, however, that your computer is safe if you ever step away from it for a brief period of time. What steps can you take to ensure the physical security of your laptop?

Professional

6. Corporate Firewall Interference You installed a new browser on your work computer because you no longer wish to use the default browser provided with the operating system. When you run the new browser, an error message appears stating that a user name and password are required to configure the firewall and allow this program to access the Internet. Why has this happened?

7. Problems with CAPTCHA You are signing up for an account on a website and encounter a CAPTCHA. You attempt to type the characters you see on the screen, but an error message appears stating that you have entered the incorrect characters. You try two more times and get the same result. You are typing the characters to the best of your ability but think you still might be misreading at least one of the characters. What are your next steps?

8. Unclear Acceptable Use Policy You read your company's acceptable use policy, but it is not clear about whether you are able to use the computer in your office to visit news websites on your lunch break. How can you determine whether this type of activity is allowed?

9. Two-Step Verification Problem A website you are attempting to access requires two-step verification. In addition to entering your password, you also have to enter a code that it sends to you as a text message. You no longer have the same phone number, so you are unable to receive the text message. What are your next steps?

10. Issue with Virus Protection You receive a notification that the antivirus program on your computer is not enabled. While attempting to enable the antivirus program, an error message is displayed stating that a problem has prevented the antivirus program from being enabled. What are your next steps?

Collaboration

11. Technology in National and Local Security National and local security agencies often use technology to protect citizens. For example, computers are used to maintain a No Fly List, which contains a list of individuals not cleared to board a commercial aircraft. Form a team of three people to create a list of the various ways technology helps to keep the public safe. One team member should research how local agencies, such as police departments, use technology to ensure security. Another team member should research ways national security agencies use technology to protect the public from threats, and the last team member should research ways that private businesses use technology to enhance security. Compile these findings into a report and submit it to your instructor.

The How To: Your Turn exercises present general guidelines for fundamental skills when using a computer or mobile device and then require that you determine how to apply these general guidelines to a specific program or situation.

How To: Your Turn ✳

Discover More: Visit this chapter's premium content to **challenge yourself with additional How To: Your Turn exercises,** which include App Adventure.

Instructions: You often can complete tasks using technology in multiple ways. Figure out how to perform the tasks described in these exercises by using one or more resources available to you (such as a computer or mobile device, articles on the web or in print, online or program help, user guides, blogs, podcasts, videos, other individuals, trial and error, etc.). Summarize your 'how to' steps, along with the resource(s) used, in the format requested by your instructor (brief report, presentation, discussion, blog post, video, or other means).

① Evaluating Your Electronic Profile

When you make purchases online, tap or click advertisements, follow links, and complete online forms requesting information about yourself, you are adding to your electronic profile. While an electronic profile may help businesses guide you toward products and services that are of interest to you, some people view them as an invasion of privacy. The following steps guide you through the process of locating online information about yourself and taking steps to remove the information, if possible.

a. Run a browser.

b. Navigate to a search engine of your choice.

c. Perform a search for your full name.

d. In the search results, follow a link that you feel will display a webpage containing information about you. If the link's destination does not contain information about you, navigate back to the search results and follow another link.

e. Evaluate the webpage that contains information about you. If you wish to try removing the information, locate a link that allows you to contact the site owner(s) or automatically request removal of the information.

f. Request that your information be removed from the website. Some websites may not honor your request for removal. If you feel that the information must be removed, you may need to solicit legal advice.

g. If the search results display information from an account you have on an online social network, such as Facebook or LinkedIn, you may need to adjust your privacy settings so that the information is not public. If the privacy settings do not allow you to hide your information, you may need to consider deleting the account.

h. Repeat Steps d – g for the remaining search results. When you no longer see relevant search results for the search engine you used, search for other variations of your name (use your middle initial instead of your middle name, exclude your middle name, or consider

using commonly used nicknames instead of your first name).

i. Use other search engines to search for different variations of your name. Some search engines uncover results that others do not.

j. If you have an account on an online social network, navigate to the website's home page and, without signing in, search for your name. If information appears that you do not want to be public, you may need to adjust your privacy settings or remove your account.

k. Follow up with requests you have made to remove your online information.

Exercises

1. What personal information have you uncovered online? Did you have any idea that the information was there?

2. What additional steps can you take to prevent people and businesses from storing information about you?

3. What steps might you be able to take if you are unsuccessful with your attempts to remove online information that identifies you?

Source: Geoffrey, LLC

✳ How To: Your Turn

❷ Update Virus Definitions

In addition to installing or activating an antivirus program on your computer or mobile device to keep it safe from viruses, it also is necessary to keep the virus definitions updated so that the antivirus program can search for and detect new viruses on your computer or mobile device. New virus definitions can be released as often as once per day, depending on the number of new viruses that are created. Antivirus programs either can search for and install new virus definitions automatically at specified intervals, or you can update the virus signatures manually. The following steps describe how to update the virus definitions for an antivirus program.

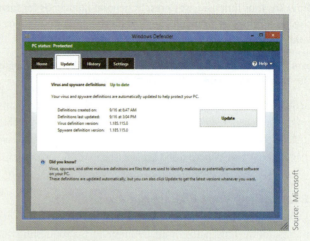

Source: Microsoft

Update Virus Definitions Manually

a. If necessary, establish an Internet connection so that you will be able to update the virus definitions.
b. Run an antivirus program.
c. Tap or click the button to check for updated virus definitions.
d. If new virus definitions are available for the antivirus program, tap or click the link to download the definitions to the computer or mobile device.
e. When the update is complete, tap or click the button to scan the computer or mobile device for viruses.

Configure Automatic Updates for Virus Definitions

a. If necessary, establish an Internet connection so that you will be able to update the virus definitions.
b. Run an antivirus program.
c. Tap or click the option to update virus definitions automatically.
d. Tap or click the option to display the virus definition update schedule.
e. To provide the maximum protection from viruses, configure the antivirus program to update definitions as frequently as possible.
f. After configuring the update schedule, tap or click the button to update virus definitions manually.
g. When the update is complete, tap or click the button to scan the computer or mobile device for viruses.

Exercises

1. What antivirus program, if any, currently is installed on your computer? Is it scheduled to update virus definitions automatically?
2. In addition to downloading and installing virus definitions from within the antivirus program, are other ways available to obtain the latest virus definitions?
3. In addition to keeping the antivirus program's virus definitions current, what other ways can you protect a computer or mobile device from viruses?

❸ Determine Whether a Computer or Mobile Device Is Secured Properly

Several steps are required to secure a computer or mobile device properly. In addition to installing antivirus software and updating the virus definitions regularly, you also should install and configure a firewall, keep the operating system up to date, and be careful not to open suspicious email messages, visit unsecure webpages, or download untrusted files while using the Internet. The following steps guide you through the process of making sure your computer or mobile device is secured properly by verifying antivirus software is installed and running, a firewall is enabled and configured, and the operating system is up to date.

Verify Antivirus Software

a. Use the search tool in the operating system or scan the programs on the computer or mobile device for antivirus software. Some operating systems include antivirus software.
b. If you are unable to locate antivirus software on the computer or mobile device, obtain an antivirus program and install it.
c. Run the antivirus program.
d. Verify the virus definitions in the antivirus program are up to date.

Verify the Firewall

a. Use the search tool in the operating system or scan the programs, apps, and settings on the computer or mobile device to access and configure the firewall.
b. If you are unable to locate a firewall on the computer or mobile device, obtain a firewall program and install it.
c. Run the firewall program.
d. View the firewall settings and verify the firewall is turned on.
e. View the list of programs, apps, and features allowed through the firewall. If you do not recognize or use one or more of the programs, apps, or features, remove them from the list of allowed programs, apps, and features.

How To: Your Turn ✹

Verify Operating System Updates

a. If necessary, establish an Internet connection.

b. Navigate to the area of the operating system where you can access the button, link, or command to search for operating system updates. For example, in Microsoft Windows, you would display the settings for Windows Update.

c. Tap or click the button, link, or command to check for updates.

d. If no updates are available, your operating system is up to date. If the operating system locates additional updates, download and install the updates. **NOTE: If the computer or mobile device you are using does not belong to you, check with its owner before downloading and installing updates for the operating system.**

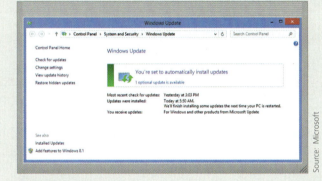

Source: Microsoft

Exercises

1. Before you began this exercise, was your computer or mobile device secured properly? How did you know your computer or mobile device was secured properly? If it was not, what actions did you need to perform to secure it?

2. Which programs, apps, and features do you think are safe to allow through your firewall? Which programs, apps, and features do you feel are not safe to allow through your firewall?

3. What additional ways can you properly secure your computer?

④ Clear Your Browsing History

A browser keeps track of the webpages that you have visited previously unless you have changed your settings. Although you can clear the browsing history on your computer or mobile device, your Internet service provider still may have logs that show a history of websites you have visited. The following steps guide you through the process of clearing your browsing history.

a. Run the browser.

b. Display the browser's settings.

c. If necessary, navigate to the settings that configure the browser's security settings. These settings often are found in the Security, Safety, or Privacy category.

d. Select the option to delete the browsing history. In addition to deleting the list of websites you have visited, you also may be able to clear passwords the browser has remembered, clear cookies and temporary internet files, clear data you entered in forms, and clear a history of downloads.

e. When the browsing history has been deleted, run the browser again.

f. Follow the above steps for each additional browser you have installed on your computer or mobile device.

Exercises

1. What are some reasons why you might want to delete your browsing history?

2. Can you configure your browser to automatically delete your browsing history? If so, how?

3. What are the advantages of keeping your browsing history? If you do keep your browsing history, how long do you keep it?

⑤ Configure a Browser's Cookie Settings

As discussed in this chapter, cookies can be used for a variety of reasons. Websites can install cookies on your computer or mobile device that can store information on your computer or mobile device, or track your browsing habits. You can configure a browser's settings to disallow websites from storing and accessing cookies on your computer or mobile device. The following steps guide you through the process of configuring a browser's cookie settings.

a. Run the browser.

b. Display the browser's settings.

c. Navigate to the settings that configure the browser's cookie settings. These settings often are found in the Security, Safety, or Privacy category.

d. Configure how the browser handles first-party cookies and third-party cookies. Some users choose to reject all cookies. To function properly, however, some websites require that you accept their cookies.

e. Save the changes to the settings.

f. Run the browser again.

Exercises

1. What is the difference between first-party cookies and third-party cookies?

2. Configure the browser to deny all first-party and third-party cookies and then navigate to five websites you visit most frequently. Do the websites display any differently now that you are denying all cookies? Describe your browsing experience while the browser is configured to deny all cookies.

3. What security risks are associated with cookies?

✳ Internet Research

The Internet Research exercises broaden your understanding of chapter concepts by requiring that you search for information on the web.

Discover More: Visit this chapter's premium content to **challenge yourself with additional Internet Research exercises,** which include Search Sleuth, Green Computing, Ethics in Action, You Review It, and Exploring Technology Careers.

Instructions: Use a search engine or another search tool to locate the information requested or answers to questions presented in the exercises. Describe your findings, along with the search term(s) you used and your web source(s), in the format requested by your instructor (brief report, presentation, discussion, blog post, video, or other means).

① Making Use of the Web
News, Weather, and Sports

Apps on tablets, smartphones, and other mobile devices are changing the delivery of the day's major news, weather, and sports stories. In one study, approximately one-half of American adults reported that they get some of their news on a tablet or mobile device. They view video and photos from eyewitnesses and fans, read analyses from investigators and coaches, and comment on stories. Men and college-educated people are the heaviest users of mobile news websites, and they are likely to read in-depth investigations and analyses. Online social networks also are a major source of information for many people.

Research This: (a) Visit two news websites or apps and locate one national event covered in both sources. Compare the coverage of the two stories. What information is provided in addition to the text, such as video, graphics, or links to related articles? Which story offers a better analysis? Which source is easier to navigate and read? Then, using another website or app, locate and read today's top international news story. What did you learn by reading the story? Were you aware of this event prior to reading the online story? Does the coverage include videos and photos to increase your comprehension?

(b) Visit a weather website or app and obtain the five-day forecast for your hometown. Include details about information that supplements the current and forecast conditions, such as a pollen or air quality index, storm tracking, travel advisories, or season summaries.

Source: National Weather Service

(c) Visit a sports website or app and read the first story reported. Describe the coverage of this event. Which sources are quoted in the story? Which links are included to other stories? Describe the features provided on this website, such as the ability to chat, customize the page for your favorite teams, or share the content with media sharing sites.

② Social Media

Sharing photos on your social media sites of yesterday's visit to the ballpark might be at the top of today's to-do list, but these images might be just the clues cyberthieves need to access your account. Facebook, in particular, is one website that scammers and advertisers use to gather information regarding your whereabouts and your personal life. Their malicious attacks begin with a visit to your timeline or other record of your activities. Searching for keywords on your page, they send targeted messages appearing to originate from trusted friends. If you open their attachments or tap or click their links, you have given these unscrupulous individuals access to your account. In addition, you may think you have crafted a password no one could guess. With your page open for others to view, however, the thieves scour the contents in hopes of locating starting clues, such as children's names, anniversary dates, and pet breeds, which could be hints to cracking your password.

Research This: In the Help section of an online social network you use, search for information about changing your profile's security and privacy settings. What steps can you take to mitigate the chance of becoming the victim of a hack? For example, can you adjust the connection settings to restrict who can see stories, send friend requests and messages, or search for you by name or contact information? Can you hide certain posts or block people from posting on your page? Can you report posts if they violate the website's terms? What are other potential threats to someone accessing your account?

③ Search Skills
Social Media Search

Search engines provide access to millions of search results by finding webpages, documents, images, or

Internet Research ✳

other information that match the search text you provide. Recommendations from people who use social media to share what they have read can be a possible alternative to using a search engine. People who take the time to Tweet pin an article or image on Twitter or Pinterest often do so because they found it useful, and hope others will as well.

To search Twitter, type the search text, search twitter, in a search engine to find the web address for the Twitter Search website, or sign in to Twitter with your credentials. In the Search Twitter text box, type the search text. For example, type the text, best mapping app, to find recommendations of links to articles or websites about mapping apps. You also can search Twitter for hashtags (a keyword preceded by a # symbol) to find Tweets about current events or popular discussion topics.

To search Pinterest, sign in to your Pinterest account and then type the search text into the search box. For example, type the search text, information security, into the search box to view related pins from Pinterest users. Pinterest users often pin links to infographics, images, and websites.

Source: Pinterest

Research This: Use Twitter and Pinterest to search for information about the following topics and then compare your results with those you would find using a search engine such as Bing, Google, or Yahoo!. (1) green computing, (2) computer virus, (3) cybercrime, and (4) malware. How are the results different? What type of information are you more likely to find on Twitter, on Pinterest, and using a search engine?

4 Security

Digital certificates and signatures detect a sender's identity and verify a document's authenticity. In this chapter you learned that many e-commerce companies use them in an attempt to prevent digital eavesdroppers from intercepting confidential information. The online certificate authority (CA) vendors generate these certificates using a standard, called X.509, which is coordinated by the International Telecommunication Union and uses algorithms and encryption technology to identify the documents.

Research This: Visit websites of at least two companies that issue digital certificates. Compare products offered, prices, and certificate features. What length of time is needed to issue a certificate? What is a green address bar, and when is one issued? What business or organization validation is required? Then, visit websites of at least two companies that provide digital signatures. Compare signing and sending requirements, types of supported signatures, and available security features. Which documents are required to obtain a digital signature? When would a business need a Class 2 rather than a Class 3 digital signature?

5 Cloud Services

Cloud Security (SecaaS)

Antivirus software offers regular, automatic updates in order to protect a server, computer, or device from viruses, malware, or other attacks. Antivirus software is an example of cloud security, or security as a service (SecaaS), a service of cloud computing that delivers virus definitions and security software to users over the Internet as updates become available, with no intervention from users. Security as a service is a special case of software as a service, but is limited to security software solutions.

Individuals and enterprise users take advantage of antivirus software and security updates. Enterprise cloud users interact with cloud security solutions via a web interface to configure apps that provide protection to email servers, preventing spam before it arrives, keeping data secure, and watching for online threats and viruses. As the use of cloud-based resources continues, the market for security as a service solutions is expected to increase significantly in coming years.

Research This: (1) Use a search engine to find two different providers of security as a service solutions. Research the different solutions they provide, and report your findings. (2) How are enterprise security requirements different from those of individual users?

Critical Thinking

The Critical Thinking exercises challenge your assessment and decision-making skills by presenting real-world situations associated with chapter concepts. The Collaboration exercise should be completed with a team.

Instructions: Evaluate the situations below, using personal experiences and one or more resources available to you (such as articles on the web or in print, blogs, podcasts, videos, television, user guides, other individuals, electronics or computer stores, etc.). Perform the tasks requested in each exercise and share your deliverables in the format requested by your instructor (brief report, presentation, discussion, blog post, video, or other means).

1. Online Gaming Safety

You and your friend frequently play a popular online role-playing game. Your friend's computer had a virus recently, which was traced back to a malware-infected website. Your friend tells you that she visited the website after following a link while playing the game. What risks are involved when playing online games?

Do This: Use the web to find articles about incidents of malware infections associated with online gaming. Research tips for increasing security when playing online games. Did you find other threats and security tips in addition to the ones mentioned in this chapter? Have you ever downloaded updates to a game? If so, how did you ensure the updates were safe? Locate a list of games that are known to cause malware infections. Share your findings and any online gaming security problems you have experienced with the class.

2. Ensuring Safety and Security Online

You work in the information technology department for a large enterprise. An increasing number of users are contacting the help desk complaining about slow computer performance. Help desk representatives frequently attribute the decreased performance to malware. Although the help desk has installed security software on each computer, users also must practice safe computing. Your manager asked you to prepare information that teaches employees how to guard against malware and other security threats.

Do This: Include information such as how to determine if a website is safe, how to identify email and other spoofing schemes, guidelines for downloading programs and apps, email attachment safety, and how to avoid phishing scams. Create a list of how organizations use common safeguards to protect other users on the network, such as firewalls, proxy servers, user names and passwords, access controls, and audit trails.

3. Case Study

Amateur Sports League You are the new manager for a nonprofit amateur soccer league. The league's board of directors asked you to develop a disaster recovery plan for its main office. The main office consists of a small storefront with two back rooms: one room is the office, with all of the electronic equipment and paper files; the other is for storage of nonelectronic equipment. The staff members — you, an administrative assistant, and an information technology (IT) specialist — work in the office. The electronic equipment in the office includes two desktops, a laptop, an external hard drive for backups, a wireless router, and two printers. In addition, each staff member has a smartphone.

Do This: Choose either a natural or man-made disaster. Create a disaster recovery plan that outlines emergency strategies, backup procedures, recovery steps, and a test plan. Assign staff members roles for each phase of the disaster recovery plan.

Collaboration

4. **Implementing Biometric Security** You are the chief technology officer of a large company. You have been reading an article about computer security that discussed several examples of security breaches, including thieves breaking into an office and stealing expensive equipment, and a recently terminated employee gaining access to the office after hours and corrupting data. Because of these incidents, your company would like to start using biometric devices to increase its security.

Do This: Form a three-member team and research the use of biometric devices to protect equipment and data. Each member of your team should choose a different type of biometric device, such as fingerprint readers, face recognition systems, and hand geometry systems. Find products for each device type, and research costs and user reviews. Search for articles by industry experts. Would you recommend using the biometric device for security purposes? Why or why not? Meet with your team, discuss and compile your findings, and then share with the class.

Technology Timeline

1937 Dr. John V. Atanasoff and Clifford Berry design and build the first electronic digital computer. Their machine, the Atanasoff-Berry-Computer, or ABC, provides the foundation for advances in electronic digital computers.

1945 John von Neumann poses in front of the electronic computer built at the Institute for Advanced Study. This computer and its von Neumann architecture served as the prototype for subsequent stored program computers worldwide.

1947 William Shockley, John Bardeen, and Walter Brattain invent the transfer resistance device, eventually called the transistor. The transistor would revolutionize computers, proving much more reliable than vacuum tubes.

1952 Dr. Grace Hopper considers the concept of reusable software in her paper, "The Education of a Computer." The paper describes how to program a computer with symbolic notation instead of detailed machine language.

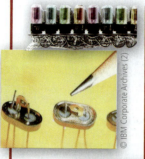

AP Images/Frederick News-Post (2); J. R. Eyerman/The LIFE Picture Collection/Getty Images

Photo: Alan Richards, from the Shelby White and Leon Levy Archives Center, Institute for Advanced Study, Princeton, NJ, USA (2)

© IBM Corporate Archives (2)

Courtesy of Hagley Museum and Library

1937 · 1943 · 1945 · 1946 · 1947 · 1951 · 1952 · 1953

Bletchley Park Trust/SSPL/The Image Works

Source: U.S. Army

S.M./Sueddeutsche Zeitung Photo/The Image Works

Courtesy Unisys Corporation

© IBM Corporate Archives

1946 Dr. John W. Mauchly and J. Presper Eckert, Jr. complete work on the first large-scale electronic, general-purpose digital computer. The ENIAC (Electronic Numerical Integrator And Computer) weighs 30 tons, contains 18,000 vacuum tubes, occupies a 30 × 50 foot space, and consumes 160 kilowatts of power.

1943 During World War II, British scientist Alan Turing designs the Colossus, an electronic computer created for the military to break German codes. The computer's existence is kept secret until the 1970s.

1951 The first commercially available electronic digital computer, the UNIVAC I (UNIVersal Automatic Computer), is introduced by Remington Rand. Public awareness of computers increases when the UNIVAC I correctly predicts that Dwight D. Eisenhower will win the presidential election.

1953 Core memory, developed in the early 1950s, provides much larger storage capacity than vacuum tube memory.

1953 The IBM model 650 is one of the first widely used computers. The computer is so successful that IBM manufactures more than 1,000. IBM will dominate the mainframe market for the next decade.

1957 The IBM 305 RAMAC computer is the first to use magnetic disk for external storage. The computer provides storage capacity similar to magnetic tape that previously was used but offers the advantage of semi-random access capability.

© IBM Corporate Archives

1957 FORTRAN (FORmula TRANslation), an efficient, easy-to-use programming language, is introduced by John Backus.

1959 More than 200 programming languages have been created.

1959 IBM introduces two smaller, desk-sized computers: the IBM 1401 for business and the IBM 1620 for scientists.

© IBM Corporate Archives

1965 Digital Equipment Corporation (DEC) introduces the first microcomputer, the PDP-8. The machine is used extensively as an interface for time-sharing systems.

Courtesy of Hewlett-Packard Company

1965 Dr. John Kemeny of Dartmouth leads the development of the BASIC programming language.

Courtesy of Dartmouth College

1968 In a letter to the editor titled, "GO TO Statements Considered Harmful," Dr. Edsger Dijkstra introduces the concept of structured programming, developing standards for constructing computer programs.

1968 Computer Science Corporation (CSC) becomes the first software company listed on the New York Stock Exchange.

© Cengage Learning

| 1957 | 1958 | 1959 | 1960 | 1964 | 1965 | 1967 | 1968 |

1958 Jack Kilby of Texas Instruments invents the integrated circuit, which lays the foundation for high-speed computers and large-capacity memory. Computers built with transistors mark the beginning of the second generation of computer hardware.

Courtesy of Texas Instruments (2)

1960 COBOL, a high-level business application language, is developed by a committee headed by Dr. Grace Hopper.

Courtesy of Hagley Museum and Library

Source: Indiana University – School of Informatics at IUPUI

Douglas Englebart

Image

Douglas Engelbart's Picture

Start Over: Profile for Englebart

1967 Douglas Engelbart applies for a patent for his wooden mouse.

© IBM Corporate Archives

1964 The number of computers has grown to 18,000. Third-generation computers, with their controlling circuitry stored on chips, are introduced. The IBM System/360 computer is the first family of compatible machines, merging science and business lines.

1968 Alan Shugart at IBM demonstrates the first regular use of an 8-inch floppy disk.

© IBM Corporate Archives (3)

1964 IBM introduces the term, word processing, for the first time with its Magnetic Tape/Selectric Typewriter (MT/ST). The MT/ST was the first reusable storage medium that allowed typed material to be edited without requiring that the document be retyped.

1969 Under pressure from the industry, IBM announces that some of its software will be priced separately from the computer hardware, allowing software firms to emerge in the industry.

© IBM Corporate Archives

1969 The ARPANET network is established, which eventually grows to become the Internet.

1975 MITS, Inc. advertises one of the first microcomputers, the Altair. The Altair is sold in kits for less than $400, and within the first three months 4,000 orders are taken.

LiPo Ching/MCT/Newscom

1975 Ethernet, the first local area network (LAN), is developed at Xerox PARC (Palo Alto Research Center) by Robert Metcalfe.

1976 Steve Jobs and Steve Wozniak build the first Apple computer. A subsequent version, the Apple II, is an immediate success. Adopted by elementary schools, high schools, and colleges, for many students, the Apple II is their first contact with the world of computers.

LongHa2006/ iStockphoto.com

© Bettmann/CORBIS

Courtesy of IBM Corporate Archives

1980 IBM offers Microsoft Corporation cofounder, Bill Gates, the opportunity to develop the operating system for the soon-to-be announced IBM personal computer. With the development of MS-DOS, Microsoft achieves tremendous growth and success.

1980 Alan Shugart presents the Winchester hard disk, revolutionizing storage for personal computers.

Courtesy of IBM Corporate Archives

| 1969 | 1970 | 1971 | 1975 | 1976 | 1979 | 1980 | 1981 |

© IBM Corporate Archives

1970 Fourth-generation computers, built with chips that use LSI (large-scale integration) arrive. While the chips used in 1965 contained up to 1,000 circuits, the LSI chip contains as many as 15,000.

Courtesy of Intel Corporation (2)

1971 Dr. Ted Hoff of Intel Corporation develops a microprocessor, or microprogrammable computer chip, the Intel 4004.

1979 VisiCalc, a spreadsheet program written by Bob Frankston and Dan Bricklin, is introduced.

1979 The first public online information services, CompuServe and the Source, are founded.

1981 The IBM PC is introduced, signaling IBM's entrance into the personal computer marketplace. The IBM PC quickly garners the largest share of the personal computer market and becomes the personal computer of choice in business.

Courtesy of IBM Corporate Archives

1981 The first computer virus, Elk Cloner, is spread via Apple II floppy disks, which contained the operating system. A short rhyme would appear on the screen when the user pressed the Reset button after the 50th boot of an infected disk.

© Rebecca Lowe/iStockphoto

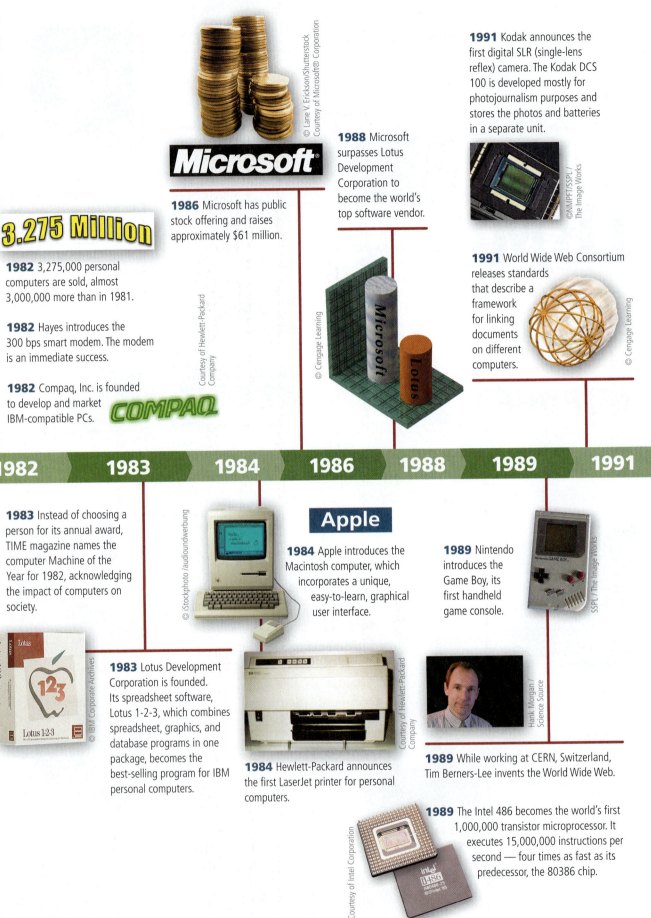

1991 Kodak announces the first digital SLR (single-lens reflex) camera. The Kodak DCS 100 is developed mostly for photojournalism purposes and stores the photos and batteries in a separate unit.

© Lane V. Erickson/Shutterstock
Courtesy of Microsoft® Corporation

1988 Microsoft surpasses Lotus Development Corporation to become the world's top software vendor.

1986 Microsoft has public stock offering and raises approximately $61 million.

©NMPFT/SSPL / The Image Works

3.275 Million

1982 3,275,000 personal computers are sold, almost 3,000,000 more than in 1981.

1982 Hayes introduces the 300 bps smart modem. The modem is an immediate success.

1982 Compaq, Inc. is founded to develop and market IBM-compatible PCs.

COMPAQ

Courtesy of Hewlett-Packard Company

1991 World Wide Web Consortium releases standards that describe a framework for linking documents on different computers.

© Cengage Learning

© Cengage Learning

| 1982 | 1983 | 1984 | 1986 | 1988 | 1989 | 1991 |

1983 Instead of choosing a person for its annual award, TIME magazine names the computer Machine of the Year for 1982, acknowledging the impact of computers on society.

Apple

1984 Apple introduces the Macintosh computer, which incorporates a unique, easy-to-learn, graphical user interface.

© iStockphoto /audioundwerbung

1989 Nintendo introduces the Game Boy, its first handheld game console.

SSPL / The Image Works

1983 Lotus Development Corporation is founded. Its spreadsheet software, Lotus 1-2-3, which combines spreadsheet, graphics, and database programs in one package, becomes the best-selling program for IBM personal computers.

© IBM Corporate Archives

1984 Hewlett-Packard announces the first LaserJet printer for personal computers.

Courtesy of Hewlett-Packard Company

Hank Morgan / Science Source

1989 While working at CERN, Switzerland, Tim Berners-Lee invents the World Wide Web.

1989 The Intel 486 becomes the world's first 1,000,000 transistor microprocessor. It executes 15,000,000 instructions per second — four times as fast as its predecessor, the 80386 chip.

Courtesy of Intel Corporation

Courtesy of Microsoft Corporation

1993 Microsoft releases Microsoft Office 3 Professional, the first version of Microsoft Office for the Windows operating system.

1993 Several companies introduce computers using the Pentium processor from Intel. The Pentium chip contains 3.1 million transistors and is capable of performing 112,000,000 instructions per second.

Courtesy of Intel Corporation

Source: amazon.com

1994 Amazon is founded and later begins business as an online bookstore. Amazon eventually expands to sell products of all types and facilitates the buying and selling of new and used goods. Today, Amazon employs more than 88,400 people.

Courtesy of Larry Ewing and The Gimp

1994 Linus Torvalds creates the Linux kernel, a UNIX-like operating system that he releases free across the Internet for further enhancement by other programmers.

1995 eBay, an online auction website, is founded. Providing an online venue for people to buy and sell goods, it quickly becomes the world's largest online marketplace as it approaches 100 million active users worldwide.

AP Images/Nigel Treblin/dapd

Oracle and Java are registered trademarks of Oracle and/or its affiliates. Other names may be trademarks of their respective owners."

1995 Sun Microsystems launches Java, an object-oriented programming language that allows users to write one program for a variety of computer platforms.

1995 Microsoft releases Windows 95, a major upgrade to its Windows operating system. Windows 95 consists of more than 10,000,000 lines of computer instructions developed by 300 person-years of effort.

/Reuters/Landov

1992   **1993**   **1994**   **1995**

Courtesy of Microsoft® Corporation

1992 Microsoft releases Windows 3.1, the latest version of its Windows operating system. Windows 3.1 offers improvements such as TrueType fonts, multimedia capability, and object linking and embedding (OLE). In two months, 3,000,000 copies of Windows 3.1 are sold.

1993 The U.S. Air Force completes the Global Positioning System by launching its 24th Navstar satellite into orbit. Today, GPS receivers can be found in cars, laptops, and smartphones.

Courtesy of Garmin International

1994 Jim Clark and Marc Andreessen found Netscape and launch Netscape Navigator 1.0, a browser.

Courtesy of Netscape Communications Corporation

1994 Apple introduces the first digital camera intended for consumers. The Apple QuickTake 100 is connected to home computers using a serial cable.

Courtesy of Mark D. Martin

© Orhan Cam/Shutterstock.com

1993 The White House launches its website, which includes an interactive citizens' handbook and White House history and tours.

1994 Yahoo!, a popular search engine and portal, is founded by two Stanford Ph.D. students as a way to keep track of their personal interests on the Internet. Currently, Yahoo! has approximately 11,500 employees in 25 countries, provinces, and territories.

AP Photo/Paul Sakuma

1997 Intel introduces the Pentium II processor with 7.5 million transistors. The new processor, which incorporates MMX technology, processes video, audio, and graphics data more efficiently and supports programs such as movie editing, gaming, and more.

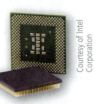

Courtesy of Intel Corporation

1999 Intel introduces the Pentium III processor. This processor succeeds the Pentium II and can process 3-D graphics more quickly. The Pentium III processor contains between 9.5 and 44 million transistors.

Courtesy of Intel Corporation

1999 Governments and businesses frantically work to make their computers Y2K (Year 2000) compliant, spending more than $500 billion worldwide.

© Cengage Learning

1997 Microsoft releases Internet Explorer 4.0 and seizes a key place in the Internet arena.

AP Photo

1999 Open source software, such as the Linux operating system and the Apache web server created by unpaid volunteers, begins to gain wide acceptance among computer users.

© Tan Kian Khoon/Shutterstock

1996   1997   1998   1999

Courtesy of Palm, Inc.

1996 U.S. Robotics introduces the PalmPilot, an inexpensive user-friendly personal digital assistant (PDA).

1996 Microsoft releases Windows NT 4.0, an operating system for client-server networks.

Box shot reprinted with permission from Microsoft Corporation.

Courtesy of Google, Inc.

1998 Google files for incorporation and is now the most used search engine, capturing more than 60 percent of the market over other search engines.

Brad Cherson / Alamy

1998 E-commerce booms. Companies such as Amazon.com, Dell, and E*TRADE spur online shopping, allowing buyers to obtain a variety of goods and services.

© iStockphoto/juniorbeep

1998 Apple introduces the iMac, the next version of its popular Macintosh computer. The iMac wins customers with its futuristic design, see-through case, and easy setup.

Source: Napster

2000 Shawn Fanning, 19, and his company, Napster, turn the music industry upside down by developing software that allows computer users to swap music files with one another without going through a centralized file server.

Courtesy of Intel Corporation

2001 Intel unveils its Pentium 4 chip with clock speeds starting at 1.4 GHz. The Pentium 4 includes 42 million transistors.

2002 Digital video cameras, DVD burners, easy-to-use video editing software, and improvements in storage capabilities allow the average computer user to create Hollywood-like videos with introductions, conclusions, rearranged scenes, music, and voice-over.

Courtesy of Intel Corporation

© Cengage Learning

2001 Wikipedia, a free online encyclopedia, is introduced. Additional wikis begin to appear on the Internet, enabling people to share information in their areas of expertise. Although some might rely on wikis for research purposes, the content is not always verified for accuracy.

Wikimedia Foundation

2002 After several years of negligible sales, the Tablet PC is reintroduced to meet the needs of a more targeted audience.

Courtesy of ViewSonic® Corporation

2000 E-commerce achieves mainstream acceptance. Annual e-commerce sales exceed $100 billion, and Internet advertising expenditures reach more than $5 billion.

2000   2001   2002

© Cengage Learning

2000 Dot-com (Internet based) companies go out of business at a record pace — nearly one per day — as financial investors withhold funding due to the companies' unprofitability.

Microsoft .net

Source: Microsoft

2002 Microsoft launches its .NET strategy, which is a new environment for developing and running software applications featuring ease of development of web-based services.

© Tatiana Popova / Shutterstock.com

2002 DVD burners begin to replace CD burners (CD-RW). DVDs can store up to eight times as much data as CDs. Uses include storing home movies, music, photos, and backups.

Kenneth Murray / Science Source

2000 Telemedicine uses satellite technology and videoconferencing to broadcast consultations and to perform distant surgeries. Robots are used for complex and precise tasks.

2002 Intel ships its revamped Pentium 4 chip with the 0.13 micron processor and Hyper-Threading (HT) Technology, operating at speeds of 3.06 GHz. This new development eventually will enable processors with a billion transistors to operate at 20 GHz.

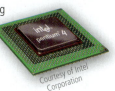

Courtesy of Intel Corporation

2004 Mozilla releases its first version of the Firefox browser. Firefox provides innovative features that enhance the browsing experience for users, including tabbed browsing and a Search box. Firefox quickly gains popularity and takes market share away from Microsoft's Internet Explorer.

AP Photo/screenshot

2004 Facebook, an online social network originally available only to college students, is founded. Facebook eventually opens registration to all people and immediately grows to more than 110 million users.

Courtesy of Facebook

2004 Sony unveils the PlayStation Portable (PSP). This handheld game console is the first to use optical discs.

ISSEI KATO/Reuters/ Landov

2004 Companies such as RealNetworks, Microsoft, Sony, and Walmart stake out turf in the online music store business started by Apple.

© Cengage Learning

2004 Flat-panel LCD monitors overtake bulky CRT monitors as the popular choice of computer users.

2004 Linux, an open source operating system, makes major inroads into the server market as a viable alternative to Microsoft Windows Server 2003, Sun's Solaris, and UNIX.

Courtesy of Larry Ewing and The Gimp

2004 106 million, or 53 percent, of the 200 million online population in America accesses the Internet via broadband.

2003

2004

© Getty Images

2003 In an attempt to maintain their current business model of selling songs, the Recording Industry Association of America (RIAA) files more than 250 lawsuits against individual computer users who offer copyrighted music over peer-to-peer networks.

REUTERS/Mannie Garcia / Landov

2003 Wireless computers and devices, such as keyboards, mouse devices, home networks, and wireless Internet access points become commonplace.

© wavebreakmedia/Shutterstock.com; ©Tom Grill/ CORBIS; © iStockphoto /hocus-pocus; © StockLite / Shutterstock.com; ©iStockphoto / LifesizeImages

Courtesy of Palm Inc.

2004 USB flash drives become a cost-effective way to transport data and information from one computer to another.

Courtesy of SanDisk Corporation

2004 Major retailers begin requiring suppliers to include radio frequency identification (RFID) tags or microchips with antennas, which can be as small as one-third of a millimeter across, in the goods they sell.

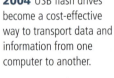

Courtesy of Intermec Technologies

Courtesy of Palm Inc.

2004 The smartphone overtakes the PDA as the mobile device of choice.

2004 Apple introduces the sleek all-in-one iMac G5. The new computer's display device contains the system unit.

/Reuters /Landov

2005 YouTube, an online community for video sharing, is founded. YouTube includes content such as home videos, movie previews, and clips from television shows. In November 2006, Google acquires YouTube.

Source: YouTube

© Cengage Learning

Video iPod

2005 Apple releases the latest version of its popular pocket-sized iPod portable media player. First it played songs, then photos, then podcasts, and now, in addition, up to 150 hours of music videos and television shows on a 2.5" color display.

HANDOUT/KRT/Newscom

LPETTET / iStockphoto.com

2006 Sony launches its PlayStation 3. New features include a Blu-ray Disc player, high-definition capabilities, and always-on online connectivity.

2006 Web 2.0, a term coined in 2004, becomes a household term with the increase in popularity of online social networks, wikis, and web applications.

2006 Apple begins selling Macintosh computers with Intel microprocessors.

Courtesy of Intel Corporation
© iStockphoto / robyvannucci

2006 Nintendo releases the Nintendo DS Lite, a handheld game console with new features such as dual screens and improved graphics and sound.

Toru Hanai/Reuters/Corbis

2005   2006

2005 Spam, spyware, phishing, and pharming take center stage, along with viruses and other malware, as major nuisances to the 801 million computer users worldwide.

2005 Blogging and podcasting become mainstream methods for distributing information via the web.

© Cengage Learning (2)

Source: Microsoft

2005 Microsoft releases the Xbox 360, its latest game console. Features include the capability to play music, display photos, and communicate with computers and other Xbox gamers.

Courtesy of Intel Corporation

2006 Intel introduces its Core 2 Duo processor family. Boasting record-breaking performance while using less power, the family consists of five desktop computer processors and five mobile computer processors. The desktop processor includes 291 million transistors, yet uses 40 percent less power than the Pentium processor.

© Cengage Learning

2006 IBM produces the fastest supercomputer, Blue Gene/L. It can perform approximately 28 trillion calculations in the time it takes you to blink your eye, or about one-tenth of a second.

ISSEI KATO/Reuters/Corbis

2006 Nintendo Wii is introduced and immediately becomes a leader in game consoles. The Wii is being used in revolutionary ways, such as training surgeons.

2007 Intel introduces Core 2 Quad, a four-core processor made for dual-processor servers and desktop computers. The larger number of cores allows for more energy-efficient performance and optimizes battery performance in laptops.

Courtesy of Intel Corporation

2007 VoIP (Voice over Internet Protocol) providers expand usage to include Wi-Fi phones. The phones enable high-quality service through a Wireless-G network and high-speed Internet connection.

Courtesy of Belkin International

2007 Apple releases its Mac OS X version 10.5 "Leopard" operating system, available in a desktop version and server version. The system includes a significantly revised desktop, with a semitransparent menu bar and an updated search tool that incorporates the same visual navigation interface as iTunes.

© oliver leedham /Alamy

2007 Apple introduces the iPhone and sells 270,000 phones in the first 2 days. iPhone uses iTouch technology that allows you to make a call simply by tapping a name or number in your address book. In addition, it stores and plays music like an iPod. Also, Apple sells its one billionth song on iTunes.

© Neville Elder/Corbis

2008 Smartphones become smarter. Smartphones introduced this year include enhanced features such as touch screens with multi-touch technology, mobile TV, tactile feedback, improved graphics, GPS receivers, and better cameras.

AP Photo/Mark Lennihan

2008 Google releases its new browser. Google Chrome uses an entirely unique interface and offers other features such as dynamic tabs, crash control, and application shortcuts.

Source: Google

2008 Bill Gates retires from Microsoft. He continues as chairman and advisor on key development projects.

Courtesy of Microsoft Corporation

2007

2008

2007 Half of the world's population uses mobile phones. More and more people are using a mobile phone in lieu of a landline in their home.

© Sean Locke/iStockphoto

2007 Blu-ray Discs increase in popularity, overcoming and replacing HD DVD in less than one year. A Blu-ray Disc can store approximately 9 hours of high-definition (HD) video on a 50 GB disc or approximately 23 hours of standard-definition (SD) video.

Helene Rogers/Art Directors & Trips Photo/ AGE Fotostock

2007 Wi-Fi hot spots are popular in a variety of locations. People bring their computers to coffeehouses, fast food restaurants, or bookstores to access the Internet wirelessly, either free or for a small fee.

© Rtimages /Shutterstock.com

2008 Netflix, an online movie rental company, and TiVo, a company manufacturing digital video recorders (DVRs), make Netflix movies and television episodes available on TiVo DVRs.

Source: Netflix

©1998-2013 TiVo Inc. All rights reserved.

2008 Computer manufacturers begin to offer solid-state drives (SSDs) instead of hard disks, mostly in laptops. Although SSDs have a lower storage capacity, are more expensive, and slightly more susceptible to failure, they are significantly faster.

© Beda / Dreamstime.com

2008 WiMAX goes live! The advantage of this technology is the capability to access video, music, voice, and video calls wherever and whenever desired. Average download speeds are between 2 Mbps and 4 Mbps. By year's end, Sprint has approximately 100 million users on its network.

iStockphoto

2009 Intel releases the Core i5 and Core i7 line of processors. These processors offer increased performance for some of the more demanding tasks. Intel also enhances its Core processor family by releasing multi-core processors, designed to increase the number of instructions that can be processed at a given time.

Courtesy of Intel Corporation

2009 Computers and mobile devices promote fitness by offering games and programs to help users exercise and track their progress. These games and programs also are used to assist with physical rehabilitation.

© Stuartkey/ Dreamstime.com

2009 Online social networks revolutionize communications. Schools, radio stations, and other organizations develop pages on popular online social networks, such as Facebook, creating closer connections with their stakeholders.

Source: Google

2009 Web apps continue to increase in popularity. Web apps make it easier to perform tasks such as word processing, photo editing, and tax preparation without installing software on your computer.

2009 In June 2009, federal law requires that all full-power television stations broadcast only in digital format. Analog television owners are required to purchase a converter box to view over-the-air digital programming.

Courtesy of Coby Electronics Corporation

2011 Netbooks offer a smaller, lighter alternative to laptops. Netbooks have screens between seven and ten inches, and are used mostly for browsing the web and communicating online.

PRNewsFoto/ Verizon Wireless)

2011 More than 200 types of mobile devices are using Google Android, an operating system originally designed for mobile devices.

2011 A new generation of browsers is released to support HTML5, enabling webpages to contain more vivid, dynamic content.

HTML5 Logo by World Wide Web Consortium

2011 E-books and e-book readers explode in popularity. Many novels, textbooks, and other publications now are available digitally and can be read on an e-book reader, computer, or mobile device.

© iStockphoto /MichaelJay

© iStockphoto /Brightrock

© iStockphoto /EdStock

2011 Steve Jobs, a cofounder of Apple, passes away after a long battle with cancer. Jobs is remembered for revolutionizing the computer and music industries.

2009   2010   2011

Source: Seagate Technology LLC

2010 Hard disk capacity continues to increase at an exponential rate, with the largest hard disks storing more than 2.5 TB of data and information.

Source: AMD

2010 AMD develops a 12-core processor, which contains two 6-core processors, each on an individual chip. Power consumption is similar to that of a 6-core processor but offers reduced clock speed.

2010 Apple releases the iPad, a revolutionary mobile device with a 9.7-inch multi-touch screen. The iPad boasts up to 10 hours of battery life, connects wirelessly to the Internet, and is capable of running thousands of apps.

© iStockphoto / hanibaram

2010 Kinect for Xbox 360 changes the way people play video games. Game players now can interact with the game with a series of sensors, as well as a camera, tracking their movements in 3-D.

Source: Microsoft

2011 Google introduces its Google+ online social network and integrates it across many of its products and services.

Source: Google

2011 Intel introduces Ultrabooks, which are powerful, lightweight alternatives to laptops. Ultrabooks normally weigh three pounds or less, have great performance and battery life, and are usually less than one inch thick.

Source: Lenovo

2012 Microsoft announces the Surface, a tablet designed to compete with Apple's iPad. The Surface has a built-in stand, runs the Windows 8 operating system and its apps, and supports a cover that also can serve as a keyboard.

Source: Microsoft

2013 Twitter users generate more than 500 million Tweets per day.

2013 Sony releases the PlayStation 4 (PS4) game console and Microsoft releases the Xbox One game console.

2012 Apple releases the iPhone 5. This newest iPhone has a four-inch screen, contains a new, smaller connector, and uses Apple's A6 processor.

2012 Microsoft releases Windows 8, its newest version of the Windows operating system. Windows 8 boasts a completely redesigned interface and supports touch input.

2013 Amazon announces it will use drones to deliver packages to its customers.

Source: Apple

2013 Tablet sales grow at a faster rate than personal computer sales ever grew.

Courtesy of Amazon

2012

2013

2012 Google's Android surpasses Apple's iOS as the most popular operating system used on smartphones. Although the iPhone still is the bestselling smartphone, competing products are gaining market share quickly.

Source: Google

2013 Samsung releases the Galaxy Gear, a smartwatch that synchronizes with a Samsung Galaxy smartphone using Bluetooth technology.

2013 QR codes rapidly gain in popularity, giving mobile device users an easy way to access web content.

© Ivan Garcia / Shutterstock

© Cengage Learning

2013 Windows 8.1, a significant update to Microsoft's Windows 8 operating system, is released.

Source: Microsoft

Source: qr-code-generator.com

2012 Microsoft releases Office 2013. Office 365, which uses the familiar Office 2013 interface, also is released, allowing users to use their Microsoft accounts to access Office apps from computers that do not have Office installed.

2012 Nintendo releases the Wii U game console.

© iStockPhoto / Mlenny

2013 Apple releases the iPhone 5S, the first iPhone with TouchID. TouchID verifies a user's identity using an integrated fingerprint reader.

2013 Many consumers prefer tablets for their mobile computing needs. Tablets provide ultimate portability while still allowing users to access a vast array of apps, as well as access to the Internet and their email messages.

© iStockphoto/mozcann

Green Computing

2014 Individuals and enterprises increase their focus on green computing. Computer manufacturers not only sell more energy-efficient hardware, they also provide easy ways in which customers can recycle their old computers and devices.

© Cengage Learning

2014 Solid-state storage is becoming more popular, with storage capacities increasing and prices decreasing.

©Oleksiy Mark /Shutterstock.com

2014 Apple releases the Apple Watch, a wearable device that runs apps and can monitor various aspects of your health and fitness.

Courtesy of Apple, Inc.

2014 Decreases in storage costs and increases in Internet connection speeds persuade more users to use cloud storage for their data. Cloud storage also provides users with the convenience of accessing their files from almost anywhere.

© Cengage Learning

2015 3-D printing decreases in price and increases in popularity.

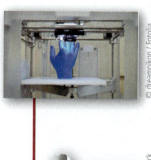

© dreamnikon / Fotolia

2015 Microsoft releases Windows 10, the latest version of its operating system. Windows 10 expands on many of the new features introduced in Windows 8, and also brings back popular features, such as the Start menu, from previous versions of Windows.

2015 Individuals and families are increasingly turning to streaming video on the Internet and abandoning their cable companies.

© iStockPhoto / xefstock

2014   2015

2014 Bitcoin continues to grow as a digital currency and online payment system.

Courtesy of Mark Frydenberg

2014 Apple releases the iPhone 6 and iPhone 6 Plus. Both devices have significantly larger screens than its predecessors.

Courtesy of Apple, Inc.

2014 Televisions with features such as curved screens and Ultra HD displays begin to increase in popularity.

© iStockPhoto / JazzIRT

2014 Google Glass goes on sale to the public in the United States.

© iStockPhoto / ferrantraite

2014 Amazon drops the price of its Fire Phone to $0.99, possibly indicating that apps and services are valued more than the device.

2015 Emerging protocols, such as LTE-A and Wi-Fi 802.11 ac, ad, aq, and ah, increase performance on mobile and wireless networks.

© iStockPhoto / Ilya_Starikov

2015 Approximately 91% of all Internet traffic is video, including HD and 3-D video.

2015 Microsoft releases Office 2016, which includes new productivity software and application updates.

Technology Acronyms

Acronym	Description	Page
3-D	three-dimensional	15
ACPA	Anticybersquatting Consumer Protection Act	64
AIO	all-in-one	114
ARPA	Advanced Research Projects Agency	56
ATM	automated teller machine	118
AUP	acceptable use policy	106
B2B	business-to-business	82
B2C	business-to-consumer	82
bcc	blind carbon copy	103
BMP	bitmap	86
BSA	Business Software Alliance	228
BTW	by the way	94
BYOD	bring your own device	35
C2C	consumer-to-consumer	82
CA	certificate authority	231
CAD	computer-aided design	164
CAM	computer-aided manufacturing	40
CAPTCHA	Completely Automated Public Turing test to tell Computers and Humans Apart	224
CBT	computer-based training	184
cc	carbon copy	103
ccTLD	country code top-level domain	63
CD	compact disc	18
CDP	continuous data protection	234
CERT/CC	Computer Emergency Response Team Coordination Center	219
CIPA	Children's Internet Protection Act	247
COPPA	Children's Online Privacy Protection Act	246
CPU	central processing unit	110
CSA	Cloud Security Alliance	232
CSC	common short code	124
CTS	carpal tunnel syndrome	142
CVS	computer vision syndrome	143
DaaS	data as a service	155
DDoS	distributed DoS	217
DMCA	Digital Millennium Copyright Act	246

Acronym	Description	Page
DNS	domain name system	64
DOE	Department of Energy	241
DoS	denial of service	217
DRM	digital rights management	240
DSL	digital subscriber line	59
DTP	desktop publishing	180
DVD	digital versatile disc	18
DVI	digital video interface	135
ECPA	Electronic Communications Privacy Act	246
EPA	Environmental Protection Agency	241
EULA	end-user license agreement	163
FAQ	frequently asked questions	94
FERPA	Family Educational Rights and Privacy Act	163
FOIA	Freedom of Information Act	246
FTP	File Transfer Protocol	24
FTTP	Fiber to the Premises	59
FWIW	for what it's worth	94
FYI	for your information	94
GB	gigabyte	61
GIF	Graphics Interchange Format	86
GPS	global positioning system	70
HDTV	high-definition television	15
HIPAA	Health Insurance Portability and Accountability Act	246
http	Hypertext Transfer Protocol	69
IaaS	infrastructure as a service	53
ICANN	Internet Corporation for Assigned Names and Numbers	63
ID	identification	222
IEEE	Institute of Electronics and Electronics Engineers	138
IMHO	in my humble opinion	94
IP	Internet Protocol	62
IP	intellectual property	240
IROC2	Institute for Responsible Online and Cell-Phone Communication	246
ISP	Internet service provider	20

Acronym	Description	Page
JPEG	Joint Photographic Experts Group	86
M2M	machine-to-machine	133
MAC	Media Access Control	236
MB	megabyte	61
MMS	multimedia message service	124
MP	megapixels	127
NFC	near field communications	138
PATRIOT	Provide Appropriate Tools Required to Intercept and Obstruct Terrorism	246
PC	personal computer	4
PDF	Portable Document Format	86
PIN	personal identification number	118
PNG	Portable Network Graphics	86
POS	point of sale	118
PUE	power usage effectiveness	241
QR	quick response	178
RSI	repetitive strain injury	142
RWD	responsive web design	84
SaaS	software as a service	105
SecaaS	security as a service	259
SLR	single-lens reflex	125

Acronym	Description	Page
SMM	Sustainable Materials Management	122
SMS	short message service	124
SSD	solid-state drive	17
SSID	service set identifier	236
TIFF	Tagged Image File Format	86
TLD	top-level domain	63
TTFN	ta-ta for now	94
TYVM	thank you very much	94
UPS	uninterruptible power supply	115
URL	Uniform Resource Locator	68
USB	Universal Serial Bus	17
VoIP	Voice over Internet Protocol	24
VPN	virtual private network	230
VR	virtual reality	87
W3C	World Wide Web Consortium	58
WAP	wireless access point	236
WBT	web-based training	184
Wi-Fi	wireless fidelity	59
WPA2	Wi-Fi Protected Access 2	236
WWW	World Wide Web	65

Troubleshooting Computer and Mobile Device Problems

While using a computer or mobile device, at some point you probably will experience a technology problem that requires troubleshooting. Technology problems that remain unresolved may impact your ability to use your device. This appendix identifies some common problems you might experience with computers and mobile devices; it also includes some suggestions for correcting these problems. If the recommended solutions in the table below do not solve your problem, or you are uncomfortable performing any of the recommended actions, contact a repair professional (independent computer repair company, technical support department at your job or academic institution, or computer or mobile device manufacturer) for additional options.

This appendix also might assist you with completing some of the Problem Solving exercises found at the end of each chapter in this textbook. Table 1 contains possible solutions for problems that might occur on your computer or mobile device.

Note: The following steps are suggestions; they are not comprehensive solutions. When working with a computer or mobile device, follow all necessary safety precautions before implementing any of these recommended solutions. Contact a professional if you require additional information.

Table 1	Problems and Recommended Solutions				
Problem	**Desktop**	**Laptop**	**Tablet**	**Phone**	**Recommended Solution(s)**
Computer or device does not turn on.	✓	✓	✓		The computer might be in sleep or hibernate mode; to wake up the computer, try pressing a key on the keyboard, pressing the power button, or tapping the touch screen if applicable.
	✓				Make sure power cables are plugged securely into the wall and the back of the computer.
		✓	✓	✓	Make sure the battery is charged if the computer or device is not connected to an external power source. If the battery is charged, connect the external AC adapter and attempt to turn on the computer or device. If the computer or device still does not turn on, the problem may be with the computer or device.
	✓	✓	✓	✓	If none of the above options resolves the issue, the power supply or AC adapter might be experiencing problems; contact a professional for assistance.
Battery does not hold a charge.		✓	✓	✓	Verify the AC adapter used to charge the battery is working properly. If the mobile computer or device can run from the AC adapter without a battery installed, the AC adapter most likely is working properly. If the AC adapter works, it may be time to replace the battery.
Computer issues a series of beeps when turned on.	✓	✓			Refer to your computer's documentation to determine what the beeps indicate, as the computer hardware may be experiencing a problem.

Problem	Desktop	Laptop	Tablet	Phone	Recommended Solution(s)
Computer or device turns on, but operating system does not run.	✓	✓	✓	✓	Disconnect all nonessential peripheral devices, remove all storage media, and then restart the computer or device.
					Restart the computer or device; if the problem persists, the operating system might need to be restored. If restoring the operating system does not work, the hard drive might be failing.
Monitor does not display anything.	✓				Verify the monitor is turned on.
					Verify the video cable is connected securely to the computer and monitor.
					Make sure the power cables are plugged securely into the wall and the back of the monitor.
					Make sure the monitor is set to the correct input source.
					Restart the computer.
					If you have access to a spare monitor, see if that monitor will work. If so, your original monitor might be faulty. If not, the problem may be with your computer's hardware or software configuration.
Screen does not display anything.		✓	✓	✓	Restart the device.
					Make sure the device is plugged in or the battery is sufficiently charged.
Keyboard or mouse does not work.	✓	✓	✓		Verify the keyboard and mouse are connected properly to the computer or device.
					If the keyboard and mouse are wireless, make sure they are turned on and contain new batteries.
					If the keyboard and mouse are wireless, attempt to pair them again with the computer or wireless receiver. Read How To 3-1 for more information.
					If you have access to a spare keyboard or mouse, see if it will work. If so, your original keyboard or mouse might be faulty. If not, the problem may be with your computer's hardware or software configuration.
		✓			Make sure the touchpad is not disabled.
Wet keyboard no longer works.	✓	✓			Turn the keyboard upside down to drain the liquid, dab wet areas with a cotton swab, and allow the keyboard to dry.
Speakers do not work.	✓	✓	✓	✓	Verify that headphones or earbuds are not connected.
					Make sure the volume is not muted and is turned up on the computer or mobile device.
	✓	✓			Verify the speakers are turned on.
					Make sure the speakers are connected properly to the computer.
					If necessary, verify the speakers are plugged in to an external power source.
Hard drive makes noise.	✓	✓			If the computer is not positioned on a flat surface, move it to a flat surface.
					If the problem persists, contact a professional.

Problem	Desktop	Laptop	Tablet	Phone	Recommended Solution(s)
Fan contains built-up dust/ does not work.	✓	✓			If possible, open the system unit and use a can of compressed air to blow the dust from the fan and away from the system unit.
	✓				Remove obvious obstructions that might be preventing the fan from functioning. Verify the fan is connected properly to the motherboard. If the fan still does not work, it may need to be replaced.
Computer or device is too hot.	✓	✓			Verify the fan or vents are not obstructed. If the fan or vents are obstructed, use a can of compressed air to blow the dust from the fan or vent and away from the computer or device or remove other obstructions.
		✓			Purchase a cooling pad that rests below the laptop and protects it from overheating.
			✓	✓	Exit apps running in the background. Search for and follow instructions how to clear the tablet or phone's cache memory. Run an app to monitor the tablet's or phone's battery performance, and exit apps that require a lot of battery power. Decrease the brightness of the display.
Cannot read from optical disc.	✓	✓			Clean the optical disc and try reading from it again. Try reading from another optical disc. If the second optical disc works, the original disc is faulty. If the second disc does not work, the problem may be with the optical disc drive.
External drive (USB flash drive, optical disc drive, or external hard drive) is not recognized.	✓	✓	✓		Remove the drive and insert it into a different USB port, if available. Remove the drive, restart the computer, and insert the drive again. Try connecting the drive to a different computer. If you still cannot read from the drive, it may be faulty.
Program or app does not run.	✓	✓	✓	✓	Restart the computer or device and try running the program or app again. If feasible, uninstall the program or app, reinstall it, and then try running it again. If the problem persists, the problem may be with the operating system's configuration.
Computer or device displays symptoms of a virus or other malware.	✓	✓	✓	✓	Make sure your antivirus software is up to date and then disconnect the computer or device from the network and run antivirus software to attempt to remove the malware. Continue running scans until no threats are detected and then reconnect the computer to the network. If you do not have antivirus software installed, obtain and install a reputable antivirus program or app and then scan your computer in an attempt to remove the malware. You should have only one antivirus program or app installed on your computer or mobile device at one time. If you are unable to remove the malware, take your computer to a professional who may be able to remove the malicious program or app.

Problem	Desktop	Laptop	Tablet	Phone	Recommended Solution(s)
Computer or device is experiencing slow performance.	✓	✓	✓		Defragment the hard disk.
	✓	✓			Uninstall programs and apps that you do not need.
					Verify your computer or device meets the minimum system requirements for the operating system and software you are running.
					If possible, purchase and install additional memory (RAM).
Screen is damaged physically.	✓	✓	✓	✓	Contact a professional to replace the screen; if the computer or device is covered under a warranty, the repair may be free.
					Replacing a broken screen on a computer or device might be more costly than replacing the computer or device; consider your options before replacing the screen.
Touch screen does not respond.	✓	✓	✓	✓	Clean the touch screen.
					Restart the computer or device.
Computer or device is wet.		✓	✓	✓	Turn off the computer or device, remove the battery, and dry off visible water with a cloth. Fill a plastic bag or box with rice, submerge the computer or device and battery into the rice so that it is surrounded completely, and then do not turn on the computer or device for at least 24 hours.
					If the computer or device does not work after it is dry, contact a professional for your options.
Computer or device does not connect to a wireless network.	✓	✓	✓	✓	Verify you are within range of a wireless access point.
					Make sure the information to connect to the wireless network is configured properly on the computer or device.
					Make sure the wireless capability on the computer or device is turned on.
Computer or device cannot synchronize with Bluetooth accessories.	✓	✓	✓	✓	Verify the Bluetooth device is turned on.
					Verify the Bluetooth functionality on your computer or device is enabled.
					Verify the computer or device has been paired properly with the accessory. Read How To 3-1 for more information.
					Make sure the Bluetooth device is charged.
Device continuously has poor cell phone reception.			✓	✓	Restart the device.
					If you have a protective case, remove the case to see if reception improves.
					If you are using the device inside a building, try moving closer to a window or open doorway.
					Contact your wireless carrier for additional suggestions.

Notes

Notes

Focus On: Web Development

Creating Webpages: Creating, Formatting, and Publishing Content Online

"I easily can create a website using an online content management system, such as Google Sites, WordPress, Joomla, or Drupal. Why do I need to know how to create a website using HTML, CSS, and JavaScript if I easily can create one using a content management system? What more do I need to know about publishing content to the web?"

In this Focus On, you will discover how to perform these tasks along with much more information essential to this course.

Objectives

After completing this Focus On, you will be able to:

1. Discuss tools for creating a website, such as text editors, code editors, and content management systems, and when to use each

2. Explain the uses of HTML5, CSS, and JavaScript technologies when creating websites

3. Discuss concepts related to web development, including static and dynamic content, relative and absolute references, HTML tags and attributes, and embedded and inline styles

4. Explain how to view a webpage's source code after displaying the page in a browser

5. Explain the unique role of the index.html page in a website

6. Use HTML tags to add a title, headings, paragraphs, images, links, ordered and unordered lists, and videos to a webpage

7. Use CSS to specify fonts, colors, and styles for text and background images or colors for webpages

8. Use JavaScript to display the current date and time on a webpage

9. Upload a website to a web server using an FTP program

Tools for Creating a Website

As discussed in Chapter 2, a website is a collection of related webpages and associated items that usually are hosted on the same web server. A web developer often creates simple websites by designing its layout, creating the content for each page, and typing the HTML codes, called tags, for each page using a text editor. When creating complex websites with hundreds or thousands of pages, web developers rely on content management systems to specify the design and content of each page.

Text Editors

A text editor is similar to a word processing program, but it lacks most text formatting features, such as fonts, colors, margins, and paragraphs, and it saves files in a text format. A browser interprets the text file and displays the content using the formatting codes specified in the file.

Operating systems typically include a text editor. For example, Windows users may use Notepad, and MacOS users may use TextEdit as their text editors. Most text editors save files in a text format automatically. Others may require additional steps to save documents in a text format.

A code editor is a type of text editor that has additional features to help web developers write the code used to develop websites and applications accurately and efficiently. For example, some code editors can display HTML code in different colors (tags might be displayed in one color, while document content is displayed in another color). In addition, code editors might improve readability of your code by applying appropriate indenting and line spacing or automatically completing HTML tags or styles as you type them. Many web developers opt to download a free or fee-based code editor with these features.

Many of the figures in this Focus On show HTML code as it appears in Brackets, a modern, open source editor built for web developers. Brackets is available for computers running both Windows and MacOS. You can download Brackets or another editor to install on your computer. Figure 1 shows several text and code editors.

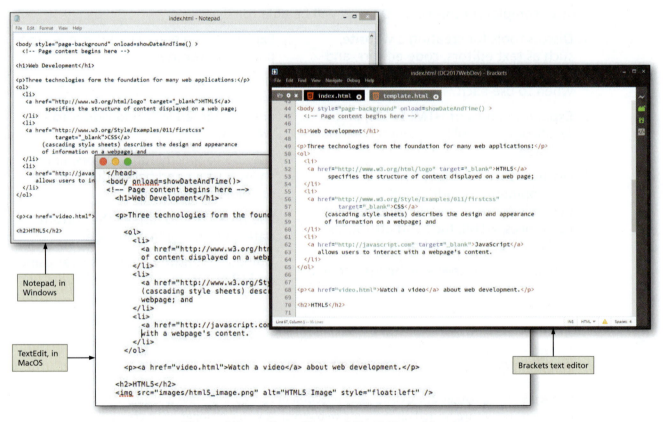

Figure 1 Text editors: Notepad, TextEdit, and Brackets.

If you are using a Mac, do you have to do anything special to use TextEdit to create webpages?
Yes. Depending on the version of TextEdit you are using, you may need to set preferences in TextEdit to save your webpage files in a text format. Ask your instructor, or consider using a search engine to locate websites that provide the instructions necessary for your computer. Consider using search text that includes words such as textedit, edit, and html.

Where can you find out more about text editors and code editors that run on your computer?
Use a search engine to locate websites that provide this information. Consider using the words, text editor web design, followed by the name of your operating system, such as Windows or MacOS, as your search text. If you are looking for only free text editors, consider adding the word, free, to your search text. If you need assistance selecting, downloading, and installing an editor, contact your instructor.

Content Management Systems

Creators of complex websites with hundreds or thousands of frequently updated pages, such as those of a university or online business, often make use of a content management system (CMS) to enter, modify, or delete content. A CMS enables and manages the publishing, modification, organization, and access of various forms of documents and other files, including media and webpages, on a network or the web. A CMS allows web developers to specify the parts of a page that are common to a website (such as a banner graphic, navigation menu, or footer information that appear on every page) so that they need to be specified only once. Many CMSs allow web developers to customize their websites by including plug-ins, which provide additional capabilities, such as displaying a slide show of images or navigation menus.

When using a CMS, a web developer creates the theme, or design of a website, and one or more website content administrators enters its content. The CMS uses a database to store both the design and content of the website. The CMS will query the database, assemble the different parts of the page as HTML code, and then send the HTML to the user's browser for display. Many CMSs provide a variety of themes from which to choose when creating a website. Often, a web developer can customize a theme by specifying colors, banner graphics, placement of navigation menus, and other characteristics. By applying different themes, developers easily can alter the appearance of a website without modifying its content. For example, one theme may be optimized for displaying on a large screen, while another theme might display only images and text, so the website displays quickly on mobile devices. Figure 2 shows options for selecting a theme or configuring the appearance of a website created with the WordPress CMS.

Figure 2 Selecting a theme for a website built with WordPress.

Table 1 summarizes several popular content management systems for creating websites. Many content management systems are open source and offer regular updates, enhancements, plug-ins, and themes for download, often at no cost.

Table 1 Popular Content Management Systems	
Content Management System	**Description**
Drupal	Powerful, open source CMS often used for large-scale websites because of its capability of being customized and its efficient use of computer resources
Google Sites	Easy-to-use website creation platform provided by Google often used for personal or small-to-medium websites, with content hosted on Google's servers; integrates with Google apps and services
Joomla!	Open source CMS often used for creating e-commerce websites and online social networks
WordPress	Easy-to-use, open source CMS combining blogging features with the capability to create small- to medium-sized websites; users may install WordPress on their own servers or use a hosted version

© 2015 Cengage Learning

Website Technologies

Hypertext Markup Language (HTML) uses a set of codes called tags to format documents for display in a browser. The current version of HTML is HTML5. HTML tags describe the structure of the content on a webpage, including headings, paragraphs, images, and links. These tags generally occur in pairs in an HTML document, one before a content item and another after it.

A complementary technology called cascading style sheets (CSS) contains specifications for the fonts, colors, layout, and placement of these HTML elements on a webpage. The current version of CSS is CSS3.

JavaScript is a programming language for creating programs that a browser can run to generate content for a website. Uses for JavaScript include obtaining the current date and time, formatting alert boxes, performing calculations, and dynamically displaying this content on a webpage.

Figure 3 shows the HTML, CSS, and JavaScript for a page on the National Zoo's website. The source code of this webpage shows that HTML tags specify the paragraphs, links, list items, and images, and a CSS file contains descriptions for how to style each of the tags on the webpage. JavaScript manages the website's navigation menus and user interaction. You can view the source code for a website by selecting the View Source or 'View Source Code' option in a browser.

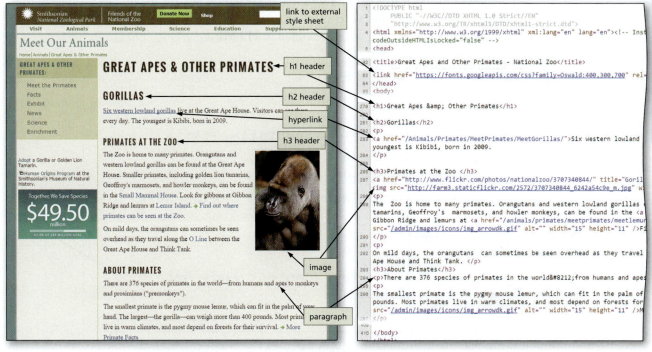

Figure 3 A page from the National Zoo website and its source code.

Because screens on computers and mobile devices are of different sizes, many web developers will create webpages that are responsive. Responsive webpages automatically adjust the size of their content to display appropriately relative to the size of the screen of the device on which it is displayed. Figure 4 shows a webpage displayed in a browser on full-size screen and the same webpage when viewed in a browser on a mobile device.

Figure 4 A responsive website, in a mobile and full-sized browser.

Structure of a Webpage

A webpage's source code contains text marked up with HTML tags that instruct a browser how to display that content. HTML tags are written in lowercase characters and are enclosed within angle brackets (< >). Almost all HTML tags are written in pairs, with an opening tag and a closing tag. An opening tag contains the tag name followed by any attributes or additional information needed to completely specify the tag. A closing tag begins with a forward slash (/) followed by the tag name. Figure 5 shows the structure of a webpage coded in HTML.

Figure 5 Structure of a webpage.

- As shown in Figure 5, the first line of code in an HTML5 webpage contains the line, `<!DOCTYPE html>`. These words identify that the document type of this page is HTML5. When viewing the source code for a webpage, if you see different values after the word DOCTYPE, or no DOCTYPE line at all, the webpage probably was written to conform to standards of an earlier version of HTML.

- The next line of code in a webpage file is always an `<html>` tag to indicate that the content is written using HTML. This is the opening `<html>` tag. The file ends with the corresponding closing `</html>` tag.

- The head section, located between the `<head>` and `</head>` tags, includes tags for the title of the webpage that appears in the browser tab displaying this webpage; it also may include styles and JavaScript. The body section, located between the `<body>` and `</body>` tags, contains the content of the webpage marked up with HTML tags.

- Sometimes a web developer will indent tags when typing them in a text editor so that opening tags and their corresponding closing tags line up, in order to make the HTML code easier for a human to read.

- The content of a webpage is placed between the `<body>` and `</body>` tags. In Figure 5, this area is marked with comments to indicate where the page content begins and ends. Comments look similar to HTML tags, except that they have an exclamation point and two dashes (`!--`) after the opening bracket and two dashes before the closing bracket. The dashes are not required, but they help improve readability. Web developers often include comments to make it easier to read and interpret the HTML code.

A browser ignores the spacing of the HTML code and any comments included in the file and renders, or displays, a webpage's content based on the meaning of the tags used to mark it up.

The World Wide Web Consortium (W3C) oversees the specification of HTML standards, and as HTML evolves, the W3C identifies some tags as deprecated, or obsolete. For example, in earlier versions of HTML the `<font>` tag was used to specify the font of text on a webpage. With the development of CSS, the W3C has deprecated the `<font>` tag. While the `<font>` tag still may display text in a particular font correctly in some browsers, the preferred way to display text in a specific font is using CSS.

The W3C provides a free, online HTML5 validator application to ensure that a webpage's HTML tags follow the specifications, or rules, for HTML5. The HTML5 validator will identify any misaligned tags, deprecated tags, required attributes, or information that may be missing, as shown in Figure 6.

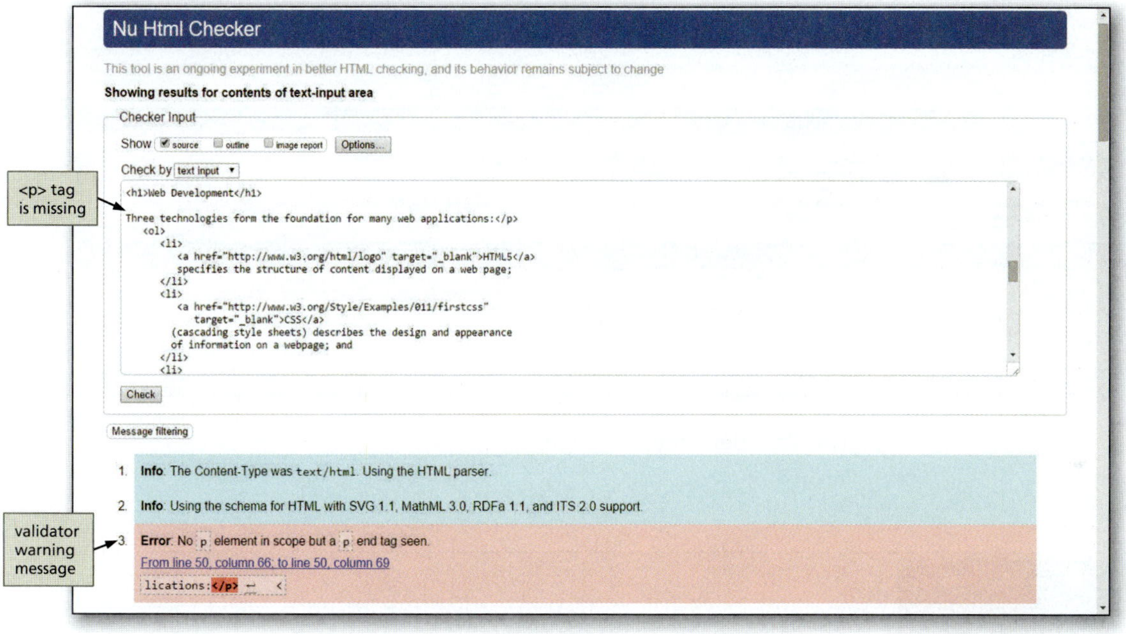

Figure 6 Code analyzed in an HTML5 validator.

How can you find and use an HTML5 validator?
Use a search engine with the search text, W3C HTML validator, to locate the W3C Markup Validator Service. Navigate to the W3C Markup Validation Service website, and specify the web address of a webpage, upload an HTML file, or paste in the HTML code to be validated. Review the output to determine any code that needs to be corrected for the page to pass inspection. Using a validator will ensure that the code complies with HTML5 standards and that the page displays correctly in all HTML5-compliant browsers.

Where can you find a list of deprecated tags in HTML5?
Use a search engine with the search text, html5 deprecated tags attributes, to locate this information.

Developing a Website

This section will guide you through the steps of creating a simple website. You will need to select, download, and install a text editor, or use Notepad for Windows or TextEdit for MacOS. The website you will create in this Focus On will include various headings, paragraphs of text, links, styles, images, an embedded video, and the current time and date (Figure 7).

Web Development

Three technologies form the foundation for many web applications:

1. HTML5 specifies the structure of content displayed on a webpage;
2. CSS (cascading style sheets) describes the design and appearance of information on a webpage; and
3. JavaScript allows users to interact with a webpage's content.

Watch a video about web development.

HTML5

HTML5 is the *current version of HTML* (Hypertext Markup Language) used for creating websites and applications. HTML uses a set of codes called tags to instruct a browser how to display a webpage's content. HTML tags specify the structure of content on a webpage, such as headings, paragraphs, hyperlinks, or images. HTML5 includes tags for playing audio and video files without relying on the use of third-party plug-ins, or modules, such as Adobe Flash, to perform these tasks. Many mobile devices and computers rely on HTML5-compliant browsers, which are capable of interpreting HTML5 tags, to handle these tasks.

Additional HTML5 features include recognizing gestures on mobile devices, performing drag and drop, creating graphics dynamically, accessing a geolocation, and storing content offline. These HTML5 features allow web developers to build applications that meet the needs of people using the web today on many different devices. Each browser implements the HTML5 specification differently and may not support all of its features.

CSS

While HTML describes a webpage's content as a collection of headings, paragraphs, images, links, and other elements, CSS allows web developers to specify how these elements are formatted in a browser. Web developers may specify the fonts and font sizes, colors, borders, backgrounds, and other styles to apply to each of these elements.

CSS provides web developers with precise control over a webpage's layout. With CSS, web developers can apply different layouts to the same information so that it is formatted appropriately for printing or viewing on computers and devices with varying screen sizes. The current version of CSS is known as CSS3 (cascading style sheets, version 3).

JavaScript

JavaScript is a programming language that adds interactivity to webpages. It often is used to check for appropriate values on web forms, present alert messages, display menus on webpages, and create other dynamic content. Some developers use JavaScript to detect the user's browser version in order to display a webpage especially designed for that browser.

Sat Aug 12 2017 13:08:23 GMT-0400 (Eastern Daylight Time)

Figure 7a index.html webpage.

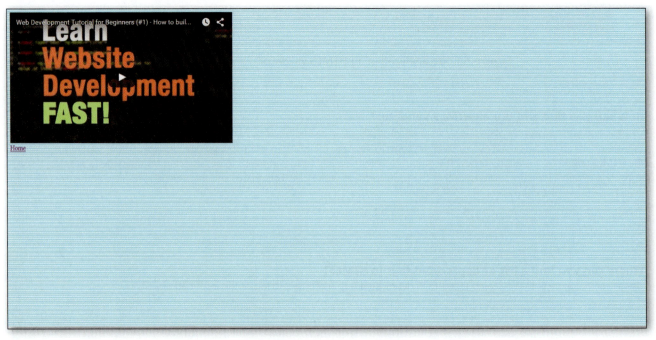

Figure 7b video.html webpage.

Are all webpages coded in HTML?

Yes. Many simple websites make use of static webpages, whose content changes only when a web developer updates the HTML code for each page. More complex websites often have dynamic webpages. Dynamic webpages obtain their content by running programs on a web server or in a browser. These programs often perform calculations or interact with a database to access requested information and then generate the HTML code to display that content in a browser.

To Create the index.html File

   To perform the steps in this Focus On, you will need to download to the starter files for this Focus On from the online companion website for this book. If you need assistance accessing these files, contact your instructor. Download and uncompress these files. Create a folder named website on your computer that will contain all of the files and images used in your website. Move the template.html, startertext.txt files, and the images folder to the website folder.

   The template.html data file includes the webpage structure. You will open this file in a text editor and save it as index.html. The index.html file usually is the first file to be displayed when you navigate to a website. ***Why?*** *The .html file extension indicates to the browser that the file stores the content for a webpage, so that it can open the file and display its contents. The webpage structure helps the browser identify the file as a webpage so that it can display it properly.* The following steps open the template.html file in a text editor and save it with the file name, index.html.

1

- Run the text editor of your choice.
- Navigate to and open the template.html file.
- If necessary, enable the word wrap feature so that you can view all the webpage text without scrolling horizontally (Figure 8).

Q&A

Can I just navigate to the template.html file and double-click it so that it opens in a text editor?

By default, most operating systems are configured to open files with an .html extension in a browser. If you double-click the .html file icon in a file explorer application, it is likely that the template.html file will open in your default browser instead of a text editor.

```
1    <!DOCTYPE html>
2 ▼  <html>
3 ▼    <head>
4        <title>Page Title</title>
5      </head>
6 ▼    <body>
7      <!-- Page content begins here -->
8
9
10
11     <!-- Page content ends here -->
12     </body>
13   </html>
```

webpage structure

Figure 8

2

- Save the file using the file name, index.html. Do not exit the text editor. If you are running Notepad on a Windows computer, change the file type in the Save As dialog box in Notepad to All Files so that Notepad saves the file with the proper .html extension.

To Copy the Starter Text from a Source File and Paste It in the index.html File

The startertext.txt file data file includes all the text the webpage will display. ***Why?*** *For the purposes of this exercise, copying and pasting text from an existing file will save you from having to type all the webpage text manually.* The following steps copy the starter text from the startertext.txt file and paste it in the `<body>` section of the index.html file so that it appears in the browser's display area.

1

• Open the startertext.txt file (Figure 9).

```
Web Development

Three technologies form the foundation for many web applications:

HTML5 specifies the structure of content displayed on a webpage; CSS (cascading style sheets) describes the design and appearance of information on a webpage; and
JavaScript allows users to interact with a webpage's content.

Watch a video about web development.                          [webpage text in startertext.txt file]

HTML5

HTML5 is the current version of HTML (Hypertext Markup Language) used for creating websites and applications. HTML uses a set of codes called tags to instruct a
browser how to display a webpage's content. HTML tags specify the structure of content on a webpage, such as headings, paragraphs, hyperlinks, or images. HTML5
includes tags for playing audio and video files without relying on the use of third-party plug-ins, or modules, such as Adobe Flash, to perform these tasks. Many
mobile devices and computers rely on HTML5-compliant browsers, which are capable of interpreting HTML5 tags, to handle these tasks.

Additional HTML5 features include recognizing gestures on mobile devices, performing drag and drop, creating graphics dynamically, accessing a geolocation, and storing
content offline. These HTML5 features allow web developers to build applications that meet the needs of people using the web today on many different devices. Each
browser implements the HTML5 specification differently and may not support all of its features.

CSS

While HTML describes a webpage's content as a collection of headings, paragraphs, images, links, and other elements, CSS allows web developers to specify how these
elements are formatted in a browser. Web developers may specify the fonts and font sizes, colors, borders, backgrounds, and other styles to apply to each of these
elements.

CSS provides web developers with precise control over a webpage's layout. With CSS, web developers can apply different layouts to the same information so that it is
formatted appropriately for printing or viewing on computers and devices with varying screen sizes. The current version of CSS is known as CSS3 (cascading style
sheets, version 3).

JavaScript

JavaScript is a programming language that adds interactivity to webpages. It often is used to check for appropriate values on web forms, present alert messages,
display menus on webpages, and create other dynamic content. Some developers use JavaScript to detect the user's browser version in order to display a webpage
especially designed for that browser.
```

Figure 9

2

• Select all the text in the startertext.txt file.

• Copy the text.

• Close the startertext.txt file.

• Display the text editor window containing the index.html file.

• Position the insertion point on blank line after the line that says, <!—Page content begins here --> (Figure 10). Recall that this line is a comment; its only purpose is to make it easier for a web developer to read or understand the HTML code.

```
1   <!DOCTYPE html>
2 ▼ <html>
3 ▼   <head>
4       <title>Page Title</title>
5     </head>
6 ▼   <body>
7     <!-- Page content begins here -->      [blank line where text will be inserted]
8  ←
9
10
11    <!-- Page content ends here -->
12   </body>
13 </html>
```

Figure 10

3

- Paste the text you copied in Step 2 (Figure 11).
- Save the changes to the index.html file.

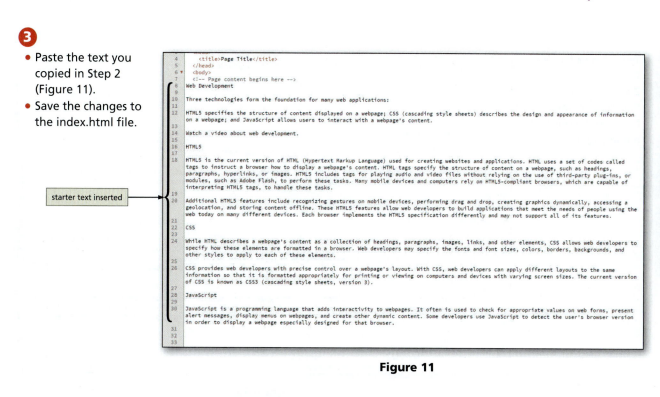

starter text inserted

Figure 11

To Add the Webpage Title

As mentioned previously, the webpage title helps identify the webpage. For example, if you have multiple webpages open in the browser, each webpage's title will appear in its respective browser tab. If you save a webpage as a bookmark or favorite, by default, the browser will identify the webpage by its title. You always should assign a meaningful title to each webpage you create. *Why?* *A descriptive webpage title can help you identify a webpage without having to view its contents and also will help search engines locate the page.* The following steps add a meaningful title to the index.html webpage.

1

- Select the text, Page Title, that appears between the `<title>` and `</title>` tags (Figure 12).

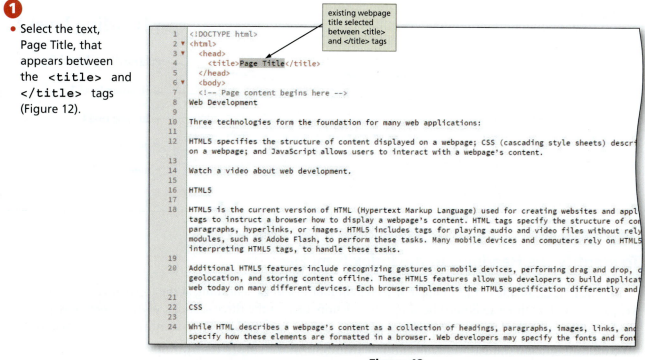

existing webpage title selected between <title> and </title> tags

Figure 12

2

• Type **Mark's Web Development Page** as the title. Replace the name, Mark, with your first name (Figure 13).

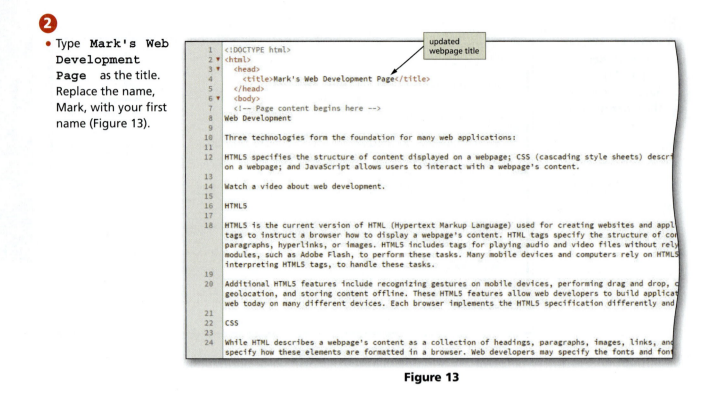

Figure 13

Headings

Headings indicate the different sections of a webpage. HTML supports six levels of headings, which are identified by the following tags: **<h1>**, **<h2>**, **<h3>**, **<h4>**, **<h5>**, and **<h6>**. The **<h1>** tag displays text in the largest font size for headings, and the **<h6>** tag displays text in the smallest font size for headings (Figure 14).

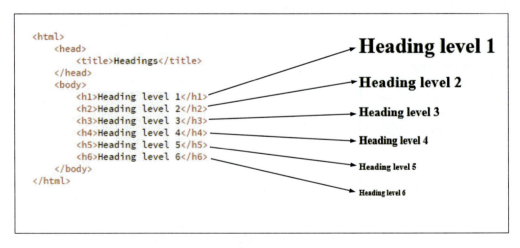

Figure 14

To Identify the Headings in the index.html File

The index.html file in this example will contain four headings: a heading at the top that identifies the webpage, as well as three additional headings that identify each of the three sections. ***Why?*** *Using webpage headings helps visitors identify the content they would like to read.* The following steps identify the headings in the index.html file.

1

- Position the insertion point at the beginning of the line that reads, Web Development.
- Type `<h1>` to identify where the heading begins.
- Position the insertion point at the end of the line of text that reads, Web Development.
- Type `</h1>` to identify where the heading ends. Although the browser disregards spacing, you may type blank spaces to indent this tag so it lines up with its opening `<h1>` tag. (Figure 15).

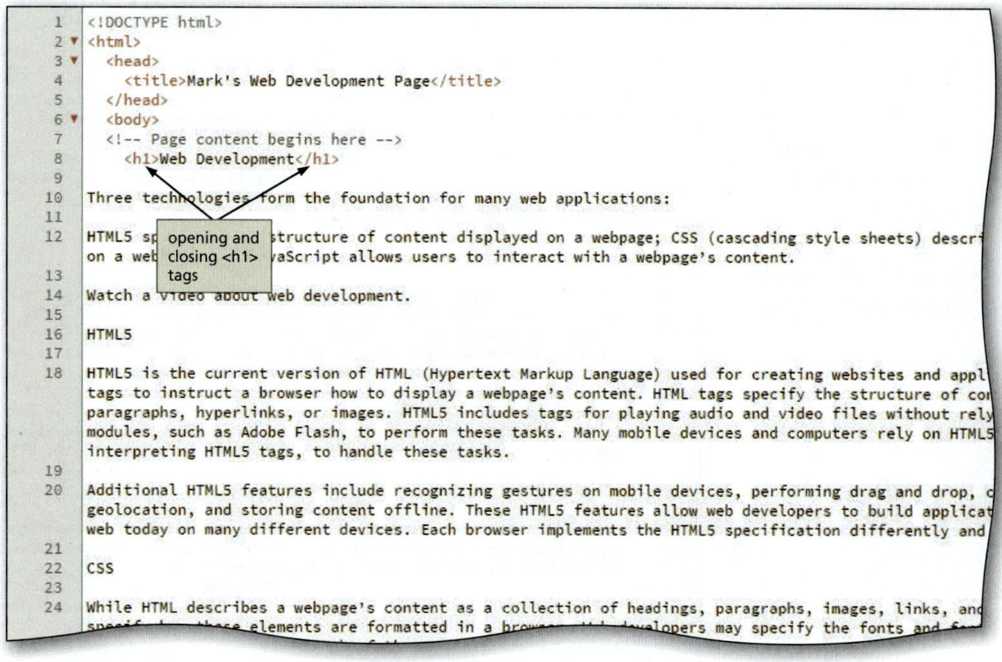

```
 1   <!DOCTYPE html>
 2 ▼ <html>
 3 ▼   <head>
 4       <title>Mark's Web Development Page</title>
 5     </head>
 6 ▼   <body>
 7     <!-- Page content begins here -->
 8       <h1>Web Development</h1>
 9
10   Three technologies form the foundation for many web applications:
11
12   HTML5 sp [opening and    structure of content displayed on a webpage; CSS (cascading style sheets) descri
         on a web  closing <h1>  vaScript allows users to interact with a webpage's content.
                   tags
13
14   Watch a video about web development.
15
16   HTML5
17
18   HTML5 is the current version of HTML (Hypertext Markup Language) used for creating websites and appl
     tags to instruct a browser how to display a webpage's content. HTML tags specify the structure of co
     paragraphs, hyperlinks, or images. HTML5 includes tags for playing audio and video files without rely
     modules, such as Adobe Flash, to perform these tasks. Many mobile devices and computers rely on HTML5
     interpreting HTML5 tags, to handle these tasks.
19
20   Additional HTML5 features include recognizing gestures on mobile devices, performing drag and drop, c
     geolocation, and storing content offline. These HTML5 features allow web developers to build applicat
     web today on many different devices. Each browser implements the HTML5 specification differently and
21
22   CSS
23
24   While HTML describes a webpage's content as a collection of headings, paragraphs, images, links, and
     specif     these elements are formatted in a browser    developers may specify the fonts and for
```

Figure 15

2

- Position the insertion point at the beginning the line that reads, HTML5.
- Type `<h2>` to identify where the heading begins.
- Position the insertion point at the end of the line of text that reads, HTML5.
- Type `</h2>` to identify where the heading ends. To increase readability, you may type spaces to indent this tag so it lines up with its opening `<h2>` tag (Figure 16).

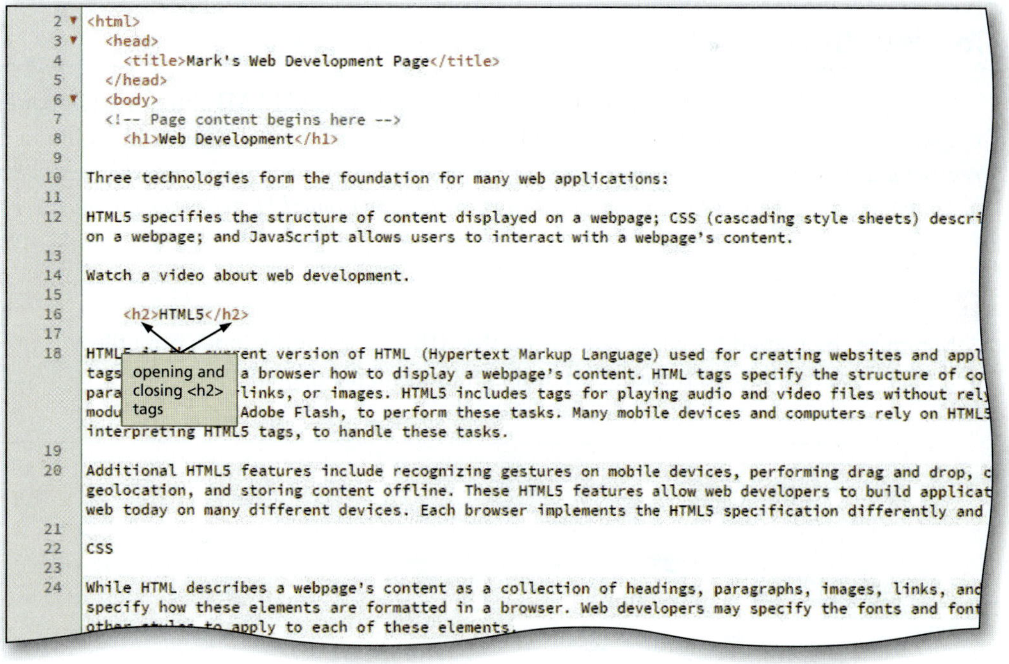

```
 2 ▼ <html>
 3 ▼   <head>
 4       <title>Mark's Web Development Page</title>
 5     </head>
 6 ▼   <body>
 7     <!-- Page content begins here -->
 8       <h1>Web Development</h1>
 9
10   Three technologies form the foundation for many web applications:
11
12   HTML5 specifies the structure of content displayed on a webpage; CSS (cascading style sheets) descri
     on a webpage; and JavaScript allows users to interact with a webpage's content.
13
14   Watch a video about web development.
15
16       <h2>HTML5</h2>
17
18   HTML5 is the current version of HTML (Hypertext Markup Language) used for creating websites and appl
     tags [opening and  a browser how to display a webpage's content. HTML tags specify the structure of co
     para  closing <h2>  links, or images. HTML5 includes tags for playing audio and video files without rel
     modu  tags          Adobe Flash, to perform these tasks. Many mobile devices and computers rely on HTML5
     interpreting HTML5 tags, to handle these tasks.
19
20   Additional HTML5 features include recognizing gestures on mobile devices, performing drag and drop, c
     geolocation, and storing content offline. These HTML5 features allow web developers to build applicat
     web today on many different devices. Each browser implements the HTML5 specification differently and
21
22   CSS
23
24   While HTML describes a webpage's content as a collection of headings, paragraphs, images, links, and
     specify how these elements are formatted in a browser. Web developers may specify the fonts and font
     other styles to apply to each of these elements.
```

Figure 16

3

- Repeat the steps in Step 2 to identify the lines that read, CSS and JavaScript, as `<h2>` headings, and indent each line by four spaces (Figure 17).
- Save the changes to the index.html file.

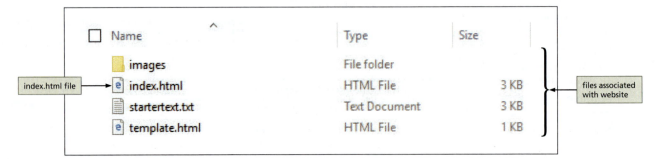

```
 5    </head>
 6 ▾  <body>
 7    <!-- Page content begins here -->
 8      <h1>Web Development</h1>
 9
10    Three technologies form the foundation for many web applications:
11
12    HTML5 specifies the structure of content displayed on a webpage; CSS (cascading style sheets) describ
      on a webpage; and JavaScript allows users to interact with a webpage's content.
13
14    Watch a video about web development.
15
16        <h2>HTML5</h2>
17
18    HTML5 is the current version of HTML (Hypertext Markup Language) used for creating websites and appl
      tags to instruct a browser how to display a webpage's content. HTML tags specify the structure of co
      paragraphs, hyperlinks, or images. HTML5 includes tags for playing audio and video files without rel
      modules, such as Adobe Flash, to perform these tasks. Many mobile devices and computers rely on HTML
      interpreting HTML5 tags, to handle these tasks.
19
20    Additional HTML5 features include recognizing gestures on mobile devices, performing drag and drop,
      geolocation, and storing content offline. These HTML5 features allow web developers to build applica
      web today on many different devices. Each browser implements the HTML5 specification differently and
21
22        <h2>CSS</h2>
23
24    While HTML describes a webpage's content as a collection of headings, paragraphs, images, links, and
      specify how these elements are formatted in a browser. Web developers may specify the fonts and font
      other styles to apply to each of these elements.
25
26    CSS provides web developers with pre        er a webpage's layout. With CSS, web developers ca
      information so that it is formatted ap        r printing or viewing on computers and devices wi
      of CSS is known as CSS3 (cascading sty      sion 3).
27
28        <h2>JavaScript</h2>
29
30    JavaScript is a programming language that adds interactivity to webpages. It often is used to check
      alert messages, display menus on webpages, and create other dynamic content. Some developers use Jav
      in order to display a webpage especially designed for that browser.
```

`<h2>` tags surround CSS and JavaScript headings

Figure 17

To View the index.html Webpage in a Browser

As shown in Figure 18, the website folder contains one HTML file for each page and a folder called images with all of the website's images. The following steps view the index.html file in a browser. *Why? When creating a webpage, you often should view your progress in a browser to make sure the webpage appears as you intend. If you find something wrong, you should correct it before writing additional HTML code for your webpage.*

1

- Minimize the text editor window showing the HTML code for the index.html file.
- If necessary, navigate to the location of the index.html file (Figure 18).

☐ Name	Type	Size
📁 images	File folder	
🄴 index.html	HTML File	3 KB
📄 startertext.txt	Text Document	3 KB
🄴 template.html	HTML File	1 KB

index.html file

files associated with website

Figure 18

- Double-click the index.html file to open it in a browser (Figure 19).

◄ What happens if the file does not open in a browser?
You may need to run a browser first and then use the Open command in the browser to navigate to and open the index.html file.

If my computer's display device is large enough, can I arrange the windows to display both the text editor and browser side by side?
Yes.

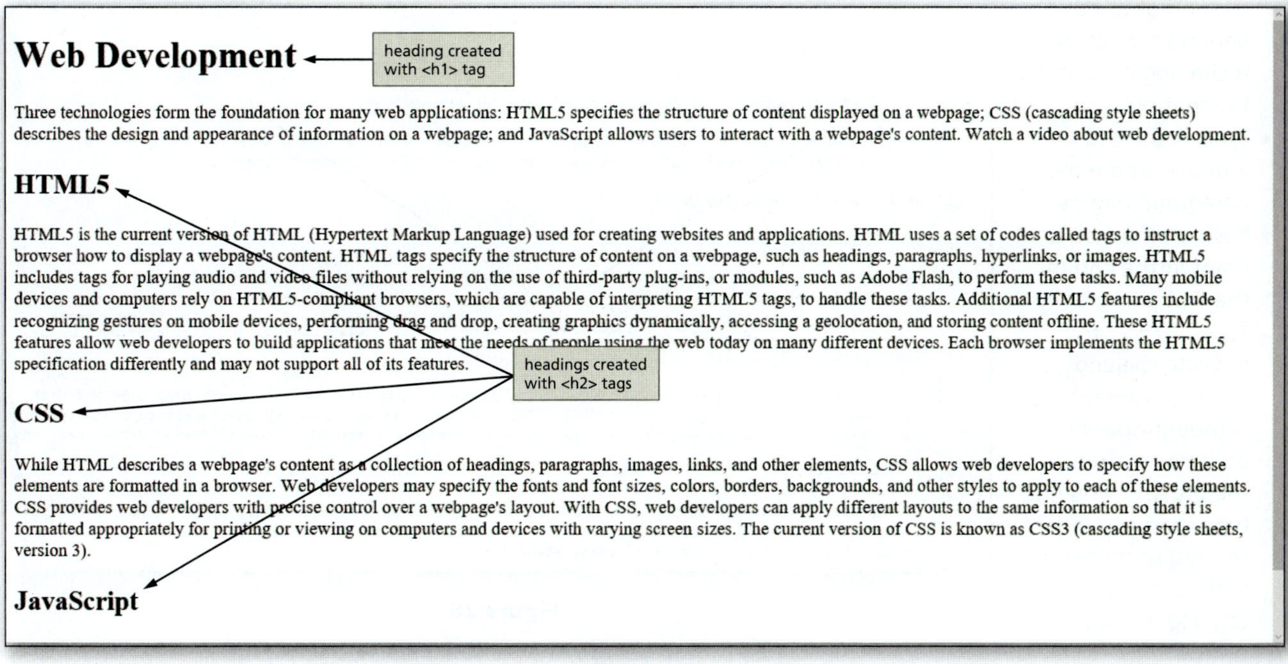

Web Development

> heading created with <h1> tag

Three technologies form the foundation for many web applications: HTML5 specifies the structure of content displayed on a webpage; CSS (cascading style sheets) describes the design and appearance of information on a webpage; and JavaScript allows users to interact with a webpage's content. Watch a video about web development.

HTML5

HTML5 is the current version of HTML (Hypertext Markup Language) used for creating websites and applications. HTML uses a set of codes called tags to instruct a browser how to display a webpage's content. HTML tags specify the structure of content on a webpage, such as headings, paragraphs, hyperlinks, or images. HTML5 includes tags for playing audio and video files without relying on the use of third-party plug-ins, or modules, such as Adobe Flash, to perform these tasks. Many mobile devices and computers rely on HTML5-compliant browsers, which are capable of interpreting HTML5 tags, to handle these tasks. Additional HTML5 features include recognizing gestures on mobile devices, performing drag and drop, creating graphics dynamically, accessing a geolocation, and storing content offline. These HTML5 features allow web developers to build applications that meet the needs of people using the web today on many different devices. Each browser implements the HTML5 specification differently and may not support all of its features.

> headings created with <h2> tags

CSS

While HTML describes a webpage's content as a collection of headings, paragraphs, images, links, and other elements, CSS allows web developers to specify how these elements are formatted in a browser. Web developers may specify the fonts and font sizes, colors, borders, backgrounds, and other styles to apply to each of these elements. CSS provides web developers with precise control over a webpage's layout. With CSS, web developers can apply different layouts to the same information so that it is formatted appropriately for printing or viewing on computers and devices with varying screen sizes. The current version of CSS is known as CSS3 (cascading style sheets, version 3).

JavaScript

Figure 19

2

- When you are finished viewing the webpage in the browser, minimize the browser window and redisplay the text editor containing the index.html file.

Paragraphs

The `<p>` and `</p>` tags are used to identify the beginning and ending of paragraphs. If you have several paragraphs of text on your webpage, these tags will inform the browser to insert additional line spacing above and below the paragraph so that the text is easier to read when displayed in the browser. The browser ignores line breaks and line spacing in the HTML file, so it is important to properly define the paragraphs using the `<p>` and `</p>` tags. For example, even if the HTML file appears to have five distinct paragraphs, each separated by a blank line, the browser will ignore the blank lines and display everything as one, long paragraph. To display the text correctly in a browser, place `<p>` and `</p>` tags around each paragraph. Each `<p>` tag must have a corresponding `</p>` tag so that the code is HTML5-compliant.

The index.html file in this example has eight paragraphs: three below the webpage title, two below the HTML5 heading, two below the CSS heading, and one below the JavaScript heading.

To Identify the Paragraphs in the index.html File

The following steps use the `<p>` and `</p>` tags to identify each of the eight paragraphs in the index.html file. *Why? Using the* `<p>` *and* `</p>` *tags to format each paragraph will enhance the webpage structure and make the text more readable for the webpage visitors.*

1

- Position the insertion point at the beginning of the paragraph that begins with, Three technologies form the foundation....
- Type `<p>` to indicate where the paragraph begins.
- Position the insertion point at the end of the first paragraph.
- Type `</p>` to indicate the end of the paragraph. Although spacing does not matter to the browser, you may type spaces to indent this tag so it lines up with its opening `<p>` tag (Figure 20).

```
1   <!DOCTYPE html>
2   <html>
3     <head>
4       <title>Mark's Web Development Page</title>
5     </head>
6     <body>
7       <!-- Page content begins here -->
8       <h1>Web Development</h1>
9
10      <p>Three technologies form the foundation for many web applications:</p>
11
12      HTML5 specifies the structure of content displayed on a webpage; CSS (cascading style sheets) descri
        on a webpage; and JavaScript allows users to interact with a webpage's content.
13
14      Watch a video about web development.
15
16        <h2>HTML5</h2>
17
18      HTML5 is the current version of HTML (Hypertext Markup Language) used for creating websites and app
        tags to instruct a browser how to display a webpage's content. HTML tags specify the structure of c
        paragraphs, hyperlinks, or image          tags for playing audio and video files without re
        modules, such as Adobe Flash, to                ks. Many mobile devices and computers rely on HTML
        interpreting HTML5 tags, to hand
19
20      Additional HTML5 features include recognizing gestures on mobile devices, performing drag and drop,
        geolocation, and storing content offline. These HTML5 features allow web developers to build applica
        web today on many different devices. Each browser implements the HTML5 specification differently and
21
22        <h2>CSS</h2>
23
24      While HTML describes a webpage's content as a collection of headings, paragraphs, images, links, a
        specify how these elements are formatted in a browser. Web developers may specify the fonts and fo
        other styles to apply to each of these elements.
```

opening and closing `<p>` tags

Figure 20

2

- For the remaining paragraphs in the index.html file, type `<p>` at the beginning of each paragraph and type `</p>` at the end of each paragraph. To increase readability, you may type spaces to indent this tag so that it lines up with its opening `<p>` tag, as shown in Figure 21.
- Save the changes to the index.html file.
- Refresh or reload the webpage in the browser window to verify the changes are displayed properly.

```
10    <p>Three technologies form the foundation for many web applications:</p>
11
12    <p>HTML5 specifies the structure of content displayed on a webpage; CSS (cascading style sheets) describes
      information on a webpage; and JavaScript allows users to interact with a webpage's content.</p>
13
14    <p>Watch a video about web development.</p>
15
16    <h2>HTML5</h2>
17
18    <p>HTML5 is the current version of HTML (Hypertext Markup Language) used for creating websites and applicat
      called tags to instruct a browser how to display a webpage's content. HTML tags specify the structure of co
      headings, paragraphs, hyperlinks, or images. HTML5 includes tags for playing audio and video files without
      plug-ins, or modules, such as Adobe Flash, to perform these tasks. Many mobile devices and computers rely on
      are capable of interpreting HTML5 tags, to handle these tasks.</p>
19
20    <p>Additional HTML5 features include recognizing gestures on mobile devices, performing drag and drop, creat
      accessing a geolocation, and storing content offline. These HTML5 features allow web developers to build app
      people using the web today on many different devices. Each browser implements the HTML5 specification differ
      its features.</p>
21
22    <h2>CSS</h2>
23
24    <p>While HTML describes a webpage's content as a collection of headings, paragraphs, images, links, and oth
      developers to specify how these elements are formatted in a browser. Web developers may specify the fonts a
      backgrounds, and other styles to apply to each of these elements.</p>
25
26    <p>CSS provides web developers with precise control over a webpage's layout. With CSS, web developers can a
      information so that it is formatted appropriately for printing or viewing on computers and devices with var
      version of CSS is known as CSS3 (cascading style sheets, version 3).</p>
27
28    <h2>JavaScript</h2>
29
30    <p>JavaScript is a programming language that adds interactivity to webpages. It often is used to check for a
```

`<p>` tags surround remaining paragraphs

Figure 21

I keep attempting to refresh, but my page does not change. What can I do?
Some browsers keep the content of previously loaded pages in local storage so that they will load faster when a user returns to them. Try pressing the CTRL key on the keyboard while reloading the page in order to clear any pages previously stored by the browser.

Images

Most webpages contain one or more images that add visual appeal. Images can be either photos or graphics. Some websites include a banner, or graphic that identifies the website, at the top of each page so that they are easily recognizable. While images can make a website more attractive, or help to deliver its message, remember that not all viewers may be able to see these images. For example, someone who is visually impaired or someone who has configured his or her browser so that it does not display images may be unable to view the images. For this reason, it is not advisable to use images as the only method of conveying information to website visitors.

Images always are stored as separate files, and references to the images appear in the HTML code using the `<img>` tag. When identifying an image to include on a webpage, choose one that has appropriate dimensions for the webpage and has a relatively small file size. Images load at the same time the webpage loads in the browser, so having images with large file sizes, or too many images, can increase the time it takes for the webpage to load. For this reason, you should use images sparingly. In addition, choose images in the JPEG, GIF, or PNG format (identified with a .jpg, .gif, or .png file extension), as they are the formats supported by most browsers.

The Web Development webpage you are creating in this example will contain three images: one under the HTML5 heading, one under the CSS heading, and one under the JavaScript heading. When adding the HTML code for these images, you will specify attributes for each `<img>` tag to provide additional information needed for the browser to display the image. Attributes are coded within an HTML tag. Many HTML tags have attributes associated with them. See Table 2 at the end of this Focus On for a summary of common tags and their attributes.

Common attributes for the `<img>` tag describe the location of an image file, alternate text for the image, and a style that indicates how to position the image. For example, the src attribute of the `<img>` tag specifies the source location of the image, the alt attribute specifies alternate text, or alt text, associated with an image, and the `style` attribute provides information regarding the placement or display of an image.

This example stores its images in a folder named images in the website folder. The `src` attribute refers to the images folder when specifying the location of an image to display.

BTW
If you are trying to display photos from a digital camera or smartphone camera on your website, you should use image editing software to shrink the photos to an appropriate size, such as 300 × 400 pixels or 600 × 800 pixels. The size, or resolution, of a photo taken with an 8 megapixel camera can be approixmately 2447 × 3264 pixels, which is larger than the resolution of the screens on many devices or monitors.

```
<img src="images/html5_logo.png" alt="HTML5 Logo" style="float:left">
```

Is it required to specify text for the alt attribute?
The alt attribute is a required part of the `<img>` tag in HTML5. Many browsers display the alternate text in place of an image when they are not set to load images automatically or the file containing the image is not found. Alternate text also helps visually impaired users, who use screen reading software to navigate a website, identify the purpose of an image. Most screen reading apps will read aloud the alternate text for each image.

CONSIDER THIS

How does the float:left style display?
The `float:left` style displays the image at the upper-left corner of a block of text and displays the text around the image.

Where is the closing tag to correspond with `<img>`?
Some tags do not have a corresponding closing tag. When no additional information is required between an opening tag and its closing tag, HTML5 omits the closing tag. In this case, the image is specified entirely by its attributes, so HTML5 does not specify a tag to close the `<img>` tag. HTML5 tags that do not require a closing tag are sometimes called one-sided tags. Other one-sided tags include `<br>` (line break) and `<hr>` (horizontal rule).

To Insert Images in the index.html File

As shown in Figure 18, this example stores images used in this website in a folder named images, located in the same folder as the index.html file. It is a good practice to store images used in a website in a folder separate from the HTML pages of a website so that they can be located easily. The following steps insert three images, which are located in the images folder, in the index.html file. *Why? You will insert these images to add visual appeal to the webpage.*

1

- Locate the `<h2>HTML5</h2>` heading in the file. Position the insertion point before the first `<p>` tag that follows this heading and then press the ENTER key to insert a new line.
- Type `<img src="images/html5_image.png" alt="HTML5 Image" style="float:left">` to insert a reference to the html5_image.png file in the images folder, set the alternate text to HTML5 Image, and style the image so that it is aligned to the left of the text under the HTML5 heading (Figure 22).

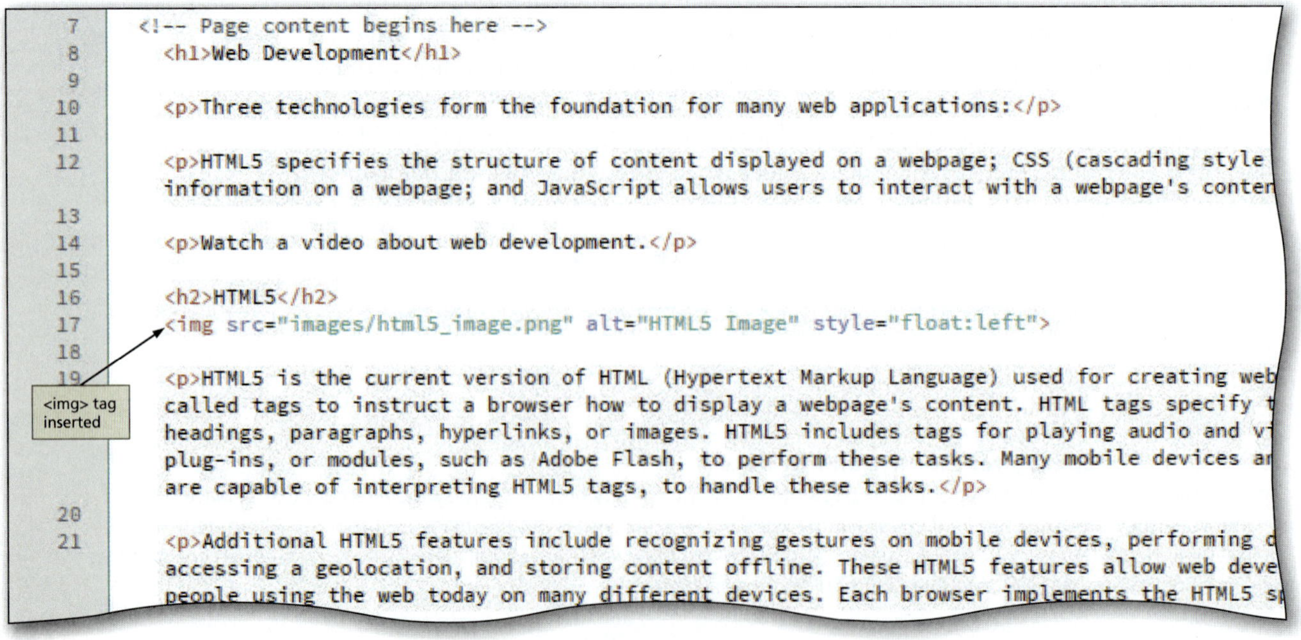

```
 7      <!-- Page content begins here -->
 8        <h1>Web Development</h1>
 9
10        <p>Three technologies form the foundation for many web applications:</p>
11
12        <p>HTML5 specifies the structure of content displayed on a webpage; CSS (cascading style
          information on a webpage; and JavaScript allows users to interact with a webpage's conter
13
14        <p>Watch a video about web development.</p>
15
16        <h2>HTML5</h2>
17        <img src="images/html5_image.png" alt="HTML5 Image" style="float:left">
18
19        <p>HTML5 is the current version of HTML (Hypertext Markup Language) used for creating web
          called tags to instruct a browser how to display a webpage's content. HTML tags specify t
          headings, paragraphs, hyperlinks, or images. HTML5 includes tags for playing audio and vi
          plug-ins, or modules, such as Adobe Flash, to perform these tasks. Many mobile devices ar
          are capable of interpreting HTML5 tags, to handle these tasks.</p>
20
21        <p>Additional HTML5 features include recognizing gestures on mobile devices, performing c
          accessing a geolocation, and storing content offline. These HTML5 features allow web deve
          people using the web today on many different devices. Each browser implements the HTML5 s
```

<img> tag inserted

Figure 22

2

- Locate the `<h2>CSS</h2>` heading in the file. Position the insertion point before the first `<p>` tag that follows this heading and then press the ENTER key to insert a new line.
- Type `<img src="images/css_image.png" alt="CSS Image" style="float:right">` to insert a reference to the css_image.png file in the images folder, set the alternate text to CSS Image, and style the image so that it is aligned to the right of the text under the CSS heading.
- Locate the `<h2>JavaScript</h2>` heading in the file. Position the insertion point before the first `<p>` tag that follows this heading and then press the ENTER key to insert a new line.
- Type `<img src="images/js_image.png" alt="JavaScript Image" style="float:left">` to insert a reference to the js_image.png file in the images folder, set the alternate text to JavaScript Image, and align the image to the left of the text under the JavaScript heading (Figure 23).
- Save the changes to the index.html file.

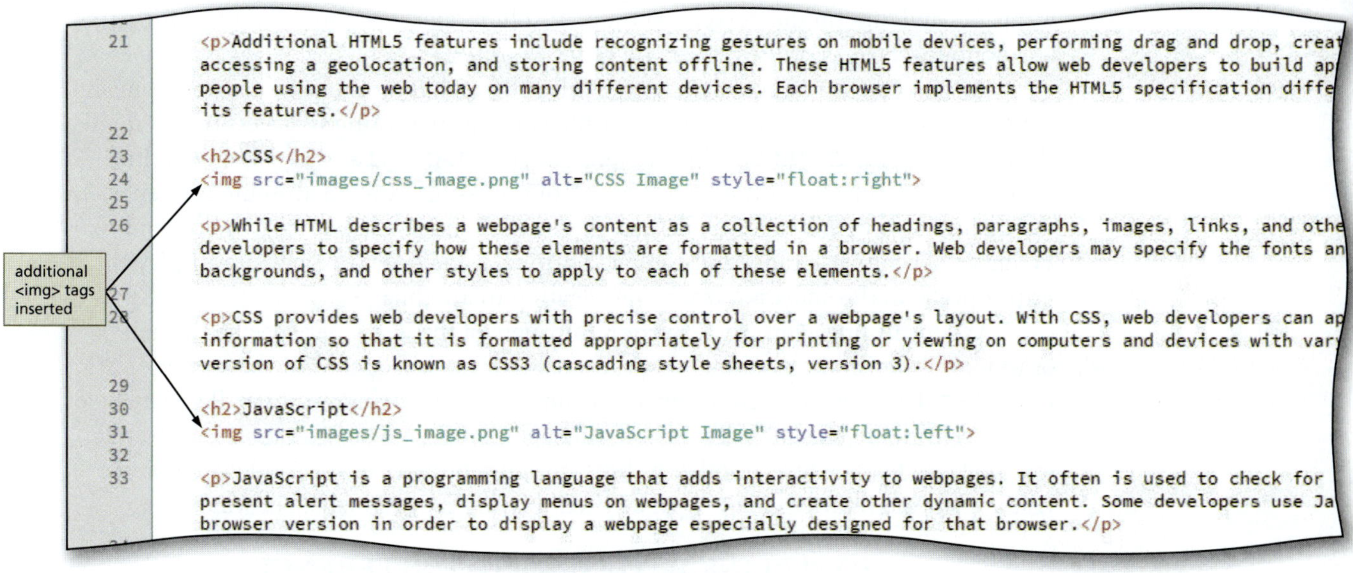

```
21   <p>Additional HTML5 features include recognizing gestures on mobile devices, performing drag and drop, crea
     accessing a geolocation, and storing content offline. These HTML5 features allow web developers to build ap
     people using the web today on many different devices. Each browser implements the HTML5 specification diffe
     its features.</p>
22
23   <h2>CSS</h2>
24   <img src="images/css_image.png" alt="CSS Image" style="float:right">
25
26   <p>While HTML describes a webpage's content as a collection of headings, paragraphs, images, links, and othe
     developers to specify how these elements are formatted in a browser. Web developers may specify the fonts an
     backgrounds, and other styles to apply to each of these elements.</p>
27
28   <p>CSS provides web developers with precise control over a webpage's layout. With CSS, web developers can ap
     information so that it is formatted appropriately for printing or viewing on computers and devices with var
     version of CSS is known as CSS3 (cascading style sheets, version 3).</p>
29
30   <h2>JavaScript</h2>
31   <img src="images/js_image.png" alt="JavaScript Image" style="float:left">
32
33   <p>JavaScript is a programming language that adds interactivity to webpages. It often is used to check for
     present alert messages, display menus on webpages, and create other dynamic content. Some developers use Ja
     browser version in order to display a webpage especially designed for that browser.</p>
```

additional <img> tags inserted

Figure 23

3

- Refresh or reload the webpage in the browser window to verify the changes are displayed properly. If necessary, scroll to display the three images (Figure 24).

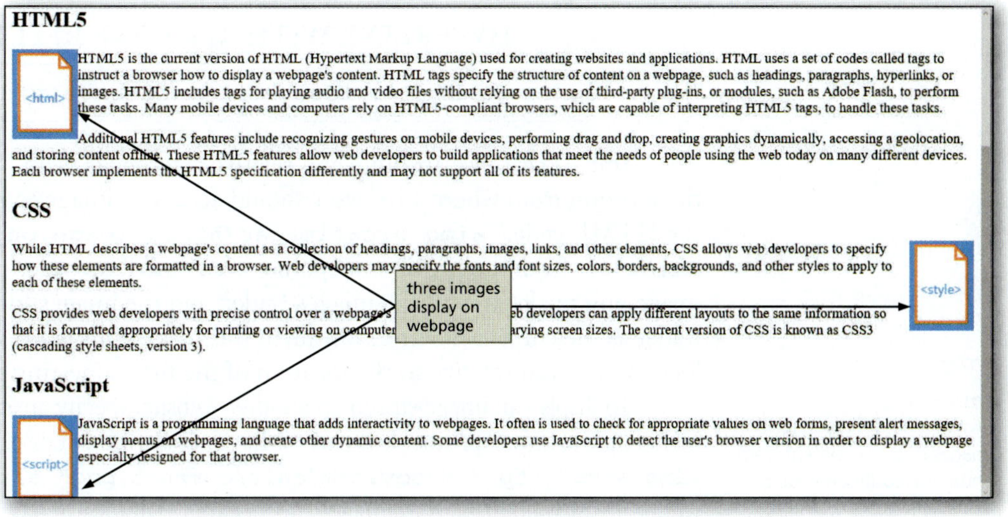

Q&A

Why are the images not being displayed? If images are not displayed, most likely the browser cannot find them. Check that you correctly typed the code referencing

HTML5

HTML5 is the current version of HTML (Hypertext Markup Language) used for creating websites and applications. HTML uses a set of codes called tags to instruct a browser how to display a webpage's content. HTML tags specify the structure of content on a webpage, such as headings, paragraphs, hyperlinks, or images. HTML5 includes tags for playing audio and video files without relying on the use of third-party plug-ins, or modules, such as Adobe Flash, to perform these tasks. Many mobile devices and computers rely on HTML5-compliant browsers, which are capable of interpreting HTML5 tags, to handle these tasks.

Additional HTML5 features include recognizing gestures on mobile devices, performing drag and drop, creating graphics dynamically, accessing a geolocation, and storing content offline. These HTML5 features allow web developers to build applications that meet the needs of people using the web today on many different devices. Each browser implements the HTML5 specification differently and may not support all of its features.

CSS

While HTML describes a webpage's content as a collection of headings, paragraphs, images, links, and other elements, CSS allows web developers to specify how these elements are formatted in a browser. Web developers may specify the fonts and font sizes, colors, borders, backgrounds, and other styles to apply to each of these elements.

CSS provides web developers with precise control over a webpage's layout. With CSS, web developers can apply different layouts to the same information so that it is formatted appropriately for printing or viewing on computers and devices with varying screen sizes. The current version of CSS is known as CSS3 (cascading style sheets, version 3).

JavaScript

JavaScript is a programming language that adds interactivity to webpages. It often is used to check for appropriate values on web forms, present alert messages, display menus on webpages, and create other dynamic content. Some developers use JavaScript to detect the user's browser version in order to display a webpage especially designed for that browser.

three images display on webpage

Figure 24

the images and that the images exist in the location you specified (in this case, the images folder). Be sure that you saved the index.html file after making the changes in the previous set of steps before reloading the webpage.

Links

A link, or hyperlink, can be text or an image in a webpage that a user clicks to navigate to another webpage, download a file, or perform another action, such as running an email app and addressing an email message. If you want webpage visitors to be able to access other webpages in the website easily, you should include links to those pages. In addition to providing links to other pages in the website, you also can provide links to other websites. Webpages always are stored as separate files, and hypertext references to the files appear in the HTML code using the `<a>` (anchor) tag. The `<a>` tag's `href` (hypertext reference) attribute often refers to the location of the file or webpage that you want to view or download.

The `href` attribute's value references a link's location using either a relative reference or an absolute reference. Relative references identify the location of webpages and files on the current website. Absolute references are used to identify the location of webpages or files stored on other websites.

An absolute reference includes the full path, including the protocol and domain name containing the webpage, image, or file you are attempting to access (for example, the code, `<a href="http://www.google.com">Google</a>`, is a hyperlink to the Google website). If the http:// protocol is missing from an absolute reference, the desired webpage, image, or file may not load. (This also is known as a broken link.) While an absolute reference must include http://, some browsers may not display the http:// prefix in the address bar when navigating to a webpage.

When creating a link, the `target` attribute of the `<a>` tag specifies the tab or window in which the resulting webpage, image, or file will open. Use the attribute `target="_blank"` to open the linked document in a new window or tab. If you exclude the target attribute, the link's destination will open in the same browser tab or window. It is a good idea to open links to other websites in a new browser tab or window so that the visitor easily can return to the webpage by redisplaying the original tab or window.

HYPERLINK WITH ABSOLUTE REFERENCE

```
<a href="http://www.w3.org" target="_blank">HTML5</a>
```

HYPERLINK WITH RELATIVE REFERENCE

```
<a href="video.html"> Watch a video</a>
```

You also can use absolute and relative references in an `<img>` tag to specify the location from where a browser should access an image to display on a website. In the HTML code, `<img src="images/html5_image.png" alt="HTML Image">`, from the previous step, the `src` attribute references a file named html5_image.png file located in the images folder, and the images folder is located in the same folder as the current file (index.html, in this case). This is a relative reference, as the location is given relative to the location of the file requesting the resource.

To display an image stored on another website, specify an absolute reference, including the http:// protocol, as part of the `src` attribute. For example, if you add the code, `<img src="http://dscov.com/quiz/correct.png" alt="Correct">`, to a webpage, it would display an image of a checkmark (indicating a correct answer) stored on the web server hosting the website at dscov.com. The image is not located in your website's images folder because it will be accessed from the website specified in the absolute reference.

The index.html page in this example will contain four links: three links to websites about HTML5, CSS, and JavaScript, for which you will use absolute references, and one link to another webpage you will be creating as part of this website, for which you will use a relative reference.

BTW

Images

Be cautious when you include images or other content from another website on your own website, as it is possible that such content always may not be displayed correctly. If the owner of the other website modifies the location or removes the content entirely, the image will not appear, or a broken link will result on your website.

To Insert a Link with an Absolute Reference

The following steps add links with absolute references to three different locations. *Why? Links with absolute references are required in this case because the webpages to which you are linking are not on the same website or web server as the index.html file.*

1

- In the second paragraph beginning, HTML5 specifies the structure, position the insertion point immediately before the H in HTML5.
- Type `<a href="http://www.w3.org/html/logo" target="_blank">` to specify the link destination and that the resulting webpage should open in a new, blank window.
- Position the insertion point after HTML5 and then type `</a>` to indicate the end of the link (Figure 25).

```
 8      <h1>Web Development</h1>
 9
10      <p>Three technologies form the foundation for many web applications:</p>
11
12          <p><a href="http://www.w3.org/html/logo" target="_blank">HTML5</a> specifies the structure of content displayed
            (cascading style sheets) describes the design and appearance of information on a webpage; and JavaScript allows u
            webpage's content.</p>
13
14      <p>Watch a video about web development.</p>
15
16      <h2>HTML5</h2>
17      <img src="images/html5_image.png"            yle="float:left">
18
19      <p>HTML5 is the current version of HTML (Hypertext Markup Language) used for creating websites and applications. HT
        called tags to instruct a browser how to display a webpage's content. HTML tags specify the structure of content on
        headings, paragraphs, hyperlinks, or images. HTML5 includes tags for playing audio and video files without relying
        plug-ins, or modules, such as Adobe Flash, to perform these tasks. Many mobile devices and computers rely on HTML5-
        are capable of interpreting HTML5 tags, to handle these tasks.</p>
20
```

opening and closing <a> tags surround link text

Figure 25

2

- In the same paragraph, position the insertion point immediately before CSS and type `<a href="http://www.w3.org/Style/Examples/011/firstcss" target="_blank">` to specify the link destination and that the resulting webpage should open in a new, blank window.
- Position the insertion point after CSS and then type `</a>` to indicate the end of the link.
- Save the changes to the index.html file.
- Refresh or reload the webpage in the browser window to verify the changes are displayed properly.
- In the same paragraph, position the insertion point immediately before JavaScript and type `<a href="http://javascript.com" target="_blank">` to specify the link destination and that the resulting webpage should open in a new, blank window.
- Position the insertion point after JavaScript and then type `</a>` to indicate the end of the link (Figure 26).
- Save the changes to the index.html file.
- Refresh or reload the webpage in the browser window to verify the changes are displayed properly.

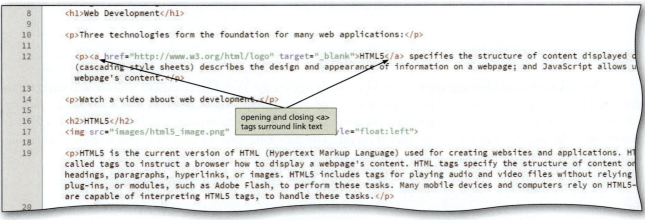

```
 8      <h1>Web Development</h1>
 9
10      <p>Three technologies form the foundation for many web applications:</p>
11
12          <p><a href="http://www.w3.org/html/logo" target="_blank">HTML5</a> specifies the structure of content displayed on a webpage; <a
            href="http://www.w3.org/Style/Examples/011/firstcss" target="_blank">CSS</a> (cascading style sheets) describes the design and appearance
            of information on a webpage; and <a href="http://javascript.com" target="_blank">JavaScript</a> allows users to interact with a webpage's
            content.</p>
13
14      <p>Watch a video about web development.</p>
15
16      <h2>HTML5</h2>
17      <img src="images/html5_image.png" alt="HTML5 Image" style="float:left">
18
19      <p>HTML5 is the current version of HTML (Hypertext Markup Language) used for creating websites and applications. HTML uses a set of codes
        called tags to instruct a browser how to display a webpage's content. HTML tags specify the structure of content on a webpage, such as
        headings, paragraphs, hyperlinks, or images. HTML5 includes tags for          files without relying on the use of third-party
        plug-ins, or modules, such as Adobe Flash, to perform these tasks.         omputers rely on HTML5-compliant browsers, which
        are capable of interpreting HTML5 tags, to handle these tasks.</p>
```

two additional <a> tags inserted

Figure 26

BTW
Webpage Names
Webpage names should contain letters, numbers, and underscores. Avoid using special characters and spaces in webpage names. Although not required, it is good practice to use filenames with all lowercase letters.

To Create the video.html File

The following steps open the startertext.txt file and save it with the file name, video.html.

1 Open the template.html file in a text editor.

2 Save the file with the file name, video.html.

3 Between the `<title>` and `</title>` tags, select the existing text and then type `Web Development` to replace the text.

4 Save the changes to the video.html file. Do not close the file.

To Insert a Link with a Relative Reference

The link with a relative reference to the Video webpage on the Web Development website will navigate to the video.html webpage you created in the previous set of steps. *Why? Because the webpage to which you are linking is located in the same folder as the file from which you are linking, it will be easier to create a link with a relative reference so that you do not have to indicate the entire path of the file.* The following step inserts a link with a relative reference that points to the video.html file.

1

- Display the index.html file.
- Position the insertion point immediately before the W in the paragraph beginning, Watch a video.
- Type `<a href="video.html">` to indicate the beginning of the link that will point to video.html, which is in the same folder as index.html.
- Position the insertion point after the word, video, in the same sentence and then type `</a>` to indicate the end of the link (Figure 27).
- Save the changes to the index.html file.
- Refresh or reload the webpage in the browser window to verify the changes are displayed properly.

Q&A How can I add an image so that a user can click it, instead of text, to navigate to another webpage?
Create the link, but include the HTML for the image tag between the `<a>` and `</a>` tags.
For example:
`<a href="video.html"><img src="images/video.png" alt="video icon"></a>`
will display a video icon for the user to click to navigate to the video.html page. Be sure the video icon (video.png) is located in the website's images folder.

```
8     <h1>Web Development</h1>
9
10    <p>Three technologies for[Web Development heading] applications:</p>
11
12        <p><a href="http://www.w3.org/html/logo" target="_blank">HTML5</a> specifies the structure of content displayed on a webpage; <a
          href="http://www.w3.org/Style/Examples/011/firstcss" target="_blank">CSS</a> (cascading style sheets) describes the design and appearance
          of information on a webpage; and <a href="http://javascript.com" target="_blank">JavaScript</a> allows users to interact with a webpage's
          content.</p>
13
14        <p><a href="video.html">Watch a video</a> about web development.</p>
15
16    <h2>HTML5</h2>
17    <img src="images/html5_image.png" alt="HTML5 Image" style="float:left">
18
19        <p>HTML5 is the current version of HTML (Hypertext Markup Language) used for creating websites and applications. HTML uses a set of codes
          called tags t[link with relative]r how to display a webpage's content. HTML tags specify the structure of content on a webpage, such as
          headings, par[reference to video.]or images. HTML5 includes tags for playing audio and video files without relying on the use of third-party
          plug-ins, or[html]be Flash, to perform these tasks. Many mobile devices and computers rely on HTML5-compliant browsers, which
          are capable o[...]5 tags, to handle these tasks.</p>
20
21        <p>Additional HTML5 features include recognizing gestures on mobile devices, performing drag and drop, creating graphics dynamically,
          accessing a geolocation, and storing content offline. These HTML5 features allow web developers to build applications that meet the needs of
          people using the web today on many diff[...]er implements the HTML5 specification diff[...]upport all of
```

Figure 27

Unordered and Ordered Lists

Two types of lists that HTML supports are unordered and ordered. Unordered lists display a collection of items in a list format, with each list item identified by default with a bullet. Ordered lists, by default, identify each list item with a number (Figure 28).

Unordered List	
`<ul>`	• HTML5
`<li>HTML5</li>`	• CSS
`<li>CSS</li>`	• JavaScript
`<li>JavaScript</li>`	
`</ul>`	
Ordered List	
`<ol>`	1. HTML5
`<li>HTML5</li>`	2. CSS
`<li>CSS</li>`	3. JavaScript
`<li>JavaScript</li>`	
`</ol>`	

Figure 28

To Add an Ordered List

The following steps convert the text in the first paragraph in the Web Development webpage to an ordered list. The list will contain three list items, each identified by a number. *Why? An ordered list will display the information in this paragraph with greater visual appeal than a long, multi-line paragraph.*

1

- The items in this ordered list will include the three links for HTML5, CSS, and JavaScript. To change the first paragraph into an ordered list, change the first `<p>` to `<ol>` and the corresponding `</p>` to `</ol>`.
- Position the insertion point before the `<a>` tag for the HTML5 link, press the ENTER key, press the SPACEBAR two times to create an indent, and then type `<li>` to indicate the beginning of a list item, and then press the ENTER key.
- Position the insertion point immediately after the semicolon in the HTML5 sentence, press the ENTER key, press the SPACEBAR until the insertion point lines up with the opening `<li>` tag, and then type `</li>` to indicate the end of the first list item. Adjust the line spacing and indentation as necessary to match Figure 29.
- Press the ENTER key so that the next list item will begin on a new line in the file (Figure 29).

Figure 29

2

- Insert the remaining list items, typing the `<li>` and `</li>` tags for the CSS and JavaScript sentences.
- Adjust the line spacing and indentation so that the HTML for the ordered list looks like Figure 30.
- Save the changes to the index.html file.
- Refresh or reload the webpage in the browser window to verify the changes are displayed properly.

Q&A

Is the spacing and indentation important?

As stated previously, browsers ignore extra blank spaces and line spaces when rendering HTML content. The spacing and indentation you are creating in the index.html file only improves the file's readability for anyone reviewing the HTML. Some text editors automatically will align or indent these tags for you.

two additional
list items

Figure 30

Applying Styles with CSS

While a main advantage of HTML is its capability to define webpage structure, it is not as easy to apply style elements such as fonts, font sizes, font styles, and colors. Although it is possible to customize these elements of webpages using HTML, CSS makes it easier to specify the appearance of similar elements in the same webpage or same website. For example, in a previous section you used the `<h1>` and `<h2>` tags to create four headings on the Web Development webpage. You can use CSS to specify the font, background color, and font color for all headings identified by the `<h2>` tag in the index.html webpage.

When you inserted the images previously in this Focus On, you used the `style` attribute of the `<img>` tag to indicate that you wanted the images to appear either to the left of the text or to the right of the text. (Recall that the HTML5 and JavaScript images appear to the left of the text in their respective sections, and the CSS image appears to the right of the text in the CSS section.) The styles you indicated in the `<img>` tags are called inline styles. Inline styles are identified by the `style` attribute in an HTML tag, and these styles apply only to the specific tag in which they are defined.

Embedded styles, which define styles in the `<head>` section of the index.html document, apply to the entire webpage on which they are defined. In this section, you will define styles for several tags in the index.html file. Figure 31 shows the styles you will define.

```
<style>
    h1 {
        font-family:sans-serif;
        color:navy;
        font-style:italic;
    }
    h2 {
        font-family:cursive;
        background-color: navy;
        color:papayawhip;
    }
    p {
        font-family:sans-serif;
        color:rgb(56,0,0);
    }
    ol {
        font-family:sans-serif;
        color:rgb(56,0,0);
    }
    body {
        background-color:#bbccff;
    }
    .fancy {
        font-weight:bold;
        color:red;
        font-style:italic;
    }
}
</style>
```

Figure 31

Where can you find more information about CSS styles and their values?

You can use a search engine to locate websites that provide complete documentation about CSS, such as w3schools.com. Consider including words such as w3schools, css, and reference in your search text.

How can you specify colors to use for backgrounds or text in an HTML file?

Most browsers recognize common color names, such as red, orange, green, and blue, along with other predefined color names, such as navy, lime green, and papaya whip. To find a list of all available color names for use on the web, type the words, web color names, as search text in a search engine.

You can use the **rgb()** function to specify colors by providing their red, green, and blue components as decimal values between 0 and 255, or you can use hexadecimal (base 16) values between 00 and FF. A value of 0 means the absence of a color; 255, or FF in hexadecimal, means complete fullness of a color. For example, black is specified by **rgb(0,0,0)** or the hexadecimal value **#000000**, red is **rgb(255,0,0)** or the hexadecimal value **#FF0000**, a shade of gray is indicated by the value **rgb(200,200,200)** or the hexadecimal value **#C8C8C8**, and white is represented by the value **rgb(255,255,255)** or the hexadecimal value **#FFFFFF**.

Is it possible to use the same styles on all of the webpages of a website?

Yes. When creating websites with several webpages, web developers often place CSS declarations in a separate text file, called an external style sheet, so that each webpage of the website can access the same style information. External styles typically are used on large websites where web developers want a consistent style on each webpage. You can find more information about external style sheets by using a search engine with the search text, create external style sheet CSS.

CONSIDER THIS

CONSIDER THIS

CONSIDER THIS

To Add CSS to the index.html File

You have added all text and images to the index.html webpage and are ready to begin formatting the page using CSS. **Why?** *Formatting a webpage with CSS makes it more attractive and is likely to capture website visitors' attention for a longer period of time.* The following step adds embedded styles to the index.html webpage.

1

- Position the insertion point at the end of the `</title>` tag and then press the ENTER key.
- Type the text in Figure 31. Make sure you pay attention to the spacing and indentation to maximize readability (Figure 32).
- Save the changes to the webpage.
- Refresh or reload the webpage in the browser window to verify the changes are displayed properly.

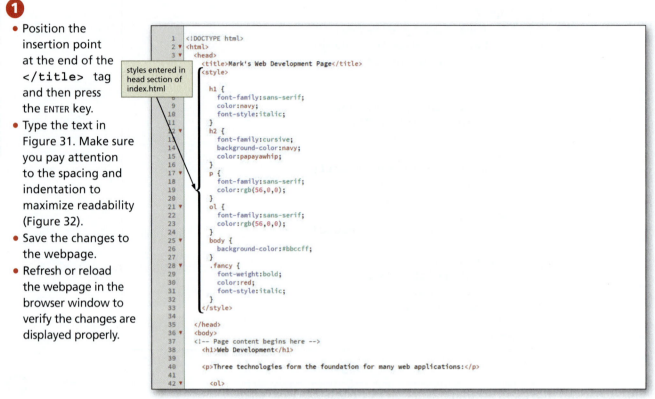

```
 1    <!DOCTYPE html>
 2    <html>
 3      <head>
          <title>Mark's Web Development Page</title>
          <style>

            h1 {
 9            font-family:sans-serif;
10            color:navy;
11            font-style:italic;
12          }
          h2 {
13            font-family:cursive;
14            background-color:navy;
15            color:papayawhip;
16          }
17          p {
18            font-family:sans-serif;
19            color:rgb(56,0,0);
20          }
21          ol {
22            font-family:sans-serif;
23            color:rgb(56,0,0);
24          }
25          body {
26            background-color:#bbccff;
27          }
28          .fancy {
29            font-weight:bold;
30            color:red;
31            font-style:italic;
32          }
33        </style>
34
35      </head>
36      <body>
37        <!-- Page content begins here -->
38        <h1>Web Development</h1>
39
40        <p>Three technologies form the foundation for many web applications:</p>
41
42          <ol>
```

styles entered in head section of index.html

Figure 32

To Add the fancy Style to the index.html File

In the previous set of steps, you specified a custom style, called fancy, which combines several styles to apply at the same time. When you specify a custom style name, you also must specify where in the webpage you want to apply this style. **Why?** *Using a custom style name allows you to specify exactly where you want to use the style in the webpage. The style is not applied automatically to specific tags, as was the case with the* `<h1>`, `<h2>`, `<p>`, `<ol>`, *and* `<body>` *tags in the previous set of steps.* The following steps use the `<span>` tag with the class attribute to specify two different phrases on the page where the fancy style is to be applied.

1

- Position the insertion point immediately before the word, current, in the first paragraph below the HTML5 heading.
- Type `<span class="fancy">` to indicate where you want to begin applying the fancy style.

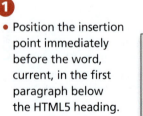

```
56    <h2>HTML5</h2>
57    <img src="images/html5_image.png" alt="HTML5 Image" style="float:left">
58
59    <p>HTML5 is the <span class="fancy">current version of HTML</span> (Hypertext Markup Language) used for creating we
      HTML uses a set of codes called tags to instruct a browser how to display a webpage's content. HTML tags specify th
      on a webpage, such as headings, paragraphs, hyperlinks, or images. HTML5 includes tags for playing audio and video
      the use of third-party plug-ins, or modules, such as Adobe Flash, to perform these tasks. Many mobile devices and c
      compliant browsers, which are capable of interpreting HTML5 tags, to handle these tasks.</p>
60
61    <p>Additional HTML5 feat                              n mobile devices, performing drag and drop, creating gra
      accessing a geolocation,                             HTML5 features allow web developers to build applicatio
      people using the web too                             browser implements the HTML5 specification differently a
      its features.</p>
62
63    <h2>CSS</h2>
      <img src="images/css_i                               "float:right">
```

<span> and </span> tags surround text to be formatted with specified fancy style

Figure 33

- Position the insertion point immediately after the word, HTML, in the same sentence.
- Type `</span>` to indicate where you want to stop applying the fancy style (Figure 33).

2
- Position the insertion point immediately before the word, Additional, in the second paragraph below the HTML5 heading.
- Type **`<span class="fancy">`** to indicate where you want to begin applying the fancy style.
- Position the insertion point immediately after the word, features, in the same sentence.
- Type **`</span>`** to indicate where you want to stop applying the fancy style (Figure 34).
- Save the changes to the index.html file.
- Refresh or reload the webpage in the browser window to verify the changes are displayed properly.

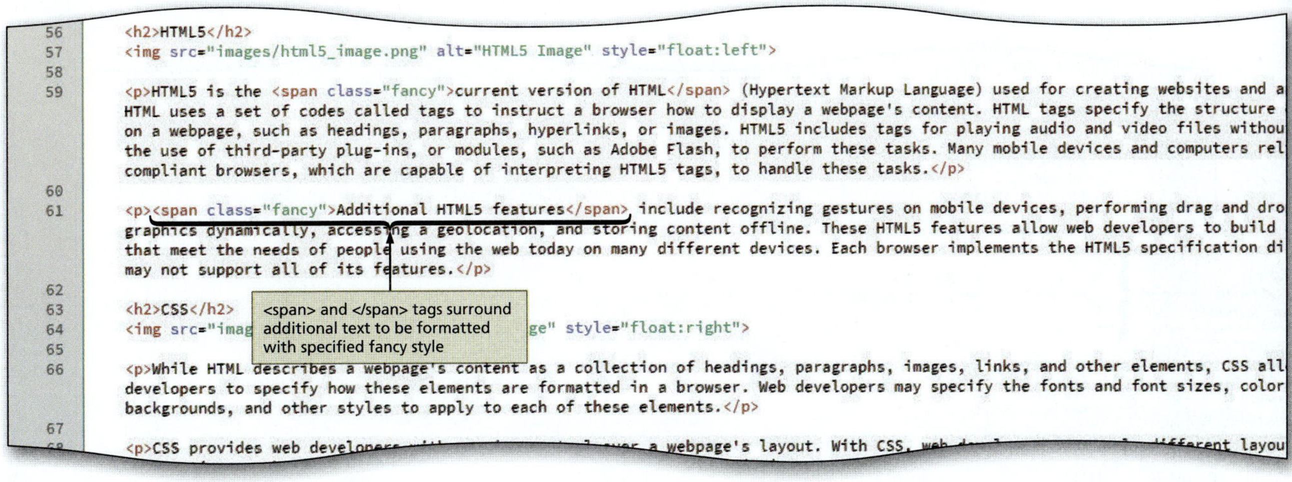

```
56    <h2>HTML5</h2>
57    <img src="images/html5_image.png" alt="HTML5 Image" style="float:left">
58
59    <p>HTML5 is the <span class="fancy">current version of HTML</span> (Hypertext Markup Language) used for creating websites and a
      HTML uses a set of codes called tags to instruct a browser how to display a webpage's content. HTML tags specify the structure
      on a webpage, such as headings, paragraphs, hyperlinks, or images. HTML5 includes tags for playing audio and video files withou
      the use of third-party plug-ins, or modules, such as Adobe Flash, to perform these tasks. Many mobile devices and computers rel
      compliant browsers, which are capable of interpreting HTML5 tags, to handle these tasks.</p>
60
61    <p><span class="fancy">Additional HTML5 features</span> include recognizing gestures on mobile devices, performing drag and dro
      graphics dynamically, accessing a geolocation, and storing content offline. These HTML5 features allow web developers to build
      that meet the needs of people using the web today on many different devices. Each browser implements the HTML5 specification di
      may not support all of its features.</p>
62
63    <h2>CSS</h2>
64    <img src="imag                    ge" style="float:right">
65
66    <p>While HTML describes a webpage's content as a collection of headings, paragraphs, images, links, and other elements, CSS all
      developers to specify how these elements are formatted in a browser. Web developers may specify the fonts and font sizes, color
      backgrounds, and other styles to apply to each of these elements.</p>
67
68    <p>CSS provides web develo                              a webpage's layout. With CSS,               ifferent layou
```

<span> and </span> tags surround additional text to be formatted with specified fancy style

Figure 34

JavaScript

JavaScript is code that can be added to HTML documents to enhance the webpage by adding interactivity or dynamic content. JavaScript can perform simple actions, such as retrieving and displaying the current date and time, to more complex actions, such as performing calculations. In many cases, the JavaScript code appears between opening and closing **`<script>`** tags in the **`<head>`** section of an HTML document. In the **`<body>`** section, you simply reference the JavaScript code where you want the resulting content to display.

To Use JavaScript to Add the Current Date and Time

Adding the current date and time to the index.html file requires you to add code in two sections of the webpage. The following steps type the code to retrieve the current date in the **`<head>`** section of the index.html file, and the code to display the retrieved date and time will be located in the **`<body>`** section (Figure 35). *Why? Displaying the current date and time on a webpage indicates to visitors that the version of the webpage they are viewing is current.*

```
<script>
function showDateAndTime() {
document.getElementById("current_date").innerHTML= Date();
}
</script>
```

Figure 35a Code to retrieve the current date and time.

```
<p id="current_date"></p>
```

Figure 35b Code to display the current date and time using the JavaScript code in the **`<head>`** section.

1

- Position the insertion point after the `</style>` tag in the `<head>` section and then press the ENTER key two times.
- Type the code shown in Figure 35a to enter the JavaScript code that retrieves the current date and time. Be sure to apply the same spacing, indentation, and use of uppercase and lowercase letters as shown in the figure.
- Position the insertion point immediately after the y in the `<body>` tag. Press the SPACEBAR one time and then type `onload=showDateAndTime()` to specify that you want to run the JavaScript code when the webpage loads (Figure 36).

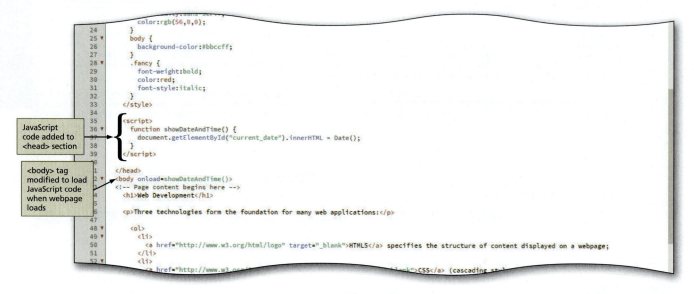

Figure 36

2

- Position the insertion point immediately after the last `</p>` tag in the index.html file and then press the ENTER key two times.
- Type the code shown in Figure 35b to specify where to display the current date (Figure 37).
- Save the changes to the index.html file.
- Refresh or reload the webpage in the browser window to verify the changes are displayed properly.
- Refresh or reload the page again to verify that the JavaScript updates the date and time that is displayed.

```
     <p><span class="fancy">Additional HTML5 feature ... recognizing gestures on mobile devices, performing drag and drop, creating
     graphics dynamically, accessing a geolocation, and storing content offline. These HTML5 features allow web developers to build applications
     that meet the needs of people using the web today on many different devices. Each browser implements the HTML5 specification differently and
     may not support all of its features.</p>

68
69   <h2>CSS</h2>
70   <img src="images/css_image.png" alt="CSS Image" style="float:right">
71
72   <p>While HTML describes a webpage's content as a collection of headings, paragraphs, images, links, and other elements, CSS allows web
     developers to specify how these elements are formatted in a browser. Web developers may specify the fonts and font sizes, colors, borders,
     backgrounds, and other styles to apply to each of these elements.</p>
73
74   <p>CSS provides web developers with precise control over a webpage's layout. With CSS, web developers can apply different layouts to the same
     information so that it is formatted appropriately for printing or viewing on computers and devices with varying screen sizes. The current
     version of CSS is known as CSS3 (cascading style sheets, version 3).</p>
75
76   <h2>JavaScript</h2>
77   <img src="images/js_image.png" alt="JavaScript Image" style="float:left">
78
79   <p>JavaScript is a programming language that adds interactivity to webpages. It often is used to check for appropriate values on web forms,
     present alert messages, display menus on webpages, and create other dynamic content. Some developers use JavaScript to detect the user's
     browser version in order to display a webpage especially designed for that browser.</p>

     <p id="current_date"></p>

     <!-- Page content ends here -->
     </body>
85   </html>
```

<p> tag contains id element to display current date and time

Figure 37

Adding a YouTube Video to a Webpage

YouTube, a popular website with more than one billion users, contains videos about almost any topic imaginable. In addition to watching a YouTube video in a browser or using the YouTube app on a mobile device, you also can embed YouTube videos directly on a webpage. When you locate a video on that you want to include on a webpage, YouTube provides HTML code you can use to add the video to the webpage (Figure 38). This section adds a video about Web Development to the video.html file.

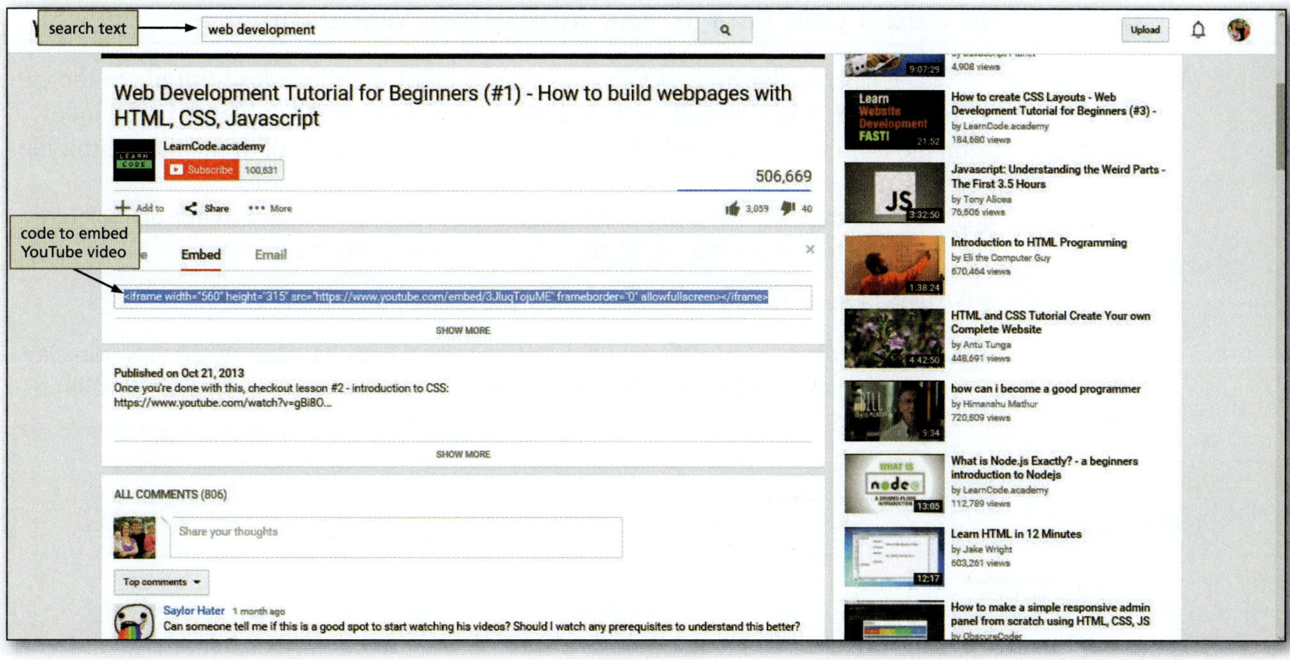

Figure 38

To Embed a YouTube Video in the video.html Webpage

The following steps locate a video on YouTube and embed the video in the video.html webpage. *Why? Embedding a video can add appeal to a webpage by presenting content in a format other than text and images.*

1

- Open a new browser tab and navigate to youtube.com.
- Use the search box on the youtube.com webpage to locate a video about web development.
- Locate the embed code. *Hint:* click the Share link and then click the Embed link.
- Select the embed code in its entirety and then copy it to the clipboard.

2

- Display the text editor containing the code for the video.html webpage.
- Position the insertion point on a blank line immediately following the line that reads, `<!--Page content begins here -->`.
- Paste the contents of the clipboard (Figure 39).

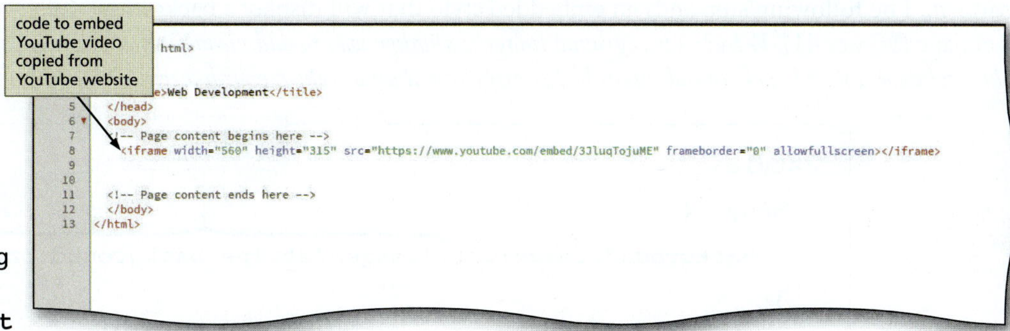

Figure 39

What other online content can you embed on a website?
In addition to embedding videos on a website, you also may include media content, such as online calendars and documents, social media posts, images or slideshows from photo sharing websites, and maps positioned at preset locations. To include this content on a website, look for a link labeled Share or Embed or an icon displaying HTML brackets (**< >**) on the website containing the content. Click this link or icon, copy the embed code displayed in the browser, and paste it at the desired location in the HTML file.

To Add a Link Back to the index.html Webpage

Earlier in this Focus On, you created a link from the index.html file to the video.html file. You now will provide a link that will navigate users back to the index.html file from the video.html file. The following steps add a link to the index.html file.

1 Position the insertion point on the blank line after the code pasted in from YouTube, immediately above the **</html>** tag, and then press the ENTER key.

2 Type **
** to add a line break after the code to display the video.

3 Press the ENTER key two times and then type **<a href="index.html">Home</a>** to add a link back to the website's home page referenced in index.html (Figure 40).

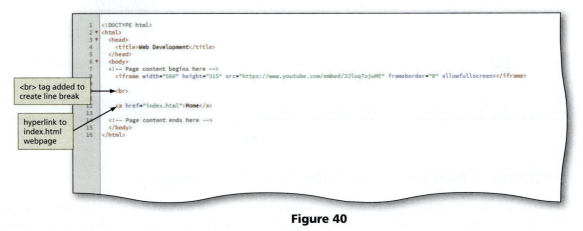

Figure 40

To Add a Background Style to the video.html Webpage

When choosing a background image for a webpage, be sure to choose one that does not detract from the webpage content. Background images create a pattern behind a webpage's content. By default, most browsers repeat the background image both horizontally and vertically in the content area to form a tiled pattern. The following step adds an embedded style that will display a background image on the video.html webpage (Figure 41). *Why? A background image is another way to add visual appeal to a webpage. A webpage with a plain white or colored background might be less attractive than a webpage with a texture or pattern in the background.*

```
<style>
  body  {
    background-image:url("images/stripe_background.png");
  }
</style>
```

relative path to background image

Figure 41

1

- Position the insertion point immediately after the `</title>` tag and then press the ENTER key.
- Type the code in Figure 41. Be sure to apply the same line spacing and indenting as shown in the figure (Figure 42).
- Save the changes to the video.html file.

```
1   <!DOCTYPE html>
2   <html>
3     <head>
4       <title>Web Development</title>
5   <style>
6       body  {
7         background-image:url("images/stripe_background.png");
8       }
9   </style>
10
11    </head>
12    <body>
13    <!-- Page content begins here -->
14      <iframe width="560" height="315" src="https://www.youtube.com/embed/3JluqTojuME" frameborder="0" allowfullscreen><
15
16      <br>
17
18      <a href="index.html">Home</a>
19
20    <!-- Page content ends here -->
```

CSS code to specify page background image

Figure 42

Where can you find images to use as textures as the background of a webpage?
You can find background images by using a search engine to locate websites that provide these. Consider including words such as webpage, background, and textures in your search text.

CONSIDER THIS

To Exit the Text Editor and Preview the Webpages

When you have finished creating the webpages, the next step is to preview them in a browser before publishing them online. *Why? It is important to thoroughly preview the webpages you create to make sure all links work, all images are displayed, and the overall webpage is displayed as you intend.* The following steps exit the text editor and then load the webpages in the browser for you to preview.

1

- Close the video.html file in the text editor. If necessary, save the changes to the file.
- Close the index.html file in the text editor. If necessary, save the changes to the file.

2

- Redisplay the index.html file in the browser window. Click the Reload or Refresh button to make sure you are viewing the most current version of the webpage (Figure 43).

Web Development

'Watch a video' link ... the foundation for many web applications:

1. HTML5 specifies the structure of content displayed on a webpage;
2. CSS (cascading style sheets) describes the design and appearance of information on a webpage; and
3. JavaScript allows users to interact with a webpage's content.

Watch a video about web development.

HTML5

HTML5 is the *current version of HTML* (Hypertext Markup Language) used for creating websites and applications. HTML uses a set of codes called tags to instruct a browser how to display a webpage's content. HTML tags specify the structure or content of ... headings, paragraphs, hyperlinks, or images. HTML5 includes tags for playing audio and video files without relying on the use of third-party plug-ins, or modules, such as Adobe Flash, to ... text formatted in fancy style y mobile devices and computers rely on HTML5-compliant browsers, which are capable of interpreting HTML5 tags, to handle these tasks.

Additional HTML5 features include recogniz... gestures on mobile devices, performing drag and drop, creating graphics dynamically, accessing a geolocation, and storing content offline. These HTML5 features allow web developers to build applications that meet the needs of people using the web today on many different devices. Each browser implements the HTML5 specification differently and may not support all of its features.

CSS

While HTML describes a webpage's content as a collection of headings, paragraphs, images, links, and other elements, CSS allows web developers to specify how these elements are formatted in a browser. Web developers may specify the fonts and font sizes, colors, borders, backgrounds, and other styles to apply to each of these elements.

CSS provides web developers with precise control over a webpage's layout. With CSS, web developers can apply different layouts to the same information so that it is formatted appropriately for printing or viewing on computers and devices with varying screen sizes. The current version of CSS is known as CSS3 (cascading style sheets, version 3).

JavaScript

JavaScript is a programming language that adds interactivity to webpages. It often is used to check for appropriate values on web forms, present alert messages, display menus on webpages, and create other dynamic content. Some developers use JavaScript to detect the user's browser version in order to display a webpage especially designed for that browser.

Sat Aug 12 2017 13:08:23 GMT-0400 (Eastern Daylight Time)

Figure 43 index.html webpage.

3

- Verify the webpage you are viewing looks the same as Figure 43. The headings and paragraphs should be formatted, the page should have a light blue background color, two phrases should be formatted with the fancy style, and the three images should have loaded.
- Click the HTML5 link to make sure it navigates to the proper destination. Then, return to the browser tab or window displaying the index.html webpage.
- Click the CSS link to make sure it navigates to the proper destination. Then, return to the browser tab or window displaying the index.html webpage.
- Click the JavaScript link to make sure it navigates to the proper destination. Then, return to the browser tab or window displaying the index.html webpage.
- Click the 'Watch a video' link to display the video.html webpage (Figure 44).

Figure 44 video.html webpage.

4

- Click the play button in the video player to play the embedded video.
- When you have finished watching the video, click the Home link at the bottom of the webpage to return to the index.html webpage.
- Close all browser windows.

To Publish a Website Online

When you have finished testing the pages in your website, you are ready to publish them so that anyone can access them on a device connected to the Internet. *Why? Websites published on a web server are accessible online for all to see.*

To transfer the files from your local computer to a remote web server, you will need to connect to the remote web server using the File Transfer Protocol (FTP). FTP specifies rules for transferring files from one computer to another on the Internet. While it is possible to enter FTP text commands in a command window to specify how to transfer files to and from a server, most users opt to download a free FTP application such as FileZilla or CuteFTP, which has a graphical user interface, to simplify the process.

You also will need an account on a web server in order to publish a website. If your school provides you with space to host a website, ask your instructor for the settings to connect to your account on the school's web server. In general, you will need to know the host or web server name, your user name, and password to publish the files, and the web address of the website's home page to view it online. You should publish only those files related to your website assignment on your school's web server.

The following steps connect to a remote web server using an FTP application.

1
- Type the host name (the name of the web server) and the user name and password for the account, or set up a profile containing this information using an FTP application.
- Click the connect button to connect to the server (Figure 45).

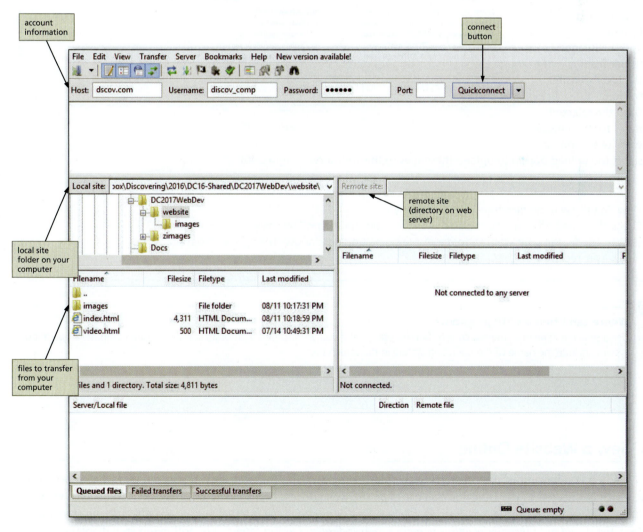

Figure 45

2

- In the local site section of the FTP application, navigate to the website folder containing the HTML, images, and other files for the website.
- In the remote site section of the FTP application, you should see the contents of your account on the web server. No files should appear if you have not yet uploaded any.
- Select the index.html and video.html files and the images folder from the local websites section.
- Drag the selected items to the remote website section, or select the upload option to upload these files to the web server (Figure 46).

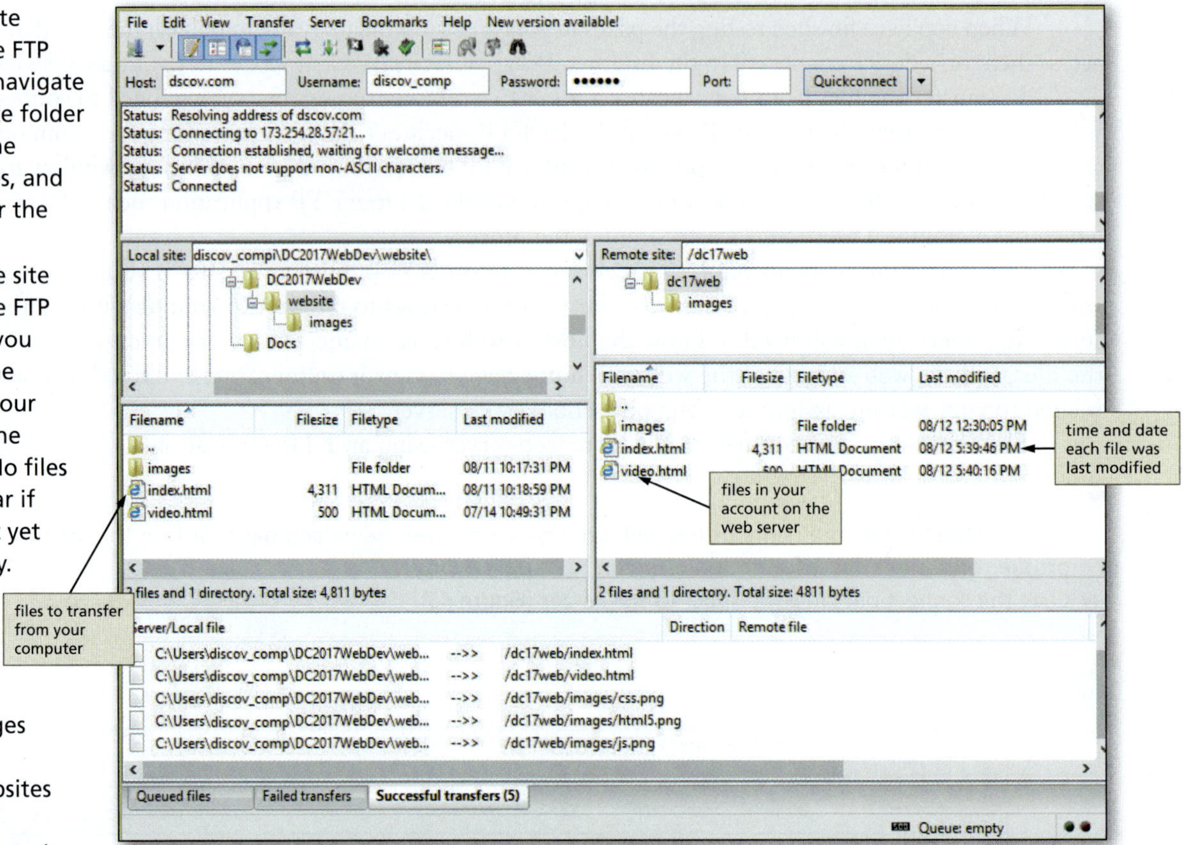

Figure 46

Q&A
How do I know if my files transferred correctly?
Check the time and date and the size of the files on the server. The sizes should match the sizes of the files in your website folder. A file's time and date shows the time and date that the web server received the file.

CONSIDER THIS

Where can I find an FTP program?
Use a search engine with the search text, free ftp program. If you wish to find a program specific to your computer's operating system, include the name of the operating system in the search text.

To View a Website Online

When you have finished transferring the files from a website to a web server, you can view the website on any device connected to the Internet. You can type the web address of a specific webpage on a website to view it. ***Why?*** *Uploading webpages to a web server allows anyone connected to the Internet to view them by entering their web address. You should view the website online to make sure it is displayed as you intend.* The following step displays the published website in a browser.

1
- Open a new browser or browser tab.
- In the address bar, type the absolute address of the website hosted on a web server. (This begins with http:// and includes the name of the server hosting the site.) The website will appear (Figure 47).

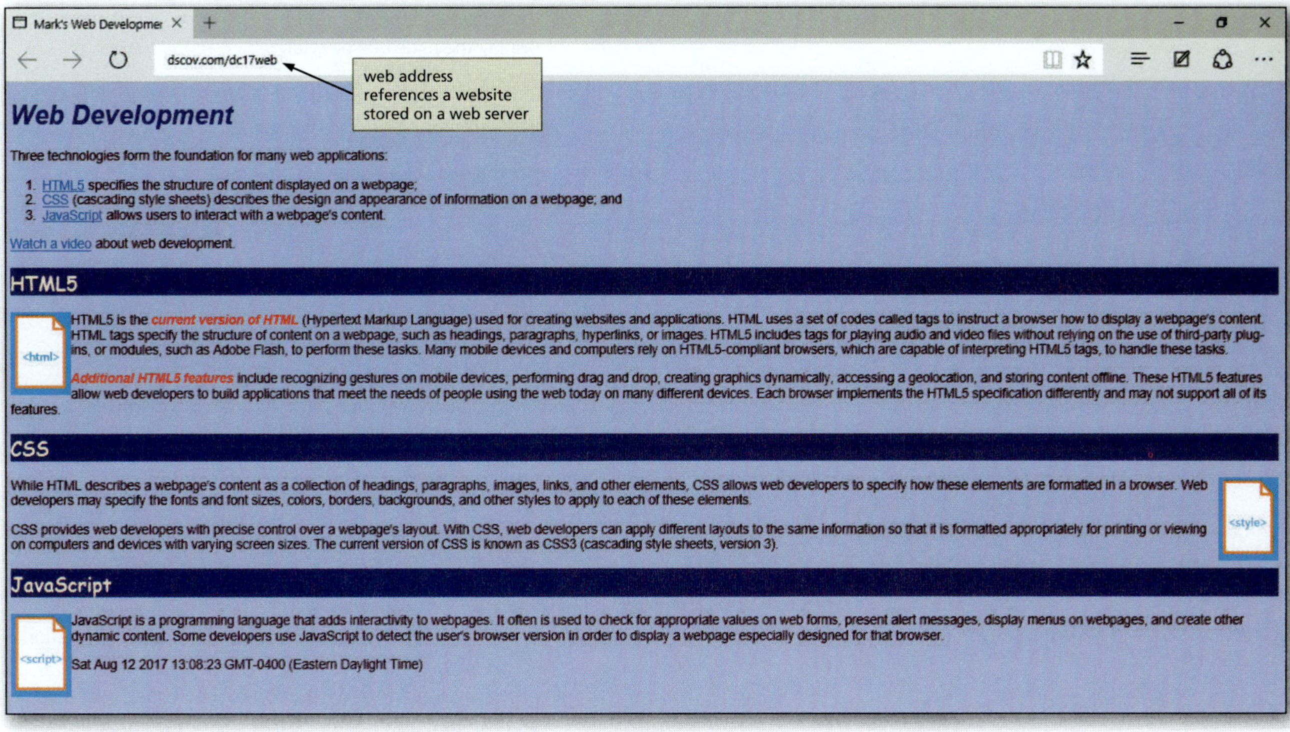

Figure 47

Q&A

Do I need to type index.html in the web address to view my website's home page in a browser?
No. You often can omit index.html when entering a web address in a browser. Because index.html often is the name of the first, or home, page that many websites display, a web server will look for a page with that name by default if no page name is specified in the request to locate a webpage.

What if I need or want to make changes to a website once it is published online?
Type the changes you want to make in the text editor, verify them locally in a browser, and then upload the changed files to the web server using an FTP program. Refresh or revisit the webpages in a browser to verify the changes were uploaded correctly.

Summary of Tags and Styles

This section summarizes tags and styles presented in this Focus On, as well as additional tags and styles often used when authoring webpages.

HTML5 Tags

Table 2 lists several HTML5 tags and notes about their usage. When a tag takes an attribute, the format is each attribute name followed by an equal sign (=), followed by its value in quotation marks, as in `<a href="http://www.google.com" target="_blank">Google</a>`. Use a search engine with the search text, basic HTML tags, to locate complete documentation online. You can add a `style` attribute to many of these tags.

Table 2 Selected HTML5 Tags

Tag	Example	Description
`<!-->`	`<!--This is a comment. -->`	Comment from web developer, ignored when page is rendered
`<a>`	`<a href="http://www.google.com" target="_blank">Google</a>`	Anchor tag, specifies a link; specify `href` (hypertext reference) and use the attribute `target="_blank"` to display the page in a new tab
`<body>`	`<body style="background-color:yellow">`	Body section of a webpage, styled to have a yellow background
` `	` `	Line break; ` ` has no closing tag
`<h1>` through `<h6>`	`<h1> This is a heading.</h1>`	Headings for content; `<h1>` is largest, `<h6>` is smallest
`<head>`	`<head> ... </head>`	Head section
`<hr>`	`<hr style="background-color:rgb(192,192,192);">`	Displays a horizontal rule (line) across the page to separate sections of content; optional `style` attributes may specify the background color or width of the line; `<hr>` has no closing tag
`<html>`	`<html> ... </html>`	Starts an HTML document
`<iframe>`	`<iframe src="http://cengage.com" width="600" height="400"></iframe>`	Includes content from another website, such as embedding webpage or an online video; use `height` and `width` attributes to specify the size, in pixels, of the iframe
`<img>`	`<img src="images/dog.jpg" alt="Dog photo">`	Image tag, `src` attribute specifies the source or location of the image, `alt` attribute (required in HTML5) provides an alternate description of the image, `height` and `width` specify the display size of the image in pixels; `<img>` has no closing tag

`<li>`	`<ol>`
	`  <li> Item 1</li>`
	`  <li> Item 2 </li>`
	`</ol>`
		List item, used within `<ol>` or `<ul>` tags

`<ol>`	`<ol>`
	`  <li> Item 1</li>`
	`  <li> Item 2 </li>`
	`</ol>`
		Ordered (numbered) list

`<p>`	`<p>This is a paragraph.</p>`	Paragraph
`<script>`	`<script> ... </script>`	Identifies JavaScript code; located in `<head>` section
`<span>`	`<span class="fancy">This text is formatted fancy.</span>`	Identifies content to apply a custom style

`<style>`	`<style>`
	`  h1 {`
	`    font-family:serif;`
	`    color: blue;`
	`  }`
	`</style>`
		Identifies embedded styles for tags; located in `<head>` section

`<title>`	`<title>My Website</title>`	Title of a webpage that appears in the browser tab; located in `<head>` section of document

`<ul>`	`<ul>`
	`  <li> Item 1</li>`
	`  <li> Item 2 </li>`
	`</ul>`
		Unordered (bulleted) list

Styles

Styles may appear in the `<style>` section or as part of a `style` attribute in almost all HTML tags, or in an external style sheet. The format for a style declaration is the style name, followed by a colon, followed by the value for the style. If more than one style is used, separate each style with a semicolon. Use a search engine with the search text, css styles reference, to locate complete documentation online.

Table 3 Selected Styles

Style	Example	Description
`background-color`	`background-color:yellow;`	Specifies the background color of elements, such as `<p>`, `<h1>`, and `<body>`
`background-image`	`background-image:url("images/stripes.jpg")`	Sets the background image of a `<body>`, `<p>`, `<h1>`, and other elements to the file whose path is given in the `url()` function
`border`	`border: 3 px red;`	Specifies a 4-sided border that is 3 pixels thick
`color`	`color:blue;`	Colors can be a web color name, a hexadecimal value, such as `#0000FF`, or an rgb value, such as `rgb(0,0,255)` that specifies the red, green, and blue components of the color
`float`	`float:left;`	Specifies whether to place an element to the left or right relative to text; often used to position an image to the left or right of text.
`font-family`	`font-family:serif;`	Specifies the font for a paragraph, heading, or other text element; use specific font names, such as `times`, `arial`, and `courier`, or family names, such as `serif`, `sans-serif`, `cursive`, or `monospace`
`font-size`	`font-size:10px;`	Specifies font size in pixels
`font-style`	`font-style:italic;`	Specifies font style; use normal, italic, or oblique as the value for this style
`font-weight`	`font-weight:bold;`	Specifies the font weight for a paragraph, heading, or other text element; use `bold` for thick characters, or numeric values `100` through `900`, in increments of 100; `400` is the same as `normal`, 700 is the same as `bold`
`text-align`	`text-align:left;`	Sets alignment for `<h1>`, `<h2>`, or `<h3>` tags; values can be `left`, `center`, or `right`

Exercises

Short Answer

Consider these HTML code fragments below and then answer the questions for each.

1. `<a href="http://nationalzoo.si.edu/" target="_blank">Zoo</a>`

   In which browser window will the page appear? Is this an absolute or a relative reference? What words will appear as the link you should click?

2. `<img src="images/cat.jpg" alt="Cat">`

   Where is the cat.jpg file located within your website's development folder? What is the purpose of the attribute, `alt="Cat"`?

3. `<body style="background-color:rgb(255,0,255)">`

   What does this style specify for the body tag? What color is specified?

4. `<style> h1 { color: blue; font-family:serif; } </style>`

   To which `<h1>` tags in an HTML document will this style declaration apply? What is the name of a font that a browser might use to display text in a serif font? Would you most likely find this style declaration in the head or body section of an HTML document?

```
<ul>
  <li>Cake</li>
  <li>Ice Cream</li>
  <ol>
    <li>Chocolate</li>
    <li>Vanilla</li>
  </ol>
  <li>Cookies</li>
</ul>
```

Consider the HTML5 code for a dessert menu on a restaurant's website. How does it appear in a browser?

How To: Your Turn

Create a website for your online resume, for a club or organization of which you are a member, or for a small business. The website should include these features:

- At least two pages, each with different background images or colors
- An image at the top of each page that serves as a banner
- Links between the home page and other pages on the website
- Styled text (bold, italics, different fonts or colors)
- Content in an ordered or unordered list
- Embedded media content (such as a video, map, or Tweet)
- Links to your accounts on online social networks
- Links to other websites (open in a new window or tab)
- An image that, when clicked, acts as a link
- JavaScript code that displays the current date and time on a webpage

Internet Research

Many small businesses host and install a content management system in order to develop their websites. Search the web for an online content management system, such as WordPress or Google Sites. Sign up for an account so that you can create a basic website and experiment with its features. Which features of a content management system did you find most useful? How does the process of creating a website with a content management system compare with creating a website by writing HTML code? Do you need to know even basic HTML code when creating a website using a content management system?

Index